THE PEOPLE vs. THE SYSTEM

vs.

THE SYSTEM

·

a dialogue in urban conflict

Edited by Sol Tax

The People vs. the System

Available from: Acme Press, Inc.

523 South Plymouth Court, Chicago, Illinois 60605

Price: $8.50 postpaid.

THE
PEOPLE
VS.
THE
SYSTEM
.
a dialogue in urban conflict

Community Service Workshop...

Proceedings of the Community Service Workshop,.,
Funded under Title I of the Higher Education Act of 1965
And held at The University of Chicago, October 1966 – June 1967

EDITED BY SOL TAX

Library of Congress Catalog Card Number 68-58488
Acme Press, Inc., Chicago, Illinois
©1968 by The University of Chicago
Printed in the United States of America

Preface

Successive "summers" in our cities reveal the basic nature of the problem which began under the symbol of civil rights: Negroes as a whole see the government in power not as their government, but rather as an establishment which forcibly maintains an economy, a "system," which does not benefit them. What happened in Detroit in 1967 — and almost everywhere in April of 1968 — was unlike what happened in Watts in 1965 (or in Detroit in 1943 or Chicago in 1919). These are not race riots in the sense that a white man need feel unsafe in the streets. In a period of two years, the movement had developed from simple individual frustration and anger to a state of warfare, albeit unorganized, with an implicit demand for complete independence from the colonialist establishment which the Negro community understood was oppressing them.

The surprise of most of us who have been part of the colonial establishment perhaps indicates better than anything else the nature of the problem. We have all lived in 1968 as well as or better than we did in 1958. We have not convinced our Congress that we must all make genuine personal sacrifices for the sake of equality. After ten years of waning hope, the Negro community has simply given up on us. We of the establishment — meaning all of us who are part of the system and hence feel that we have or can get what we want — assumed that it was beloved as the source of security and well-being by all the right-minded. We did not understand — and they were too insecure to tell us — that (to paraphrase Browning) we who had gold to give were doling out silver. We are like the Dutch who were so surprised and hurt that their enlightened colonial policy served them no good in Indonesia. The white racism that the Kerner report pinpoints as the cause is simply the acceptance by whites of the historic establishment. To whites such acceptance is somehow "natural," to blacks it is an inhuman outrage that is greater, not less, because it has lasted so long.

The trouble that has come especially to cities is due partly to the migration of Negroes from country to city. The trouble comes specifically from the circumstance that the cities which had promised a better life have demonstrated an inability to provide it. Mayors and chiefs of police, as well as the private and public organizations, education, welfare, health, and housing — even Urban Opportunity Committees — were revealed as part of a tight establishment whose highest goal seemed to be the protection of the establishment, of "law and order." It proposed, in effect, to do what every colonial administration does: "prepare people for independence" while protecting the establishment. That the analogy would act itself out and that the colonized would be unwilling to wait might perhaps have been expected from historical experience.

When I proposed the Community Service Workshop, I understood poorly the nature of our real situation. It was the Workshop which rapidly made

i

evident the great hiatus between the perceptions prevalent within the system and the needs and drives of the people. We had depended upon Negro civil rights leaders to be a bridge; but these found themselves following, rather than leading the people; like other middle-class people, they were part of the system, and only a little ahead of others in changing their perceptions before they could interpret the people to the system. The Workshop was designed precisely to get understanding between the established power and the people at the grass-roots. Initially, it did not focus specifically on the Negro community, but was designed to bring together Negroes, Appalachians, American Indians, and many others. It soon became evident that the Negroes were a special group of the disestablished and as their independence movement proceeded, their views dominated the discussions in the Workshop. That the Workshop took place at a critical time in the history of the movement is reflected in, among other things, the shift during its course from the term "Negro" to "Black." It is not surprising that the Workshop turned out to be a "happening" and that those of the establishment who participated learned in part by shock. What came out of the Workshop, therefore, was (1) a realization of the hiatus in communication and the need to overcome it, and (2) a common new understanding of substantive urban problems especially as they affect Negroes.

The Community Service Workshop was conducted by the University of Chicago with a grant from Title I of the Higher Education Act of 1965. It brought together all levels of staff in public and private agencies, religious institutions, educational institutions, and community organizations. They were removed from their usual workday problems and particular conflicts to an academic atmosphere. The relief was great from the usual frustrations of the grass roots leaders in trying to get government and private agencies to do their will, and from the frustration of the well-meaning agency people to enlist the cooperation of the citizenry. For those present the experience was so positive that they determined to maintain themselves as an organization with continuing communication.

It almost seems incidental that all of the participants learned a tremendous amount about the substantive problems of urban life. Yet, by bringing together knowledgeable people, speaking from different vantage points, the Workshop indeed produced a wealth of material on the problems facing urban communities. It is not the scholar's encyclopedia that is here published, but a rich sample of the cream that surfaces in the process of first creative communication. Whether or not this record will educate agency staff members and grass roots workers in the way that the confrontation did for the few people in the Workshop, it surely confirms the growing realization that unless we can bridge a great hiatus that we hardly know exists, we are not likely to resolve the problem.

The Workshop was designed to deal with urban problems generally, and participants were deliberately drawn from beyond the Chicago area. But Chicago inevitably became the overpowering center of discussion. This was the more interesting as it became evident that Chicago is a polar extreme among American cities. In most places power is diffuse, and people are frustrated because even when agreed upon, nobody is able to effect change. In Chicago there is a single focus of power. As the Workshop progressed, this came to seem the overwhelming fact. At one point, near the end, I was asked to get "Washington" to assure grass roots participation in planning for the Model Cities Program. I gave up when it became evident that nobody's clout equalled that of our mayor. At least then, President Johnson needed Mayor Daley more than Mayor Daley needed the President. This book therefore highlights the plight of the still poor who are helpless against a strong government which — because it wins its votes on election day — believes it successfully represents them.

The eight-month program was designed to provide a heterogeneous group of people with an opportunity for candid discussion of current urban problems and issues; to promote understanding among people from agencies and community organizations; to increase the effectiveness of people involved in social change activities; and to provide new opportunities for communication and cooperation. A variety of methods were used to achieve the Workshop's objectives. Plenary sessions with selected panelists were developed to provide opportunities for varying points of view to be presented on the specific topics being discussed and, on some occasions, lectures were arranged for topics to be considered in greater detail and depth. In order for the participants to discuss the issues raised and their implications, discussion sessions followed panel presentations and lectures. In addition, small discussion groups were scheduled to provide opportunities for continued discussion. Feedback sessions followed the small group discussions thus enabling the small groups to share their ideas with the total group of Workshop participants. In addition, work sessions were scheduled so that the participants could focus on specific problems, develop concrete models, and suggest solutions.

This book reflects the Workshop program and content. The panel presentations (except for the opening orientation session) are included in their entirety and the discussion sessions following them have been summarized. The book therefore owes most to the participants who were willing to maintain an honest dialogue on real issues and who listened and were genuinely responsive to the guests from all over the nation who joined them to discuss various topics. It is also a special pleasure to note that the guest participants almost always fell quickly into the spirit of the Workshop, and regardless of their positions, were candid and open in their discussion. The Workshop might have been ridden with mutual defensiveness or unyielding formality. In that case, it would have ended prematurely because the participants are too busy and too committed to be satisfied with polite or meaningless talk.

A residential Workshop requires a special kind of meeting place with the facilities, services, and staff to make it run smoothly and successfully. The staff of the Center for Continuing Education, the interns, and adult education students contributed much to the Workshop's success. None, however, rivalled in effectiveness my assistant, Maryl Levine, whose tireless care made the Workshop possible, and earned for her the affection and the admiration of all the participants.

A Workshop of this nature needs intellectual help as well as the legwork of staff. From the start we had an interdisciplinary advisory committee composed of members of the faculty, and especially our cosponsors, the Center for Urban Studies and the School of Social Service Administration. Dr. Leonard Borman helped with the planning as the "participant evaluator" of the whole program.

Finally, and most of all, my editing this book hides the fact that it was made possible by staff experienced in grass roots community organization, including Robert Rietz, who took leave as director of the American Indian Center, and Earl Doty, who had just completed five years work as associate director of the Chicago Youth Development Project. The selection of Earl Doty became critical as urban Negro problems became the Workshop focus. His personal involvement with, and understanding of, the Negro community were a sine qua non.

The book itself owes particularly to Stephanie Michel, who collected, edited, and summarized the material from the tapes, with constant concern for capturing the spirit of the Workshop as well as the heart of the issues discussed.

Beyond the Workshop and the book, it may be worth a moment of the reader's time to reflect on the University's first use of Title I funds. The idea of the Act is simple: American universities have done so much for agriculture and rural development — cannot they be enlisted to help solve our urban problems? Colleges and universities were therefore invited (75% at federal expense, reduced now to 50%) to experiment with new ways of relating their special knowledge and capacities to community problems. Our University of Chicago experiment was this Community Service Workshop, to face indigenous grass roots leadership with the public and private agency people concerned with community problems. What use we were to these leaders and agencies (or to constructive action in the urban setting) the reader of the book will judge for himself. What use we were to the people who actually met face to face, they know best. Many of them report that they will never be the same again; it was a great experience in their lives, and some of them have organized similar programs since. Whether the Workshop developed a pattern which can be followed elsewhere (as Title I foresaw), perhaps the book will indicate. Whether the new knowledge which was produced in the Workshop will spread to others in the nation will depend upon the success of this book.

The one answer I have — whether this was foreseen by Congress — is that the university participants learned much from, and were greatly inspired by, those remarkably wise, talented, honest, down-to-earth neighborhood folk. I most of all.

The University of Chicago

Sol Tax
July, 1968

Contents

PART IV Youth and the Community

Critical Issues in
Community Organization

Critical Issues in Community Organization

EARL DOTY

The initial phase of the Community Service Workshop must be viewed as having been qualitatively different from the ensuing series. Unlike the others, its focus was not on dealing with specific issues and the concomitant "exposure of self." Rather, the task that the Workshop selected for itself was to achieve a working definition of *community organization.* The focus of the group on this task was in part generated on the basis that it was non-controversial; it did not require a major exposure of self; it helped to provide a frame within which ensuing sessions would be run.

The program was as follows:

1st day:

  Plenary Session 1: Orientation

  Plenary Session 2: The Community in Historical Perspective

      Richard Wade

2nd day:

  Feedback from participants on previous presentation

  Plenary Session 3: Introduction to Community Organization

      Irving Spergel

  Plenary Session 4: Federal Government and Equal Opportunity

      John McKnight

  Plenary Session 5: Power and Responsibility – Case Presentation and Analysis, The Woodlawn Organization

      Solomon Ice

      Rev. Thomas Ellis

      Rev. Lynward Stevenson

  Plenary Session 6: Power and Responsibility – Team Discussion

      Victor DeGrazia

      David Greenstone

      Theodore Lowi

3rd day:

  Feedback from participants on previous presentations

  Plenary Session 7: Social Service and Social Change – Case Presentation and Analysis, Chicago Youth Development Project

Hans Mattick
Gerald Suttles
Nathan Caplan
Dennis Deshaies
Plenary Session 8: Social Service and Social Change – Team Discussion
Alan Wade
Clyde Murray
Herbert Thelen
Edward Riddick
Tour of local Urban Progress Center

4th day:

Freedback from participants on previous presentations
Plenary Session 9: Political Conditions for Effective Indigenous Leadership
Paul Peterson
Group discussion on relevance of the case analysis to back-home problems
Plenary Session 10: Indigenous and Professional Leadership – Case Presentation and Analysis, Mobilization for Youth
Ezra Birnbaum
Edward Pitt
Daniel Morris
Plenary Session 11: Indigenous and Professional Leadership – Team Discussion
Irving Spergel
Archie Hargraves
Sol Tax
Elaine Switzer
Daniel Morris

5th day:

Feedback from participants on previous discussions
Plenary Session 12: Integrative Session – General review of relevance of Workshop experience to back-home problems; orientation to next phase
Workshop Staff

   Movement and interaction of Workshop participants during this phase was of a staccato pattern. The "feeling out" process was overtly operational and the overwhelming majority of participants were guarded in their comments. This relative absence of interaction was at two levels: between participants, and between participants and discussants. The very fact the *the* University had brought together such an active and heterogenous group made it immediately suspect and contributed to the protracted testing-out period. It was the consensus of participants that the University was engaged in some type of covert research program geared to: (1) a study of social cynamics of participants; (2) an attempt to gather information and documentation of activities of community organization in order to share the same with the city administration.

As a result of the above, the only item that the group felt comfortable enough to deal with was "the nature of community organization." The tapes for this session were not complete enough to furnish a formal record of the presentations, but the following rendition of the conception of community organization that arose out of the discussion may now provide the reader with some orientation to the chapters which follow.

The concept of community organization is an extremely varied one and the form which it takes will, in part, be determined by how one defines "the community." For the purpose of the Workshop the concept of community was viewed as a geographical one as opposed to a community of concern, a community of thought, or a particular ethnic community. Community organization ought to be viewed as both a field and a process which is practiced both horizontally and vertically at the national, state, and local levels. Throughout history community organization has been engaged in by such diverse entities as political parties, convention bureaus, chambers of commerce, special-interest groups, churches, and local indigenous self-help groups. Although the importance attached to such efforts may be primary or secondary, any given agency had to engage in it in order to survive and operate in the context of the social systems of the community. For the sake of simplicity, the Workshop defined community organization as an effort to mobilize resources around certain needs based on a theory of either cooperation or conflict. Ordinarily, community organization proceeds on the theory that cooperation will prevail, but if there are powerful interests involved or there is lack of agreement about objectives, then the potential for conflict exists.

The involvement of local adults in community organization activities affords an opportunity for the direct engagement of indigenous people in a socially rewarding and noncompetitive effort and serves as a testimony to the American tradition of "self-help." Unfortunately many people have a stereotyped notion about the nature of community organization, which they envision as a group of people brought together in a place of assembly who elect a chairman, select committees to effect a division of labor, and discuss problems with a view to formulating plans of action. There is no doubt that this stereotype reflects a common form of community organization, and one that the community organization team will strive to bring about, but it is not the starting point in community organization work.

The realtive success in bringing about a more viable form of community organization is based, in part, on the emergence of a particular work style(s). Some of these work styles focus on: *issues and individuals; independence, anonymity, interdependence; realities of power.*

Issues – Individuals

Which is of primary concern? Should issues be imposed or developed? What of the dilemma of manipulation and leadership?

Independence – Anonymity – Interdependence

What are the consequences of isolation and amalgamation? Should the decision-making apparatus be maintained or vested in others? Private frustration or community action?

Realities of Power

Assigned or assumed? Cooperation or conflict? How does power work or make itself felt? What are the consequences of its use? What is the relationship of power and shared leadership?

Issues – Individuals

Among practitioners of community organization the concern over issues or individuals, strategies or tactics, platform or program, has fostered a false dichotomy. It is our contention that this question, historically expressed in terms of "either/or," ought to more properly be viewed in terms of degrees. The community organization effort ought to blend these two foci and articulate a style of community organization which emphasizes the building up of relationships both with and between the indigenous as opposed to a focus of organizing professionals of various agencies for purposes of communication and coordination. Problems of articulation are more directly related to the economically depressed and conceivably they, rather than professionals, should be brought together for such purposes. The style of work for our community organizers has been to work from the bottom up with primarily a "people" as opposed to an "agency" focus and is in part akin to the first and third Newtonian laws which pertain to change and external force – a centrifugal force acting outward from the center and designed to come to grips with "consensual concerns." Such concerns arise out of an interaction between people and are not issues which have been arbitrarily imposed. Issues which have been imposed in such a fashion tend to make people intellectually dependent and not self-responsible. Were one to focus primarily or exclusively on the issues, one would obtain only a superficial view of the community, and people would be relegated to the background. The obvious danger in such an approach is that it is overly sterile and that while issues may be isolated (to mobilize around slum housing-abandoned housing) people remain very much uninvolved and uncommitted by not having participated in the decision-making process. A much more prevalent and subtle danger is that the "established" community organizations and agencies charged with articulating the issues may themselves be victims of the prevailing system. Thus what is articulated may well be change   enveloped in mediocrity.

The forte of community organizers has been to relate directly and intensively with people of the community with a view to bringing about constructive dissonance on an individual and group basis. It has been our experience that dissonance properly worked through and channeled can stimulate the involvement of people in community concerns. In working toward this goal, the worker is obliged to assume a good many roles. He functions as enabler, stimulator, arbitrator, educator, caseworker, counselor, organizer, and "social generalist." The worker functions as a communicator who serves as a bridge between different segments and elements of the community which without him, would tend to remain isolated from each other and alienated from the social welfare system. Regardless of which role the worker assumes at any point in time, his greatest tool is "talk." Relations which the worker builds up are with both the indigenous and the professional. At the professional level (police, school authorities, social welfare practitioners), workers have been obligated to form multiple relations with various personnel from the same agency. This serves not only to give the worker a more comprehensive view of any developing situation, but also acts as a safety valve should singular relations become strained. Through the vehicle of talk and "the conscious use of self," patterns or subsystems of communication begin to crystallize which represent the incipient stages of community organization.

Independence – Anonymity – Interdependence

In thinking about community organization activities, the worker in the field has to make a start somewhere. Traditionally, the "block" is conceived of as the "natural" unit for organizing local adults. Regardless of the starting point, the essence of organization is that it take place around the "relevant community." It is the experience of community organizers that initially the relevant community must largely be defined by those who are the objects of organization and not the organizer. Thus, the concept of relevant community runs the gamut from a single building to a block or a much larger geographical area. The usual pattern of operation is for the worker to organize or affix himself to a series of block clubs which may be viewed as "structure formations" and range in size from 8 to over 100 people. While there is a tendency for a practitioner new to the field to wallow in disenchantment at the "minimal" response of his organizational efforts and label those who fail to respond as "bad," the reality factors of the situation must be constantly held before him. The reality factor is that the eight wonders of the world will not erupt overnight after years of systematic exclusion from participation. The reality factor is that a participatory democracy places the onus of involvement on those to be organized as well as the organizer. Finally, the reality factor is that meetings (community, P.T.A., professional community organizations) held at noon or the early afternoon are in fact designed to exclude the disenfranchised. There is the further danger of the novice attempting to impose his need for structure on the group (officers, constitutions, by-laws). One consequence of this is to end up with elaborate structure and very little function. Thus, the worker must learn to tolerate ambiguity. Community organization by its very nature is ambiguous. Nothing is permanent or static.

While in the early stages of community organizing it may be tactically sound to work with a series of isolated structure formations, strategically one's effectiveness is limited and energies exhausted by building upon such narrow bases of support. Such singular supportive structures are much more likely to be victimized by stagnancy and atrophy. Most life styles follow a pattern of development which is characterized by ever-expanding relations. Movement is through a logical series of systems designed for socialization — home, school, the neighborhood, work, Chicago, and the larger society. It is one contention that such a centrifugal pattern of involvement is likewise imperative if indigenous groups are to be effective in articulating their concerns. A significant contribution to society is difficult, at best, if involvement of the masses is marginal. Consequently, the worker, after stabilizing and nurturing the independence of a series of structure formations, seeks an increase in group sophistication and effectiveness by expanding their individual concepts of community. Such an expansion makes possible a more realistic alignment with the political, economic, and social realities of the situation. In effect the worker brings about a more viable form of community organization through the amalgamation of a series of previously isolated groups. Such an organization can more effectively mediate the relations of the individual and the larger community. Through the pooling of energies, talents, and the inherent cross-fertilization of emotions, a broad base of support is built up that can deal with the causes of "situational dependency" as opposed to the symptoms. An attitudinal set for action, based on the cognitive dissonance generated within the group, is firmed up. Although the process of solidification brings into being an overarching body, the autonomy of the individual member groups must be maintained as they meet a variety of strategical and psychological needs. Interdependence is essentially mutual dependence which in turn means if we are to utilize other resources, somehow our own resources are also to be utilized by others.

Realities of Power

Power is a major element in any social system. Its exercise is a factor of obviously great importance in the workings of any organization and in community decision-making. It may be viewed in terms of individuals who exert it, situations within which it is exercised, and social systems within which it exists. It is the experience of community organizers that for maximum effect, power should be channeled through a social system that provides for continuous expression. Should it not be so channeled, it is likely to be diffused and its effects diluted. Power is not something that can be functionally assumed. It must be assigned and is generally assigned on the basis of social action skills and competencies as opposed to numbers of continually visible group participants. Further, it is our hunch that it is assigned as a result of action and interaction between the group, influential individuals, institutions, agencies, etc., both within and outside of the community and may be more a product of the imagination than a reality. Consequently, from time to time and in order to reinforce these delusions of grandeur, it may become necessary to mobilize large segments of the community. However, aside from the process involved in the assignment of power, which may be akin to the "self-fulfilling prophecy," it is important to bear in mind that its longevity will be determined by the way in which it is utilized. Ways in which it has been utilized and therefore concretized have been:

Conferences among policy makers and other influentials

Special task forces or committees that seek to influence the decision-making process

Interviews to mass media

Personal confrontations of persons to be influenced.

In closing let me suggest that power is neither good nor bad, but is essential to the operation of any social system. Values, judgements about it should be based on a realistic appreciation of the way in which it is used and the objectives toward which it is aimed.

In summation, community organization should not be viewed as an end in itself. Rather, it has been our experience that it is the beginning of an emotional rekindling, fired by the process of group catharsis and achievement, and the sophistication and success of the group brings about a strong identification and a sort of positive transference. Individual members of the group feel, in fact, that they can control those forces that help to shape their lives. Consequently there are a series of individual sortees to enhance the self. Many members have been encouraged to seek employment and others to continue their education formally or informally. In fact, community organization is a type of broadening or educational process wherein the group takes on the role of the academic institution, and the particular project being worked on, the curriculum. It is both socially rewarding and noncompetitive.

Finally, the communities in which we thrust ourselves are not disorganized. On the contrary they are tightly organized, but along different lines and for different purposes. One of the consequences of this type of organization was that the disenfranchised tended to function for the economic and psychological gratification of the larger community. Consequently, the charge of a community organizer is to change the relationship of situational dependency that existed between the target population and the larger community. It is our impression that some success can be attained.

PART 1

Politics and the Welfare System

1

The Welfare System:
Politics, Policies, Practices

EDWARD SCHWARTZ

One of the more pronounced and promising developments in the welfare field during the 1960's has been the rapidly growing consensus concerning the need for a fresh and thoroughgoing analysis of our social security system, and particularly our provisions for the treatment of mass poverty. The history of the public assistance programs in the twenty-five years following the passage of the Social Security Act in 1935 was characterized by the dogged and ill-fated struggle of the public welfare bureaucracy to administer a program which was designed to meet the conditions of the 1930's. The chief causes of poverty during the Great Depression were seen as interruption of earnings because of unemployment, and the loss of earnings because of old age. Reliance was placed on the social insurance programs to deal with these problems. All other causes or types of poverty were seen as of relatively transient and minor importance, and their treatment was relegated to the public assistance programs. These programs were to be aided financially by the federal government but their administration was to be in the hands of state governments. Federal controls on state administration of federal grants in all were quite limited in the Social Security Act of 1935 and were further weakened over the years in subsequent legislation and informally through the higgling and jiggling of the political process.

The intent of the founding fathers of the Social Security Act was that the public assistance program was to be a residual program and that with the extension of coverage of the social insurances that public assistance would be reduced to a program of modest proportions. Whether or not this analysis of the nature of poverty and of the potentialities of the social-insurance, income-maintenance approach was correct for the 1930's, it is now crystal clear that it was incorrect and in some respects irrelevant to the social scene of the 1940's, the 1950's, and the 1960's. Certainly, for more recent times poverty must be seen as a more complex and persistent phenomenon and its treatment objectives as differential, including not only income maintenance but, even more important, income creation and assurance.

During the decades of the 1940's and 1950's public interest in the treatment of poverty was spasmodic and almost universally negative, and was habitually expressed in the form of ancient ritualistic chants about high costs, failure to reduce the relief rolls, lax administration, chiseling, illegitimacy, malingering, and other alleged demoralized behavior – à la Newburgh. The reaction of the public assistance bureaucracy and particularly of state

13

and local welfare departments to this kind of vulgar criticism and pressure has been defensive, limited, monotonous, and self-defeating. Resources of manpower time and energy have gone first into tightening procedures for determining eligibility and amounts of assistance granted that is making these procedures increasingly more restrictive and punitive – and then into stereotyped management surveys and administrative reviews aimed at shifting organizational structure around and increasing operating efficiency by reducing costs at the margin through changes in procedure. Such efforts have characteristically started off in a flurry of activity and then have petered out in a whimper of manualizing, moralizing, and staff turnover.

The 1957 and 1962 amendments, widely heralded as the most important changes in the public assistance titles of the Social Security Act, focused not on the key problems of lack of adequacy, equity, or dignity in the administration of financial assistance but rather on largely unrealistic goals for the expansion of so-called rehabilitative services – and these legislative proposals were supported with promises, since proved to be unfounded, that they would produce significant reductions in the assistance rolls. This kind of emphasis on service may or may not have represented frustration at the federal level with the persistent inadequacies, inequities, and disgraces in the administration of financial assistance in the various state and local welfare departments, but in any event the recent federal legislation did little to deal with the central issue of providing enough income to the destitute and the poor to lift them out of poverty.

During the last five years and for the first time in almost three decades, a dialogue has begun concerned with ways of designing a system which would assure enough income to every person in this country to lift him above the poverty line. For the first time since the early 1930's we have widespread public discussion of methods for improving the economic position of the poor and recommendations being made by influential bodies to those in high places calling for study and reappraisal of the social security system and especially the treatment of mass poverty. Among the names best known to the informed public of those connected directly or indirectly with the resurgence of interest in this subject are John Galbraith, who pointed out that this is an affluent society; Michael Harrington, who pointed out that despite our unprecedented   affluency, mass poverty still exists;   Robert Theobald, who pointed out that the market system alone can no longer be relied upon to meet the totality of human economic need; and Milton Friedman, who popularized the suggestion that the federal income tax system can be utilized as a mechanism for direct payment of benefits, as well as for collecting taxes.

A universal federally guaranteed minimum income policy and a program to implement it are urgently necessary now. Our present two-deck social security system, consisting of social insurance and public assistance, should be expanded to become a three-deck system. The top layer would consist of the present social insurance programs. The new middle layer would be a federally administered Family Security Benefit program that would guarantee the difference between what a person's income would otherwise be and the financial requirements of his family and himself as indicated by the national minimum-income schedules. Federal administration of a Family Security

Benefit program would be designed to meet the objective of adequacy, comprehensiveness, and equity of payment in the meeting of financial need. The use of the Internal Revenue System as an administrative device is suggested to insure dignity and equity in treatment as well as efficiency in administration.

The bottom deck of the social security system would be a program of last resort to provide financial assistance to those found to be unable to manage on their guaranteed minimum income because of catastrophes or personal incapacities. The persons to be assisted by this program would be numbered in the thousands rather than in the millions as under the present public assistance program. In effect, the present public assistance program would be reduced to the scope originally contemplated by the framers of the Social Security Act.

Arguments in opposition to the proposal for a federally guaranteed minimum income center around the work issue – that is, the argument that if people are assured enough money to live on, their incentive or motivation to work will be destroyed or seriously weakened and that this will be ruinous to the economy and demoralizing to the individuals involved.

The argument that a federally guaranteed minimum income would weaken work incentives is essentially not an argument against a particular proposal but against any proposal providing adequate assistance. Karl deSchweinitz has pointed out that the function of the English Poor Law was not to help the poor but rather to force them to work. This was attempted through the imposition of the principle of less eligibility; that is, that relief payments must be less than the lowest wages, and through other deterrents so brutal and degrading as to make any employment no matter how dangerous, dull, fatiguing, and ill-paid seem preferable to undergoing the rigors of the classic means test.

The charge that manpower needed for production of goods and services would be lost if the needs of people are met other than through their own earnings has been leveled throughout the centuries not only against improving the adequacy of financial assistance but also against many other proposals for improving the condition of the poor. For example the nineteenth-century movement in this country for universal education through a free public school system was met with the question, "If the education of his children is assured would not a man's incentive to work be weakened?" If this kind of argumentative question directed against attempts to improve the condition of lower economic groups had any relevancy in the nineteenth century when the demand for common labor to produce the necessities of life was high, it certainly has less today when common unskilled labor tends to become a drug on the market.

The pertinent questions that have to be asked today about the nature of the allged work disincentives involved in an adequate income-maintenance system are as follows:

1) What are the values and the specific objectives behind the demand for negative work sanctions and enforced labor?

2) Would a significantly large proportion of the labor force essential to the economy be vulnerable to the disincentives produced by a guarantee of income just above the poverty line? How does the value or benefit of the goods thus lost to production compare with the social and human costs of policing their production? To what extent does the withholding of needed income from poor families result in forcing the earnings of the needed income? To what extent does it result in deprivation and the handicapping of children and other innocent parties?

3) Are we concerned with the societal need for labor or with the morals and the mental health of the work-shy individual? If we can validly insist that persons who are able to work should do so either because of the socioeconomic necessity or the moral imperative or both, then why do we not find and apply sanctions against all persons who do not work, whether thay are rich or poor? Or do we believe that the rigorous, stern tenets of the Protestant work ethic should apply only to the poor?

The approach to the work question through negative sanctions appears to be inevitable accompaniment of the so-called residual view of social welfare — the view that the function of social welfare is to patch up rents and tears in the social fabric. The institutional view on the other hand is that social welfare has a unique function to perform in enhancing the relationship among people and between people and their environment. The residual view in the area that we are discussing focuses on the treatment of the problems of hard-core families, desertion, illegitimacy, malingering, and chiseling. The functional view of social welfare focuses on ways of meeting the needs of persons. The institutional or functional purpose of an income assurance program is to meet the basic financial needs of persons for food, clothing, shelter, and those amenities of life which make it possible to enjoy the society of one's fellows. Maslow's theory of the hierarchy of need holds that basic primary needs must be met before the individual can mobilize his strength to seek the satisfaction of higher level needs. Basic adequate income must be assured before the individual can take advantage of better education, health and welfare services, and better employment opportunities — and certainly before he can participate in planning for the general betterment of his community.

JOHN BALLEW

There are, I am certain, as many opinions on the subject assigned to me today as there are persons in this room. I hope, and I expect, that my remarks will be provocative for I have formulated them without the usual qualifications and have presented opposing views at their extreme. I have done this in the hope that it will give substance to your deliberations during the next two days.

I express them as my personal views and opinions and not as a policy statement of the Cook County Department of Public Aid or of public welfare in general. As far as particular goals and policies are concerned, I can only refer you to the well-defined statements of the American Public Welfare Association.

We are living at a time of critical decision for public welfare in the United States. Programs, policies, and plans of the past thirty years are being measured with unprecedented severity against the urgent social problems of today. Both conscious evaluation by informed and influential people, as well as the more general impressions gained by the public at large, have led to harsh judgments about the welfare system. Some of this criticism has reached the state of proposals to abolish the entire welfare structure and replace it with some other mechanism for dealing with poverty. There are some, for instance, who believe that the case for a negative income tax or some sort of guaranteed minimum income is a statement of the case against public welfare. It is not, and in fact such proposed changes assume the continued existence of that which welfare wishes to eliminate and which society should eliminate: poverty.

It is the goal of public welfare to ensure the creation of conditions that will provide all persons with an equal opportunity for self-realization and self-support while, at the same time, ensuring him a decent standard of living. The guaranteed minimum income, on the other hand, puts the cart before the horse; it assumes that poverty must become an accepted and hence subsidized way of life for a large proportion of the American population rather than a reducible evil. It is defeatist about our ability to prevent rather than alleviate most forms of poverty.

To all too many people and to these people poverty seems to mean merely the absence of money. This is a definition influenced, perhaps, by the belief in American society that if money is lacking, work and determination will provide it, and that in our affluent society no one need starve. But it must also be remembered that poverty is not merely a question of food, or of money, or of determination. We would like to think so because then we could ignore it or appropriate it out of existence. A Chicago newspaper in a recent editorial discussing the War on Poverty spoke directly to this point:

> If "poverty" is merely the condition of an economic income below a certain level, then, of course, poverty could be abolished by 1976 – or by the end of 1966, for that matter – either by changing the definition so that it applies to nobody or by giving everybody enough money to meet the minimum conditions.

> But no problem that can be solved by playing with words is real; and no real problem that can be solved merely by appropriating money is very deep. And poverty is both real and deep.

> The poverty that matters is not of the pocketbook but of the mind and the spirit. It is the lack of human, social, and economic qualities and skills that are necessary for living a life that is satisfying to one's self and useful to others.

Thus poverty deprives the individual not only of material comforts but also of human dignity and fulfillment. Its causes are much more complex, and its cure requires more than merely a check or the creation of one or two programs of training and retraining. It must be realized that, because of the growing complexity of modern society, the disadvantaged, in particular, more and more lose the very ability to make choices, to be responsible, to know what must be done, and to take action. In short, poverty has today become a complex interlocking set of circumstances, caused by and in turn reinforcing each other, that combine to keep the individual without money, without help, without hope, without work. It can truly be said that today those people are poor who can least afford it. They can least afford it because modern technological changes combined with inequality of opportunity and cultural and educational isolation affect those least capable of adjusting and defending themselves. It is this isolation and this defenselessness that must be understood.

It cannot be emphasized often enough that people do not remain in poverty through an act of will; they remain in poverty through a lack of education, of training and of knowledge in the demands of our modern urban society. People do not merely help themselves; they must frequently be helped to help themselves. The fact that people cannot lift themselves by their own bootstraps is a fact that must be explained again and again. Unemployment compensation or, where that is unavailable, general assistance may be all that a man may need when he is between jobs; but a man whose only skill is no longer needed, needs more than money – he needs a new skill. The mother and family in a home without a husband and father will need money to feed, clothe, and house themselves. But this same mother will also need to learn the facts of urban living if she comes from a rural area, she will need to learn the fundamentals of good housekeeping if she has never been taught these, and, in fact, she will often need to be taught some fundamental educational skills if she is to be the help and mentor of her own children who are in school.

In short, public welfare is not a question of money alone; it is not a question of some minimum level. It is not a simple question of alleviation of need, but rather the elimination of the need. A check is not enough and a guaranteed annual income will not solve the problems of poverty and of the poor. Each person has a right to the necessities of life, but he also must have the necessary knowledge and skills that will make that life fruitful and meaningful.

In order to appreciate this fully, it is necessary that we realize the magnitude and complexity of the problems of welfare today, that we understand the nature of those in need of assistance and, at the same time, the need for improvement and change, rather than the simplified approach of elimination and replacement.

The problems to be faced today can be seen here in Cook County as in any other urban area. As the acting director of the Cook County Department of Public Aid, I was responsible, during the month of November 1966, for a program serving some 249,326 persons in 94,563 families and spending in assistance some $15,665,554. In carrying out this program the Department employes 4,914 persons, the vast majority of whom are directly concerned with the needs of the recipients. But it is also not the responsibility of the Cook County Department of Public Aid merely to administer the spending of these huge sums; rather it is its responsibility to help these people help themselves and return them to a productive and fruitful role in society. Thus, the Department during the month of November had 10,852 persons enrolled in special education and training programs. This included 2,978 in the basic literacy program, 2,051 in the high school program, 315 in the special training programs, 1,107 in the skill maintenance and development program, 903 in training under the terms of the Manpower Development and Training Act, 3,498 enrolled in the counseling and placement program, and 572 enrolled in the home economics and family improvement programs.

What are the needs of these families? These needs can best be seen in the nature of those receiving assistance. Of the 249,326 persons receiving assistance 40,724 were receiving either old age assistance, blind assistance, or disability assistance. I do not believe that it is the goal or desire of the citizens of Illinois to force the aged, the blind, or the disabled into work that they cannot do; although it is the goal of the Cook County Department of Public Aid to give them the assistance and training and education necessary to lead a fuller and happer life.

In addition to these there were 171,245 persons in 36,261 families receiving Aid to Dependent Children assistance. These families consist of mothers raising an average of three to four children each. The question of their employment is one that totally depends upon the circumstances of the case. How old are the children? Are they in school? Can proper day care be found? This is not to say that mothers should not work for they do in modern American society. But if there is any doubt, the welfare of the children must have first consideration. But this is also not to say that these mothers should not be given needed education and needed training. Such education and such training are a part of her role as mother and her role as mentor for her children.

Of the remaining cases there were 9,067 persons in 1,287 families receiving Aid to Dependent Children of Unemployed Parents Assistance. In this group the father is present and these 1,287 men represent a group, in many cases, with high employment potential. And finally, there were 28,290 persons in 16,291 cases receiving general assistance. These 16,291 cases are also generally employable. So, we have a maximum of 17,000 to 18,000 employable men or women. But, they are persons who are potentially employable; their ultimate employment depends primarily upon the continuation and expansion of needed education and training programs; it does not depend merely upon money.

This then is the picture of those in need of welfare today, and a picture that implicitly states the true goals of public welfare, and gives the true perspective on public welfare.

I believe that I can quite briefly summarize these goals and I shall summarize them in terms of a dichotomy between what some have called for and what I am calling for.

First of all I am not in favor of a guaranteed annual income. I am in favor of a guaranteed job, and the guaranteed education and training to prepare for that job. If necessary, I am in favor of a public works program to provide those jobs. I am in favor of an adequate wage for everyone who works and, where needed, a system of family grants to aid the parent in the early expenses of raising his children.

I am not in favor of the automatic issuance of checks by some machine without consideration for those needs that exist beyond money. We do not exist by checks alone. I am in favor of a program of welfare that combines financial assistance with social services, with health services, with education, with training, and with counseling and guidance where needed. I am in favor of a unified program of welfare to which the individual and family, with all their complex problems, can turn as a single source for help.

I am not in favor of a minimum guaranteed income, for that assumes that poverty must become an accepted and hence subsidized way of life and that millions of Americans must settle for a minimum level of living dependent for its financing on the more affluent majority. I am in favor of a program of welfare that will attempt to eliminate poverty. I am in favor of an adequate program of social insurance benefits which is an earned but deferred return on labor which replaces earnings lost by reason of old age retirement, sickness, disability, and motherhood, vacation periods, premature death of the family breadwinner, and unemployment. Such a system if adequate and broad enough would care for the aged, the blind, the lame, the widow, and the orphaned child and would be something received as an adequate right and not a minimum gift.

And finally, where all else fails, I am for a system of public welfare based upon the concept of individual rights and not a system based upon a privilege bestowed by society. Life itself is the first human right and life is not given by society. This recognition of help as a right implies a revamping of the administrative structure but not its replacement. It implies the elimination of existing artificial barriers of categories and abolishing such criteria as age, residence, employability, family composition, relatives' responsibility, and the like. In short, there should be a simple national program based solely upon need. This concept of needs and rights also implies a much-needed simplification of administration beginning at that point at which the person first comes for help: the application procedure. The affidavit should be used, thus eliminating the degradation of a lengthy investigation. It also implies maximum speed and efficiency in administrative actions.

These are but a few of the most obvious needs and the most obvious areas for improvement. They are not new. Those in public welfare have called for them for many years. Most recently the Advisory Council on Public Welfare summarized these needs and improvements in a report entitled "Having the Power, We Have the Duty."

It is easy to be a critic. It is something else to administer a vast and complex program that has grown slowly over the years from the repressive concepts of the early poor laws and poor houses to the present recognition that the citizen has the right to help from his nation, his state and his fellow citizens. History — short of the biblical miracles — has never provided a one-stroke solution for a pervasive social problem. In the words of an ancient Chinese proverb: "A journey of a thousand miles is made one step at a time." Many of these first steps along the road to the Great Society have already been made by public welfare. It is by a further accretion of such steps that poverty, ignorance, and social maladjustment can be banished. Clearly, the best way to achieve the good society is to prevent need before it occurs. This means persisting in our efforts to give needy citizens the means of self-support as well as adequate physical maintenance. Only on the solid ground of educational improvement and social integretion can a program to eliminate poverty succeed. These are the politics of public welfare, the policies of public welfare, and the procedures of public welfare.

MATTHEW SCHERER

I. What is the Cook County Department of Public Aid?

It is a system of distributing money to the unemployable and the employed. It has criteria to determine which category an applicant falls in. According to its stated policies, it provides services to retain and find employment for those considered employable; and it provides supportive and rehabilitative services for those considered unemployable, to increase their potential for future self-support.

Unfortunately, the Welfare System is many other things.

1) It is a system that does not trust the client's word or have faith in his ability to lead his own adult life.

2) It is a system that makes its staff members into verifiers and investigators — a system whose administrative procedures make it extremely difficult to provide real social work services.

3) It is a system whose staff is poorly paid and whose clerical help is so underpaid that many of them are themselves recipients of aid or eligible for food stamps and free medical care under the MA-NG program.

4) It is a system many of whose training programs prepare people for jobs such as nurses aides and domestic help, jobs whose low pay does not free people from dependency on the welfare system and which reinforces society's stereotypes of Negroes. (In Chicago, 85% of the Department of Public Aid's clients are Negro.)

5) It is a system that maintains its clients on grants below the poverty level.

6) It is a system whose low rent ceilings for clients only perpetuate slum conditions and make it impossible for clients to find adequate housing.

7) It is a system that does not provide any incentive to obtain employment since there are no adequate provisions for income exemptions. A family who receives any assistance at all to supplement their wages cannot save any money. The system perpetuates their state of poverty. The budget of a family where the husband is employed is the same as the budget of an ADC family.

8) And it is a system that perpetuates dependency.

The welfare system is founded on the assumption that if a person is unemployed, it is somehow his fault. There is a moral stigma attached to being on welfare. Although it is a right guaranteed by law, it is administered as a privilege. This mistrust of the welfare recipient is imbedded in the State Public Aid Code which makes it clear that if the client does not do what the Department of Public Aid wants him to, his assistance must be stopped.

The present assumption of the CCDPA that if someone is able-bodied he should be working is often no longer valid. The Department of Public Aid does not yet seem to realize that people are becoming more superfluous in the area of production of goods and that radically new skills are required; and that people may be out of work because there is literally no work for them to do.

Can a Department of Public Aid really provide sophisticated training programs with long range social services to those for whom it now provides unskilled, underpaid jobs?

These are some of the features of the CCDPA welfare system. It is a system in which the staff though told to be professional, cannot relate professionally or humanely to the clients, and in which the clients are mistrusted, inadequately supported, and poorly serviced.

Two statistics are pertinant here, reflecting the gross deficiencies of the present welfare system. One is that the turnover rate of personnel in any year is over 50%. The other is that 56.3% of general assistance applications are reapplications.

II.   The Independent Union of Public Aid Employees

The IUPAE was organized as a direct response to these realities of the Department of Public Aid. It was organized to provide adequate salaries and increments, social security, and other related fringe benefits, and it was organized so that it could bring the changes to the welfare system necessary to provide adequate professional services to the clients.

We in the IUPAE are frustrated professionals. When the agency trains new personnel, it teaches them to think of themselves as social workers, as professionals — teaches them to plan with the client, to understand his needs, and to provide services for him. Since the Economic Opportunity Act of 1964 and the national drive for more social workers, the status of the social worker has increased. So it is easy to expect that the position of caseworker will be a professional one.

Once immersed in the realities of working in the Department of Public Aid, however, it becomes very difficult to fulfill these professional aspirations. Too often assistance is delayed or stopped when financial and social needs still exist. Those who cannot work around this or who balk at the complex paperwork or unnecessary demands to "prove the client's eligibility" before services can be provided represent a large proportion of those who leave the agency every year. Last October, over 20% of the caseloads had no caseworkers.

How can any continuity of services to clients be maintained under such conditions? When the staff complains and suggests changes, they are ignored. The IUPAE is the one organization for the staff of the CCDPA where the employees' professional concern can be voiced, and through which the much needed changes can be brought about.

What are the changes the IUPAE wants to bring about within the present welfare system?

The IUPAE'S contract proposals include the following demands, whose effect will be (1) to decentralize the administration of assistance, to give the caseworker and his supervisor more power to administer assistance, and thereby to provide speedier services to clients and (2) to make automatic those provisions that now are discretionary and thus unequally provided to the clients.

In the latter category, the contract calls for automatic additional clothing allowances twice a year to all clients, an up-to-date housing list for the clients, and a list of available doctors and dentists. The IUPAE also asks the support payments from a husband or wife or putative father to his or her family be made directly to the agency so that even if the support payments are not made promptly or in full, the family will continue to receive full assistance.

In the first category, the contract calls for emergency checks to be issued from the district office on the same day the client applies for them, with only the approval of the supervising caseworker being necessary. Currently no emergency currency can be issued in the district office, and the assistant district office supervisor must approve any issuance of emergency assistance.

The IUPAE is also proposing that a community organizer be assigned to each district office and that a trained group worker be assigned to every fifteen caseloads.

To ease the burden of coping with paperwork while trying to provide service, the union is also demanding the immediate instituting of a unit clerk system, and the maintenance of no more than sixty cases (by the HEW standard) to each worker instead of the eighty to ninety they now have.

Also, the union contract is calling on the CCDPA to formally acknowledge the right of client groups to represent the client from and including the day of initial application.

III. Clients and Welfare Unions

Those features of the welfare system that caused the formation of the IUPAE operate in a similar manner on the client. Many client groups and welfare unions have been organized, such as WSO, JOIN, and KOCO, to organize and represent the welfare recipient.

Because the IUPAE sees the employees of the CCDPA as being treated by the welfare system in as disparaging a manner as the clients, the IUPAE feels it has close ideological ties with client groups and has a real concern for the position of the client within the welfare system. The IUPAE has prepared a recipients' handbook, which we hope can be printed very soon, which states explicitly the rights and obligations a client has under the present system of welfare. We hope that the welfare unions and community organizations will distribute them and use them; for these organizations are in the best position to understand and interpret the agency's rules and regulations to the clients in the most meaningful manner possible.

IV. Strike

Before even the modest proposals the union is presenting will be agreed to, it is almost inevitable that we will have to go on strike again. A strike by the IUPAE alone, however, while perhaps achieving some benefits for the clients, would not fundamentally affect the position of the client with respect to the agency. He may be dealt with more considerately, but basically control over his life would still reside with the agency.

In a strike, only a coalition of client groups and the IUPAE can hope to lead to any sort of redistribution of power within the Department of Public Aid that will mean more autonomy and control over the decisions that affect the client and the employee.

It is my hope that such a coalition of forces will hasten the day when a true guaranteed income is a reality and when we all will be able to develop as individuals fully and freely.

LEONTINE LEMON

The Public Assistance Program is governed by laws – state and federal – which are translated into policy by the Illinois Public Aid Department. The state law provides that in counties of over 500,000 the public assistance program will be administered by the County Department of Public Aid under the supervision of the State Department of Public Aid. Thus, the employee in the Cook County Department of Public Aid finds himself a county employee, subject also to laws and policies set by the state.

For example, we participate in the Cook County Employees' Annuity Fund. Our vacations, holidays, sick leave, and working hours are set by the Cook County Board of Commissioners. Our office hours and the policies of the programs under which we work are set by the State Department of Public Aid. Our salaries and staff allocation are set by the State Department of Public Aid in conjunction with the State Department of Personnel. The laws which govern the program, the retirement system, and the appropriations for grants and administration are made by the state legislature. Furthermore, the federal Health, Education, and Welfare Department has authority in setting the standards for qualification for federal funds. So, if you think we are mixed up, maybe now you understand why.

Many problems beset our staff, and, as you can see, the level at which a problem can be resolved may involve more than one agency. Adequate salary levels, and a fair and equitable means of moving within that salary level, are problems that have been with us for many years. At the present time, inequities within and between classifications are our greatest grievances in the salary area.

Probably the biggest frustration to our staff is the red tape and paper work which interferes with getting things done. We have fragmented the casework job to such an extent that frequently the left hand does not know what the right hand is doing. For example, to provide a bed for a client, three approvals are needed – the caseworker, the supervising case-worker, and the assistant supervisor. Until recently we also required the approval of a home economist at the central office level. A supervising caseworker said recently, "In adjusting budgets and setting up assistance, a caseworker can issue thousands of dollars by just signing her name, but she can't authorize an eight-dollar bed even if she has seen the mattress setting on the floor."

The amount of paper work required to take an action is fantastic. I brought with me a bulletin on change of address and transfer procedures. There are twelve pages which describe how you change an address or trans-fer a case. At the end is a list of the *twenty-six* forms referred to in the bulletin.

Since we have become mechanized – the machines are in Springfield – we have been plagued with IBM cards. Every time we turn around, we have another set. We are told to know policy, what is behind the making of policy, and that we should never say "it is just policy." I heartily agree with this concept. However, policies and procedures change so fast that it is difficult, if not impossible, for staff to keep up with the changes. In 1966, ninety-two official bulletins were issued by the State Department of Public Aid and twenty bulletins by the Cook County Department of Public Aid. Approximately the same number of memoranda was issued by the two departments, and this does not include manual releases and interoffice memoranda.

I brought with me one of the ninety-two bulletins issued by the state in 1966, O.B. 66.71, which will give an idea of the volume of reading re-quired. This consists of 109 pages of procedure and exhibits. Another bul-letin, O.B. 65.73, related to the Medical Assistance Program. It consisted of forty-three pages. It was subsequently supplemented by seven releases and amended by three between the date of issue, December 5, 1965, and June 14, 1966. This document became obsolete on September 21, 1966 and was replaced by a manual section of thirty-one pages.

We employees are as concerned about our public image as the administra-tion, if not from a standpoint of dedication to the job or individual status, then from a purely economic standpoint. How can we ask for more salary if the community and those empowered to increase salaries feel we are not worth what we are presently receiving? If you, the community, find a work-er to be abrupt, impolite, or offensive, and you project this onto all our staff, then we all stand indicted.

We are as concerned about that worker as you are, but before you pass judgement, try to decide if you or the workers are being unreasonable. The most honest answer a new worker can give you is, "I do not know, I will have to talk to my supervisor." Give the worker the opportunity to give you a correct and considered opinion. Do not demand from the worker what you know he cannot give. We are frequently contacted by representatives of elected officials who decry a restrictive policy when it affects a constituent, yet they have participated in instituting the legislation on which that policy is based. I say to them, "I agree with you. This is a bad law. But you make the laws; all I do is carry them out. I suggest that you point out to your fellow lawmakers how this affects your constituents so that the law can be changed. This is your responsibility." If this is a local official who says he is not in the position to make laws affecting our program, I point out that he is in close contact with legislators who are.

Rent ceilings set at the time of the last General Assembly are still in force and are completely unrealistic in the city of Chicago. The policies regarding relative responsibility, stepfathers, and employed children in ADC families require changes. The present appeal procedure is anything but a fair hearing as required in the federal law. The responsibility for changing these and other restrictive policies rests not only with us but with you because until there is community concern, there will be no change.

Recently much has been heard about social workers organizing public assistance clients. Everyone today is seeking answers to our social problems, but we cannot say that we have the answers simply because we are social workers. I would like to know what qualifies the social worker to organize the client group when, in all these years, we have not been able to organize ourselves. Let's lay our cards on the table. When we talk about public assistance clients, we are talking about Negroes, since the large majority of persons on assistance are Negro. I feel that the Negro today is suspicious of those who want to do "for" him. People have been doing "for" us for many, many years, and we have found that we are done "to" more than we are done "for." I think what we are interested in is the freedom to make our own decisions. If social workers really want to help people on public assistance, then I suggest they help in those areas that will develop skill and confidence in decision making.

EDWARD SCHWARTZ

I suggested that there were three major factors underlying the organization and structure of our present public assistance system, the system which we currently use to treat, rather than to prevent or cure, mass poverty. We have heard a rather dramatic demonstration of the difference between the overt goals of an organization as very forcibly and eloquently presented by Mr. Ballew, and the latent goals the actual behavior of an organization, as described by the two union representatives. The reference to the paper work, to the incredible amount of detail that workers are presumed to master while taking responsibility for rehabilitating a large case load, seems to be due to the basically poor design of the public assistance system. The system is at fault. There is no use looking for devils in this set-up – it is not the administrator and it is not the workers. It is the system.

My proposal is for each state and the state would have to accept it in order to receive financial assistance from the federal government. The federal government would also make up the difference between what the states are now spending and what the liberalized program would cost. I think we would all be in favor of this. I would be in favor of it if it were the best we could get, but I do not think it is.

One of the fatal difficulties in the proposal is that it is still necessary for a state to submit a plan. The federal government under this proposal could not absolutely guarantee a minimum income to everyone in this country because it would be necessary for the state to take the initiative and submit the plan. We tend to rely on the fact that it would be to the financial advantage of the states to do this. But I am suggesting that states like individuals, to quote Mr. Ballew, do not live by bread alone. Some states place certain values, such as the value of controlling their minority populations, above money. So if the federal government established adequate standards of assistance throughout the country, there is no assurance that the southern states, for example, would submit the plan to be approved by the federal government.

I do not think that this is a radical consideration. The history of the passage of the Social Security Act indicates that the very limited control placed with the federal government in the first instance was not accidental. It was the result of a compromise between southern reactionary members of the Democratic party and the Roosevelt administration. The southern Democrats supported the social insurance features of the Social Security Act in return for maintaining state control of public assistance. In our public assistance systems, we are suffering from – and I suggest that what we will continue to suffer from – state and local control.

2

Politics and the Great Society

THEODORE LOWI

This is an attempt to evaluate the Great Society in its most spectacular manifestation – the War on Poverty. I feel warranted in the attempt despite the protestations of official and unofficial personnel that it is too early for evaluation. I think now is the time to judge it philosophically and as a question of general public policy. If we wait for the long run, either most of us will not be around, or the program will have become too committed and bureaucratized to allow for any options. I think it is part of the role of good citizenship to act prematurely; in that sense, I will try to act as a good citizen.

Let me get defenses up right at the beginning. My evaluation ends on an extremely negative note, so negative that it makes me wonder why so many good liberals – especially members of the Negro movement – could be so in favor of this program. It is all the more incredible to me that they are also willing to salvage it with not $1.8 but $18, and $28, or $38 billion or whatever the situation is. This kind of sentiment calls for evaluation.

I will briefly review my impression of the poverty program in five cities. For the data I wish to thank my colleagues, Professors J. David Greenstone, Paul Peterson, and some of their students, as well as other scholars from other parts of the country. Of course, they do not necessarily agree with my interpretation of their data.

First, the New York City Community Action Program. It has turned out to be largely a fight for recognition among groups the government helped to create in some instances. It has been primarily a fight for formal recognition and access ending in widespread battles to create peace. The result is maximum participation by all kinds of leadership, and modest appropriations of funds to the poor. A real "culture of poverty" may be in the making.

Chicago, a second illustration, has a poverty program that is the extreme contrast of New York's. Here there has been maximum appropriation of funds – on the average two or three times as much per capita as in New York. However, there has been minimum feasible participation. Furthermore, though there has not been a sense of futility, because monies do seem to get around, there has been a sense of the program's illegitimacy because, in maximizing its administration, there has been a minimum espousal of the values contained in the federal legislation.

I gather that in Philadelphia the situation is between the other two, somewhat closer to that of Chicago. That is, there has been some appropriation and some participation. However, it seems only to combine the worst features of New York *and* Chicago. To a great extent there has been a sense of the lack of the program's legitimacy, due to the amount of discretion exercised at the center. But there is also a sense of futility as to the degree to which individuals can .participate directly. Thus, Philadelphia's is the program with the most direct participation by individual members of the poverty class; yet when it comes to voting, only two to three percent at the most turn out. To me this is an indication of their sense of futility, not of their ignorance, alienation, or anything else. The connection between representation, taxation, and appropriation seems, to say the least, not entirely established. There is also evidence that the program has mainly served the "representatives" and their friends and families.

In Los Angeles, a city of extremes in all respects, and one which obviously had the greatest need, there was very, very low appropriation of federal funds. After the Watts demonstrations, the appropriations increased, in an interesting and rather spectacular expression of representation. However, it appears that very little actual representation has taken place with the increase of funds. It is a bit like chasing one's tail. After Watts, increases of federal funds appear as blood money, or the homage that vice pays to virtue, because the *sympatico* of the program was destroyed. Thus, any response the government makes seems to be interpreted as buying off rather than as an instrumental part of the program. It became a case of "damned if you do and damned if you don't."

The Syracuse program, last mentioned here, was actually the first instance in which efforts were clearly made to exercise discretionary appropriation of welfare. In other words, individuals were empowered to decide on the spot where the money should go and for what purposes. It was in Syracuse where we first began to learn the difference between the "poverty program" and the old-fashioned welfare program where assistance is simply open to a class of people without regard to individual variation. It seems to prove, better than any of these other cities, that a poverty program, a Great Society concept, can create inconsistencies between the poor and the power structure that did not exist before and that are not necessarily natural. In a sense it created a conflict in the mayor's mind about how he should work. Previously, through voting and the normal forms of political vulnerability, conflicts had existed on some occasions; but the poor and the powerful are not necessarily on opposite sides. It depended on who the powerful were. The new program tended to create permanent conflict of interest where it did not exist before.

Admitting some oversimplifications if not outright misrepresentation, I am trying to evaluate a poverty program that is a new kind of welfare state. It is not a welfare state based on the routine and bureaucratic giving of funds to whoever fits a certain class. The War on Poverty, it is clear, is a new concept which intends to add the factor of discretion to the welfare concept. But more. It will allow people to adminster those particular amounts of money *to themselves*. As far as I am concerned, an effort to do this with the welfare program has resulted in one of two alternative consequences, or perhaps in both together.

On the one hand, it has tended to encourage cynicism and a sense of illegitimacy toward public objects. For instance, in Chicago, a sense of illegitimacy is felt, not only by the recipients and the nonrecipients, but also by those of us observers who fortunately do not have to depend on these funds. There is cynicism because the whole thing depends on the strength of the congressional delegation, and because access depends on who you know rather than what you need. To me this sense of cynicism tends to get associated with almost any totally discretionary program. On the other hand, it can be an exercise in futility. In establishing mass participation and allowing for discretion, you simply reduce the flow of funds until such time as everybody can live with others in peace. Instead, they go to pieces in stalemate and frustration.

I would like briefly to evaluate some of the values and characteristics that underlie this new welfare concept and seem to make these outcomes almost inevitable. Then I will try to suggest some of the alternatives the Great Society administration might consider.

The problem is the result of trying to do more with welfare than it can do. The War on Poverty is like trying to stuff four pounds of corn in a three pound bag. It just will not go. It is characteristic of Americans to try to make one kind of public policy serve several functions. Rather than have a national plan, we take the income tax and try to encourage industry by tax rebates. In other words, we try to get the revenue system to serve as incentive as well as revenue system.

In like fashion, the welfare program was taken over to serve more than simply the alleviation of poverty. In the 1930's it was created to make the march to the grave a bit more comfortable for those who are uncomfortable. That's what welfare is, has always been, and always will be. Classic welfare works through the routinization of aid, and it tends to work toward those who do not have anything. Make a *discretionary service* program out of it and you are likely to end up with neither welfare nor service. Ironically you are most likely to end up with an extremely conservative force. It will tend to be conservative in the sense that it does not change the injustices that exist in our society nor create the capacity for others to change those injustices. It only diverts attention from the real problem.

In other words, the problem of the 1960's is a problem of injustice to Negroes. To think that it sounds more egalitarian to say you are responding to it by eliminating poverty is nonsense. You are answering injustice not with justice but with indemnification. It starts by taking a poverty program and then pretending that the ill is not race but poverty. It ends up being conservative in the sense that it creates no institutional capacity for change to take place, because poverty will always be with us. You cannot get rid of the poor. You can elevate the poor, you can artificially and arbitrarily take one or another poor person and say "from now on we will fix it so you won't be poor anymore"; but you cannot eliminate the poor. It is a relative phenomenon. The poor exist as long as the rich do. Furthermore, we require the poor; Gilbert and Sullivan had the right idea: "If everybody is somebody, then nobody is anybody." Whatever the reasons, of preference or of definition, you cannot get rid of the poor.

The issue is poverty only insofar as it makes the march to the grave more comfortable. The new issue of the 1960's is not poverty; it is injustice; and it is attacked by *changing the rules so that poverty is a random rather than a nonrandom thing.* Poverty in the United States is unjust because it is not random. Poverty has to become a universe for the cruel, the lazy, the stupid, the irresponsible, and the accidental. Other characteristics were not meant to be punished or sloughed aside by the system. Just a glance at the racial composition of the poor will tell you what I mean.

Certain features of our poverty program tend to be additionally conservative, therefore. While it will fail to eliminate the poor it will further block change by falsely focusing the attention of responsible people interested in social change. It is no coincidence that the demand for civil rights has declined as the demand for poverty money has increased. One cause is deserted for the other. The poverty program will further demoralize and block change because of its pattern of implementation. When you set up a poverty program run by private groups, certain groups must be recognized for purposes of official representation. In so doing the emergence of other groups tends to be discouraged. We are impressed by the number of groups that the organizers are helping to bring about. However, once the situation becomes stabilized, the groups that get official recognition will tend, by their existence, to discourage the emergence of new groups representing new values. As far as I am concerned it is legitimate to compare an officially recognized group to a gang – take the Blackstone Rangers or any other. The gang goes to a child and says, "You belong to my gang or we will beat your head in." Ten years from now when the poverty program is stabilized and the groups have been organized, the government will say, "We recognize you." Then the leader of that group says, "Now we are official." Then he goes to community residents and says, "If you do not belong to our group, you won't have any access. Your lives, your community activity will not pay off as well as if you stay with our group." Social relationships tend to congeal at whatever level and in whatever lines were established during the first round of organizing activities. This differs from the Blackstone Rangers only in the subtlety of the coerciveness of membership recruitment. The Community Action Program is setting up new privilege without even destroying the old.

Finally, I think it is a conservative idea because it is ineffective. It is ineffective in the basic sense that it does not appeal to any moral sanction in society. As far as I am concerned, the poverty program does not allow the Negro revolution to use its resources in the most effective way. It asks that the Negro revolution demand alleviation of the poor. This is simply a desirable thing to do. I am not for eliminating the poverty program, but I am suggesting that it deprives the Negro revolution of its moral authority. The War on Poverty, with its emphasis on cash and access, is literally demoralizing.

So, not necessarily with any evil intent on the part of the federal government, or Mayor Daley or anybody else, the War on Poverty has tended to refocus a large proportion of the fevered interest of the reformist community, Negro or white, away from its national obligation and its sense of citizenship. It has tended to weaken the Negro's political power by removing the one lever that expands his resources into something irresistible. Political resources – including numbers, organization and "green power" – are important. But with resources more effective, they cashier into more effective power, when the moral claim is strong. Given the strength of the Negro's moral position and the guilt of the white community, the revolution is selling out cheap for merely a war on poverty.

I suggest that the real secret of influence of the Negro movement in this country is the moral authority it possesses. The Negro's discomforts create cause, but discomforts do not create rights. Certain rights exist, and these are being deprived. The discomforts of poverty did not create those rights, and the attack on poverty will not necessarily expand them. It is most likely to reduce the enjoyment of rights by defining them away in a flourish of temporary prosperity.

RICHARD BOONE

A friend of mine who lives on the Cumberland Plateau of Eastern Kentucky, recently said, "Somebody told me that if you matched every poor person against all the money the government put into the poverty program, each person would come out with about $3." Then he said, "I'm still looking for mine." I think that many others share the sentiment expressed in that statement.

Temporarily putting aside the chronic lack of funds in the current antipoverty effort, let me share with you a bit of history still being written.

There are three unique features in the Economic Opportunity Act. First is the concept of local community action programs, the mandate for local rather than state or federal administration of efforts to deal with poverty. Soon after the passage of the Economic Opportunity Act, the Vice-President referred to the Community Action Program as a unique program which put authority for program development and management into local hands. This reflected a belief that local people could do the job. The second unusual feature of the Economic Opportunity Act is the mandate to bring together public and private resources at the federal, state, and local levels in support of a coordinated, substantial attack on poverty. Its third unusual feature is the charge that residents of the localities affected by the antipoverty program are to participate to the maximum feasible extent in the development and operation of those programs.

For a few moments I would like to concentrate on this point of maximum feasible participation. Three major considerations dictated the inclusion of this idea in the Economic Opportunity Act. The first was the impact of the Civil Rights Movement and its principle of one man, one vote. The second was the deep concern felt by the architects of the Community Action Section of the Act over the dangers of entrenched professionalism. Too many professionals in the human service professions had advanced the notion that only professionals could work effectively with the poor. Only certified teachers could teach; only certified health workers could work with sick people; only professional social workers could hold administrative and executive positions in local "helping" agencies. The demand for maximum feasible participation of the poor was a demand that the poor be accorded an opportunity to work with the poor in their own neighborhoods, bypassing the credentials trap.

The third, and by no means least important, force for inclusion of the maximum feasible participation section was the existence of what I will call "Kennedy's Washington." Though it has not been adequately reported, the "self-help" approach received widespread support among the younger people then working in Washington. And these were the people who were so often recommending policy, developing administrative guidelines, and writing the major speeches for key officials of the Kennedy administration. This force was best represented by the Peace Corps. And it was stated in the early days of the Alliance for Progress. Maximum feasible participation of the poor as a basic concept within the Economic Opportunity Act was a part of that tradition.

But what about the advocates of that principle within the Congress? Was there pressure from that quarter for such participation by residents of the areas in which the programs were to operate? Absolutely not. In fact, there was almost no testimony on the subject. Was there pressure from the grassroots to support the idea? There was very little. In discussing politics and poverty, it is interesting to remember that the phrase came into the Act without the effort of any organized support for its inclusion in the Act. Nationally, there wasn't even a coalition of liberals in support of it.

Effective policy level representation of the poor in local community action programs is still not a reality. In many cases, the so-called "representatives of the poor" have been hand picked by parts of the local establishment. For the most part, where there have been attempts to hold fair elections the poor have not been organized to take advantage of the electoral process. There have been no parties. The relevance of the process has been dubious and foreign to most of the poor, and it has required an extraordinary organizational effort and commitment for even minimal voter turnout.

Once elected, the representatives have more often than not found themselves responsible to no organized constituency. Thus, the process of subtle co-option by forces mirroring institutional priorities other than those most clearly associated with basic needs of the poor has been encouraged.

The second form of resident participation, that of employment of the poor to work with the poor, is probably best described in the book, *New Careers for the Poor* by Frank Reissman and Arthur Pearl. Today, every local Community Action Program has nonprofessional workers. While many problems beset projects embodying this approach, the idea is promising. It holds the possibility of meaningful work and money in the pockets of poor people. As more power is developed from within low-income areas, the demands will increase for more and better jobs of this type.

However, the promise of maximum feasible participation as a right of the poor has little hope of fulfillment if it is based alone on administrative decrees of representation in local CAP's and nonprofessional employment in human service projects. If the right of participation is to be implemented more fully, at least two basic needs must be addressed. First is the need of the poor for quality education. The second is their need for strong organization.

The plight of the ghetto poor was dramatically illustrated not too long ago in a Harlem meeting at which the mayor of New York City asked residents to express their grievances. Midway in that hearing a man arose and said, "I have five kids in the Harlem schools. You people who do not have kids in this school system don't know what it is like. I will tell you about that system. It is a system of designed retardation."

I would submit that in our slums, the average big city school system is just that, a system of designed retardation. That system could be construed as a conspiracy against the have-not's, particularly as one looks at the future and at the quality of education necessary to move into and upward within our sophisticated technological labor market.

The need for solid organization is nowhere better exemplified than in the Civil Rights Movement. It is one thing to fight for new laws. It is another to get them fairly implemented. The civil rights laws of the last ten years were the product of a coordinated national movement. The just implementation of those laws occurs only as there is strong organization to take advantage of these new rights. While there are various kinds of organizations, I will speak about only one, that of local community organization. In the context of the politics of power it is a disservice to limit ourselves to "unitary" neighborhood organization. Standing alone, it is an artifact. It is disfunctional to the needs of poor people. It is beside the point.

We will continue to witness the growth of the urban complex, the probable development of city-states and certainly of regional urban authorities. The megalopolis is the future for most of us. One will stretch from Boston to Washington and will contain over 21 million people. Another will stretch from south of San Diego to south of San Francisco and will probably contain nearly 19 million people. A third will be in the midwest, embracing the whole area from St. Louis through Chicago to Milwaukee. At least 15 million people will live there. Unless the millennium arrives soon, these megolopoli will contain large enclaves of poor people. If there is going to be effective organization through which the poor gain a fair share of resources, organization is going to have to transcend independent and unconnected neighborhood organizations.

For instance, if there is going to be effective organization in Chicago, it is going to have to be bigger than The Woodlawn Organization. This is in no way a criticism of that organization. The Woodlawn Organization is one of the few outstanding examples of local organizing by neighborhood residents. I am suggesting that many Woodlawn Organizations must be linked into a confederation of substantial "people power" in the inner city. Otherwise the galloping growth of the urban structure and its changing political design will sorely limit the possibilities of doing much for the vast majority of have-not's in our inner cities. While the neighborhood is a vital component, the base for action must be broader than the neighborhood.

In Rochester, Saul Alinsky has helped to establish a program which goes beyond the neighborhood. FIGHT (Freedom, Integration, God, Honor, Today) is a confederation of over one hundred local groups within Rochester. FIGHT has developed a power base which, while dependent upon local neighborhood groups, is an inner-city organization holding the allegiance of a substantial portion of Rochester's inner-city population.

Rochester is a company town. Kodak is the principal employer of adult males in Rochester. FIGHT thought it had negotiated a contract with Kodak through one of its vice-presidents. Under that contract, Kodak was to have hired approximately four hundred Negroes, using FIGHT as a principle recruitment and screening instrument. The president of Kodak repudiated the agreement. There will be a serious confrontation between FIGHT and Kodak, unless Kodak backs down. In any confrontation FIGHT will draw its basic strength from a population of inner-city size. No corporate enterprise in recent history has faced this degree of strength from poor people in its own backyard.[1]

Another example of power beyond the neighborhood is illustrated in the Child Development Group of Mississippi. This is a child development program stretching through twenty counties of Mississippi. While it is based upon locally controlled community units in each of these counties, each local group is part of the larger system. CDGM hires over 3,000 people. It directly affects about 20,000 people and indirectly affects up to 100,000 people. It has a real base of people power.

Because of its large base and the fact that it has the potential of a mass movement within the state of Mississippi, CDGM has become a clear and present danger to the status quo, including the entrenched political forces of the state. Currently, there is extensive pressure against the refunding of this

---

[1] Subsequently, the management of Kodak agreed to hire a group of unskilled Negroes immediately, and to play a major role in the establishment of Rochester Jobs, Inc., a cooperative effort by about forty local industries to act as a future clearinghouse in finding jobs for otherwise unemployable persons.

program by the Office of Economic Opportunity. But there is reason to believe that CDGM will be refunded, notwithstanding the opposition of Senators Stennis and Eastland, the tacit opposition of many of their fellow Senators, some members of the House of Representatives, silence on the part of the White House, and even resistance to CDGM from within parts of the Office of Economic Opportunity itself. CDGM can marshall thousands of poor people to its support. And due in large part to this mass allegiance, it is being defended by church, labor, professional, and civil rights organizations at the national level.[2]

One last point. As we look at the question of politics and poverty and the various devices which might be set forward to eradicate poverty, I hope we keep before us a fundamental challenge. That challenge is not simply the eradication of poverty; it is the eradication of poverty in ways consistent with the protection of individual freedom. With this country's tremendous wealth, it would be possible to move people out of grinding poverty and still deny them freedom. It would be easy to create a new army of consumers, but consumers who have little or no economic and political independence. As we begin to move forward, dreaming, as we always do, of great new ways to solve our problems, we must ask ourselves whether our new plans and programs will stand the test of making people free.

Let me express my concern in this way: Some years ago, well-intentioned people advocated a public housing policy. Look at its results today. Look at your own city, those of you who come from Chicago. Look at the modern high-rise public housing ghetto on South State Street. Look at who gets into that ghetto and how he gets in. Look at the conditions under which he stays there or is forced to leave. The system is controlled by bureaucratic gatekeepers influenced by their own rigid bureaucratic policies and the "suggestions" of representatives of a powerful political machine. This perversion is possible through devices which place new power in the hands of people who are committed not to the eradication of poverty but to its containment and the manipulation of its victims. In our new programs will we inadvertently create a new, insidious kind of poverty which strikes at the very roots of the society which says its wants to be free, or will we advance policies and programs consistent with economic and political freedom?

<hr />

[2] In January 1967, the Office of Economic Opportunity announced that CDGM would receive $8,000,000 to continue its child development program in Mississippi.

3

Politics of Legislation and
the Welfare System

WILLIAM ROBINSON

The topic "Politics and Public Welfare" and how we get public welfare legislation is an intriguing one. In 1965, an Advisory Council on Public Assistance was appointed by the President and the Secretary of HEW. A copy of their report is available from the United States Government Printing Office and costs one dollar. The principal observation of this report was that public assistance operates to guarantee and nail down poverty for about eight million people in this country. Public assistance perpetuates poverty.

I would like to make another observation as we approach this problem of welfare legislation. Who proposes it? How do we get it? What are some of the political implications of welfare? From the beginning, we have to remember one significant fact: the majority of people on welfare in Illinois are Negroes. They are Black, and as the politics of welfare flows from the fact that, since most of the people on welfare are Black, certain liberties may be taken with the welfare system throughout the program. Thus one of the weaknesses of welfare, at both the state and county level, is that emphasis is placed on how many people will leave the rolls at the end of each month, and not on the volume of services rendered to people on public assistance which will produce a climate of rehabilitation and dignity.

The politics of using people on public aid to produce political power is a fact of life in Chicago. This means that there must be a change in the direction of the program so that the people on public aid recognize that they do not get their money from City Hall, or from the politicians. People must know that it is a federal-state program, and that they have rights as recipients.

Recipients are citizens and not disfranchised because they are the dependent poor.

The goal of welfare is to help people to help themselves. This process of helping must recognize the dignity of each human being. Human services must be delivered in a climate of dignity and self-respect.

DAVID GREENSTONE

I would like to begin by considering the role of legislative activity in the context of the development of the War On Poverty which our previous speakers have mentioned.

There are many reasons why the War On Poverty is at this very moment struggling for survival. One is the attitude of the highest officials in the Johnson administration itself. Another is the Vietnam War. Let me suggest still a third which relates to a statement Mr. Boone made at the beginning of his very interesting remarks. He said that there were two unique elements in the Economic Opportunity Act. One was the maximum feasible participation of the poor; the second was doing the job locally.

I would like to suggest that the two are mutually incompatible. When you do the job locally you give it to the established local authorities. I suggest that an attempt to stimulate, indeed to subsidize this kind of radicalism, by the Federal government is very difficult under any circumstances, but is even more difficult if you attempt to do it locally, through the established local authorities.

What can we learn from this? Among other things, we can learn that you must look for allies. If by "established local authorities" you mean administrators, then who are your natural allies? I suggest that, to some extent, it is legislators; it is just the way their job is structured. Legislators like to investigate and have something to say about how policies are run.

It seems to me that therefore this panel's topic is particularly important. Much could be done in terms of legislation and in terms of structuring programs to eliminate administrative discretion. And I think the need to explore this kind of legislative activity has been revealed by many of the comments in this and the preceding sessions which reflect discontent with existing patterns of welfare and other programs designed to aid the poor.

But what do you do when you look at the problem of legislation? How do you become an effective legislative group? Not by organizing a single neighborhood. The most effective legislative groups, such as postal workers, railroad clerks, or, in its heyday, the Brothershood of Railroad Trainmen, had a few people in every congressional district. This is impossible given the pattern of segregation by income and race, but it is of foremost importance to increase the coverage that any protest organization has in different congressional or legislative districts. In terms of legislation this means a very systematic effort to find every conceivable ally; there will then be that many more legislators who may be at least bothered when they find pressure arising from their constituents.

It is true that many of the poor do not vote, but the first step is to get something started in as many districts as possible. The second step is to develop a program which is specific and concrete. For this reason, the possibility of a negative income tax has to be very seriously considered. It seems to have many advantages, one of which is that it is specific or can at least be made specific. Another, which Mr. Boone mentioned, is that it eliminates certain kinds of administrative discretion. I would add that it opens up the potentiality for building alliances.

On the basis of some research I did in Washington, I can tell you that there is a very respected lobby of a group which is largely, but not exclusively, poor. I refer to the aged, the senior citizens. They are extremely respected, because without exception they exist in every congressional district in the country. When they put through Medicare, they won a major victory over one of the most powerful lobbies in the history of the United States, the American Medical Association. For a variety of reasons, they do not have much money, and it seems to me that a very fertile field for an alliance would be that between the aged and others who are deprived economically.

Nor are the aged the only group that can be reached. If one looks at liberal groups and asks which have the largest staff of skilled legislators, the answer is the trade union movement. This is the largest staff of skilled legislators among possibly sympathetic groups. I recognize the difficulties with the trade union movement. I know that some unions are lily white and some are not; I know that those which are not have almost lily white staffs of hired officials. I realize all these things, but this is an imperfect world and one has to try to find allies where one can.

As I understand it, when the fight was waged about CDGM in Mississippi, there was an antiunion business man on the competing group. Partly by accident, his presence allowed the labor movement to step in and help support CDGM. This is not going to happen every time, but this kind of alliance has to be considered as well.

Obviously legislation is not going to solve all the problems. I recognize the enormous problems that come with the implementation of some kinds of legislation but not others. For example, if the guaranteed annual income program went through, the problems of implementation probably would be much smaller than in other kinds of programs. However, I am suggesting that we must think through in conclusion a theme which kept reappearing in Mr. Robinson's comments: that there is no lobbying or letter writing by the people who need the help, that the legislation comes from some bureaucrats or a few liberal legislators.

ABNER MIKVA

When we were introduced, I noticed a distinction between Representative Robinson and myself. He was introduced as having current employment which implies that I am unemployed. I guess I am, and therefore, perhaps I can talk about the problem a bit more seriously.

I would like to pick up something that Bill Robinson said and talk for a moment or two on this numbers game. There is no question that the ultimate aim of everybody (and, at least on the basis of the content of our speeches on the floor of the House, I have to include myself and I think

Bill Robinson) who introduces or proposes new legislation in the welfare field is to demonstrate how much money it will save for the state. We talk about it either in the short run or in the long run.

This has bothered me for some time. When, for example, the Bureau of Fraud and Complaints of the Attorney General's office makes its report to the legislature, it boasts about how many people it has served that year. When the Citizenship Division of the Board of Education makes its report to the Board, it brags about how many people have been enrolled in classes that year, how many have been taught to speak English and assume the responsibilities of citizenship. I can go up and down all of the other governmental agencies who take how many people they have served as a mark of their success. But in public aid it goes just the other way. The successful administrator is the one who can show how many people he has kicked off the rolls, how many less people have been served that year.

This is an important and meaningful distinction because it goes to the root of what is wrong with most of our thinking about public aid. It seems to get into the whole problem that underlies the notion of guaranteed annual income – we still have this so-called Protestant ethic. Thus we are suspect of anybody who goes on public aid because we all think that we really would like to go on public aid. We are not, for a variety of reasons, but we are suspicious of anybody who obtains any kind of assistance. Unless we keep the lid on, clamp down, and tighten up on it, unless we do this and do that, we think we will end up a society of indolents where everyone will receive the dole.

This just is not true. I have been involved in public aid problems for at least twelve years and have yet to find one recipient who enjoyed being on the rolls. It seems to me that we must somehow communicate to all, including the people in this room, that this problem of having to keep the lids on and having to move people off in natural and unnatural ways is just not a real problem. We have to make it clear to people that if public aid is treated as a service in the same way as education, citizenship, and helping people out of legal difficulties, then people will take the service when they need it, but will not come in and freeload when they do not.

In part I suppose these suspicions arise because we are dealing with the subject of money. We assume that people will do things for money that they will not otherwise do. Unless we have these lids on, unless we put in all these restraints, restrictions, means tests, investigators and so on, we assume that people will just run riot on the public aid rolls. The other part of the problem seems to go back to what both Mr. Robinson and Mr. Greenstone said, that the people who know most about the field of public welfare legislation are never involved in the process. Everybody else from the Chamber of Commerce to the Taxpayers' Federation to the social workers gets involved in it – everybody except the recipients. I have yet to know of a bill where the recipients were consulted about the drafting, the implications, the potential success, about how it would work, and so on.

Let me give a few illustrations of how the combination of these two factors works. Senator W. Russell Arington is now president pro-tem of the Illinois Senate, and what this may mean in the public welfare field should be of some significance to the people who live in Illinois. In 1957, my first term in the legislature, he led an organized campaign against the welfare program and made no bones about it. I do not think I am misrepresenting him as publicly stating several times that he was out to "straighten up" the public aid programs in Illinois.

Among his straightening-up proposals, there were four that I would like to mention. One was fixed ceilings on all assistance programs which, as you may know, meant a recipient would get so much money, no matter how many children she had over a certain number, no matter where she lived, and no matter what the circumstances of her family. But that was the mildest of the proposals. He had another called "the one mistake bill" which said that we would provide for the first illegitimate child but the rest could starve. He had a five-year residency requirement which said a recipient had to live in the state of Illinois five years (and there was talk of amending it to up to ten years) before he or she could be eligible for any kind of assistance. Finally, he had a bill which said that anyone who was on assistance would not be allowed to vote as long as they remained on assistance and for six months thereafter.

Those bills were being treated seriously. Many of them, as I recall, passed the Illinois Senate, although they were all ultimately defeated in the House. Not once during that legislature did we ever have any visits from the people involved in the program. Not once during that period did I receive a single letter from a recipient expressing opposition to the proposals. Not once did I receive a letter from anyone who was really directly involved in the process – not just as a recipient but as an administrator.

Though some of the social workers and a few of the more enlightened administrators were very concerned about them, rather paradoxically, the bills were beaten finally by representatives of the Metropolitan Welfare Council who came down in a successful eleventh-hour effort. Most of them were Senator Arington's constituents, the board members of the various agencies that made up the Welfare Council and lived in the north, south, and west suburbs. They finally got the message from their own executives that, if these programs passed, their own private charities would be inundated to pick up the slack; and they defeated the bills.

It is interesting that (though the message did not get through to the legislature) these others finally realized that, if you look at the public and private sectors together, clamping down the lid on public aid recipients does not save any money or really eliminate any of the needs; it merely shifts the burden around between the two sectors.

As Bill Robinson said, if the category is need, the need remains. If you say only the first illegitimate child will be fed by the state, somebody is going to have to feed the other illegitimate children. Our consciences are not so callous that we will allow them to walk around on the street with distended bellies. If you say they have to live here for five years before they could be eligible for public assistance, somebody is going to have to feed those people who have lived here only four and a half years. If you say they should only get so much as a ceiling, somebody is going to have to make up the difference between that ceiling and the amount that is really necessary to live. Somehow that message never got through to legislature.

In 1963 we put on fixed ceilings, and we are living with them now. They are ridiculous. We say that in Chicago, an assistance family can get only $104.00 a month for rent. Everybody knows, or I hope at least everybody in this room knows, that for $104.00 you cannot get adequate, semiadequate, or even inadequate housing accommodations for large families in Chicago, especially if you happen to be Negro and on public assistance. So, we have created a category of exemptions. We allow one hundred cases a month to go above the ceiling. I will not needle the Cook County Department of Public Aid, but I know that there are more than one hundred families that cannot live within that ceiling, and I am convinced that those cases are rotated so as to pay the rent for one hundred families one month and skip them the next month to get another one hundred.

Because we do not really believe that the problems exist in the first place, we still assume that if we just tighten up on these things, the problems will go away. One thing we do not have in this country is an inventory of the problems of the poor. We have some nice Fourth-of-July phrases about the one-third or the one-fourth of the nation which is underfed and underclothed. I have used them too, but we have never taken an inventory of the real problems and needs of the poor. What is this category of needs of poor people? The category of need of food, of legal services, of training and of assistance in becoming self-sufficient. Again I read an element of force in almost every one of them. We tell the people: We are going to teach you how to be literate, and if you do not accept this program, if you do not attend these literacy classes that we give to ADC mothers from 6 to 9 P.M. (a wonderful time for a mother to get away from her family) we are going to throw you off the rolls. Once again, there is just no communication with the people in terms of their real needs and what really will permit them to do what they want to do in the first place, namely to get off of that sickening, rotten, debilitating, humiliating public assistance roll and take their place as a regular member of the society.

Some years ago one of the educational channels decided to put a literacy program on television. We do not even have an inventory of how many of the illiterate families have TV sets. We think we know but nobody really knows. We say everybody on ADC has a TV set, but it's not true. Let me mention one item about the format. Of course, it was a typical white, suburban family with a carport and the children rushing out to greet the father coming home from work. Most parts of the program were like this. What really stuck me was their method of distributing information about the programs. They did not know how to get in touch with the people who needed help, so they placed big ads in the newspapers: LEARN HOW TO READ – WATCH CHANNEL so and so. It sounds ridiculous, and yet there are dozens of other examples like it.

What does it all lead to? Does it have to be that way? Of course not. Do we have to continue accepting our notions about what these programs ought to be from people who can only know vicariously what the needs are? Of course not. Do we have to continue operating our public aid programs on the notion that we must be strict, tough, and mean in order to keep these indolent people from running away with our budget? Of course not. Some striking examples of success have proved it can be done the other way.

Let me give a few more examples. The great Orange Juice Fight of 1964 was one of the great victories for the poor in Illinois. After the ceilings went on as the result of 1963 legislative action, the Department of Public Aid in Illinois, and I do not mean to be derogatory here, was faced with the responsibility of administering an unadministrable budget. They were told by the legislature: this is the amount of money you have to feed all the hungry. They and a few others knew that you could not feed all those people on the amount of money they had been given, but they had to go through the motions.

So they called in some home economists and nutritionists who sat down and figured out a theoretical food budget. A real expert on shopping, cooking, and nutrition – who never burned a meal, who never had to buy from a credit grocer (who charged a little extra to take care of the credit function), and who could do all of her shopping on the loss leaders that the various chain stores engage in – such an expert could get by nutritionally on so much per day. One of the results was to substitute grapefruit juice for the orange juice that had been a part of the previous theoretical diet. Another was to substitute dried skimmed milk for whole milk.

These nutritional experts, who were scientifically correct I am sure, never stopped to find out whether kids on ADC liked grapefruit juice instead of orange juice. They certainly never found out whether kids liked dried skimmed milk instead of whole milk. It set off a great controversy.

I even put my own family on the public aid diet for a week. My wife failed miserably. On the fifth day she miscounted her money and thought she had enough to buy a chicken which was going to be our one good meal that week. She went out and bought a chicken, but when she came home, she realized that she would not have enough money to feed us the other two day. So she put the chicken in the freezer and we had something else. When she told me about it I said: "Zoe, that is exactly the way any ADC family would handle it. When they saw that they had overbought, they would just put the chicken in the freezer, reach into the reserve money supply, and buy something else."

We had a Goldwater student living with us at the time. When we asked him if he minded going on this diet for a week, he said he would be very pleased to do it. He wanted to satisfy himself that all these people were living high off the hog as he suspected. So he tasted every horrible tasting thing that my wife put in front of him and said, "This is great, just fine." He was not about to let his philosophy go down the drain until the first time we tried the dried skimmed milk. He took one sip of it, put it down, made a most awful face, and said, "Well, not bad." At that point, my ten-year-old daughter glared at him and said, "You like ti, you drink it."

Let me get back to the Orange Juice Fight. Finally the subject was brought up before the legislative advisory committee which Bill Robinson mentioned. A group of West Side ministers, many of them from the West Side Organization and the West Side Federation, brought a group of ADC mothers to the legislative advisory committee. I do not remember whether Bill was on the committee at the time or not, but it has to stand as one of the red-letter days in Illinois history. It was the first time that most members of that advisory committee had ever seen an ADC mother and they were shocked. One of the mothers, happened to be white, and it had never occurred to a couple of my downstate brethren that anybody on ADC was white. They just assumed that everybody on ADC was Negro.

They could not withstand the very simple, inarticulate, inexpert, but very sincere, assault by these mothers. The mothers explained that they could not get their children to drink grapefruit juice and dried skim milk. Many of them were continuing (and, of course, this is the ridiculous thing about the whole notion of a food budget) to feed their children orange juice and milk. Therefore, they did not have enough money to buy the children clothes, so they could not send them to school and were keeping them home.

The conservative, reactionary members of the legislative advisory committee not only voted for, they *moved* to increase the food budget by five cents a month so we could restore orange juice in lieu of grapefruit juice. That may not sound like very much, but it seems to me to be an indication that this is the role that has to be followed if we are going to try to get legislation and programs that work in this field. We have to get the people involved. Is it more effective to get them involved on the congressional level? Sure it is. Would it be great if we could get up a welfare union of all these people in the country? Of course it would be. But even if it is on a block-by-block basis, a single parish basis, a single household basis - - somehow the recipients of the program, in their own inarticulate ways, have got to get pulled into the process so that the programs, the administration, and so on, involve them.

I see some hopeful signs in that direction. The welfare union idea is an exciting one. I am glad to see the church groups get involved on a parish basis rather than sending money to the poor in some anonymous way. I am glad to see some of the results that come out of this.

One West Side organization arranged a sit-in at one of the welfare offices. Unfortunately, the ministers and recipients went to jail (I suspect that some of them are here), but after they went to jail, the head of the office, who was apparently a gal absolutely unsuited to handling the office, was quietly transferred out. The Public Aid Department gave the sit-in no credit for having moved her out, but it has been admitted to me that this was the reason. Interestingly enough, even the jury and the judge who sentenced the ministers and recipients to jail were deeply touched when they heard the plight of the recipients under this woman's administration. Several of the jurors cried, and the judge wrote letters to the Corporation Counsel of the City of Chicago and to the head of the Public Aid Department, saying that something had to be done about the horrible administrative conditions that exist in the welfare office.

We have got to get a camaraderie with the poor. We have got to know and understand the problems they really have, not the ones we like to think they have. We have got to understand that they really are not anxious to stay on the rolls, but they are going to have to tell us how to solve their problems. We cannot begin to solve them by talking only to each other, and that means we have to get rid of some old ideas.

Sometimes the social workers, who I love dearly and who have been helpful in so many things in Illinois, are the worst enemies of the poor. They insist on hanging onto the ideas they learned in college. For example, perhaps one of the best things you could do for some poor families would be to manage their financial affairs for them. Not because it is going to teach independence to the parents but because it might get the kids out of a pattern of three and four generations growing up with the same problems. Yet, every time I talk to a social worker about that possibility, I hear the old shibboleths of the 1930's. "It must be cash, it cannot be this, it cannot be that."

I would like to see more responsible people talking and thinking about guaranteed annual income because I think it is at least a potential major breakthrough on the real solution to this problem. We once and for all must eliminate the notion that these are people who are feeding at the public trough and instead start looking at them as people with problems of the poor. As Mr. Dooley said, "The poor, who need money the most, seldom have it." Basically, the guaranteed annual income says, "Let us give money where it is needed."

Finally, we have to start realizing that the people on the various assistance programs can be articulate even though they cannot speak the king's English. We must let them talk to us and with us rather than always telling them what they need and what's good for them. We have to help them organize, but in helping them organize, I think we can take a few pages from Saul Alinsky's book. Help them organize, yes, but then let them tell you the direction they want to go in, rather than superimposing on them our fixed notions of what they should do. Abe Lincoln once said that God must have loved the poor people because he made so many of them. Well, if that is true, then I would say that, at least in Illinois, the Lord's point of view is a minority one.

HENRY McCARTHY

I am a product of this university, and I came here the same year as Robert Maynard Hutchins. Once, after he had been here a while, somebody asked him, "Mr. Hutchins, how would you compare the University of Chicago with all the other great universities in the world?" Mr. Hutchins stopped and thought a minute and then he said, "Well, we are not very good, we are just the best there is." If I were asked how the State of Illinois Public Aid Administration Program compares with that of all the other states of the Union, I would give the same answer, "We are not very good, but we are the best there is." I would like to give some illustrations of that.

Seated to my right is a representative from the state of Ohio, a man who represents public aid. In Ohio they have a budget standard which is roughly comparable to that of Illinois, and they pay 78% of their budget. Similarly in Pennsylvania, and at last accounts, they paid 62½% of their budget. But we pay 100% of ours.

The modern welfare department has three objectives. The first is that it shall provide adequate economic support on a standard needed to maintain health and decency, and I will have something to say about that later. Second, we have the responsibility of restoring people to self-support. Though Abner Mikva says that we kick off people, I would say that we help them get to the point where they can be self-supporting. When we brag about the number of people who have gone off the rolls, we are bragging because we have helped them get rid of the terrible burden of being on relief. We are not interested in kicking people off relief, we are interested in helping people to become self-supporting. The third responsibility is the newest concept and really has not been generally implemented or accepted. It is the prevention of dependency, and we are just at the beginnings of that.

On this last point, for the last two sessions of the legislature the Department of Public Aid has introduced a bill which unfortunately has not passed. It asks the legislature to authorize us to extend our services to former and potential recipients of relief. At the last session of the legislature, I testified before the committee that was conducting hearings on that bill. I was asked, "Who are you trying to reach here?" I said we were trying to reach one group who had gone off relief, gotten jobs or employment, or been restored to self-support, but who, through some mishap, had to come back to us as repeaters. The other group, which we thought even more important, were those who were on their way to dependency, potential recipients of relief who had not gotten there yet but who, inexorably, were moving toward dependency.

As for some facts on that, we close 2,000 ADC cases every month of the year. Year in and year out we close an average of 2,000 cases. These cases are closed for a great variety of reasons – because a family is reunited, because people have been made self-supporting, etc. Unfortunately, at the same time, we open very nearly 2,000 cases a month. It has been a little less on the average because the case load has been going down.

Of these 2,000 cases that are opened every month, a full half of them are cases that were never on relief. In other words, a thousand brand new ADC cases come to us every month. The gestation period of movement toward dependency has been going on for months and months. As we sit here now, some family that never was on relief is getting ready to come and apply for assistance a month, or two or three months from now. The causes of dependency are at work all the time. You know what those causes are: for example, the broken home situations, the alcoholic breakdown of a family, which by the way, is one of the growing causes of dependency. All the families on their way toward dependency and relief are of concern to us, and we think they are a frightening concern. We ought to be able to extend services to them, reach out to them, offer them the kinds of services that the department is equipped to offer, and thus help prevent dependency.

I also mentioned trying to restore people to self-support. We have been unique in Illinois compared to the rest of the country. I think you all read or heard the Governor's statement before the legislature the other day. It shows that we had gone down in our relief rolls from 460,000 people three years ago to 400,000 people today. We are the only major industrial state in which this has occurred. Of the thirteen largest industrial states, we are the only one where the case load has gone down. As we were going down, the others were going up an average of 10 to 15%; New York went up 60%, and California went up 90%.

When you ask why, the answer is not that economic conditions are better in Chicago or Illinois than in New York or California. Those states have participated in the general prosperity too. The answer is very simple. In this state, and we are the only state in which this has occurred, starting in 1963 the legislature gave us $5 million for adult education and training, in 1965 they gave us another $8 million for adult education and training, and in the next budget we are asking for $12 million for adult education and training. And this adult education and training has paid off.

We have representatives of Cook County here who I think can testify that through it we have conducted classes and educated people, not in a dead-end way, but toward specific jobs: we have gotten thousands of people jobs as cab drivers, we have gotten people jobs as checkers in supermarkets, we have gotten people jobs in filling stations, we have gotten people jobs as typists and as keypunch operators. All this has been done through the training programs initiated under the $5 and $8 million appropriations for training. In our department we emphasize the idea that anybody who is remotely employable will be trained and helped toward self-support. That is of the essence of our whole program at this time.

As far as legislation is concerned, I certainly agree with Bill Robinson that we do not get much substantive legislation from any outside source though we should be getting it from a lot of sources. Most of the legislation is introduced by the Department of Public Aid.

Two kinds of legislation are introduced. You might call the first administrative legislation. It is brought about by the pressure of experience within the department, from the staff, on the director and ultimately on the legislative advisory committee, to improve our administrative processes. That is a proper kind of legislation. It comes out of our experience; we know which things are working well and which are working badly and which need to be improved, and we do try to get adminstrative improvements.

But, we do not get much substantive legislation unless there is pressure for it, and that pressure has to come from the community. Substantive legislation is that which will change the policies, the philosophy, and the practices. We have not been very fruitful in this because there have not been the kind of pressures from the community that I think would be helpful in improving our situation.

We are talking about 400,000 people on relief. Of these, 58,000 are over 65 years of age, 30,000 are permanently and totally disabled, 2,000 are blind. Add those up and you have 90,000 people in what we call our AADB category, Aid to the Aged, Disabled, and Blind. Using round figures, it costs about $100 a month per person to take care of this group of people. None of them are employable. The average age of the aged is over seventy, and they are not employable; the permanently and totally disabled are not employable; the blind are not employable because they are the needy blind, the lowest percentage of blind on relief in the whole nation.

The next group is 210,000 children under eighteen years of age, and they are not employable. Some of the 50,000 mothers taking care of those children in the ADC program are employable, and, wherever it is a good plan for the family, we are concentrating on training those mothers and getting them into placement.

Then we have about 50,000 to 60,000 on general assistance in what we call "receiving" townships or counties; Cook County is one. The amount of money raised locally on the one-mill levy is not sufficient to pay the relief load in the township or county, so the state takes over that cost and insists on the state standards being observed in the administration of general assistance.

Among those 50,000, there are some employables, but I would like you to know what kind of employables. Among that 50,000 employables on general assistance, there are the single people and the couples without children. They are not old enough for old-age assistance, not disabled enough for aid to the disabled, and are not eligible for any other category. At the best, they are marginally employable because they are the people of about fifty-five or sixty years of age who have never had much education or constructive work experience. They are the hardest to place, and yet we have tried to train and place as many of them as possible. Among them are the dischargees from mental hospitals and prisons who are also hard to place. Yet, we try our best to place them. We have the alcoholics, the narcotics addicts, and the psychological misfits who are to be found in any community, and they are the hard to place.

The general public has the notion that the average person on relief is a big, husky, six-foot young man who would rather loaf than work. Nothing could be further from the truth. Going down the composition of this case load, I think I have demonstrated that by far most of them are completely unemployable. At any given time, we never have more than 5,000 currently placeable people on our roll. The 210,000 youngsters who we hope will become employable some day are not employable now.

What should be our main concern? It seems to me that it sould be to see that they share in the tremendous growth in national prosperity which is occurring in this country. This year we are up to a gross national product of nearly $700 billion, and it is estimated to go up to $720 billion next year. Yet at no time in this state, and to a much worse degree in other states, have the poorest of the poor shared in the increase in gross national prosperity. They have been the forgotten men.

I always remember Lester Granger talking about the war on poverty. He said that his greatest fear was that in the march towards the Great Society, we left the battered and bleeding corpses of the real poor lying by the wayside. And this is what has been happening.

As I said, we take care of the aged, blind, and disabled at the rate of about $100 a month. We take care of the ADC at the rate of about $45 per person per month. Do a quick calculation: on the average, a mother of three children gets $180 a month. That is about $2200 a year which is far below the $3,000 minimum that the War on Poverty set as a rule of thumb, benchmark for the poverty line. We are far below that in Illinois. How much further are we below it in Ohio, Pennsylvania, Mississippi, Missouri, Indiana, and Michigan? All these states have ceilings. We do not have ceilings in Illinois, except on rent, and that is in process of adjustment.

We not only have a 100% standard, but we have a standard that compares well with that of any other state. In fact, Minnesota is the only state that is above us in the actual standard. As I pointed out to you, even Minnesota is still far below the poverty line. But about legislation I would like to say, at this point, that we would welcome suggestions, even pressure, from the community as to what they think ought to be done at the state level. I emphasize at the state level here because in dealing with the problems of the relief poor, it seems to me that the biggest part of our problem is getting revision of federal laws.

Moynihan recently testified in Washington that the only answer he could see was not the guaranteed annual income, not the negative income tax, but the family allowance system as they have it in Canada. Personally I also think this would be one of the answers for the mitigation, if not the elimination, of poverty in this nation. The biggest problem we have is the family with small children who is on ADC. They will only move up and receive a share in the general prosperity if there is a family allowance of so much per month for every child, regardless of economic status.

We have done some things in Illinois of which we have a right to be proud. We have emphasized the training program and the 100% budget; we have emphasized as decent a budget as is possible under present conditions. We have also liberalized some aspects of our laws which we think would be helpful to the poor. For example, we have added $5 a month for every child who is a junior or senior in high school. We have exempted $62.50 of income for any teenager who stays in the household while he is earning money. He has $62.50 in his own pocket in addition to expenses of employment which provides an incentive for him to work, to help, and not leave his family. We have exempted $50 of income for ADC mothers in work. We have exempted up to $85 in income for the blind and $50 for the aged. We have provided scholarships for youngsters on relief who may be eligible for higher education.

We have done a great many things in the way of offering services to the people who are on relief, expanding our services to take advantage of the 1962 amendments of the Social Security Act. In the 1962 amendments we were offered the incentive of 75% federal reimbursement of services in addition to the usual services that are offered to families. And we have been trying to expand those. We have reduced our case loads so that we can give more individual attention.

I would like to hear several things from Mr. Robinson and Mr. Mikva particularly, and I hope that our discussion will permit that. For example, I would like to hear what kind of legislation was introduced by Mr. Robinson, and by Mr. Mikva when he was in the legislature, that was not passed and that they would like to see reintroduced. I would like to hear from anybody in the group about the kinds of state legislation we ought to have now.

We talk about having a single category of needs. We are all for that, but it has to be done on a national basis. Improvements of the standard of assistance also has to be done on a national basis. So far the national government has not seen fit to adopt either one of these proposals. We hope that they will someday, and we certainly would go along with it. When you contrast the $45 per person on ADC that we now have in Illinois, with the $9 per person on ADC in Mississippi, you can see how broad the discrepancy is and why we need a national standard.

In Florida, to give yet another example, the maximum for a person on old age assistance is $66 a month, regardless. That covers rent, food, clothing, household replacement, personal care – everything. The maximum for a family on ADC in Florida is $81 a month regardless of the number of children. In Indiana, they give $100 to the mother with the first child and then $23 a child. In Missouri just to the south of us, they give $63 to the mother with the first child and only $23 for every child after that. However, my guess is that even if a national standard is adopted, it probably would not be more than the present Illinois standard because even that would bring Mississippi way up.

(At this point, Mr. McCarthy's presentation was curtailed, in the interest of time, by the chairman, who then called for general discussion.)

4

Politics of Administration:
Differential Perspectives

JOHN WEDEMEYER

I may be here under some misunderstanding. I cannot talk with you mainly about city problems and must base what I have to say on experiences at the state level and as a county welfare administrator.

No person comes to recognize more keenly what Martin Rein and Miller recently pointed out than the administrator at any local level who has been given the task of carrying out some legislation enacted to aid the poor or disadvantaged. Certainly it is not new to you here that each of us has a private agenda for poverty reduction. We would be dissatisfied if income insufficiency were reduced and other goals were not. As Rein and Miller[1] point out, we are each concerned with poverty *and* something else which represents a social value significant to us. So we tend to talk about poverty in terms of "poverty *and* social control," or "poverty *and* civil rights," or "poverty *and* social engagement," or "poverty *and* equality," or "poverty *and* mobility," or "poverty *and*" some other value or purpose. What follows these "ands" generates the conflicts over public policy and public administration. Furthermore, it creates difficulties in developing programs which, as well as being acceptable, have a maximum potential for cooperative, interprogram coordination and effectiveness or interprogram coherence.

I suspect that these "ands" are as different among the poor as they are among the affluent. The differences become immediately apparent when the administrator begins to put a new law into effect. There are immediately important matters with which the administrator must deal. Most of them have not been clearly or openly considered as legislation is in process. Too often the legislation expresses a system which necessitates compromise between some of these "ands" so that the legislative product may be subject to all sorts of interpretations, depending upon the "ands" of the particular persons who are involved.

I think it is also necessary to realize that the matter of coherence is primarily a political matter and one that extends well beyond legislation into

---

[1] Rein and Miller, "Poverty, Policy and Purpose: The Axes of Choice," *Poverty and Human Resources Abstracts*, vol. 1, no. 2 (March – April 1966).

administration. The local administrator or the state administrator is frequently involved, first of all, as a power in himself. That is, his views often become of critical importance, whatever his governmental unit, whether it be the state which basically governs the enactment of the welfare program, or whether it be locally in terms of some of its applications. He is called upon to express his views; then, once having stood for what he thinks it ought to be, he is called upon to defend the result of what it turns out to be. Very often he also has a substantial hand in the legislative work which receives the enactment of laws. As you know, often his views are sought, and he is expected to represent not only the administration, but also, to some extent, the persons who are involved. What he personally stands for is important.

Once enacted, the peer involvement becomes of major importance and is again largely a matter of intra-administrative politics. The coherence between the way in which the public welfare program is carried out and other programs depends to a great extent on the political abilities of the administrator in working with his peers. Disparities are often more the result of struggle for power and of conflict between different administrative goals than of ignorance, as Rein points out.

When looking at the welfare system in this country, it is also ·important to recognize that in the states comprising the most heavily populated areas, the actual administration rests wholly upon the local subdivision, except for some standard setting and a substantial amount of funding provided by the state administration. The key funding in fifteen states rests with the locality (which in this country is the county) for the public welfare system. Federal and state support flows only as the locality is willing to put up a share (usually small) of the total cost. Thus the adequacy of local funding becomes the critical element in the adequacy of state or federal funding.

So when a state director once has the law, he is not himself always in control of or responsible for what happens in all instances. There is a vast amount of interpretation, a vast amount of political activity involved in the negotiation that goes on with the subordinate groups, the county, the city, and in some places, representatives of various pressure groups. Very often, as a result, a whole new set of values is injected into the interpretation of the law. In many places there is a strong organization of local county supervisors' associations or local welfare directors' associations. They function on their own politically, both in connection with the enactment of legislation and in connection with its interpretation and application.

In view of this, there are certain key things which have a distinct relevance to the adequacy of the public welfare programs in the first place, and, second, to the forms it takes in administrative practice. To my knowledge, there is no legislation in this country which treats public welfare as a matter of right. There is a lot of terminology in the laws and in bureaucratic talk where many public welfare administrators and others express the view that welfare benefits should be a right. But to my knowledge, none of our legislation – federal, state, or local – lays this out as a flat right. Nor can it be so as long as the key money provisions depend absolutely on closed-end appropriations, as is the case in most places.

Perhaps central to this, and central to the major problem of the relations between welfare and the whole attack on poverty, is the fact that certain elements of public welfare legislation were added to the basic legislation as an afterthought. These have to do with the heart of the poverty problem – with the people among the poor who are the key element, the families with children. The program for families with children was not part of the initial and key design of the system which we have. It was sort of tagged onto a system primarily created to deal with the aged. The fundamental differences in needs, goals, and problems have never been squarely faced on their own merits. Thus the whole set of values with which the administration and the poor, particularly among the family group, get involved, have not, at least until very recently, been thoroughly exposed to serious public debate in terms of finding some resolution and some basic guide lines.

I believe, on the basis of my last seven and one-half years, particularly in the California program, that the lack of an involved constituency in welfare is most important. Among welfare administrators and certainly in my own experience, there has been a great deal of confusion as to what is the constituency or whether there *is* any. Consequently the welfare administrator develops views of what his constituency is which most often do not include those with whom the programs deal. He knows the taxpayer's association, he knows the county supervisors' association, he knows the chambers of commerce, he knows the farm bureau. Very often he knows little of the basic group, in any political or organized sense, from which those with whom he deals as an agency administrator come.

This is important because most progressive public welfare legislation is in the areas in which a constituency has become commonplace and effective – the aged and the blind, for example. During the last year a good deal of fear of organized constituencies of the younger poor has been expressed. But this has not carried over to the aged and the blind. As recently as fifteen years ago, organized groups of the aged were considered a great threat. But under leadership of such people as George McLain of California, and people who had to do with other forms of pension organization, the aged, in many places, have found an effective voice and a very substantial power, and they know how to use it. The legislators respect it, know how to deal with it, and find no fault with it. They deal like the transportation interests deal, or the medical profession, or the landlords, or real estate dealers. That is understood, and what is understood is not feared.

They are also able to do this because it is among this group that the most adequate basic underwriting of maintenance is provided. Thus individuals can more easily afford to belong to a membership organization. One of the mistakes being made is assuming that organization is achieved by direct financing or subsidy to the group rather than by looking at how adequately the needy are maintained. When maintenance is sufficient, then, if there is something that they wish to do, like the aged have done, they can participate without starving. That is the way the aged have succeeded.

This, of course, brings me to the matter of adequacy of aid. Regardless of all the other "ands," I firmly believe that unless provision is made for the basic maintenance of the poor, nothing else can prevail. Having said that there is no right, I would like to mention something said by one of the participants. I think that there is only one right and it is a right we all share: a right to be treated like a human being. This is the right that in my profession is violated most often. It is the only right around which some other things can happen.

I would like to point out that many of these things do not depend on revamping the entire system. The system can be and is being, to some degree, modified. More could be done with the stimulus of an organized constituency. There must be many changes within the system. If these occur, you would have a very substantial alternative base from which you could move from matters of immediate concern about deficiencies of the welfare system to ways to accomplish some of the other "ands" about which we need to work.

One of the problems that, as a state and local administrator, I have come to look at very differently is the type of staffing pattern typical of most communities throughout the country. That is, the orthodox public welfare agency uses a type of organization which assumes that the only avenue for delivery of service is the caseworker. In many cases this goes further because, for many directors, the caseworker is the only avenue to understanding the people with whom the agency deals or the issues which grow up between those people and the administration trying to serve them.

I have come to believe that every administrator must have lines to the group he serves other than those which come through the casework line. I question that the system of case load allocation is an appropriate system. I know from my own experience that simply changing the system of application investigation, from its present scheme to one of affidavits, can and will create a whole new system of relationships. It makes it possible to begin to structure services which have some meaning in terms of product and which create opportunities for the use of many resources other than those of a caseworker. Most importantly, these can include the services of many among the poor themselves.

There is a real issue involved in the greater use of personnel recruited from the poor. One of the constructive elements in welfare administration throughout the country, as far as I am concerned, has been the development of the union movement. But unions may face some problems as this sort of change is engendered. They may begin to function rather like the old institutions and become unwilling to accept the poor as competitors if the changes threaten some elements of the existing staffing arrangements.

Improvement in the public welfare system entails many changes – some small, some quite substantial. Such major elements as revision of the standards of aid and standards for consideration of income and resources from other sources are important, not just from the standpoint of adequacy, but also because of the impact upon motivation and incentive. Not only do processes need to be simplified – they need also to be based on more realistic consideration of common family expenditure patterns. They need most of all not to confiscate the results of efforts to achieve. It is the way in which the means test is applied, rather than the test itself, which infringes on rights of people. The means test is not abandoned under any other alternative as far as I know. Even the income tax is a form of means test, and as Dr. Haziltine Taylor of the University of California has pointed out recently, it is doubtful that any alternative system is going to do without a means test. In my mind, it is only a question of the way we go about administering it (which is really mechanics) and the matter of treating people as human beings that will determine whether the basic programs will be good, bad, or indifferent.

WILLIAM ROBINSON

I do not know whether I can speak for John Ballard, or not. I can speak for Bill Robinson; I can share some of my reactions to John, since I was on the committee that helped to select him.

We are focusing on the city government and have with us the very distinguished Alderman Despres who is really the authority. This morning we talked about welfare and politics, and now we are looking at the city. We are a little handicapped when we talk about the city and welfare because the city of Chicago does not have much to do with welfare except to levy a one-mill tax for general assistance. However, there is the County Welfare Department which involves all of Chicago. In talking about the political establishment, we can hardly escape the discussion of welfare.

In order to discuss the establishment and welfare, we need to look at some of the folklore of welfare practices in this metropolitan area, and how it relates to the political structure, thinking in terms of the legislature, the advisory committee, the legislative advisory committee, the advisory committee to the Department; the Cook County Department of Public Aid (which ought to be Public Welfare), the advisory committee to this department, and the way these advisory committees have been used (or more appropriately not used); and finally the relationship that the Welfare Department has had to the political establishment in Chicago. And here I mean both Republican and Democrat.

Let's take the Republicans first: The chairman of a Public Aid Advisory Committee is John Carroll – a very good friend, and a fellow party member. The Public Aid Advisory Committee is the most powerful group in public aid in Illinois. It sets the tone. As a matter of fact, if you really examine the minutes of the Public Aid Advisory Committee from month to month, you might conclude that it is more administrative than it is advisory because many of the pronouncements of the administration of public aid in this state are those cleared through the Public Aid Advisory Committee. This committee is very peculiar because the chairman of the Public Aid Advisory Committee is a Republican. He was appointed from a Democratic House, and the Democratic Speaker of the House agreed that he would be chairman. Of course this could have had many implications: It could have implied the Republicans would get onus, or it could have implied that the Democrats and the Republicans both decided on having a certain system of welfare in this state, and that it does not make much difference who is chairman. Mr. Carroll comes from the suburbs, and it is interesting how often, politically, the downstate territory and the suburban territory seem to vote alike. Though they have cornfields downstate and lawns in the suburbs, they seem to have a point of view on welfare that is quite similar.

In Cook County, as in every county, there is a Welfare Services Committee. I read through the list recently, and there are not many people from the power structure on the Welfare Services Committee. Most of them are very conforming people. Some of them are professionals who are related to the welfare establishment. Some of the heads of agencies on the committee are doing business with the juvenile court and with Public Aid and of course, you just cannot disturb the waters because they are part of the status quo of welfare. And this is not the crass politics of the forum: this is the politics of welfare itself. It is very interesting that several years ago, when I introduced a bill to investigate and study the Family Court of Cook County, it passed both houses and was vetoed by the government. It was vetoed twice – once by Stratton and once by Kerner. There were certain large agencies which could not support even the study of the Family Court because some of their budget depended very largely upon fees paid by the Family Court for children who were cared for by these agencies. Many of these agencies were receiving their children through the General Assistance Agency of the Childrens' Division. The point I am trying to make here is that the very politics of welfare itself is a barrier to reform and to change. They only loaded on the bandwagon for change when the political structure had decided that the heat was so intense that something had to be done with the Family Court. Then, of course, they appeared in the picture. Then it was perfectly respectable to say to the Family Court without endangering at all their relationships to the economic system of which the Family Court fees were a part, that change is needed.

How does politics itself fit in? We have civil service for caseworkers in public assistance itself. However, I would invite any of you to examine the personnel of the Court Service of Cook County, and make an evaluation of the kind of preparation and background of the workers in Court Service, and determine how we are living up to a system of standards for social work. I invite you to take a look at this. If you saw the payroll you would perhaps understand why you have people without college degrees supervising people with college degrees, and they are making much more money than those who have college degrees. This is just an off-the-record statement.

You might also discern some idea of how patronage can work and affect services in a situation like this. The average person on public assistance in Illinois, in Cook County, in the Robert Taylor Homes, Ickes Homes, Cabrini Homes — in any of the low-income housing projects — feels that his whole existence depends upon allegiance to the political machine. He lives in the machine's house and eats the machine's food, and the machine sends him a check. Therefore, in order to live at all, he must have allegiance to the machine. Precinct captains know this very well. They become peddlers of fear, and if fear does not do it, they become very threatening and hostile to the people on public assistance.

This invites a kind of urban peasantry, in which people feel that they are dependent upon a system, a dead-end system that they cannot by any means risk. Therefore when Martin Luther King came to the Robert Taylor Homes last summer for a rally, here were the poorest people, the most needy people, and yet it was the poorest rally in the city of Chicago. The machine had sent its angels around a few days before and suggested that it might not be well to attend the Martin Luther King rally in the Robert Taylor Homes, and we, the movement, lost money on that spot.

This shows up in the primaries and in certain Republican townships in Cook County: You get some of this same attitude. But because it is so massive in Chicago, it has a tremendous effect upon the political decision-making in this metropolitan area. I have said to many people in Winnetka that "you do not make decisions for Cook County, they are made down in my ward," where you have tremendous voting majorities.

Of course, the people who work for the system know this kind of thing goes on. On my desk at this moment, I have a statement from a girl that has epileptic seizures (and there is a nine-year old daughter in the home) who has been asking for a telephone for two months. The only reason she does not have it: The caseworker told her it required too much work to get her a telephone, despite the fact that she has epileptic seizures and had one two nights ago in the hall of the housing project where she lives. People who are callous, people who are untrained, people who are not professional can take this kind of risk and this kind of position because they know the climate within which this system is operating.

Because it operates in this fashion, it becomes part of a paraphernalia of political activity, of political assessment, of political planning in Cook County, and in Chicago. And take the precinct, and precinct by precinct: If you look at the return cards of election day, you can almost count the precincts where you have a high caseload of public assistance. Any so-called social change in this city must free the people on welfare, so they know that their political rights are respected, that they do not have to vote one ticket or the other simply because they are on public assistance, that they cannot be evicted from a housing project without the legal process of a court, that their grant cannot be cut and taken away without a right to an appeal and a right to have the facts known in their case. And finally, that they have the right to know what their rights are.

We have here heard the case of a mother with the $5 for her kid in junior high school. Two years had passed; she did not know anything about it. Then she finally got it; the girl got a job, and they deducted the $5 all at once from the budget. But during the previous two years when the right was there and the person did not know it, nothing happened at all.

This is the kind of political operation one sees in the welfare picture. What is the answer? The answer is in doing what we try to do at the West Side Organization, what we try to do at Committee on Community Organizations. The answer is to organize welfare recipients, tell them what their rights are, explain to them what their budgetary allowance should be, so they become knowledgeable people about the system. Then if they need to march, march; if they need to sit, sit; but most of all, they need to know that they can vote like they darned choose, against the administrators who are not free either. Neither the administrators nor the caseworkers are free. If we are going to make welfare a meaningful and viable system that ministers to human need, this change will have to come in this system long before we get annual income. Until the ideal time comes, we better get some guaranteed bread and butter now and use this system to help people.

LEON DESPRES

You have asked me to talk on the politics of the administration of city programs, that is, how city programs are administered, and what the underlying politics of administration are. From taking part as alderman and neighborhood representative for the last eleven years, I think I can say that in each city department, the administration of city programs has two aspects: service and manipulation.

Under service I would include the publicly acknowledged program of the department: the inspection of buildings, the enforcement of codes, the establishment of mental health centers, the sending of rat killers up and down alleys, that is to say, any function described in the city budget or the annual departmental reports, or the mayor's budget message or the publicity announcements about what the city is going to do or has done.

Service is a very important function but the second function, manipulation, which is not discussed very often, is of prime interest here, especially to those of you who belong to community organizations, have to deal with city administrative programs, are interested in them, and want to develop them. Manipulation can be summarized best as the function of the department which insures that at all costs nothing the department does shall result in the independent organization of people. The manipulation function is extremely important, and I am sure all of you have come across it. The more directly the service program of a department is connected with people in the community, the more important it is for the department to be successful in its manipulation function, that is, in preventing the program from resulting in any kind of independent organization of the people it serves.

Mr. Wedemeyer put it very well, in somewhat more sober terms, when he said of a welfare administrator, "He develops notions of his constituency which do not include the people with whom he deals." The departments consider their public to be persons who ought to remain in the background, and proceed to develop notions of their constituency "which do not include the people with whom they deal." And how do they effect this? In a great number of ways. First of all, they do not regard the people as their true clients. They divide the people against each other. If there are popular organizations, the departments try to hold them off and, if the organizations persist, divide them against each other. And then, when the departments find they cannot avoid organizations of the people with whom they deal, they often try to create compliant shadow organizations.

The more closely a department's service program depends on the people of the community, the more energetically it tries to prevent the people of the community from organizing effectively. Unfortunately, the manipulation function impairs the service function. When a department is involved with the people of the communities of Chicago and fails to allow them to organize independently or acts affirmatively to prevent their organization, its service function falters even though its manipulation function succeeds. In other words, manipulation is supported at the expense of service.

I would like to take a few examples; not a great many, because I think all of you have often had experience with this kind of activity. The purpose of the examples is to insure that we are all thinking about the same thing. I suppose the most dramatic example is the antipoverty program because the statute expressly states that the program must have maximum feasible participation of the people of the community. Since this was an embarrassing directive for administrators who desire minimum and not maximum participation, the manipulation function became urgent. On the service side of the antipoverty program, the department is trying, as hard as it can, to send the largest possible part of its funds into the perfectly safe portions of the program such as Head Start, job training, or any other program which is insulated from the groups of people it serves, highly structured, and highly technical, and does not call for community organization.

But in the community action portions, the antipoverty program has to deal with people. So it creates shadow organizations and advisory councils in the community. It goes into the community and selects the existing organizations which seem to be the least dangerous, the most reliable, or the safest. It brings them in large numbers into the advisory council. Then, grudgingly, it introduces a few other people from the community so that the advisory council will be weighted as strongly as possible against independent citizen participation.

From that point on, the administration of the program is directed toward manipulation so that the people of the community will not organize to advance themselves, because if they do you never know what might happen; they might even really work their way out of poverty. If people on the advisory council would begin to ask the antipoverty department, "Do you mean that we really are free to examine these programs, that we really can propose programs of our own, that we can call on you for staff, that we really can share in the administration of the antipoverty program?," the classic answer of the department would be the old nursery rhyme: "Mother, may I go out to swim? Yes, my darling daughter, hang your clothes on a hickory limb, but don't go near the water." That is really the message the department gives to the citizens' advisory council.

I can document this much further because in Woodlawn, which I have observed intimately and where I belong to the advisory council, I watched the antipoverty program. I guess that I can say this without expecting any official contradiction because no one from the antipoverty office is here. You would expect the antipoverty program to have half a dozen representatives here to meet with important community organizations from poverty areas, but since that would be an encouragement of independent community organization, nobody came, for the very reasons I have just mentioned.

When the Woodlawn antipoverty community progress office opened, it was obsessively concerned with preventing The Woodlawn Organization from having any influence on the antipoverty program. I am not even sure that The Woodlawn Organization was interested in having influence, but that was the obsession of the first two directors of the antipoverty program in Woodlawn. The advisory council began meeting in a sterile manner but finally did begin to take action on some of the programs. The administration had such confidence in the makeup of the advisory council that it did not bother to order its reliable members to attend. It assumed that enough of them would. So at two successive meetings (I could understand the first one, but then they really slipped up on the second one) the advisory council took the initiative, referred programs to committees, conducted hearings, and then disapproved some of the programs. I assure you that this action brought the roof tumbling down on the advisory council, and at the next meeting every single administration member was present. Every safe member was there, and, of course, at the third meeting, the actions of the second meeting were completely reversed. And the advisory council was completely squelched. We made some other efforts after that, but I think they were almost entirely for the record because the demonstration of administration domination was so crushingly complete.

I am sure you can repeat that experience elsewhere, but I would like to give you some examples from other departmental programs because the antipoverty program is well known to all of you and well documented and dramatized.

The building department is another example. On the service side, the building department has an elaborate program for the enforcement of the building code and the protection of housing standards. It is useful, and it is better than it was. But there is one step that the building department will never, never take: it will never stimulate *any* kind of effective organization of the victims of the violations, who are, of course, the tenants. One never hears, because it never happens, of an inspector calling the tenants of the building together for a discussion, much less organizing them in any way.

You never hear of an inspector walking down the street, taking the initiative, and making a complaint when he sees a rat-infested or roach-infested slum, because that would be stimulating initiative on the part of the people.

A large auxiliary building inspection program was turned over to the antipoverty office, under the direction of the building department. The orders were that under no circumstances were the community representatives to do anything which would amount to organization of the tenants – the victims – not even call them into a single meeting in the front room of one of the apartments of the building. Thus the service function was carried on along with the manipulation function, but the manipulation undermined and weakened the service and made it much less effective.

Urban renewal works the same way. In urban renewal, as Mr. Wedemeyer said, notions of the constituency do not include the people with whom the department deals most closely. Of course there is a constituency, and the law requires the formation of citywide advisory councils and community conservation councils. Again, the "mother, may I go out to swim" illustration applies.

You may remember that, at a meeting of the citywide advisory council on urban renewal, Monsignor Egan (of the Archdiocesan Office on Urban Affairs) and Dr. Edgar Chandler (of the Church Federation) began asking questions and raising objections to what was going on. The meeting was quickly adjourned. I was reminded of that incident a few minutes ago when Mr. Doty called for reports and said, "Is there a minority report from the B group? No? Fine!," and that was the end of it. Monsignor Egan and Dr. Chandler also never tried it again. Yet we know that urban renewal, the attacks on the problems of the city, all the service programs of the city, would be infinitely better if the citywide manipulation were different.

I could give you other examples. We could talk about the rodent control program, the Board of Health, or the mental health centers. We could talk about the clean-up program which leaves Chicago about the same each year as it has been, but which is glorified by awards given by the large supply firms and passed around among the major cities. Each year Chicago is able to get a "cleanest city award" from some association somewhere, while 63rd Street or Roosevelt Road remain indistinguishable from what they were the year before. We could talk about the current police-community relations program – a laudable effort which is intended to give an appearance of community support and create some dialogue, but under no circumstances organize the communities to do the job.

I want to end with a little note of encouragement. After this discussion of the politics of administration, I do want to say that a community organization should not feel totally discouraged, because it can make effective demands on the service portion of the city administration programs, such as the building department programs, and the health programs. Those service portions, even though impaired, even though not as strong as they ought to be, are nevertheless responsive to demands and should not be ignored. You can organize a community, you can make demands, and you can even win small victories and achievements for community organizations. These achievements are important to the life of an organization.

What is the cure for the unexpressed manipulative discouragement of citizen organization? In a broad political sense, the solution of the basic problem of administration is political. So long as people who make a living *off* politics operate government, they find it absolutely essential that people not be allowed to organize because the independent organization of communities and of people is a threat to the people who live off politics. You have to see that government is run not by people who live off politics, but by people who are interested in running government to advance the community-oriented policies for which you work. Achieving that is definitely a political problem.

EUGENE BORUCKI

I would be glad to add a few comments of my own now that I have oriented myself.

I have no high-level position in any program but I teach in a school on the West Side which, for some reason, has produced some amazing individuals such as Warner Saunders, Al Raby, and Mr. Cash. These are all fine individuals. Al and I have discussed the problems of the West Side neighborhood for hours on end, after school, before school, and during school.

Most depressing about the question of welfare is that I must look at it every day. I see what is being created; I see what is not being produced. I teach at the Hess school which is supposedly an upper-grade center. Poverty and education are so entwined that they cannot possibly be separated. The neighborhood itself is depressing.

I live just eight minutes from the school. Most of the teachers drive there, to and from the suburbs. The district superintendent lives so far out of the city, I am not sure he knows how to get there each morning. The principal lives far out on the north side. Most of the administrators live so far out of the district they must travel an hour and a half (they are still within the city). Thus the people who are working in the school, and many of the people working in the welfare section in that area, are not really aware of the problems or what they are creating. They are dealing with human beings, delightful, beautiful children who can and must be stimulated.

At one time Ben Willis and the Cook County Department of Public Aid ran an after-school or evening literacy program to teach people, who never did get an education, to read or write. To me this seemed an endless task. About 80% of the 1000 each year that graduated from the Hess school did not finish high school. As far as I was concerned this was self-perpetuating; you could never end it. If each semester in the evening, you educated 250 or 300 adults, the next and following years, another 700 who could not read or write came in.

I think that what we are talking about here today is basically a problem of administration. Do the administrators know what is going on in the neighborhood? I am almost convinced that the Welfare Department is strictly a political being. At one time the Board of Education was a political being. A terrific scandal was necessary to change this particular Board of Education. Now it is so divorced from City Hall that it is difficult to understand who is running which. The next in the city was the police department. It was an entirely political being, and a tremendous scandal was necessary to wake people up, to let it become an independent branch of government. In the welfare situation, and its complete tie-in with politics, perhaps this must happen again.

You can talk all day about what is going on, see it, feel it, and know you have to witness it every morning. It is a depressing sight to walk into a school that is filthy. The school itself has no relationship to the community, the people who work there have no relationship to the community, and I am not too sure the children or the parents have a relationship with the community.

Start from scratch. Children are suffering. We are creating generations of welfare recipients, and the whole idea of welfare is an educational policy. If you cannot read or write, how can you work? If you cannot work, how do you eat? So, then you go on the welfare rolls. We are perpetuating this within the schools, and no one seems to be disturbed about it. My principal is not disturbed about it. The district superintendent is not disturbed about it. The administrators downtown are not disturbed about it. It seems that no one will be disturbed about it until, as in the previous board of education or in the police department, somebody presses the panic button.

Perhaps we are in a social age today where people do not care about one another; they are not interested in human beings. We are interested in the people of India; they are starving. We are interested in the people of Vietnam; we are going to get democracy for them. We are interested in Europe. We are interested in Latin America. But we are not interested in the human beings who live within a fifteen-minute drive of this area.

It is shocking to me. Perhaps we are in an age where there are too many statistics, too many administrators, where there is not enough self, human dignity so that one person gives to another. Until, as the alderman and Mr. Robinson said, we set the program down to where the people know their rights and know that they do have rights, we will continue to create countless generations of welfare recipients.

Whatever effort you can make, to a large extent you will have to tie in the schools with the poverty program. Perhaps the social workers could work out of the school. Instead of setting up the poverty offices outside the neighborhood, they could be set up within the school.

Representatives from the various county agencies might even come and speak to the children. You either educate the very old or the very young. Head Start is doing this; it is giving them a start. Let the children know what is available, so they can go home and tell their parents. Many of these children in the seventh grade have a better knowledge of worldly affairs, can speak, read, and write better than their parents who came from the South.

You might have to draw the school in as a center of activity because there is none in these areas, except the ward headquarters. Then we go back to what Mr. Robinson and Mr. Despres said; we are back to the political structure again. I would like to see the schools participate more. I know there are services available to me, but I do not have the time, nor the energy, nor the power to seek out a social worker. The people in those neighborhoods understand four particular agencies that the county or city provides in the city: Cook County Hospital, the Welfare Department, Cook County Jail, and the local police station.

If more people took an interest in human beings, and if every day they saw what is going on, I suspect that eventually they might get religion. It is a touchy subject; everybody runs from it, no one will face up to it. The greatest facing up to it is just to drive through the neighborhood, talk to some lovely, charming faces who will be adults, and know that before they even get started, they are lost.

JOHN WANER

I did not know the exact reason I was to come here tonight. I am not prepared to make a formal presentation. To a degree, I feel something like Anthony when he walked into Marie Antoinette's boudoir. I did not come here to make a speech.

One reason I am here is out of curiosity. As you know, in the last three weeks I have been busy trying to organize some facets of what many refer to as a hopeless campaign. Perhaps some of them speak with authority based on the past performance of Republican candidates in Chicago.

However, I do feel that if some of the Republican principles that used to exist within the Republican party are carried back to the people, perhaps they will give it another look. I was not picked by any special group in Chicago to represent the Republican party; I went before the slate-making committee, and for about three weeks I fought like the devil to be the candidate. I felt that for the last thirty-six years we have not had any real effort on the part of any Republican in Chicago to go after the office of mayor, perhaps with the exception of the one race by Bob Merriam, which was an honest effort to wrest the mayority from the Democrats.

When I announced my candidacy for mayor, I said that services to the people of Chicago are actually a right to which they are entitled, not a privilege granted only to those who do business with the city or those who are subservient to the system. I am very much in favor of community control. In fact, one of the first talks I gave before the press stated my belief in rebuilding our communities, giving them the greatest possible right to express their opinions and, to a degree, govern much of their destiny. This has always been a Republican principle and, now more than ever, it represents the new look within the Republican party.

I believe that if we rally the people around the candidate we can be elected and, when elected, I intend to change the system which has been allowed to grow unchallenged in this city for the last thirty-six years. Of course, this has also been the situation for the last twelve years under Mayor Daley, who is a creature of the machine he heads and to which he is obligated. If there were a decent conflict-of-interests law in Chicago, the D'Arcos, Dawsons, and Keanes of this political machine all would be in the penitentiary, because most of them carry on direct dealings and are purely profit motivated.

As FHA director, I listened to Rennie Davis talk about the Urban Renewal program and I regret that I must agree with him. The Urban Renewal program is a mystery not only in Chicago, but all over the nation. It is a shame that it has not been allowed to work as intended by Congress.

Perhaps I am the leading authority in Chicago on that particular question. I spoke to one of my aides, Phil Crone, a young man who is here with me today, and I said, "Phil, I do not know what the devil to talk about." He said just talk about what you have been telling everyone and what you think.

The moderator mentioned that in 1960, under President Eisenhower, I was appointed the Federal Housing Director for Northern Illinois. A good many of you remember that in 1960 the Federal Housing Administration in Chicago was completely bogged down. There was absolutely no activity in the Chicago office. Since the construction industry is one of the major sectors of our economy, many builders, contractors (heating and ventilating contractors included), and many sponsors wondered why the office was even allowed to exist. While the FHA was not or is not making any direct loans, it was established in order to make available mortgage money in what would normally be considered high-risk areas. By insuring the mortgage against a loss by the lender as such, it was intended to be an important factor primarily in the areas where private money was not intending to move. The element of risk kept private money out.

I called my assistant director who was a long term ... I was going to say bureaucrat ... but I won't; he has been there for some thirty years. I said, "What have we got in the office?" He said, "Well, Mr. Waner, to tell you the truth, we have nothing." I said, "What in the devil are you operating on?" And he said, "Well, we have got a lot of projects here that we did not final out, but we are keeping the files open because if we final them out, we will not have anything left in the office." I thought this rather unusual and, knowing that the entire building industry in the area of urban renewal was complaining that no programs were emanating out of the FHA, I called a meeting of all the builders, lenders, and people interested in urban renewal. Among them were Julian Levi from Kenwood-Hyde Park and Winston Kennedy from the University of Chicago.

We met at the Sherman Hotel, and the meeting went something like this: I asked my staff, the underwriters, appraisers, and mortgage credit men to join us, with all interested sponsors and builders, asking them to let their hair down, and tell us why they do not do business with the FHA. Without exception everyone told us in detail why they did not do business with FHA. Basically it amounted to the fact that everything was bogged down in bureaucracy. Projects, to bring a program out of FHA, required six, seven, eight months before they were even looked at, and then another year or two to process. By then either the sponsor died or the land was no longer available, or the money market changed, and so on.

Immediately after this meeting, I called the staff together and said unless we get off the ground, I will have no recourse but to insist that Washington close the office. I asked them to all cooperate in every way. I intended to cut red tape and run projects out of the office as fast as we could.

I went back to all the sponsors and told them, "Now we are ready for business." If you remember from the local press at the time, the Chicago office processed more applications than any other office in the country and was accredited the number one office. We put through the first urban renewal at 54th and Blackstone under section 220. We put through the first 220 University Garden's projects, Prairie Shores; the first section 213, cooperative housing; and section 232, nursing homes. Marina City was processed downtown under section 207 by a slight variation of the rules which previously called for families with children. A request on my part from Washington changed section 207 to read "for family living" which made it possible to bring out Marina City. While some will complain about the aesthetics of Randolph Street East, it was the first air-rights leasehold project processed by the FHA in the United States. We prevailed upon builders to come in and work under section 221 of the National Housing Act relocation housing.

It amazed me that the city administration under Daley issued a list of accomplishments, one of which was that they had knocked down some 50,000 dwelling units due to land clearance, urban renewal, and other causes. Not one single dwelling unit was built or made available under any of the sections of the National Housing Act existing at that time. In fact I talked to Mr. Mackelmann who was then in charge of the urban renewal division in the City Hall. He had not issued one single relocation certificate for new housing in spite of the fact that fifty thousand people were dislocated through the aforementioned government action. Certainly this was extremely poor planning; you do not knock down fifty thousand dwelling units without making provisions for building new buildings to house those you displaced.

Since then I have been extremely critical of the fact that, after the government has paid 50% of the costs for clearing urban renewal land, the land is sold back to private developers at an exorbitant price on which the city makes a substantial profit. Low rent, market land should be sold back to private developers for approximately a dollar or two per square foot so that they can make a profit on the economics of the building, to keep the rent low so that people who have been displaced can return to the community they have been displaced from into new low-rent or low-cost, long-term small mortgage payment housing. If we use Sandburg Village as a criteria, the land after clearance was sold for $9 per square foot. Many people who have been dislocated by government action cannot even afford the security deposit, much less afford the rent to move back into the area from which they were displaced. Where Sandburg Village now stands, where did these displaced people move? With no new housing at low cost available the answer is easy: the ghetto.

Of course, this made me very aware of why the critical housing shortage exists in the Chicago area. In 1960, I called in the Chicagoland builders and the Chicago mortgage people. I cautioned them that the Chicagoland mortgage people must pay more attention to the so-called "area of declining values" – incidentally, that is a term which I picked up when I was with the government – it is used by government officials to describe an area where they will not encourage the making of mortgages. I have always insisted that the government will have to step in and demand that the lending institutions in metropolitan Chicago carry a fixed percentage of mortgages in the areas of declining values in their portfolio or lose their Federal Deposit Insurance. All of these areas are ineligible for a mortgage unless they are specifically designated as urban renewal areas. Of course, the legal or elected representatives of many areas in Chicago will not have their area declared one of urban renewal. This would invite federal funds which they do not want because federal funds mean no segregation.

We are very aware of the fact that, in the areas where the Appalachian whites, Negroes, or Latin-speaking peoples are currently housed, it is physically impossible for them to get a mortgage at a long-term or a decent interest rate or, for that matter, without paying exorbitant rates under the table. This is a result of the fact that all of the Chicagoland mortgage people, every one of them carrying a Federal Deposit Insurance Corporation label on their window, are reluctant to move into these areas to make long-term mortgages.

I do not want to harp on it too much, but I realize that we must make mortgage money more readily available, even in the areas of 221(d)3. Today 221(d)3 money is going out of Fannie Mae – the name given the Federal National Mortgage Association – at a seven point discount. This means that the property must be overappraised by at least 7% in order for the mortgage to be handled. Thus the tenant, buyer, or sponsor must own a piece of land or equity which in mortgage circles is referred to as a "declining equity mortgage."

There was an alleged instance here in Chicago recently where a private developer embarked on a 221(d)3 program. He bought one building and presented it to FHA under Section 221(d)3. He worked on the economics for a month or two and found that it did not pay because the property cost too much. So he tabled it, even though it had lost him something like $25,000 for engineers, appraisals, architects, etc. Then he moved on to another building, and after spending some $25,000 found that that did not work. He tried a third one, and that did not work. He had $75,000, so finally he bought a fourth one. It worked, but the $75,000 he had lost on the first three was put on the fourth which in turn resulted in a higher rental to the tenant.

This is certainly not conducive to sound lending practice and, in fact, I believe it is illegal. I recognized what shortcomings existed in 1962 when I left the FHA. I was asked by leading Democrats to stay in the FHA after I resigned, in spite of the fact that I was a Republican. They said they would like for me to stay there; I had done more for Chicago than any other official in the field of housing. I told them that it had always been my opinion that a director in the city should reflect the thinking of the administration and that by no stretch of the imagination could I reflect the thinking of the Democrats.

I resigned from the FHA, a civil service post, and one of the first things I did was to go before the State Legislature. I asked that they empower the city of Chicago to issue municipal bonds in order to form a mortgage pool of money within Chicago so that anyone who received an insured commitment from the FHA could go to the city with this commitment and get money on its face value without paying exorbitant discounts. Julian Levi of your community, myself, and a number of others worked on this. Subsequently this bill was presented as a bipartisan bill by Noble Lee and others, and signed into law by Governor Kerner.

Today, the city of Chicago is empowered to sell municipal bonds, at the going rate of about 4%, to provide money on long-term FHA mortgages, in some instances up to forty years, to anyone, so that he may rebuild, alter, modify, repair, change, and so on, without paying exorbitant discount rates, or going to where this exorbitant discount fee is paid. As of today, not one bond has ever been sold by the city of Chicago and no mortgage pool exists for the people who are building in the areas of declining values, or — another term that I learned in FHA — the "areas of transition." There is no mortgage money available at par, in spite of the fact that Daley was given this power by the legislature. Today it is part of the Villages and Municipalities Act of Illinois. Why isn't this pool set up?

These things, among others, incensed me all the more, and I   said, "Darn it, I am going to run for mayor, and do something about it." And here I am.

5

Para-Politics: Techniques and Strategies

RICHARD FLACKS

I guess that much of the formal and informal discussion – much of what people are thinking about – has to do with how we can affect the structure of power locally and nationally. What most of us think of when we begin to think of strategies for change is the use of the ballot box and the power of the vote.

That the title of this panel is somewhat obscure is my fault. I am not sure there is such a word as "para-politics," but I think we have in mind the fact that in addition to the conventional political process there are other ways to influence the structure of power, ways that are outside conventional politics.

There are several problems with conventional politics, and perhaps the poor know that better than most of us in the middle class. One problem is that the poor are a minority and particularly a political minority. Therefore, even if they achieve effective political representation, which they do not have now, they would still have difficulty influencing the legislatures and city councils. The second problem, as our history shows, is that those who claim to represent the poor often get absorbed into the established political structure and cease to be effective representatives of the people for whom they claim to speak. The third problem is that the conventional political process is inherently a process involving compromise. There must be ways for people to express themselves outside that framework of compromise if large-scale social change is to take place.

All these factors, as well as others which could be mentioned, suggest to me the proposition that deprived communities must be organized at the grass roots, independently of any established power bloc or political party; such organization must be effective at mobilizing disadvantaged people to action in their own interests, and such action must include techniques and goals which are para-political as well as political. All of these things must happen if poverty is to be abolished and democracy survive in this country.

At the tactical level, I mean by para-politics the series of techniques, based on mass action, which both the civil rights and the labor movements have demonstrated to be effective instruments of changing the structure of

69

power. Mass marches, picketing, direct action, civil disobedience are essential tactics for forcing a recalcitrant power structure to respond to the demands of the poor.

However, I think that, when we talk about para-politics we mean something more than just effective techniques of protest. I think we mean developing within communities, organizations which can become stable institutions and which strive for a situation in which the community has more direct control over its environment and the forces which act on it. Judging from the activities and discussions going on in a number of cities among people involved in various types of community organizing, it seems to me that there are at least three functions that I would call para-political which community organizations ought to consider. And I hope that the other discussants will be able to make these more concrete by describing particular situations.

First, such organizations can act like a trade union, that is, defend against the exploitation of people in the community and demand better services. There are many examples of organizations in the community acting like trade unions. The most obvious are tenants' unions and welfare rights organizations, but one could add the organizations which act against police malpractice, which try to work to protect consumers, and so forth. The techniques these groups use – such as rent strikes, boycotts, demonstrations, the exposure of malpractice, the use of the courts – are also similar to the techniques of the trade union movement. This is activity which is going on now, and undoubtedly there are people in this room who know more about it and the problems it involves that I do.

It seems to me that this particular set of activities comes up against a series of problems which are often not very visible to people outside of those communities. They can be boiled down to this: when people try to organize community unions, they come up against a situation much like that which the labor movement confronted when it tried to organize the industrial workers – that is, a kind of fear or unwillingness to take a risk, especially when the payoff for that risk is uncertain. I think that in the very near future we will need a Wagner Act for community unions, similar to the Wagner Act for the trade union movement, which will protect the right of poor people to organize. Along with that we will need an effective program of legal aid to the poor to assist these organizations in winning such rights. Such legal support is essential if the community union idea is to take root. But the community union concept, as far as I can tell, is only one type of function, which can be served by the kind of para-political or insurgent organizations that I am talking about.

A second type of function has to do with the electoral process and conventional politics. Community organizations can become highly sophisticated political organizations, making candidates responsible to the community, serving as a constant monitor of representatives' performance, and writing the platform and defining the issues for representatives. In other words, it is not enough to get behind a man who seems good or speaks the right rhetoric or is talking the right way. It is more important to have an organization which can select the candidates, define the issues, write the platforms, and bring him home when he is not doing his job.

In the absence of real representation in the official legislatures, a notion is arising in some places of developing a kind of parallel political structure, one which can serve as a model of how the official structure could operate. This is what the Freedom Democratic Party did in Mississippi when it began to organize. It created a political party for people who had no political voice and it held elections even though these were not officially recognized. And in New York, a number of organizations have recently gotten together and formed a "People's Board of Education." This is not the official Board of Education but it has held hearings and is trying to define a school program for that city. And I understand that in Chicago, a group of people have begun to form a police review board which would have a similar kind of function.

In the third place, we have what I think is the most farreaching thing that is happening or at least being discussed. This involves moving beyond simply the notion of community unions or of getting some control over the political process, to begin working for direct community control over a great variety of services and resources. First, this can be done by trying to achieve a degree of decentralization of certain public functions such as the school system, the public housing system, the police, and so forth so that the people in neighborhoods can begin to control them. Second, a degree of community self-determination can be achieved by striving for community voice in the administration of public programs such as the war on poverty and urban renewal. These two programs have been the focus for an enormous amount of activity along these lines around the country. Finally, we have the extremely important idea of beginning to develop within the community, within the neighborhood, institutions that people own and control cooperatively.

On the one hand this means developing from within the community what people see as their own institutions: stores, credit unions, community centers, theatres, etc. More ambitiously, this means beginning to establish foundations or community corporations under the control of the people in the community itself. Now, there are a number of plans along this line. One which is well known is apparently sponsored by Senator Kennedy in the Bedford-Stuyvesant neighborhood of Brooklyn. It remains to be seen how these will work out, but the theory is that the people in the community can form their own corporation, their own foundation, or whatever you want to call it. They receive funds from outside, but do the planning and shape the direction of their community themselves. It seems to me inescapable that that redefintion of community government is what we must have if there is to be anything like an effective abolition of the slums or an effective notion of democracy in cities.

The problem is that all of these potential directions for community organization, from community union to people's foundations, strike at the heart of existing sources of profit, and bases of property, and political power in the city. The result is that whenever people have begun to undertake this sort of activity, they have been met by all sorts of reprisals. These are too numerous to mention now, but I hope that some of our speakers will give some examples of them. I do not know whether the incipient movement within communities for self-determination, which takes the variety of forms that I have described, will be allowed to take shape and gain strength. If it is not, then I think we all have to be extremely pessimistic about the future of our society.

JAN LINFIELD

Until a few months ago, I worked with the Kenwood-Oakland Community Organization, and while I am at the moment at Billings Hospital, I will soon be in a storefront clinic, the Woodlawn Children's Health Center on 63rd Street.

I interpret "para-politics" to mean something that exists outside the framework of the existing welfare system, in a sense a counterforce to the existing system. It reminds me that, in the Welfare Rights Organization in California, workers in the organization are known as "counter caseworkers."

As a professional social worker, I have always worked within the welfare system, although I have never worked for the welfare department. I have spent many hours on the telephone with a welfare recipient sitting by my desk, trying to straighten out some tangle that had resulted in her being without any funds. Over the years, I have become thoroughly discouraged and frustrated with this case by case approach. The individual's problem was eventually solved, but the whole process had to be started over again for the next person who had a similar problem. Nothing in the system was any different, and any social workers in this group know exactly what I mean.

I first heard what the West Side Organization was doing from Bob Strom. He described what was again a case by case approach to the solution of welfare grievances, but one which goes a very important step further, into the area of organizing the people who had been helped to form a pressure group that could work toward bringing about some real changes in the welfare system.

When we began organizing in Kenwood-Oakland, knocking on doors, and talking to people about what they saw as their problems, one of the major things people kept telling us about over and over again was the problems they were having with the welfare department – how they got what they called the "welfare run-around." They told us about people who apply for assistance and wait three or four months without any kind of emergency aid before they are given any help, people whose checks are cut off or whose checks are reduced by $30, $40, or $50 a month without any kind of an explanation. When the person on welfare tries to find out why this has happened, he is told, "I will look into it," "I will have to ask my supervisor," "I will see what I can do," or "I will take care of it," but nothing happens.

We found that 30.9% of all people living in Kenwood-Oakland are receiving some kind of public assistance. From the point of view of organizing, this appeared to be one of the most effective issues that we could begin with.

We started with eight of the most difficult problems we could find and took them into the district office. We had the help of Bob Strom, Bill Darden, and Ralph Henry of the West Side Organization. The problems covered a wide range. There were women who had applied for assistance when their husbands deserted and had been waiting for two or three months. A woman, who had applied for assistance and had been referred to a job which paid considerably less than her budgeted grant would have been, was told that she was eligible for supplementary assistance which she never received. There were women who had been budgeted for child support which they have never received. Budget deficits amounted up to $60 or $70 a month.

What happened in the district office was somewhat electrifying. Supervisors began running around the office; emergency checks suddenly appeared. One woman who had applied for assistance three or four months earlier and had been waiting for her caseworker to come all those months was told that he would come to see her the following day, a Saturday. All the eight women had been trying to get their problems settled over a period of months and had talked with their caseworkers many, many times. At the end of the day, they left the office with a total of over $800 in emergency aid and disbursing orders.

Possibly the only unique thing about this experience is the fact that we did this with eight people at once. This is something the West Side Organization had been doing for at least a year or two before we started, and it is something that the women in KOCO repeated over and over again in the succeeding months. After the first few times we went into the office, the ADC mothers in the Kenwood-Oakland Community Organization carried this operation completely by themselves and continued to do so after I left the organization. Basic policies concerning eligibility and how to figure a grant are easily learned. Any ADC mother who can figure her grocery bill can do nine-tenths of what the Public Aid caseworker does and in many ways do it better.

The KOCO Welfare Union (and I think the same could be said of the other welfare unions) has never lost a case they have taken into the district office. This seems like an extravagant claim, but it is true. It is true because the welfare department constantly and repeatedly violates its own policies in dealing with welfare recipients. When the welfare union goes into the office with a welfare grievance, it simply points out this is what the welfare policy says and you have not done it. We know that the cases we bring in are the ones in which gross mistakes have been made. We have no idea how many more there are because only a few get to welfare unions.

By any definition you suggest, this kind of activity on the part of people – welfare recipients on behalf of other welfare recipients – getting this kind of redressive action is power. We need to look at and try to understand the ingredients of this kind of power. Certainly it is not the so-called expertise of a professional social worker because no social worker can do this by herself. It is not the power of the clerical collars of the ministers who sometimes accompanied us. Such power comes rather from the name and reputation for militancy of the organization – KOCO, WSO, JOIN, or whatever group. The supervisor being confronted sees a vision of the thousands of people believed to be behind this organization, known to have been treated unfairly and unjustly by welfare policies or by the failure to observe welfare policies.

One source of this power comes from its association with the civil rights movement. This was demonstrated in one of KOCO's encounters with the welfare office. We were sitting with the head of the welfare office and her four assistant supervisors. One of our negotiators was Father Jones, an Episcopal priest who is on the staff of KOCO. In this conference, the head of the district office repeatedly addressed Father Jones as "Dr. King" – a slip which revealed how she saw the group confronting her. A group's reputation for militancy usually has to be established initially by a show of direct action, but once they have proven they are willing to go to the lengths of submitting to arrest, this kind of power seldom needs to be displayed again.

Welfare unions operate by confrontation – as opposed to concilliation. Most of the groups I have known, not only in Chicago but across the country, have found it necessary, in the beginning months of their negotiations with the welfare department, to sit-in at the welfare office with a women who was to be evicted the following day. All of them knew the fear of being "set out" and, when the woman was refused emergency aid (a decision clearly against agency policy), they refused to leave the office and were arrested for "criminal trespass."

Being arrested is not particularly noteworthy these days, but what was interesting about this particular incident was the extreme lengths to which the welfare department went to persuade these seven mothers from being arrested. The mothers were told that if they were arrested they ran the risk of having their children taken away from them. For this group of mothers who had a total of forty-five children, this was the most terrible weapon that could be used against them, but none of them changed their minds; all of them stayed. The next day one of the mothers with twelve children was visited by her caseworker and told that if she ever showed her face in the district office again, except on her own business, she would be cut off assistance.

The case against us dragged on for months, with one continuance after another, in the apparent hope that the group would pay its fines and not go to trial. We *were* going to trial, however, and to jail if necessary. But the morning we appeared in court – seven mothers and forty-five children, and reporters waiting to find out what was happening – the Welfare Department quite suddenly and with no explanation dropped the charges against us!

This suggests another source of power inherent in welfare unions: by and large people on welfare are children and mothers, aged, disabled, and sick people. When they are allowed to tell their story, to be seen as they really are, not separated by all the myths about welfare, the misconceptions and stereotypes that are portrayed in the public press, they create sympathy for themselves and their cause.

There are two things that happen in the welfare system that I see as parallel because they are things that happen to people. One is that case-workers and administrators in the welfare system reach the point where they see less and less of what really happens to people. They become in a very real sense desensitized and immune to the stories of human suffering which they hear over and over again.

This was most graphically illustrated in a case we took to the welfare office of a young mother who had a deficit of about $40 in her check. This meant that after her rent was paid she had $34 on which to support herself and two children for a month. Her electricity had been cut off because the agency had not paid her bill. She did not have lights; she did not have refrigeration. She had just come home from the hospital with a two-day-old baby. She borrowed money to buy milk, and stretched the milk by adding water, but she did not have any refrigeration for the milk, and the baby died when it was four days old. Upon hearing the story of the baby's death, the supervisor's only question was, "How did you get money to pay for the funeral?" Although she admitted a mistake had been made, it took several days, in spite of the family's desperate need, to get emergency aid for this mother.

The parallel part of the "What happens to people?" is "What happens to the person who is receiving welfare?" People get on welfare by one of two paths. Either you are born into a family that is on welfare, grow up in a family where money comes from the welfare department, and move from this to receiving a welfare check of your own; or, by a long series of defeats in life, you end up at the point where there is no alternative to applying for welfare. Having gotten to this point, you go through a long, humiliating, degrading experience of proving that you are a failure, that you have no money, no resources.

Then, having been beaten into submission, all the policies of public assistance conspire to keep you in this state. You are not really allowed to make any decisions for yourself: where you live, how you spend your money. You are given food stamps, not cash; rent is often paid by disbursing order, your utilities and medical care are paid directly by the agency. You accept what the caseworker tells you because you really do not know what your rights are. The caseworker assumes a tremendous power in your life because he can cut off your means of existence.

I believe that we will not see an end to the Frankenstein monster that the welfare system has become until the people who are the victims of this system in ever-increasing numbers rise up and demand their rights.

But having spoken of the potential and the *necessity* of welfare recipients organizing themselves, it is also necessary to at least mention some of the difficulties involved in welfare organizing.

People on welfare are often injected with the same picture of themselves that the rest of society holds of them – as worthless, depreciated people who have no rights and should be grateful for the pittance society doles out to them. The most pervasive feeling is *fear* – fear of becoming too visible, fear that someone will discover the few dollars of unreported income, fear of the caseworker's real or imagined disapproval of their belonging to a militant group. The experience of the people in the Poverty Rights Action Center – the national organization of welfare rights organizations – suggests that most of the welfare groups they knew in this organization had reached a certain plateau in organizing. There was a central core or cadre of very dedicated, committed, knowledgeable people, who worked very hard in the organization, but this was a very small group. Beyond it, there was a peripheral group of possibly several hundred or more who were only very loosely affiliated with the organization. While the peripheral group has unquestionably been touched by the fervor of the core group, the question of how to organize on a mass basis is still largely unsolved.

Another problem faced by many groups is whether welfare recipients can be most easily organized as welfare people per se, or within an organization representing all the interests of the community. Mr. Flacks suggests that the latter is most effective. I would agree in theory, but the experience of groups attempting this – KOCO is one of them – has been that the welfare group is forced to fight the same prejudiced attitudes within the organization that they do in the community at large.

Resistance and direct opposition to welfare organizing comes from many directions, not the least of which are the political forces in the community which are threatened by the emergence of any grass roots organization not under their control. Reprisals are sometimes subtle – a visit from the precinct captain is often all that is necessary – and sometimes very direct – an office ransacked and records destroyed. The remarkable fact is that in spite of these difficulties welfare unions continue to move ahead. They are, in my opinion, the fastest growing and potentially the most powerful movement in America today.

RENNIE DAVIS

My remarks here will be directed to caseworkers and poverty warriors, liberal professors and "concerned" public employees, and those well-meaning people who generally hold that all is not right in Chicago or the country. Somehow my association with JOIN – a rather unique organizing venture in a poor white Appalachian migrant community – has given me a ticket on Chicago's "panel circuit" and the opportunity to meet many of Chicago's most progressive-thinking citizens. The people on these panels are usually close friends, and we carry roughly the same critiques and prescriptions to auidences who usually share our values, our criticisms, and our hope for a new direction in Chicago. Those of us on this ride down the social critic's panel circuit should, I suppose, be encouraged by the variety and numbers of people who want change in this city. It would appear that the allies of the freedom movement had penetrated Chicago's institutional activities at many levels and that we had significant support in the very places we seek to change – the welfare department, all-white segregated communities, the police and urban renewal departments, the schools, poverty programs, private social agencies, the universities, and even city council.

But what is the reality? Behind the thousands who count themselves progressive, what is the power for real change?

Consider an issue such as urban renewal. Plans are being developed for every Chicago community that harbors an independent base of power of poor people – in Kenwood-Oakland, the Near West Side, East Garfield Park, Lawndale, Uptown, and Englewood. These are the communities of KOCO, the Oakland Committee for Community Improvement, the West Side Organization, the East Garfield Park Community Organization, the Lawndale Union to End Slums, JOIN, and the Englewood Action Center. These are also the communities that will become the victims of "redevelopment" schemes designed to build apartments that low-income families cannot afford and create lucrative contracts for supporters of the political machine. Now, many well-meaning Chicagoans will speak out on urban renewal with declarations for "community participation" or for "serving the interest of all our citizens." But who will help track down the major contractors, community by community, and help to discredit and ruin their operations? Who will risk their job for a serious fight against a federal housing program that does not have the tools to "save" poor communities even if the will was there? Where are the architects and planners who will volunteer their time to help community organizations develop alternative plans against the city's land grab? We need lawyers to tie up the city in the courts at every stage of urban renewal development and professors who will turn their research towards translating urban renewal decisions from an abstract, impersonal system into a list of known men and women who make decisions about specific resources. Where are these people?

Or consider welfare. Jan Linfield described powerfully and accurately the importance of a welfare recipients union to an ADC mother who has no protection against an inhumane, understaffed, poorly directed, and pitifully budgeted public aid system. Where are the caseworkers who would turn their union – the Independent Union of Public Aid Employees – into more than a group of recent college graduates with a few clucking old women "fighting" for higher wages and smaller "case" loads? We need a union of people who would risk their job, their so-called professional reputation, and an unblemished court record to confront and to change a system of public aid that is immoral and indecent to recipients.

Or consider Chicago's "finest" – the police department. Not too long ago, a blue ribbon committee was appointed to consider the merits of a civilian review board in Chicago. The freedom movement had demanded this study committee be established during the summer marches. Its mayor-backed architects saw it as an opportunity to whitewash brutal police actions last summer. Many of us had an opportunity to testify at this committee hearing. And many of us politely measured the pros and cons of a needed change as if some English chess tournament was about to be launched. In Uptown, police stick revolver butts down the throats of young guys and scream, "We're running all you motherfucking hillbillies out of town, so move, motherfucker, move." Who got up in their fancy suit and told the committee what was really happening?

There is no movement, no risk-taking, and little program, organizing, or courage among our Chicago progressives. We are strapped down by our own institutions. While we call for organizing unions in the ghetto, our own strength depends entirely on our individual strength. We look to others to change this city. We have no complimentary program to the Chicago free-dom movement. There is no independent base of power among Chicago's well-meaning people nor are there organizers attempting to bring it into being. Until we find a way to break through this powerlessness, we will advance little beyond liberal conferences, proclamations and characterizations of Chicago's progressives as "well-meaning people."

What is required to build an "independent" base of power in a city? What is required for an established individual to make a psychological break with the establishment? How could we create the basis for the well-meaning friends of the movement to join it, to feel that their lives were also bound up in a major collective force that was seeking real change in a city and country? To me, these are the critical questions. Answering them is no abstract, intellectual game but a practical move toward the possibility of a renewed, humane city.

Let me attempt to explain what those questions have meant for me personally. My education was spun out of a liberal family and several of the "best" colleges. I always believed what people told me: that I could "get ahead" and "be somebody." Somehow in the back of my mind that meant becoming a famous university professor. There was nothing in my back-ground that would have lent itself toward wanting to generate new forms of power independent of myself or deciding that it is more important to change the rules of American politics than it is to play its game, or that I should attempt to live and act out a set of values that ran against the dominant theme in American advertising, ideology and ceremonies.

It was a small group of people – university friends on the whole – who helped me begin to explore the assumptions behind my own career aspirations, the truth behind most public pronouncements, the logic behind a foreign policy of anticommunism, the meaning of democratic life in our universities, our corporations, and our communities. Developing a commit-ment to a group of honest friends in search of the truth behind the phoniness — to me, that was an important step toward personal and political independence.

Next, I moved to a community in Chicago, a community of 35,000 other migrants, though most of them came from poor families and the hills of Kentucky, West Virginia, and Tennessee. Here I started to work as an organizer. I learned the incredible importance of independent organization in freeing people to consider new perspectives and alternatives to the status quo. Poor whites in America have something in common with the well-meaning middle-class people I have been talking about. Both complain about issues and problems, though, of course, from very different vantage points. And both feel powerless to confront those problems. Both are swallowed by the same system. Neither can view or understand that system. There is no reinforcement for developing an independent understanding or strategy or movement to deal with that system. Both the liberal and the hillbilly have earned a set of blinders that restrict their vision of the possible and reduce their "concern" to petitions or conferences, wife beating or mean drunkenness. Only a significant part of the Negro population has created the kind of independent organization and movement that has allowed people to develop an independent relationship to American life. In Uptown Chicago, we went to work attempting to create this kind of independent organization for poor whites that could lift the blinders.

Uptown is next to impossible to organize, yet against the impossible, JOIN, the organization that was created, has made considerable advances. It is particularly impressive when measured by the number of people who have been personally and politically freed by a process that reinforces the individual to think and feel honestly.

Jan Linfield, in her description of the welfare recipient union in the Kenwood-Oakland Community Organization, summed up the activities, style, and purpose of one of the JOIN operations — the welfare union. But JOIN was conceived not as merely a welfare program. We call the organization a "community union" and define its constituency as poor and working class people. The organization both attempts to serve its members and the people in the community, and to raise broad social and political questions about who represents Uptown and how does a man go about controlling a brutal policeman and shouldn't the hillbilly school be as modern as the fancy school several blocks east along the lakefront?

This community union has several parts. First, as I mentioned, there is the welfare program. A second is the tenant unions — people living in bad buildings who use their collective power to get a landlord to improve instead of sap a building's condition. JOIN was the first organization in the city, and perhaps the country, to develop a collective bargaining contract with a landlord. Increasingly, our housing work is being directed toward developing an alternative to the urban renewal plan that will displace our people with luxury apartments and rehabilitated, higher rent housing.

A third component of JOIN is a group called the Uptown Goodfellows. Comprised of about one hundred young men, most of them from the

South, this group represents an important power in a developing poor white movement. The group organizes around social activities and a common enemy – police brutality. Last summer, about 250, most of them in their late teens, marched on the Summerdale Police Station to demand new citizen checks on police brutality and the dismissal of one officer, Sam Joseph.

A fourth and central part of JOIN is its alternative precinct captain system – neighborhood people who call themselves "stewards." They represent over a hundred people who distribute a weekly newspaper to 3000 people, provide communication to the community and service people who have specific welfare, job, housing, and other problems.

The significance of JOIN is that it cannot be bought out or reduced to quiet by a call from the mayor or a "boss" or a bishop or a dean. It provides a framework for people to consider alternative ways to organize a community, alternative priorities and alternative power. It was not organized to be a part of an established program or system, but to be independent and to reinforce independent thinking and planning. I believe that this kind of organizational framework is needed across this city if we are ever to develop the kind of power and program that can make a dent in the machine's way of running things.

I am not just calling for the creation of 30 or 40 WSO's, JOIN's, or KOCO's in Chicago, though that must happen. I am thinking that we must somehow build new frameworks for professionals, teachers, caseworkers, and city planners where it might be possible to politically and personally grow outside the forces that restrict thinking, planning and the creation of new power within rigid institutions. We need an intelligence network in this city that is responsive to the needs of a broad social movement – people who supply information and analysis about what is happening "inside" the shells we seek to change. We need the kinds of professional organizations whose fundamental purpose is to examine the program and policy of the welfare, sanitation, urban renewal, and police departments. We need to develop alternative programs for our major public and private institutions, programs that people can think deeply about, organize around and push for. If there is to be a new government to replace the Daley machine, if there is to be a new ethic and purpose in our churches and corporations and courts, a deliberate effort to organize an independent framework to which people can come to think and plan and develop strategies for change must be created for every segment of our urban society. While we may decide not to damn the well-meaning conference goers, perhaps we should at least raise the organizer and those who would *work* to create programs and power for a city of shared abundance and democratic life. Only a very few people will begin to do this kind of organizing. But it is those few that can turn remarks such as these from absurb projections into real and felt alternatives.

6

Politics of Coalition

ALVIN PITCHER

Any organization that hopes to achieve much power must include people with varying social philosophies or with varying views of what the ends and means of social action are. In any such coalition the units of the coalition will be more or less independent. Thus it is that when we speak of coalition, we speak of an organization in which there is no agreement on the fundamental targets or fundamental goals and the means for achieving them; or to put it another way, we mean an organization in which there are a variety of views of what ought to be done and how it ought to be done. Sometimes we refer to these views as ideology. Thus it is that in a coalition there is no common idealogy, no common agreement on ends and means. In most coalitions there will be no way to force various elements or units of the coalition to agree upon a common action; therefore it will be necessary to arrive at a consensus. It will be necessary to find some program of action that can be agreed upon without a common ideology or without any sanction on the basis of which rewards and punishment can be used to force agreement.

I want to set forth a view of political action under such conditions that could possibly work for a more satisfactory form of organization. At the theoretical level, then, it is necessary for those who are leading the coalition to understand the alternative ideologies or the alternative philosophies of social action. This involves a careful study of the statements and actions of men in order to understand the grounds upon which they justify what they do. In some cases the philosophies of social action will be very clearly stated. In other cases it will be necessary to infer from statements and from actions what it is that forms the presuppositions or the fundamental ground for the assertion of particular programs of action.

The second phase of the theoretical basis for the coalition or for work with the coalition involves the framing of a program that can be supported for a variety of reasons. Thus it is that one who works in a coalition must be able to formulate a program of action and to justify it on several different grounds. Knowing well the differences of approach within his organization, the leader will be able to rationalize or to justify a program of action on different grounds with different people.

Now there are certain practical considerations that follow in carrying out

81

this understanding of the approach to a coalition. First, the leader will never insist upon establishing one reason for any action. Second, he will establish the public debate on any action in such a way as to avoid long argument on the validity of different fundamental analyses or different social philosophies. He will focus on the program of action and a debate about whether or not it makes sense from several points of view; he will not focus on the different points of view. This means, in fact, that he will work privately with different people, with different factions of the coalitions in order to establish the grounds for understanding the validity of the program of action. He will attempt to point out how the proposed program of action fits into the fundamental understandings of different factions for different reasons. By doing this privately, he is able to bring about support for his program of action and in part, at least, to avoid debate in public on the basic differences in social philosophy. A third practical consideration is an inclusion of all the vocal factions in policy making. For if it is true that a coalition includes a variety of understandings of ends and means, it is also true that people of one faction will be very suspicious of a program set forth by people in another faction. In other words, there is built into a coalition a suspicion of programs set forth by anyone who differs from one's own position fundamentally. This built-in suspicion makes it necessary to include different positions in the decision-making process. For it is only after it is clear to different people for different reasons why a program makes sense that this suspicion will be removed; or if it is not removed people will privately think, perhaps, that they are achieving their own ends at the expense of other persons' goals. Of course, I believe, that it is possible for a program to fulfill the requirements of several different fundamental points of view. A fourth practical consideration involves the amount of time necessary to establish a consensus. If there is a fundamental agreement on the ends and means, the debate, then, involves a consideration of the way in which a program fits into the fundamental presupposition point of view. This is a matter of intelligent perception or practical wisdom. It involves a judgement as to whether or not a program makes sense. However, in a coalition it is necessary to establish the rationale for a program from several points of view. This compounds the problem and makes it necessary to explain the reasons that justify any given program at great length until different people for different reasons come to see the program as a valid one. This involves a great deal of patience, for many persons will resist suggestions made by another faction in principle. They will not accept such a program until their own reasons for support can be made clear.

Another problem of a coalition involves the way in which individual factions are expected to act once a consensus has been determined. There are three alternatives. One may insist that everyone support everything that is supported by a majority of the coalition. The second approach is to insist that no public opposition to a position be stated. A third approach seeks support for the consensus but does not insist upon it. In the latter case individual organizations or members of the coalition may actually take public stands against the position of the majority of the coalition.

Thus having stated a theory of coalition, I would like to illustrate how it works in a given situation by discussing the open-housing action during the summer of 1966.

It seems to me that there were several different reasons for engaging in this particular action. The action involved moving into all-white neighborhoods in which real estate agents had refused to show, rent, or sell housing to nonwhite people, in order to make clear that there was a denial not only of a moral right to equality of treatment, but also an illegal action on the part of the real estate agents. Many different purposes motivated people to participate in this action. Some actually believed that it was important to get the real estate agents to show this property in order to provide opportunities for people to move into the all-white neighborhoods and therefore integrate them. In other words integration was the end — the purpose of the action. Others felt that the action of the real estate agents was a direct affront to the humanity of the Negro people; thus the fundamental purpose of the action was to establish the fact that Negroes are people. The effort to gain respect took one of two forms: to achieve it either by virtue of the behavior of the real estate agents, or by virtue of encouraging the nonwhite, the Negro, to stand up and be counted, hence to establish respect in himself in the face of opposition and rejection. In either case the concern for respect might have taken place with a view of integration or without any concern for integration. The third purpose in participating in the open-housing marches and actions was to relieve the pressure in the ghetto. This position did not express a concern for integration particularly but a concern for relieving the pressure that provided the landlord in the ghetto with the kind of market that made it unnecessary for him to keep up his property and that made it possible for him to charge more than in other areas of the city. The fourth purpose for engaging in the marches was to create tension that would lead to a power that would achieve several different goals including open housing, more housing, and better housing among other things. On setting forth the program for the marches, therefore, one might have appealed to all of these reasons.

Similarly, when we think about the summit agreement that ended the marches, we find various reasons for participating or coming to the conclusion that the agreement ought to be accepted. Some persons felt that the open-housing program was one that could not be won; ultimately there was no way to achieve a victory. It was a poor target; hence it was important to take whatever victory was won and to get out and move into some other area where the targets were concrete and the victories more tangible. Second, some people felt that the injunction brought about by city actions set up a situation that was impossible to challenge. It so circumscribed the marches that they were virtually ineffective, and therefore the troops that would help to bring about the confrontation with the city of Chicago were too few. As Martin Luther King said, "It would take two years and two hundred thousand dollars to take the case to the Supreme Court." It was assumed, of course, that in all other courts the control of the city would be such that the foregone conclusion would be that the injuction would be sustained. Other people felt that there was a need for a victory and that the summit agreement did represent the achievement of accommodation and adjustment on the part of the power structure of the city. Other people thought that the threat to the powers that be was at a maximum height and that we ought to take advantage of it before we lost it.

Similarly there were different reasons for opposition to the summit agreement by civil rights people. Some would have opposed any terms of agreement because they were suspicious of the people representing the civil rights movement; any agreement by those people would be interpreted as a sellout to the powers that be. Others opposed the agreement because they were not consulted; the process of ratification did not include the rank and file of the civil rights movement. Still others were dissatisfied with the actual terms of the agreement; they felt that nothing concrete had benn agreed upon no time had been set, no standards had been established by which to measure results. These three different evaluations resulted from different orientations. It was not a matter of judgment regarding the situation, but a matter of different perspective on the basis of which to evaluate the summit. In addition judgment entered in the opposition of still others. Some felt that we were just beginning to cause sufficient creative tension (or disruption) to bring the powers that be to real negotiation; a few more weeks of action would have brought them to the conference table willing to make real concessions. Others felt that the tension had to be extended to other cities in order to bring the federal as well as the local government into the picture.

Thus it is that one can see how important it is to separate differences that occur because of differences in basic orientations and those that result from arguing about fundamental differences in perspective. There is every reason to examine carefully and to discuss at great length differences of judgment. No amount of argument would convince those who opposed the summit agreement because of a faulty process of decision making that the results were desirable. In civil rights coalitions the different orientations have to be organized. Without a program approach as a basis of coalition, the civil rights movement will be continually fragmented. This does not mean that there is not a place for debate about the fundamental grounds for action and for the attempt to win people to a new understanding of the issues, but the coalition, in this case, is not the right place.

CHESTER ROBINSON

I think we have been making a lot of mistakes, especially in our organizations. I want to start off with Negro culture, and the question, "Does the Negro really have a culture of his own?" A lot of people talk about bringing the Negroes into the white man's culture, whatever that is. If we study history, we know that the white man stole the Negro's culture from the old country, Africa, etc.

But my problem with organizations like the Welfare Council, and with professors, and middle and upper-middle class people in general, is that they do not know what the Negro really wants.

When people call me for meetings in those big offices, I turn them down because they do not want to meet in the ghetto, in the poor people's neighborhood. This says to me that they really do not want to be identified with the poor people, Negroes in general. We have to ask each other, "What do Negroes really want?" We cannot sit in a big office and figure that out. We have to come down into the ghetto and deal with people.

A lot of Negroes do not want to move to Gage Park or Cicero. I know I don't. And so we have a problem. We have people trying to get Negroes to do things they do not want to do. A lot of Negroes do not want to work, so you cannot make them work. In one organization in Chicago, when you hear one person talk, you hear them all talk. All of them think the same, so they do not have free minds, and this is a problem. Whenever one or two hundred people think and talk the same way all the time, something is wrong. A person should be free to think for himself.

Often people ask me what is black power. I say it defines itself. You do not need to go into anything, just use the term and that is it because there is black power in Chicago already. The Dawson machine has black power, and it probably has more power than the average organization in Chicago. They are independent and have independent black power. Many people think the Dawson machine is a Daley machine, but they are wrong. They are independent and they do what they want to do. I found that out six months ago.

We were talking about the Welfare Council. I had some dealings with them last year. I do not see how anyone can have meetings on poor people's lives, how someone can say we are going to write up legislation and try to get it passed for the poor people down in the ghetto. Those people have never been there so they do not know what the people are thinking about, what they want, what kind of jobs they are qualified for. Any legislation they pass might not help the people at all and thus might hurt the people they are trying to help.

Who are the big organizations? Civil rights organizations? What do they know? Most of them want to be white. They have moved into the white culture, so to speak. They try to talk, eat, and dress their houses up like white people. This is not a Negro, because the majority of Negroes want to be different from white people because they are different. You might think they are uneducated, but they have that much sense.

I do not want to hurt anybody's feelings, but I just cannot help it. I know that some Negroes love to build around each other. I know I do not want to integrate. I live in an integrated neighborhood now and the only time I go there is when I go home and go to bed. It is not that I dislike white people. It is because I am used to being around my own people. I am used to what we have been doing all of our lives. It is the same in an Italian or Irish neighborhood; they each have their own culture, and they bring it to America. I do not know what they call their big parades and parties, but they are always in the style of the old country.

The Negroes have Bud Billikan parades, and that is white-oriented. It comes from the white man. If a Negro comes dressed like an African, everybody looks at him; he is something different. But he inherited some of that culture, while some of his culture comes from slavery.

So when we say coalition we are going to run into a lot of trouble until we realize that Negroes are different and until some Negroes realize that we are different.

REV. ALBERT SAMPSON

To talk about coalition is really to talk about where people are going if you have united these political forces that are concerned about social change.

One of my problems is that political forces in or out of a coalition across the nation refuse to understand that throughout history revolutions have been waged regarding land. Black people have never gotten land nor Abraham Lincoln's political promise of forty acres and a mule nor proportionately own the land they live on. Yet another problem is that Negroes in the North are over concerned with politics. They do not understand that, though politics was the instrument that held back people in the South, it is economics in the North. Therefore, when we talk about coalition, we are actually talking about the philosophy of nonviolence implementing an economic movement. Many of us are concerned about the plight of the Negro urban man, as in the past we have been concerned about the plight of the rural Southern Negro.

As background, we must realize that some of the instruments we attempt to use for social change really are social gimmicks of interpersonal ego-organizational institutionalized prostitution. Community organizations sometimes become institutionalized financial corporations and in the process they become sterile. They become diversified and fail to relate to the needs of the people.

Understanding men receive their value system from institutions, we are dealing with a man who at a particular moment in history came from Africa with 100% frustration, with no opportunity unlike the Diasparo Jews. Coming to the South he dropped fifty per cent of his frustrations, but he landed in the South with fifty per cent more added on because he did not bring any institutions with him to redress his grievances. So he ended up in the South with 100% frustration.

Through the Moynihan report, the federal government substantiates that the Negro is the only group of people in the world who never had a mommy and daddy. Their family structure was ripped asunder due to the perpetuation of segregation utilizing the tools of economic exploitation.

Negroes found themselves rejected from several institutions. The church became the only social institution to which they could address their grievances. Negroes never had a family, so they could not address themselves to the family. Negroes talked about schools. Schools were not designed to educate people; they were designed to perpetuate. So the Negroes are still learning "Dick and Jane. Here comes Spot. See how Spot runs. All apples are red." They have not changed that yet.

Look at what shapes our value system. At one point we were under the historical impression that social institutions like the family, the church, and the school gave us our value system, but from the way America is structured now, our value system is revealed as shaped by racist institutions like militarism, government, and economics. Our society spins on one thin definition: that you have to work in order to eat because Adam made a mistake in the Garden. We never go to the New Testament where "Jesus says take no thought for your life, for what you eat, for what you wear. . ."

The tragedy of Black Power is that the average white person now assumes that they have decision-making power that they never had which in turn covers up the real sickness – racism. A man named Ferdinand Lundberg wrote a book entitled *America's Sixty Families* and pointed out that sixty families in America own and control 84% of the nation's capital.

The Negro found himself involved in the underground railroad which was his vehicle of escape from the South which represented Hell, to the North which represented Heaven. When coming to the North, he could not answer urban questions like, "Do you have a family?"

"No, no, I do not have any mommy and daddy." America testified to that via the Moynihan report.

"Do you have education?"

"No, don't need a Ph.D to say 'whoa mule, whoa'."

"Well, do you have an economic base?"

"No, no, Abraham Lincoln gave me Emancipation of Proclamation, but he did not give me forty acres and a mule." Just like the constitution gave some the right to vote and none the right to eat.

"Well, do you have a trade?"

"Yes, I can build houses."

"I am very sorry the building trade union in Chicago is segregated."

So, when a man comes North, he adopts 100% frustration based on the urban life, plus 50% from the Southern life which means that you have got a man walking around the ghetto with 150% frustration. And because he wants to be like President Johnson when he grows up he attempts to solve his social problems through violence.

We talk about levels of participation and get caught up in a certain theological sickness. Many of us in this room function under the Good Samaritan premise that when we see a man lying on the ground, whether he is lying there because of the welfare system, or because of the educational system, or whatever, he is there. We come riding through with our institutionalized social service donkeys, pick him up, and we bring him to "x" theory and commence to intellectually operate.

The question "Who is our neighbor?" was raised, but we never raised the question "What is our problem?" I would like to believe that the Good Samaritan went back to Jerusalem and redefined seemingly necessary institutions so profoundly that one man no longer would have to rob another man in order to steal the resources of the universe.

Instead we play the Good Samaritan role and end up being like Tom Sawyer. We whitewash the fence and convince people, theoretically and intellectually, that this is the answer, that this is the way to go, and everyone should go that way. Basically we do not want to be radical because that means getting at the root. It does not mean carrying a picket sign. It means being able to use all of your creative resources to get at the root of racism.

I would never take a black woman or poor white man down to anybody's welfare office because by definition I would be saying "Thank you for paying these people to stay out of society." They do that to the elderly; they give them a social security check, a payment to stay out of society which says, "you are of no value to us anymore."

Instead of admitting that and accepting that check, I would demand that every institution accept me as a person, train me and equip me with enough tools so that I will be able to ride down the road to Jericho without having somebody rob me because the resources of the universe are denied or restricting another man.

What is the solution? How do you deal with this? When SCLC first came into town, they said we have to find the definition of a slum. We asked a lot of people, but no one knew the definition.

First level of nonviolence is seeking information. We discovered the definition of a slum is that certain economic and psychological resources march into a Negro community: retail outlet store, banks, FHA, urban renewal, school system, welfare system, slum landlords, and the real estate board. Whether you are in Gage Park, Lawndale, or Rhodesia, whether you are in India, South America, or South Africa, this is the way our racist institutions function. We bring our institutions and resources into a community, and the same people who bring these psychological and economic resources in take them straight out again. This is basically what happens in the ghetto, the slum, which actually equals a colony, utilizing the tools of economic exploitations.

Some folks call it segregation and some call it discrimination. Black people talk about "the man." I used to work with gangs. The gang does not know who the man is. What man? Postman? Milkman? What man? We do not realize white people think in terms of the Jim Crow. I am better than the Negro. Regardless of whether you are white or black, you function by the academic economic credit card system, which says "five dollars down, forty months to pay just for one's food, clothing, and shelter." That means our society has never said, "What is a man?" We have gone from

Huckleberry Finn to Tom Sawyer to Louisa Mae Alcott's *Little Women* and *Little Men,* then inferior to superior. Now we have gone to Superman, Batman, and James Bond's 007.

Historically speaking, we have never sat down and demanded our institutions to say, "What is a man?" Consequently we have come to believe that the resources in the universe are more important than man which is my definition of racism. And every decision that is made in America's institutions today is based on racism. It is not based on the dignity of men. The white farmer in Wisconsin and the black farmer in Mississippi get paid not to plant food while people starve in India and in Chicago. That is because resources are more important than man.

Seymour Melman, in his book *Our Depleted Society,* points out that America has enough military power to destroy any nation one hundred and twenty-five times. He says that if we are really threatened by communism, we could carry on an economic revolution. For on one hand, Russia chastises us, and, on the other hand, turns around and borrows wheat. How do we break up this economic exploitation? There are a lot of forces in the movement who believe that if you are going to talk about coalition, it must be on the basis of a nonviolent philosophy. That profoundly, radically, and sacrificially comes to grips with the question, "What is a man?"

Then how do we break up the kind of economic exploitation that goes on in the ghetto? It does not make sense for us to play the Good Samaritan role and bring the best kind of education on structures in the nation into the ghetto, or set up tutoring schools if the related school system fails to say, "What is a man."

We built an experimental project in Alabama, and discovered that we could give high school graduates "programmed learning" under Science Research Associates. After three weeks of math, three weeks of English, and three weeks of social sciences, we sent them to 170 colleges across the nation. We succeeded because we brought in the best educational material necessary and set up the kind of educational bank where a man could come in with a deficiency and leave with an efficiency.

How do you break up this economic exploitation? One of the ways we have done it is through Operation Breadbasket. We say that if retail stores are not going to put some of their resources back into the Negro community through jobs or other programs, then we are going to withdraw from this illicit relationship. This has very theological implications. It is saying what Peter and John were saying in front of the temple: when the beggar said, "Give me some alms," Peter and John answered, "I do not have any alms; all I have got is Jesus."

When segregation gets too expensive, retail stores will let it go. The Operation Breadbasket program has gotten to the point where it has put jobs back into the community and demanded that the economic institution say Negroes are people and people need jobs.

It also has said to retail stores, rather than take your resources downtown, we want you to make deposits in Negro banks so that Negroes can be released from contract buying and get mortgages and rehabilitation loans. As the present system stands, urban renewal comes in and moves Negro homeowners out because, one, they do not want Negroes to own property, and two, they know that Negroes cannot get loans from institutions downtown. Consequently the property will deteriorate and another segment of Negro community becomes transient, irresponsible, and open to further economic exploitation. But by demanding that retail stores put the money back into the Negro banks, and with the real estate board functioning along with the slum landlord on the supply and demand theory, you give Negroes an opportunity to lift, divert, and dissect economic exploitation.

Starting the building program, one of our constructions is going to be cooperative housing; another is going to be the condominium for low-income people. What this means is that when a Negro comes up from the South, he now has a choice between moving into a condominium, a coop, or a slum building. If he chooses one of the first two, he attempts to cut economic exploitation because he takes the economics out of the bad building.

There are other programs that we know can break up economic exploitation which I do not have time to go into, but our thesis is that, if we are really concerned about this man with the 150% frustrations, we will not get caught playing the Good Samaritan role. We will get at the root of the problem. When we talk about coalition, we are talking about free men, able to use their intellectual, organizational, and economic resources to break up the pattern of economic exploitation. Otherwise, we are spinning our wheels and participating in interpersonal ego-organizational institutionalized prostitution which negates any possibility for politics of coalition.

7

Planning Concepts and
New Directions – Welfare*

RICHARD CLOWARD

Nearly eight million Americans depend on public assistance checks for their sustenance, including 4.4 million children, 2.1 million aged persons, and 700,000 of the blind or otherwise incapacitated. And this nearly eight million are less than a quarter of the poor (urban families of four with an annual income under $3,100, or rural families of comparable size with no more than $1,860 a year). So the public welfare system today leaves millions of the poor unaided. It may, however, be made to do considerably more. Favorable rulings in test cases now before the courts or in preparation could double or treble the number of people on welfare rolls.

On June 19, a three-judge federal court in Connecticut rendered a historic decision, declaring unconstitutional the state's residency requirements for welfare assistance. These requirements, some variation of which exists in every state, generally restrict welfare payments to people who can prove that they have lived in the jurisdiction for anywhere from six months to six years. The plaintiff in the Connecticut case had been receiving public aid in Boston, moved to Hartford to be with her mother, applied for welfare and was turned down. The majority of the court held that "the right of interstate travel also encompasses the right to be free of discouragement of interstate movement. Denying ... even a gratuitous benefit because of her constitutional right effectively impedes the exercise of that right."

Nor is this the only instance in which constitutional issues have been raised in public welfare. New York's highest court has ruled that social welfare laws do not authorize the jailing of male welfare recipients who refuse to work under terms dictated by a welfare department. Any other interpretation, said the court, might result in violation of the Thirteenth Amendment and the Federal Anti-Peonage Act, which prohibit involuntary servitude.

In situations where fraud is suspected, welfare recipients are often told

*This presentation was later published in *The New Republic* (August 5, 1967) as "We've Got Rights! — The No-Longer Silent Welfare Poor", co-authored with Frances Fox Piven, At Dr. Cloward's request the printed version has been here substituted (by permission of *The New Republic)*for his recorded remarks.

that if they refuse to answer questions which might incriminate them, their benefits will be cut off. Cases now being prepared in several jurisdictions charge that this threat — frequently carried out — is a violation of the Fifth Amendment. Mass searches without warrants (e.g., midnight raids) have recently been declared unconstitutional by the California Supreme Court.

This new concern for developing a rule of law in programs of the welfare state owes much to the legal scholarship of Jacobus tenBroek, a blind professor of political science at the University of California in Berkeley, and more recently to Charles Reich, a Yale law professor. TenBroek has spent the better part of his career exposing America's dual system of justice — one for the affluent, another for the poor.

A leading strategist in the current assault against "poor law" agencies is Edward Sparer, director of the Center on Social Welfare Policy and Law, sponsored by the Columbia University School of Social Work and financed by both the Stern Family Fund and OEO. Sparer and his six-man legal staff give advice on tactics and help to prepare briefs for other organizations taking test cases. Representation in the courts is being performed by the Neighborhood Legal Service agencies sponsored by the Office of Economic Opportunity (one of which handled the Connecticut case), the NAACP Legal Defense Fund, the Scholarship Education and Defense Fund for Racial Equality (formerly affiliated with CORE), the American Civil Liberties Union (and its special division, the Lawyers Constitutional Defense Committee), as well as the Lawyers Committee for Civil Rights Under Law. Here and there, lawyers affiliated with the more traditional legal aid societies are also becoming active. The Law Students Civil Rights Research Council recruits law-student volunteers to provide information on legal rights and subsidizes research for attorneys representing recipients.

The growing number of court challenges deal with two areas of grievance: violations of the civil liberties of welfare recipients, and arbitrary denials of benefits. Our discussion focuses on the second area.

Many state laws work to the disadvantage of the very poor. A prime example is the requirement that every new resident wait one year before applying for benefits. In a few states, like New York, there is no specific waiting period, but a test of "motive" can be applied. If welfare officials believe that the applicant came in order to obtain welfare, they may deny benefits and issue a bus ticket to get the applicant out of the state. In practice the applicant must disprove the allegation to the satisfaction of welfare officials, which is usually impossible. The Connecticut decision casts doubt on the constitutionality of both types of residue laws. Similar cases are pending in federal courts in half a dozen states.

If the Connecticut decision is upheld, the consequences will go far beyond affirming a constitutional right of indigents to travel. The effect of residence laws has been to deny aid to the most economically depressed, such as rural people driven into urban ghettos by rapid agricultural mechanization and by federal agricultural subsidies which favor large landholders. One sizable group — 2.5 million migrant workers — remain untouched by the

Connecticut decision, for the court did not extend the protection of its ruling to persons who do not intend to establish permanent residence in the state. So long as welfare aid remains unavailable to migrant workers, they will be compelled to accept jobs on terms dictated by farmers in each locality.

What Mothers Must Do

Then too, there is some form of "employable mother" rule in about half the states, designed partly to keep taxes low and to ensure a labor supply which can be driven by the threat of starvation to do any kind of work at any wages. For instance, a Georgia regulation requires that to be eligible for Aid to the Families of Dependent Children – a program intended to help needy youngsters – mothers whose children are over three years old must accept "suitable" employment when it is deemed to be "available." The rule also prohibits county welfare departments from paying supplementary benefits to mothers who are employed at wages lower than what they would normally receive on public assistance. Finally, it directs county welfare boards to deny *all* applications and close *all* existing cases of AFDC mothers who are deemed able to work during what the board calls "full-time employment" periods in communities with seasonal employment (e.g., cotton chopping). A group of mothers are now bringing suit in Georgia, claiming racial discrimination because the rule is used to exclude Negro mothers far more frequently than white mothers (picking cotton is not deemed "suitable" work for white women). They also claim that denying supplementary benefits to mothers who are employed for less money than they would get on welfare is contrary to the purpose of the program. The fact that a mother works, they contend, is an arbitrary basis for classifying the beneficiaries of federal aid, in violation of the equal-protection provisions of the Fourteenth Amendment.

These Georgia AFDC mothers are also asking for the right to rebut the presumption that they can get jobs merely because a welfare official says they are employable. They base their challenge on a prior ruling of the US Supreme Court, "that a statute creating a presumption which operates to deny a fair opportunity to rebut it violates the due process clauses of the Fourteenth Amendment." A panel of three judges has been appointed, and trial is pending. It is estimated that AFDC rolls in Georgia will double if the employable mother rule is struck down.

Traditionally, benefits have been denied to families if the husband is present and "employable" (whether or not he can get a job). Unemployed husbands therefore "desert," and mothers may then get on relief (if they agree to sue for nonsupport). But often the men remain near their families, despite the danger of being apprehended and jailed for nonsupport. Welfare departments maintain squads of investigators who track down these men, sometimes by invading homes between midnight and dawn without warrants.

Not content with driving husbands away, the system has also traditionally disqualified mothers who appear, on investigation, to have a conjugal relationship with a man. In Alabama, for example, children can be denied assistance if their mother "appears" to have a relationship with a "substitute father," defined as a man who either (1) lives in the home, (2) "visits frequently for the purpose of cohabitation," or (3) "does not frequent the home but cohabits with the child's natural or adoptive mother elsewhere." (Cohabitation is defined by the Alabama welfare department as sexual relations.) These rules, attorneys believe, violate the equal-protection clauses of the Constitution by establishing an arbitrary and unreasonable basis for distinguishing among children: whether their mothers do or do not have intercourse. In a case now being taken in the federal district court, the plaintiff is an Alabama widow with several children whose benefits were terminated after she admitted that a male friend visits in her home.

An especially vicious feature of these rules is that if a caseworker judges that such a man "appears" to exist, the burden of proving that he is not a "substitute father" falls on the mother. A Texas woman and her five children lost their benefits because of the mother's alleged association with a man who was not the children's father and was not helping to support them. A state hearing officer reversed the local departmental decision on the ground that the evidence concerning the man's presence in the home was insufficient. However, the administrative appeals board reversed the decision again: the reason it gave was that the mother had failed to *disprove* the allegation.

The welfare applicant who is not excluded by statutes and rules does not automatically get on the rolls, or then stay on. Far from it. According to a *New York Times* editorial of May 18: "New York City Welfare Commissioner Mitchell I. Ginsberg reports that there are nearly as many eligible families *off* the relief rolls as there are on. The welfare budget for the year starting July 1 is estimated at $913 million, up to $207 million over the outlay for this year; yet that staggering amount will take care of only half of those who could qualify for aid if every eligible applied."

This vast discrepancy results from the fact that welfare functionaries everywhere, responding to community pressures to hold costs down, try to keep people off public assistance. If information about eligibility were widely disseminated, claims would rise precipitously, and so welfare departments do nothing to advertise the availability of benefits; indeed, they try to keep potential recipients in ignorance. A survey in Detroit uncovered many families in dire need, but more than half did not know about public welfare or erroneously believed that they were ineligible. To remedy this situation, groups of recipients are preparing to sue for access to welfare manuals, on the ground that these are public documents.

Those who do know about public welfare must run a grueling bureaucratic obstacle course in order to qualify. In effect, the applicant must prove his poverty to functionaries who are at best skeptical. HEW, having surveyed procedures in a number of cities, reports that applicants are "being required to assume too much responsibility for substantiating their own eligibility." Several cities require that applicants produce documents to support information of birth, past places of residence and employment, income and the like. Frequently they are forced to answer questions about their sexual behavior, open their closets to inspection and permit their children to be interrogated. To resist any of these procedures is to risk rejection for "failure to comply with departmental regulations." Rather than submit, many withdraw or do not apply.

To overcome this pattern of intimidation, some applicants are demanding the right to bring an advocate to the intake cubicles — a friend, a representative of a welfare recipients' organization or a lawyer. A recent suit established this right in New York, but elsewhere welfare administrators still resist, claiming that they have a legal obligation to "protect applicants" by holding transactions "confidential."

Furthermore, many of those who do apply and endure all of the investigatory procedures are turned down. In Phildelphia, for example, half of the applications are rejected, and lawyers estimate that half of the rejections are not expressly justified under existing statutes. In 1962, the Moreland Commission of the New York State legislature noted that a great many "rejections are arbitrary," for only 35 percent of the denials were based on the contention that the family had "sufficient income."

Perhaps the cruelest exercise of discretion by welfare department functionaries is in the arbitrary suspension or termination of benefits. Taking a sample of poor families headed by women, the New York City Community Council found that only 12 percent had received assistance continuously for 18 months following childbirth. Some 29 percent had had their cases closed and reopened at least once during that period despite continual financial need. Some investigators close as a disciplinary measure, knowing that when the affected families ask to have their cases reopened, as they usually do, they are likely to be more compliant. Other cases are closed because the investigator has noticed a new item of clothing or furniture and has not received what he regards as a satisfactory explanation as to where the money was found to make the purchase. Still other terminations are the result of administrative errors in a system burdened by fantastic paperwork and haphazard procedures.

The practice of summarily terminating people from the rolls without a written reason or an opportunity for a hearing led Boston recipients to stage a sit-in. When the police beat them, the demonstrators screamed out the windows of the welfare department, and rioting erupted in the streets for three nights.

No Rights If You're on Relief

What makes these practices possible is the absence of any tradition of legal rights for welfare beneficiaries, as is illustrated by a recent court ruling in the nation's capital. When a group of AFDC mothers sued for declaratory and injunctive relief against unreasonable searches, harassing surveillance, eavesdropping and interrogation concerning their sexual activities, the district court not only ruled against them, but rendered the astonishing opinion that welfare benefits are a gratuity, that statutes governing welfare agencies merely define who is *not* eligible for benefits and do not impose the obligation to grant benefits to all those who meet eligibility requirements. Which of the eligibles are actually to get benefits is, the court held, within the absolute discretion of administrative functionaries and therefore is not a proper subject of judicial review. During the courtroom argument, the judge commented on an allegation regarding illegal search: "Any recipient has a perfect right to slam the door in the face of the investigator. Of course, he runs the risk then of being cut off the rolls." In other words, the welfare system can treat people as it sees fit; if people don't like it, they don't have to take the money. (On appeal, however, a higher court directed that the welfare department hold a full hearing on the mother's charges preliminary to further court review.)

The main thrust of the legal attack on arbitrary terminations of benefits is in public housing. In two cases now in the federal district courts, tenants allege that public housing authorities violated their rights under the due-process clause of the Foureenth Amendment by evicting them without a written reason or an opportunity for a hearing. In a third case, taken against the public housing authority in Durham, N.C., the US Supreme Court had agreed to a review. Before the case could be argued, however, officials of the federal public housing agency issued a bulletin stating that local authorities must inform tenants of the reasons for evictions and give them opportunity to rebut. The Supreme Court ordered the case back to the state courts.

An important challenge is also developing in Mississippi where, in early April, a beneficiary under the Aid to the Permanent and Totally Disabled program was abruptly notified that he was no longer medically qualified for assistance. No specific reasons were given, nor was a hearing offered prior to the termination. The client, a 30-year-old Negro father, secured affidavits from prominent doctors confirming that his right hand had been amputated and that he had both pulmonary tuberculosis and sickle-cell disease (a type of anemia which leads to progressive weakening and, in this case to a short life expectancy). The day before the court hearing, welfare officials visited the plaintiff to say that a mistake had been made and would be rectified. Nevertheless, the plaintiff insisted that a hearing be held, arguing that his benefits might be arbitrarily terminated at some later time unless the constitutional issues raised by welfare procedures were ruled upon. Despite protests by attorneys for the state, the judge agreed that serious questions of due process were involved and held the matter over for trial.

The number of people who would be affected by successful court challenges to termination procedures is suggested by experience in the District of Columbia. There, under the iron rule of Senators Robert Byrd (D, W.Va.), chairman of the Senate subcommittee on appropriations for the District of Columbia, the department of welfare has been forced to acquire nearly as many "fraud investigators," bent upon cutting people off relief, as "social investigators," who are responsible for passing on initial eligibility. In speeches on the floor of the Senate, Byrd has reported that under his aegis AFDC case loads fell from a peak of 5,628 in November 1961, to 3,823 by October 1963. His request for appropriations with which to hire additional investigators was struck out on a technicality in a House-Senate conference. As a result, he says, "the AFDC case load has gradually crept back up, and by August 1966 had recorded a total of 4,767 cases." Bad though he believes this is, he observes that without the investigators who were available, the case loads would have reached 9,600 — double the present rolls. (The Senator reacted to the recent tide of legal appeals with these remarks: "I'm not against fair hearings, but I'm not going to sit by and watch our agency attacked. What business do [these lawyers] have to question [the Department's] regulations?")

And What Do They Get?

Once on the rolls, recipients get very little. In large part this is because of the low grant levels set by state legislatures; annual AFDC payments to a family of four range from an average of $388 in Mississippi to $2,700 in New York, or about $1,800 nationally. More than half the states do not even appropriate enough to neet their own "minimum standards" for welfare payments. Some limit the amount that can be given to any one family, to discourage the poor from having large numbers of children. (The notion persists that the poor have children in order to obtain additional welfare allotments — an extraordinary idea considering the size of the increments.) As a result, a child in a large family may get less to eat than a child in a small family. The constitutionality of this arbitrary and discriminatory classification is being challenged by the parents of 10 AFDC children in Maryland, where the law increases aid only up to seven family members. In this case, the complaint follows an earlier and successful suit taken in Iowa.

It is characteristic of the American way of public welfare that people on the rolls are regularly cheated out of such benefits as the law provides. As a consequence of the high turnover among welfare employees, many of them never learn the complex regulations governing allowances or master the equally complex administrative procedures. And recipients, as we have noted, are rarely permitted to examine the regulations. The result is underbudgeting, which is estimated to deprive recipients of about 20 percent of what the law says should be included in their regular biweekly or monthly checks.

In addition to these regular checks, public assistance recipients in many places are entitled to receive special allowances, as needed, for clothing, household equipment and furniture. A study in central Harlem found that two-thirds of the AFDC mothers interviewed had never been informed by their investigators of the availability of such funds. There are 650,000 recipients in New York City. Informed observers estimate that it would cost an average of $100 to bring each recipient up to standard. In other words, the department has saved a total of $65 million in this fiscal year by not providing grants to which people are lawfully entitled.

Groups of recipients in New York City have become alert to these deprivations and have been circulating check lists of the items which welfare regulations define as entitlements. The completed check lists are submitted to the welfare department in bulk. As a result of this tactic many families have received special allotments, although sometimes after a long delay, and sometimes for only a few of the items requested. The client groups are now beginning to back up requests that the department meet "minimum standards" with applications for "fair hearings." This is likely to compel far more expeditious handling of the original requests, if only because of the expense and travail "fair hearing" procedures involve for government. In Washington, D.C., the chief of the welfare department's investigative arm recently protested the rising volume of appeals against the department's decision: "Our costs have gone up at least 25 percent because of this type of activity." The true purpose of these challenges he said, "is to increase the cost to the point where it is better to leave clients on the rolls."

Live Alone and Like It

Recipients are also cheated by techniques of computing other sources of income which are presumed to be available to them. Even where state law permits fathers to remain with their families without disqualifying them for benefits, the traditional "man-in-the-house" mentality persists: if a man is about, even though he is not a legal spouse, and even though he is not the father of the children, the presumption is often made that his income is available to the family, and their welfare payments are correspondingly reduced. If the man refuses to disclose his income, the mother and children can be dropped from the rolls.

One such case was recently heard by the New York State Department of Social Welfare. A 66-year-old recipient of Old-Age Assistance allowed a man of similar age to live in her home. Her benefits were terminated when the man refused to disclose his income. The state hearing officer agreed with the recipient that the mere fact that the man lived in her house did not demonstrate support, and that her grant should be reduced only by the amount of the man's actual contribution to the household expenses. As a result of another case recently heard in New York, the state has acknowledged that the "man-in-the-house" regulations are ambiguous, and that local welfare departments have exploited this ambiguity to impose an unlawful obligation upon men to support children not their own.

A more fundamental challenge is now in the federal courts in California. At issue is the constitutionality of a state provision which requires that the income of a stepfather be considered available to his stepchildren in computing the mother's AFDC benefits. But a man has no legal obligation to support his wife's children by a previous union; therefore, an AFDC mother deprived of a portion of her grant because of the stepfather's income cannot sue to compel him to contribute his income. This case is of more than passing interest to AFDC mothers, for welfare regulations in effect make them ineligible for marriage unless they can find a mate who is both able and willing to take over the support of their children. Such men are not in abundant supply, especially among the poor. In the California stepfather case, the desperate mother instituted divorce proceedings, and thereupon became eligible for AFDC again.

Recipients also lose funds because of the general reluctance of welfare departments to make any form of retroactive payment, even when they admit that benefits were unlawfully denied. A court action is pending in the District of Columbia, where an applicant for Aid to the Disabled was forced to wait 85 days for a decision, and then was not given retroactive payment although the department's regulations appear to authorize it.

As a consequence of the laws and practices we have described, only one in four of America's 32 million poor are now receiving public welfare — their aggregate benefits represent a mere .7 percent of national personal income. One reason is that federal enabling legislation leaves great power to the states and localities, which are typically harsh in dealings with the poor. Since most welfare laws and regulations are made by the states, or under the authority of state officials, they are designed to keep expenditures down — usually by seeing to it that as few people as possible obtain as few benefits as possible. Successful attacks in the courts could do much to alter welfare practices and to increase the volume of benefits available to people, provided that welfare departments comply with new regulations. Pressure to compel compliance is now beginning to be exerted by recipients' organizations springing up all over the country, as part of a new National Welfare Rights Movement which staged a series of demonstrations June 30 in more than 40 cities.

The growing legal assault is also helping to build a case for some new and federally administered income program. Each legal challenge reveals new abuses by the present system of locally administered public assistance. It thus adds to pressure for a federally administered income program (such as family allowances or a guaranteed income), which would provide uniform and decent grant levels based on need as the sole criterion for eligibility. The "poor law" still stands, but its foundation is beginning to crumble.

Reaction and Reconsideration

Four major ways of looking at the problems surrounding the system of public welfare, primarily as it exists in Chicago, emerged from the dialogue among welfare administrators, local politicians, various city and state officials, and others who assumed the role of "advocates" of the welfare recipients: (1) the flaws inherent in the system and its administration as it now exists; (2) the feasibility of implementing changes in the system through legislation and through coalition of forces working for change both inside and outside the welfare system; (3) possible alternative approaches; and (4) ways and means of implementing change through coalitions of power among the poor.

Administration

Opinions were expressed about the effectiveness versus the ineffectiveness of the system, procedures surrounding grievances and appeals, administrative frustrations, and the goals of compulsory education and training programs.

> The Cook County Department of Public Aid is one of the best in the nation. [local politican]
> There is plenty of room for improvement, and that shows how bad off we really are. [unidentified participant]
> We must examine three types of evidence. First, with regard to the decrease in the number of people on the rolls, we must examine both the cases that come on the rolls each month and those closed. Second, if everyone received assistance who was entitled to it on the basis of existing standards, the Public Assistance budget would at least double. Third, it seems that given the choice, an overwhelming number of people in Illinois would vote to discontinue ADC. [local politician]
> We should also consider the number of people rejected before they even get on the rolls. One of the main reasons for the rolls being down is the rigidity of the process of getting on them in the first place. [welfare administrator]
> Since there is a 50-55% acceptance at intake, I would suggest that the decrease in the number of people on the rolls is a sign of greater effectiveness. [another welfare administrator]
> The fact that 50% of those who go off the rolls return cannot be

100

taken as evidence of the effectiveness of the system. A major problem is the lack of channels for communication from the poor to those within the system. [community organizer]

Grievances and desired changes should be made known to the Department. The problems involved in the present situation are extremely complex. [welfare administrator]

Legislation concerning the continuation of grants while cases are being appealed was introduced but not passed. With regard to appeals, the director of a department is the one who not only makes the policy but also the one who has the final authority in ruling on an appeal. Two important problems are the understaffing, and the quantities of paperwork that frustrate caseworkers to the point where many of them leave. One reason for the paperwork is the Department's focus on reducing caseloads by getting people off the rolls. [welfare administrator]

But this paperwork could be greatly reduced by restricting and simplifying the rules regarding the legal responsibility for support by "relatives," which involves a lot of work for caseworkers, to a spouse and parents of children under eighteen who are living at home. [welfare administrator]

There is much within the existing system that indicates its ineffectiveness. Among other things, recipients who participate in relief programs often receive lower wages for the same job than they would on the regular payroll which certainly does not help them become self-supporting; and there are other problems that result from people not being made aware of that to which they are entitled. [participant working with community organizations]

Special training and educational programs are geared toward increasing the welfare recipients' potential for self-improvement as well as his or her job qualifications. [welfare administrator]

Since acceptance of available employment, rehabilitation, and training programs is compulsory, recipients must seriously consider having their assistance terminated if they do not accept what is offered to them. Furthermore, it is at the caseworker's discretion to decide if the job or training offered is suitable for the recipient. [community organizer]

But I would point out that of the many thousands of recipients, only 5,000 attend classes. Social workers attempt to motivate recipients to attend, and in only a minority of cases has it been necessary to withhold assistance due to lack of attendance. [welfare administrator]

Whatever vocational training is carried out by public welfare is the dead-end type and costly. Other and older organizations could do this training more cheaply. In basic education the teachers are tired after a full day's work in the regular classroom. Instructional materials are lacking or not speedily distributed. Basic education void of a vocational objective is worthless. Those graduates of welfare classes are the very few exceptional people who are put on display. The dropout rate indicates the program is not effective. Welfare could farm out their educational programs and give justice to the trainee and save the taxpayer's money.

[confirming state vocational & rehabilitation worker]

Legislation

Several discussions focused on what could be done to improve the current welfare system through legislative changes and coalitions of the poor and members of the establishment.

It is apparent that legislation which has been passed and court rulings which have been made in the direction of civil rights are only very slowly implemented by federal and especially state and local governments. What role can recipient organizations and unions of Public Aid employees play before and after court rulings have been made and laws passed? [public aid employee]

If we acknowledge that there is corruption within certain City departments, in the last analysis, enforcement rests with community organizations, aldermen, and local officials. For example, in the area of housing, citizens' fears about swearing out warrants seriously hampers just enforcement and is a matter to be dealt with by community pressure. Furthermore, since overenforcement can also be a problem, we should work toward selective enforcement and concentrate on slum areas. [city official]

But manipulation of individuals is often the result of collusion *between* departments as well as corruption *within* them. For example, when one department decides to schedule an area for urban renewal, inspectors from another department begin to strictly enforce housing regulations. [community organizer]

The present situation in Chicago is a very serious one and many aspects of the administration impair the effectiveness of programs. The administration of services from City Hall involves political manipulation, sometimes to the point where services as well as the recipients become incidental. Although a lot of money and effort are fruitlessly spent, such programs should not be abolished. Rather changes are needed to expand and humanize, strengthen and improve those programs which presently are failing to accomplish their stated aims. [city official]

To be effective, the training of Negroes for jobs in apprenticeship programs would have to involve the coalition government in this City which would mean working with corporations heads, big businessmen, etc. The fact that this has not happened indicates that the necessary good will has not been manifest. [staff member of a private agency]

Community organizations are rendering services that no city agency offers and achieving things that are not achieved by working with the City, businessmen, etc. It is important to actually do something about the immediate situation rather than simply develop theories about it and future, long-range possibilities. [community organizer]

In addition to considering the relationship of the welfare system to the recipient, it is important to consider the relationships of those who function at different levels within the system, particularly with regard to how legislation is developed and by whom. It is the legislators, rather than the welfare administrators, who are developing laws on the basis of political considerations rather than the actual needs of the people. [community organizer]

Changes are necessary at both state and federal levels. The welfare department has played an important role in trying to change legislation by lobbying, etc., but as with other legislation, the breakdown has resulted from lack of support from the voting population. [welfare administrator]

Yes, there is no indication that the general public is ready to admit that the problem exists must less respond to it. There is a great need for changing the climate in the country so that a larger investment can be made in the public sector. [unidentified participant]

How can groups of lay people learn more about the legislative process and how can they become more effective in introducing legislation? [participant from a government agency]

The first step is to decide whether your objectives are to be revolutionary or pragmatic (or, as someone else put it, concerned with the ideal or the mundane). A fundamental approach to the problem of legislation would be to get the administration to start talking about public assistance as a right. It is necessary to probe and push at the power structure that influences the legislative process. For example, representatives of organizations in the Welfare Council have not used the powers of the decision-makers on their boards to help them reach senators. Instead, they have concentrated their efforts on fighting them. [lawyer]

It is also important to work with people who make appointments in the state administration since a lot can be changed administratively without changing legislation. If legislative changes are to be made, it is necessary to develop a wider coalition including legislators and the people who influence them. [welfare director]

I believe that the impetus for new legislation must come from powerful recipient and social worker unions sparked by the Welfare Department. [community organizer]

I agree that a court decision will not necessarily result in compliance by local departments, but I do not think there is much either welfare groups or public welfare employees can do in advance of such decisions. However, there is a great deal they can do afterwards. Using demonstrations and other nonviolent tactics, welfare recipient groups and those few employees who are willing to ally themselves with welfare groups can exert political pressure to try and get compliance by local departments. Certain issues can be dealt with best through the courts when action is backed by political pressure; for example, the literacy and job training that is made a condition for receiving benefits. There are other issues, such as recruitment, that welfare groups can deal with effectively outside the courts. The welfare system will not do it, and there are a lot of people who are not on the rolls and could be without any changes in the law. It is partly an information problem. What is needed is a broad advertising campaign backed up by a vigorous movement to insure that those who apply, get on and receive full benefits. [professor of social work]

Alternatives

Several discussions focused on the necessity for fundamental changes in means of distributing income so that poverty can be eliminated without destroying the self-respect and motivation of the poor.

As long as the system is predicated on administrative discretion that involves one set of people having power and control over another, administrative injustices are inevitable. Therefore, it is futile to devote energies to trying to improve or patch up the existing system. We should be concentrating on how to either abolish the welfare system or how to legislatively change it entirely. [political scientist]

With regard to how people in this country are thinking about welfare and about changing the welfare system, nobody is satisfied with the present public assistance system which fails to even help people get enough money to live on. [faculty member]

We must stop defending the present system which will fail to help people in any significant way until recipients are respected as human beings. [community leader]

Though a guaranteed annual income has been suggested as an alternative to the existing system of welfare, it still would not deal with the more pressing problem of the nature of the relationship between administrators and recipients. [community leader]

It is also significant that the guaranteed annual income does not provide for education and training programs. [welfare administrator]

Money should be distributed as a right. Those things which are a matter of right must be bureaucratized and routinized so that individual choice and discretion is no longer involved, as with income tax, for example. The present legislation imposes categories in terms of which caseworkers must make their decisions. Furthermore, caseworkers should not be concerned with the administration of money; rather they should function as social workers in the fullest sense, offering social services. A way must be found to focus on social services. [university faculty member]

Poverty is a syndrome and lack of money only one small aspect. I suggest that poverty is a syndrome caused by the ghetto structure, substantially caused by absurdly low allotments. If a person is exposed to measles, one uses vaccine to hit the cause – one does not solve the problem by surgical excision of every sore. Likewise, it may well be that stopping the lack of money may substantially reduce the other factors welfare administrators among others see in poverty. None of this is to deny that voluntary services are needed. [unidentified participant]

It is a truism that "giving a ghetto dweller a nice new home (a good job, a good school, etc.) will not do any good; he will just ruin it." The advocates of this truism have little ground for so believing, for it has never been tried, unless one considers the Robert Taylor Homes a "nice new home." [community organizer]

Coalitions of the Poor and Change

The dominant issue in the discussion of "Politics and the Great Society" involved the question of how to break the cycle of poverty. Attention focused on the problem of the poor gaining the power needed to secure their deserved rights. Despite general agreement that the ultimate goal is breaking the poverty cycle and that organizing the poor is necessary to gaining political power, there was disagreement as to whether mobilizing the poor on the basis of their common poverty or around the rights they have been denied is the best strategy.

A confederation of groups is of political importance. [director of a national program]

In Chicago, there still exists the problem of getting neighborhood communities sufficiently cohesive to become effective. This must be achieved before a larger confederation, whether of groups within the city of Chicago or between cities across the nation, could become a meaningful reality. However, even if creating effective links remains a long-range problem, it is essential to the gaining of power. [community organizer]

Since the passage of the Economic Opportunity Act, harm has been done by diverting attention from the moral issue of citizens' deprivation of rights to a concern for gaining power by organizing people. [political scientist]

You don't organize anybody around their status – but around their denied rights (your morality). For example, you don't organize poor people – you organize people who are denied their rights. [unidentified participant]

However, rights deprived extends beyond the black masses, beyond the unwashed masses, and include the great washed masses, the middle class, who are being deprived systematically of their rights by an incredible array of forces with whom those who make poverty the cause celebre cooperate. For a mess of pottage we sell our birth rights! Long live the liberal cause! [unidentified participant]

As evidenced in the civil rights movement, people only surrender so much on conscience alone, and despite the hope that morality could prevail, unfortunately this is a world of power. [former community organization leader]

The thesis that poverty is not worth crusading about unless the poverty is distributed according to economically irrelevant categories (such as race) is debatable. Even granting the validity of that contention, it is debatable that race constitutes the most important economically irrelevant category operative today. I would argue that, among others, being born of parents not of our own choosing is an irrelevant category. Yet this applies to most people, and since the child has no way to alter this condition, I would argue that poverty as a phenomenon *is* worth a crusade. [unidentified participant]

Emphasis on the need for power coupled with insistence on a moral mandate for use of that power provides a good model for all social action. [community organizer]

It seems that lack of credulity or sabotage by city government centers account for the failure of CAP'S. [unidentified participant]

It is important to consider the reactions of the people who are being organized. Many groups ·in this country do not admit to being poor or realize that they are being denied rights, and it is necessary to educate them about the rights they are being denied. [participant from a local community]

It is a great tragedy that the poor do not vote. [unidentified participant]

The political reality of the two-party system does not often provide the poor with alternatives which reflect their interests. [community organizer]

A poor man will not risk his vote in form of a demonstration against the ruling powers; he should, but he won't. The poor know that if they gamble with the vote they have been giving to the Dems and lose, they have had it for four or more years! Therefore they cling to the one weak bit of life-giving flotsam they trust and have been historically conditioned to depend upon, the Democratic party, which they take to mean ample relief, favors dealt to them through a precinct captain who can get things done, etc. Losing hold of that plunges them in either the abyss of fury when the pinch is felt or into the yawning chasm of a level of even less tolerable suffering giving rise to a series of neuroses, but mostly to a seething but diabolically patient anxiety for the next election so they can return them, the Dems, to power. [unidentified participant]

There are important side effects which the poor derive from organizing. These include learning what it means to have the ability to effect changes in the community as well as learning how to make those changes. [community leader]

We have to distinguish economic as opposed to political power. Individuals who belong to minority groups are poor as long as they lack power, whether or not they have money. Poverty and the deprivation of rights are closely interrelated in terms of any action to be taken. The poor cannot break the poverty cycle as long as they do not have the capacity to exercise their rights. [community leader]

The Republican and Democratic parties want more or less the same sort of Public Aid system that we now have to prevail in Illinois. What are the political alternatives possible for those interested in changing it? [unidentified participant]

I could offer two suggestions. One, to develop strong community organizations to fill the gap left by "vicious bypartisan dealings" and the other, to encourage liberals from both parties. [welfare administrator]

Schools can be effective with regard to many social problems, not only as centers for education but also as focal points for community organization. Perhaps now would also be a good time for a third force to emerge along with efforts to get out the vote. Changes in government personnel and policy do not necessarily mean change in the structure of government; and, to some extent, this would also be true with regard to the formation of a third party within the existing structure. A different distribution of power is necessary if there are to be significant changes, although organization of communities is crucial. The people in these communities must be made ready for change. [community organizer]

The discussion on para-politics focused on the organization of communities, but there was disagreement between those who viewed separate community organizations as most effective, and those who took the view that a coalition of forces was essential.

With reference to the possibility of community organizations effecting responsiveness from elected officials, how could a city official respond to a situation that involves two different positions taken by two strong community organizations from different areas of the city? Further, how are those who are not organized, who may represent a sizeable number, receive justice if office holders respond only to those who are organized? [community organizer]

Although it is desirable to have conflicting interests represented, it is not yet the case that the organization and power of the white, middle-class communities is counterbalanced by powerful community organizations from ghettos representing minority groups. The constitution of our political system necessitates anyone running for office being a broker among competing groups which means that we need sources of power in addition to the ballot box. If community leaders seek political office, they begin in the City Council where as aldermen they would represent a specific neighborhood rather than as in Congress where they would represent a wide range of interests. [sociologist]

It has been suggested that cooperatives be formed by ADC mothers, and other poor, but where would such groups get the financial resources to start a cooperative that may or may not benefit them? In any case, wouldn't this serve to perpetuate the ghetto situation? [community person]

Most communities of the poor also include people who are not so poor. If more attention were given to organizing people as communities, institutions such as cooperatives could be developed. For example, some ethnic groups have been able to achieve political power because they were able to get those of their members who had been successful in business, etc., to channel some of their resources back into the community. A similar process could begin in ghetto communities. It is important that businesses within the community serve the community not only in terms of the services they offer but also by channeling resources back into the community. Finally, outside resources in the form of subsidies from both private and public sources could be utilized. [sociologist]

I doubt that the government would fund an organization that might stand up against it, perhaps forcing it to change its point of view. Organizations seem to be wasting a lot of time by operating individually rather than collectively; racial barriers have to be eliminated and cooperation has to be achieved before anything effective can be done. If all those groups presently without significant power would join together, they would be able to change the status quo. [unidentified participant]

Although poor Negroes are held down by many of the same problems that hold down poor whites, there has been very little organization around issues. However, where parallel movements of poor Negroes and whites (such as Appalachians) have developed, groups have been able to find some common meeting ground, as well as some ability to deal with their racism. However, these organizations only represent a small percentage of the community and though they have begun to deal with their racism, the majority in the community still have terrible racial problems. Decentralized community control of resources could provide a commonality of interests in terms of which separate communities could be brought together to more effectively deal with "the man downtown." Although this may sound feasible, the big problem, of course, would be to actually carry it out. [community organization leader]

Most Chicago communities are segregated on racial and ethnic grounds, and there is little contact between them. This situation furthers bigotry and prejudice, hatred and fear. [Chicago politician]

The divisions that exist between ethnic groups continue to be exploited so that any attempts to build a broad base will run into conflict with the administration's control and the existing political parties. [participant from a private social agency]

During the discussion of the politics of coalition there was general agreement from all sides that the ultimate goal is to increase the American Negro's freedom of choice, but disagreement on whether this could be best achieved by emphasizing integration or separateness.

The facts are that the Negro in America is part of the white man's world. [unidentified participant]

If he were, he would not be economically and politically separated as he is. It is wrong and dangerous to preach separatism and the hate it engenders. [unidentified participant]

Organizing around the fact of being Negro can be very effective. [community organizer]

It is important that neither Negro leaders or white liberals dictate what it is that the majority of Negroes want, or should want. We must find that out from the large majority of Negroes who are not speaking out, whatever the reasons. [unidentified participant]

How do the people (the poor) that you organize feel about being organized by you? [unidentified participant]

This is one of the problems that has to be faced by many honest middle-class, liberal professionals, whether Negro or white. [unidentified participant]

If coalition means mutual advantage, how can a coalition between Negroes and whites in this country be broadened to include more than people of good will? [staff member of a religious council]

The basis of any coalition would have to be self-interest; people could work together so that each gets more of what he wants. [unidentified participant]

There were many levels of self-interest, and for me the one most important, and the main reason I am in favor of a coalition between Negroes and whites is the hope that my children will be able to live in a world centered on love rather than hate. [participant from a government agency]

During all the discussions on welfare, a general feeling of anxiety was generated by the participants' dual concern for both dealing with the immediate situation and developing a new system which would effectively meet the needs of the people. Despite agreement that it was necessary to deal on both these fronts, specific priorities were not established. However, as a result of the discussions there was a fuller realization of the urgency and complexity of coping with urban poverty.

PART 2

Dominant Issues in Urban Education

8

Breaking the Poverty Cycle

GERALD FITZGIBBON

It is a common and justifiable complaint that schools in low-income areas have tended to turn inward, to give the appearance of imperviousness to the communities they purport to serve, and to cut themselves off from inter-action with outsiders. The reaction of community residents to this splendid isolation of schools – which are in the community and not of it – ranges from quiet indifference to loud protest. Both extremes have captured public attention; their effects on students' attitudes toward learning have been re-searched and documented. But what seems to have escaped notice is that alliances newly forged between schools and antipoverty agencies have begun to improve community relations and to increase the constructive participation of local residents in the affairs of their schools.

Coordination is required between local education agencies (LEA) and com-munity action agencies (CAA) in the planning and implementation of proposals submitted under Title I of the Elementary and Secondary Education Act (ESEA) and Title II-A of the Economic Opportunity Act. This provision has led to fruitful dialogue that has afforded the poor them-selves the opportunity to contribute to the improvement of educational pro-grams. Such coordination, which derives from the ESEA, is governed by procedures developed jointly by the Office of Education and the Office of Economic Opportunity and promulgated in parallel memoranda. Briefly, there are three parts to the procedure: collaboration between applicant agency and advisory agency early in the planning of a proposal, sign-off by the advisory agency on the final proposal to be submitted by the applicant agency, and appeal to the funding authority in the event of serious local disagreement between the two. For example, a public school system applying for Title I funds would meet with representatives of the community action agency (CAA) serving the area, and, after developing the proposal with them, submit it to the CAA director for his observations and his signature. The comments of the CAA director represent one of the factors to be taken into account by the State Education Agency (SEA) in its decision to approve the proposal. Substantial objections by the CAA call for mediation by the SEA in conjunction with the State Technical Assistance Agency, the SEA counterpart for economic opportunity at the state level. This procedure, which is known as the checkpoint procedure, has increased the involvement of community people in local educational planning and programming. .

The experience to date indicates that in the vast majority of cases, despite the pressure of deadlines and the unfamiliarity with the process, CAA-LEA coordination has been carried out without delay and without conflict. However, in some communities the zeal to avoid conflict has resulted in CAA passivity, pro forma compliance, or an exchange of signatures rather than a continuing dialogue. The regulations governing coordination are intended to encourage the establishment of working relationships in a framework which preserves the legal prerogatives of educators. Consequently, "checkpoint" can be a durable vehicle for the systematic expression of community sentiment, for the airing of differences, and for the effective coordination of programs for the disadvantaged. The uniqueness of this arrangement is that the CAA is entitled to this advisory role as a matter of right. However, the right entails the serious obligation to bend every effort to make coordination effective.

Let me draw upon the summary report of a pilot study of the checkpoint procedure which was jointly undertaken by the Office of Education and the Office of Economic Opportunity. The findings have been reinforced by subsequent reports and information. It is significant in this connection to observe that the Head Start follow-through program will attempt to build on the partnerships which in many cases can trace their origin to this procedure.

Our investigations confirm the practicability of the checkpoint procedure for achieving the limited objective of launching and legitimizing dialogue and avoiding programming conflicts and duplication. The sign-off provides potentially effective monitorship of the coordination mandated by Congress while at the same time preserving the prerogatives of communities to work out a local modus operandi consistent with the guidelines and of the states to assume a leadership role in fostering cooperation, determining the degree of compliance, and the adjudication of disputes which may jeopardize successful execution of the federal project. As such, the procedure stands as an example of federal, state, and local partnership.

The checkpoint procedure has not, however, worked miracles. False expectations and a lack of understanding of the real meaning and purpose of the procedure contributed to the few problems that did arise during the first year and a half.

Our findings underscore the folly of expecting from this unprecedented experiment in collaboration the solution of deep seated differences between schools and the poor. That the interaction between the LEA and CAA was not free of conflict should come as no surprise to an observer of the American educational scene. But the conflict of ideas may represent an index of successful coordination insofar as it represented the surfacing of the divergent points of view heretofore unexpressed.

Consultants who made site visits found the kind of conflict that checkpoint sometimes creates as salutary and long overdue. The required coordination procedure effected some beneficial changes that hold promise of improving the education of the disadvantaged. In particular, the procedure increased the accountability of schoolmen to a long neglected segment of their constituency. The procedure has facilitated the fulfillment of the spirit of Title I by encouraging dialogue which can help surmount the problem of communication between school and the poor.

Lack of early involvement sometimes exacerbated local disagreements. The CAA which had been excluded from the planning process was placed in the position of signing off on a completed proposal. Receiving the proposal at the eleventh hour, the CAA could not make a positive contribution without risking accusations of obstructionism. The pattern in such instances was for the CAP Director to affix his signature rather than suffer the political repercussions of seeming to jeopardize important services by delay or by sharply negative comments. But by and large both agencies attempted to bring programs into phase and did so with very few incidents. Many of the problems encountered in early tests of coordination can be traced to the unfamiliarity of participating agencies with this process. The federal agencies launched the procedure through the issuance of guidelines. The state agencies in the midst of a hubbub of new activity tended to assume a passive role. LEAs in the absence of evidence of concern on the part of state and federal agencies tended to act in the fashion to which they were accustomed.

Prospects in the immediate future are that education will increasingly be the focal point of activity in community groups in poverty areas, as they come to recognize the connection between education and opportunity. It is timely and essential, therefore, that mechanisms for channeling community concern be improved and strengthened. The checkpoint procedure is rooted in the principle of community involvement. It goes beyond the mere avoidance of overlap in programming, for the language that originally gave rise to it spoke of genuine working relationships and dialogue. And for good reason. The wealth of studies in community development show how difficult it is to implement change over the resistance of affected groups. But the justification of involvement does not derive solely from a fear of blockage and resistance. The evident lack of success of schools in poor areas was a prime factor in the decision of Congress to enact Title I. The procedure implicitly endorses an alliance between school and community which allows the poor to contribute their own insights to the development of educational projects. The CAA-LEA dialogue represents one important form of involvement, a vital concept in the War on Poverty.

RAPHAEL NYSTRAND

I would like to address myself to relationships between school districts and Community Action Programs (CAP). My comments are based upon three case studies in medium-size cities and some observations that were made in one large city.[1] This is a very small sample which limits the conclusions

[1] This research was supported by a grant from the Office of Economic Opportunity under the provisions of Title II of the Economic Opportunity Act of 1964.

that can be drawn from it.

Community Action agencies have the funding capacity to establish educational components. The legislation of the Economic Opportunity Act (EOA) was quite clear on this point. It initially suggested that a good part of the effort of the Office of Economic Opportunity should be directed to providing educational benefits. The passage of the Elementary and Secondary Education Act (ESEA) has modified this somewhat. It provides another funding vehicle which, in many ways, has become more attractive to school people. Many Office of Economic Opportunity officials would like to see ESEA funds directed more specifically toward children of the poor in poverty areas and not simply to schools which qualify on the basis of gross socioeconomic statistics.

The EDA and ESEA guidelines provide for local community action agencies to review and cooperate in the development of educational programs which are to be funded under the Elementary and Secondary Education Act. If community action agencies were to participate meaningfully in the development of education components, this would mark a significant departure from the traditional decision-making processes in most school systems. Local boards of education have been charged traditionally with the responsibility of making community educational decisions. The functions of school boards are well known. Local Community Action Boards supposedly are to perform the same functions with respect to poverty-related matters.

The Community Action Legislation required that people who are poor, people who represent the areas to be served, must be represented on the Community Action Policy-Making Board. The extent to which these people are effective in developing policy and implementing programs is one of the questions that has surrounded this legislation. My observations in four cities indicated that neither the Board of Education nor the Community Action Policy-Making Board had much effect on what ultimately became education programs. In no case did board-type groups suggest program components; the program components were developed by experts, staff people within the school system or within the community action agency. This suggests that the road to establishing almost any kind of educational program change is not through boards but through administrators, people with the technical competence to develop programs.

I found three patterns of relationships between school systems and community action agencies. One can be characterized by high school access to the Community Action Board. The CAP staff did not have the manpower or the professional capability to make suggestions for educational programs. The programs that came out of decision-making arrangements such as these looked very much like traditional school programs. They represented ideas familiar in the educational literature and, in most cases, were merely extensions of what these particular school systems were already doing.

The second pattern was a situation in which the community action staff was very strong and worked very effectively with its own board as a legitimating group and where the school people had no access to that board. Here the prevailing pattern was one of conflict. Community action people were dictating unilateral educational policy to the schools, saying, if you want Economic Opportunity money or Elementary and Secondary Education Act money without our making a fuss about it, then you must do certain things.

The third pattern, and the one we are most interested in, was one in which the agency staff was strong and the school people did have access to the Community Action Policy-Making Board. Here truly innovative programs seem more likely to develop because the CAP staff, people in the program who are not necessarily educators, serve as a check on educational traditionalism. However, it is important that at the same time there is the professional expertise of the educators to temper ideas brought in from the outside.

My observations indicated that very important community linkages can be built when school and CAP agency personnel work together. One of the programs developed made use of urban agents outside the school system. Though they were not employed by the school system, they worked very closely with the school people. They served as, what may be termed, "conflict-mediating agents" in cases where conflict between the school and the community appeared imminent over trivial things such as Johnny saying he was sent home from school because the teacher does not like him. Because they are outside the school system, these urban agents could go into the neighborhood and say, dispassionately, "Look, the school system is not always wrong and the school people want to help. They are trying to do the best they can. Let's see if we can resolve this thing."

I wish I could say that when school and CAP agency personnel cooperate, the results will always be effective but I cannot. My observation in the larger city, indicated that the school people and the community action people talked to each other often and were very cooperative, but they simply could not agree. It came down to a difference of philosophy. It is difficult to be optimistic about the cooperative route to educational innovation under such circumstances. It becomes very much a political process, the matter of access being of great importance. One possibility worth testing is that the most effective route to the development of programs in the big city is on the individual building level, working with building principals or district superintendents rather than trying to approach the system in its entirety.

I will briefly mention three conclusions that I would be happy to discuss in the remainder of the session. First, I suggest that these patterns of operation, as well as the effects that I think go with them, might be applicable to the relationships between school districts and agencies other than Community Action agencies.

Secondly, I would say to you as community service people that, if you want to influence school programs or use education as a route to breaking the poverty cycle, it is incumbent upon you to become knowledgeable about educational affairs. Probably most important here is recognizing the expertise of professional educators which is available to you and working with them to develop cooperative programs. Your goal should be to supplement rather than replace their expertise. Implicit in this suggestion is my rejection of the conflict model which purports that prevailing school programs must be destroyed before anything workable can be developed. Not everything that should be done by professional educators has been done, but they are eager to do what they can, and you will find more and more school people eager to work with community people. In this context, I cannot overemphasize how important it is that you come to them as representatives knowledgeable about education.

Finally, I would caution that a welfare or social-service orthodoxy has no more to recommend it than the traditional educational orthodoxy that many persons are so ready to denounce. Community involvement by itself is not the answer. Nathan Glazer had a fine article in *The New York Times Magazine* last spring in which he suggested that the poverty program represented a revolt against professionalism.[2] Merely to seize upon fifty slogans or a new orthodoxy is not the way to break the poverty cycle. What is needed are people willing to work continually to define issues, identify problems on the grass-roots level, articulate these problems to school officials, suggest strategies for ameliorating them, and serve as a sounding board for the ideas they may want to feed back to you.

CURTIS MELNICK

Let me orient you as to how I fit into this scheme. I am district superintendent of one of twenty-seven geographically oriented districts in Chicago. My district happens to be the one in which the university is located. It is small and compact, three square miles in area, and runs roughly from 47th Street to 71st Street, and from Cottage Grove to the Lake.

A lot of people and a lot of schools are packed into this district, but I want to focus particularly upon the community of Woodlawn because I think it is the area in which you are most interested and to which today's topic is most relevant. Let me say that in answer to the question, "Can education break the poverty cycle?," I would have to give you an unqualified "yes." I would have to go "out of business" if I could not answer "yes."

What is the community of Woodlawn? The portion of Woodlawn which is within my particular district runs from the Midway primarily to 76th Street, and from Cottage Grove to Jackson Park. The population in this area is declining. In 1960 there were 81,000 people; in April, 1966, it was estimated that the population was down to 78,000. My guess is that now it is even less. The people of Woodlawn are finding that they can live

---

[2]"The Grand Design of the Poverty Program," *The New York Times Magazine*, February 27, 1967, p.69.

elsewhere and not pay high rates for poor services and residences. According to the statistics that I have, there has been a drop of about 3,000 people. On the other hand, the population is increasingly becoming Negro. In 1960, close to 90% of the population was Negro, and in 1966, it was estimated at 98%. Within one square mile, I have eight administrative units at the elementary school level and one at the high school level. I have a school "around the corner" from just about everybody, almost one on every block.

What are the characteristics of some of these youngsters? Our population is very transient and there is a lot of movement in and out of, and between, schools in the area. A year ago the dictum came down from the central office that when youngsters, particularly those in the upper grades, moved out of one attendance district and into another, it was not necessary to transfer them from one school to another. About three years ago, we found it expedient, in Woodlawn, to stop such interschool transfer. It involved too much paperwork and was not doing the youngster any good. If a youngster registered at one school and moved across the street into the boundaries of another, he was to be permitted to stay in the first, at least for that school year.

I have mentioned the high transiency of most of our population and can cite a statistical study we carried out in a school that opened after a great deal of preparation for its opening. Accurate records were kept and we know that, within two years, 50% of the youngsters who had registered in this school in the fall of 1963 were no longer there. You can see that such a situation makes education difficult. We do not have the youngsters long enough to make a lasting impression on them. I think that these figures are comparable in other schools in the Woodlawn area.

Someone might ask, if you are going to attack the problems of the disadvantaged where do you begin? Do you begin with the very youngest children, do you take care of those now in school, or do you work with adults? My answer is that you try to work at all levels, and this is the philosophy we have tried to adopt in the Woodlawn area.

Four years ago we opened a night school at Hyde Park High School which is not far from this building. It has been a very flourishing night school, growing to the point where its student population is probably one of the largest in any of the city's twenty-five evening schools. Its principal believes in being flexible enough to offer the kinds of program the community wants. For example, he started out by offering a traditional high school program. Soon he saw that some of the people could not read and write properly, and for those who were functionally illiterate, we offered basic adult education. About a year ago, when some of the high school students graduated and asked for a college program, three college-level courses were included for them. Thus we have tried to meet the needs of the adult population.

Most of you are aware that Head Start has been operative in most of the disadvantaged areas. During the summers of 1965 and 1966, our Head Start was a large program, serving about one thousand youngsters. However, we need what we now call Child Development Centers, that is, the same type of pre-school programs throughout the year. I am sorry to say that we do not have the facilities. We have tremendous need for this in Woodlawn. We have two programs in the adjacent portion of District 14, Hyde Park-Kenwood, where there are several vacant rooms. But we do not have the facilities in our Woodlawn schools now.

This year we have had a school population which, for the first time, has not caused all the schools to bulge at the seams. I attribute this to several factors. One is a very acute sociological problem which broke out sometime last spring and is continuing – the so-called "teenage gang warfare." It has caused a number of families and teenagers to leave the area. The other is the fact which I have already pointed out, namely that more and better housing has become available. People are leaving the poorly maintained homes in Woodlawn for "greener pastures," and in my opinion, this is all to the good.

For example, this fall we lost many of the youngsters in Hyde Park High School due to the gang warfare. This immediate area was divided up; we had turf. There was one gang on one side of Woodlawn and another gang on the other side, and one would not permit youngsters from the other to cross into its territory. As a result, Hyde Park High School became the territory of one of the gangs and youngsters belonging to the other simply disappeared. Some went to other schools, some moved, and some dropped out of school. We still have not solved this problem at the Wadsworth Upper-Grade Center. This is the facility for the seventh and eighth grade youngsters in Woodlawn, where we have an almost equal number of youngsters from each gang, and we have not been able to effect a lasting peace.

We have also tried to help these youngsters by taking advantage of almost any program the community and educational agencies have offered to us. The University of Chicago has been most helpful particularly since Roald Campbell has become Dean of the School of Education. We feel that we can serve the University by being a research lab for the professors who want to work with disadvantaged children. In our Woodlawn schools, we have a number of projects which are being conducted by professors of education at the university.

On the other hand, we make use of the university's resources to a great extent. For example, some of the bright youngsters at Hyde Park High School are allowed to use the Harper Library at the University. To my knowledge, we are the only school in the city with this advantage. A number of professors at the University come to speak on their special fields to youngsters at Hyde Park High School. Professor Janowitz and Professor Bettelheim conducted a very successful seminar on Behavior Characteristics of Disadvantaged Youngsters. Dan Lortie, a professor in the School of Education, conducted a seminar for principals. The University High School conducted a special summer school for twenty–five apathetic youngsters who were capable of doing better work. This has had a very salutary effect and there are quite a few published reports of what the Stern Summer School accomplished. We often use their museums, libraries, and collections. Thus we have greatly benefited from having the University of Chicago as a resource in our district.

In Woodlawn we also have the first fieldwork unit of the School of Social Service Administration at the university. Six social service fieldworkers serve the schools in Woodlawn. Last year they served only two schools but this year they are serving almost all the schools and are invaluable to us. One of their instructors has an office in one of our Woodlawn schools and we get the benefit of a number of social workers. Furthermore, we have our own Board of Education part-time social worker as well.

We are looking forward to even more cooperation with the university. For example, a health service building in which people from the university will be the dominant staff members is planned. I hope the Department of Education will also sponsor an Urban Education Center, an Early-Childhood Center, and the like. There are other programs which we are quite happy about. The Woodlawn Mental Health Center Program is a Board of Health program but is unique in that the psychiatrists who run it actually conduct an intervention program by working with first-grade youngsters in our schools as well as their parents. For the last two or three years, they have been working very well in our classrooms.

Rather than belabor you with the extent of the federal programs of which we have taken advantage, I will just list a few. In several schools we have been able to reduce class size. A physician has been assigned to the Wadsworth School to work in the areas of nutrition and family-life education. We are going to have a closed-circuit cluster television program for six Woodlawn schools. Several special summer schools were organized on a basis that we would like to see for our schools during the school year. In one school, we have a tutorial program for emotionally disturbed youngsters who could benefit from a one-to-one relationship. Next week some of our youngsters will participate in an outdoor camping and education program, and throughout the spring the rest of the Woodlawn sixth-grade youngsters will participate in this program.

We have had a number of cultural experiences for them such as field trips, and have brought in orchestras, bands, ballets, and the like. We have conducted a large instrumental music program throughout the Woodlawn area and have had a huge after-school program in reading, arithmetic, and guidance. At the high school level, we have had teen tips for girls, typing and the like. We have had a program in speech improvement, which is not speech therapy but helps the youngsters learn to use standard American language.

It might be argued that, particularly in areas like Woodlawn, we should put more federal money into reducing class size. I do not disagree with this, but we cannot find the people. We have a teacher shortage, not only in Chicago, but throughout big cities. We have enough people in Woodlawn for our established and authorized teaching positions, but we cannot get day-to-day substitutes. We get less than half of what we need while some of the more privileged areas get as high as 90% or 95%.

Like all other districts, we are held to a strict 33:1, pupil-teacher ratio. I argue unsuccessfully that this is in a sense penalizing Woodlawn because teaching thirty-three children in Woodlawn is not the same as teaching thirty-three children in Chatham, Beverly, or Rogers Park. Furthermore, when we do not get all the substitutes to which we are entitled, we have to break up the rooms, and in effect, drive up the average pupil-teacher ratio or the class size.

I think that most of you know that we have so-called non-quota teachers, adjustment teachers, or counselors. We have librarians, teacher-nurses and are doing more in the provision of such services. We are greatly in need of psychological services which have been reduced to the point where they are almost non-existent. We have two full-time psychologists to serve the entire district of seventeen schools when we could use one full-time psychologist in *each* school. This is the result of our salary policy, and steps are being taken to correct it. When we begin to pay psychologists better I think that we will be able to attract more of them. We have not been able to get full-time social workers either. We have one now and could use many more, but as I have indicated, the School of Social Service Administration of the University of Chicago has helped in taking up the slack in that particular area.

In summary, the schools of Woodlawn are doing as good a job under existing conditions as they can. But they are basically not meeting the educational needs of most Woodlawn children. Perhaps a new philosophical approach is needed. Certainly massive amounts of money, manpower, and material are needed now and will be needed for the future.

Yes, I must reiterate the claim that if any force can break the poverty cycle, it will be education that will do it.

PHILIP HAUSER

It is inspiring to hear the kind of report that Mr. Melnick has just presented in an effort to utilize and increase educational resources for a community such as Woodlawn. But I am afraid that having said that I must also say that what is being done is inadequate. If we turn to the question of "Can education break the poverty cycle?" there are two elements that we must bear in mind in attempting an answer. One is the quality and character of the education and the other is the quality and character of the society into which the person with such an education emerges. Presumably, the function of education should be to provide people with certain basic skills, saleable skills (which, of course, include vocational skills), and citizenship skills so that he can assume the full obligations and rights of citizenship in these United States.

Looking at what is actually taking place, and considering the Educational

Establishment as it exists today in metropolitan United States, including Chicago, it seems to me that the question "Can education break the poverty cycle?" must be answered (and I am afraid that I must disagree with Mr. Melnick) with a resounding "no." Education is just one element in the process of socialization which converts the infant into a human being. Education alone, no matter how excellent, will not produce either a person prepared to accept the obligations and rights of American citizenship or an opportunity to escape poverty. It must take place in the context of general socialization which, among other things, equips the child to take on his education.

This is not the case today. In fact my major quarrel with formal education is that it has operated in a vacuum. It has operated as if it were a separate principality, divorced from the rest of the social order of which it is a part. It has remained separated rather than integrated. I am not here referring to integrated in terms of the color line, but in terms of being tied in with other programs such as housing, recreation, employment, preschool education, and the rest. Let me make this observation: despite all the advantages and contributions of Head Start, I think that until the schools are reorganized to build on what Head Start tries to do, we are just pouring money down the sewer. I submit that public school education in this country, including Chicago, is not so organized now.

Let me say, these beginning observations should not be interpreted as in any way a condemnation of Mr. Melnick, his colleagues, the present Board of Education, or other agencies now operating in the city of Chicago. The inadequacies are the result of the sorry situation into which our society has drifted over the last several decades. Our social order, including among other things its technological complexities, simply have passed by the education establishment which itself has largely been asleep. This is not necessarily true of everyone in the educational establishment. Some have not been asleep, and from what I read and know, Mr. Melnick is among those who have not been asleep.

However, those who have been asleep have contributed to a situation over the years in which the faculties, principals, district superintendents, and superintendents today, if I may use an analogy that I think is appropriate, are at bat, facing Sandy Koufax with a banana stalk for a bat. They simply have not been given the resources with which to do the job. This is the situation today and we should not kid ourselves about it.

Perhaps I can be more concrete and specific. At present in our society educational opportunity depends on what – with your permission I will use a concept that I have invented – "the preconception IQ" of the child is. The child with a very high preconception IQ – that is, an intelligence quotient before he is even conceived – who is smart enough to pick white parents who live in the suburbs, by that very astute act automatically guarantees unto himself a much larger dollar input for his education in a public school than the child with a very low preconception IQ who is stupid enough to pick Negro parents who live in the inner city. I might complete the continuum by pointing out that the child with an intermediate preconception IQ who is smart enough to pick white parents, but not smart enough to pick white parents who live in the suburbs, automatically receives intermediate educational opportunity and quality. He has something better than the Negro child in the inner city but considerably worse than the white child in the suburbs.

If you think about it, this is a pretty serious indictment of the American educational system. We speak about equality of opportunity in a democratic society, but for reasons I do not have time to go into we have drifted into a situation in which our public school education is actually contributing to the establishment and maintenance of a society stratified on the basis of social and economic status, and, in the present circumstances, also stratified by race. The educational system in the United States undoubtedly is contributing to a caste society.

"Can education break the poverty cycle?" My first answer is that education as it is organized at present certainly cannot. Without going into great detail, it cannot primarily because it does not have adequate resources. As a society, we have not allocated enough federal, state, and local monies for public school education.

Second, it cannot because it does not yet have the necessary basic objectives. The most fundamental of these is giving every child an opportunity to acquire the basic skills, the saleable skills, and the citizenship skills which give him at least an equal start in the race to climb the social, economic, and political ladder to a level limited only by his own capacities. This is not an objective of American society today, and until this is made an explicit goal, education will not break the poverty cycle.

To carry this a step further, what would be adequate resources? The White House Conference "To Fulfill These Rights" took place about a year ago. It was my privilege to serve as director of the task force on education. If you read the chapter on education in the report of that conference, you will find that one of the recommendations is that a floor be established of about $1,000 per annum per child for public elementary and secondary school education.

Now this is a floor. When I say that we do not now have the basic concept of what education requires, I also include this notion. We find Superintendent Melnick reporting that in Woodlawn there is pupil-teacher ratio which is average for the city as a whole. On the face of it, and I choose my words carefully, this is just stupid and inept. It is not Mr. Melnick's fault, but it is stupid and inept because, presumably, we are proceeding on what I regard as a blind concept. We say that every child is entitled to an equal input, as represented, for example, by a teacher-pupil ratio. This is a crazy notion in a society which believes in equality of education as a bridge for equality of opportunity.

If the objective were to give every child the opportunity to acquire the basic, the saleable, and the citizenship skills, then it is a question of giving every child whatever he needs to achieve this objective. Of course this is essentially why such a notion as "compensatory education" is meaningful. It is not Mr. Melnick's fault, but it is stupid to say that every child is entitled to an equal input, as represented, for example, by the teacher-pupil ratio. If the objective were to give every child the opportunity to acquire the basic, the saleable, and the citizenship skills, then it is not a question of giving every child an equal number of dollars for his education. It is necessary rather to give each child whatever he needs to achieve the objective. Of course this is essentially why such notions as "compensatory education," "enrichment," and so on have come into the picture. But compensatory education, enrichment, Head Start programs, and some of these very nice things of which Mr. Melnick speaks still constitute inadequate resources – these things do not begin to do the job.

I think that public school education in Woodlawn today will produce a generation of Woodlawn high school graduates who will still have eighth-grade reading ability. They will have been put through the school system because, among other things such as Mr. Melnick's inadequate resources, the teachers are compelled to promote 98%, or whatever it is, of all students who enter the class at the beginning of the school year. The object is to get them through the school system because there is a budget and so forth. But this is not the objective that I am talking about; this is not giving the child the equipment to stand on his own feet so that the poverty cycle can and will be broken.

What must be done? I do not have adequate time to elaborate this now, but let me quickly put it this way. It is one thing to listen to me and to say, "He is attacking the Chicago school system again." But that is not my idea at all. The school system is a victim of our society which in this respect is just plain sick as far as I am concerned. I did attack the previous Superintendent of Schools because I thought, and the passage of time demonstrates it, that he was the best nineteenth-century superintendent Chicago ever had. The trouble is that we are past the middle of the twentieth-century. He not only did not have the concepts I am talking about, he would not even open his mind to them.

However, that is another matter, and fortunately it is water over the dam. Now we have a Superintendent of Schools whose ears are at least attached to his brain. Among other things, he is apparently competent to think about these problems and to try and face them instead of ignoring them or even denying their existence.

The State Legislature is also made up of predominantly nineteenth-century minds, which will become increasingly clear as the legislature session proceeds in Springfield. They continue to refuse to provide Mr. Melnick and his associates with adequate resources to do the job. He and many others in the educational establishment know how to do the job. There are dedicated people in the school system who want to do the job. However, they cannot take the tack I am taking at the moment, which is a privilege of university professors. I not only have the right to say these things; I think I have the obligation to say them. I do not work for the establishment; Mr. Melnick does. We have a State Legislature that lives in the nineteenth-century and will not provide adequate funds.

Let me document that. In 1965 this great state of Illinois, of which I am a native, ranked 45th among the states in the Union in the allocation of monies in relation to income for education per child. I blush to admit that in 1966 my great home state changed its rank from 45th to 46th among the fifty states. This is what Mr. Melnick and his colleagues at the Board of Education have to contend with.

Incidentally, this is why federal monies must be obtained. It is true that even if Chicago had enough money for education, we do not have enough qualified personnel. This is another indication of how what I have been calling the establishment has been afflicted with rigor mortis. We need more money not only to train more teachers but also to train them to know something about the areas into which they go and to acquire more substantive knowledge instead of just learning the techniques of teaching.

The last observation can set off another discussion, but I think many forces in this direction are already in motion. Moreover, the school teachers who are available now are not necessarily being used as effectively as possible. In addition to classroom teaching, they are still doing a lot of clerical, patrol, and other work. This is not because Mr. Melnick wants it this way, but because again he does not have the resources to get other personnel who would enable his teachers to teach instead of doing all these other ancillary duties.

To state the case in negative terms, I am convinced, and I think you will be, that you cannot break the poverty cycle without adequate education — certainly not in a society such as ours which has very little use for anybody who is not literate and who does not have specialized skills.

On the basis of 1960 census figures, the fact is that as recently as 1960, 78% of all Negro adults in this country had not completed high school, 23% had never finished fifth grade and were functionally illiterate. This was their preparation for metropolitanism as a way of life. Basic and central facts such as these go along with the fact that within fifty years the Negro American has been transformed from 73% rural to 73% urban. He has only recently been able to move from the rural slums of the south and is now more urbanized than the white population.

But he has had little or no preparation for urbanism as a way of life. In consequence, new needs and demands upon the educational system of a completely unprecedented character have arisen. It is perfectly absurd for the educational establishment to assume that the budgets, techniques, and textbooks they have had in the past will be adequate to the new needs. A basic change in concept as well as in the allocation of resources is involved. It adds up to the fact that education is a necessary but not sufficient condition for breaking the poverty cycle. To enable the child to get out of the poverty cycle, in addition to education you must have a community, a neighborhood, a family, and all the other bolstering institutions that play a role in the child's socialization. As long as our public schools operate as separate, independent principalities and the program does not approach the child in a holistic fashion, education, as it exists in the United States, in Chicago, and in Woodlawn, will never break the poverty cycle.

One final thought about the inadequacies of present education. A recent report of the Office of Education on *Equality of Opportunity* for education, prepared under the supervision of my former colleague here, Jim Coleman, points out that, even before he starts school, the Negro child is disadvantaged in relation to the white child. And then for every year that the Negro and white child stay in the public schools in the United States, the discrepancy between them increases. That is an astonishing fact. Every year that the Negro child is exposed to public school education, he becomes increasingly handicapped in relation to the white. Given these facts, I find it just a little bit difficult to talk about education as it now exists breaking the poverty cycle.

One other word. I said that the character of society is also involved. I mentioned this with all that it implies. There are other fights to be fought in the United states. I have pointed to the inadequacies of education. But it is also true that the more education and the higher the occupation the Negro gets in the United States, the smaller is the proportion of his income relative to that of the white with similar education and occupation. Thus, if the Negro American gets more education but has made the mistake, by reason of a low preconception IQ, of picking a black skin, then, although he can get a better job and higher income, the discrepancy between his income and that of the white with the same education is greater than if he had no education at all. I make this observation about our social order as a general challenge to our society, including Chicago.

9

Vocational Education and Apprenticeship Training for Urban Youth

DANIEL REID

I work for the United States Department of Labor in the Bureau of Employment Security. Previously, I worked with the Illinois State Employment Service for ten years where I was the community coordinator for the city of Chicago. Prior to that, I was a youth worker. I owe most of my success to Earl Doty who, when he was with the Chicago Boys Clubs, took me under his wing and taught me the ins-and-outs of community service. I feel that this morning I should give you some background to the problem of the construction industry as far as Negroes are concerned. I will take you all the way back to slavery days and bring you up to the present.

However, before I do that, I will tell you just how our bureau is involved in the Apprenticeship Information Center, which we call the AIC, and the Urban League, and apprenticeship program. The United States Department of Labor has jurisdiction over all the employment services in this nation, and the Illinois State Employment Service administers the AIC in Chicago. The AIC does recruiting, testing, and referring to the joint apprenticeship councils, and the Chicago Urban League – Special Project Program does the recruiting and provides the supportive services for bringing young Negro boys into the apprenticeship program. As minority group representative, my job is to assist and advise the Urban League and the Employment Service in this program.

As for the background, prior to the Civil War, most building and construction labor in the South was performed by Negroes as slaves. As plantations grew larger, slaveowners trained more and more Negroes in the crafts. This division and specialization of labor was not only economically necessary for the owners but, for obvious reasons, it was also profitable – *the slave craftsmen drew no pay.* White craftsmen from the North saw no advantage in coming South for work, and those that were there already were antagonistic and resentful. They readily perceived that the employment of slaves in skilled occupations was a real threat to their own economic and even their social status.

With emancipation and its massive and historic social upheaval, the Negro freedman's favored status in the skilled building trades *suffered drastically.* He had always worked under a master, without concern for costs of materials or experience in negotiation with contractors or employers. Thus, he was in no position to compete with the white craftsmen who, remembering only too well their disadvantageous position of slavery days, instituted, promoted, and maintained a racially-based exclusionist policy, which, aided by the economically and politically powerful former slaveholders, was *tragically effective.* The segregationist alliance, plantation owners, and other elements of the Southern power structure, along with the growing labor unions, caused the proportion of Negro construction workers in the South to shrink to less than one-third by 1890. One handy device used was the tactic that led the unionists to designate Negro jobs as "white man's work." Although southern Negroes in the nineties held their own in bricklaying, plastering, and cement-finishing, some losses occured in carpentry and painting.

In the North, general exclusion of Negroes from skilled-craft jobs came from employers who were under the thumb of white partisans. Color barriers in the large industrial areas effectively prevented Negro freedmen from working in the trades for which they had been well-trained in the South. In addition, they were prevented from developing skills in newly emerging trades and occupations, such as electricians. Moving northward, racial exclusion took on increased significance, and resulted in displacing Negroes from a variety of skilled occupations. The construction industry was the example of this trend.

The first major breakthrough in the pattern of discrimination occured during World War I when thousands of Negroes migrated to the North. In many instances, Negro craftsmen were employed as laborers and helpers; they were allowed to observe the job content and procedures of northern union workers. During the 1920's, some advance in skilled, construction employment was accomplished, but this was offset by the depression which triggered the reactivation of exclusionist policies, removed skilled occupations from the job possibilities of Negroes, and instituted a self-perpetuating pattern of racial discrimination in the building trades. Massive manpower shortages arrived with World War II, and the skilled-craft barrier was subjected to its second major breach. It was characterized by a desirable trend toward equal opportunity for minority group workers in skilled-craft employment. When the war ended, fairly significant numbers of Negroes were able to retain their recently achieved positions in the ranks of organized construction tradesmen.

Since World War II, the overall picture in the construction industry has been mixed but by no means egalitarian. As a result of government pressures and the influence of civil rights organizations, chiefly the NAACP and the National Urban League, the traditional wage differential has almost disappeared in jobs covered by union contracts. However, areas of conflict remain which include formal and informal union discrimination, segregated seniority rosters, licensing laws, which when administered function as devices of discrimination, and the imposition of many other unreasonable and anti-Negro restrictions.

Recently, the number of international unions having formal racial barriers has declined from at least 22 in 1930 to 2 in 1965. Negro membership in unions has increased from about 56,000 in 1930 to between 1½ and 2 million. According to a study recently published by the Labor Committee of the NAACP, there is a significant correlation between the relative absence of Negroes in skilled-craft employment and their almost total exclusion from apprenticeship training programs. This is also born out by a National Urban League research report which documents major impediments to apprenticeship training opportunities for Negro youth in most building and construction occupations in major urban centers.

The Federal government recognized this situation, this inequality of opportunity, this covert, devious, and often blatant segregationist policy. They recognize it as a danger to the growing economy, an obstacle to the realization of the goals of the civil rights movement, and as the perpetuation of second-class citizenship for a significant segment of Negro youth who must perforce accept dead-end jobs, most of which are in the unskilled or marginal category.

Another aspect of the problem is that young Negroes are not being apprenticed even to the extent necessary to offset and counterbalance natural losses. This means that, at present *Negro journeymen who die or retire are not being replaced fast enough by new Negro apprentices.* Moreover, these youngsters do not have the primary role models (fathers, uncles, and other adult relatives) in skilled trades, who could give them information about job content and apprenticeship openings, or at least inspire them to choose a skilled trade as a career.

As a result, the United States Department of Labor has set up a high-priority program for recruiting eligible young Negroes living in Chicago into the building and construction trades. This campaign is an implementation of the intention of President Lyndon Johnson and Secretary of Labor Willard Wirtz to crack barriers and achieve maximum feasible integration of the industry. As I said earlier, the two agencies involved are the Illinois State Employment Service and the Chicago Urban League.

What are the selling points, the attractive features of this program which concentrates on Negro youth? There are many, but I will discuss the four features that are most vital and possibly most easily understood.

1. *Life-time security:* A journeyman's skills are specialized, and thus he can reasonably expect steady work throughout his active life.

2. *Pay and advancement:* The hourly wage of an apprentice in the construction trade usually starts at 40% to 50% of the craftsmen, journeymen rate. According to the present rates, this is between $2.50 to $3.00 an hour in some cases, which is half the journeymen's rate. Pay increases regularly throughout the apprenticeship training period. In fact, the youngster gets five days' pay for four days' work because one day of each week is spent in school.

3. *Education:* As we said, one day per week is spent in regular classroom study. This consists of subjects having a direct relationship to the trade or occupation the apprentice selected. Even in the preapprenticeship period, remedial education is available in subjects such as English and mathematics which enable the candidate to prepare for the entrance examination.

4. *Exemption from military service:* After 1,000 hours of apprenticeship training, favorable consideration for exemption from military service may be requested. Usually after 2,000 hours the apprenticeship trainee is entitled to full exemption.

As an occupational class, construction workers earn more money per year than many white-collar workers, laboratory technicians, bookkeepers, and most school teachers, social workers and middle-echelon state and federal government workers as well as many others, including some managers and businessmen. Is it any wonder then that there has been such a long and determined effort by white locals to exclude Negroes? Is it any wonder that rigid barriers based on race and color have been maintained by segregated locals since emancipation?

Herbert Hill, Labor Secretary of the NAACP writes, "Prior to the formation of viable craft unions, organizations of artisans sought to restrict the skilled-employment opportunities of Negroes and were, in some cases in the North, even opposed to emancipation." Add to this persistence of the exclusion policy the clear prediction that the entire American economy will be faced with a serious crisis in the next decade because of the lack of skilled manpower. A major factor contributing to the economically and socially harmful operation of the nation's apprenticeship program is *color discrimination and racial exclusion.* For years, the union locals have been saying, "Sure, we are going to integrate." But either they receive no applications from qualified Negroes or they make token admissions to their training programs in the hopes that such action would exempt them from some of the heat directed against them by the liberal community, the civil rights organizations, and at times the Federal government.

Why do we feel that massive mobilization is necessary in our area now? Because, if we can confront entrenched union resistance with a roster of qualified young Negroes who are willing and able to successfully complete an apprenticeship training, all the evasive generalizations, specious arguments, and formal and informal restrictions will be exposed for what they really are.

White Collar vs. Blue Collar: Some will ask, does not this work against and possibly negate the arguments for higher education for disadvantaged youth? Is not this a possible reversal of the theory, long held and expounded by many of us, that a college education for the bulk of our great and growing population of young, underprivileged Negroes is an answer to economic and social discrimination?

The answer is no. Certainly, we are woefully short on doctors, dentists, lawyers, teachers, engineers, architects, and scientists. Certainly big businesses are frantically scrambling to recruit or "shanghai" Negro college graduates for management trainee programs or as public relations men. Lately, in the Spring, Negro college campuses have been swarming with corporate recruiters looking for Bill Berry's "Instant Negro." There is ample evidence that many parents, as well as counselors in Negro schools, work to instill in the minds of the young the concept that nothing less than a college degree will insure them with adequate means to escape from second-class citizenship.

Practically speaking, this line of thinking is unrealistic. It does not take the basic fact of individual difference into account. This fact is true of members of a family as well as of ethnic groups, white or Negro. Each person on this earth is endowed with individual aptitudes, abilities, talents, and responsibilities. An architect who designs a modern building very likely would starve to death if he had to earn his living installing the plumbing in that building.

It is time for us to realize that not all birds can fly, not all horses are race horses. We need to broaden the base of the Negro middle class. We need to reach out now for a better economic life which is ours by right. We need to give hope and motivation to our youth by proving that doors can be opened even to those who have little more than utilitarian aptitudes. We need to restore and reinforce the stability of the Negro family by providing thousands of young Negro future fathers the job security that craftsmenship brings.

WILLEY KLINGENSMITH

Many of our urban problems are the result of the industrialization of the rural areas of this country. When we look at the national picture, we see that certain technological factors have made quite a change in our thinking and will make quite a few more changes in the years ahead. Technological changes and the impact of automation along with its technological operations are tied in with educational problems, with opportunities, and with population changes of the last few years.

Several years ago, Mr. Charles Shuman who is president of the American Farm Bureau commented that through experimentation at our University Agricultural Experiment Stations, we now know that within five years after it is planted, one particular strain of oats will be susceptible to a certain type of rust. So we developed a new strain of oats that will not be vulnerable to this type of rust but will be susceptible to a new type of rust and then we have developed a new strain of oats which is immune to this new rust. Each few years a new strain of oats will be developed. Therefore, agriculturalists today know which kind of oats we will be planting in this nation fifty years from now. That is how far ahead these experiments are, and this is one implication of technology in the rural area.

We also know that today in the Corn Belt, two men running two, four-row, picker-sheller machines in a corn field, along with another man hauling the corn to a nearby elevator, can pick, shell, and haul 10,000 bushels of corn in one day. Twenty years ago, one man, working with two horses was lucky if he picked, shucked, and put in a crib one hundred bushels a day. This means that one man can do more in one day than forty men and eighty horses could do in a day twenty years ago. This is technological change and you can see what it does to the farm labor supply.

Changes are also taking place in the field of home economics. An electronics institute on the north side of Chicago is experimenting with a new method of electronically baking a cake mix. Take the cake mix out of the box, mix the batter, put it in an electronic oven, and in sixty seconds, the cake is baked. I am told that soon these ovens will be available to the general public.

In the field of business education, automatic electronic data-processing machinery can do bookkeeping, write checks, and provide total information centers. When properly programmed, these machines will give out information at a dazzling speed. Certain companies in this city have communication centers where executives can dictate letters on tape recorders, move the recorders to the communication center, attach it to a machine, and copies of what he said go to sixty of their offices across the nation in thirty minutes. You can see what this will do to reduce the amount of secretarial help needed.

The machinery in the coal mines of southern Illinois is now almost entirely automatic and has replaced the man who used to dig coal there. One machine can dig as much coal in a day as 150 men used to dig. Again, this is displacing human labor.

These are just a few of many technological developments, but they illustrate what modern machinery is doing and is going to do in the future. We have reached a point in our economy where one person out of about fifteen, that is 7% or 8% of our population, can produce all the food that we need to adequately feed the nation. Furthermore, a decreasing percentage of our labor force is going to be engaged in the production of clothing and housing. Thus increasing numbers in the labor force will not be needed to produce the basic essentials for living, namely food, clothing and shelter; and their efforts are being devoted to producing items or performing services which a few years ago might have been considered luxuries. Barring devastating wars, of course, we can expect more luxuries in the future.

Another aspect is the changing economy that goes with these technological factors. In the United States in 1970, according to the best estimates, there will probably be 87 million people working full-time in the labor force. In 1940 there were 58 million. This is a tremendous increase in the labor force, and these people will have to keep pace with the changing economy. They will need training, and re-training to keep up with all the new technological changes. During the next decade, 26 million young workers will join the labor force on a fulltime basis, and 3 million women will change from housework to the labor force. These young wives, mothers, and widows will need marketable skills if they are to become competent workers.[1]

[1] U.S. Department of Labor, *Manpower Challenge of the 1960's*.

It is estimated that only two out of ten pupils now in elementary school will graduate with a four-year college degree. This means that 80% of these students will have to earn their living with less than a baccalaureate degree. Of course, many of them will go on to junior or business college, technical institutes, trade evening schools, or through job training courses to receive the skills and training which will give them the ability to earn a good living. But the rest will not be adequately prepared for a highly industralized or technical society. This is one of the basic reasons why the new 1963 Vocational Act was written. Many of the changes in this act are changing the vocational picture and vocational education across the nation.[2]

I would like to say that there are also some changes in neighborhood patterns within our urban society which affect the types of programs schools offer in the city. Neighborhoods bring to bear a great deal of pressure, and the type of neighborhood, the type of parent in that neighborhood, and the background of that parent has a great deal to do with the kind of program the schools offer. In a residential community where nearly all the parents have a university education, the youngsters are almost compelled by home and community pressures to take a college preparatory course in high school and go to college. Thus, in these communities, it is difficult to get enough youngsters to fill even one industrial arts shop at the high school level.

Of course, the program in that community will be very different from the one in a semiindustrial community. Many of these parents earn their living through labor, in either skilled trades, semiskilled trades, office work, or store-keeping, and the schools in such communities must provide more vocational offerings. These schools have more shops and drafting rooms, and offer more in the way of home economics and business education. Most vocational schools are located in highly industrial areas. Though there are exceptions, in general the cultural background in the home and neighborhood are important factors determining the education that parents want for their children.

There are ethnic groups in the city where the parents do not believe in sending their children to college. In our office we can hire secretaries who are nearly all high school valedictorians or in the upper 5% or 6% of their high school graduating class basically because they belong to this ethnic group. This is another problem, and the girls turn to business education to earn a living, the boys elect shopwork in the high schools.

Now I would like to shift to what we offer in terms of practical arts and industrial education. In Chicago, this program is, of course, administered by the Superintendent of Schools through the Department of Vocational and Practical Arts Education. This department is in charge of an Assistant Superintendent of Schools and within the department there are several bureaus. These include business education, home economics, industrial arts

---

[2]*Education for a Changing World of Work,* summary report of the Panel of Consultants on Vocational Education Requested by the President of the United States.

(which I added to technical subjects), and vocational education for girls. We also work very closely with the manpower group which is not actually in our department. A number of supervisors are assigned to this department to assist the schools in each special area.

I have already indicated that the kinds of programs we offer vary with each locality, but for example, in the elementary schools, we have two types of offerings. In residential areas, we continue to offer the home mechanics program which was initiated in the depression years of the late thirties. Many of the youngsters live in homes and, in this type of community, they do a great deal of their own home repair jobs. Communities with a higher population density have a different administrative set-up. In the Upper-Grade Center, we have industrial arts shops which go into the manipulative skills a great deal more than in the home mechanics classes, and similarly home economics courses which go into greater depth.

At the high school level, in the general high school we offer business education, home economics, and industrial arts. The industrial arts is a broad area involving several different materials and tools. We want to give the youngster basic training in the use of tools and an acquaintance with materials and industrial processes so he can be flexible enough to shift from one job to another. The same is true for business education and home economics. All of these industrial arts, home economics, and business education subjects are elective and not required. Going into each of these areas more specifically, in business education, there are courses in office practice, typing, stenography, bookkeeping, and distributive education which is basically the distributing of merchandise and really a vocational course. In home economics, there are courses in home management, clothing, and foods. In the industrial arts, we have the general shop, the wood, metal, electric, print, and auto shops as well as mechanical and architectural drawing, and machine drafting.

In addition to the general high schools, we have two technical high schools in the city. The one on the north side is Lane and the one on the south side is Lindbloom. These schools have curricula designed to prepare youngsters going on to either engineering school or technical institutes or into industrial careers. I will just add that a youngster going into engineering must have a background in a number of shops. However, he is limited to two years because he must also acquire a certain number of courses required by colleges.

In Chicago there are nine vocational high schools. In the first two years at a vocational school, we offer two years' basic education, and in the final two years, the youngster concentrates on his chosen area of specialization. This is true for all vocational high schools except Jones Commercial High School which does not accept students until their third year and specializations start immediately. Open enrollment is in effect at all vocational schools; thus any student may attend any vocational school in the city. Whether he elects to go to a vocational high school or the general high school is voluntary with the student and his parents.

Areas of specialization in the third and fourth years include: business education, office occupations, stenography, typing, transcription, distributive education, beauty culture, practical nursing, health occupations, foods, clothing, home economics, aviation, auto mechanics, drafting, architectural drafting, machine drafting, welding, machine shop, sheet metal shop, foundry, graphic arts, electricity, electronics, carpentry, cabinetmaking, upholstery, woodshop, and cooperative work training programs.

The one trade school operated is the Washburne School for apprentice training. Students attending the school come from the entire city and come upon recommendation of the joint-apprenticeship committee. They are persons employed four days per week on the job and attend school one day per week and are paid by the employer for the five day week. The length of time they attend depends upon the trade to which they are apprenticed.

ASHBY SMITH

I do not have too many problems because my speech has already been stolen. I am left with several observations that grow out of the efforts over the years of the Chicago Urban League to actually recruit young men and women for jobs in the Chicago area. Our ability to recruit young people from the minority community for apprenticeship jobs is subject to several considerations.

One is the state of knowledge within the Negro community about particular jobs, especially apprenticeship jobs. Let me mention a few of the apprenticeship offerings and you see what you know about these trades. What do you know about structural iron work or sheet metal work? Do you really know what a carpenter does? If you do not know, how can you direct a youngster toward these occupational endeavors or careers? There is an information gap at this level.

Second, Mr. Reid gave you a rundown on the history of the Negro in the construction trades. He told you that in the 1920's the Negro situation in the construction trades regressed and, in the Negro community, knowledge about the construction trades also regressed. Apprenticeship in the construction trades gained a negative context for Negroes. Those who knew about apprenticeship said Negroes were not wanted. Negroes felt there was no point in looking into it and turned their backs on the trade. When the Negro community turns its back on particular programs, it does a good job of it. It starts to channel its youth in other directions, even those who know something about apprenticeship and might want it. The community turns them into ministers, school teachers, and social workers because that is where jobs are available and a living can be made by Negroes.

The task of the Chicago Urban League is to reverse that pattern. After we assure ourselves that the openings are there, we must assure others. It is not only the Negro community that turns its back on these opportunities but also the institutions that service the Negro community. Schools, youth-serving agencies, and the State Employment Service adopt the attitude that

Negroes cannot make it because there is discrimination in that area. Generally, these agencies refer Negroes to the areas that are known to accept Negroes, the traditional job areas. We must get the Negro community and these agencies that service the Negro community to recognize and take advantage of new opportunities.

Third, the kinds of educational offerings that are available in the school must also change. Crane Tech is no longer a technical institution; Tilden changed from being a technical to a general high school when the technical high school moved to Lindbloom. Through our recruitment drives, we found that the best candidates for apprenticeship jobs or highly skilled, on-the-job training programs came from the general high schools of this city, not from the vocational schools. I am concerned with the mediocre youngster, and I do not understand why, in terms of the educational courses he has taken, the mediocre youngster from the general high school is better prepared than the one from a vocational high school.

I think that Mr. Reid told you about the pay that skilled people make once they have acquired their skills, but he neglected to tell you that some tradesmen earn more than either he or I do. This comes as a shock to the youth-serving agencies in the Negro community. As we go to them in our recruiting jobs, they become curious about these jobs and begin to reassess their activities. They do spot bright students and direct them as well as the dumb ones. But the bright students are directed on the basis of what is known to the agencies, teachers, shop teachers, counselors, and principals. If they do not know what opportunities are available or are about to emerge, they cannot do the best job of selecting and directing their youngsters.

The community becomes extremely important to our program because we have a supportive-services component which is aimed entirely at the retention after recruitment of youngsters entering the building trades. This program was established partly because most of the building trades are open only once or twice a year for selection and placement, while we recruit year-around. The gap between the time a youngster is recruited and the time the program begins its selection and placement procedures is crucial for a youngster who initially knows little about the trade he is trying to enter. His environment knows even less, and other opportunities which operate faster are competing for his attention.

We have to hold these younsters, which is not an easy job. We get involved with everything from marital problems to budget mismanagement to lack of self-assurance in handling the selection procedures, i.e., the aptitude tests and oral examinations that are involved.

On the other side of our door is a trade and a life to which they are not accustomed, one they have seldom seen in their own community. They have not really seen what the carpenter was doing, what the plumber was doing. They could not tell a plumber from the janitor who knocked on the pipes. We are increasing their knowledge about the trades, and we are increasing their communities' knowledge so the community, too, can support their endeavors to succeed in the apprenticeship of their choice.

10

Dominant Issues and
Proposed Solutions

OSCAR CHUTE

I cannot offer a solution for any community other than Evanston, unless you can find one in what I have to say. Every community has its unique qualities and a different mixture of cultures and leadership. I can only tell you about the direction and steps being taken in Evanston looking forward to the integration of its schools.

I went to Evanston in 1946. Evanston has had a Negro population for sixty or more years, and the percentage of Negroes in our school district is not very different today from what it was twenty years ago. People say that we have many more Negro children in our schools, and we do. We also have many more white children. Even though it seems to some that Evanston was well-developed in 1946, in two decades we have grown from some 5,000 elementary school children, K through 8, to close to 12,000.

Another image of Evanston is that everybody is rich, white, Protestant, and Republican. It is not true. I am a living example of one anyway. I am not rich. Over a period of years, I served on committees with one of the Chicago Assistant Superintendents and sometimes when I spoke he would say, "but after all, that is Evanston, a rich community. You can do things that Chicago can not do." They believe in education, but they pay for it. It has one of the highest school-tax rates in Illinois.

When this Assistant Superintendent told me how rich Evanston was and how poor Chicago was, I looked at the statistics. The City of Chicago has about $19,000 of assessed valuation behind each public school pupil. If the elementary and high schools are put together as in Chicago, the assessed valuation behind each school child in Evanston is less than $25,000. Yet, in comparison to the City of Chicago, we spend well over twice as much per capita out of local taxpayers' dollars. Furthermore, when Operation Head Start came along, we looked at the 1960 statistics and found that an amazing number of people qualified under the poverty program. We found 150 to 175 children without any trouble and did not even begin to tap all those who would have been eligible, had we been able to enlist the cooperation of the parents and the government in this problem.

Over the years, we have been committed in Evanston to a so-called "neighborhood school policy." The school boundaries have not been changed for a very long time. This made relatively little difference because we had a very fluid transfer policy. When a parent came to me with what I thought was a good reason for moving her child to another school where there was an empty seat, my philosophy was to give the lady what she wanted. Because we had no school bus service the parent had to assume the responsibility of getting the child to and from school.

I would like to talk briefly about the role of community groups. We have them; we have more darned organizations in Evanston than you can shake a stick at. I do not mean that they are all darned. The people are wonderful, and some of the groups have been rather significant in this area of integration. When I came into Evanston in 1946, the Dewey School had about 10% or 12% Negro children. This grew to 30%, 40%, 50%, 65% and finally to 70%; and during that time, the Negro and white neighbors in the school vicinity got alarmed. They organized into a Dewey Community Conference. They liked integrated education, integrated living, and integrated housing, but they did not want to let one rule the other. So they organized what might be called a pressure group to work on the city authorities and the School Board, to see what could be done to maintain some kind of racial balance in that school and neighborhood.

In another neighborhood that was changing rapidly, a group, which called themselves The Westend Neighbors, organized to stabilize their racially integrated community and schools. Another group, The Northwest Property Owners, was all white and some of the leaders wanted to maintain white segregation. I do not want to castigate the entire membership because not all of them felt this way. A Human Relations Office which had been set up by the City Council was helpful during certain critical periods. It was an interracial council which was organized before I went there, and I think later came to be called a human relations council. The National Organization of Jewish Women have done great work in operating a preschool program before the advent of Operation Head Start. The NAACP was a kind of burr in our saddle but turned out to be a constructive force. All these groups are pressure groups, and I approve of pressure groups. In fact, I have organized some down through the years.

The Urban League was, and still is, very helpful. They organized adults in the community to run evening tutorial programs in churches and schools which are opened for that purpose. The teacher group was also a pressure group. At certain critical periods when they anticipated the need to express themselves on the subject of integrated education, they stood up and were counted. Some statements they delivered to the Board, the Superintendent, the press, and the community made me very proud of them.

In 1946, the schools were largely white with the exception of one de facto segregated school. There were perhaps one, two, or three white children in this Negro school. However, at that time, out of some fifteen schools, two had about 30% Negroes, and they still have about 30% Negroes. These two schools represent a cross-section of the entire community, rich and poor, and a variety of ethnic backgrounds, and they are prime examples of how integrated education is good for not only Negro children but also for white children. In these particular situations, the white and Negro families, the whites more than Negroes, not only chose to live there but even sought that kind of neighborhood because they thought that education in a multiracial school setting was better than in an all-white setting.

Gradually Negro families have broken out of the boundaries set for them by the white man, though that is not to say that we have open housing in Evanston. We do not, but they began moving to other neighborhoods. I presume these other neighborhoods were rather prescribed by what you have been calling the "white power structure." I do not put all the blame on realtors because remember, they are working for us. They will do what their customers want them to do over the long term, and so, I think, they are reflecting what the people important to them want them to believe.

We began to integrate our faculties long before the time that I arrived in Evanston, and yet in the all-white schools there were no Negro teachers until the 1950's. About ten years ago our faculty began to examine the human relations content of textbooks, which some of you spoke about this morning, and the teachers' attitude toward minority groups and others who were different. Beginning in the late 1950's we began faculty in-service programs with the National Council of Christians and Jews, and others, to develop a long-term faculty climate that would be helpful to all children.

In the 1950's Negro teachers began to appear in schools other than the Foster School. During the planning of a recent bond issue, it became very evident that it was necessary to consider what could be done about more fully integrating our schools. The Board of Education passed a resolution on December 14, 1964 which was just prior to the bond issue which was to come up in the latter part of January. We were greatly helped by a Negro member of the board, Dr. Grant Shockley, who was a member of the staff at the Garrett Biblical Institute. The white members of the Board asked him to help them interpret the civil rights revolution, with particular reference to integrated education. I think he did more than any other person within Board circles because the Board sincerely wanted to learn something, and he was able to be our teacher.

On December 14, 1964, the Board passed the following resolution: "Whereas the Board deplores the condition of de facto segregation that has come into being because of housing patterns developed over the years, whereas the Board, being concerned with the welfare of all of the children in the schools and continuing to subscribe to the neighborhood school concept, recognizes the psychological and sociological disadvantages to which the children are subject because of the condition of de facto segregation. Whereas the Board recognizes that not all of the factors contributing to the condition of de facto segregation are subject either to direct control or even direct influence by law. Therefore, be it resolved that the Board does hereby resolve to eliminate de facto segregation in this school district . . . "

Meanwhile, the Foster School Committee, a staff-citizen group in the neighborhood of this one de facto segregated school, was invited to recommend something to the Board of Education, a platform and basis for effecting greater integration in our schools, and especially at the Foster School. On several occasions during this time, informal meetings were held, initiated by Dick Nelson, who was then chairman of the Human Relations Committee of the city, and including Mr. Graton, their Executive Director, together with representatives of the NAACP and the Urban League. They were not representative in the sense that they were not officially selected to represent any group. They met with the President of the Board of Education and with me during two or three fairly long sessions. All appeared to be people of good will. None of us were happy with the situation at the Foster School and wanted to do something constructive about it. Mr. Nelson offered to pull together the main points of what had been said over a three- or four-week period and come up with a second resolution.

Finally it came to the Board. The Foster School Committee had become rather inactive though in time they could have worked something out. However, the timing was important because we were faced with the bond issue. If the bond issue had passed with de facto segregation as one of the issues it might have seemed to some of the more conservative members of the community that the community really did not want to integrate its schools. But, if the Board passed a further resolution perhaps giving more substance to their December resolution, and the bond issue passed, this would indeed have been indicative of the community's willingness and desire to eliminate de facto segregation.

In January, the Foster School Committee unanimously adopted a resolution that was then passed on to the Board: "That supplementing its resolution of December 14, 1964, to eliminate de facto segregation, that the Board of District 65 direct the Superintendent of Schools to develop specific plans for implementing its resolution. This plan so be submitted to the Board at its regular meeting in May, 1965, three or four months hence. It shall include an over-all time table for the integration of the District 65 schools, developed in conjunction with building plans. The plans shall also provide . . . ", and then some more specifics. The Board of Education adopted this second resolution unanimously. The bond issue passed successfully and had the support of most groups including civil rights organizations.

I reconvened my committee of advisors from the NAACP, the Urban League, and the other groups. Again, this was an ad hoc group, but perhaps here was a desire on the part of the Superintendent of the Schools to learn something, and I believe that we taught each other. This confrontation continued for three or four months; every Saturday morning from about 9 o'clock through lunch. We sat in the board office and just let our hair down. In the end, I felt prepared to write my report as directed by the Board. My report went to the Board on time.

It recommended the development of a sixth, seventh, and eighth grade middle school. Since we are already building a fourth, seventh and eighth grade junior high school, and this is an elementary school district, rather than building junior high schools, we decided to have the middle school. This concept is a reasonable one and more popular across the country today than it used to be. Educationally nothing is wrong with it, and it achieves a kind of integration one year earlier.

I also proposed to reduce the Foster School by using any and all vacant seats available in other schools. This reduced the size of Foster, but a pocket of de facto segregated children remain. Educationally, I could not quite understand why so many systems start the integration process at the high school level and then work down. By the time students who have been segregated all along reach the high school level, it is too late for integration. I draw this from the conclusions of Ben Bloom and others at the University of Chicago, with the respect to the effect of early learning.

I also proposed that the Foster School could be phased out as a neighborhood school and replaced by a demonstration school that would cut across all levels of society and all the cultural and racial groups within the community, that there should be other boundary changes, and that the Negro population of the Dewey School would be reduced at least 50%, and hopefully 40%.

Another recommendation was that a Citizens' Commission on Integration be convened, and that, in advance, each of its members should be dedicated to the proposition of integrated education. I thought this reasonable because the Board had already committed itself, and there was no reason to choose a debating society to decide whether integration was a good thing or not. I have been out of touch since I retired in July, but I believe that our Board is devoted to the idea that integrated education is *better* for both whites and Negroes than an all-white or all-Negro situation.

The Citizens' Commission is a distinguished panel of people from across the community. They received a bit of publicity because some people in the community, who worked in the computor center at IIT, used a computor to help them draw the school boundaries which were to be recommended to the Board of Education. The commission issued its report early this fall, and the Board adopted it. By September 1967, it should result in an integrated situation in each school, such that every one will have at least a 5% or 10% Negro population and none will have more than 25% to 30%.

I would like to reemphasize something that has been said here in a number of different ways: a racial mix is not integration. All of us would like simple solutions to social problems, but just mixing children, whether they be Jewish and gentile, rich and poor, Negro and white, Puerto Rican, Mexican, Indian, or whatever — just putting them side by side in a classroom is not integration. It is only the beginning. The remaining problems are educational, social, family, and community related.

Through the years in Evanston, we have been trying to attack this educational problem on several fronts such as materials of instruction and textbooks, as we heard here earlier. The Negro-white, first-grade textbook is only a very small part of what has been going on in this field. Incidentally,

I might remind the university people that though these textbooks are written by university people, they portray the minority in anything but favorable light. Even historians do not always stick to pure history when they are writing textbooks for junior and senior high school youngsters.

I would like to also suggest that parents have a major role to play. Certainly faculties need a strong in-service program because again the universities do not train teachers to accept children from backgrounds different from their own. College professors do not have time to give adequate attention to human relations because they are too busy teaching the academic prerequisites for the baccalaureate.

Community groups, such as the ones I mentioned and others, as well as the churches, need to continue their concern for integrated neighborhoods and education. The schools can not do the whole job. The ultimate solution to a wholesome racial mix in our schools is integrated housing. Until then there will be a generation of children going through our schools. These children should not have to wait for us to get around to doing something about open housing. At least in Evanston the children will have integrated education under teachers who understand and accept the challenge.

Two and three years ago, programs for parents were started so that all-white schools, schools with very few Negroes, and even the Negroes themselves, would have a better perspective and healthier climate for their children. Prejudice is not all with the white community, as you know, so we need parent education for Negro parents, white parents, all parents.

Another thing that concerns us is that we also have some Jewish segregation. What are we going to do about that? There is always something over the horizon to worry about. Some of our schools are 90% Jewish, and some thoughtful Jewish leaders are not too happy about it. They do not think it is good, and I think this will be the next round. I suppose that later we will be worrying about too many Methodists, Baptists, or something else in a particular school.

I have found that historically communities have been ahead of school boards, or superintendents, and teachers are one step ahead of superintendents.

A great deal more can be done in every school system represented in this room. We talked about freedom, and yet not one school in the United States has used the freedom it has. Instead of worrying that the hierarchy of administrators and boards of education won't permit us to move, many individual schools are developing constructive programs in school systems that appear to be rigidly controlled. If a faculty really wants to do something, a lot can be done, even in schools where there is a strict, rigid, hierarchical structure.

Some people predicted that Evanston would be all Negro if we started to integrate the schools. I know some people in Evanston that I would like to encourage to move out if I could have some Negroes move in, but it is interesting that the parent group in our community is changing. White families are competing for residences. Not that they are lined up, a block deep at each real estate office, but, in the last two or three years, I have known scores of white people who have come to my office, picking out Evanston and an integrated situation for their new home. I think this is the hope for our community over the long run. We will attract both Negroes and whites who view integrated education as something to be desired for their children.

BRUCE McPHERSON

Last Christmas my sister gave me the Tom Lehrer record "That Was The Year That Was" which some of you may have heard. I am strongly influenced by that recording, particularly when I am asked to talk to a group of any size. As you may recall, Lehrer points out that people seem to be having a lot of trouble communicating these days. I think I quote him correctly as saying, "If a person can't communicate, the very least he can do is shut up." Taking that advice, I will proceed as briefly as possible.

I would like to talk about a few things that get under my skin and make me think a bit as I observe urban schools here in Chicago. I was a high school teacher and principal at one time and how have two sons in Chicago public schools. I want to highlight several issues and make a few comments. I will not apologize for the fact that the issues are on different levels because they are the ones which interest me most now.

As a professional, I am very concerned about the question of collaboration. Today we hear a lot of loose talk about collaboration, at community or institutional levels, in federal, state, and local relationships, or whatever. It is loose talk because we have not faced up to the fact that collaboration is extremely difficult and apparently we will have to go much slower than we once thought.

If you look at the Elementary and Secondary Education Act of 1965, you will find a tremendous challenge to collaboration. But if we look at what has happened under that act, we find as much failure as success. You may recall that the Act assumed that parochial schools would be deeply involved with public schools in a wide variety of programs. Universities at last were going to be working very closely with public school systems. Under Title III, we were going to define education so broadly that it would not be simply the realm of the professional educator. Museums, art galleries, and the people who work there would be involved too. But we have found that it has been very difficult for people to get together, and I don't think we can minimize that fact. The Title IV regional laboratories that were formed under that act are having trouble even getting started. The successful Title III programs have been too few.

Why this failure in collaboration? One thing we fail to do when we try to identify an educational problem is getting down to the grass roots. I defy you to find evidence that a community organization has been deeply involved in any of the Title III and IV programs. The community has been cut out in the small village as it has in the city. Furthermore, we have given more concern to administrative mechanisms and programs than we have to dialogue. You cannot collaborate unless there is something to collaborate about, and we have not identified either problems, or, through dialogue, questions that interest people.

In thinking about collaboration, we must also recognize that people in institutions have constraints upon them. They have primary responsibilities, and it has been extremely difficult, as an example, for scholars who are used to working as researchers to think about working actively with a community organization or the public school system. I am not talking about hit-and-run research in this instance but about the collaboration that results from real dialogue and that can produce meaningful research in education.

Collaboration must be thought of in terms of mutual interest as well as pay-off. I do not think we have been smart enough politically, when we try to tackle educational problems in the city, to think about pay-off. What is the pay-off for the university researcher, the person in the community, the principal and the teacher in the school? A good politician makes sure that there is a pay-off, but we do not. And, of course, the pay-off to the child has always been at the bottom of the priority list. In too many situations that pay-off seems to be very low on the priority list of the federal government as it moves in to collaborate with public school systems and universities on a variety of programs.

Therefore, I am a bit more pessimistic than I was two or three years ago about the realities of people getting together to work out problems that certainly demand their getting together. Instead of giving up, we had better face up to our failure and move ahead with the knowledge that collaboration is quite difficult.

The second question that haunts me more today than it did ever before is how to persuade urban school administrators and teachers that they actually work for a community. How are we going to insure that they will act with dignity as professionals in the inner city and preserve the dignity of the people of the community? It seems to me that we have hemmed and hawed too long about how communities get involved with the schools. It is time for public school administrators to take the lead and to insure that the necessary mechanisms are available inside the school system.

You may recall that in Chicago within the last few months, Superintendent Redmond said, "The schools do not belong to me. The schools do not belong to the school board. The schools belong to the communities, and it is a privilege for us to work with communities in educating their children." It is a nice statement. Nobody has said it much better, but there is not much evidence to suggest that this position has been translated into action within the system.

It seems to me that it is easier to talk about taking the first few steps toward decentralizing the Chicago school than it is to actually think about how to improve Scott School which is in a very difficult section of Woodlawn. The parents do not have very much money, the quality of education is low, and the children are isolated from everything we like to think of as the best in American life. When we talk about decentralization, we should talk not only about decentralizing to the district level, but also to the school level. We need administrators who can tell District Superintendents and Principals that they must have a Board to which they are responsive and one which helps make decisions at the individual school level. Otherwise we will never begin to crack the real problems or have the necessary dialogue but, instead, will continue having a school system holding the people it serves at arm's length.

While this is an intensified problem for the inner-city school, I suggest that it is a problem not only for urban schools but for all schools. I have lived in suburbia and in villages, and the schools hold people at arm's length in both these situations too. This is a professional error, and as a professional, I deplore it. Ironically, questions regarding community control of the schools are now being asked in low-income areas and school people have a chance at the site of the most devastating educational problems to begin relating in a more relevant manner to the people of the community. The question is asked by the people who are receiving least and asking for most, as well they should.

My third concern is a question of personnel. We often hear about the high mobility of teachers in urban school systems. We know that many teachers not only leave schools in low-income areas and segregated schools, but they also leave the city to go to suburban schools, or quit teaching entirely. There is a lot of loose talk about combat pay, but I do not think that is the answer at all. Whether we are talking about long-range integration of city schools or, in the short range, trying to do the best possible in schools that are segregated and may be segregated for years, we must talk about substantially improving the conditions of work and life in those schools, not for just teachers and administrators, but for children. And I think good school personnel and parents are ready to meet the challenges, where they exist.

We have evidence from our own students at the University of Chicago that vastly increasing numbers are ready to do their best to become good teachers in the city. We are proud of that but we are not as proud of our programs. I would agree with Mr. Chute that at the universities we are not doing the job we could and should in working with our students, communities, and with the public school system. I think that people are ready to work in the city, and if we can set good conditions of work, people will not only stay, they will make great contributions. In Chicago, at least, we vastly underestimate the number of truly competent people now available and working in the school system. It is easy to deplore the quality of urban teachers, but in part I think we are dealing with a myth. There are many good people at work right now. The best teachers and principals that I have ever seen at work are in the city of Chicago. And the worst.

I am also concerned about curriculum. It seems that the professional curriculum makers will take the reins. And it is about time, whether we are talking about Woodlawn, Evanston, or Hyde Park. I think that more than ever before we will turn to the children as we develop curriculum. The children and the people of the community are the givens. Particularly in communities that are in the process of renaissance, striving for change and improvement, we can do no better than to start thinking about how the community gets involved in making a curriculum for its schools.

I would like to read something from a meeting which was recently held involving representatives from the University of Chicago and from public schools in Chicago and in The Woodlawn Organization. The minutes of this meeting quote a Woodlawn housewife. She is commenting on an announcement made by a public school representative who said that there is to be a new, educational television, closed-circuit network in the district next year. She said, "I hope we are going beyond the Dick and Jane readers. Our children don't understand what they see in the Dick and Jane readers. Our children see sidewalks in our daily life and not the beautiful parks. I hope that we will gear the educational television programs to what our children know and see, and let them go from there." There is a phrase I like, — "and let them go from there," because kids can go if we can make the education relevant to them. They can achieve almost anything they want or that we as professionals and observers want for them. Most inner-city schools and most schools in the low-income areas of Chicago are irrelevant as institutions. They do not mean anything; they do not relate in any way. I keep looking at Joe Rosen across the table. Thankfullly he is one of the exceptional principals in one of the exceptional Chicago public schools. I am talking about somebody else and somebody else's school.

The last question I want to turn to is that of funds. As Mr. Chute has also pointed out, there just does not seem to be enough money in the cities. That is a tremendous problem for boards of education, but I would add that it is a tremendous problem for a community, a subcommunity, a neighborhood. The question of how funds get allocated, how responsibility is brought down to the district level, is terribly important. As you know, in most cities, very little of the money is equitably transmitted down to local schools, and very few decisions regarding money are made by anybody who is outside the hard core of the downtown central staff. We have to go outside the available resources, and I would suggest that we are going to need more general aid, federal and state, not only for the school programs but for construction as well.

Though I would argue in many instances for unrestricted aid, it must be categorical with regard to questions of segregation and integration. Most of the money that gets poured into new construction should be poured into city schools that will be integrated and will further patterns of integration in the city. There will be exceptional cases where we will expend money in segregated schools that will remain segregated while the community decides what it wants and how it is going to get involved.

For a long time we have attempted to cope with the either/or dilemma, enumerated by Stokely Carmichael on one side and Roy Wilkins on the other. I refuse to be polarized. In the long run, we have to work for integration, and in the short run we may have to do something in those schools that are going to be segregated for awhile. If we believe that we have a choice, we are kidding ourselves and copping out. It is time to stop doing that. We all know what the goal is, and if we want integrated schools, we must push as hard as we can for them. People cannot remain isolated if they are to move ahead.

The I.S. 201 experience is only the beginning. The challenge coming from low-income neighborhoods in the city is the most important challenge to education that has been posed. We are very fortunate in having Mr. Wilcox here and having a chance to learn more about the I.S. 201 situation in New York. It has a tremendous lesson for all of us, and I only hope that we are smart enough to learn that lesson and act upon it.

Let me just reiterate one point. Our real opportunity to understand the key issue in education will come if we listen to the people from Woodlawn and Lawndale. They are telling us that a school cannot survive if it is not related to a community in every dimension. I think they are telling us that unless the communities are in charge of the schools, we might as well fold up our tents as educators, as workers in community organizations. I firmly believe that the schools hold tremendous promise for children, for adults, and for communities. Outside the framework of the community, outside the contexts that control the community, we do not have a chance.

It is most interesting to me that when you talk to people in Woodlawn, they really do not want to take much away from professional educators. They do not want to make what we would call "professional" decisions. They do not want to teach the children, but they do want the schools to be theirs because the children are theirs.

BERNARD BERKIN

I want to talk about the strategy for change. This year I have had the fortunate opportunity of being able to deal with these issues on a national level. Bruce McPherson and I worked together for a long time, and I am not sure that it is possible to achieve what he wants without some other, bigger issues being solved. Somehow, despite the fact that it is many years since the Supreme Court decision, it seems to me that the question of separate education still has not been accepted. The critical question is can it be equal?

We continue talking about the possibility of making a separate, racially-isolated school equal. We imply that we could make it better than equal if we do some things in communities, improve teachers and principals, and increase expenditures. The net result of such remarks leave the impression that we could march out of here and do something significant in Woodlawn. I maintain that you can do very little in Woodlawn. The isolated school experience cannot work.

The structure of American education is quite clear. In our society, schools function for two critical reasons: one, to perpetuate the society with all the democratic ideals we can articulate; and two, for the child's self-actualization, for personal growth that he needs in order to earn a livelihood as an adult as well as just to live, personally fulfilled.

The first educational goal, the perpetuation of the society, is clearly not being accomplished today. We cannot take children in American schools in isolation and teach them how to live in a democratic society. Every school board in America has the stated objective of preparing their students for this goal. To show movies of Negro children in order to prepare children in their suburban schools to live in a democratic society is an inadequate educational experience. There is very little we can do in these schools to provide the experience American children need in order to live together as adults. Newspapers bring that home to us every single day.

This is quite obvious for the Negro child. For him the isolation is not just isolation; it is a negative experience, negative because it denies him his position. It is certainly far worse for him than for the white child. The experimental evidence of the recent Coleman report clearly illustrates that. In order to feel part of American society, the Negro child has to be in a school situation which looks like it is American society. That is the goal of our society, and it cannot be served in isolation.

With regard to the individual — his growth and development — again the Coleman report clearly indicates that the greater the integrated educational experience, the more realistically the student's interpretation of it and the greater his academic achievement. Incidentally, there is a parenthetical statement in the report which indicates that similar results are achieved for the Negro student who attends school with middle-class Negro students. The critical variable seems to be middle class, but there are not many middle-class Negro students in America who are part of American society.

I have to stress again the question of isolation. I do not believe that there is anything we can do to a Negro child in the ghetto school to get him to feel that the educational program in which he is participating is relevant. No matter how much money we spend, and no matter how many integrated textbooks we give him, he will not feel that he is being prepared for American society as long as everything he sees around him in his daily experience tells him that he is not part of that society. Once that criteria is established, then I cannot accept any educational experience that is less than an integrated one. Even though as responsible adults we have to make the interim experience as nice as possible, it is doomed to fail.

As a matter of fact, the ghetto experiences of other groups in our society are nowhere near as difficult as the ghetto experiences of the Negro given the historical situation in America. Nevertheless, the ghetto experience for other groups had many detrimental factors. The Jewish groups, for instance, though they appear to succeed in reading in ghetto schools, have revealed other harms. Many Jewish children grow up to live as adults only within Jewish experience. They work in Jewish firms with Jewish fellow employees; they shop in Jewish stores and live in Jewish neighborhoods. I would not accept that experience as an indication that they succeeded in school despite their isolation. I would say that this aspect of their experience in isolation reveals a serious limitation.

Once integrated experience is established as the criteria for educational success, then it becomes top priority for any educational program I would propose. Clearly the residential patterns in our communities are not going to change quickly. Even if they changed, I think the problem would only be changed from a Negro-white discrepancy to one of the haves against the have-nots. The middle-class Negroes would move to middle-class, white neighborhoods, and the ghetto child would still have an isolated educational experience.

Therefore, I must look to education for a change to what school populations must look like. It seems to me that, since housing patterns will not provide a good student "mix," the only alternative left is to expand the attendance area. Whether you call the school facility that results from the expanded attendance area an education campus, a university, a park, or whatever, it must cover a large attendance area.

I should quickly add that the bussing solution is a very poor one. The notion that we can bus Negro children out of ghettos into suburban schools is racist on the face. Even the Evanston plan, which has great merit in comparison to how slowly other communities have moved, retains the neighborhood school for white children. The Negro children must move out of their neighborhood school. Ultimately, if the goal of American education, as far as equal education is concerned, is to leave the Negro child with the same feeling of being part of society as the white child, his school experience has to be the same as that of the white child.

Thus, instead of Negro children being bussed out of their neighborhoods, I would advocate what has been frequently called the "education park." It brings many students, from many communities, neighborhoods, or however we designate geographic areas, together in a central location where ten or fifteen thousand can gather. Considering the problem of the small unit, those fifteen thousand students can be divided into groups of any size we wish. It does not matter what we decide is the unit the child needs in order to feel a sense of individuality. Whether it is schools of 100, 500, or 1,000, the campus plan can provide it.

Once we establish the criteria of broadened attendance areas which enable all students to attend the same campus on an equal basis, the next issue we must face is one that people have been emphasizing the last few years. It is the question of *quality* integrated education. Clearly, the campus plan merely desegregates; it merely solves the numbers problem. However, as some of you have already experienced, though certain large schools with large attendance areas have solved one segregation problem, they resegregate because the students are ability-grouped and tracked. It would be folly to trade one form of isolation for another. I think American education can use this situation very effectively. For many years, we have talked about the need to improve the educational program in our society, but we have not made much progress. However, given this situation, we have the chance to make fantastic strides.

I want to explain. One of the side problems that has developed is that, in our move to equalize education, we have developed a concept of compensatory education which says that we are going to do something special for the students who need it. Frequently the compensatory program itself has become stigmatized. Many families, when they hear that their school is going to become a center for compensatory education, believe that this means the educational program will be geared to lower academic levels, and they do not want any part of it. Compensatory education must really mean, and quality education must ultimately always mean, a move toward individualized attention. Upon analysis, the good suburban school program ultimately reveals that they have a better "fix" of their individual students' problems. Then proceed to develop improved programs to deal with those problems.

Thus, it seems to me that compensatory education has been the wrong handle to use in education. A far better handle is the move toward individualized attention toward identifying individualized educational needs. Once a school system moves in that direction, no distinction between the educational program for Negro and white students has to be made. All students need programs which are geared to their problems, strengths, or however we want to define it. Moving in this direction, the question of ability grouping becomes far less important for a large educational center.

I am convinced that school systems now propose ability groupings largely as a strategy to serve the anxieties of the white middle class who say, we will permit you to integrate schools if you can guarantee that the quality of the educational program will not decrease. Most of the school system's critics add that you had better show me that, in fact, it is going to improve. The strategy in Evanston is quite clear. To sell the program, Foster School had to become a lab school. Some guarantees had to be given to the white middle class that something magically different was to be done. Stick with us and you will see that it will work better. In some communities, this strategy to guarantee improvement became ability grouping, tracking, and, as I indicated earlier, ultimately resulted in resegregation.

There was another reason that the school system had to move in the direction of the quality program. Quality came to be defined for the white middle class as the maintenance of the educational program. But the disparity between the Negro ghetto student and the white, middle-class student is a real one. After all, the ghetto student's educational experience has been a bad one. Therefore the new, integrated school obviously must have a considerably improved educational program. Aside from the strategy of maintaining the white population, the Negro student, or any student for that matter, really needs this quality program.

The strategy for change does not seem to me to be so difficult if we move in the direction of individualized attention. Industry has a tremendous stake in what education will do. We have been talking about computer technology, about increasing the roles in education, about new personnel, and now we are talking about a giant financial enterprise. Rather than the strategy of a small, local community agency trying to improve the quality of its educational program, it would be far better to move toward helping industry see the fantastic profits they will derive if we truly move in the direction of a revolutionary program which will require vast expenditures.

The expenditures clearly cannot be supported by the local community. I am convinced that the federal government has not given the kind of money that the school systems need to conduct their new programs essentially because educators have indicated to the federal position-makers and establishers that they really did not know what to do. They merely indicated their need for more money without establishing a program.

On the other hand, if educators went to Congress, indicated that they had a program costing, for example, $3,000 per student, and for the 50 million students in America it would cost $150 billion, which could be spent at the rate of $15 billion over ten years, then I think that Congress would give them the money. Rather than the civil rights people having to provide the impetus, I believe that the civil rights people can gather together such organizations as Lytton Industries, IBM, SRA, North American Aviation, General Learning, etc. They can reveal to them that there will be great profits when education moves toward individualized attention. Then I think we will see a new kind of lobby in Washington – one with considerable power.

11

The Teacher's View

THREE TEACHERS FROM
URBAN PUBLIC SCHOOLS

TEACHER I

I am a third-grade teacher in a transient area of a large city. Our school meets the qualifications of the provisions of the Federal Elementary and Secondary Education Act and the Federal poverty program. Because of the transiency of the area (within five months I have had ten children transfer out and six students transfer in – my enrollment is 37) and language problems (almost one-third of the student body come from Spanish-speaking backgrounds), we have many academic problems.

It is the purpose of this talk to discuss the effects of the Federal programs upon student achievement in our schools. Among the programs which are in effect are Head Start, after-school reading, and teaching English as a second language.

Head Start is probably the best of the existing programs. Through it the children's medical and dental deficiencies are detected, and some are treated. The child, because of pleasant initial contact with the school situation, will hopefully develop a positive attitude toward school. But close examination of the program has revealed that while, at first, children who attended may have shown themselves to be ahead of those who had not, eventually many fell behind. For some children it is a traumatic experience to be put into a completely different type of situation in the regular school program. Whereas the Head Start program had fifteen children with three adults, a regular class in kindergarten and first grade may have from 34 to 39 children with one adult.

The after-school reading program poses a number of problems. The students and teachers are tired by the end of the day, and many students do not want to attend. Much of the clerical work in connection with the program requires time from the class. Attendance reports and other reports have to be sent to the office (a child is the messenger); milk cartons must be picked up and returned (a child acts as milk messenger). The initial organization of the program is done during the regular school day often by a regular faculty member who may have to take the time from his regular class.

Little is done to evaluate the teaching in the program. Teachers are given a great deal of freedom. While freedom to teach in an individual way is a desired condition, more extensive evaluation of the program is necessary.

Often inadequate teaching materials are available. Stress is laid upon novelty and how the program differs from the regular day program. There is not enough stress on that which the program can best accomplish – and individualization of instruction. Field trips, movies, radios, phonographs, and tape recorders are motivational and stimulating, but they do not get to the roots of the learning problems. Many children are truly interested in reading, but they are lacking the basic tools.

Teaching English as a second language should be a program of great merit. It operates for the most part during the school day. It provides individualized help to children who do not speak English. The program, however, deals only with the most severe language problems. There are many other children who are in need of specialized help in order to function comfortably with curriculum in the English language. In many cases teachers in this program are not adequately prepared.

We have been experimenting with many programs, but, it seems, with few guidelines. Most of the programs have been instituted too rapidly and without teachers being properly prepared. We are often satisfied to know what the schools are teaching, what teachers are teaching, and what various programs are designed to teach. But do we know what the students are actually learning?

TEACHER II

I shall make a few general observations about my experience teaching in one of Chicago's inner-city high schools, and then mention briefly an interesting experiment in community-school relations which grew out of the youth service program which we developed at Crane High School.

However, first it may be helpful to tell you something of my background. I did not get into teaching through the usual channels. I did not come from a teacher-training program, but rather from a general liberal arts program. Sometimes I still have trouble distinguishing my roles as a lay person and a teacher. Some of the views I shall express are those of a lay person who feels some surprise and bewilderment at what he has found inside a large city school system.

I have been teaching for four and one-half years in Chicago, the last three and one-half of which have been at Crane. This is a predominantly Negro high school located on Chicago's West Side near Western Avenue and the Congress Expressway. Enrollment now is about 3200, about 98% of which is Negro. The teacher ratio is about 50-50 white and Negro. As in most other inner-city schools, there is a high teacher turnover rate. Only two-fifths of our total teaching staff are certified; the others are either full-time or day-to-day substitutes.

Like most lay people coming into the teaching profession, I had certain preconceptions about what schools were doing and what they should be doing. These were undoubtedly influenced by my previous experience as a group social worker where I had gained considerable knowledge of volunteer work projects, recreational activities and travel programs.

First, as a new teacher entering the Chicago school system, I was surprised at how little help I received from the principal of the school to which I was assigned. In fact, it was practically nonexistent. That which I did get to survive in my first year in North Lawndale came primarily from the other teachers, most of whom were new and inexperienced like myself.

Secondly, there seemed to be very little concern for the teaching that was going on in the classroom. There was concern only for the discipline that was maintained and that the clerical work assigned us was turned into the office on time.

Thirdly, it seemed to me that principals in the Chicago schools were not really expected to be principal *teachers,* but rather principal *clerks.* From what I could see much of what I saw principals doing could be done just as well, if not better, by competent clerks. In the area of disciplining unruly students, I suspect that this time-consuming chore could have been handled better by a well-trained social worker.

Fourth, I was struck by the highly authoritarian attitude of the administrators toward the teachers. This was not only true for the elementary school to which I was first assigned, but also for the first two principals at Crane. Incidentally, during my first three years at Crane there were also three different principals. These first three principals did not seem to be engaged in a joint, cooperative endeavor with the teachers to educate their young people as much as they seemed to be preoccupied with their climb up the administrative ladder. Indeed, there was a definite attitude of working "over," rather than "with" the teachers, and an undisguised use of fear and intimidation to make teachers do what was wanted.

It also struck me as rather odd that the substitutes were not expected to teach but to babysit – at least that seems to be the most accurate description of what day-by-day substitutes do. I also observed an appalling misuse of valuable teacher time and training – and what is worse, the teachers' acquiescence in this.

Furthermore, as the elementary school teachers have pointed out, classes are frequently interrupted by parent conferences and, at the high school level, by club meetings, special rehearsals, and athletic events as well. This afternoon, for instance, my ninth and tenth period classes were cancelled for all intents and purposes because of a varsity basketball game. In the Chicago school system, most varsity basketball and football games are played on weekdays, not on Saturdays.

An observation of a more general nature is the failure – and the lack of concern about it – to prepare inner-city students for the life they will face after graduating from school, that is, if they graduate. This is evident in Crane's high drop-out rate (which is fairly typical of inner city Chicago high schools) of 65% to 75%, and in the poor achievement level of many who do obtain diplomas. We receive frequent complaints from employers that our graduates are often unable to fill out job applications correctly!

My final observation is the apparent inability or unwillingness – I am not sure which — of many school administrators to develop the new approaches, techniques, or methods which we somehow must devise if we are going to change the attitude of inner-city students toward school and education. The most common attitude I have found among my students is that schools are a type of jail, and that education is something to be endured rather than enjoyed. Overcoming these negative attitudes strikes me as being one of the greatest challenges we face if we expect our schools in the inner city to turn out young people who can be considered "educated." As I am sure most of you are aware, the traditional teaching methods — and even some of the new experimental ones being used successfully in the suburbs — somehow have not seemed to work in our inner-city schools.

As a result of the foregoing observations, I have been forced to conclude that in Chicago, and perhaps in other large cities as well, public schools are regarded more as *custodial* rather than as *educational* institutions. Perhaps this was best epitomized in the period just before the threatened teachers' strike last January. The Superintendent called upon parents, or anybody, to come and help man the schools in the event of a strike. "What would we do with all of those children running loose on the streets," he said, "if they were not in school?" Hardly any mention was made of the education they would miss! It would appear that perhaps one of the reasons so little of the educational process takes place in our inner-city schools is that the administrators' expectations are so low in terms of educational results.

Sometimes one is also forced to conclude that in many respects our Chicago school system has become a self-perpetuating bureaucracy. Its chief concern seems to be the protection and enhancement of the jobs of its staff, rather than the attainment of the best possible education of the city's young people. So much for my observations on school administration.

Insofar as the students are concerned, most of those who come into our high school are not prepared to do high school level work. In the study we made for the statement by "Crane's Concerned Teachers" issued a year and a half ago, about 65% of the Crane student body were reading at the 6.5 grade level. This included freshmen, sophomores, juniors, and seniors.

Another fact which has caught my attention is that most of the incoming students seem to be conditioned to rote learning methods and extremely strict classroom regimentation. In my history classes I try to involve them in discussions or other group interactions, but most seem completely unprepared for this. As you would expect, most are apathetic. This, rather than discipline, is the main problem we face. Actually, we have only minor discipline problems at our high school in comparison to what most people think is the case in inner-city high schools.

Regarding teachers, as was pointed out earlier this afternoon, some of the best and some of the worst teachers can be found in the Chicago school system. In my limited experience, I have observed that those who seem to be doing the best job in the inner-city schools think of themselves as social workers as well as teachers. They are not afraid to get involved in the community and with the children outside, as well as inside, their school.

This brings me to the community-service project I started when I arrived at Crane. It grew out of a civics class unit designed to give young people some tangible, concrete experience of what it means to be of service to one's community. The project started off with cleaning and painting jobs for churches, settlement houses, and other community-serving agencies. Later, it branched out into volunteer work at nearby hospitals, recreational leadership help at parks, errand-running service for elderly people, and tutoring programs for grade school children. All of these activities, it should be pointed out, were done after school or on Saturdays.

Initially, I thought it would be necessary to hold out the incentive of better grades and the further reward of being taken on trips to induce students to participate in the program. Soon, however, I discovered that the students obtained so much satisfaction from the work projects themselves that they showed more concern for the date of the next service project than that of the next trip, or for the extra credit they were to receive in their civics class.

Since 1963, when the program started, it has branched out to include joint work projects and social activities with students from Evanston and New Trier High Schools, both located in Chicago's North Shore suburban area.

A detailed description of this youth service program, and what it has accomplished, would take much more time than I have here. However, to those who are interested in obtaining more information about it, there is available a written summary which I prepared recently for fund-raising purposes. You see, we were not able to incorporate this program into the regular school program, so we had to go outside the school system and obtain help from local community agencies to carry it out. Today, it is incorporated as a not-for-profit Illinois corporation called the West Side Youth Service Corps.

In concluding I should like to make one final point. The small amount of contact this program has provided us with people in our community around Crane has convinced us that there is a tremendous potential of undeveloped community leadership among our public school staffs. Teachers and administrators have many of the leadership skills that are needed, and because they are still held in great respect by most inner-city parents, they can – if they want to – exert a tremendous influence first, in building up a sense of community in the neighborhoods around many of our inner-city schools, and second, in going on to help make these communities a better place in which their students can grow up to become self-supporting, responsible citizens. One has only to work a brief time in any inner-city neighborhood to discover that a sense of community is almost totally lacking there.

If the limited experience provided by our small program is any indication of what ordinary classroom teachers can accomplish in the community around Crane, what might a principal – or even a District Superintendent –

accomplish if he were inclined to provide some leadership in the broader community outside of his school?

TEACHER III

We have twenty-six assigned teachers and seven substitutes on a full-time basis who are filling a vacancy. We also have eight provisional teachers with a degree in another area who are taking their education courses at night. Right now, twenty-eight of our teachers are white, eleven are Negro, and three are Oriental.

As for academic ability, there is not one single room in any grade in our school where all the children are working at grade level. This involves the 1300 children in the school. There are five second-grade rooms. Less than half of my children are working at grade level, and there is not one child above. These children were drawn from about 160 first-graders.

Studies have shown that by the end of kindergarten, there is very little difference between the test scores of children in the inner-city schools and those in schools in other parts of the city, including suburban areas. But with each year, the gap grows wider and wider because the tests become increasingly verbal. Even children who score at grade level on the standardized test do not work to that level in the classroom because the curriculum calls for other abilities such as different language patterns, abstractions, creative writing, and so forth. Coupled with this are the children's poor work habits, lack of perseverance, and reduced inner controls.

One of the factors which contributes to this low achievement seems to me to be that teachers are not held accountable. A teacher is sovereign in the classroom, which is very good under ideal conditions. It is more conducive to creative teaching while it is stifling to have someone down your back all the time, but we should be held accountable for teaching. Children go from one room to another and nobody knows what they are doing. No one worries that at the end of the third year, a child may know less than he did in the second year because he had not been taught anything in between.

We have a continuous development program in which the children should be working at the level at which they can function. For example, E level would be the first part of second grade, and F level, the second part of second grade. When you see the records a month after school has started in September, many a child who had left the E level has been put in the third grade, G level. He skipped the F level because, instead of the teachers taking the children at the level at which they are functioning, they work with them at their grade level. No one seems to do anything about that.

Another contributing factor is the difference between the disciplinary philosophy of Negro and white teachers. I have spoken with many teachers in various schools, and in their schools as in ours, the Negro teachers as a group believe in physical force, and there is a great deal of hitting at the schools. It is very difficult for a child to go from a very controlled atmosphere to one that is structured. It may be permissive but there is such a thing as structured permissiveness. The only means of punishment they know is to be whipped, and that is what you must do. If you do not, then you do not have control of them, and you cannot teach.

I very seldom hear anyone talking about how much a teacher is teaching and how much children are learning. It is rather what control the teacher has over the children. A premium is placed on control and quiet in the classroom. It does not matter whether the child is learning, as long as you walk into a room and everybody is quiet. It is very easy to keep children quiet if you want to give them a lot of busy work. They love to sit and copy from a book or board, or do something that they have learned before. I suppose they feel secure in going over the same thing. They will be quiet. The noise comes when you try to have some discussion or have them learn from doing things.

The problem is complicated by the fact that many of the parents feel the same way about punishment. Many of them have told me, in front of the child, that the only way his child will behave is if he is whipped. When I tell them that we are not supposed to whip the children, they offer to come to hit the child. They come with a belt ready and want you to hit them in front of the other children. They say, this is my child and I give you permission. I don't care what the Board of Education says. I will put it in writing for you. You hit the child. Well, you cannot teach like that.

I find it interesting that a speech therapist told me that she finds it very difficult to help correct the speech of children with Negro teachers. They have been so controlled and are so passive that it takes a long time to get a response.

12

School-Community Relations

JOSEPH ROSEN

I think that you have heard enough to know my position very well. The question is, "Can effective school-community relations be achieved?" I say yes, although over the years my head is bloody, but unbowed. On the basis of my experience, and perhaps on the basis of feeling even more than fact, I believe that achievement of the relationship we want will depend upon the concern, realistic, everyday, very, very, tangible concern, that we demonstrate for children. The educator can be selfish in the expression of these concerns because in the end he is helped. The task we must perform is to present a child with an educational program in which he can participate. This, of course, is the primary function of the educator.

In this task one will find obstacles to the child's participation, and a secondary function then often replaces the primary job. The primary function may thus become the one that will help overcome the obstacles to children's participation in the school's programs. For a school to develop good community relations in our situation, i.e., a school located in a distressed community, the school has to take on the tone of what I call an "academic settlement house" with the object of reaching out and seeking solutions to the problems that face people.

There must be a total concern for the child. We must be concerned with his physical well-being so he can participate in our educational programs. That is the keynote. The only reason I do anything is so he will be able to participate in school life. Practically speaking, this means that you feed people if you must. I maintain that no child on ADC can receive adequate meals in the course of a day. Our community has the highest incidence of TB in the city, which is related to poor nutrition. The child living in our community will fail the vision-screen examination at the rate of one out of four, partially due to poor nutrition. Apathy may result, or there may be irritability due to low sugar and this may cause behavior problems.

Food is important. I have been feeding some five hundred children without charge but not capriciously. The mother must come to the school and indicate, on paper, her income, the size of her family, and the rent she pays. We stack it up against an assistance figure. When parents come in, there is no shame or embarrassment of any kind. Unfortunately, children have to wait for their food. But they wait, and the waiting is indication of their need. I am involved in a battle downtown because they have cut me down to three hundred. We have had this kind of fight right along.

I was in New York City in I.S. 201 in which every child gets a free lunch. In New York City schools, unlike ours, 50% to 60% of the children get free lunches. On the basis of the New York City form and the statistics upon which a child can receive a free lunch, a family of four with an income of $87.00 or less per week is entitled to free food for their children. If I were in New York City we would be feeding one thousand out of two thousand.

I have been challenged for feeding the number of children we do, but by taking my papers downtown when challenged, I have repeatedly proven that we do not do this without a system. At the moment, the system may be inadequate in terms of the cost of living, and I have before me, a letter from the ADC people that exhorted the school system not to say that a child on ADC is not eligible for free lunch. In Chicago, we do not have a standard about free lunch. The principal certifies that, in his opinion, on any basis he chooses, children should or should not be fed, that they should take care of themselves, and so on. He can say that simply because they are on ADC, they do not get fed. In Chicago we have no policy; it is the will or the whim of the principal that decides.

Clothing for our children is important to me if the child stays out of school for five days; think of the cost in state aid and if he does this two or three times a year; the chance of success in school is limited. The cost of failing today is probably $500 because now we have a yearly, rather than a half-yearly, plan of promotion. To me, just economically, it is wise to do everything possible to see that the child is in school. Furthermore, a relationship is developed between you and the community. The child walks in with his feet sticking out of his shoes and goes home with a pair of solid shoes; this is telling the parents something extremely important – that the school is concerned.

Again I say that it is concerned for a selfish reason. Whatever the school's program and however successful you are, it cannot be achieved if the child is not there. We have a dentist. Teeth hurt, and when teeth hurt, you know you cannot work. We are very concerned about the children's health. We do our own vision screening. Instead of the school system, we screen each child every year. The school system policy is to screen children in the first and fifth grades only. In the outer-city schools, such as Rogers Park, if a child in the first grade needs glasses, you tell the parents on Wednesday, and by Saturday they have gone to the doctor. You cannot do that with our children. Eye testing in the first and fifth grades is inadequate. If he is not there at the time of the test one year, he does not get it again for four years. We need a flexible policy. In some schools, the first and fifth is fine. In our schools, this is necessary every year.

We think that this demonstration of concern for the child's physical well-being indicates a total concern to the community, and things happen between you and the community. People come to us with problems that are not obviously related to our function: concerning the halting of an ADC check, a cold flat, the cutting-off of gas, and so forth. We put community workers to the task. We call the community agencies and try to help. Parents come to us because they think we are concerned.

We are concerned with emotional well-being. We do not suspend children at all. A teacher does not say he wants a child out of school because of something he did. We may change a child's situation by trying another teacher, or holding the child in the office for awhile, or putting him in one of our three social adjustment rooms, which are probably one of our greatest assets. In general, we try to give the child a sense of security in school he might not have.

We think that our staff of teachers, gathered over the years, demonstrates this understanding. We believe that if a school works in this way, then teachers who are compatible with this kind of thinking begin to gather around. An outstanding strength in your staff is developed. Teachers demonstrate their concern when they bring a child in difficulty to me and tell me about his home and his reaction to other children. The other day a boy would not stay in the classroom. We do have homogeneous placement, but that room was not for him. He felt very uncomfortable and we made an adjustment. The teacher did not say the boy does not want to stay in the room, he runs out, so send him home. Instead, we sat down, talked, and so forth.

I think that this kind of demonstrated concern by teachers for children is reflected in the child's communication with the home. You know how often your children tell you about a teacher, good or bad. And you know that the best communication between the home and the school is the child, not the nice little school newspaper you may send home, not the P.T.A. meetings where the school tells parents what it is doing, but what the child tells the parent, and that parent tells other parents. An aura of good will develops around the school. Best of all, when you work in this way and gather the staff the school needs, the children are most adequately served.

In terms of schools' relationships with community organizations, we must become sensitive to the nature of the organizations with which we develop a contact. We would rather be actively associated with community groups, which in the eyes of the parents of our school really are significant. The perspective of the people must be considered and in Lawndale we have certain organizations that are more meaningful in the minds of the people than others, and the organizations that are significant are not necessarily those that have the best financial support. This implies that school personnel must have an awareness as to what people really think, and when this awareness is not present and the wrong organization is supported by the school, then trouble develops.

We have believed in home visits for a long time and now have a school community representative who makes these contacts in the home. We have a liaison with the University of Illinois School of Social Work. One of their master's degree candidates deals with half a dozen of our most difficult home situations; he works with the child at school and the parents at home.

We are sensitive to what is written in the daily newspapers and want the teachers to discuss the civil rights issues and other problems in their classes. We use newspapers constantly and subscribe to the *Sun-Times,* the *Daily News,* and even the *Tribune.* The *Sun-Times* is free daily. We give every child in the school a copy of *Weekly Reader.* It allows for the differences between high-interest and low-achievement levels; the third-grade *Weekly Reader* even interests sixth-graders; these are current event papers that discuss what is happening in the nation and the world.

Thus, in terms of community, we try to keep before the children things that are pertinent to the community. In the fifth and sixth-grade classes, the children discussed the 16th Street riots that swirled all around the school last summer. We want such things to be talked about. For a long time we have been involved in teaching Negro history in relation to ongoing school activities. There is no question that such things affect the community, and the school has demonstrated its interest in problems pertinent to the people.

We were given some $50,000 for a summer school program. We wanted to develop our summer school program for the hard-to-reach. There were certain conditions for children who went to the regular summer schools; The mother had to come to the school and sign a paper and the child had to be well-behaved. He might be an underachiever, but he had to be fairly adjusted. We could not get the hard-to-reach child to go to summer school, so we tried to develop a special program with the $50,000 we received.

We engaged four Community Action people for OEO. The first month before summer school opened, we recruited on our own, but were short about 75 to 80 pupils, so we used our OEO representatives as recruiting agents. We sent these women into the homes to persuade parents to send to summer school the youngsters we wanted, the lowest achievers and poorest behaviers.

In the summer school, for the first four grades, the maximum in a class was twenty. The fifth and sixth grades were tutorial, with a maximum of five children, per one and a half hours, for each teacher. The children could stay on but five pupils were concentrated on for one and a half hours. The school ran from 9:00 until 2:30 and was only a six-week session, which we thought might be an added inducement to attend.

Two of the components we tried to add were objected to by the school authorities. They did not allow us to serve breakfast and lunch.

They also objected to an experimental reward system. For 95% attendance over the summer, a child could get a transistor radio, a ball, a doll, or other prizes. For 100% attendance, a child could get other and better rewards. If in the six weeks, a child worked hard enough to make a gain of six months in reading, he would get another reward. In other words, I was trying to apply some of those bad middle-class values; strive for something concrete, give the children an immediate goal.

MEYER WEINBERG

It was suggested to me that I concentrate on the research activities of the CCCO Education Committee and how these relate to the federal government. The topic today is "how to bring about more effective school-community relations." This can be brought about only by mobilizing all community resources on behalf of better relations between the community and the school.

In Chicago, research is potentially one of the most valuable resources in the community. However, its value is rather ambiguous. When members of the civil rights movement are marching and actively organizing, they hardly ever think of research as another asset or resource. They tend to think of research when nothing else is happening. In this way, the civil rights movement reflects the role of research in American culture at large.

In other words, I have not found that the civil rights movement is made up of many sensitive scholars dying to do research. There are very few such persons in the civil rights movement as well as in some of our universities. On the other hand, the issue of school integration has become involved with government, with complex legislation, administrative regulations, and the like. In order merely to make your way in the subject requires a good deal of specialization, and the CCCO Education Committee has taken that task upon itself.

Before I describe our work, I want to point out that the kind of research which is done depends on the local problems, or so it seems to me. In Chicago, getting a few facts out of the school system has been a big problem. We have never been successful in getting principal information directly from the school system. This is partly because it does not always have it and partly because it is reluctant to give us the information it does have. Much of our work has been pure digging, and I think in that we have been successful.

On the other hand, I think Mr. Preston Wilcox does a different kind of research. There are very enlightened people in New York. Though New Yorkers might deny it, their school system releases certain information more readily than the Chicago system. It seems to me that in New York the problem of research in the civil rights movement is not one of digging but of how to maneuver the super-sophisticated segregation that exists. I think a man like Mr. Wilcox is an excellent example of someone with a bright idea – which I also call research. He put it forward in the spring of 1966, and, of course, it became related to what is now the I.S. 201 problem.

In Chicago such an imaginative approach does not typify our research. On the other hand, shortly after their arrival here in October 1965, the SCLC staff went on a retreat in Williams Bay, Wisconsin with the CCCO people. There was a marvelous feeling at the time. James Bevel spoke, or rather he preached, and one of the things he preached about most enthusiastically was the situation in Alabama. "We cannot go to the University of Alabama and say, 'fellows, how about doing some research for us?' However, there would be no problem here." He is now a wiser man because, as far as research is concerned, the universities in our community had not been very helpful.

In what has our research consisted? In July and December 1965, CCCO submitted, on behalf of some forty-five affiliated organizations, two official complaints to HEW, the Office of Education. The first charged that segregation in the Chicago school system was not a matter of de facto segregation but of deliberate intent. We illustrated this charge with a study of gerrymandering school and attendance boundaries, and a number of the system's other practices. I think we provided ample documentation for this charge.

The second complaint, of December 1965, related to the Chicago school system's misuse and abuse, as we saw it, of Title I of the Elementary and Secondary Education Act. Again, I think we offered great detail and support for our charge that Chicago's money was not being spent in accordance with the law, and how that which was being spent in accordance with the law was highly ineffective. Primarily, it was being put into after-school programs; the same ineffective practices that were prevalent during the day now were practiced by tired teachers and tired students.

As a result, since July and December 1965, the federal government has been variously investigating these two complaints. In June 1966, we still had no response. Of course, I am skipping over that well-known episode of the four days in October 1965, when the then U. S. Commissioner of Education Francis Keppel deferred funds on the basis of our charges of deliberate segregation. But that was quickly undone by Mayor Daley.

In June 1966, we went to Washington to meet with Commissioner Howe and several others. We said, "Where is the action?" He said that by August he would be able to tell us. Very late in July he wrote that he would not be able to tell us by August. In August, word reached us that the answer to our first complaint would be issued very shortly, but, as you know, it was not issued shortly. Finally, last month, on January 6th, 1967, a partial report was issued in response to our first complaint. It supports a number of our charges, but it does not accept our charge of gerrymandering though it does not reject it either. Apparently we are in for a long career in this matter; these complaints will go on and on.

I do not want to go into the details but to draw what I see as a lesson. The fact that the federal government has waited this long reflects the weakness of the civil rights movement in Chicago. I do not think it reflects the intellectual problem of discovering whether or not our charges are correct. We have had a lot of informal indication from way down the line – not from the top – that the investigators have found that our charges are more or less correct, but, in Chicago, at this time, the political power behind our research is minimal. At this point in the movement, research permits the movement to hang onto the issue, and the researchers hang onto the organization, hoping that, in the future, it will become strong enough to enforce our research. Perhaps those who regard research as something abstract and distant will not understand this, but if you have ever been involved with the federal government, you will understand it very quickly.

It is said that when H. G. Wells asked Stalin about the role of the church, Stalin asked Wells in reply, "How many divisions does the Pope command?" When you go to Washington with a complaint, that is precisely what they want to know: "How many divisions do we command?" And I am afraid that most attention is paid to the research of those with the most divisions. Those of us within the movement who do this work do not feel belittled by this fact. We think it is very, very important work to do, but we do wish that we had more cooperation from the various other institutions in the community than we have had.

According to a recent interview, CCCO has not achieved its end. We do not know if conditions in this city will be any different next year from what they have been in the last three years. The change in school administration and its meaning are not at all clear. In December 1966, the CCCO Education Committee had three meetings with an administrative committee. The superintendent was not present though some assistants and associates were present. We tried to bargain on a very specific matter, the location of the sites for the school provided for in the 1967 budget. We met in December because that was one month before the budget was to be adopted. We not only criticized their choice of sites, but, in almost every case, we made an alternative suggestion. Every single one was rejected, and rejected in the manner in which we in Chicago have become accustomed.

Thus, as of this moment, there has not been one specific, concrete step taken by the new school administration that suggests to us that we are coming to a point where children will walk into school not knowing how to read and come out knowing how to read. There is no reason yet to think that there will be any change in this respect. I am not here to tell you a success story — we have our work cut out for us.

WARREN BACON

In answer to the question that is posed for the panel, "Can effective school-community relations be achieved?," I can answer right off, yes and no. I think that covers the whole problem, but I would like to qualify my answer by saying that I look at this question in terms of two levels.

First, can we, as individuals and citizens of the community, have more pleasant, interpersonal relations with the Superintendent of Schools and some of the people on his staff? I think the answer is definitely yes. Anyone who followed the previous General Superintendent was bound to be an improvement in terms of personality and willingness to respect others. I think our present Superintendent, Dr. Redmond, is a very fine person in this regard. He is affable, nice, easy to work with, and even says, "Yes, sir," "No, sir," "Yes, Ma'am," and "No Ma'am." He strives to get the information you ask for, and I have no doubt that he is interested in making a substantial change in our school system.

However, there is also the other level which Mike (Weinberg) and Joe (Rosen) have mentioned, can we expect children to walk into our schools not knowing how to read, write, and do arithmetic, and come out knowing how to read, write, and do arithmetic? My answer is no. If this is what the community is looking for, I do not think we will get effective school or community relationships unless some very substantial changes take place, not only at the school administration level, but also at the political and business level of this city.

Earlier in the discussion Mr. Berkin was telling Mr. Rosen that perhaps the good guys should say, since we cannot do the job as it should be done, we will leave. I think there is some merit in that, but I would be afraid that they would be told to get the devil out and then there might not be anybody in the system that really cares whether or not these youngsters are learning.

There are good community relations on the number one level with principals like Dr. Rosen and this is important. However, it has been pointed out that the children coming out of his school do not read very well either. If anyone has any illusions that things have changed substantially in the city of Chicago as far as education is concerned, they might be in for a surprise. At least, I have not seen it. We have changed the administration and, as I said, a fine man is superintendent now; but he alone cannot make the changes which the community should expect and desire. There cannot be effective school-community relations where the community says above all else, educate my child, until the business and political interests of this city create the climate, and provide the tools, money, and willingness to make the substantial change in our education system that the conditions demand.

Despite the great myth that, in this city, politics (in the good, not the bad, sense) and education never meet, the School Board and the school system are not their own masters. I will cite four instances.

The first occurred in the fall of 1963 when Superintendent Willis resigned. I was very new on the Board but had the opportunity to sit in on the deliberations that took place. That was a very politically oriented session. There were members on the Board of Education who made no bones about the fact that they would get him (Willis) back, at all costs, because of what it meant to the city. I translated that into what it meant in terms of votes in the city.

The second instance was the deferral of funds at the time the Office of Education was going to withhold funds from Chicago. Undoubtedly the big stick was used, and I guess even President Johnson had to stop and think about the machinery in Chicago – if we alienate that organization, will the votes be deliverable when the time comes?

The third instance took place in the fall of 1965 when teachers threatened to go on strike for the first time in recent years. All the good board members who normally vote as a block with the establishment were adamant against granting the union the right of collective bargaining. As far as the union was concerned, that was the major issue in the fall of 1965. In addition to wanting more money, they also wanted the right to hold an election to determine the sole bargaining agent. Bill Lee, and one or two other top leaders very closely identified with the so-called "power structure" of this city, were sent over to the Board meeting, and those Board members who were adamant against granting the union this right changed just like that.

I hardly need mention what happened in May 1965 over the extension of Dr. Willis's contract. Even before the Board members had taken official action, one of the newspapers wrote a story portraying precisely what would happen at the afternoon meeting. That paper was in our hands at noon and the meeting took place about two o'clock.

So, with regard to school-community relations, when you arrive at the substantive end, requiring major changes in our system in order to educate youngsters, we will have to do more because, for the most part, we are not doing the job now. We will have to create the climate and provide the tools and money. That cannot be done by the Board of Education alone.

Early last year, Jim Clement and some others of us wanted to float bonds for new school buildings. The President of the Board of Education told us that we should not put the remaining $25 million bonding authority on the ballot in the primaries because that was not a good time. Two weeks later, the Mayor announced that the $195 million, physical building bond issue for the city was going to be on the June 14th primary ballot. This means that now we have to return as we did in November and ask for our $25 million pittance. Then we will have to turn right around, return in the aldermanic, and ask for another $15 million. We are going to have to return again and again in a petty way. I think the public will get tired of our returning to ask for little handfuls instead of sitting down and figuring out what we need and presenting it in a systematic, organized fashion.

I have gone over all this again to reinforce the notion that if you expect good relationships between the community and the school, and if you expect the school to teach children to read, write, and do arithmetic, then you had better refocus your attention. You had better concentrate not just on the Board of Education, but also on the politicians, starting with the mayor, the power structure, and the business interests of this city because, in my judgment, that is the only way to get results.

13

Case Presentation: I.S. 201

HELEN TESTAMARK

First I would like to correct Mr. Rosen's statement that all the children in I.S. 201 receive a free lunch. My daughter, Ann Therese Testamark, does not. He should have said almost all the children in I.S. 201. Also, I received the impression from him that the children were receiving lunch because of need. It is another story.

It is rather mandatory that the children in I.S. 201 stay in during their lunch period, not because they are hungry and in need of food, but because the Board of Education is using them to maintain a staff of lunchroom people and what-have-you. There are 560 children in a school originally built for 2100 students. To maintain staff, they need a certain number of children to eat lunch in school everyday so they made it a mandatory situation where all the children must eat lunch. (This is called a captive lunch period.) Also, there is no yard or playground.

Unfortunately, many parents do not realize why their children must stay in. I do and I insisted that my daughter come home for lunch. So, I am going to speak to Mr. Rosen about it, and if he tells anyone again, he will have to say, "except Ann Therese Testamark."

The situation at I.S. 201 did not just happen. It was the result of many years of frustration on the part of the parents. They were bandied about by the so-called "power structure" which, in New York City, is our Board of Education.

In 1954, the United States Supreme Court made the decision about segregated education and its effects. The parents took a forward step, demanding integrated education for all children. Since I am from Harlem, I am speaking for Harlem, New York City, U.S.A. The children in the Harlem schools were not receiving a good education. Indeed, their education was quite inferior, and many parents went to court to bring about a just solution and get what is now called a "quality education" for their children.

In 1958, the New York courts agreed, in the case of Skipworth vs. Board of Education, that Negro parents had the right to insist that their children attend the best available schools. Since we do not have a best or a good school in Harlem, parents fought for the right to send their children into other schools in white communities where they could receive a much better education than they were now getting in Harlem. For many years, as parents, we have fought for a good education for our children, and the kind of treatment we have received forces us to believe that we do not count as far as they are concerned. Therefore, we decided to take a step and try to show that all our children do count and, indeed, are educable just like white children.

Because nine parents fought to send their children to other communities for a good education, the Board of Education suggested that a junior high school be built in Harlem that would be the utopia of our education. Realizing that the trend was toward integrated education, that all of us were living in what is commonly called a "ghetto," and that white parents would not want to send their children to our schools because we did not want to send them there ourselves, the proposed site for Junior High School 201 was rejected. It was suggested that the school be located where it would be easily accessible for white as well as Negro children.

The Board of Education countered, saying that they had chosen a location for Junior High School 201 that was easily accessible, close to all major transportation arteries, and that would not pose any problem to integrating the school once it was built. Parents knew full well that this would not be done, and for many years they fought to keep the school from being built there. But, as usual, the voices of black people were heard but not acted upon, and, ignoring our pleas, the Board of Education built the school at 127th Street on Madison Avenue.

Meanwhile, many schools had many problems, and most parents shifted to fight for other things and other schools, never forgetting I.S. 201. In those schools, we managed to get many things done. In the school where I was the president of the P.T.A., we had a principal who did nothing. Every year for seven years, he had less than one-third of the youngsters graduating with an academic diploma. He sat in his office reading the *New York Times* all day. By now he should be the best darned educator anywhere because it is said that, if you read the *New York Times,* you can get a good education. We fought for his removal and for the removal of many people in our area who were not producing, who showed through their daily behavior they did not care.

I am speaking about School District Number 4 which has twenty-four schools for a population of approximately 45,000 children. Over-all, about 65% of the teachers in each school are certified, and in certain schools, it is even less. The teacher absence rate is very high, and everyday an average of fifty to seventy-five classes are uncovered in these twenty-four schools.

A gentleman here stated that information is readily given to people in New York City, but I do not think it is easily given. There are many ways in which we get information. Sometimes we gather it undercover, to testify, like the teachers who have spoken here. The information that is given out usually makes the system look great, but actual reports are never given out.

Out of the 45,000 children in this district, 85% are up to five years behind grade level in reading and mathematics. On the basis of such information, the parents decided that we could not allow another school producing less-educated youngsters to open in our district. Our children were being crippled everyday. All the interested people in the community met in the school where I was president of the P.T.A. I stated the facts as I knew them, and there was a more or less spontaneous reaction on the part of the parents that I.S. 201 should not be opened without certain guarantees. The major guarantee we sought was that, when I.S. 201 opened, it have an integrated student body and staff. It was after being told by the Board of Education that I.S. 201 would not be integrated that we then demanded Professor Wilcox's Community Council.

We knew that of all the New York City principals, there was not a single black face to which we could point. We were constantly being told that our children did not have any motivation, and we felt that seeing a black face at the head of a school which was supposed to be a model school (a school, by the way, that we call a $5 million monstrosity) would have some kind of motivational value for our youngsters. Previously someone here spoke of Negro children in other terms. In our school, we have what are usually called behavior-problem children.

Parent and community organizations and ordinary individuals gathered together and decided that once-and-for-all a stand would be taken. We had many, many meetings of all kinds: street meetings, church meetings, school meetings; we went to organizations. By the way, we had meetings with the NAACP in New York City and to this day they have not told us whether or not they support us on this. We poured out everything to them but they never told us anything.

At this moment, the children in I.S. 201 are not receiving the quality education which the Board of Education says they are getting. The children are faced with many problems. One of their major problems is lack of good administration. The teachers in I.S. 201 are more or less on their own to do and say as they please and, in return, the children do likewise.

The teachers feel that all the children are psychological problems. They call in psychologists whenever they please and make appointments for the children without parental permission. If you ask the principal about it, he says that it is wrong and should not be done unless the guidance counselor calls in the mother, but, he does nothing about it. I know five parents who are very upset because their children were psychoanalyzed without their permission. Some are suing the Board.

We have many fights in the course of a school day. Yesterday, a gentleman told me that he visited 201 and found a harassed principal. He might have found a harassed principal because parents constantly complain about the variety of things that are being done to their children everyday. I am sure he also found a bunch of uneducated children who have never been taught the basic skills. Saying that the children in I.S. 201 do not know anything is used as a crutch. They did not know anything when they got there, and they probably will not know anything else when they leave. In 201, they lose everything they might have learned elsewhere.

My daughter is in the sixth grade in what is called I.G.C. class, and she is pressured into doing high school and college level work. I do not know why they do this to the children in that class. It does something to children when a teacher tells them that, in seven days, they must turn in twenty pages on Egypt if the children have never been given any background information on Egypt. I stopped my daughter from writing that kind of report. There is no continuity in the children's education. If a teacher wants the children to write something on Egypt, they do it, even if it has no relation to what is being taught. If you tell the principal about it, he says that she probably has an idea which she wants to follow through. I would call I.S. 201 an experiment. If you want to try out an experiment, come to I.S. 201 because it seems to be in order there. Teachers and children do what they want.

As far as the parents are concerned, we are just tired. Parents and community people have fought battles. We have gotten a big institution like the Board of Education with their backs more or less against the wall. This was done without help from educators and professional workers in our community. The only professional who helped us all the way was Professor Wilcox who will speak later. Of all the thousands of people in our community who would have come to our aid, Professor Wilcox was the only one that stayed with us. Everybody else thought we were kooks.

I understand Mr. Wingate has spoken here. Har-you is a big community organization in our community, but Har-you did not even come to the aid of the parents. For weeks Mrs. Edwards and I tried to get in touch with Mr. Wingate for help. Everything we did at I.S. 201 was done without so much as a penny. We had no money to get the things we needed. Work was done mainly by parents, information passed by word of mouth, and those of us who were working in antipoverty organizations got what materials we could. The Board of Education found themselves threatened with having a big $5 million school which the parents planned to boycott on September 12th. Ten days before the boycott, they went to the Har-you office and enlisted Mr. Wingate's help to stop the parents.

Some might not agree with me, but I would say that organizations such as Har-you did what the Board of Education asked them to do, and because of their involvement, everything got sidetracked away from that for which we were fighting. On the one hand, the organization had to show that it was supporting the actions of the people in the community, and, on the other hand, they had to work with the white power structure, which was also partly responsible for most of their financial agreements. I believe things got confused because we were totally unprepared for this kind of impact; I.S. 201 turned out to be a nation-wide concern. We simply assumed this to have been a community problem. We were told by many people that we were not professionals, that we were troublemakers, that we did not know what we were doing, and that it was time for better educated people to take over the fight. We had done something for which they had been paid large salaries to say they were doing. They were not doing it and could not do it. People without much formal education were doing the job and doing it without funds. Although the parents did win their fight and did reach an agreement with the Board of Education at the time, it was forces other than the parents who stopped the agreement from being implemented. The teachers rebelled without knowing the issues. The papers turned it into a racial problem and called us racists. If it is racist to want your child to have a good education and to have it in the best way possible, I am a racist. My daughter believes that everybody in the United States is a certified racist whether they like it or not.

The issue and selection of a black male principal for I.S. 201 had, in our estimation, the image and motivational element that is lacking with continuous "other" leadership. In our original demands this was not at that time the important request. It was after being told by the Board of Education that they were not about to integrate the school that this became a major demand of the parents.

E. BABETTE EDWARDS

I must say that coming to Chicago has my shoulders sagging even more. This is my first time in Chicago, and the school system here seems worse than New York. However, we share common consequences: the wholesale crippling of black children. Multiply that by all the other states, and what emerges is the systematic holding back of a whole race. We have a board in New York City that is unable or unwilling to dispense education equally to black children. On either charge the board disqualifies itself. In light of the present situation, black people must begin to relate to new structures, not to the same old tired corrupt framework that continues to perpetuate illiterates.

Our fight in New York City is the breaking up of an overcentralized bureaucracy that only owes allegiance to its vested interests. This must be replaced by a structure which will be responsive to our children's educational needs, and accountable to the community it serves – a redistribution of power.

This morning I have heard repeated references to de facto segregation, as it relates to schools in the North. If we are talking about deliberate, politically inspired segregation, then the North must accept its rightful label – de jure.

Even though it is now thirteen years since the 1954 Supreme Court decision, the Board has not moved on integration, and the federal government has continued to subsidize segregated schooling – they have responded to white power. The Board has been so busily engaged in manipulation and deceit, that it's had little time to address itself to excellence in education.

Most of the Board's highly touted programs have had no appreciable impact on the education of the majority of black children who are still failing, and still being blamed for not learning. If the Board follows its own reasoning about the effectiveness of their programs, then the logical conclusion is that black children are in fact inferior. Since we know black children are not inferior, something is radically wrong – criminally wrong.

Are the children disadvantaged, or are the teachers and administrators disadvantaged? They are the ones unequal to the task. We have been reminded often enough that they are the professionals. I view the whole ghetto school situation as an educational wasteland where a new educational system must be created to replace the system that has failed.

The I.S. 201 crisis was the "moment of truth" for the New York City Board of Education. The implications extend far beyond East Harlem, New York City, raising serious questions nationwide.

Is the N.Y.C. Board of Education going to implement its policy on quality integrated education? Given a nonfunctioning segregated situation, do parents and community have the right and obligation to participate in the affairs of its schools? With an overcentralized Board of Education, should there be controls by community over key areas of school policy and operation to insure a system of accountability and maintenance of standards? Would this result in a change of attitudes on the part of administrators and staff? Would this lead to an improvement in achievement levels?

I.S. 201 was chosen as a focal point to test the seriousness of the Board's reorganization plan in providing integrated education; to challenge a so-called merit system where four black (all female) principals, and no Puerto Rican principals emerge out of 800 plus; to spotlight the educational breakdown in our existing schools; to make 201 a model school to be duplicated in similar communities.

Since 1954, glorious pronouncements and policy statements have come from on high announcing the Board's commitment to integrated education. Boycotts, bussing, pairings, tons of recommendations, plans for educational parks, and finally the Allen Report, which proposed the famous 4-4-4 Plan.

Today segregated schools are increasing, and achievement levels are spiraling downward in our ghetto communities. Two years ago 50% of our children were two to three years behind; today it is 90%.

The first rumblings around 201 started in 1958 and were later intensified in 1965-66. When hard questions were asked concerning administration, staff, programs, zoning, and desegregation of the school, no satisfactory answers were forthcoming. When the assistant superintendent, Daniel Schrieber, was asked if the school would be integrated, he said yes, 50% Negro and 50% Puerto Rican. The fight for desegregation was taken to all levels of officialdom in the Board, city, and state, culminating in a meeting with Federal Commissioner of Education Howe in Washington, D.C. on August 5, 1966. Frustrated at attempts to make I.S. 201 more than just another ghetto school and appalled at the bad faith and indifference shown by the Board, parents and community representatives asked the Board to turn the school over to them; hence the cry, "Total Community Control." The community could not do any worse. We would have to do better for we have the largest stake – our children.

Today 201 is still an unresolved issue. Parents in other schools across the city are also asking for meaningful community participation, e.g., P.S. 125-36. In Brooklyn and the Lower East Side, parents and community have actually set up independent school boards. The trend today is definitely decentralization for local control. The Board has proven its inability and conceded its failure to deal with the needs of black and Puerto Rican children. The community has no choice but to define its own needs, and determine the processes to resolve them.

Black children must move from a base of blackness, knowing their past didn't begin within the confines of these boundaries called America, but extends back to Africa, and feeling secure in the knowledge that their community has some controls over their lives. These things have a great deal to do with a youngster's perceptions of himself and have a great deal to do with the education process.

We regard a black or Puerto Rican principal necessary not only for the image value, but as an educational tool, motivating children to aspire to a higher level of achievement. The need for black and Puerto Rican principals extends to other areas, but especially in ghetto communities.

The existing school system structure is not responsive to our children's educational needs; therefore, we feel local control is needed to insure accountability, set standards, determine over-all policy, and direct personnel and budgetary matters. Any lasting solution must come from the community and not be imposed upon it. Mistakes will be made in the process, but the difference will be commitment. Black people are tired of aliens sitting in ivory towers programming lives without any understanding or sensitivity, saying to black people: substitute my agenda for yours because *I* have the solution to *your* problems.

The New York City People's Board of Education is another manifestation of community disgust with the New York City Board of Mis-Education. The People's Board, headed by Dr. Milton Galamison, acts as a catalyst or model encouraging local communities to set up their own boards. Our emphasis has been to stress the power inherent in local communities, raising the level of awareness of the constituencies.

Any significant action around schools today must be relevant – which means radical. Radical problems require radical pressures to bring about radical changes.

In New York City today there are still forces which urge moderation, translated – preserving the "status quo." They still believe in endless meetings, and denounce any kind of demonstration or confrontation spotlighting the crisis situation and chaos our children live with daily.

Would such moderation be urged in a white area if 90% of the children were underachievers?

These same people deplore the use of the boycott as a weapon when statistics show that the longer a slum child attends schools, the lower his achievement level becomes.

What are the children missing? What is desperately needed is a full scale mobilization of community for a sustained effort to bring about basic changes in the New York City school system.

The effect of federal funds on achievement levels has been practically nil. The effectiveness of Head Start, the most widely acclaimed program, has been canceled out by the inadequacy of the schools. Parents of Head Start children must begin to make the school system ready for their children.

Any action connected with education must of necessity be directed toward change – not accommodation. We must stop measuring progress in terms of the educated few, and start measuring it in terms of advancement for the majority of black children.

We are now fighting for our youngsters' educational survival, but without black people being involved in the decision-making process, there will be no significant change or any chance for equal educational opportunity.

PRESTON WILCOX

Whenever I go someplace with Babs (Edwards) and Helen (Testamark) I learn more about their ideas on the movement in which we are involved. Believe it or not, at home, we never have a chance to talk this way. We are too busy going from one activity to another.

I will try to fill in some things they did not mention and give you some insight into what this movement is about. One of the first things we learned was that all the ghetto's enemies did not live outside of the ghetto. We spent a great deal of time "isolating" the people who wanted to speak for us but who had never spoken to us. We call them the "clean power gang;" those who say black power is dirty power are fighting for the right to be white while passing for Negroes. Part of our job has been to help people in the community learn how to keep those people *responsible* and responsive to them. In a sense, part of our job has been to try to de-brainwash the community. Many had come to believe that the Board of Education had the total responsibility for educating their children. So, we deliberately had picket lines in order to give visibility at the local neighborhood level. This action was designed to convince local residents, not particularly the Board.

To get the Board of Education to just sit down with us, we had to become involved in absolutely fantastic activities. About three hundred people picketed the office of the District Superintendent. At two in the morning, we picketed the home of the Board of Education staff person. To get a meeting with the Board of Education, we had to tie up traffic on Madison Avenue from 127th to 42nd Street at about 5:00 P.M. one day. When the deputy inspector came by, we had him call the mayor's office. He wanted to go back to his precinct to call, and Helen (Testamark) said, "No, there's a phone booth here on the corner. You call from right here." While Helen was pushing him into the booth, youngsters were playing hopscotch on the street. This is *their* movement too. We also had to deliberately walk out of the meetings in which they were not respecting us. We would not sit there while people tried to convince us that they were our masters.

On one level, we tried to get the people in the community to believe in what they could do. We also knew that the Board of Education could make many mistakes which we could turn against them. It is rather like the relationship between Martin Luther King and Sheriff Clark. We needed each other and we needed the bumblings of the Board of Education in order to mobilize the community.

Getting the community involved in the "game" of naming the school was one of the worst things they did. The committee did historical research, selected an honoree, and went to the meeting only to find the Board had already named the school.

As Babette (Edwards) suggested, when the Board came up with the new school population, they "gerrymandered" *within Harlem* to come up with a population that was 50% black and 50% Puerto Rican. Then, they had the nerve to try and convince us that this was integration. The day before "integration" in New York City was defined as "Negroes, Puerto Ricans, and others." They said it as though they actually expected us to accept it. This was the blatant disrespect.

I think all of us recognize the validity of sustaining the crisis. We are trying to tell the ghetto youngsters that we care about them and that they do not have to sit next to a white child in order to feel important.

What were some of the thoughts that went into the effort? Helen (Testamark) says it was my proposal. I say it was their proposal. I put on paper what I heard them talking about, and, in January, I wrote a thinkpiece which I called "To Be Black and To Be Successful." I dedicated it to a local organization, the Community Association of the East Harlem Triangle. They reprinted and circulated it and held meetings to discuss it. We had a meeting then with Dr. Donovan, Superintendent of Schools, and he liked parts of it. Then, on April 1st Mayor Lindsay came to Harlem and all the parent associations met before him and the local school board. Each parent association spoke about their own problems and, at the end, said they wanted a *community committee* for I.S. 201. The idea became theirs and they began to work on its behalf.

I am involved because I wanted those little black youngsters in Harlem to know that at least one person with credentials will stand up for what they believe in and will not allow himself to be used against them. In fact, I began to realize that we had power when I saw how others tried to get me to sell the people out. They would say, "Professor Wilcox, we would like you to meet with us on Thursday morning." I would say, "You call Mrs. Edwards and Mrs. Testamark, and, if they can be there on Thursday morning, I'll be there if they say I should be there. If they say I should not be there, I will not be there." I have gotten rather used to their calling me a kook. It is part of who I am, and they should call me a kook, as long as they fail to educate the kids and I continue to try to help them to do so.

For about seven years, I had worked on a cooperative basis with schools in East Harlem. I have come to believe that cooperation is a waste of time.

In most cases it meant that the master-servant relationship was maintained, and the people just adjusted to it. Similarly with integration; they applaud it and deny it to blacks at the same time. So Harlem youngsters come to feel that they cannot get a good education unless they are sitting next to whites. It is a continuation of the anitbellum thesis, "If you're white you're right; if you're black, get back." All integration was outside Harlem; the black kids moved to the whites. It is a very subtle thing. We ought to be telling our youngsters that they are important because of who they are. We are focusing on the youngsters who have been "left behind." I am not convinced that the Board of Education ever intended to educate the black ghetto youngsters. I think they literally have conceded their inability to do it. For all intents and purposes, many schools in the ghetto are becoming teacher employment agencies.

There is another issue, it relates to the ghetto school being essentially an island in the midst of a colony. I have seen youngsters who could learn on the streets but not in the school. In Harlem, there is a proliferation of Cadet Corps. Youngsters learn all the army procedures, first aid, hygiene, parades, and so forth. I used to sit in on some of their classes and watch them teach each other. A corporal would teach privates, and a private would teach his peers. They went through oral presentations and read statements to one another. They asked questions of each other to make sure they knew it. When these same youngsters walk into school, they turn off this ability because there it is not recognized as appropriate.

I studied one of these Cadet Corps. In 1966, I interviewed six seventeen-year-olds who were going to college in September that year. Not one of their guidance counselors knew they were going to college or that they were involved in the Cadet Corps. I asked them why, and they said that guidance counselors only talked to them about getting out of high school.

So much positive potential in the community is not being exploited by the schools. It has no access to the school. In order to get into any of the six Cadet Corps I studied, you have to be in school and bring your report card to your company commander. A value is placed on education. Helen (Testamark) is part of one which has about two thousand youngsters in it. They have about sixty-five basketball teams, their own adult leadership, and the schools are the only places they cannot use on a regular basis. When we talk to the principals, they use the term "our schools." I get upset every time they say, "our schools." The principals are deciding what should happen in the educational life of these youngsters as well as in their informal lives, weekends, and what-have-you, since they have the "keys" to much needed community space. Few principals have seen a ghetto on weekends unless driving through on the way to the country.

We tried to bridge this gap with the Community Committee. We wanted people other than parents to have some access to the school. Helen (Testamark) has been a leader on her block for the last fifteen years, and anybody who went into that block and did not talk to her did not have a chance. On other blocks, there are other people who have tremendous power to legitimate the educational experience and the school. But, they have no access to the schools. I think that if we could get the principals to respond to these people as people, and the youngsters saw them do it, the school would take on a very different meaning.

We also wanted access to the informal channels of influence; I got this idea accidentally when I was working in East Harlem. I asked one of the parent leaders to meet me for lunch at Joe's Bar and Grill there. The principals, housing managers, and social workers have lunch there, and many important decisions are made across the lunch table. This mother came dressed up like I was taking her to the Copacabana. This was right in her own neighborhood, and she did not have access to the very important decisions that were being made. Most transactions between school and community are on a formal basis with no effective, two-way communication. The principal sits on one side of the desk and interprets administrative procedure. This was one aspect.

The second is what I see as a master-servant relationship between professionals and nonprofessionals, like that between a welfare investigator and a client. The welfare investigator expects the client to behave like a poor person. The client learns to wear an old dress because if she wears a new one, the investigator could not deal with her. He would think that she had a man in the house or was working. People get conditioned by this.

If you work around Harlem you see that, when whites drive up to 96th Street and Third Avenue, which is the Mason-Dixon line between Yorkville and Harlem, they automatically turn up their windows, put down their buttons, and speed up. The police wave them on through the community. The youngsters in the community see the police letting the winos drink on the streets, but when we picket the schools, a whole pageant of police are there. One day I counted 168 police at I.S. 201. The youngsters learn inferentially that if you are black you get back, and I do not believe that should be the case.

Many youngsters we are trying to educate in the urban areas are much more *rural* than *urban* in life style. Whenever a friend of mine who works in Mississippi and I talk about our work, we find that there is very little difference, except that he is talking about Mississippi and I am talking about New York. In many cases we are trying to help youngsters become *urbanized* and *middle-class* at the same time.

I distinguish between a middle-class youngster in school who spends all of his energy learning and a lower-class youngster, with a different life style, who has to learn school behavior as well. The major focus of the school is on his behavior, not on his learning. We wanted to create a community-school concept in which the school was reponsive to what the youngsters felt was important. Rather than having cake sales, let's have some chicken fries, something that is indigenous to the community. We wanted the youngster to feel he belongs in the school, that people who are important in his life are also important in that school. In these areas, principals and welfare investigators are VIPs. They have tremendous power over people's lives, and we are trying to break that stranglehold.

Third, we wanted leadership with the proper psychological approach to our youngsters. If you say "white power structure" often enough, you begin to believe it, and soon you are complying with it. Someone has to say to those youngsters that just by their behavior, they count. Things are not true simply because Dr. Donovan, Mayor Lindsay, or President Johnson say them. We want someone who is appropriately angry, someone who will advocate on behalf of the youngsters. The principals talk about the youngsters coming from poor homes, but I have never known them to do anything about those poor homes.

We also felt that it would be important for that person to be a black person. We were not afraid of being called racists because we think that when a black community begins talking about having *black leadership*, it is a positive minority group action. We would like more of it. We wanted the youngsters to see someone who looked like them and really cared about them in a position of power to help them exploit the system. We were not trying to make our youngsters better than anybody else, but we do want them to acquire the skills necessary to manage their own lives.

Some of the enemies have been mentioned. I think Babbs (Edwards) and Helen (Testamark) mentioned the United Parents Association (UPA), the Public Education Association which gives the illusion that the public is involved in education. Among the enemies are the thirty white principals who came out with a statement accusing us of being racists because we were pushing for a black male principal. We think they were pursuing their own selfish interests, the same way we were pursuing ours. We also think the black Anglo-Saxon members of the staff helped to turn our victory into defeat. In the newspapers, it was the black principals who were quoted as saying that a person should be named on the basis of competence, not race. These statements were used repeatedly, and, in fact, the use of statements by blacks against us was racist in itself.

In conclusion I will mention what we saw as some of the important functions of the Community Committee. First, we felt, and still feel, that the Community Committee should select the principal. In fact, we feel that the people of the community may be able to discern those intangible qualities which make the difference between a mediocre and an outstanding principal. We know for a fact that the examination does not test for these factors; it tests the ability to write an essay or answer a question about a school management problem. We also know that the merit system has not produced creative principals. The test reflects the ability to pass a test, not the ability to provide creative leadership in the black ghetto. We feel that the parents should be involved in the selection process, and we are going to continue fighting for this. This has another kind of pay-off. If the parents are involved in the selection of principals, they will have to use their own energies to make him and the school work.

Second, we feel that the parents and the community groups ought to be involved in the development of curriculum. We would like to know how many schools in Harlem have discussed the attempted castration of Adam

Clayton Powell. We think this ought to be discussed in every Harlem class-room. I took my son to Washington this year. We walked through Mt. Vernon and saw the main house where Washington lived. We walked a bit further and came to a place that was not labelled. My son asked me what it was, and I told him that it was the slave quarters. I happened to mention that Lincoln stopped slavery, and he said, "Why didn't Washington stop it?" He knew that Washington was the Father of our Country; he knew about the cherry tree and the slave master. That should have been an integral part of his education.

It should not have taken a civil rights movement to get Negro history into the New York City schools. We want youngsters to know that they have a right to have their ideas heard at the market place. This should be a part of the educational process. They are not here just to defend the existing society, but also to question it and try to make it work on their behalf. We see this as part of the whole educational process.

Third, we want to have a role in evaluating the educational process. Let's evaluate whether or not the teachers are teaching.

PAUL PETERSON

The I.S. 201 situation, first of all, shows what is possible in a city which is not controlled by a powerful political organization. I made the same point the last time a group of this kind gathered, and, as some of you may recall, we discussed the differences between machine and nonmachine cities. In New York, where the machine is considerably weaker, parents were able to organize and make educational policies the focus of a major issue – even though they did not succeed in every respect. (Helen Testamark said, "We did win," but certainly she would agree that not everything is the way she wants it.) However, the success that this organization had in raising this issue to the public's attention and winning at least some concessions is due not only to the parents' courageous efforts but also to the vulnerability of public officials to community pressures in a city where the strength of the machine has declined.

Second, I am all in favor of community organizations and their directing attention to the schools and the welfare bureaucracy. It is an excellent approach to the problems of the urban city. Something has to be done to break down that tyrannical relationship between the bureaucracy and the clients which has been testified to again and again in these presentations.

But in order to provoke discussion, I would like to examine the limitations of the I.S. 201 effort. What was the group not able to do? Rather than this group being a most radical and kooky outfit, I think that, in fact, the demands they made were narrow; the changes in the educational system which they called for were not as major as is necessary. Precisely because they are a neighborhood group, which must focus on their own neighborhood, they are unable to develop support for significant citywide reforms.

Let me give two illustrations of this point. The East Harlem organizations, first of all, have called for decentralization of power within the educational system, which would involve parents and community people in decision-making for East Harlem schools. Although this proposal may have the virtue of reducing the distance between teachers, parents, and students, it has one severe drawback as well — the program would have to be implemented in all areas of the city. There is no reason for giving preference to East Harlem, Harlem, or Bedford-Stuyvesant over other areas of the city. But if you decentralize control over school policy in cities like New York and Chicago, undesirable policies are likely to be the consequence. Segregated teaching staffs will increase, as white communities use local power to turn down the applications of Negro teachers. Such a system would provide little opportunity for increasing student integration. In curriculum matters, Negro history would scarcely be taught anywhere except in Negro schools. Neighborhood control implemented throughout the entire school system seems an ineffective tool for reaching the goals long proclaimed by the civil rights movement.

Secondly, though the symbolic significance of asking for a Negro principal at I.S. 201 is important, changing the entire recruitment pattern for principals within the entire city is a more important consideration. Neighborhood organizations find this very difficult to do because they want to focus on their own problems and schools. Who will raise these questions about changing recruitment patterns for principals, assistant principals, and superintendents throughout the entire city? Somebody must focus at the citywide level.

In this regard, increasing federal interest in education may well be an essential adjunct to community organization. The Elementary and Secondary Education Act is a beginning, but it must be expanded to a much larger scale. Federal regulations will have to be much more specific so as to control the ways in which funds are spent at the local level. Federal policies leading to educational reform are thwarted by the political realities in Washington, but there may be more hope for future political support at that level than in the city. Community organizations, in becoming concerned with their own neighborhood, should not forget the importance of developing support for political leadership at the national level that will support educational reform. Through participation in regular, democratic, political processes, we can seek to develop leadership in Washington necessary to bring both financial support and specific policy requirements that will improve city school systems. I think this may generate those general policies within cities which are necessary to implement needed radical changes. Neighborhood organizations, focusing on particular schools in their own community, cannot do it by themselves. It takes pressure from an outside source, i.e., the federal government. Consequently, attention must be focused not only on our own neighborhood, but also on city and national political processes.

14

Case Presentation:
Child Development Group of Mississippi

PEARL DRAINE

I am a Mississippian. I was born in Lexington, Mississippi and have spent most of my life there. I am proud to say that it was advanced education and civil rights involvement that took me out of Mississippi. I am married and have three children, two in college to support, one in tenth grade, and am trying to adopt a five-year-old. I have a daughter at Tougaloo College who is presently on exchange at Oberlin College in Ohio and is driving me crazy because she has two majors, chemistry and mathematics. I have a son who has transferred from Paul College in Waco, Texas to Alcorn College, a tenth-grader, and this small youngster. I have little enough sense to believe they love me even though I am gone most of the time.

I have spent seventeen years in the public school system. On Monday, I will celebrate the one-month anniversary of my resignation from the public school system. I resigned in order to do exactly what I am doing, take chances to advance. The film* portrayed a lot of my feelings. I also wanted to be free enough to do as I chose as long as it did not infringe on anybody else's rights. I could not do that with the Jackson public school system. I am not angry with the school system; I am proud of those officials; they made me what I am. As long as I was with them, I was not myself because I did most of what the public school system wanted me to do. Then, a month ago, with my husband, I decided not to do it any longer; I was going to resign. I cannot even tell you what we discussed. We were in debt, as many people are, and we said: "Where do you go now?" As for my over-all feelings, my trust in not in Man, so I have no worry. I just quit.

I did not quit to go to CDGM since I had been affiliated with them since June 11, 1966. I had served as a field consultant and will leave material to tell you what that is. Presently, I am the associate director for the Child Development Group of Mississippi which serves 14 counties, 5000 children, 2000 employees, and has 74 centers and 393 units. I am responsible for a program to instruct people on the development of a program for these many children. This is the greatest responsibility I could ever have, for if I fail, I fail many people.

*Head Start in Mississippi

The film shown is a true one. It would be impossible to make a film long enough to sit through that would really tell what I have seen in Mississippi. I truly solicit your whole-hearted support. Say CDGM and say it loud and long — it is the greatest program that I know. I certainly hope that you feel the same way about it.

Today I was to be on the stage in Jackson, Mississippi at the Eighth District Educational Teachers' Association. I had to choose where to go? You can guess what I chose since I am here.

Let me briefly tell you how the program operated. I am going to leave some material for the Workshop with Earl (Doty) and you can discuss it. It really will matter what you say because I am going to take a plane shortly and will not be able to hear what you say. I will also leave job descriptions. You ought to know about jobs with the Child Development Group of Mississippi. I have some material entitled, "Position Available: Field Program Advisors." We need field program advisors in Mississippi. They can come from anywhere, be of any color as long as they have the qualification entailed in this paper which I will leave with Earl.

Field program advisors are responsible for developing a program in the field. For example, in Stone County which will have three centers, ninety children and three teachers per unit of fifteen, the field program advisor will help people do the things you saw in the film. Without some professional involvement, the program could lag, they just do not get done. We do not go into areas and plan a program, and pass it out to the people in the communities. We go there in such a way that they will be relaxed enough to say whatever they want to say. On that basis, we have developed programs for the children in particular areas.

I am also leaving some information on resource teachers. Most resource teachers come from the area itself, and their educational qualifications are not quite so high. I do not think that this should even be compulsory. Many rural people do not have much education and should not be denied the privilege to hold these positions on that account. In many instances, they know much more from their experiences than the Ph.D.s shipped in from other places to work with children in this poverty area.

We are in desperate need of energetic men for the program. I am also leaving some material on what men can do in the program. We have only cited eleven things, but there are many more. We seriously think of children who come from broken homes, who have not had a chance to hang onto daddy's arm, ride his back, and really get the feeling that there's a man who loves them. We must realize that children need to have that manly image around. There are things that men can do in the program with 5000 children. We treasure them because they can travel long hours, long distances, stay up late, drive cars, lift big boxes, swing the children in the trees, tie the rings around the ties and help with other activities you saw in the film. We do hope to have many men working with the preschool children. Area teacher guides, known as ATGs, will be responsible for a designated area within the fourteen counties. I will leave the qualifications with Earl along with the position description for the Associate Director for Teacher Development and Program for Children. I dare you to apply – that is my job. But I will leave the description so you will be well-informed as to the terms in which we work.

I will also leave our preplanning for January 15 to March 1. It includes all our week-by-week plans for getting the schools open by March 1st. This might be a pattern and it might be something to enlarge upon. We have to submit our plans to OEO from the day we were granted our money to, say X number of weeks, Y month. Then, every so often after March 1, we will again have to submit our plans from that day for four or five weeks in advance, or whatever they say. They are our bosses.

I also have about a dozen proposals for you to fuss over. I had to check with several persons in the office to be sure that I had the right to give them out.

I want to give you a short excerpt from the proposal which is in keeping with a portion of the film. I love it because it expresses so well what I said and what I have tried to be. I was born and reared in the country, on a farm, and while I was working with the proposal, I was asked bluntly, "Draine, how do you feel about rural children? You were born there; tell us what your life was like." I will not read it, but the feeling is, "How bad it is to be a Negro in the backwoods of Mississippi, to live on a white man's farm, turn a white man's soil, pick a white man's cotton, and go to bed in a white man's house. And then, to have nothing. How bad it is to be told what to do from the cradle to the grave."

People in Mississippi feel this strongly. They are not willing to be told how to get out of this, but they are willing to stay up all night to find their own ways out of it. They are very conscious of this, and I do not think you saw anybody in that picture that wanted any sympathy. They wanted people to get out of the way and let them try things. We want your support and good faith.

There are books created by people in CDGM. The people in them are real and as you read you will find what they have to say about the CDGM program. I will leave some of the booklets with Earl, and if you need more, we can send them. There are too many to bring, but I did want to share some of this material from Mississippi with you.

You were talking about books for education. CDGM makes its own books. One is called "The Pond," it was actually done by people in a Head Start project and it is about children on a trip, what they saw and said. They treasure this book. We have them in the schools and every child can have one. He can take it home, and the parents can have them. The children can actually see and remember their trip which was responsible for the little book that was created.

There are two other things which I want to share with you. One a "CDGM for a Year in Pictures." It includes projects from most of the centers, and I have put many hard hours into it. The other is Tom Levin's report a true story of Mississippi.

Before concluding, I want to tell you about the conditions of the grant. One is concerned with religious activities while the children are in the centers. This is one of the conditions that governs our getting the grant, governs the employees, the use of money, and the time we work. One plainly says that no CDGM employee can participate in any civil rights activities during working hours, from eight to five. You can do as you please after five, but nothing to deal with voter registration or the like while you are employed. If you go to a house to see a mother about her sick child, you cannot even ask her if she is a registered voter. This is in the book, and I want to leave it for you to read. It is just too much to push down your throat, but we do have conditions. At our meeting last week people said, "conditions, conditions, conditions," but we had to go through with them. I do not feel badly about it. You have to take certain things to win others.

We have what we call a "built-in manual for operation." It starts with the very first visit in the community when you ask for a children's center. The community is called together. No officers are elected because you must give notice seven days prior to any election. Fifty percent of the elected officers must be parents of children enrolled in the school. This gives poor people a governing power because they become the decision-making body.

The central CDGM staff does not dictate, dominate, or interfere with the community people as long as they are following the OEO guidelines, and we make sure that they know them. They are free to call on us, and we try to stay out in the field. We do not sit in that office behind those big desks, smoking cigarettes and drinking coffee. Very few people in the program stay in that office. Central staff personnel (FPAs) are supposed to be out in the field with people.

How do I know you are there? You write up a day-by-day report of what is happening. I can pick up the Watts-Line and call to make sure you are out there. I really want to know what is going on. If you are not really dedicated, either you get dedicated or you get out. That is the only alternative. Nobody gets fired, you just vacate your place.

I hope I have thrown some light on CDGM. Might I just tell you that next to Jesus Christ is CDGM with me.

15

Upgrading Education in the Inner City

DOXEY WILKERSON

We are addressing ourselves to a problem that needs little documentation. It is simply the fact that the schools in the inner city, if you prefer that euphemism, or schools in the ghetto, are failures. By any reasonable criteria, they are not doing what we expect schools to do with the children involved. I take it that we are concerned with what can be done to make them successful.

Since prescription should flow from diagnosis, let me begin by briefly suggesting what seem to me to be the main factors causing the failure. Why aren't the schools effectively educating the children in the slums? As you know, these days it is customary for those of us in the profession to say that the big explanation is that these children are not educable. We do not put it so crudely. Rather, we point to the deficiencies in the socialization of youngsters brought up in the awful poverty and discrimination of the ghetto. We cite their early experiences which were limited, their language patterns which were distorted, their lack of the cognitive development which children get in other circumstances. We rattle off a whole list of handicaps, and say that they are "culturally deprived," they have been so scarred by their social circumstances that they are not ready and able to do effective school work. I think this is the prevailing rationale for failure that one now finds in the ghetto school.

Let me first say something about the child from the slum and his characteristics as the explanation of our failure to educate him. Undoubtedly, being nurtured in poverty and discrimination does not contribute to academic excellence. These youngsters are indeed scarred by many of their social experiences; and hence they come to school with certain deficits as measured by norms which prevail generally among children with more fortunate beginnings. These pose special educational problems. I do not think we can deny this.

At the same time, it has never been established that the fact of children not having in their preschool experiences certain socializing experiences which we think would better equip them for school work *precludes* their doing effective academic work once they are in school. Those who have been following the literature on this certainly know that, in many times and places, it has been demonstrated that if children from slum neighborhoods, with all the deficiencies we have been talking about, are provided with appropriate school experiences, they can perform satisfactorily in their school work. The socially-induced deficiency surely is a part of the explanation, but what we do about it is generally missing in the analysis.

This brings me to the second part of the diagnosis, if you will, the school itself. In the profession, we are very prone to predicting. We can measure a child this way and that way and predict that in the sixth grade he will be two years behind in reading. We are good at it, but sometimes we are so enamored with the importance of being correct in our predictions that we do not try to foul them up. We really need to recognize that a large proportion, though not all, of the children from slum environments do lack some of the important experiential background characteristics of children from more advantaged classes. This would seem to call for whatever modifications in the school program are necessary to overcome those deficiencies, and thus move these children forward in their development. Failure to make such modifications is tantamount to malfeasance.

It is not customary for us in school work to say this. I often feel that our profession is one of the most defensive. Whenever it is suggested that the products of our institutions are not what we would like them to be, we look everywhere for an explanation but at ourselves. Many things about the way schools are run, which I do not need fully to document for you, suggest that certain characteristics of the schools themselves are much more important in their failure to educate than the deficiencies with which a child from a slum environment comes to school.

Perhaps most important is the point of view with which we approach these youngsters, our expectations for them. You must be acquainted with some of the interesting studies relating to what Clark calls the "self-fulfilling prophecy." If we begin with the notion that these children cannot learn, we communicate that fact to them. When they do not learn, our predictions are fulfilled. We bring them into and try to run them through a school situation which was patterned for children with different preschool experiences and perspectives. If they do not make it in what to them is quite an alien environment, it is just too bad for them. We seldom say to ourselves, "Is this the kind of school experience they should be brought through? Does it fit the youngsters in the ghetto schools?" Rather, we subject them to meaningless experiences which have no real tie with their lives, no real significance for them. Then, of course, we are upset when they rebel, which is the only healthy thing they can do.

We tend to rationalize our failures in terms of the child; rarely do we explain them in terms of our own professional deficiencies. Ten years ago it was convenient, customary, and respectable when a child did not learn in school for the teacher to say, "Look, he's got an 80 IQ, so what do you expect of me?" But, as you know, the IQ has lost its aura; this explanation is no longer respectable in professional circles. However, we have something just as good: "His parents are uneducated, his home is broken, there is no father there, he has been impoverished," and on and on. "He's culturally deprived; therefore, I can't teach him," and I'm off the hook again.

I think that here we are dealing with something which runs deep in ghetto education. It is much more important in explaining the failures of the ghetto school than the characteristics of the youngsters themselves. I remind you of the fundamental fact that the school is an integral part of the larger society, an interacting unit of the culture; and it tends to reflect the social relationships and values which prevail around it. This is inevitably true, in our society, in any society, and in all times; and our schools today are operating in a social structure which is deeply racist. The decisive forces in the community look with derogation upon the lower classes, the poor people, particularly if they are of a racial minority. Ours is a society in which we profess democratic values, but when it comes to ghetto children, we really do not mean it. Moreover, the people of the ghetto have little or no significant say in shaping their children's education; they are in a more or less powerless situation.

I submit that it is illusory to think that we can make good schools for ghetto youngsters as long as their parents are powerless to influence what goes on in the school. I suspect that this is quite fundamental to many of the other things we relate to the school's lack of success.

If this is a proper or at least partial diagnosis, what is the prescription? First, if our schools are to serve the developmental purpose we want them to serve, the curricular experiences they provide will have to change markedly. I use "cirriculum" broadly to refer to all the pupil's experiences which are guided by the school. This means many, many things, all of which cannot be detailed here. It means smaller classes, and much more individualized instruction geared to the youngsters' particular needs. It means curricular content and materials relevant to their lives and meaningful to them. It means textbooks and readers which do not show the characteristic biases now found.

It means living in a school in which you are genuinely respected by everybody, even though you are black and poor. You must be an important human being to every person in that school, and that fact must be communicated to you. It means going to school under the guidance of teachers who expect you to learn, who think you have the potential to develop and seek to realize it, not to rationalize their failures. It means going to a school where the Negro and poor are not segregated, but where they benefit from associating with children of different socioeconomic and ethnic backgrounds. We must make considerable changes in the nature of children's school experiences. This is but a sample of what we need to do.

Of course, we will not do that unless we make some rather important changes in the people who are guiding the learning of these youngsters. I am talking about the teachers. My field is teacher education. I have been fooling around with it for some four decades; I am unlearning many things I thought I know as well as learning some things I once did not suspect. It is increasingly clear to me that very many of the people who are responsible for instructing ghetto youngsters do not have the general educational insight and understanding, professional skills, or even the humanistic values essential for doing the job.

Sometimes I despair when trying to lead teachers who come from our typical teacher-education programs into more effective school procedures. They lack even the educational background in the behavioral sciences that would enable them just to comprehend the problems we face in ghetto schools. The professional skills which they learned in teachers' colleges were seldom directed towards the problems involved in teaching disadvantaged children. Their social experiences did not equip them with the attitudes and values which are essential for effective work with children of the poor. I think that we have done and are still doing a very poor job of teacher education. I wish I had time to tell you about an innovative program that we are trying to develop at Yeshiva University. Obviously, we must do much reeducating of teachers.

We can write the best possible experiences in curriculum bulletins, but nothing happens unless we change teachers' behavior, perceptions, and approaches in the classroom. To change the curriculum, we must change the teachers; and this calls for vital pre-service and in-service education programs. When I refer to in-service education programs of teacher education, I am not talking about the formal, superficial "courses" for which teachers come together for ten sessions, listen to somebody lecture, go home, and nothing happens. I mean really vital programs designed to transform the character of the teachers' behavior in the schools.

Modification of teachers' insights, skills, and behaviors is an obvious second requirement if we are to make the ghetto schools effective; but neither this nor the first will be achieved unless we also effect rather important changes in social relationships, and particularly in the distribution of power as it affects the school program. This is the third element of the prescription.

There has been a lot of discussion on this point already and I am not going to press it unduly. We have here already discussed I.S. 201. I am happy about what is happening around I.S. 201, and now around another junior high school in Harlem as well as several other schools. I do not know whether similar things are happening in Chicago, but parents and community leaders in the ghettos of New York City are beginning to demand some effective control over the policies and programs of schools that serve their children. I am firmly convinced that such controls are a prerequisite if we are to modify the curricular experiences of the children or substantially modify the behavior of teachers.

It is of the nature of any bureaucracy, including, par excellence, our education bureaucracy, that it tends to go the way it has been going and is incapable of regeneration from within. If there is to be a significant change, it must come from external pressures. One of the most hopeful things I see now on the educational horizon, as it affects ghetto areas, is the rebellion of parents who are organizing and who I think will win. In New York, I think we will win a Board of Education policy which will lead to rather substantial local influence over educational personnel and program. This is fundamental to the prescription about which I am talking.

In summary, it is clear that we do no service to the children who are brought up in poverty and discrimination by saying they are "just like any other children"; they are not. They have been scarred, and they have special educational needs. But our big error lies in placing the burden on the children rather than on the schools. We need to recognize that, in the profession, it is our responsibility to cope with those problems. Supposedly, that is why we are professionals. Undoubtedly, the big target of change is not so much the child as the school itself. Finally, we will not be very successful in our efforts to modify the schools along the necessary lines unless there is some restructuring of social relationship, some redistribution of power, giving considerably greater influence to the parents of the disadvantaged youngsters who are now being failed by our ghetto schools.

TIMUEL BLACK

Mr. Wilkerson has just about said it. The day before yesterday I made a similar plea to his in Kalamazoo at Western Michigan University to three different levels: the Job Corps teachers, the undergraduates, and the professors and instructors at the university. Though the language was different and not as eloquent, the ideas were somewhat the same, and I will probably repeat much of what has been said.

Perhaps my topic should be, "How to become a man as a Negro male in a competitive, capitalistic, racist society" or "How to make a joke out of the oky-doke." If you do not know what an "oky-doke" is, ask one of the brothers and perhaps he can tell you what it is and how we get to the point where we make a joke out of it. Or perhaps we ought to have a conference between Negro men and Negro women on "maleness," and entitle it, "Never have so many wanted so much in so few."

It was suggested that I deal with three major areas: One, "What can teachers do?" This may be the cutting edge of what Mr. Wilkerson has already indicated. Two, "What can the middle-class Negro do?" I have not found out exactly what the middle-class Negro is but maybe we can make some definitions. Third, "What can I do as an individual?" I will speak to these points as I see them without going into detail. Perhaps in the discussion we can get into more detail.

Unfortunately, what Mr. Wilkerson has said about the teacher is so true that perhaps we need a conference for those of you who do not know what kind of teachers we have in the schools. However, for those teachers who have come to grips with the deficiencies in our education for all children, but especially for ghetto children, I could suggest the following:

When we talk about black power, white power, or whatever power, I think of the ability to get the job done, whatever that job may be. One can hardly get it done without some area of power which he can affect, control, and direct. So, as far as the first issue, "What can teachers do?," I would make the plea that teachers should join those organizations which have some power. Teachers who are really concerned could infiltrate the union so as to take part in the union's decision in a bargaining agreement with the Board of Education.

It was only a few years ago when, in the Chicago Teachers' Union, I was almost alone in raising the race issue. I was booed, hissed, and gavelled down many times. My fellow teachers would say, "That's not our problem. Let's move on to the order of the day, Mr. Chairman." The chairman would gavel me down and sometimes my fellow teachers would boo me down because to them, the race issue was not the order of the day. Since then it has become the order of the day, and, perhaps, if more teachers, who knew which order of the day was on the way, had been within the framework of the union, some of the catastrophic developments that have occurred since then could have been avoided. Perhaps we could have made a difference in the way the union felt.

Teachers should be active and get into such other organizations as NEA and professional groups such as the National Council for Social Studies which does have some effect on curricular materials. There are other pressure groups such as the Teachers Committee for Quality Education of which I am a member, Teachers for Integrated Schools, and caucus groups such as the Teachers Action Committee (TAC) which affects what goes on from within the union. These people are making decisions in an attempt to gain some level of power. Teachers should do this.

They should join and participate in community groups around their schools, not as leaders but as fellow participants in the community, taking their cues from the indigenous leadership and helping to strengthen those groups. They should join and be active in the PTA since it exists and has some influence. Teachers who will give meaning to the in-service and pre-service training programs should organize in their schools to see that these programs are honest and intelligent, and that they deal with the issues at hand.

They should help students learn to organize. It is good to teach a group of students what it is to develop a petition, circulate it, and demand that reasonable action be taken. In fact, this is a normal part of social studies. Perhaps, at some point, teachers can even encourage students and their parents to protest against some of the evils of the system.

Teachers can be friendly with the people they now look down upon and thus create a better climate for themselves within the school. The engineer could be a very useful person for certain things in the classroom. The lunchroom heads, cooks, and others can be very useful. I have been fortunate enough to use their good services in behalf of my students, and other teachers have done so as well. This should be an ongoing, conscious thing. Janitors can move things around when necessary if they feel positively toward a certain teacher. Clerks can expedite or block many things. Teachers can enhance a good educational program with their help. I cannot go into the specifics but this has its effect.

What can the Negro middle-class do? They can begin to think of themselves as what they are and what society sees them as being – that is as Negroes. Not just Americans, but American Negroes. They can identify with the problem of racism and the contradictions in the American ideal, and begin to deal with that problem honestly. They can become more active and vocal in community organization and take special interest in pressure groups such as the NAACP, which we know does not fulfill all its claims. They can become a part of organizations such as CORE and SNCC. They can join political action groups such as Americans for Democratic Action and IVI on the local level, and begin to become conscious of the candidates they select to run in these areas, and possibly become candidates themselves. Children like to see their adults active in things. It gives a sense of pride that is hard to describe. Children see their parents actually doing what they say the children eventually ought to do.

They can join groups such as SANE because the war issue does affect our local economy. If a lot of war materials and money must go to Vietnam and other war efforts, then it will not be applied to local situations, and the poverty areas are certainly the first places from which it will be taken. If we fail to understand that, then, of course, we do not understand the realities of our economic and political systems. Get into SANE and other groups which protest the sometimes useless expenditure of money and lives.

The middle class should lend the benefit of their training and their class to increasing identification and knowledge, and to gaining allies. As I have heard so often, they should help build bridges, create for the oppressed communities a sympathetic and empathetic understanding of their problems. Then the people who have or can at least effect power will be able to deal realistically with the problems, not as philanthropists or missionaries but as participants, fulfilling their obligation as American citizens and as human beings. Often the middle class has an entree to these areas and fails to use it to benefit those who need it most – for their own people, in fact.

What can I as an individual do? It is almost repetitious. In our family life, we must occasionally let our children understand their responsibilities as social human beings. To some extent, we must exemplify that by participating in things that are, in fact, the order of the day. To effect these things, we must become participants in school and community affairs. Individuals in the community, though they may not be teachers, will have to pay the price for the deficiencies of the poor school system. Volunteer, become part of things that are power.

If people will actively deal with the problems that need to be dealt with, then the details of the educational program that need to be changed, can begin to be changed. The solutions will begin to arise out of understanding the need and of placing the resources, not only to deal with the need but also to reduce the problems of education which are vexing our communities today.

The alternatives are horrid to consider. Summer is coming and, speaking symbolically, the alternatives will keep us all so busy that, year 'round, we will not be able to have any conferences. Summer will shade into autumn and winter. To that extent, there is an action program in which we can become involved and make ourselves useful. Then, conferences such as these can give us the stimulation and the information that will help us do a better job.

DAVID STREET

The previous two speakers have done an excellent job of stating some of the problems and goals of the kind of education we want in the inner-city. I want to talk about a perspective and strategy for implementing some improvements in inner-city education. With a colleague, Morris Janowitz, who is also in the sociology department, I have been involved in a study of the organizational characteristics of large city school systems. We are focusing on Chicago but have gained some perspective by visiting other cities.

In looking at the big city school systems, we see what we call a "second crisis in urban education." The first crisis, the one we have been talking about here, has been recognized for at least ten years by many people who have been trying to produce a change in the inner city. The second crisis is the failure of the innovations we already have. That is, if you go from one city school system to another, you see numerous attempts at innovation, projects which are exciting at least for a short time. You see a variety of attempts to do something for ghetto populations.

One way to put it is that, though there is a great deal of innovation, there is very little change. Educators have greatly increased their understanding of things such as the biases built into the IQ test, cultural deprivation, and the inner city. However, there has been little meaningful improvement, perhaps with the exception of reductions in the numbers of students on double shift in most large cities and changes so that we now have very little overt gerrymandering of school districts. Why have we not seen the production of major change?

Our perspective leads us to look at what we call the organizational character of the big city school systems. We try to discover what in these systems permits them to do certain things and not others. Then we ask, "What kind of realistic demands can we make upon the school systems as they are currently set up?" And, "What are we asking for that is likely to be unrealistic, given the character of these organization?"

One could go into considerable detail about the organizational character of large city school systems, but I would briefly suggest that, in many of these systems, one sees a very bureaucratic operation with a tremendous number of built-in constraints and relatively little flexibility in operating practices. When one looks at innovations in these school systems, one frequently sees temporary, ephemeral change which does not ripple out to other schools in the system. A number of legal, quasilegal, and traditional restraints and bases of operation are built into the system. Joseph Pois has written a book called *The School Board Crisis*. It is about the Chicago School Board and illustrates a number of the constraints which face a board member when he tries to think about how to produce some meaningful policy decisions in the schools.

Second, a number of constraints are tied to a commitment to universal treatment of all pupils. In the history of the large city schools, the commitment to universalism was a triumph. That is, the image of the comprehensive school, the school which would serve all social classes and which could not discriminate by race, ethnicity, or religion, and so forth, was an important one. However, at the present, the commitment to universalism — which requires that, if possible, there be identical numbers of teachers for identical numbers of students and the same kind of curricula in schools with quite different clientele — creates a number of rigidities in the school system.

A third kind of constraint is that, in comparison with other large-scale organizations, the school system tends to lack the various control devices that insure that things really will get done. In the Chicago schools, especially during the ten years of the predecessor to the present superintendent, the prevalent notion has been that the system was overcentralized and could not work because all decisions are made at the top. This kind of diagnosis seems to be relevant to most big city school systems, but it is an oversimplification. If these systems were as overcentralized as we tend to think they are, then we would expect that any new change that the people at the top of the organization wanted could be introduced rather readily. This is not the case. On the one hand, these systems are overcentralized in that they have standard curricula, standard textbook selection, and standard ways of allocating personnel and facilities. On the other hand, they are under-centralized in that they are rather inflexible; there is little control over what can be done from the top of the system.

The fourth kind of constraint might be characterized as the ways in which personnel are recruited and kept in the system. In large city school systems, except sometimes for the man in the top position, one sees a great degree of inbreeding. Personnel come up through a traditional system with very little interchange among systems. Frequently suburban systems work on ideas which may be twenty years ahead of those in the inner city.

Fifth, one sees many rigidities in the division of labor of the school systems. Personnel resist flexible operations to such an extent that, in many cases, the teacher organizations, along with the administration, oppose the introduction of subprofessionals into the system. They hold that this would jeopardize the roles and rewards of the teachers. I think that, given the limited facilities and the limited numbers of good personnel with teaching certificates who could be brought into the big city school systems, some derigidification of the division of labor is necessary.

I will mention two other constraints in the school system. As I am sure you all are aware, there are many difficulties in relations between the schools and the community, especially in the ghetto neighborhoods. Schools frequently operate so as to set up great barriers, even to parents who want to inquire about their children. Obviously, these can be barriers to political or meaningful citizen action by members of the community.

Finally, there is the obvious weakness of research and development and of ways to monitor changes in the school systems. The lack of research poses the question of whether or not any of the some fifteen front-page headline experiments of large city school systems which have been talked about in the last ten years, have accomplished anything important at all.

Thus, we have large, bulky, bureaucratic school systems, and we must ask what is the potential for change? As the Negro populations of the cities increase, the Negro populations in the school system will increase disproportionately, as is the case in Washington, D.C. It seems likely to me that without some major changes in the school system both the white and Negro middle classes will continue to withdraw from the public school systems. We face the danger of the schools being operated very much like public assistance agencies, perhaps to a large extent on federal money, probably with quite a bit of direction and federal legislation from the Office of Education, and probably with not very much effectiveness.

Could some effective changes be made in the organizational character of the large city school system? Yes – at least a number of things could be done which could make a difference. We assume that there is the capacity for doing the good teaching which is necessary, and for stimulating personnel to do a better job in the ghetto areas, if the system somehow can be changed in ways which will permit and encourage it.

We have worked out a statement of a variety of strategies for producing change. It would take quite a while to go into this, but let me mention a few things which seem necessary. First, and following from what I have said, it is necessary to produce a greater flexibility in the division of labor, by bringing in large numbers of subprofessionals, both paid and volunteer.

Second, in these systems, it is necessary to greatly increase and improve the quality of in-service training as well as opportunities for teachers, principals, and middle-level administrators to have meaningful professional, collegial contact with each other. We can compare education to social work in terms of on-the-job relationships. In social work, there are many on-the-job relations with colleagues. They talk about ideas, discuss what they are doing, gossip, complain, and build a sense of identification. They convince themselves that what they are doing is worth doing, and this has positive effects. School teaching on the other hand, is by and large a solo practice. Except for the children, it is practiced alone. We assume that a useful model would be to build in a higher level of professional contacts and more opportunities for retraining and retooling teachers.

A third strategy for producing change in these systems, and the last I will mention here, is an attempt to produce a genuine decentralization of the large city school systems. Obviously, the systems are too big and bulky to be wholly operated from a downtown office. Furthermore, those of you who are in cities which have district decentralization probably have seen that, in most cases, it is relatively ineffective. In Chicago there are now about twenty-five districts, each with a superintendent who is told to "run his own area" and talk with people in the community. But he does not have personnel to help him and he does not have control over his own budget. He has to continually call downtown in order to operate his district.

Our image of decentralization would be to develop pieshaped sectors in cities, four or five "super-districts." Only if there are relatively few districts can there be enough staff to operate the relatively autonomous system, develop local Advisory Boards of Education, and decentralize decision making from the top of the organization down to sublevels. We would suggest doing this in such a way as *not* to have socially homogeneous districts. There should not be a lower-class Negro district, a middle-class Negro district, and a working-class white district.

What is needed is a smaller, manageable set-up that can involve more of the local citizenry. The over-all formula is not to decentralize the school system to citizen control at the level of the individual school. Though this may be useful in a crisis such as that of New York's 201, obviously most staff operations cannot be decentralized to that level. Many local attendance areas are very small, and a leadership vacuum may result. In trying to have citizen control, a city like Chicago might have more precinct captains than leaders to fill the available positions.

In conclusion, I would like to suggest that such strategies necessary for changing the large city school systems are not entirely utopian. On the other hand, as I have suggested, one does not see tremendous change in these systems. We must face the fact that the cry for the schools to become more humane, take on more social welfare services, and function more in the interests of their students, is decades old. To simply make the cry is likely to be ineffective. One must learn from the experience of the Mobilization for Youth's, attempts to get cooperation with the New York schools, from the difficulties of the Chicago Youth Development Project, and from the fighting, hemming, and hawing between social workers, school systems, and politicians in Detroit, Cleveland, and elsewhere when cooperative ventures were tried. At some point, one has to conclude that you cannot keep putting all these demands on the schools – not because it is unfair to them, but because they are not equipped to handle them.

Therefore, my last point is that, in some cities, if there is to be a humanistic high school, it may have to be developed as part of a social welfare service or a community action program, one that excludes the public school people and the education professionals. Too much federal money that is envisioned for experimentation in education goes to the educators. You know the old line about the war being too important to leave to the generals. The problems of education in the inner city are too important to leave wholly to the educators. Other professional groups and the citizenry must be brought in as well.

REV. ARTHUR BRAZIER

I think the first thing that has to be done to upgrade education in the inner city is to rid many people of the notion that schools in black communities cannot be good schools unless there are some white children around. Too many of us have become afflicted with the idea that good education and integration are synonymous. Most of you must know that is not true. I have many problems now with the tremendous push for school integration. Having said that, I do not want to get caught in the box of being quoted as saying I am against integration. I am in favor of integration, and I do not want to get caught in the old, separate-but-equal bind or be accused of gilding the ghetto.

But there is only one way to upgrade education in the inner-city schools and that is to start upgrading education in the inner-city schools. In the past few years, great emphasis has been placed upon getting schools built in areas where there can be maximum integration. We have wasted a lot of time with the School Board trying to get boundaries redrawn so as to have a certain amount of integration.

The integration door, which was cracked in 1954, is opening very, very slowly because white people control it and can open it at whatever rate they choose. They can open it rapidly, they can open it slowly, or they can close it. At the rate the door is opening now, it has been said that we will have integration in about 975 years which is a little too long to ask anybody to wait. There seem to be deepseated, behavioral patterns in the white population that will not be changed overnight. Plans to achieve integration, such as cross-town bussing, must have the support of the white population. Otherwise the white population flees, and the goal of integration is defeated.

Though we want integration to come, and should support all citywide organizations that work for integration in the public school system, I think community organizations should begin to take a somewhat limited view of the school situation. They should work for better education and better schools in their communities, laying aside dreams, goals, and ideals. The children in the first grade of these schools will graduate from the eighth grade in all black schools.

Since in Woodlawn, we know that Scott, Wadsworth, Fermi, and Tesler will not be integrated in the near future, we feel that one of the only ways to begin upgrading public school education in this community is to have some control over what is happening in the school system. In order to get control, we need power. It is not necessary to dream about this control or to look for psychological and philosophical ways of gaining it. The only way to get power is to take it, and I am a firm believer that black people must organize on a basis of power and become, not partisan, but political.

This society is based on the body politic and the boards of education are responsive to the political forces of the cities in which they operate. It seems to me that we have to begin to take a meaningful look at exactly what is going on in our public school system and make certain demands. We ought to be demanding a meaningful voice in what happens to the local school in our community, and we do not have that voice. To put it another way, the school is in the community, but it is not part of the community. A school takes its cue from the principal, and we just do not have any voice in who becomes principal.

We ought to begin an effort to upgrade our schools and organize parents, above, beyond, and apart from the local PTAs. We can call our organizations Parent Organizations, Parents For Better Education, or anything we like, as long as they are organized above, beyond, and apart from the system. Then demands can be made on the system. We can say that we want to interview every new principal coming into this district, not necessarily on a basis of their educational qualifications, but we do want a say. We want some background on their psychological orientation and their attitudes toward the children they will be in charge of teaching. We want to know if they have the syndrome that black children from ghetto communities cannot learn. Are these black children "things," or are their parents "those people?"

We ought to have a say in the kind of power structure that has been built up around the teachers' unions, principals' unions, and tenure laws that keep flooding and inundating our Negro communities with the least experienced principals and teachers. The time has come when we should be demanding that our Boards of Education handle our school system in the same way that a corporation handles its far-flung network of factories.

If a corporation is having labor or production troubles in a New Jersey factory, they do not go to Pennsylvania, get some guy just out of college who is beginning to move up the industrial ladder, and send him into a tough situation, with tough union stewards, and tough labor bosses to solve union problems and clear up hamstrung production schedules. They get their old-line, experienced men who have proven themselves. They send them into the field of battle, as it were, to do a job. Instead of the Boards of Education sending the most experienced people to deal with the difficult problems, they send those who are least experienced. Then, as they gain experience with our children, they use the tenure laws to make rapid exits out of our community. We do not like it, and we are tired of it.

If we are going to upgrade education in our communities, we must stop telling ourselves that, historically, segregated schools have been inferior. Negro schools do not have to remain inferior. To some degree, it might be our fault that we have been getting inferior education. As parents, many of us are lacking an educational background. We have felt that merely by walking through the school door, our children were getting a good education. It is only recently that the eyes of black parents have been opened to the fact that their children are getting an inferior education. It becomes increasingly apparent that the key to our situation is the sweeping changes that will affect schools with difficult problems.

The Boards of Education seem to take great pride in saying that the pupil-teacher ratio in all our schools is now 33:1. Many of us are beginning to wake up and understand that they are only giving us a big public relations campaign. If our schools are designed to give everyone equal opportunity and equal education, it seems that a 33 to 1 ratio all over the city is not really what we want. If it is desirable for a teacher in a middle-class community to have 33 children, it seems to me that in our schools we need a 20 to 1, or 15 to 1 ratio.

In order to upgrade education in our communities, instead of being proud that $500 a year is spent on every child in Chicago, we ought to have $1,000 spent on our children. In other words, if we have more difficult problems, then more money should be spent dealing with them. We should not think that our children are getting an education equal to that of the children in Rogers Park because the same amount of money is spent in all communities. This is a very sorry position for our boards of education to take.

In conclusion I would like to say that, at some point, we will have to stop trying to change the personnel on these boards of education. We do not really know what we are getting when we change, except a lot of delays. They will fall back on the excuse that they need at least two years to become acquainted with what is happening. Then they will ask for $400,000 from the federal government to restudy the system and come up with some new ideas.

In order to upgrade the education in our school system, we in the city of Chicago ought to blow the whistle on Mr. Redmond and say, "You have been here long enough; now let's get some things done." Those of us in community organizations see that, in many cases, the man at the top is locked in by all the subordinates upon whom he must rely for his information. Recently there was a big change at the top, but everyone deep down in the administration is still there. I do not think there was a metamorphosis when Mr. Willis resigned.

In order to really upgrade education, we must have sweeping curriculum changes. We need more money spent in our schools, even if it means asking for more federal money along with federal guidelines. I do not think that we should run from these federal guidelines as many people are. The states do not have enough money to adequately meet the needs of education, or build adequate roads with all the federal guidelines on the fitness of the roads and the materials to be used, and they take the money gladly.

We who are putting money into the federal government should not rely upon a state like Illinois that is controlled by downstate legislators who have no understanding or desire to understand the problems of Chicago's inner city. Stop waiting for these people to raise Illinois from 46th to 45th on the list of per capita spending per pupil. Try to get more federal money into the school system so that we can make the changes that are so necessary.

We have had Head Starts all along. If I understand it correctly, kindergarten should have been a kind of Head Start. We put a Head Start on top of the kindergarten Head Start, and we may put a Head Start on top of that Head Start.

I would suggest that we call a conference of local community organizations to decide upon a goal. Let TWO, WSO, WFO, and the Mile Square Federation, let all of us decide on one thing we want. Then all our organizations can promote it, and when we get it, we can push for number two and number three, rather than each one of us pushing for separate, different things and destroying our basic power. We need power. The answer to upgrading education is more power in the hands of local people so they will have meaningful control over their local schools.

16

Planning Concepts and
New Directions – Education

ROBERT HAVIGHURST

Instead of starting with the usual prayerful analysis of the problems of the large city, I will focus on some concrete and practical, if general, remarks about the relation of the public schools to the remaking of the city. I think we all agree that the city has to be remade. I usually use the term "social urban renewal" since physical urban renewal has been so badly mismanaged in Chicago and elsewhere that it has made the problem of social urban renewal even greater. I will first talk generally about the relations between the school system and the other agencies that are trying to improve the city, and then I will consider some specific areas in Chicago.

The school administrators of a preceding generation learned to mistrust governmental agencies in the big city and concluded that there could be no useful cooperation with them. The history of public education in Chicago between 1920 and 1945 reveals the basis for their mistrust. The Republicans under Mayor Thompson and the Democrats since Mayor Kelly exploited the schools for political purposes. Therefore, those who have been running the school system have tried to do so on their own without getting involved in politics. Their view is that they can do the job of educating children better by avoiding entangling alliances.

Five or six years ago, Chicago had the opportunity to get substantial amounts of federal money to work on problems of juvenile delinquency, and Mr. Livermore was brought to Chicago to develop the city's program. There was a chance to receive money like that which went to New York for the Mobilization for Youth program, and it proved impossible for the public school people, the city organizations for youth, and the private organizations to agree on a plan that the federal government could support. Though this was not entirely the fault of the school administration, it indicated their mistrust in people who worked for other organizations. In Chicago and elsewhere, the law says that the location of new school buildings should be decided in consultation with the City Planning Commission, but this has been kept to the very minimum until quite recently.

School administrators are slowly changing, which can be seen by comparing those under forty with those over fifty. If you asked them whether it is desirable for the public schools or the School Board to cooperate with public and private welfare agencies, the public library, the Planning Commission, and so on, those under forty would, for the most part, favor this cooperation, while most of those over fifty would be against it. Those people who are working at the basic problems involved in remaking the city must insist on substantial and substantive cooperation between the Board of Education, public planning agencies, the public library, parks, and others.

A variety of government organizations should be brought together for planning purposes. Though it is necessary to be alert to exploitation of the schools by political organizations, the situation is different now than it was in the 1930's and 1940's. The federal government has put so much money into big city programs through the local city government that it is no longer possible for any big city government to use government money for its own purposes to any significant extent. There is too much public attention fixed on local government. In other words, as city government has become increasingly responsible for welfare in the broad sense, its possibilities for operating in its own narrow interest have decreased. It seems to be as safe as anything is in modern urban life for the city school systems to cooperate with other systems concerned with the welfare and general education of young people. That is my first general point.

The second has to do with the actual work on the problems of the city by the educational system. The best approach seems to be a decentralization of the city's program to allow for the development of programs that fit a given area in the city. It is worse than useless to develop a citywide program with identical procedures for all sections of a city.

Though one might quarrel about the actual geographical boundaries, the Planning Commission's division of Chicago into sixteen regions seems sensible. Here it means an average population of 200,000 per region which is about right in terms of the architecture of the great city. There should be an attempt to divide the city into areas that have some natural unity in the light of local feeling or of physical factors such as rivers, canals, or hills. These subdivisions or regions should be encouraged to work on their problems and to develop their own plans which fit into an over-all plan as far as the school system is concerned. This would necessitate a district regional superintendent with the authority to develop a school program for a population of 100,000 to 300,000 and it would allow for a number of different regional programs.

For example, in Chicago, the Near North Side seems to be such an area. It has a population of about 300,000. The Lincoln Park Organization is one of several major community organizations in the area. There are enormous resources available. There is the lake shore, the park, good transportation, easy access to the Loop, and this is an area with a fairly good balance among various ethnic groups. Thus, I would see the schools cooperating through a regional superintendent with substantial authority to locate school buildings and allocate resources, staff, and so on, in full discussion with private citizens and organizations as well as other governmental agencies in the area. It even would be possible to at least consider an "educational park" for the region.

Another area is that just south and southwest of the Loop. What will happen there and who will go to live there largely depends upon the schools. The Chicago Board of Education could define this as an area of interest, and, working with other organizations in the City make this area into a model for the development of urban living. The Planning Commission and the Housing Authority should agree to severely limit low-cost public housing in this area and to do what we now recognize should have been done on South State Street, namely, widely distribute small units in the area. Literally tens of millions of dollars from private real estate interests would flow into this area for building middle-income residences if there was any assurance that the school system and governmental agencies would support a program of economic and racial integration in the area. This could be a model for all big cities in the country. The problem would be to start it.

The area which includes South Shore, Woodlawn, and Hyde Park-Kenwood is another area of similar size, 200,000 to 300,000. In some ways this is an easier area in which to work though it, too, has major problems. It should be treated as a unit in planning Chicago's development, and the school districts should be treated as one unit instead of two as they are now. Instead of creating new districts here, one larger district with subheads should have been created. An organization should be developed that considers the welfare of Woodlawn, Hyde Park-Kenwood, and South Shore as a unit. Though Woodlawn obviously will not become integrated very soon, unless plans for Woodlawn are made in relation to plans for South Shore and Hyde Park-Kenwood, there is little chance of real progress there. Woodlawn must be part of a larger whole.

A big city can be defined in terms of reasonable units for development, and each unit can work out its own future in relation to the others. Certain areas of the city would lag behind, but as long as they do not interfere with progress in other parts of the city, I think they should be left alone. The problems of a big city cannot be solved with one big plan, and I would argue here for a considerable decentralization of planning to speed up progress on the real problems. On the other hand, a city like Rockford which itself is a unit of 200,000 should remain as one, but large cities such as Detroit, Chicago, and New York need this new approach. It would not be difficult for the schools to fit in. A plan has been proposed for the decentralization of Chicago schools which would be divided into three large regions which could easily be further subdivided down to the size I have been considering.

BERNARD BERKIN

I am interested in practical efforts to select areas for the development of models, and in that sense, I agree completely with Mr. Havighurst. However,

I think that any plans that we develop for different sections of Chicago must be seen in relation to an ultimate plan for 1980. I am convinced that if we seriously intend to have integrated education, then our plans will have to be metropolitan; if we are going to think in terms of segments, then they must be good representations of what an integrated society can be. The communities that Mr. Havighurst pointed out are more or less like that now, and the history of our city tells us that they may be difficult to maintain. We need some very dramatic models and very soon. I think we can use the advantages of these communities so as to bring a new texture to them. I find the notion of the education park so exciting because it is a truly different educational concept.

The imperative for integrated education is a given. It is absolutely crucial that young children of different classes and races have experiences together. Starting with that as an imperative, any educational setting that is developed in light of the existing population distribution absolutely must draw from a large attendance area. There is no other way to get a good mix of races and classes in a school setting. This means we must talk about an educational facility to replace the neighborhood school.

The other imperative for the education we need is that the new educational program must be truly superior to anything we have ever had. I do not think it is possible to do this with small schools as presently constituted. Even if we could motivate children and work with parents, teachers, and principals, I do not think that we could achieve what will be needed. With the special mix, the education park could make possible the education we dream about. Let me dream with you a bit.

As you know, libraries in small schools, for example, are quite inadequate, but in this large center we could combine fifteen schools into a library, the potential of which would be considerably greater than that of the small school. Furthermore, we could combine the resources the community has allotted for adult library facilities with those allotted to the public schools. That would mean the resources of fifteen schools and perhaps three small libraries combined into a super library.

Given this notion of using other resources, we can begin to talk about health services, legal aid, youth activities, golden-age programs, job corps. Without any new legislation, various government agency programs which the schools have almost completely ignored could be utilized. Proponents of the education park have discussed the new relationship of this educational center to the community. It is for the entire community, not just young people. The efforts of various agencies that offer services, monies, etc., can be coordinated, becoming powerful programs for the community in terms of adult activities.

Furthermore, young people would have the opportunity to become involved in a great variety of activities within their own center. In our schools we now offer young people obsolete occupational programs. However, a Golden Age Center immediately adjacent to or within the learning center as well as the other community agencies I suggested, would mean that, in addition to the so-called academic work, high school youngsters could spend part of their day working within these other social institutions. In terms of strategy, it would be impossible for any suburban school system to compete with that kind of an education program. There is power in young people being able to deal with this complexity of agencies, services, and people. Strategically, we have a chance to involve suburban school systems in our educational plan when we begin to offer programs like these.

Urban planners often speak about the educational park in relation to physical environment, and there is a negative reaction from some, the point being that there is too great a reliance upon the physical. When David Lewis made a presentation at a conference held by the education department on the educational dimensions of the Model Cities program, there was this reaction. Like it or not, the physical environment determines which activities are possible. Therefore, Lewis is suggesting that we can create a new environment on a scale that permits doing all that I have suggested. I desperately need his grand environments in order to develop grand educational programs.

In the Civil Rights Commission report, the latter part of the "Remedy" chapter presents the education park as the way to achieve an integrated educational program as well as a great education. Most feasibility studies regarding the need to desegregate education, after indicating which procedures will be used to desegregate, end by stating that the new situation will include quality integrated education. They do very little in the way of discussing how this can be obtained. The Civil Rights Commission report departed from that in that it discussed possible educational experiences, problems that would develop, and how to go about answering those problems.

The first problem that the report discussed is the question of size. John Fisher, president of Columbia Teachers College, was asked to write a position paper addressed to this question. He indicated that there is no need to be concerned that people will lose their identity because 15,000 people are brought together in one facility. Identity is what we do with the people when they are there; it is not that size in itself must necessarily force the child, teacher, and others to lose their individuality. Therefore, Fisher suggests small-unit subdivisions. After bringing children together to achieve a good mix, we can easily divide students into units of 500, 300, or 25, whatever we decide is important for children to feel a sense of identity, and we can do the same with teachers, administrators, and other personnel.

Dan Lortie, who wrote a position paper on the role of the teacher in the education park, told us that teachers' needs can be served. Critics have frequently cried out that if only the teachers were better, all our problems would be solved. Yet teachers operate within the context of what the school has to offer, and at present they are tremendously harassed. We need a new institution that will free them. It would be possible to develop resources within the education park that would be exclusively for teachers. Those of you who have had experience in the schools know that it is very difficult for a teacher to find the space to operate as a professional. Given the resources that this new center could provide, there could be a building exclusively devoted to the professional activities that teachers need in order to be better prepared to meet the needs of young people. This is very difficult to achieve in the small school.

In-service training programs could be developed in a large center that are limited only by the extent of our ideas. It is very difficult to achieve a good mix in a school with twenty-five teachers, but a center with a large number of teachers would present the opportunity for an in-service program that could be superior to anything that a great university could develop. All of the teachers would be located in a central area, and world-famous experts could be employed. In a center of many teachers, for example, it would be feasible to employ a Jerome Bruner to spend considerable time helping teachers improve their program. Though there might be an initial reluctance to be part of a large center, since so much could be offered to help teachers grow professionally, and since there would be small subunits within the large center, we felt that teachers would participate.

As to the question of grouping, large schools resegregate. The Evanston High School is a development of the education park notion in that four schools are subunits of a total high school unit. Yet it has resegregated in terms of ability groups. John Goodlad, a proponent of new notions with regard to grouping students, prepared a position paper. He told us that many so-called "ability" groupings have no educational basis but are developed for administrative convenience. He explained that it is possible to group students of different levels, teach reading, and at the same time serve other needs that schools have.

I think that, however clever we might be with regard to groups, given the past experiences our young children have had, it is inevitable that some form of grouping will separate children. We concluded that we will never obtain what our educational enterprise has to offer until we reorganize for individualized attention. When a child enters school, he and his parents must know that any educational activity that is not ultimately organized to serve him as an individual will be gravely limited.

Two constraints exist as long as we are oriented to the group's progress: the amount of time and the number of methods that will be used with children. If the child hasn't learned by the time these two constraints are played out, we say he has failed. (We even have tests to prove that he does not have the intelligence.) If one has appendicitis and needs surgery, the doctor doesn't group him with thirty others explaining that the typical operation takes two hours and there are a set number of methods he will use. He does not indicate that some will not come through, some will do very well, and most will do fairly well. We accept individualized attention for the medical profession, and I maintain that we can accept it in education as well. We can teach any child if we are willing to expend the time and vary the methods.

I am suggesting that ultimately, the educational program must be organized so as to serve each individual. Two more position papers in the

Civil Rights Commission report are addressed to this. We have always had the resources to provide individualized attention for students, but we did not have the technology. Now we do have the technology to organize, administer, and program educational activities in schools for individualized attention. Once every child in the school is identified and a program is developed for him, we can decide if that program will be carried out in large, medium, or small groups, or individually. In any case, it will develop out of attention to his specific educational needs, and the final two papers discuss new available technologies – most of which are based on computer-based systems.

Reaction and Reconsideration

Though many of the recommendations for change and improvement suggested during the discussions on education pertained to Chicago schools specifically, the majority of problems and issues raised face every urban school system in the country. Much of the problem was seen as related to a lack of constructive attitudes toward the use of available resources. Education parks and the need for fundamental changes in the educational system were also a major consideration.

Financing and Planning

Although we are facing many problems in Mississippi, you threw me for a loop when I heard about the Chicago situation. [teacher from Mississippi]

Not only are we not spending enough in inner-city schools in comparison with other large cities but we should be spending more than the suburbs, not half as much. We should be spending $12,000 to $15,000 per child instead of about $500 as we now are. We should, and to some extent do, employ every possible community resource but, in order to improve the quality of education in the inner city, we must also assess the latest technological advances, increase the number of textbooks per year per child, and restrict the pupil-teacher ratio, ideally so that class size would be limited to about eight or ten. [administrator in Chicago school system]

To a great extent the problems in the educational system are economic ones – the powers that be operate in terms of making do with the least amount of money possible. [teacher]

Administrators of public programs such as principals have a great deal of latitude that they are not using. [social worker from out-of-state]

In addition to there not being sufficient resources available, in many cases those which are available are inadequately used. [teacher in Chicago school]

What can be done to help children receive a better education, given the limited resources available? [community mental health worker]

Special Programs

What could be done to insure the effectiveness of the Head Start program? [community worker]

Changes in the first three years of public school are necessary if the input of Head Start is to be maximized. [sociologist]

At this point, school boards, etc. are not working on the follow-through but in light of its importance, everything possible should be done toward this end. [teacher]

Contact between Head Start and public school teachers is one way to instigate the continuation of benefits from preschool experiences. [faculty member from the Department of Education]

One of the common problems with after school programs is that the children do not want to attend. One reason my daughter did not want to attend was that she had the same teacher during the day. Since she could not learn from her between nine and three, how could she be expected to from three to five? As for the teachers, I am surprised to hear that in Chicago, they must be coerced to stay for after-school programs. Where I come from, teachers want to stay from three to five to make the extra money. [teacher from out-of-state]

With regard to Title I and money being spent on after-school programs, the council of which I was a member was advocating concentrating educational funds on the regular school day when all or most of the students are present. If the teachers are inadequate, the real cutting edge lies in the school system set-ing up programs to make them more effective. [school principal]

The problem of children not wanting to participate or stay in school begins in kindergarten when public schools first fail to give the child an opportunity to say what he wants to say and do what he wants to do. In order to find ways to get children to want to stay in school, we must look at who controls who. The child must control the teacher in the sense that the teacher should be reacting to the child. This requires a deep familiarity with and concern for the child and his social situation. [teacher in a preschool program]

We know this is not usually the case. For example, a Ph.D. dissertation on a school in Chicago revealed that while the teachers thought most of the students were on ADC, in fact only 22% were. [former school administrator]

Textbooks

How many of the books used in slum schools are integrated texts? [participant from a neighborhood center]

Each year more and more are being used. At first publishers did not see the necessity or desirability of producing these books, but their attitude has changed within the past two years. [school administrator]

Many communities are demanding that integrated texts be used; what are administrators doing about increasing their use in the schools? [participant from a community organization]

The situation is a very complex one which sometimes involves a legal question. According to the law, new books can only be adopted once every four years and no school can order books that are not on the official list of approved books. Attempts are successfully being made to change the law so books can be adopted more frequently. [school administrator]

In view of the experimental nature of many of these books, how free are public school people to adopt them? [theology student]

More red tape than necessary is involved. [school administrator]

The use of integrated texts is only one way to promote meaningful social change which is necessary if education is to contribute to breaking the poverty cycle. However, ghetto communities cannot do this on their own. For example, there must be some meaningful changes in the freedom that individual principals have in deciding which texts are used in their schools. As a result of the rule that this choice is up to the principal, integrated texts are increasingly being used in ghetto schools but this will not necessarily be the case in all-white schools. Furthermore, while Negro students are learning about the Negro contribution, this is omitted from what white students are learning. This can only serve to widen the gap between races and set the stage for future conflicts. [leader of a local community organization]

One way to attack this is by including contributions from minority groups in all approved texts. Principals are increasingly realizing their responsibilities in this regard and this will probably happen eventually. [school administrator]

It is important to evaluate the effects of integrated texts to be sure they were worth fighting for. Has there been any feedback from teachers or students on the effects of using them? [mental health worker]

Although parents seem to appreciate their use, very little has been heard from either teachers or students. I think the impact is there, but they are not verbalizing it, at least not through official channels. [school administrator]

The difficulty in verbalizing is important in itself. Furthermore, although the color of skin has changed, the context of the material has remained middle class and thus the contents of these books still is not relevant to these children. What can be done by administrators, community-active people, and others to influence publishers to make the basic changes that are necessary? [participant from a private, national social agency]

We have to remember that the real world includes both the ghetto and the middle class, not one or the other alone. [educator]

It is difficult to find people who are competent and interested to write these books. [former parochial school teacher]

In our school we are using a new approach for developing texts. Starting with pictures of their own community, students in grades one through six make up stories about everyday situations which interest them. By writing and reading them, they are not only working with material based on their own experiences and interests, but are also learning to write and read their own language first. [elementary school principal]

Student Promotions and Failures

Are children who are not up to grade average promoted? [community worker]

In the school where I work, over 40% of the children in third-grade are more than one full grade behind and, by the time they are in sixth grade, almost 68% are at least one full grade behind in their reading and mathematics scores. [community organizer]

Children are promoted whether or not they meet the standards in all Chicago schools. This is particularly the case in the first three grades when there is the "continuous development program" in which no child is failed before reaching the third year. Though this is supposedly an innovative program, despite changes in terminology, such as "failures" being referred to as "retainees," there is nothing significantly different about it. [teacher]

Though one of the teachers here said she thinks children are emotionally secure when they repeat familiar work, in my experience many of these children are extremely emotionally disturbed. [mother working with elementary school children]

What does it mean to a child when you tell him that he has failed, especially at the beginning of his school years; what damage can this do to him in the long run? [sociologist]

Teachers have a great deal of leeway in interpreting standards. Although this has a positive aspect, in light of the minimum of supervision, it often results in more demanding teachers failing students who might be passed by other teachers. [high school teacher]

With regard to high school students, I question the presumption that the standards set should be the same for all students, regardless of their background. For example, if a Negro child does not speak like he is white, he is presumed to be defective. [community organizer in a citywide group]

In my experience many of the parents become upset when they are told their child was retained because he was not working up to his ability. We have to start considering whether children should be passed or educated. [community agency staff member]

I agree the question which needs to be addressed is not so much one of passing or failing but of what can be done so that a child passes? And if he fails, will there be changes to enable him to meet the demanded standards? To simply keep a child back is purely punitive and will not in itself contribute to his improvement. [public school teacher]

The teacher's concern should be with assessing the child's capacity and helping him learn to that capacity by motivating him and placing him in situations where he can achieve. [sociologist]

Holding Power of the Schools

Has the schools' holding power increased as a result of new texts, programs, etc? [participant from a state board of vocational education]

What is currently being done in high schools is not conceived in terms of the students' perspectives, does not meet their needs as they see them, and thus does not hold them. The high schools on Chicago's West Side graduate only 30% of their students. [discussant familiar with high school vocational programs]

Apprenticeship programs seem to have greater holding power than the high schools. Our program started with less than 100 and has been built up to the point where now some 300 are involved at various stages. During the year of operation, there have been only 64 dropouts. I think the program's greater success is due to its being a service rather than an educational program. Though the youngsters are not paid, the program focuses not only on increasing the youngster's knowledge about the trade but also on developing their interest in it. The services are basically motivational and a concentrated effort is made to deal with personal problems which keep these young men as active recruits for apprenticeship. [director of vocational programs for a private agency]

If high schools are to increase their holding power, they must move in a new direction. Perhaps instead of concentrating academic studies in the first two years and training in trade skills in the second two years, this order should be reversed. [participant from a state board of vocational education]

Vocational Training

Perhaps academic studies and vocational training could be "mixed" rather than separated. These youngsters need job counseling at the beginning of high school rather than after they are out of school. [mother active in community programs]

When the child is in the eighth grade, his parents are contacted to discuss possible educational programs. [vocational education administrator]

Courses in home economics and machine shop were removed from the school curriculum in one school I know about when it became all Negro, even though there were industrial arts shops and home economics facilities in the building. [the mother active in community programs]

I know this happens but it is due to the overcrowding which results from the great increase in school population and staffing problems. [vocational education administrator]

How many teachers and principals in the vocational and commercial trade areas come from the industry and how many shops are being closed because they cannot get staff? Why should a skilled and experienced person have to return to teacher's college for education courses? [high school teacher]

To my knowledge, every trade shop and drafting room in the city is staffed with a competent person. However, I agree that there are shortages which is probably due to the fact that, though trade teachers can be used in the third and fourth years, those teaching in the first and second years must have a bachelor's degree as well as other qualifications, and it is difficult to interest these people in teaching. [vocational education administrator]

Can the building trades guarantee a man the opportunity to obtain the skill he needs to become a journeyman? [participant doing job placement in a settlement house]

If he complies with the available program. [discussant from the Building Trades Council]

What is the proportion of Negroes and Spanish-speaking participants in these programs? [teacher]

Out of 2,400 apprentices in the building trades in Chicago, 130 are Negro and 20 are Spanish-speaking. In one vocational high school out of a total of 1,000 to 1,500 enrolled in apprenticeship programs, 138 are "minority youth," and 125 of them Negro. [vocational education administrator]

Do the building trades guarantee employment which in itself would serve as a motivating factor? [participant doing job placement]

Employment can be guaranteed to the maximum of eight hours, but since the men are journeymen, they must be prepared to carry their marketable skills wherever they are needed. Their security is their skill and their mobility. [council member]

We must also consider the fact that these youngsters will be competing in a racist economy, and if they really understand the situation, not much can be done to build their trust in those who are supposedly offering them the opportunity to become journeymen. [counselor in a settlement house]

Do all who complete the program receive journeymen's cards? [teacher]

Yes. [vocational education administrator]

The Teacher's Voice

Have the teachers in Chicago ever gone on strike against the inadequacies of the school system here? [teacher from out-of-state]

No! The teachers' union in this city has been nothing more than an extension of the Board of Education. If it were not for an insistant group within the union at the present time, there would not have been even the threat of a strike. [member of Chicago Teachers' Union]

The union does not support teachers who speak out against the school system. However, for the most part, the teachers do not speak out against the school system because they seem to think money is the most important thing. [teacher and union member]

We have heard some teachers' criticisms of the school system which are serious indictments. That other teachers are not interested in striking seems to indicate their lack of dedication to teaching and their strong interest in money-getting. [community leader]

It is significant that some teachers do want to be heard. The tragedy is that within the schools there is no way open for communicating their distress with school administration procedures and school administrators. Teachers should be encouraged by the head of the school system to openly express their views in faculty meetings, formally or informally, or these festering sores will surely continue. It is healthy for a school if teachers meet together and express their opinions. Principals should be encouraged to see the importance of teachers being able to express themselves as one step in improving education for children. [school administrator]

Attempts have been made to get principals to work with teachers rather than use fear and intimidation to control them. Despite some success, in my experience a major obstacle has been that teachers seem to give even higher priority than principals to the pressures put upon them. [teacher]

For most principals in the Chicago system, it is of the utmost importance not to let anything seem to be problematic. Furthermore, in most cases it is taken as a reflection on the teacher if, for example, his students do not pass, and most teachers cannot stand that. It appears that both principals and teachers want rewards from the system, and the way to get them is by appearing successful, whether in running a school or in educating children. Consequently, problems are hidden, children are passed before they are ready, etc. [teacher]

Though I am not satisfied with the way the union is functioning, it is the only vehicle for expressing teachers' feelings and having them considered. [teacher and union member]

This is a problem in all schools, not just those in the inner city. [teacher in a suburban school]

School Administration

Are the superintendent's actions controlled by the Board of Education? [community leader]

Yes, but the Mayor appoints the Board, and various groups and ideologies must be represented. [School Board member]

Despite the recent appointment of a new Superintendent of Schools, the subordinates are the same as those under the former superintendent, and there has not been one substantive change in Board policy. This is due either to outside forces that were preventing the new Superintendent from implementing changes or to his subordinates who are the ones really in control. How can the internal problems of the Board's administrative structure be dealt with to improve its effectiveness in supporting rather than destroying those few administrators who are attempting innovative and constructive approaches to education? [community organizer]

Though I agree that nothing of real significance has happened yet, there is a slightly different climate. Despite the mess he inherited, the new Superintendent does want to do an honest job, but his time is running out. The Board plans to make a thoroughgoing study of the school system's administration. Though they expect to make some very drastic recommendations for change, I do not know whether or not they will be adopted. [School Board member]

The Board of Education seems to be pretty efficient when viewed in terms of political control of people. Those who explicitly or implicitly say they seek cooperation with the Board of Education while pointing out its ineptitude imply this when they say they have to rely on the political and business spheres for influence. How can effective cooperation be expected from institutions that would be working against their own interests? Since controls are so tight, it might be necessary to take a more direct approach and go elsewhere for assistance. [settlement house staff member]

Progress and change depend not on research but on strengthening the Movement in the city. We must continue to ask for things we cannot get because if we stopped asking, we would be sending the message to the power structure that we are not even watching them. [leader in a citywide organization]

Instead of criticizing administrators, we have to focus on developing strength given the processes available. We need to organize the political power we have and we need to develop more political power in order to obtain the ends that we want. Votes are the big stick you carry when you go to politicians. [School Board member]

Are there any plans to develop this "big stick" among community people to put on the pressure in support of the drastic administrative changes which supposedly will be suggested by the research consultants? [Community psychologist]

I do not know of any such action that has been taken, but I think it would be a good idea. If the school system is to be made effective, a vast reorganization will be necessary, and I would give top priority to decentralization. [School Board member]

Since a liberal, bottom-up program poses a threat to the power structure, the most feasible way to promote it is by working through that structure. [worker in an antipoverty program]

We must accept the fact that segregated schools exist and get down to dealing with the issues. We know what is going on and do not need more research, which becomes an end rather than a means. Segregated schools could become quality schools and the focus must be on what kind of education they should offer and who is teaching. [settlement house worker]

Changes in the system will have to insure that administrators will no longer be able to pass the buck, that they will be forced to listen to the voice of the people. [community organizer]

It is important to recognize that the people they are listening to, if they are listening at all, are not saying what you want said, and those who are saying what you want said do not have the numbers behind them to make what they say important to those who make the decisions. [School Board member]

In view of the facts that there is a real crisis in the social situation and that education must play an important role in dealing with it, why do Northern Boards of Education take so long to do what we all know is right? [leader of a community organization]

One of the problems is that administrators in the public school system have not figured out who they are working for. They must be ready to say to students and parents, "Here we are; what can we do for you?" [social worker]

What goes on in a school depends on the principal and faculty there, and thus there are wide variations. [school administrator]

The Professional and the Community

There was general agreement that the attitude of professionals, including administrators and teachers, toward students and education in general accounted for much that was wrong in the educational system today.

Why aren't professionals offering the kind of help needed from them? [state mental health worker]

Professionals set themselves apart from and above the parents and community people with whom they are working. If they do not even speak to us, how can they speak for us? [community leader]

Though they might say they want to work with us, in a sense they want us to work for them. They approach us as if what they say is law. It is important for professionals to support the parents in the community and abide by the ground rules set by them. [community leader]

Many professionals, including teachers, seem to be ready to get involved but need to develop confidence in and rapport with the community. They must be able to tell parents, "I can do a lot but you have to help me." Instead of starting with a kindergarten class, start with a group of parents of children in kindergarten. Ask them what they want you to do with their children and then do it. I do not think that this approach would cost any more than what is now being spent on unsuccessful approaches. [social worker]

With regard to the question raised earlier of how to insure the continuation of the positive effects of preschool educational programs such as Head Start through parent involvement, community organizations should help parents get involved in the public school system which would put them in a position to follow through with their children. [teacher]

Efforts along these lines have not worked in the past. [community organizer]

It is difficult to open lines of communication between parents and teachers despite parents' efforts and appeals to the Superintendent. Letters go unanswered and there is a general lack of familiarity with the local situation on the part of Board of Education administrators who do not even visit the schools. [president of a community organization]

Although the system is responsible for what is going on in the schools, it is important to realize that many parents are not aware of the situation in which their children are placed each day. For example, many do not know that their children are coerced by threats of spanking; many do not understand the testing program or the "levels of achievement," etc. Furthermore, the PTA seems to be merely an extension of the Board of Education and allows for only very limited action. In one school, the principal was supported by the Board of Education's own rules when he decided to refuse certain parents their right to come into the school as members of the PTA. Though he said he wanted a PTA, he also said the parents were not sophisticated enough. The PTA has been barred from functioning in the school because of its activities in the community, and the PTA State President has supported the school's position on this. We must find a way to let parents know what is going on in the schools, and they will not find out by sipping tea and eating cookies at 1:30 in the afternoon. They must come into the schools and see for themselves. Parents are not apathetic – they are interested in Johnny, but they are turned back when they try to find a way to help. [PTA president]

Teacher-parent relationships in our school are very different from those described for Chicago. In PTA meetings, the importance of knowing how to get along with those working within the school system is stressed. Once a good president gets appointed, and parents get through to her, and she gets through to the principal, many things can happen. This was our approach. Politicking which gets to be politricking has to be used until something can be done to change the existing set-up. This has to be changed but such changes can only be achieved at the national level. [teacher from a southern state]

Some PTAs in Chicago are achieving some degree of success. [community worker]

It is important for parents to stick to their guns and not just resign. Parent organizations are very important. In our school, many of the parents were not willing to organize, so we solicited the help of community people, which proved to be a workable alternative. [parent from out-of-state]

Education Parks

What do you think of having 15,000 children together in one primary school? [social scientist]

I can see no reason why it could not work if the campus was large enough and the units small enough. Furthermore, any model, experimental school would be a strategy in itself. Just as many white as Negro children would be bussed there, and it is already known that many parents are willing to send their children long distances to parochial and private schools because they think they will receive a better education than if they attended their local school. Since parents are willing to do this, any school which offers something other schools do not will function as a deliberate strategy, pressuring other schools to improve and incorporate its special features. [school administrator]

I agree, but the main problem with that approach is it is too slow. [proponent of the education park]

What are the specific advantages of the education park as compared to, for example, the Evanston plan? [community worker]

A very important aspect of the Evanston plan was its involvement of the total community which is not the case in most other attempts to integrate schools. However, Negro and white students do not come together as equals in Evanston because the school was not located to avoid discrimination with regard to which racial groups must take busses to school. [discussant who worked with the U.S. Commission on Civil Rights]

An educational park can soon achieve the same stigma for those children who will have to go back to the ghetto. [community organizer]

Of course, problems such as these will have to be faced, and the first and foremost concern must be to address the problem of racial isolation. The Commission could find no evidence that any ghetto school had really worked. [discussant who had worked with the U.S. Commission on Civil Rights]

In an attempt to evaluate some of the specific gains that could be achieved from an education park, participants presented various other examples of attempts to improve the quality of education.

One Chicago school which is located in a ghetto area has excellent facilities, teachers, and virtually all else that is recommended to provide for quality education. However, the problem remains that it is segregated which, I think, accounts for its lack of success in improving the effect of education on the students there. [former school administrator]

In the Banneker School in St. Louis, despite all community efforts and changes in role expectations on the part of teachers and parents, the children in that school still have the lowest achievement scores in the city. I think this is due to their being isolated and not involved with the total community. Likewise, the problem of providing equal education in Chicago cannot be solved without a metropolitan plan. [proponent of the educational park]

In the case of I.S. 201 in New York, the people in the community took charge of their own educational destiny, which in itself is important. Not only does it affect self-image, it puts you in a position to make your own decisions instead of having them made by some abstract bureaucracy that does not know who you are. [community organizer]

I do not think the Negro students at I.S. 201 are being prepared for the larger society in which they will be forced to find a place. What they are learning is applicable only in that isolated situation. The New York educational plans cannot be totally successful as long as there is more than one. [proponent of the education park]

Integration is an ultimate goal, but in light of my primary function, which is educating the children in our school, I can not wait for integration. My immediate concern must be to provide those youngsters with the most suitable condition for participation in an educational program. In my experience, I have found that, if a school functions in certain ways, the right staff will be attracted to it. I do admit that ghetto schools face difficulties when competing with suburban schools for certified teachers. Many of the suburban schools have long waiting lists of teachers, but the principal must take the first on the list. He can only reject that teacher on the basis of inadequacies observed in the classroom. Unless the principal can prove that the teacher is inadequate, he must keep him, even if that teacher is not conducting the class as the principal would like him to. Our school has a secret weapon. Since most of the teachers are unassigned, coming to me on the basis of a friend's recommendation or the like, and because they do not have tenure, I have the option of rejecting any teacher that does not suit me. As a result, I have a hand-picked staff. And still, 65% of the teachers in our school are fully certified and assigned, and we have no vacancies for September. [principal of a ghetto school]

In Chicago, 65% certification does not indicate a fair allocation of teachers. [educator]

I do not consider most of the so-called "certified" teachers in suburban schools qualified to teach in our school. The teachers in our school who are not certified are proving themselves in the classroom even if they have not passed the exam and are not considered qualified to teach in the suburban schools. Although the teachers in our school must try to get certified, certification in itself does not prove someone is a good or better teacher. [principal of a ghetto school]

As far as I am concerned, this approach to inner-city education relies on the hope that there will be good principals and that things will improve. Since even good principals cannot do their job given the present structure, they must put the pressure on superintendents and the School Board if there are to be significant changes in the structure of the education system. As long as they are not allowed to say, "I've got to do my job the best I can," they do not have to face the real issues. Any action-oriented group must accept the fact that you have to forego certain things for today in order to get what you ultimately want. Given a system like Chicago's which is spending about $400 million a year, a system with 20,000 teachers and 550 administrators, there could be a far more equitable allocation of resources, both in money and personnel. We should work toward setting up the institutionalized procedures whereby this can be achieved. I'll just give two examples to illustrate the kinds of inequalities that pervade the present system. First, it is well known that teachers have the right to transfer schools and that the majority of teachers in ghetto schools are not certified. Furthermore, schools in middle-class Chicago communities have long waiting lists of teachers wanting to transfer into them. Despite the limitations of the system of certification, we must depend on it to select those people who we believe will be better for our students. Second, the principal with a long waiting list of teachers does have options that the principal in the slum neighborhood does not have. In the process of trying to provide teachers for all his classrooms, it is well known that frequently the principal in the ghetto school has to eliminate adjustment services, a gym teacher, or a library, in order to place someone else in the classroom. Though we should never pull back from a position of doing everything possible to improve teachers and assist principals, at the same time we have to build certain guarantees into the institutional character of the school system in order to insure that available resources are allocated equitably. The only way I know for achieving this is to make sure that the educational program of the ghetto child is locked into the educational program of the middle-class child. Thus we must make sure that we have integrated educational programs whereby we can begin to get at least some guarantees that the ghetto child will share in the goods a big city system can offer. [proponent of the education park]

Even in good ghetto schools, children cannot read when they go into the classroom and they cannot read when they get out. [discussant]

This is true to a degree, but IQs, medians, and the like are often misleading. If we look at our achievement in relation to IQ, we are on the same level, and in one area of reading, we are above the IQ level. [principal in a ghetto school]

The previous school superintendent concluded that since the closest relationship between IQ and achievement was found in ghetto schools, the Chicago school system was doing its best job in those schools. The Hauser Report made the error of measuring both IQ and achievement with the same ruler which of course leads to the conclusion that they are pretty close together. Whatever flaws there are in the Coleman Report, it clarifies the fact that, among other things, children are going into and coming out of these schools without knowing how to read. When reading achievement, instead of so-called "ability," is taken as the indicator, it is evident that we are doing the worst job in these schools. [discussant]

Posing a grand solution such as the education park is the wrong end of the stick. I agree that the ghetto has to go out of American life, but the approach which will do most to eliminate the ghetto must be one that works from the inside out. [social worker]

Many problems would continue even if, or because, children would be attending an integrated school while living in segregated ghetto areas. [community organizer]

The education park is no panacea – life in and out of school must be considered together. [teacher in a predominantly Negro high school]

Integration itself would not necessarily have the positive effects predicted; perhaps the conflicts that would arise from children being in an integrated situation during the day and in the ghetto after school would prove to be too paradoxical and traumatic in terms of self-image and identification. [community leader]

One can never predict the problems that will result from a revolutionary situation. The children are the key concern, and although the ghetto is a sick social situation which breeds problems not only for those living in it but for the total society, as long as children receive a meaningful, individualized education, they will be better off even if they have to stay in the ghetto than if they are thrown into a very unrealistic, autocratic oligarchy. [community leader]

These problems will have to be dealt with even if an education park is built. We live in a racist society, and if we are prepared to divide into two segments, then we can talk in terms of developing two separate educational programs moving in similar directions. On the other hand, if we intend to work toward an integrated society, then at the same time as we develop educational programs, we must do everything possible toward that end. [proponent of the education park]

How can this dream, even if it is a good one, be made a reality? Integration may be more feasible through housing than through education. [community organizer]

I am amazed at how good people are willing to settle for so little, so quickly. If you look to where the power is, when decisions are made, those activities get carried out for the most part. It is necessary to get aligned with the power structure to get what you want, and it is possible to find ways to work together, serve each other, and get things done. The only alternative is revolution, overturning the establishment, which I do not think we expect to happen. [proponent of the education park]

Since black people are asserting themselves and attempting to gain control of their own schools, perhaps the concept of an education park is a rationalized reaction, based on racism, to keep that control from them. [community worker]

The way bigots avoid the educational park idea is one indication that this is not what is happening. Whatever the educational destiny of America, all children should have their equal share. [proponent of the education park]

That is misleading. Education does not necessarily result in control as evidenced by the position of the Negro middle class today. [community organizer]

The middle-class world is no more real than the ghetto world. [community organizer]

The goal of the education park seems to lie within the larger white society. [Negro parent and critic of the education park]

I disagree with the assumption that the two goals of education are to socialize youngsters and to perpetuate the society. Education has been perpetuating the society that a large group of people want; this keeps certain people in a particular state of ignorance and non-knowledge. We need to look for a way to restructure society so that it is fulfilling for everybody, whether or not everybody wants that to be the case. [community organizer]

Members of minority groups need to know the value of being people, and in an integrated school the differences between groups may be lost along with the appreciation of their culture. It is important to maintain the differences between groups while doing away with the inequalities of the present system. [community organization staff member]

A lot must be done and immediately because black children are consistently being destroyed. In existing segregated situations, students' achievement scores would go up and their sense of worth would increase if their community had some power over its destiny. [community worker involved with educational problems]

We have enough trouble trying to get parent involvement in neighborhood schools; how could you get it in an educational park? [staff member of a regional government agency]

The larger size of an education park could make that more difficult, but ways to maximize parental involvement could be built in from the very beginning. The concept is so broad that almost anything is possible; we would have to talk about a totally new kind of administration. Individualized attention means that community adults and young people will have to be employed. Furthermore, the other activities and agencies that would operate in that center mean that it would not be just a school for children but a community learning center. Community people would be going there for a variety of activities which would result in a kind and extent of involvement that we have never yet been able to achieve. The education park only provides possibilities; we would still have to work to achieve our goals. Involving community people could be very easy; we just have not done it. [proponent of the education park]

The question asked poses a major problem and that is not an adequate answer. Parents prefer having their children in a school within walking distance from their home, although, because of the importance of integration, we may have to change our ideas on this. In any case, achieving parental involvement in schools that are not nearby will be just that much more difficult. We do not want either a single center or to maintain the status quo. We need a compromise between the ideal of complete social integration and the ideal of local responsibility and participation. This will involve a considerable use of the neighborhood school for younger children with some expansion of its function along the lines suggested by advocates of the education park. We also have to think in terms of relating the local elementary schools to a larger unit to get as much advantage as possible from integration while recognizing psychological and practical considerations. [community leader]

The Need for Fundamental Changes

Given the present situation, is it possible to make any real changes in education? [community leader]

The big issue for 1967 is who should control the Negro's Peter Rabbi and the white man's Shakespeare? Though I agree that what is needed i organization in Negro communities, I do not want to orient the Move ment around capturing the white man's curriculum. It is necessary t produce an alternative to participation in a racist system and involvemen in power politics with the establishment. [civil rights worker]

It is even more important that the community has the power t decide which direction it will take, even if the direction it chooses i becoming a part of this society. With regard to education, the communit should determine the curriculum and who the administrators and teache will be. [public school teacher]

Nobody is saying, "fit into the status quo," but I am not sure tha we want to throw out 200 years of progress because of current problem It is not necessary to forsake the entire school system because we hav not been getting the kind of education we want. We must effect som meaningful changes in it. We have helped to create this society, if onl by our passivity, and we all agree on the need for change; but I do nc think separation and destruction are the ways to achieve the desire changes. We must use the techniques and tools that other ethnic grou have found successful. Furthermore, we need to understand how to us power in order to get whatever it is that we want in the school system and I would set top priority on a curriculum that meets our need [community leader]

How do you think agreement and cooperation between communit organizations can be achieved? [director of a citizen's council]

I doubt that there has been sufficient meaningful communicatio between community organizations to warrant the assumption that w cannot get together. There has been agreement on major issues. In orde to achieve fuller cooperation, a specific issue must be pinpointed, an each community must take whatever action it sees as desirable. If w start at the same point, a citywide federation of black people's organiz tions moving on the same issue eventually will develop. Though this ma take a long time, if it happens, then you will see power beginning t generate. [community leader]

Suggestions made here for effecting change in the Chicago publ school system have been too conservative. Changes can not be effected long as you play the game by their rules. You have to make them pla by your rules. I am wondering how a young child would feel if he hea us talking about problems in the schools in the tone we are. I think v ought to be angry about the present situation. Instead of appealing t the Board of Education, community people must look for ways to u the power they have and thereby put pressure on the Board to comp with what the community wants. The better white communities do n have any more formal power than we have in the black community, b they know how to use their informal power to get what they wan Anger is cooled out of children by the schools. I want my child to sta a little angry so the causes for his anger can be removed. We must try to get these children to believe in themselves instead of relying on teachers to stimulate them. [social worker]

PART 3

Major Developments in
the Field of Housing

17

Housing Programs and Discrimination

JOHN McKNIGHT

The United States Commission on Civil Rights has been concerned that federally supported housing programs be designed and utilized to decrease urban residential segregation. Therefore, I have been asked to describe the various kinds of federally supported housing programs and how they might be utilized to nondiscriminatory ends.

When talking about these programs, most of us in the federal government say too much about basically unimportant details without describing adequately the essential elements. Thus we do not convey the message. Therefore, we are going to take the risk of telling you about the essential elements while leaving out the details. If you are interested in these housing programs, I am sure that you will get the details.

Basically, we want to discuss the low- and moderate-income housing programs which are federally supported and require nondiscrimination. First, several things must be said about most of these programs. In our national dynamic, there has to be a special reason for the federal government to become involved in the housing field. The essential reason for this involvement is that, presently, the private market is not structured or, under existing law, able to deal effectively with the problem of providing adequate standard housing for city people who have moderate and low incomes. That is almost a given under our present system. The federal government becomes involved because the private market is not. That is not to say that we could not change our legal structure so that the private market, instead of the federal government, could be providing adequate housing in the inner city. Indeed, there is considerable Congressional interest in various plans to involve the private market in this area.

Since the federal government is directly involved, it must very carefully define programs that do not interfere with the private real estate industry. Therefore, federal programs may sound extremely obtuse to you — as if they involve some very special and contrived controls and requirements. This is frequently because the program was built on the premise that it could not threaten the private market.

Second, it should be made clear that the availability and nature of these federal programs at the local level are controlled by the local elected government. Generally, there can not be any federally supported housing programs in a community until the local governing body adopts a "workable program." A workable program is a plan submitted by a local government to the federal government. It says that the locality agrees to do seven things in return for which it will be eligible for federal housing programs. Rather than enumerate those seven things, let's just say they relate to the development of the capacity to engage in community planning. Thus, the local community is assuring the federal government that it will engage in community planning and guarantee that the federal money will not be used on a particular program which will be negated by a lack of planning for everything that is around it.

A workable program must be approved by the local government before it is submitted to the federal government. About 95% of Chicago's suburban governments have not adopted a workable program. Therefore, these communities cannot develop any federally supported middle- or low-income housing programs. The workable program is the key that opens the door. If a community does not have that key, the door is closed to all the programs that follow.

The workable program includes one requirement of particular interest to us. It is that community participation in the development of the community plan is required. A community advisory committee must be established and must have a subcommittee on minority group housing. If you have a workable program in your community, you might be interested in seeing how the minority group housing subcommittee is operating and how the community advisory committee is involving minority group interests in the planning process.

Public Housing Authorities

A local Housing Authority is the entity that the City Council usually establishes as the community's recipient of federal funds for low income housing. We usually think that the only thing that a Housing Authority does is what we will call "new construction." The Housing Authority directly supervises, controls, designs, and establishes the type of public housing which will be built.

However, there are two other possibilities that are not so well known. There is a program called "turnkey" housing. Rather than the local government completely controlling, designing, and building typical public housing, turnkey allows the local Housing Authority to purchase and rehabilitate existing structures and use them for people who are eligible for public housing. They may also contract for the purchase of a unit which somebody else plans to build, or contract for land on which a developer will build a structure which the Authority will buy when it is completed.

"Turnkey" means that an existing unit, in the control of either a developer, a builder, or an owner, is sold to the Housing Authority. The "key" is "turned" over to the Housing Authority.

The second program is called leased housing, which means that the local Housing Authority is authorized to lease apartments in existing units to people eligible for public housing. When we think about public housing, we usually consider only new construction. In fact, it is possible to do with public housing what can be done with private housing – build, buy, or rent (lease). It is very important to be aware of these three possibilities. The most appropriate alternative should be utilized. The Commission is concerned that these choices be made so as to eliminate discrimination and promote desegregation.

Not-for-Profit Corporations

There is another series of federal housing programs that are actuated not by local housing authorities but through local not-for-profit corporations. These not-for-profit corporations could be developed from nucleus groups such as the boards of settlement houses, industrial associations, local unions, local churches, church federations, and community organizations. There are three particular programs that local not-for-profit corporations may be especially interested in.

The first is "221d3." 221d3 allows you to build or buy and rehabilitate buildings in order to provide what is called moderate-income housing. Though there are exceptions, most of these buildings must have five or more contiguous units. In large cities, the land cost is such that a seventy or eighty-unit building is frequently necessary because until there are that many units on a piece of land, the cost per unit is not low enough to meet the standards of the Act.

Generally speaking, 221d3 allows a not-for-profit corporation to build new or buy and rehabilitate with a loan which is provided through FHA. There is no down payment and a long-term loan is provided at 3% interest. The FHA will say that these operations should not be entered into, however, without some "seed money" to cover the original costs.

In order for the 221d3 building to be built, or bought and rehabilitated, by the not-for-profit corporation, help may be needed from lawyers, architects, land planners, engineers, building managers, and financiers. The federal government does not provide this help. Therefore, a not-for-profit corporation composed of church people will have to do all of this on their own or seek the aid of commercial developers or "packagers" who can help and make some money providing the service.

Once the 221d3 structure is completed, people who are judged to have a moderate income are eligible to live in it. These standards vary from one community to another. As an example of the standard, in Chicago the maximum income for one person in a 221d3 structure is $6,000; for two it is $7,250; for three or four it is $8,550, and for five or six it is $9,850. In general, these standards for maximum income are considerably above the maximum for public housing.

From the point of view of most not-for-profit corporations, 221d3 presents some very real problems as a social instrument. In essence, the federal government will insist on controlling occupancy, rent, and tenant income. The FHA oversees a 221d3 structure in a way that will control the maximum rental, limit the number of occupants per apartment, and set maximum incomes for tenants.

The second possibility for a not-for-profit corporation is a new program called 221h. It allows a not-for-profit corporations to buy five or more single-family units which do not have to be contiguous, rehabilitate them with an FHA loan that is no-down payment, long term, 3% interest, and then resell them to people whose income meets public housing standards. In essence, the loan received by the not-for-profit corporation to buy and rehabilitate the home is directly transferred to an individual with an income low enough to qualify him for public housing. This program has outstanding potential in those cities where ghetto families live in five and six unit wooden structures. Often, tenants in these properties are renting from a large holder of these properties. The not-for-profit corporation can often buy these deteriorated structures from the holder, rehabilitate them, and sell the homes back to those who were previously renting them but at a monthly mortgage payment less than the rent used to be. Thus, the corporation can often provide renters of deteriorated homes to become purchasers of decent homes at less monthly cost.

"Rent supplement" is the third significant possibility for a not-for-profit corporation. Funding for this program has been very limited by Congress. Basically, the rent supplement program allows the not-for-profit corporation to build, or buy and rehabilitate, a building or buildings of five or more contiguous units. While the loan is for no-down payment and a long-term, unlike the 221d3 program, it is a market-rate 6% loan. When the building is ready, an arrangement is made with the federal FHA, rather than the local Public Housing Authority, on how many units in the building will be rented to people whose income makes them eligible for public housing. Not all, or even most of the tenants must be public housing eligible – although the building must always house some people in this income bracket.

In a rent supplement structure, the FHA says to the not-for-profit corporation, you, not the local Housing Authority, select the tenants in- cluding some public housing eligible people who will pay 25% of their in- come in rent. The FHA will pay the corporation everything over that up to a maximum of about $50 a month. For example, if the rent on a unit is $150 per month, and the income of the man who lives in it is $400 a month, he pays one-fourth of his income or $100 a month toward the rent. Each month the FHA will send a check to the owner for the $50 difference.

One of the advantages of a rent supplement structure is that if the income of tenants eligible for public housing increases such that they are no longer eligible, they do not have to move out of the building. They can remain and pay the regular rent. In a 221d3 or public housing structure, if one's income increases beyond the maximum income level, the family has to move out.

It should be noted that the rent supplement program is meagerly funded and little used. For example, there are no rent supplement structures in Chicago.

Code Enforcement Areas

Finally, you all know about federally supported urban renewal programs. There is now a new program called Code Enforcement Program. A Code Enforcement area is designated by a local government and, if accepted by the federal government, given special treatment in the same way as an urban renewal area. However, the area receives intensive housing code enforcement rather than major clearance. The federal government helps finance this code enforcement on a matching basis by putting in much of the money to get code enforcers into the area, process the paperwork, and help move the housing courts along. The federal government attempts to do everything possible to begin to upgrade a neighborhood by providing a foundation of basic property maintenance at minimum code level.

Many cities can no longer afford, financially or politically, clearance-type urban renewal. However, cities can cover many more neighborhoods for less money with the Code Enforcement Program. As this program develops in old neighborhoods, people in these areas will begin to feel the bite as code enforcement pressures owner-occupants to upgrade their property. To alleviate this financial pressure, there are two potential benefits that go along with the Code Enforcement Program.

First, there is the Section 115 grant. If a code enforcer finds someone who owns a house and is in the poverty income group, Section 115 declares that person is entitled to an outright grant of $1500 to bring his building up to code. Not many urban people would be in that condition, except for the possibility of retired people who might have an actual income of less than $3,000 and own a building.

The second benefit in a Code Enforcement Area is the Section 312 loan. If a person's income is above the poverty level, or if there is enough code work so that a poverty income owner needs more than $1500, either person is eligible for a Section 312 loan to bring the building up to, but not beyond, minimum code requirements. The Section 312 loan is a 3%, long-term, no-down payment loan which is certainly the best rate available anywhere.

18

Housing and Urban Renewal

PHILIP HAUSER

I will speak on housing and urban renewal in historical perspective. Government is now concerned with both but, in general, most of our urban plant, including residential housing, has been produced through the operation of the free market. The free market has determined where and when individual units were erected in the city and has, in the main, determined housing patterns. To be sure, the free market always was supplemented by government regulations and provisions. Construction codes and zoning appeared early in the history of our urban areas. But I think it is correct to say that many aspects of housing codes were honored in their breach throughout most of the history of our cities. They were not enforced nor, for a variety of reasons, could they be enforced.

In general, the operation of the free market was largely responsible for determining land-use patterns and population distribution; and it produced by far the highest mass level of living for Americans that any people has enjoyed in the history of man. However, the operation of free market also produced problems. It precipitated the slum which became an international disgrace. Though I do not have time to elaborate, it precipitated the slum primarily because, in our system of free enterprise, profit can be made out of slums. It is possible that new slums are still being generated as rapidly as urban renewal and public housing are eliminating the old slums. Throughout most of these United States, it is still profitable to have slums, and I suspect it is safe to say that we will be generating slums until we develop and implement policies that would take the profits out of slums.

With that historical overview, I will try to provide another quick perspective. My second point is that public housing and urban renewal are relatively recent programs. To my mind, they represent the determination of the American people to clean up the mess created in the rush to get where we are. A partial explanation of slum formation and the degeneration of the inner city is to be found in the very rapid rates of population growth and the exceedingly rapid construction of our urban plants. Furthermore, frictions in the operation of the free market frequently resulted in the construction of an urban plant without regard to the general welfare, even though the developments were consistent with private property rights.

Being a relatively new policy, it is not very surprising that the programs

234

which have emerged, public housing on the one hand, and a general urban renewal on the other hand, have been accompanied by many major mistakes. Though the federal government did not plan it this way, in effect, its programs in the entire housing and urban renewal field have made it easy for middle-class, higher-income, white populations to live in suburbs and flee the central cities. It has also frozen low income, disproportionately Negro populations in inner cities into segregated public housing projects which are massive monuments to human stupidity and cupidity. If you want to see an example, observe South State Street.

The third point I want to make is that although the programs are relatively new the mistakes are already being recognized. It is heartening to know that new perspectives are emerging which may result in new policies and new programs. These new programs may make more sense than what we as a nation have done to date in public housing and with at least some aspects of urban renewal.

Next I should like to focus on urban renewal as such. In my judgment as a sociologist, the single main deficiency in urban renewal policy and program has been the extent to which it has been preoccupied with *physical* planning and renewal. In years to come, urban renewal policy will be supplemented by a policy which has not yet emerged. It is one which I think reflects the status of the development of our civilization with respect to housing and of community development in general. Our culture has demonstrated its competence to build an urban plant and to bulldoze and rebuild it once it has deteriorated, but we have yet to demonstrate that we are competent to maintain an urban plant once we have built it. I think "urban maintenance" will become a major program which perhaps will make it lucrative for financial organizations and the construction industry to have as much activity in renovation, modernization, and maintenance as they now do in new construction.

To return to my main point, the greatest deficiency of urban renewal has been its concentration and focus on physical renewal. It is becoming increasingly clear that a physical plan, without regard to the social, economic, and even the political, may create at least as many problems as it resolves. It does little good to bulldoze the inner slums and erect public housing when, under public housing regulations, we, while creating better physical quarters for families, also create the most abnormal types of social communities. Moreover, urban renewal is carried out by an urban renewal administration operating as a separate principality. It is not fully integrated with the other basic aspects of urban living, namely education and the public schools, welfare, safety and security, recreation, and other public services. Thus, I repeat, urban renewal has created as many problems as it has resolved.

In Woodlawn, for example, there is little advantage to a better physical plant if it does not simultaneously get public schools with the resources and competence to educate the Woodlawn youngsters, giving them the basic, saleable, and citizenship skills that would enable them to assume the obligations and rights of American citizenship. It would be of little avail for Woodlawn to get new houses if, in addition to education, there are not also training or re-training programs for people too far down the line to be affected by public schools, so that they can achieve an adequate and steady income flow.

There must be some income maintenance either through labor-intensive work suited to the limited skills which these people by reason of their pathetic share of American life actually possess, or by forms of welfare other than the inadequate and indeed ridiculous ones represented by ADC. Let me say that among other things, I think ADC is designed to prevent the Negro family from ever coming together again. This is the only industrial nation in the world which does not have a family allowance plan which would be a much more effective form of maintaining income flow among the poor, white or Negro, than any of the forms of welfare we now possess.

I can conclude by observing that any fundamental consideration of housing and urban renewal must be in the context of the community and its problems. Unfortunately, in our society, again largely by reason of the play of the free market, we have slums that are not only deteriorated physically but also represent tremendous human and social problems. As a civilization, we will accomplish little if we attack only one facet of the problem, namely the physical problem. We cannot continue to ignore, but must fully integrate and coordinate, the general approach necessary to enable the deteriorated communities in this nation to take their rightful place and assume the full obligations and rights of American citizenship.

Perhaps that is a sufficient introductory diatribe, and hopefully my colleagues here will be more helpful in putting things together for you.

JACK MELTZER

Let me briefly share with you some of the issues that I think are involved in refashioning many of the programs under discussion.

It seems to me that two main points are being made by this panel. First, there is the need to retain an historical perspective which recognizes that programs do not have lives unto themselves. This is to say that we should not develop chauvinistic attachments to urban renewal, public housing, or any other public program. What we need to address is the usefulness or lack of usefulness of these program opportunities.

From this vantage point, programs require assessment in terms of the degree to which they are serving that part of our population which needs societal reinforcement, or demand shifts in their environmental impact, or basic changes in our political responses. In other words, we should avoid special loyalties or identifications with any program as it exists or has existed. Those who are associated with these programs should recognize this fact and avoid the build-up of resistances associated with excessive identification with existing program structure. This is an important point because our core purpose ought to be the enhancement of our capacity to deal with problems, and indicated changes should flow in response to experience.

Second, we are increasingly recognizing that we have to reconcile two historical threads in the approach to city problems. There is a social welfare thread. As has already been pointed out, throughout history there have been people who were concerned with tenements and housing conditions, and a long series of public actions, codes, ordinances, etc. have been tied to the social welfare response to city problems.

Concurrent with this thread, there has been another largely environmental thread which has viewed problems in relation to the physical environment. This latter thread has been concerned with zoning and with the early forms of slum clearance. These two threads are now being reconciled, although we are in the early stages of reconciliation. At some point in time, the threads will become indivisible, related in the ways that Professor Hauser has described.

It seems to me that this is what our panel has been discussing, and it raises a whole series of specific questions in my mind. We are all concerned with doing more than paying lip service to urban problems, but I have a hunch that to make progress, one starts by paying lip service. That is, after we verbalize our concern, we can discover where to go from there. At this point, we are only at the threshold of this process.

Clearly, there are a variety of dimensions in which we could examine public programs. We could do so in programmatic, administrative, and political terms for instance. Yet we all know that, in order to progress, we will have to relate all these dimensions, each of which in their own right create added problems. It is very difficult, for example, to talk about solutions to housing or school problems within current political jurisdictions.

We have to do more than pay the usual deference to the "need for metropolitan government." In order to solve certain problems in the inner city, we must recognize their relation to the outer city. We will have to deal with this fact and not delude ourselves on this score. Even if overstated, I would say that no mayor of any major city, no matter how well-intentioned, has the capacity to resolve most problems that he faces within the city in the light of current rigid and artificial governmental jurisdictions.

Now I recognize that there may be merit to small jurisdictions as is frequently claimed by those who fight any metropolitan response, as reflected, for example, in the urge for suburban identification. If such merit exists however, it should exist in the central city as well. In other words, I think there is a clear relationship between the defense of local jurisdiction outside the central city, and the demand for neighborhood and community identification within the city. In the central city we call it community organization and community areas; in the metropolitan universe, we call it suburbs and village government, as if these were different.

Similarly, I think we have to reconcile the notion of "status quo" and "open city." Many programs, including urban renewal, have been used to reinforce the status quo, not with malice but in response to emotionally charged words such as, to prevent the flight of the whites, and to stabilize, conserve, and prevent population out-migration. On the other hand, we are greatly concerned with enhancing mobility, accelerating change, and with an open society. I think we have to begin reconciling these terms and issues, and avoid the conflict among alternative program purposes.

On a more technical level, which also concerns me with my practitioner background, if there are relationships between human needs and environment, what is the character of those relationships? How does one begin to devise a plan which grows out of a concern with "people" or to use my colleagues' phrase, with "social needs?" How is a plan prepared today with this purpose uppermost, different from the one prepared yesterday without this purpose paramount?

A series of other questions could be elaborated, but in the final analysis, it seems to me that in a variety of ways, we are moving toward diminishing the importance of housing and toward an approach which views housing not as an independent factor, but as a critical tool in a larger program with overriding social and economic purposes. Thus if as a society, we seek to enhance the mobility of population, we will adapt housing activities to achieve this purpose, rather than viewing housing (and related activities) as end programs in their own right.

ERWIN SALK

As the only banker on this panel, they sat me on the right. I don't know whether or not this is significant, but I think it is only fair to say that my university training was at the University of Chicago.

I am here as a mortgage banker. Mortgage bankers are very actively engaged in working out financing for properties, not only in Chicago, but throughout the United States; however, it is important to clarify a major point. A mortgage banker functions as a conduit, if you will, seeking out and recommending investments for the funds of insurance companies, banks, pension funds, savings and loan associations, and other similar organizations. We are not the direct and primary source of funds. We can only make loans based on the policies of the financial institutions who control the funds. However, we do have a responsibility to counsel and advise these institutions as to what should be matters of major importance for consideration; not that they will necessary take our advice; nor do all mortgage bankers as yet recognize this as one of their responsibilities.

I have been asked to address myself specifically to the social, political, and economic obstacles in securing financing and in purchasing or rehabilitating property in inner-city areas as well as what has been or can be done to alleviate these obstacles. This is not easy to do in ten minutes or so, especially for businessmen who come directly to the point after perhaps two hours of negotiations.

I will not be discussing the source of funds per se, even though this, I realize, is a most important consideration. However, I am reminded of a story where a rather large contribution was offered to a major religious order from a gambling casino. There was considerable debate as to whether or not to accept this gift. It was finally decided in favor of acceptance on the grounds that it was brought by the Devil but sent by God. In solving urban problems on housing, we are not primarily concerned with the source of funds – as long as they are available.

There are a number of dimensions – perhaps philosophical concepts – that are very seldom raised, either in the business, religious, academic and even, if you will, in civil rights-oriented communities. I will attempt to briefly raise some of these for your consideration. I believe they represent some of the social, political, and economic obstacles in securing financing. First and foremost is that a problem has absolutely no relationship to what one likes or dislikes. This is fundamental in the business community, in application to business problems. Businessmen tend to forget this when they talk about social problems and they tend to forget the direct relationship between social and economic problems.

Another important point is that virtually no consideration is given to what builds the strongest basis for a healthy society. As already touched upon, business, for example, as well as other sectors of our community has never established the fundamental, inescapable relationship between business and social matters. I cannot see how any business can plan without paying full attention, not only to the existence, but also to the solution of social problems since social stability is essential for sound economic development. I sometimes feel that I am the only banker on LaSalle Street whose actions are directed towards preserving our system. In so many instances the actions or inactions of the business community seem to be directed towards the destruction of this system, even though not necessarily on a *conscious level.*

We business leaders are considered extremely important in our society and we owe our society the obligation of reciprocity. We are expected to create new dimensions in thought and action and provide leadership in solving problems. If our business community does not provide leadership and direction in seeking solutions of both social and economic problems on a realistic and practical basis, then we are abdicating our responsibilities, have no basis for tardy complaints, and must live with the consequences of our inaction.

Another very fundamental point that affects every range of our community – government, business, religious, academic – is that very few people or institutions understand the nature of social change or, if you will, social revolution. Social change and/or social revolution is not something one is in favor of or against, but it is essential to understand what is going on throughout our own community and elsewhere. This may sound strange coming from a banker but, unfortunately, in our country we have come to equate the understanding of a social problem and/or social change and social revolution with being in favor of the problem or the change.

Unfortunately, the same thing happens when you try to discuss, with the business community as well as others, these social problems, these social changes, and the economics thereof. As aforementioned, these questions are totally irrelevant to what we are for or against. I cannot emphasize too strongly, as I mentioned above, that this is an important dimension – social change occurs whether we are in favor of it or not. The business community must recognize that whatever their preferences, we will never again live in the world of Wilson, Roosevelt, Truman, Eisenhower, Kennedy. That was the world of yesterday. We can only live in the world of today and plan, as we do in the business community, for the world of tomorrow. If we awaken in the morning to find that our inventory is obsolete, we have no choice but to get a new inventory. We can cry, tear our hair, beat our heads against the wall, but we must get a new and saleable inventory. The same thing pertains when social change occurs.

Another important question to which I have alluded but which has not been thoroughly enough examined, is what constitutes the true strength of our society. Has our concern been too much with material concepts? wholeheartedly agree with Phil Hauser's comment that, in urban renewal, we primarily emphasize the physical plant development without full consideration of the people who will live within the physical plant. There is only one major resource which fundamentally represents the true strength of any society, and that is the human resource. Our true strength does not lie in the number of bombs we possess, the size of our destructive arsenal, the number of our soldiers, nor even in the number of autos per capita, the miles of highways, the kilowatt hours of electricity we produce. Our true strength is basically in our human resources – the physical, economic emotional, and educational well-being of our citizenry.

The weakness of our country lies in not providing the opportunity for every individual to develop his growth potential to the maximum. Whenever an American is excluded from these opportunities, our community and our country suffer. Our society as a whole is then deprived of its maximum growth potential and is susceptible to decay and destruction, as has happened to great civilizations in the past. When this occurs, then you and I as well as public and private coffers are robbed of their rightful due and are not maximizing our potential growth.

We have learned well to spend billions for destruction, but in comparison spend virtually pennies for construction. We prepare for destructive efforts like giants and for building of a good and great society like pygmies

We must ask ourselves time and again – do we have a great society or an aimless society?

I have been asked about funds for housing. I am on the board of the Chicago Conference on Religion and Race, and we have employment office which cannot get funds because the poverty program is being cut. Yet in talking about housing, people fail to relate the spending of $80 billion year on war and defense with not having sufficient funds for urban development and all of the accompanying unsolved problems. Certainly many of you have seen statements to the effect that $125 billion would be sufficient to tear down all the slums in the United States and replace same with new housing. This is not a great deal. It used to be a two-year federal budget, and now it is a one-year federal budget. If we have these commitments to destructive efforts, we will not and cannot have funds to develop our country. Many businessmen are becoming concerned about this as they slowly realize that if necessary, the world can manage economically in trade, development, and so forth, without the United States. It may not sound as if I am talking directly about the urban problem, but if we thought about it we would know that we must get to root causes in order to find solutions. I am often surprised that more mayors are not more vocal on this subject since they cannot get the federal funds to enable them to carry out their responsibilities, vis-a-vis, their cities.

In any problem, there is too much planning and decision making in downtown offices and not enough conferences in the ghetto areas and with the people themselves. Fannon, in *The Wretched of the Earth,* cynically points out that, "If you think you can manage a country without letting the people interfere, if you think the people upset the game, slowing it down by their mere presence, or sabotaging it by their natural ignorance, then you must not hesitate to keep the people out." Obviously, you cannot keep the people out, but so many of our discussions about bulldozing the West Side, clearing 31st Street, etc., hardly take into consideration what the people want or what happens to them.

In the final analysis, most social change occurs when the people finally insist on change. There never has been a historical instance where social change has resulted from a legislative body saying, "Yes, it is good. It is time to pass this" — whether it was the right of women to vote, the eight-hour day, or whatever struggle; social change only came about after the people decided, worked, and acted to achieve it. I do not think we should be afraid of people. I think their instincts are basically good.

As I pointed out, the business community, and the religious community as well, never have thought in terms of the relationship between the social and the economic, and I think this must be done. The old-fashioned, pioneer frontier spirit has dominated our thinking without taking cognizance of the debilitating effects. Many of the people who rush out to the suburbs do not realize that inner-city problems do not stop at Harlem Avenue or Howard Street. You cannot run to Barrington to escape the effects of the city. Many people fail to see that what is happening within the city is very much like a cancer inside the human body. The Outer Drive and the development of 75 acres of air rights on the lake might result in a healthy looking facade, but if the gut is being eaten away by a cancer, the results can only be economic and social ruin.

We have had some success in getting downtown bankers and industrialists to think in terms of the totality of their investments in the city and what can happen to these investments if we do not take care of social problems.

The banking groups and savings and loan associations have talked about setting up a fund of some $20 million to buy FHA loans for rehabilitation on Chicago's West Side. The stymie to this has turned out to be how to bring the people who need these loans together with the source of funds. It appears that one of the biggest problems is how to develop the conduits.

As referred to above, the business community is by far not the only sector that has been derelict in their understanding and action – so have the religious and academic circles. It is only within the last couple of months that there has been some recognition in religious circles that they must speak strongly to their local congregations in the all-white, noncontiguous areas. It is true they have all filed their amicus briefs with the courts but were all intimidated by their local congregations. They were afraid to talk to them, pound the pulpit, and say, "You cannot buy fire insurance here anymore."

Of course, there is .the problem here in Chicago of where we can place public housing or other types of low-income housing without the approval of the local alderman. Consequently, we have a continued environment of discouragement. We not only have ghettos by color, but economic and cultural segregation as well. There is almost a new concept that, "black and white together, we will stand against the poor." I am not convinced that the basic problem is whether we build high-rise or low-rise, but that unless we have these total environments of encouragement for people, then the finest or worst facade will not alleviate the environment of discouragement.

In closing let me just touch on a couple of additional problems. Our firm has been very active in the FHA 221d3 program, having, for example, financed all the Kate Maremont Foundation rehabilitation projects. One of the problems that we have encountered is with the land costs – how to justify the low-income apartment structure against the land-cost structure of the North Side, far West Side, far South Side. If we are forced to restrict these types of developments to the environment of discouragement which I mentioned, we will have new housing, but not a new humanity.

Another problem is in terms of being able to take over certain buildings and being able to procure enough funds from the FHA for both the purchase of the building and for the rehabilitation or the tearing down of the building for a new structure. This is created by perhaps an existing first mortgage which leaves an additional financial burden on the existing structure.

The question of sources of money, whether for the seed money or for the final money is, of course, fundamental. There is little question that there are sufficient funds available in our nation, providing we are able to think in terms of national priorities on needs – a subject long overdue for examination.

I realize there are many points which we have not had time to cover. If you will indulge me, I will conclude with a little story which I think points up one aspect of our dilemma of understanding. In 1948 I was a general observer to the UN General Assembly in Paris. At that time, Senator Austin was our representative. There was a debate on the partition of Palestine, and Austin pounded the table saying, "We must get the Jews and the Arabs to sit down and settle this problem in a true Christian fashion."

19

Public Housing

HAROLD BARON

If the order of speaking is such that we start with a critic of the Chicago Housing Authority, followed by one of its administrators, Mr. Humphrey, I might as well get in my licks first. In order to be brief, I will just touch on a number of points which I think are essential to comprehending the nature and effect of public housing. Hopefully, if some of these prove interesting or controversial we will discuss them later at greater length.

Since I see several of my friends from the Public Housing Authority here, let me start with one disclaimer. I am not talking about the individual intent of those who administer the housing program which I think is fairly irrelevant to the points I will make. I am talking about the effects of the total system and am not attacking individuals working in that system.

Because I am an historian, I always make my ‘ audiences go back in history with me. As an historian, I am amazed when I read the speeches of public housing proponents in the 1930's or even the early 1940's, and when I talk to people who were in public housing during that period. In the 1930's, public housing was more a movement than an institution. It was envisioned as the great solution to urban problems. Its enthusiasts saw it combating slums and delinquency. They thought it would provide an instrumentality for upward mobility, a waystation out of poverty. Many of the people who went into the public housing movement were crusaders who considered it a tremendous instrument of social change.

The public housing system, as it exists today in this city and in most other large modern cities, is no longer an instrument of social change, but has become an integral part in the making of racism into an urban institution. I think the questions we must ask are: What accounts for this change, and what lessons does it have for today's crusaders? I often ask myself if everything we in the civil rights movement are working toward now will turn out like public housing. Will it turn out that after we win what we seemingly want, its effects will not be those that were intended?

We of the Urban League have studied the nature and development of the Chicago public housing system, and there seem to be three periods in its development. There was the early period of the crusade. Though there had been some state-sponsored public housing in the earlier 1930's, the big

243

beginning was with the first federal Public Housing Act that appeared in 1937. The New Deal objective was to replace the slums, give people decent housing, and change the environment. World War II brought about the second phase. Public housing became an instrument for meeting manpower needs. It was built for war workers to be near war plants. In the third phase, Chicago's public housing was to become a virtually Negro institution, forming an integral part of the web of urban racism.

Let us look at how questions of race were handled in these different phases, because this is such a key issue in the nature of the public housing system today. Some 142,000 persons live in Chicago Housing Authority facilities. Roughly, 4,000 of them are elderly persons. Of this 142,000, 90% are nonwhite and 97% of the nonwhites in Chicago are Negro. This means that about 125,000 Negroes in Chicago live in public housing, or approximately one-eighth of Chicago's Negro population. The Negroes in public housing are effectively segregated – 90% of them living in projects that are 90% or more Negro. Therefore, I want to trace the thread of race, historically.

In the first period of public housing that aimed at slum clearance, the rule was to maintain the racial composition of the area. When you tore down buildings, you maintained the exact racial ratio that existed before. Where white slums were removed there were white projects, where Negro slums were removed, there were Negro projects. On the land on which the first Jane Addams homes were built, there had been forty Negro families; and forty Negro families, plus or minus two, lived in this project over a ten-year period. During this period, the construction of any public housing for Negroes was considered a race victory.

Then during the war, workers were needed, and some public housing projects were built on vacant land to provide quarters for them. Altgeld homes in the far south part of Chicago was constructed specifically for Negro war workers. During the first two phases, the system was basically for low-income whites with a Jim Crow section for Negroes. It was mainly made up of all-white projects, but there were some all-Negro projects plus a handful in mixed neighborhoods that maintained the preexisting Negro-white ratio. This situation prevailed into the postwar era as long as housing was at a great premium.

Then between 1948 and 1955 several things happened. One, the housing shortage in the city decreased, at least for whites. Middle-income housing in all-white suburbs was built with large government subsidies in FHA and VA mortgages. This relieved much of the housing deficit for whites. The government then subsidized expressways so that the suburbanites could get to work. Two, in this period, a great number of urban renewal programs came into being. With uncanny uniformity, they were located in Negro neighborhoods. This situation led to the commonplace that "urban renewal is Negro removal." Government action in this case was adding to the deficit of housing for Negroes. Public housing began to function as a place where people who were displaced by urban renewal and expressways could be moved. Instead of functioning to eliminate the slums or meet wartime manpower needs, it became the catch basin for Negroes dislocated by the process of rebuilding the city and making it accessible to suburbanites' automobiles.

In every major city, urban renewal has generally functioned around influential institutions which sought to upgrade the surrounding neighborhood by removing real or potential slums. We have seen this occur around the University of Chicago, the Michael Reese-IIT complex, and the downtown area. The primary thrust of urban renewal has not been a housing thrust, but an effort to save certain large prestigious institutions through changing their environment. For Negroes, urban renewal has been a thrust out of their homes. Public housing has provided a safety valve for urban renewal by taking in many of these dispossessed. The Chicago Housing Authority has been scrupulous in seeing to it that this safety valve function did not diminish the effectiveness of the ghetto boundaries. In Chicago prior to 1950, some public housing sites were located in Negro areas, but in fact, most were in white areas. From 1950 on, of some thirty-three sites that had been proposed by the Chicago Housing Authority, thirty-two were proposed in predominately Negro neighborhoods. In other words, between about 1949 and 1955, public housing changed from an institution that eradicated the slums and served the poor in general to an institution for Negroes.

By the way, one of the most fantastic political fights in the history of Chicago was between the City Council and the Chicago Housing Authority over the latter's suggestion that some public housing be located on vacant land in white areas. The City Council said no, and Miss Elizabeth Wood, who was then head of the CHA, was forced to resign. Since then, the CHA has not proposed housing outside the ghetto.

When the Chicago Housing Authority became a Negro institution, other features of public housing also changed. The style and design of public housing shifted. Prior to 1950, there were many row-house and garden-type public housing buildings, with proportionately few high rises. There were no seventeen- to twenty-story buildings. The projects were more scattered. After the transition, the buildings got higher and the size of the projects got greater, such as in developments that extend some five miles along State Street. They grew into tremendous concentrations of public housing, with dense land usage and high ratios of persons per acre. The effect was that Negroes who were dislocated from some portions of the ghetto by urban renewal or highway construction were relocated in very compact areas within other ghetto sites. In other words, the public housing development pattern reinforced the distinct separation of white and Negro residences. The ghetto lines were made tighter.

Given the operations of the over-all system of northern racism, this intensified public school segregation and employment segregation. Obviously, if you make the residential boundaries between Negro and white sharper, with a neighborhood school policy there will be an increase in educational segregation. If you restrict Negroes to housing within the ghetto at the time the jobs are moving further and further away from the ghetto, you eliminate Negroes from many of the jobs.

Further, because of these large concentrations of people in vast projects with high-rise buildings, there was a great destruction of social relations. Except for a few churches, virtually every existing institution, every line of familial and personal stability, and every semblance of formal and informal organization was cleared out and had to be started over again. It is like going into the wilderness. Those chosen to go had little means, came in large numbers, and were treated like outcasts. Under these conditions, public housing creates a great burden upon municipal services. For example, it puts a strain on the schools when all at once Robert Taylor Homes are opened up for 20,000 persons. It is especially trying when there are hardly any other institutions around to assist and give support.

I have tried to sketch how the pattern of public housing development in our city has fitted into the over-all web of racism and the various subsystems that make up that total system. One other point I would like to make is that something happens within the housing complexes themselves. The physical design and the style of management in high rises intensify the pressures from the outside. Isolation and anonymity are reinforced.

When I have visited the various housing projects, I have noticed a great deal more social interaction in the row houses. People know their neighbors and a certain amount of local leadership is possible. This is diminished in the high rises. There a huge, impersonal system is providing shelter for a large number of persons who are at the bottom of the social ladder. They are tucked in these housing projects behind the color curtain, and they are at the lowest income levels. Thus, when a family gets on its feet, very often because of income ceilings it can no longer stay in public housing and provide stability and leadership. Once you earn enough money you have to move out. The Chicago Housing Authority has concentrated together the vulnerable targets to be at the receiving end of American racism.

Finally, we should look at the manner in which the residents in public housing are treated by the large, impersonal administration. There are two important distinctions between obtaining services from the standard housing market and obtaining services from the public housing administration. The purchaser or user of services in public housing lacks, first, effective alternatives and, second, an independent power or ability to influence decisions in the society at large.

People who own and manage housing in the private sector treat their tenants as clients. Obviously a real estate management firm tries to please its clients, otherwise they will move. However, within the public housing sphere, the tenants do not have much of an alternative. People who live in public housing perceive their alternative as going back to rats, roaches, and fires. At least the housing projects are fireproof and do not have rats and roaches. Not having a real alternative of withdrawing their patronage, they are treated not as clients receiving a service and sought after by the management authority, but as wards of the management authority.

The lack of independent power can be seen in contrast to the manner in which the Federal Housing Administration operates. The Federal Housing Administration acts as an intermediary in the mortgage market guaranteeing home loans. The Administration seeks out the real estate brokers, developers, and mortgage brokers. FHA is hypersolicitous to the needs, requirements, and demands of the politically powerful housing industry. In effect, FHA sees itself as part of the industry with the private sector as its clients.

In contra-distinction, the local public housing authorities at best operate as benevolent and paternal colonial administrations. They operate on a one-way street — from the top down. The tenants do not have the power to affect significantly the operation of the public agency. Accordingly, their status is one of being wards rather than independent agents. The tenants' alternatives are about nil, and in such a situation a reaction of frustration and hostility can be expected.

Therefore, there are intense social problems within the large public housing projects. Not only are the tenants segregated, not only are they at the bottom of the income ladder, but they are constantly at the receiving end of this big, impersonal, administrative structure. They feel hopeless, helpless, and totally manipulated.

C. E. HUMPHREY

Since I was asked to talk about the physical, social, and economic problems in public housing in fifteen minutes, I will restrict myself to some facts as I see them today.

As most of you know, the Public Housing Program started in 1937. The program's objectives were to provide decent, safe, and sanitary housing for families of low income; to help clear slums and blight; and to aid residents in elevating their standards of living and developing their talents. Since that time, the Chicago Housing Authority has cleared slightly more than 900 acres of slum land and developed it with about 33,000 dwelling units. Of these, 10,000 are walk-ups. About 3,500 of those completed were designed specifically for housing elderly families.

Despite what some might say, the developments have always been well below the zoning requirements of the neighborhood. The number of units in the project as well as the type of construction have been based on the maximum government allocation per housing unit. I would like to mention that, since long before my time, there has been a government regulation which says that the cost cannot exceed X dollars per dwelling unit. You are faced with this unit cost whether it is a one- or five-bedroom unit.

During the early work in the Housing Authority, most of the units were one- or two-bedroom and predominantly two-bedroom. About the time the Taylor Homes were built, larger three- and four-bedroom units were needed to balance the program, which is still not balanced. Today a low-income family that applies for public housing, needing a one- or two-bedroom unit, and willing to locate in any available facility, can have a housing unit within a few months, whereas the family that needs a three- or four-bedroom unit has to wait for two or three years. Statistically, a family that wants a five-bedroom unit would have to wait thirty-five years.

In connection with the construction of public housing, we are authorized to provide ten square feet of community space for each dwelling unit built. This community space cannot be operated by the Chicago Housing Authority or any other housing authority but must be turned over to a public or private agency which operates a program. Though we are not supposed to, in several places we have had to operate elderly programs because we could not get other agencies to operate them.

At the present time, we have about 1,900 units under construction, most of which are for the elderly. We have 2,500 units in the design and land-purchase stage. In addition, we have about 1,650 under contract with the federal government, for which we do not have sites because the federal government recently increased the cost limitation. As soon as this was done, we revised our programs to place less units on a site, cut down building heights, and build more walk-up units. As a result, we need new space for the 1,650 units we have under contract.

Last year, after a three-year demonstration conducted by CHA on the leasing of apartments in private buildings, we received an allocation for 500 units, about 400 of which are now under lease. In this case, the housing authority leases the unit from the owner of the building and then subleases it to a low-income tenant. Nearly all these units are occupied by elderly families and are efficiency and one-bedroom units. One reason for this is that, in Chicago, the primary vacancy rate in standard units is in efficiency and one-bedroom units. In fact, they approach a 3% vacancy rate. According to federal government regulations, where the vacancy rate is less than 3%, the only units that can be leased are substandard units which have been brought up to standard.

As you know, in this particular program, like any other program, it takes quite awhile before people realize that we might have something here. We have been working on it, and now have enough people who want to participate in the program. Therefore, we are preparing the necessary data to add one thousand units to the leasing program, which I think everyone favors.

As for the social end of public housing, we want to house a cross section of the lowest one-third income group. Presently, about 143,000 people live in Chicago's public housing, of which 93,000 are under twenty-one years old. There is an average of 4.4 persons per family and of 2.9 minors per family. Several types of families are housed in public housing: there are 12,400 normal families; 11,300 broken families; 1,500 are childless, nonelderly; 7,400 are elderly. As for their source of income, 15,300 families are self-supporting, 6,400 are on ADC, and the remaining 10,900 or so are either on Social Security, Veterans' benefit, old-age, blind, unemployed, or general assistance.

The racial occupancy in public housing today is 12% white and 88% non-white. In the elderly program, there are 52% white and 48% non-white. This is obviously because the influx of Negroes into Chicago is primarily of younger people, and there are not many elderly Negro families. Though two or three years ago we received almost no applications for elderly Negro families, now we receive nearly the same number of applications from Negroes and whites.

As far as the community relations end of our program is concerned, CHA has always considered it basic to the operation of good public housing program to provide tenants with opportunities to improve their living standards and their potential, and to participate in community activities. To accomplish this, we have over seventy community and tenant relation aids on our staff who, along with other management personnel, help organize and coordinate work in the various programs. This involves over fifty public and private social welfare agencies operating in 97 CHA locations. They occupy all our authorized community space, and we have converted 260 large apartments to make more community space available.

Of course we start all our programs, both outside and inside, with an orientation of our tenants. They are taught how to take care of their houses, how to clean the floors, wash the walls, de-ice the refrigerator, use the range, and so forth. Anyone who quickly passes the test does not have to continue, but those who do not receive help from our own people as well as outside agencies that we call in. Only about ten families per year are put out of public housing because of poor housekeeping; and usually there are additional, very serious reasons for giving up on them.

There are homemaking programs at four locations run by the Board of Education, the University of Illinois Extension Service, and private agencies. The Board of Education operates health services in twelve of our fourteen management operations, and we have programs run by the TB Institute, the Red Cross, Planned Parenthood, and the like.

We have given space in one building to the Illinois State Employment Service so they can talk to the people living in the projects. We give them the names of people who by our records are unemployed, and they call in prospective employers to interview these people. Last year they placed about 500 people, who were on welfare, in skilled and semiskilled jobs.

We have preschool training in all our programs. About 2,000 people who are having trouble in school are in the tutoring program. They are assisted by approximately 1,000 high school and college volunteers as well as housewives, career girls, and some organizations such as Montgomery Ward, Illinois Bell Telephone, and others. Last summer in our Neighborhood Youth Corps, we employed about 150 high school and college youngsters. Now we have about 150 on a year-around basis who are school dropouts and learn to operate switchboards, do filing, general clerical work, stock clerking, and the like. The Chicago Housing Authority is the largest single institution in the nation that sponsors a scouting program. We have over 200 troops and 1,260 leaders who are tenants in the projects. There are 4,000 boys and 1,700 girls in scouting who live in public housing.

The median income of the people in public housing is approximately

$3,600 per year, and for the elderly it is slightly less than $1,700. The annual subsidy we receive from the federal government can be used only for debt service, and all operating costs must come from rental income.

Last year the average rent was $63.37, and in fact, we operated at about 50c in the red. The total rent last year was slightly less than $24 million of which all but $59,000, or .3% was collected. In this we had a very low rate of loss. Last year, our payment in taxes, which is 10% of the rent charge, was about $1,625,000. Incidentally, this is comparable to the slightly more than $700,000 which the same property was paying in taxes before it was acquired and developed with public housing.

MONSIGNOR JOHN EGAN

Some time ago, Winston Churchill said that if we fashion the homes, the homes will fashion the people, and I think this is a basic problem facing public housing. I doubt that anybody in this room would say that, as a concept, public housing is not a blessing. If it had not been created in the thirties, we would have had to create it in the forties, fifties, or sixties. However, I would say that public housing as an institution in Chicago today is a monument to the community's ineptitude to face its long-existing social and housing problems. It is also a monument to the CHA's fear and lack of leadership in facing serious resident social problems which could have been foreseen in the housing built by CHA over the last twenty years.

Look at the history of public housing as Mr. Baron delineated it and, in lesser detail, in terms of the CHA's competence. Look at the charts and graphs, and you see a constant effort which depended, it is always alleged, solely on economic conditions to increase the size and height of public housing from 1937 to the present, absolutely disastrous, 22-story apartment building on Cermak Road and State Street. Much has been said in theory and principle about the social effects of public housing. The danger here is that we can be entirely too theoretical, if not utopian, and continue to make the same mistakes.

I would submit that this is equivalent to an inhuman procedure of experimenting with the lives of individuals and families. The true assessment of the social issues and problems connected with public housing must be post factum empirical investigation. Furthermore, those most competent to speak to the social issues are not Colonel Humphrey, Mr. Baron, or myself, but people living in public housing. I think that they would do a far more competent job on this question than any one of the three of us.

There has also been a lack of leadership on the part of the Chicago Housing Authority in presenting specific and general facts about public housing to a public that supports it and to this distinguished group which has demonstrated its concern with housing by the time spent on it during this Workshop.

I was alone about four years ago when I pleaded with the Chicago

Housing Authority, in the face of some of their future plans, to have an outside, objective study of the effects of high-rise public housing on the mental and physical health of individuals and families. It seemed like common sense that there would be serious effects from asking a mother to care for a large family of young children who need recreation and other amenities in such a situation.

I do not know what those effects are and I do not believe that the Chicago Housing Authority knows. Four years have passed and to my knowledge that investigation and study have never been carried out or even attempted. It was passed from the Chicago Housing Authority to the Chicago Renewal Program and, again I say, to my knowledge it has not been carried out from that day to this. All of us here, including the managers of public housing, will be talking only in theory until we truly investigate the effects of high-rise public housing on family living and on the lives of our most disadvantaged people.

We will be talking pure theory until we look at public housing, with its 143,000 people, as a challenge, not only to the Chicago Housing Authority, but to the entire community, and demand the objective research which will give us the facts we need to determine the programs we must have. I believe this is a reasonable demand upon the CHA and sincerely hope that it will come from this Workshop.

A large amount of money is and will continue to be put into public housing, and I think we will continue to be faced with inadequate architecture, which I think reflects a starvation diet on the part of the people who design public housing. We, not as a welfare agency, but as a contributing force interested in the design of public housing and in the amenities surrounding it, must bring all the city's forces to bear upon the amenities which should be in the neighborhood, from shopping to recreation.

I believe that in public housing we have created, if you will, "instant community" rather than what I think all of us want, a natural community. There are pros and cons. Mixed income, ethnic, and racial groups are possible, and neither the community-at-large nor the Chicago Housing Authority has provided the leadership needed to break the ghetto pattern of public housing in the city and suburban areas.

There has been a failure on all our parts to prepare adequately for ownership and integrated neighborhood living. As Mr. Baron mentioned, public housing reinforces the ghetto and will continue to do so for years to come. The building shapes the family rather than vice versa. Public Housing willynilly generates teenage gangs.

I also plead for the leadership which leads to true consultation with the indigenous community. I feel that the Chicago Housing Authority has operated silently which reflects the total community's silence and lack of concern, both when the housing was built and at present. I was present at the City Council meeting of the Committee on Housing and Planning when members of the Chicago Housing Authority presented plans for a housing site. I felt that those plans and designs were dishonest in presenting a building without any reference to the surroundings. The aldermen present did not seem to be affected by the fact that 20,000 people were living in the public housing surrounding the building to be built.

Colonel Humphrey rightly said that recently the height of public housing has been diminished. This occurred in the face of some, though not great, public demand, but again I ask Mr. Rose, Why was this decision made? Why was the height of the buildings lowered? On the basis of what objective study was this done? What is the rationale behind this kind of decision? From time to time, you have all considered building on selected blocks rather than tracts in order to provide for different income brackets which the entire community would demand.

Though some civil rights groups and other individuals and organizations have tried to break the ghetto pattern of public housing, in my time I have seen no leadership from the Chicago Housing Authority on this question. This certainly would be a key to open occupancy.

Again, if proper research had been carried out, larger families would have been provided for before the demand arose as would community services, recreation, and other social services. Rehabilitation as an alternative to new public housing is an old concept. If I am not mistaken, it was tried years ago near Ashland and the Congress Street Expressway. Whatever the reasons that particular project failed, rehabilitation as a substitute for public housing has not been seriously considered until very recently, though it was an alternative all along.

In conclusion I want to mention specifically for your discussion the question of the safety of those living in public housing, the recreational facilities provided for the 93,000 children out of 143,000 people, the concentration of people, the management procedures, the inaccessibility of management personnel, the danger of open elevators, and the absence of special arrangements to soften the bureaucratic procedures.

I think these are all very serious problems which indicate a lack of sensitive leadership, first of all on the part of the total community because it is easy to make the Chicago Housing Authority the whipping boy. However, in all candor and honesty, I have not and do not see the leadership coming from the Chicago Housing Authority to the rest of the community which would enable us to intelligently respond to the many problems of these 150,000 people. In the Judeo-Christian tradition, they must be considered one of our most precious heritages.

20

Open Occupancy

ROBERT MANN

Together with my colleague, the distinguished State Senator Dick New-house, I want to speak with the orientation and perspective of a state legislator representing a great urban constituency which includes this university.

In Springfield at present we are considering a number of fair housing proposals as well as a number of ethics bills which would regulate the moral and fiscal integrity of legislators in Springfield. For some it is difficult to say whether there is more need for an ethics bill or a fair housing bill. I am inclined to say that we need both, but it is ironic that we probably will come out of the session with an ethics bill regulating the conduct of legislators but without a fair housing bill despite the moral and the pragmatic need for such legislation in Illinois.

Briefly, I would like to tell you about the work of the Legislative Commission on Low-income Housing of which I am privileged to be chairman. In the past eighteen months the Commission has been holding hearings in the state of Illinois with a view toward compiling data and making legislative recommendations, and we are scheduled to present our report to the legislature very shortly. We have held about twenty hearings in Chicago, south Cook County, and downstate Illinois. We have talked to landlords, tenants, public aid recipients, academicians, public housing experts in Illinois and Washington. This has all been against the background and goal of trying to reintroduce the State as a meaningful factor in the Illinois housing picture.

Due to the rural control of our legislature, mayors in Illinois cities have increasingly felt the need to go to Washington for the help they should be getting in Springfield. To wit, in the Land of Lincoln it took us fifteen years to get an FEPC Law. As a result, some federal-city relationships have developed around the needs of the urban areas. We have no quarrel with these relationships to the extent that they meet the needs of the urban areas, but we also feel that the State must be introduced as a factor in this picture unless it is to be nothing more than a funnel and a rubber stamp for the federal money and programs that come into our cities. Therefore, those of us who feel strongly about this regarded the reapportionment decision by the Supreme Court, in Baker vs. Carr and the cases that followed, as a mandate for the states to begin relating to the urban scene and doing something about housing.

The plain fact of housing for the poor in Illinois is that it is uniformly bad. There is almost no decent housing for poor people anywhere in Illinois which is true of large sections of Chicago neighborhoods. It is true of south Cook County where suburban life should be the good life. In Chicago Heights and Robbins, more than 60% of the housing is substandard. It is incredibly true in downstate areas like Danville, Cairo, and East St. Louis. In the Denver-side section of East St. Louis, a community of 13,000 Negroes are living in inadequate housing.

Our commission just completed a tour of Danville and I remember visiting a certain house there. When I stepped onto the porch, my foot went right through. I remember a little shack where nearly three tons of coal a month was not enough to keep it heated. The impact on children is fantastic. In Cairo, Illinois we visited a day care center which we built recently. I asked one of the supervisors about the bunks stacked up against the wall, and she told me that this was the first chance that more than half of the children had to sleep in a bed by themselves.

The housing is bad, particularly for public aid recipients, because of two factors. In Illinois there is a $90 rent ceiling plus $14.50 for utilities which, together with the segregated pattern of housing in Chicago, has created a situation which enables the landlord who specializes in the management and ownership of substandard housing to gouge the public aid recipient. Because of the segregated housing pattern, the recipient has nowhere to go, and because of the ceiling, even if he had somewhere to go, he would be stuck in slums and ghettos.

Ironically, this makes the state of Illinois, with taxpayers' money, the largest subsidizer of slum housing. My colleagues in the Illinois General Assembly zealously guard expenditures of money, and yet we spend about $70 million biennially in rent payments for public aid recipients. With the exception of the money that goes into public housing, almost none goes into housing that is anywhere near being adequate by any of the accepted standards. The commission will certainly take the position that the maintenance of a $90 ceiling is unrealistic.

In downstate Illinois we found almost no utilization of the rent-withholding statute. This permits the Department of Public Aid to withhold rents, upon certification by a building department that the premises are not up to code, and intervene in an eviction suit against the tenant on the same basis. In East St. Louis we were told that this was not done because property owners would walk away from their properties leaving people out in the street. In Cairo we were told this was not done because they do not have a building code. Interestingly, they have 9,500 people, all their housing for the poor is dilapidated, and they have one 76-year-old housing inspector.

We have found that no matter what is done to provide new housing or rehabilitate existing housing, the landlord-tenant relationship is central if housing is to be improved. Historically, in Illinois and many other states, there has been an imbalance in favor of the landlord. This not only impairs the slum tenants' rights in the courtroom which is, of course, most important, but also in the marketplace.

Thus, we feel that legislation to strengthen tenants' rights is of extreme importance as is legislation to provide state grants to local communities for code enforcement. While we certainly want to make the landlords bring their properties up to code, we feel it is unrealistic to do this without providing some financial means and tools for meeting acceptable living standards. Therefore the commission will propose legislation to provide state financing for rehabilitation, and seed money for the building of low-income housing with not-for-profit sponsors initiating the projects.

You may think this is all somewhat far afield from the discussion of open occupancy which I am billed to speak on, but I really do not think it is. Roger Nathan, the distinguished director of the Illinois Commission of Human Relations, is as familiar with what goes on in Springfield as I am. He will verify and confirm for you that in Springfield today there is a lag on the whole question of open occupancy, despite reapportionment. The Speaker of the House has introduced a bill which, in effect, would permit a citizen to tell a broker or a real estator that it is all right to discriminate, and this is supposed to be a step forward. As far as I am concerned it would be noxious to have a law which, in effect, says that it is all right to have segregated housing patterns as long as you tell your broker. Yet, this is perhaps the only law which will be passed. Senator Newhouse has introduced several measures which I am sure he will tell you about.

The Legislative Commission on Low-income Housing was not charged to provide a specific recommendation on open housing. However, the question of freedom of residence has been central to every aspect of our inquiry; it arises at every turn and bears upon every consideration and recommendation of our commission. The public housing authorities downstate, in Danville, East St. Louis, and Cairo are not complying with the 1964 Civil Rights Act. They should receive applications on a nondiscriminatory basis and, as some of us read the Act, should take affirmative steps to integrate public housing. However, with the exception of one project, there are not integrated housing units in any of these three cities. Though they take applications from Negroes, it is incredible that the housing continues to be segregated.

It seems to me that somewhere along the line someone from the Public Housing Authority should be presenting an explicit statement of the federal and the state governments' interpretation of the 1964 Civil Rights Act. In my view, more is required than a statement by a local Public Housing Authority that they will abide by the 1964 Civil Rights Act and receive applications from individuals regardless of race, color or creed. To achieve integration in existing sites and in future site selection, the 1964 Civil Rights Act requires affirmative action on the part of the local housing authority.

In all three of those cities, it is a matter of local policy to exclude unwed mothers from the Housing Authority. Many of these unwed mothers are receiving ADC grants. It is an incredible kind of morality which, by the way, is how they justify it. It produces a policy in state-assisted housing which denies these people adequate housing on the grounds that it would be immoral to do so while the state is giving them ADC money, paltry as it is. It seems incredible to punish these children. Interestingly enough, in some of the communities, when the mothers happened to be Negro, this was also used to get around the intent of the 1964 Civil Rights Act. There are other methods too, such as using two lists as well as ploys and dodges.

In conclusion, I would like to say that segregated patterns are present in Chicago but are not endemic to Chicago. They exist all over the state of Illinois. Where there is a dual-housing market, and especially downstate, we tend to find that housing is bad for the poor whites as well as the Negroes. We find that the very people we are trying to drive out of the housing business, namely the so-called "slum lords," are exacting great profits out of this continued system of segregation. We find that the state has a public policy against discrimination and segregation and, as a part of this system, it pours $70 million into housing biennially.

I would submit to you that, though we need an ethics bill in Springfield, there are strong moral and economic reasons why we need open occupancy. No matter how much public housing we build, we need more of it. However, it does not matter how many government programs are initiated; as long as these patterns of segregation exist in housing, the outlook for improving housing for the poor will be bleak indeed.

EDWARD HOLMGREN

In his comments Representative Mann emphasized the physical quality of housing and the desperate need to improve that quality, especially for the low and moderate income groups. The legislature and other entities within the state, specific communities, and, of course, a variety of private organizations and individuals are increasingly concerned with this problem. I want to talk with you about another aspect of this problem which is certainly interrelated with it, as Mr. Mann has suggested. It is the question of the availability of existing housing and housing that is to be built, the question of equal opportunity and equal access to the housing market.

We are all very aware of the events of last summer which precipitated the summit agreement. The creation of the organization which I represent and of which I am executive director followed on the heels of that agreement. It is the Leadership Council about which I will talk most in the few moments I have.

The events of last summer provided an important confrontation with the system on which housing had historically and still is being marketed in our community and state. Significant progress has been made in other areas of civil rights. The right to get a cup of coffee, to secure employment on an equal opportunity basis, in most instances, and many other aspects of the so-called civil rights struggle have been established and rooted in law.

However, with the housing issue we encounter an entirely different response on the part of the community at large, one which makes achieving the quality that we are concerned with a much more difficult problem.

This is precisely because the system under which we operate demands the segregated process that we find. As Mr. Mann has suggested, a considerable profit is realized from the management, control, and ownership of slum properties, which is related to the fact that, in the housing market, there is also profit in segregation itself. We all know that, at every income level, Negroes, in this and other communities throughout the country, pay more for their housing and get less. This fact alone quite conclusively indicates the profit in housing segregation under the present system. Hopefully the kind of confrontation which occurred last summer will result in a basic change throughout the system.

There have been a number of significant efforts to develop techniques for the construction and management of low- and moderate-income developments throughout the state, but for the most part these have been halting and miniscule in proportion to the need. Of course, as a corollary effort, there must be an opportunity to make existing housing available without discrimination. From this comes the role of the Leadership Council as an organization dedicated to the establishment and maintenance of the principle of equal opportunity in the housing market throughout the metropolitan area. This is a big task as all realize who are aware of the various aspects of the system with which we are dealing.

It is significant that the summit agreement, which was the first response to last summer's demonstrations, and the creation of the Leadership Council, which was the next response, represent the recognition and acknowledgement by the leadership elements of this community – political, business, religious, labor, and so forth – that this is indeed a very serious problem and one which demands priority attention from the leadership of this community. When I say "this community" I am talking about the entire metropolitan area, six and one half million people and the housing which makes up their domiciles.

It is important to point out that, as an institution, the Leadership Council is concerned and dedicated to the prospect of creating a single housing market. Mr. Mann also referred to our dual housing market. It is very significant that of all the elements and commodities bought and sold in the vast American economy, the only one that is marketed on the basis of race is the very basic one of shelter. Anyone in this room can go into a shop and buy a pound of meat, a suit of clothes, or an automobile without his right to make that purchase being questioned. On the other hand, if one seeks housing and wears the badge of color, this right is not free and absolute. Negroes are often rejected or rebuffed in their selection of housing.

Therefore, across the board, the programs of the Leadership Council are dedicated to this goal. These programs include the need to establish techniques for developing low- and moderate-income housing, again throughout the metropolitan area. This is not to suggest that we will be involved in construction as much as in promoting such housing through various agencies, non-profit sponsors, and the like.

The way in which the market operates is even more important than the physical aspects of housing needs. At present, controls are exercised by the gatekeepers who are, in effect, the real estate, mortgage-banking, and building industries. In terms of who gets what, where, and how, these represent a very substantial means by which the market place is controlled.

In a host of areas, community attitudes considerably reinforce the broker who represents himself as protecting or as maintaining community characteristics because of the community's desires. It is necessary to create programs which will develop the understanding and acknowledgement of the community at large as well as of the housing industry people. They have a primary responsibility to shift the system so that it develops and operates on the basis of nondiscrimination.

Another very important aspect of the role and goal of the Leadership Council is directed by the summit agreement itself. The Council is responsible for evaluating and reporting on the progress of the commitments made by the four public agencies in the city and county which have responsibility in the area of housing. I am referring to the Chicago Housing Authority, the Department of Urban Renewal, the Commission on Human Relations, and the Cook County Department of Public Aid. Three of these agencies are limited primarily to the city of Chicago itself. Of course, the Cook County Department of Public Aid is responsible to its clients and their housing throughout the entire area.

These agencies made specific commitments to programs in which they could engage immediately upon the adoption of the summit agreement or soon thereafter. We have been responsible for systematically inquiring into their progress, or lack thereof, in responding to the demands of the summit agreement. We are in the process of attempting to determine the degree to which these individual public agencies are in fact living up to the spirit as well as the intended objectives of the agreement.

In addition, a host of other organizations and groups within the metropolitan area have continuing commitments to foster and extend the concept and actually create the reality of equal opportunity in housing. For instance, the savings and loan associations committed themselves to the policy and practice of providing housing loans to anyone qualified for such loans on a nondiscriminatory basis. The religious community has embarked on a series of ambitious programs, again to extend equal housing opportunity as broadly as possible. Some of these programs are oriented denominationally and some are engaged in community areas on an ecumenical basis. Various elements of the business, trade union, and other communities and so-called "leadership" elements have made commitments in support of the concept of equal housing opportunity. It is the function and responsibility of the Leadership Council, which is made up of representatives from these various segments of the community at large, to make these programs mesh and get off the ground.

The truth of the matter is that very little progress has been achieved since the time of the summit agreement. There have been a number of move-ins by Negro families in previously all-white city and suburban communities which for obvious reasons cannot be pinpointed. In several instances the Leadership Council or constituent parts of it have been involved in the success of these move-ins. In the final analysis, the acid test of the summit agreement itself is the reality of the Negroes' opportunity to seek housing wherever their choice or their dollars may lead them. We also recognize the very important need of achieving substantial, tangible, and visible progress without undue delay. The tensions of last summer were significant and very meaningful in the sense that they resulted in the summit agreement, and unless there is substantial and meaningful progress, it is possible that what we saw last summer will be repeated.

A very significant aspect of the Leadership Council is that it consists of perhaps the most diverse and representative spectrum of leadership elements within the community, ranging from the freedom movement to the highest echelons of the business community. This represents an acknowledgement by all these community elements of the importance and urgency of this issue. We are very conscious of the need to establish substantial and meaningful progress in this area in the very near future. We are hopeful that progress is and will be made toward a real change in the system in which housing has been marketed.

S. T. SUTTON

As I look around, I can see that some of you might be more intelligent or handsomer than I am but none of you are balder.

Listening to Mr. Holmgren, I could not help but think that one thing I like about the friend of the Negro is that he always gets a decent job and pay to worry about and patronize the Negro. I have before me a headline from the *Sun-Times:* "Housing Chief Fears a Black City" — that is the head of your organization, Mr. Holmgren. It does not matter whether the city is black or white if the Negro is equal.

I have always felt, as I have stated time and time again, God bless those who want to live in integrated communities, but those who want to live in an all-white community have that right. Those who want to live in an all-Negro community have that right and should not be interferred with by the law. This is an individual's right. I continually hear the term "racial justice." There is no such thing as racial justice; there is only individual justice, and this is the only way it can be.

We are here to discuss open occupancy and I have heard Mr. Holmgren say that all elements of the city were present at the Judas Conference. He forgot the most important element — the white homeowner. There were no representatives of the white homeowner.

The heads of two organizations in areas where Marty King marched are here with me today. He came in and got trouble. After all, it would be un-Christian if we did not give him a little trouble wouldn't it? That is what he was looking for and that is what he got. If he comes back this summer, I promise you he will get even more. I would like to introduce Mr. James Hoffman of West Elston and Mr. Rich Fort, president of the Southwest Council of Civic Organizations which includes Marquette Park, Murray Park, Gage Park, and Chicago Lawn – the areas in which Marty had his fun this summer.

I assure you that if he comes back this summer, he will have even more fun because the people have had it. We are tired of troublemakers coming into our law-abiding, peaceful communities to create tension. Any Negro individually can walk through most of those areas without being molested, but a group is going to get trouble. And trouble we promise you.

Open occupancy itself has not solved problems in other states, and it is not going to solve a problem in this state. As long as people can run, they will run. It is clear that not many Negroes are that interested in living with whites. Why should they be? If we follow your own doctrine, whites are not superior. Why would they want to live with us? If they are equal, they do not care. I think this is the greatest weakness of your approach.

It would seem to me that, after five years of an approach with which you have created more racial hatred, distrust, and mistrust, you would try another. I can see it in our communities and organizations. There is more distrust and dislike of the Negro today than there was five years ago. People resent force and subterfuge. If you are going to take that approach, you must deal with whites and Negroes as individuals. If you come in as groups, make demands, and beg the white man, "Please let me live next to you. I cannot educate my children with my own. I need your children." – then you know there will be troubles. It cannot be any other way.

Few white parents will accept the responsibility for raising Negro children which the Negroes evidently feel they cannot raise themselves. We are not going to take it, and there is no good reason why we should. If, in fact, your Negro schools with your Negro students are inferior because they are Negro, then you have no right to put that on us. We have enough problems with our own children. Let us be honest, we cannot even solve the problems of our own children much less attempt to solve your problems. It cannot be done. These are the resentments that build up.

Mr. Partee's latest bill is a beauty, and it is typical of the proponents of this type of legislation. Section 34 provides for discriminatory practice – you may discriminate. In the previous bills, only one group was allowed to discriminate, the churches. They were exempt. Now exceptions have been made. Anyone may discriminate providing they file with the Commission a plan for a quota system to maintain a racially balanced neighborhood. I defy you to define a properly racially balanced neighborhood.

This calls to my mind the South Shore Commission with which we are all familiar. They have battled with the Board of Education. They know Negroes are equal, up to 40%. After that, you are niggers. They do not want you after 40%. Now, as I have indicated, if you are equal it does not matter whether the community is 99% Negro or 99% white. You Negroes are dealing with hypocrites. You are dealing with the worst elements of the white society. They have lied to you, misled you, and take our money to do it.

Next week we have our first dealings with the Negroes on the other side; we are inviting them in for the first time. We could not have done it a year ago; we would not have dared to make the approach because we cannot get too far ahead of our people. We think that now we can make the approach without getting too much kickback. We told the three Negroes who are coming in that we will try to treat them with the same utter contempt with which we treat each other. Let us face facts. The first half hour of the meeting will be a song and dance as everybody pretends there is no difference. We know there is a difference, but everybody will be polite when there is no need to be polite. If we are going to deal with this problem, we have to deal with it honestly.

The peripheral areas are a problem in metropolitan Chicago. Those areas adjacent to Negro communities cannot take Negroes because they become inundated and cannot survive. If Negroes are to go someplace, they have got to come out to where I live, to DuPage and Kane County. They cannot go to the peripheral areas because, unfortunately, those areas adjacent to the Negro community have been destroyed by the inundation of Negroes. Those are the facts with one or two minute exceptions. There is no reason why those who have worked so hard for their homes should be compelled to give up their homes or their neighborhoods, so, if you are going someplace, you have to go someplace other than the peripheral areas.

To refer again to Mr. Partee's bill, he allows legal discrimination, and as I look at the proponents of this legislation, I am convinced that it will not help the Negro, it will not improve race relations, and it will not do justice. It is an attempt to destroy the middle class. The very basis of the middle class is private property, and private property means that you have the right to exercise dominion over it. If you cannot, you are a serf on your property. We are returning to the eleventh century as Mr. Mann said, and, Mr. Mann, I would rather live in the eleventh century than go toward the 1984 to which you are leading us.

If a man is to have property and is to be free, he must make some decisions for himself. Certainly one of these decisions is to withhold property from whomever he wishes. This type of legislation uses the government's power of eminent domain solely because of race. You say to the owner, "We are taking this from you because of race alone." That is racism. We are often accused of being the racists but we are reacting to racists. Your whole doctrine is race: "regardless of race, creed, or color." Race, race, all I heard from the other speakers was race, race, race. We are reacting to racism, and when you react to racism you get racism.

The Roman Catholics here know our position on the clergy who participate in this type of activity. We have urged our people to cut off funds. We know that in certain areas we are hurting the church, and in other areas we have not been too successful. There is no reason that those with certain political or racial beliefs, particularly beliefs which I do not think are founded on doctrine, can take our church away from us too.

I have the feeling that you cannot wait to get at me. I shaved my head because that makes it more difficult to scalp.

Another earmark of the middle class is that we earn and pay our own way. We are tired of being told that there are people who cannot do that. The greatest incentive to work that I know is the fact there is no food on the table. Work. The only way any Negro will get ahead is to work. If to get ahead you have to depend on your white liberal friends, you are still a slave. You are dependent. Slavery is dependency.

I have read many statements by Catholic clergy condemming the middle class. I use Catholic because I am a Roman Catholic. I feel that they condemn us because, one, we are not on relief, and two, we only have one father in the home. We pay our way and expect others to pay their way. This is the story of life. You cannot continue forever robbing us to do something else. And once again, if the Negro is dependent on us, then he is not equal. If he is equal, then he does not have to be that dependent on us.

To go on to the next question, that of equal opportunity, there is no such thing as equal opportunity, and there is no obligation to give the Negro equal opportunity. I work hard not for Negroes' children, or Jim Hoffman's children, but for my children. Jim Hoffman works hard for his children and his family and not for my family. This is the way to get things done. Any other system has failed in the past and is failing presently. If you are going to do it, you must do it yourself. I hope I have made myself clear on that point.

To return once again to private property, St. Thomas Acquinas said, "The indicias of private property are the right to dispose, the right to withhold, the right to the fruit, and the right to the use of property." If you take these away, you do not have private property. As I have indicated, you have returned to serfdom.

In cities there is little you can do with your property without gaining permission from some government agency whether it is putting in wiring, adding a room, taking down a room, or building a new building. You cannot put up a three-story building in residential sections; you can put up a one-story building. If you own rental units, to be told that you must rent or sell to somebody in spite of their religion and their race is an evil in itself. This is a decision that only an individual can make.

You may not agree with his decision, but the essence of freedom is the fact that you and I may not agree about who our associates are going to be. Association is a mutuality. I do not have any right to demand your association in certain areas and you do not have any right to demand my association. I have the right to refuse and you have the right to refuse. Of course there are exceptions in areas such as public streets or public parks. I use the word "public," but "private property," no. I have the right to reject you for whatever reason, good or bad, brilliant or stupid. This is the right of the individual.

RICHARD NEWHOUSE

The last time Mr. Sutton and I were on a platform together was about two years ago. I guess neither of our views have changed very much since then. At that time, in jest I opened my remarks by saying to Mr. Sutton that I would not want him to move next door to me and throw his garbage in my yard. It is hard not to respond to a talk such as his, but I will try to keep any response that I make within the context of what I have planned to talk about.

It is necessary that certain things be clarified because a lot of patriotic words have been used which serve to confuse the issue before us. For example, we talk about rights of individuals, the control of property, and I suggest that nothing in the open housing legislation of either party is contrary to those rights. Once you decide to make a sale, the character of a home changes. It is no longer a home; it is a house, a commodity on the market. To suggest that a commodity on the open market should be passed along or withdrawn according to the whim of the seller who is looking for a market seems to me to be specious reasoning. As far as living in homes is concerned, there is nothing in law or logic to say that, if I buy a house at 1776 East Damen, I will control 1778, 1780, 1782 and all the other houses on the block.

It disturbed me slightly to hear a lawyer who is an officer of the Court refer to, as "fun," such things as aggravated battery, property damage such as the turning over and burning of automobiles, and similar activities. It is a little more disturbing to hear him promise us more "fun" this summer. And I do not understand the nature of the threat, but if there had to be such a threat, I would rather not have heard it from an officer of the law or an officer of the court.

To return to the subject matter at hand, open housing, I would like to discuss shortly the high costs that we pay for a segregated system and say something about the sorts of bills that are in the hopper in Springfield, and the kind of expectations we should have for what comes out of the legislation this year. I think that Chicago is a showcase of what usually happens in a neighborhood when it turns over. There are several things. One is that the supply of mortgage money is shut off. There are reasons for this. Generally, the community is at least fifty to sixty years old. The buildings need new roofs, new heating plants – major capital improvements which the seller will not make before he sells and which the purchaser cannot possibly make because of the high cost of the structure to him.

How does the cost of the structure rise all at once? When neighborhoods begin to deteriorate and are about to turn over, there is usually a change in the rental structure. For example, twenty-four units in a building might be converted into forty-eight or seventy-two. By the ordinary real estate rules of thumb, the purchase price comes to about four times the gross income. It is readily apparent that the gross income from a 72-unit structure is a good deal higher than from a 24-unit structure. Thus the purchase price may be three or four times what the building is actually worth. Cost, then, bears no relation to the value of a physical structure.

Consequently, in order to get back his money, the purchaser must use up the building as fast as he can before it falls apart. That is the game, it is a business. For example, three times the number of families might be using the building as formerly used it. In many cases, the family units are larger than when the structure had one-third the number of families, and consequently the building continues its downward trend at an accelerated pace.

The building depreciates so fast that the new owners' taxes go down, but the cost of services to that building (police protection, fire protection, garbage collection, and everything else) go up. This is inevitable due to the increased number of people in the dwelling and the accelerated use. The landlord takes his profit out of the middle, depreciates the building, and, when it falls apart, he simply walks away. He wants no further responsibility, but as taxpayers you pay the cost.

First of all, you make up the substantial difference between the actual cost of service and the taxes paid by the landlord. After the building has deteriorated, you must pay to acquire it for demolition, then you pay again for that demolition. Subsequently, urban renewal will cost billions of dollars. You will have to pay for having land that has been acquired using public monies turned over to private entrepreneurs to build new structures. These are where the cost factors enter.

The ideal way to approach the question of open housing would be on a voluntary basis. In this country, we are operating on a theory that we have never really proven, and the fact of the matter is that we have not worked very hard at the matter of making free enterprise work. If we talk about self-policing, which is the atmosphere in which we would like to conduct our affairs, then we are talking about people who recognize that they have a responsibility to the system of democracy. Once one subverts that responsibility to private feelings (whether for money, self-aggrandizement, or whatever), then the government (state, local, or other) has some responsibility to legislate what people have not done of their own free will. Such action is necessary if society is to survive.

Legislatively, there are several approaches to the problem. One is to frame legislation which will provide sanctions against a seller who wants to discriminate. Another is providing sanctions against a broker who wants to discriminate or will cooperate in discriminatory acts.

Bills covering both these phases are in the hopper in Springfield now. At this stage, Senate Bill 155, which is the Partee bill, is probably the most palatable. Presently it is in the Registration and Miscellany Committee on which I sit. To my knowledge, this is the only committee that has had only one business meeting since the session began, and I do not have very high hopes that 155 will come up or pass. You may have read that I dropped in a fairly severe open housing bill, but it was not an open housing bill at all. It was a piece of omnibus legislation that codified under one heading most of the laws that pertain to race relations in the State of Illinois. It had a good deal more bite to it than some of the other things that have been put in already, and, as a matter of fact, I am amending it so that the teeth will be even longer. I do not expect that bill to pass in the next twenty sessions, but as a tactical matter, it might jar some people into recognizing that the Partee bill is a livable one.

Even as a freshman, I say that a peculiar situation exists in the present legislature. I am not talking partisan politics but am simply explaining a situation as I view it. The Republican majority is sufficiently large so that they have absolutely no problem in passing out as a party matter any type of legislation they choose. So the facts of life are that a bill could be passed next week if the Republican party so desired.

The Smith bill has come out very recently. As you know, Representative Ralph Smith is Speaker of the House of Representatives. Let me tell you what it says and what I think will be a practical consequence of this proposed legislation. In effect, it says that if a person wants to discriminate in the sale of a house, he simply has to say so in writing, and he and the broker will be protected in the process. There are two separate bills on this. One permits the seller to discriminate and the other protects the broker who participates in the discriminatory sale. Though I have framed it in its worst light, it is a true light. Not only do I think this is not good legislation, I think it is regressive and very possibly unconstitutional.

As a practical matter, if a bill like this passed into law, this is what could happen. The standard form of real estate sale contract has many paragraphs that pertain to most of the situations encountered in the course of an ordinary sale. I suspect that very shortly after a bill such as this is passed, there would be a new form of contract with an additional paragraph which would authorize discrimination. If, as a conscious matter, you did not cross out that paragraph, you would have an automatic discrimination clause in every contract. I am sure that those who framed this legislation know this.

Three Republican Negro representatives signed that bill, and now they are probably dancing around like a cat on a hot tin roof. I doubt that they realized how bad this bill was before they put their names on it and probably thought that this was the best they could get out of the legislature this time around. They may be right, but the problem is that this bill not only condones segregation, it actually encourages it. We will probably be in a worse condition with this kind of legislation than without a bill at all. The Partee bill is couched in terms of persuasion, conciliation, and mediation, and is by far more desirable.

My bill is not couched in these terms at all but in terms of fines, and as an extreme case, jail sentences. If we try to legislate open occupancy, we have to do the same thing as Mr. Sutton, but I hope we do it in a slightly different manner. We have to negotiate from our toughest point. It seems ridiculous to talk about a bill that is nothing more than a statement of policy which is what we have gotten in the past. It makes no sense at all to talk in terms of a bill which says, "The bad guys will not sign a paper saying I want to discriminate and that way we will accomplish the goal of open occupancy."

I suggest that it makes a great difference whether Chicago or any other city is an all-black city, an all-white city, or whatever. We are failing on the world scene in an area of which we should be in the forefront. We have always been good in the area of selling. We are without peer in the sale of ideas and commodities all over the world, but the one thing that we fail to sell is our system. In half the places around the world, we are trying to shoot people into believing what we profess to believe and it is utterly ridiculous. If ever we need a sales job done, we need it now.

We must start by perfecting our system so that people will want to do what they see us doing. The availability of housing to all people is certainly basic to promoting the idea of a democratic society and a true capitalistic system in which you expect that the best man for the job will get the job and the person who is equipped to buy the house can do so with impunity. As a legislator and citizen of Chicago, I suggest that much must be done on both sides in the area of education. We cannot do without the kind of education necessary for the kind of society I think we all want.

We are now in the awkward position of having to legislate the concept that all men should have equal access to housing consistent with their means. I hope that the vote on stop-and-frisk was not a real indication, and I shall do everything in my power to bring out a sensible open housing bill that we, as well as Mr. Sutton, can live with.

21

Federal Housing Programs: Opportunities for Innovation

JOSEPH BURSTEIN

This is a hard act to follow, but let's try to set aside what we've just been discussing because I will be dealing with this problem from an entirely different standpoint. I will be talking about the practicalities of putting low-income families into decent housing. I met Dr. Tax in connection with his work with Indians, and the very sorts of things that are taking place on Indian reservations, as far removed as they are from here, can serve as prototypes for city problems.

The Housing Assistance Administration is the successor to the Public Housing Administration, and the change in name is significant. It indicates a change in the type of assistance provided by the Federal Government for low-income families through public housing agencies that in many ways have nothing to do with public housing as we know it.

The Housing Assistance Administration finances two very important programs. For example, the present leasing program provides subsidy to low-income families for any housing in which they can be placed including privately owned housing. These may be apartment houses or individual houses. A family may have the option to buy if their income increases, or substandard housing may be brought up to standard through the provision of assistance, and so on.

An entirely different aspect of this type of assistance is for housing that comes to be owned by a housing authority such as the Chicago Housing Authority. There has been a major administrative, rather than a legal, change in producing this kind of housing in order to reduce costs and increase the possibilities of private enterprise in rehabilitation and new construction. This is the turnkey method of producing housing. We coined this term which means that housing is either built or rehabilitated by private enterprise with private financing for sale to a housing authority. Its purpose and effect are to make many more sites available. We hope that private enterprises that want to sell land, finance construction, or maintain their labor force will become interested in producing public housing rather than the Housing Authority having to beg, borrow, and steal.

So far our experience has been very, very good, and I would like to go over some of these more specifically because the specifics are what is important. Somebody here referred to "spinning of wheels." In my opinion, the worst thing anybody can do is speak in generalities which in some respects both sides here have been doing in our discussion. It is most important to accomplish a particular project, development, or scheme in one place or another, in the country or in the city, so you can say "it's been done, and this is the way to do it."

This is especially important when we get involved with private enterprise, that is private ownership, leasing, and financing, where the private entrepreneur's money is on the line. In order to interest private enterprise rather than beg or ask for special favors, you have to show that you have something they can use — financing, subsidy, the means whereby a reasonable profit can be made. We are doing this with essentially the same type of financing which has been in public housing for the last thirty years. It is basically a subsidy to low-income families which ranges from about $50 to $80, and for very large families perhaps to $90 a month.

We are using this subsidy in a variety of ways, and interested groups can help. In the first place, under the leasing program the Housing Authority can find vacancies in any decent housing in the city which does not need repair. Normally, the Housing Authority leases these units from the owner at the rent he specifies, moves in an eligible, low-income family, and makes up the difference between the rent and what the family can afford to pay, as I mentioned, up to between $50 and $90 per month depending on family size and other factors.

Though this is the typical situation, there are alternatives. For example, a Jewish old-age home in Houston that was not interested in any more long-range financial commitments could not house all those who applied. Some of the elderly who applied could live independently and use its services, but there was no room for them. Therefore, it was suggested that this non-profit organization lease units in nearby, available apartment houses, go to the Housing Authority for applicants who qualified as low-income elderly, and place them in these apartments. I suggested this in a speech in Philadelphia, and it took a year and a half for it to actually happen. Nevertheless, it has happened, and people across the country have been asking this organization, "how do you do it?"

Let me translate this particular situation into some others. If the members of a church are moving away because the area is deteriorating, and the church and its membership are interested in maintaining the community, the church organization can do exactly what the old-age home has been doing. The leasing program could be used if the industrial and teaching institutions around the University of Chicago were interested in keeping low-income students, low-income faculty members, or whatever in the vicinity.

To take this a step further, an organization interested in promoting integration can locate apartments or individual houses within the city with very few funds because it is using Housing Authority money rather than its own. This is a voluntary program; I assume that many apartments can be found on a voluntary basis. Whether this organization is non-profit or whatever, it can find such places and put the appropriate families in the appropriate locations. Thus, it is not the Housing Authority alone. Incidentally, the applicants themselves, the people on the Housing Authority rolls who are waiting for apartments, can find decent apartments and ask the Housing Authority to qualify them for these apartments.

In other words, an array of interested individuals and organizations in their own self-interest and for their own objectives can use the leasing program. It is a very flexible program because it provides a one- or five-year lease with options to renew. If the organization is interested in promoting home ownership, it is possible that the owner can be persuaded to lease with an option to buy. Unlike traditional public housing, the leasing program has the advantage that a family does not have to move from the leased apartment if their income increases. The subsidy is reduced accordingly and when they can afford to pay the going rate, they merely become regular tenants. If there is an option to buy, they can do so and continue paying on the mortgage. Thus, from the standpoint of flexibility, and of some of the problems I've been hearing about here and others that I know, I suggest that you look at the leasing program in particular.

Now I will turn briefly to units that are not in standard condition, substandard housing, and what the leasing program can do. Those of you who are familiar with the problems of code enforcement and the problems of the slum owner will find that, though sometimes the owner's bad intention are involved, the economics of the situation are more relevant. It costs so much to bring housing up to standard that, in the first place the courts do not force an owner to do it, and second, the resulting rents would be so high that the families who would live in those areas simply cannot afford it. Therefore, some subsidy is necessary.

Last week in the *New York Times,* it was reported that in New York, a non-profit organization, whose motives cannot be questioned, undertook the experiment of rehabilitating housing to see if they could make it pay. This was not a slum landlord but a do-gooder organization trying to prove something, and they did. They proved that it cannot be done. In other words, the expense of rehabilitating a slum and of maintaining property in a slum area, meaning tenants who do not keep up their property properly, vandalism, and so forth, is not a paying proposition. A subsidy is essential to make it work.

The Housing Assistance Administration, working through a housing authority, has the subsidy. I might say parenthetically that, technically, we do not have to work through a housing authority in the leasing program. We can work through any public agency which is authorized to provide housing for low-income families or slum clearance. Though this is a possibility, we have yet to find our first customer of this type. Of course, through the years we have been working through housing authorities because our permanent program requires the sale of bonds and so forth. I am just mentioning this as another possible area where problems might arise.

As I said, we have the subsidy, and thus the means, to make effective what the New York non-profit group could not. We can rehabilitate a slum and make it available to tenants who would live in those areas. The Housing Authority does this in a manner similar to what was done experimentally in Washington, D.C., for the first time. Owners of fifty three-bedroom row houses scattered throughout the city were induced, on the basis of only a five-year lease, to invest in each house about $1500 (one was about $4000) and lease to low-income families. In other words, the Housing Authority said, we will lease your house for the next two years at, say, $150 per month.

If necessary, the owner can use the Housing Authority's commitment to lease for the purpose of financing. He can go to a bank with this commitment for a fixed rental of $150 per month and ask for a loan with which to fix up the house. Very often the answer is yes. The Washington experiment was on the basis of a two-year lease, but the law permits leasing up to five years and continued optioning for longer periods. Thus, this can result in a commitment that is quite substantial, one with which an owner can get the necessary financing from a bank to bring the housing up to code. Furthermore, this is a commitment to pay a fixed rental, but it includes the $50 to $90 subsidy to the low-income family that will occupy the house. Thus, with the same subsidy, we provide both the means with which to rehabilitate the house and the means whereby a low-income family can move into that house.

As far as I know, the most extensive rehabilitation to date in this brand new program was the conversion of a hotel in downtown Holyoke, Massachusetts into housing for the elderly. This involved substantial capital expenditure and was possible only on the basis of a long-range commitment to lease which enabled the bank to lend the necessary money.

I will suggest some thoughts on which you can use your imagination again. In a program which I believe is in Rochester, the FHA insures housing for which the participants themselves do the repairs. Under these circumstances an equity credit can be provided. Incidentally, as against conventional financing at 6%, this is 3% financing which means a rent reduction of $20 to $30 per month, and the families involved, I understand, still cannot afford it.

Under the leasing program, if a tenant organization undertook the responsibility of maintaining or even fixing up these houses, it would be possible to lease this property; then the units could be subleased to individuals with the subsidy covering the expense of rehabilitation. Again, a commitment of fixed rental is necessary, and it would be possible to house families who could not otherwise afford to live in that situation. Thus, here is a good device for tenant organizations that are willing to undertake the responsibility of maintenance and so on.

I mention this in particular because, as you know, very often slum properties are owned by absentee owners. Many of them would welcome the idea of an organization such as the Housing Authority sharing the responsibility with tenants' organizations, and of these two entities taking over the burden of fixing up and maintaining the property in a decent condition. In the New York experiment, because rental property was involved, the individual tenant did not have a personal financial interest in the result. If an organization can be devised where, by way of rent reduction, equity, or whatever, the tenants, in their own self-interest, become personally involved in preventing vandalism and seeing that things are properly maintained, then much can be done which is acceptable both from the standpoint of the community and of the financial interests involved.

I've tried to cover the leasing program as rapidly as possible and, as you can see, only your imagination sets the limit on what can be done with it and with indigenous groups. In this connection, I would like to mention the impact of legislation of Senators Kennedy, Javits, and others which involved indigenous labor in a target area. The leasing program is a natural here because, in a very simple way, it can involve participation by the neighborhood groups in their own housing and in their own self-interest.

In the leasing program, housing is not owned by the Housing Authority, whereas the turnkey program results in rehabilitated housing or new construction which is owned by the Housing Authority. Turnkey is important because it fully involves private enterprise in producing housing, and the more you invite private enterprise, the further ahead you are. This is because, with all due respect to the efforts of non-profit groups, not many are ready to undertake construction of a forty-year mortgage, especially with respect to housing for low-income families. In my opinion, in order to create a large volume of housing owned by the Housing Authority, it is essential to involve private enterprise.

Furthermore, only by involving private enterprise is there any possibility of overcoming the burdens that the Housing Authority faces in getting sites, designing projects, producing at reasonable costs, and matching what is being done by private enterprise. By that I mean producing housing in a year rather than three, four, or five years as is now being done. This is possible under turnkey because the developer goes to the Housing Authority with a site and says he will build for sale whatever they want on that site.

Though I will not go into the details, the developer contracts to produce the specified housing at the specified price, and the Housing Authority agrees to buy the finished product. The contract and guarantees are such that banks are willing to finance the construction and development of that housing. This involves the entire business community, banking, land, and construction interests, in the production of housing for low-income families owned by the Housing Authority. They are doing very well; we are flooded with requests and cannot handle all that come in. I think we have to persuade the Chicago banks, as we have persuaded financing institutions all over the country. We are always ready to talk business in order to produce this kind of housing.

I am not talking only about high-rise, new construction, but also about rehabilitated units. Incidentally, it is likely that within the next two or three weeks, we will approve a program in Philadelphia for 5000 row houses. Three thousand are to be rehabilitated and 2000 are to be replaced by new row houses under the turnkey method. By this summer, we will complete 1000 rehabilitated houses there, and over 400 others are already occupied.

We are using turnkey there as we use it on Indian reservations, for example, where the Housing Authority agrees to buy prefabricated housing. The production of the finished product involves a combination of labor, assisted under manpower and training by the Labor Department, an apprenticeship program, self-help by the families themselves on a mutual help program, and other assistance. The Housing Authority purchases the finished house under the turnkey program which makes possible the combination of all this desirable activity in the production of housing.

Perhaps it is difficult to translate this into the urban situation because of such things as labor union problems. Nevertheless this prototype now exists over the entire country. Whether you can make it work here or anywhere else in the country is a matter of your imagination, initiative, and your getting to the specifics and practicalities.

22

Tenant Unions

MARTIN BAKER

I would like to briefly delineate two dimensions along which an organizer thinks of tenant unions: the modes of organization, and the purposes for which a tenant union is brought into being.

The first dimension is that of the tenant union for itself, i.e. the modes of organization, not mechanics. In other words, how to provide for, or ameliorate, housing conditions that allow people to live in at least semidecent surroundings. Everyone here who has been organizing knows the kind of problems which exist, but I will run through them briefly for the others. The first is to get people brave enough to organize. In one apartment building after another, people will tell you their problems and that something is wrong with the building, but, at first, it is very difficult for them to come out publicly and work together. Once they begin to tell the organizer their problems, it is hard to stop them from pouring their problems out. Steve Bracker, who is our tenant union director, could use twenty-five men working 100 hours a week as he does to take care of housing problems alone, without dealing with the important underlying problems and, the causes of poverty.

The second problem is to help them to understand how groups communicate – work together. Many of these people have no group function experience.

Once a tenant union is established, it is almost impossible, especially for amateurs, to run even one building. We have had experience with this, and the people on the West Side have had some experiences. They know how hard it is to manage a building when, especially as amateurs, they face many of the same problems the landlord faced.

This brings us to the next problem for a tenant union and an organizer, pressure from the landlord to keep such an organization from ever coming into existence. The landlord is not always acting from cruel or misguided motives. He may be pushed to the wall economically. When Dr. King took over the building on the West Side and a court injuction ordered him to stop the rent strike in the building and return the money, I think he was happy. He could not afford to run that building and put it in a habitable condition on the rental revenue obtained. We have had the same experience with our buildings. It takes a tremendous amount of money and time to

273

put a building into decent shape.

One of the main reasons for this is a lack of cooperation from the people in the building and especially in the surrounding area. A building cannot be divorced from the community. Mrs. Robinson will talk about a building in which an astounding portion of the monthly income was spent replacing the light bulbs in the halls. The gangs took out the light bulbs and used the halls as a hotel at night. The winos and the gangs had an arrangement. The gangs got the second floor and the winos got the first. The tenants cannot control the environment outside the building, and in many ways the tenant union is not equipped to handle the impact of the neighborhood on their building.

Who does the tenant union organize against or around? In the traditional labor pattern, either you organize around a craft and let all those who work against you, the managers and employers, come to you, or you organize around a particular industry. In tenant unions, we can choose to organize around a building, or against a particular realty firm and deal with all their buildings, or on a community-wide basis, including all the buildings in the area and dealing with the various realtors or owners. A choice has to be made. Frankly speaking, we have had two experiments in this city. Mr. Feldman probably will tell you about dealing with one realtor who controls a large number of buildings, and in Englewood we are finding it most convenient to deal with individual, small owners, one at a time. It is probably simply a matter of the amount of energy available.

External to the building and the community, the major problem an organizer faces is from the city government. Many hours are spent fighting with building inspectors who do not inspect or who inspect superficially, and many hours are spent in the court. We have gotten to the point where we can very quickly get demolition and condemnation proceedings, but it takes a tremendous amount of energy to overcome the inertia of the bureaucratic structure. I think some of Dick Newhouse's questions about the Department of Urban Renewal point to the lack of interest in human concerns on the part of the bureaucratic structures.

The organizer's last problem in involving people is that they see that the laws favor the landlord and not the tenant. In this city, when a lease is available, it is a standard lease form which provides standards lower than those set by the city building code. It also includes a hold-harmless clause. Though I do not think it is legally valid, supposedly, a person who is injured as the result of building mismanagement is precluded from suing the landlord. The tenants are constantly pushed about by the law and all the structures.

Probably the most difficult part of organizing is getting together people from different parts of the community. Everyone is so concerned with their own problems that they find it very difficult to move outside them. However, once you are successful with one building, people begin to realize that there is a community of problems on which they can work together and find solutions.

Though I am supposed to speak on organization, I think we all know that to organize takes many hours of talking and working with people, literally of being out on the street. There are no pills, no magic solutions, and I think that those involved in community organization know what to do. The question is whether you will go into the streets and do it. That is the first dimension.

Let me briefly run through another dimension which is beyond that. In and of themselves, tenant unions are important in providing proper housing and in getting people together. They are, however, only one particular means to the end of total community organization. Tenant unions, welfare unions, or any one of a number of devices can be used. Tenant unions are a very good device simply because people spend so much time at home that, in many ways, they form a permanent community. They have an exact location where you can work with them.

Tenant unions do get people together, and they see that they can work together to solve problems. Whether or not they are totally successful is a moot point. Today we hear many people talking about Negroes moving into the suburbs or into different neighborhoods. As an organizer, I am not sure that I want that to happen. I agree with Stokely Carmichael and Representative Dawson that, if I want a strong community politically, I want to keep the Negroes together. I want to keep them impacted where I can control and utilize their political energies to whatever ends I have, whether they are Stokely Carmichaels or Representative Dawsons. Integrationists may be trying to force all the smart Negroes to move our because when they disappear, again there will be no leadership. It might result in a Negro "brain-drain." If all the Negroes move around and integrate all over the city, they are no longer a factor. This is what, in the long run, destroys the power of the Negro community. If you drain off by allowing only the leadership to escape, you keep the body thrashing around without a real head. In the past this has worked against the Negro very well.

Finally, we must understand that tenant unions, at least on the West Side, were a product of the Industrial Union Department of the AFL-CIO which was very interested in the unions of the poor. Norm Hill has spent a great deal of time working with his tenant union on the West Side. I have real reservations about the relationship of organizations of poor people to the traditional labor structure on the basis of the history of the trade unions and the labor establishments in this country. I can well understand the problems that Norm Hill and Charlie Chiakulas have in, if you will pardon me, putting themselves in a position to help the poor. In this city specifically, how can the Chicago Federation of Labor support the poor and the labor movement when Richard J. Daley, Bill McFetridge, and Bill Lee have been playing ball together since they were small children? Many of the poor see the unions blocking their chances for a better life. Perhaps it is necessary that Reuther is trying to force the labor organization into admitting the problems and working actively toward solutions.

Summarily then, there are two dimensions. The first is the problem of organizing, of realistically facing the problems, and the second is the strategic problem of what to do after you get people together – what are your ends? The poor people in the slums have very little energy, and they spend most of it fighting rats, a bad political machine, and other problems. They do not have the surplus energy of the nice white liberals or the fighting white homeowners. First we must solve what might not seem to the poor to be the little problems, fixing light bulbs in the halls and getting the building together so that energy does not have to be wasted in trying to stay warm and whole at night. Then people will have much more energy with which to solve the long-range goal of restructuring society which is what I think tenant unions eventually will have to do.

GILBERT FELDMAN

As Marty Baker has indicated, the term "tenant union," by which this session is designated, is not altogether appropriate. Tenant unions are a means to desired goals and not ends in themselves; hence, "community organization" might be a more adequate term. The significance of the proper use of terms was impressed upon me by an anecdote I read recently which you may have seen. It involved a Russian factory worker who said to her superintendent, "Madam Superintendent, I would like to get off a little early tonight to go to the opera." The superintendent rather gruffly said, "Do not call me Madam. We are all equal here and the correct term is Comrade. Call me Comrade Superintendent." So the worker said, "All right, Comrade Superintendent," and the superintendent said, "By the way, what opera do you want to see tonight?" The worker replied, "Comrade Butterfly." "Comrade Butterfly" impresses upon me how very much terms can be misleading.

I would like to briefly outline some of the factors which I think were significant in the development of the institution of tenant unions in Chicago over the last two years. Six factors will be discussed and undoubtedly others could be named.

First and foremost is the existence of so many poor people in an otherwise affluent society as reflected in our northern industrial cities.

Second, many of these people are segregated according to race and live together in ghetto slums where existing political and economic institutions parasitically take advantage of, and thrive upon, their situation, exploiting them and perpetuating their adverse conditions.

Third, in Illinois and in many other northern industrial states, the relationship of landlord and tenant within the judicial structure is archaic; it is an appendage of an age when industrial cities as we know them did not exist. Of course, basically, this acts to the detriment of the tenant, specifically the tenant who does not have the option to move about freely, the tenant who must face the landlord without the necessary tools with which to confront him.

Fourth, motivation and inspiration for the development and emergence of tenant unions in Chicago came from the early activity of SCLC in late 1965 and early 1966.

Fifth, certain forces within existing labor organizations are now faced with serious problems threatening their continued viability. I refer to those forces that are still interested in organizing and assisting poor people. I note in passing that many existing labor organizations are not interested in and may actually be adverse to organizing the poor. But those forces within the labor movement that still cast their lot with the poor found that their customary methods of organization during the last two decades no longer worked effectively, and they became interested in finding new ways to reach and organize poor people.

Finally, in this industrial society, there is simply no institutional or other constructive way to resolve the real conflicts and real conflict of interests which exist in areas such as the Chicago ghettos. This has meant that these conflicts were either being pushed under the table and ignored or that they were met in other ways incompatible with the interests of the larger society.

I shall now briefly mention four simultaneous but rather independent historical events of early 1966 that played a prominent role in the development of tenant unions. First, Dr. Martin Luther King established an organization called the East Garfield Park Union to End Slums which in its inception was not a tenant union, but rather simply an organization to face community problems as they might arise and exist. The SCLC–furnished staff began meeting and discussing problems with people who lived in the community. Later I will discuss what sequence of events then transpired in East Garfield Park.

A second branch of King's movement was in the Lawndale area where representatives of SCLC and a number of other young people, some of whom are present here today, engaged in certain activities with resident tenants to see what could be accomplished. At a very early stage, this resulted in a gigantic rent strike which involved a community of about 400,000 people and led to some significant developments.

A third independent event was taking place at the same time on the North Side of Chicago. It involved an area occupied not by Negroes, but by Appalachian whites. This is the Uptown section of Chicago where an organization called JOIN, which is operated primarily by the Students for a Democratic Society, began engaging in social activities in an attempt to resolve some of the problems of the poor there.

Finally, the fourth significant event that was taking place at the same time, and completely independently of the others, was the organization of residents of a large, building complex on Chicago's Near North Side. This was at the Old Town Garden Apartments where the tenants were attempting to resolve the problems confronting them as management was replacing white tenants with Negro tenants.

Discussion of these events in slightly more detail is warranted. First, let us examine the East Garfield Park situation. Initially, there was basically protest activity. Residents living in the neighborhood related their problems to the staff; there was picketing and there were rent strikes. A major focus of this organization soon became a real estate agency, Condor and Costallis, that operated buildings in the community. A major rent strike ensued, and tenants were asked not to pay rent to this agency. There were sit-ins in the agency office and attempts to discourage people from renting from the agency. A full-scale economic war was under way against this agency which, at the time, was unwilling to meet with the tenants or their representatives to discuss their problems.

Most of you are probably familiar with East Garfield Park which is an area on Chicago's Near West Side. About 40,000 people live in the area which was built to house 20,000. Both small buildings and large apartment complexes are subdivided and there is extreme overcrowding. Services are inadequate, and it is significant that not one new building has been constructed in that area since 1924. The buildings are run down. In short, it is a typical ghetto situation.

In early June 1966, Condor-Costallis decided to resist the activities of the tenant organization by resort to the courts. They brought a suit seeking injunctive relief to stop the tenants' organization from engaging in the ongoing activities. This led to a highly publicized hearing for a temporary injunction. A great many people attended the hearing; there was newspaper and television coverage. Rather than engage in this type of conflict covered on television screens and depicted in the newspapers, nationally as well as locally, Condor-Costallis decided to negotiate with the tenants and their representatives.

Within about three weeks, there had been negotiated a collective bargaining contract. This was a unique and historical document, an agreement essentially like an industrial union labor contract, containing a number of significant terms. It provided for recognition of the union as the representative of those of its members who lived in buildings which were operated, owned, or managed by the agency. The agency agreed that all parties for whom it managed property would come under the terms of the agreement or be dropped by the agency as a client. It provided for certain short-term improvements in the buildings themselves such as code compliance, fixing doors, hallways, and apartments. It contained a grievance procedure and required that grievance meetings were to be held between representatives of the real estate agency and stewards to be elected from the various buildings involved.

It provided for fact finding in the event a dispute was unresolved between the union and the real estate agency, and it named a permanent fact finder. It further allowed that, in the event of a dispute, rent could be withheld by tenants and placed in the hands of a third party pending compliance by the landlord, and the union was given the final say as to whether or not there was compliance.

I will not go into further details in this area except to say that this contract was executed at a very early stage. In the history of tenant unions, effecting compliance and administering a contract has been an extremely complicated matter, and the union is still at an early stage in organizing the tenants and working out the details to make the contract work.

Lawndale is a large ghettoized slum area with about half a million people living in extremely run-down buildings which have not been maintained for years. Negotiations for collective agreements transpired with several small landlords, and soon an agent named Atlas, who owned a number of buildings, was encountered. Atlas proved to be extremely intransigent, and the people in the Atlas buildings went on strike in June. As a matter of fact, they are still on strike in some of the buildings. Eviction cases were filed against them and withdrawn. Meetings were held and negotiations ensued. At one point, an interim agreement was worked out which provided for certain basic corrective items as well as further negotiations. The eviction cases were reinstituted and are still pending. They will be coming up in court shortly.

The Maremont Foundation came into the picture at one point. The union took the position that Atlas was so intransigent that it was impossible to deal with them and that a working relationship could never exist between them. Atlas took the position that they would rather withdraw from the picture than have to deal with organized tenants, tenants with bargaining power. Presently, negotiations are in progress to see whether Maremont will acquire the properties and rehabilitate them with the tenants ultimately purchasing the rehabilitated property in the form of co-ops. I will not go into detail on rehabilitation or not-for-profit foundations which engage in this activity because Irv Gerick, a representative of one of those foundations, will be speaking here as will Vic DeGrazia, a representative of the other.

JOIN on the North Side did not limit its activities to the housing question. This organization was devoted to handling social, political, and economic problems of people living in the area. As it turned out, housing was but a minor item in their activities. The first collective contract of the type we are discussing was actually executed by this organization. However, it and several others which they executed later were on a single small-building, one-landlord basis. They did not provide for rent withholding, but for compulsory arbitration. Due to the complexity of details and problems that arise from handling disputes through compulsory arbitration on a building-by-building basis, these contracts proved to be unenforceable and largely unworkable. JOIN has moved on to other areas because the tenant union concept was not as workable in the Uptown area as it hopefully might be in others.

The Old Town Garden activity on the Near North Side was interesting in that it also did not initially emerge as a tenant union. Rather, the residents of that building complex viewed themselves as individual tenants, negotiating with the landlord for an improved lease. The landlord was a very large New York holding company that engaged a local manager of slum properties within the city to milk the property without providing maintenance or repair. From January through May, negotiations ensued with various representatives of the owner of this building, and the tenants accomplished little. There was much talk but very little else. A rent strike was called in June, 1966, and the tenants began seeing themselves as a tenant union or community organization. Approximately 50% of the tenants in the 650 apartments withheld their rent. As a result, there were some very dramatic, eviction court proceedings: 137 people were evicted in a single day and three families were physically evicted by the bailiff. Large-scale demonstrations followed, a number of court suits were filed, and everything reached crisis proportions.

About this time Irv Gerick and the Community Renewal Foundation entered the picture. They had been negotiating with the owner for the purchase of these buildings, and at the time the strike reached crisis proportions, these negotiations reached a climax in an all-night session where a three-party agreement was worked out. Community Renewal Foundation agreed to eventually purchase and rehabilitate the buildings, the tenants agreed to call off their strike, and various other items were involved which I will leave to Mr. Gerick to explain in more detail. The result was that a framework was established within which an effective community organization could work with a foundation interested in rehabilitation. In combining these two forces, the hope was for a smooth transition period during which community assistance and participation could effectuate the renovation of a decaying building. The result is still unknown as Mr. Gerick will explain.

During the summer a great deal of publicity about the activities of the four groups discussed above filtered down to various areas in the city. Resulting was the formation of some marginal and some rather substantial community organizations. They ranged from community groups of a particular ethnic origin, to tenants in a building which was not being maintained, to tenants in a group of buildings within the same neighborhood. All were interested in the developing concept of tenant unions. With the assistance of the Industrial Union Department, a very loosely formed federation was established whereby representatives of these organizations began to meet every other week. The Federation lacked decision-making powers, but met primarily so that the people engaged in these activities in their various areas could communicate with each other, exchange information about what they were doing, and render assistance if needed. During the summer, the tenants federation was quite active on this informal basis. In the early fall, these activities lessened and regular meetings are no longer held.

To indicate what is developing in terms of laws and court action, I would like to briefly mention some of the litigation which has ensued or is pending. A number of eviction cases were filed against people who went on strike. When things reached crisis proportions, most of the cases were dismissed and negotiated settlements between the parties were effected.

This may or may not take place in the Atlas situation, and a number of questions may be tested in currently pending eviction cases. For example: What defenses are available to slum tenants when the landlord evicting them refuses to deal with them, refuses to abide by the building code, or maintain the building? What is the effect of welfare withholding? As you probably know, sometimes the Welfare Department will withhold rent from a landlord who is not complying with the building code. Are building code violations a defense to an eviction? There are numerous unanswered constitutional issues. For example: Is it constitutional for a court to evict Negroes who cannot move out of the slum area when the landlord refuses to abide by the building code, deal with the tenants, or maintain a decent place in which they can live?

A second form of legal action which we encountered were the injunction suits brought by the landlords to enjoin picketing, striking, and most other activities by the tenant unions. In the East Garfield Park area, a law suit is pending which will determine if a landlord can obtain an injunction, enjoining tenant unions from engaging in activities which interfere with the operation of his business. There are also a number of criminal trespass cases which resulted from striking, picketing, and other activities. One suit was filed in South Shore which touches upon the question of relocating while rehabilitation is taking place, and the applicability of urban renewal provisions to pay moving costs and find decent living quarters for people who are forced to move. A significant question which has not yet been determined is whether or not the Federal Government has the obligation to find new housing in other nonsegregated areas for Negro tenants forced to move because of condemnation of the property or rehabilitation.

MARY ROBINSON

I am a tenant of an apartment building located at 6327 South Stewart. It is a fourteen-flat building, and each apartment has three to five rooms. I have lived there since 1959, and every year the building's condition has worsened. In 1966 a new manager was hired to take over the building. He became a tyrant and just took over. We were given heat only when he decided to give it to us. He cut out extermination and shot rats with rifles in the basement, and everything else. So we decided to get together and see what we could do.

Some of the tenants along with the community representative of the Urban Progress Center called a meeting in which we decided to start withholding our rent. We felt this would get faster action than anything else. We were advised to ask Chicago CORE for some help and composed a letter stating our problems, demands, and finally our goals. A letter was sent to every important official in Chicago: the mayor, congressmen, aldermen, the Building Department, and everybody that we thought should know about it.

On the basis of these letters, the city filed a suit against the owner for twenty-two major violations. In June, 1966, the court dates began. We still did not pay any rent and were threatened with eviction. The manager was going to get us out without due process, but we still would not move or pay any rent. Finally, we went to court and were faced with a very, very "wonderful" judge who was a personal friend of the landlord's lawyer. This meant that we had more problems. He ordered us to pay the rent and we refused. Then he ordered us to deposit it with the court and still we refused. He ordered us evicted but we had turned to ECO (Englewood Civic

Organization) for help. Rev. Dick Lawrence, the president, assigned Steve Bracker, his staff worker in charge of tenant unions, to work with us.

We decided to fill the courtroom with as many community people as possible. On Saturday mornings we picketed the owner's place of business, a meat company, and on Saturday afternoons we picketed his beautiful home near Rainbow Beach. He did not like this at all, and we felt that if we continued to picket and hold the rent something would come of it. Every Monday we were threatened with evictions. In the meantime we had gotten rid of the manager who was shooting the rats and mixing his own extermination products. This time an alcoholic was sent to manage the building. We did not want him and decided to get rid of him, too. So we still did not pay any rent or do anything we were told to do, but we filled the courtroom on court dates as the judge kept trying to discourage us with continuances and threats.

Then the judge made us parties to the city's suit against the owner because we would not sit down and shut up. He felt that he could frighten us into paying the rent by telling us that, if we did not pay, we would be held in contempt of court. This did not work either. We had made up our minds that we wanted a better place to live and were entitled to decent management if we were going to pay the rent. We were paying whatever he charged. Every time someone moved out of the building and someone new moved in, they were charged more rent. He wanted the older people out so they could not tell the new ones what was happening. We decided that would not work because we were part of the building and would have to stay there. There were many discussions, trips to court, threats, and so on.

In the meantime, Steve contacted Mr. Newmar, a lawyer from the Freedom Movement who had been sent to us. He decided that the judge just did not care for us; we just were not his type of people. We asked for a change of venue which was granted. This frightened the landlord and his attorney. We had never been able to talk or bargain with them, but after they faced a new judge, they decided to talk with us. Steve Bracker from ECO and our attorney talked with the owner and his attorney and decided that what the tenants wanted was right. They just had to have their way. Mr. Bracker asked us what we wanted. The owner was so tired and was losing so much time from his business that he wanted to get this cleared up and out of court. We decided that we had him in a spot and that he had to do just what we wanted.

We decided on a tenants' union. At first I thought this was the way to get what you wanted, but we might have gotten out of this without forming a tenants' union. I am not sure if it was the right thing or not. We still did not give in, and he saw that we meant nothing but business. Nobody was paying rent. Most of the people in the building were on aid, and we had gotten all their rent stopped. Only about four families were not on aid, which was not enough to keep the building going. Every way he turned, we cut him off so he had to come back to us.

After much discussion and many trips, our lawyer and his lawyer drew up a contract giving the tenants at 6327 Stewart the sole bargaining agreement. They collected rent, paid bills, fired and hired all the people called in to do work, and they OK'd all the work. All the building's profits are to go back into the building until it is rehabilitated the way we want it.

People must stick together. We had quite a problem with this because many were afraid that they would be evicted. Those on aid were afraid that they would be cut off because workers came and threatened some of them, and some checks were held up for a while. Others felt that you had to fight for what you wanted, so the few of us who would fought for all.

Because of the bad weather, not much has been done since the contract was signed, but next Wednesday the owner, Mr. Bracker from ECO, and the union stewards will meet to start the contractors on rehabilitating the building. We hope that by the summer it will be a much better place to live in.

23

Private Resources and Public Problems

JEAN WHITE

I am going to discuss what TOC is doing in Near West Side public housing. TOC stands for Together One Community. We are a group of tenants that are working in a public housing community called ABLA. In all, there are about 14,000 people residing in the complex, distributed (some say jammed) among fifteen-story high-rises, seven-story buildings, four-story walk-ups, and row houses. After it was in operation for six months, TOC decided to readdress itself to three main problems in the area: a public library, an A&P store, and public housing. Every Monday we called together tenants who were active in the community to plan strategy sessions on certain community problems, primarily the three just mentioned. The sessions were closed and only members of TOC and people in CHA housing were invited. From these small meetings, larger and more open meetings developed.

On September 1, we invited Mr. Harry Schneider, Director of Management of the Chicago Housing Authority, to work on certain proposals we had compiled from complaints that tenants felt were important. Our first proposal was for better security in high-rise buildings. We wanted them to close in the first floor lobbies, and install buzzers and an intercom system with a guard. We wanted laundries put back in the basement. We wanted rent assistance for senior citizens who received social security and were paying flat rent. Mr. Schneider said he would put our proposal for rental assistance for the aged to the federal government, and it is now in effect. The senior citizens are now receiving rent assistance and we feel that we played a major role in accomplishing this by bringing it to his attention.

CHA did not respond to the other issues, and they just ignored them entirely. CHA does not seem to be able to act on its own or be creative in planning for housing of families.

The next issue we mentioned in our proposal was decoration. The tenants wanted their apartments to be decorated every three years instead of every five years. Next, we wanted recreation facilities on the first floor with a staff to provide adequate activities. We wanted more guards. In a survey of the community, we discovered that there were only about eight guards in the area. We insisted on more guards; Mr. Schneider said he would get them, and he did. We wanted more janitors, but he did not react to that. We wanted exterminators for the rats, roaches, and mice. We wanted him to emphasize the elimination of apartment overcrowding, particularly in the high rises where in some cases there were thirty-five children on one floor. From this meeting, Mr. Schneider was not convinced that these were true problems. To convince him, we conducted a survey. We drew up about fifty questions, called in student volunteers, and on Saturdays we went out in crews. We chose different areas and canvassed the neighborhoods, interviewing the tenants. Most of the questions could be answered "yes" or "no" but additional grievances were included. We did this for about one month and continued having our small Monday sessions which we called our strategy meetings. We invited professionals to advise us on strategy or approach, long- and short-range goals. After about a month, we decided to discontinue canvassing. We threw away our questionnaires because we knew what the problems were, and we spontaneously began putting all our effort into improving the conditions of the public housing tenants. A tenant told me about her children living in a two-bedroom apartment, five in one bedroom. She asked what I could do for her, and I said that I would take her problem to the manager. A group of us went to the office and demanded to see the manager. We told him that we could not tolerate having five children living in one bedroom while there were two vacant apartments next door. Though he would not give her either of these because outsiders, such as people displaced by urban renewal or other emergencies, have priority over insiders, he did give her the next available vacancy.

We held an open meeting and decided that we could not handle the A&P issue. It was too broad an issue and for it to be handled effectively, a citywide boycott was necessary. A previous A&P boycott had not accomplished much, and overcharging, bad service, and uncleanliness continued to exist. We dropped that issue and the issue of the library to concentrate fully on public housing. In the meeting, the people said they could buy their food in other areas of the city where it was cheaper, but they could not live elsewhere. They wanted to concentrate all their efforts on public housing. We had started something and wanted to continue it. We were demanding reconsideration from management and giving the tenants a voice in deciding public housing policies. We told our manager that we wanted to see him every two weeks to bring in tenants' grievances and solve these problems and other issues. Though he agreed, at the time he did not believe that we could do it.

We have been seeing him for about four months, and we have grown steadily. Our small, Monday night meetings were changed into open meetings. Every Monday night, up to twenty-five people attend these meetings, and our grievance meetings with our manager, Mr. J. J. McGrath, are also growing. People come whom we have never seen before. It has passed by word of mouth that TOC talks on grievances. In our February meeting, we told our manager that we had seen families sitting outdoors and that we would no longer tolerate this eviction policy. We wanted a list of all nonpayment and any other imminent eviction cases mailed to me. He agreed to send me the list, but again, he did not believe that we could handle it because there are so many eviction cases. However, we have been able to handle the job and have saved families from having to sit outdoors.

An example of eviction for other reasons was a mother who lived alone. Her son was in the service and her daughter was living with her husband. The daughter and her husband separated and the daughter moved back into her mother's house. The mother told the caseworker that she and her daughter wanted to stay together. Since the daughter was working, she would support the family, and the mother would come off welfare. The caseworker told CHA officials, and they replied that the daughter could not stay. They actually wanted the mother to go back on welfare and move to a smaller unit. The daughter was considered an "unauthorized" person who must move or be evicted. The mother went to WSO and they gave us the case (because they had worked on it as much as they could but could not get anywhere, and it was directly within the type of work we had been doing).

We took the case and solved it in one day. A group of us went to the manager and said, "This is ridiculous. Are you trying to perpetuate a welfare system here? This lady is trying to help her daughter, and you tell the daughter she cannot help her mother . . . ." He said that things had been misinterpreted, and communication had broken down. The matter was finally satisfactorily resolved and the daughter was allowed to stay, although we were required to produce written evidence of the daughter's separation.

Another family was three months behind in their rent payments, and we were able to arrange for the back rent. Welfare was quite cooperative in this case and paid $260. Welfare is now giving us cases and asking for our help. We call in the CHA lawyers and tell them that we have money for a family. We ask them if they will stop the legal procedures and not send out bailiffs if the rent is paid. They agree, if we get an okay from Welfare. Welfare generally agrees, the rent is paid, and that is the end of the eviction case.

Now we are also working on excess utilities. Bills are paid directly to Edison, and in some high-rise buildings, bills for a one-bedroom run from $10 to $30. In one high rise, we are collecting all the tenants' bills, will compile them, and possibly call in the federal government. We will call in Edison and the CHA to get to the bottom of this. I might add, we use legal, welfare, or any agency that will help us.

VICTOR DeGRAZIA

I will first describe how the Maremont Foundation entered the housing business. Its official name is the Kate Maremont Foundation and it was originally established as a charitable family foundation. Arnold Maremont, who is the Foundation's president, was chairman of the Illinois Public Aid Commission in 1962. During his short and happy tenure, in addition to learning about birth control, he learned that the state was subsidizing slum housing with welfare payments, particularly in Chicago. Looking into it more deeply, he found what everybody here today knows, that the poor, and particularly the Negro poor, pay more rent for worse quarters than the middle-income or white families.

It was decided that something should be done, and Dr. Weaver, who was head of HHFA before the Department was created, suggested that the Foundation go into 221d3 rehabilitation. It was Weaver's idea and he wanted to see somebody do something about it. So we did. During the first two years or so of the program, most of our time was spent acquiring any property in Chicago that the FHA would accept and tried to work out a rehabilitation program on it. The rehabilitation was in accord with FHA standards as they interpreted them for a moderate- and low-income family program.

A little digression here. Part of our original problem with 221d3 rehabilitation was that the FHA viewed it as a middle-income housing program while we viewed it as a low-income housing program. Since they are the ones with the right of approval, they won, and all our original buildings in the program were middle-income buildings.

Then, about two years ago, we got involved in our two best developments. One is with The Woodlawn Organization in Chicago where for three years we worked on developing plans for the urban renewal section. The bidding was opened several weeks ago for Cottage Grove between 60th and 63rd. In addition to The Woodlawn Organization and the Maremont Foundation, we have established the new KMF-TWO Development Association with six board members from TWO and five from the Foundation. Since this new group was the only one to bid on all of the residential land, unless they throw out all the bids, it will probably be awarded to us. We did it together. The community organization worked with our architects and with the builders to develop the kind of housing they believed was necessary and best for the community. As a side benefit, the expertise of a planner, an architect, and a builder was available to them which enabled them to reinforce their resistance to high rises or whatever else the Department of Urban Renewal might want which the community opposed.

You might be interested in this latter aspect, When the city proposed the plan for community review, it had no restriction on the height of the buildings. It had some pious language about how the housing should be related to the ground, but there was no prohibition on high rises. A meeting of the Woodlawn Citizens Committee was held, and Lou Hill from DUR presented a plan. Then about eighty-eight groups all testified that they wanted an absolute prohibition against the high rise. The DUR heard the people's voice and changed their draft, banning buildings of more than five stories. This was put into the official plan and approved by the City Council.

We are still enthusiastically working with another development which is in East Harlem, New York, in an area called Metro North, and our particular province runs from about 100th to 106th. It combines a number of things, and I assume Jim Phillips will tell you some of the ways U. S. Gypsum is involved in that area.

Our goal here is different than with TWO. In Metro North, we had a good group of natural community leaders which had developed over the last few years in the face of problems in the area. It came into existence to resist the city's urban renewal program which was going to tear down the buildings and produce another high-rise, public housing project. The community and the businesses in the area resisted and stopped the city, but found themselves in the position similar to that of many other communities. They had been negative; they had stopped something and then did not know what to do.

A number of institutions in the community, one of which was the Union Settlement Association, advanced money to hire Bill Conklin, one of the best architect-planners in the country. With the community organization, he produced the Metro North plan. Several weeks ago, Mayor Lindsay referred to it as the Plan for Metro North. Although it has had no official action, all the city agencies know it and understand what should be happening. Therefore, officials, including the mayor, refer to it as the plan for the area which shows that it is possible to develop popular support for a locally generated plan and get the bureaucratic hierarchy to go along with it.

With Metro North our objective was to develop a self-sustaining housing program, and I expect that in about two years it will be that. Now we are rehabilitating five tenement buildings on 100th street and have established a new corporation in New York called the Metro North-East Harlem Housing Society. It consists of the settlement house, a Catholic and a Protestant Church, and the Foundation. We are each equal members, and the advanced funds for the staff have been provided by the Foundation. The Housing Society owns and operates these buildings, and, as I am sure you will hear, we have an agreement with U. S. Gypsum that when they are finished, the Housing Society will take over the twelve buildings they are rehabilitating in the area.

In addition, the New York City Board of Education recently designated the Housing Society as the sponsor for a new New York program which combines the construction of a new school and housing on one site. As sponsor, the Housing Society will develop a beautiful site on the East River between 100th and 102nd, providing approximately 350 new housing units.

We believe that Metro North and TWO represent what is needed to make a viable housing program. First, local leadership must be present. Though the best leadership will not always be apparent at the start, there must be some vigorous local activity. In Metro North, new resident leadership soon began to emerge which, in fact, was better than some of the original leadership. Second, community institutions with a long-term stake in the community should be present and interested in participating. Third, a financial catalyst must be provided as the Foundation was in both TWO and Metro North. And fourth, professional expertise is necessary to get a job done in housing but it comes very easily once you have the first three.

In conclusion I will briefly mention a basic problem that is met within local governmental agencies. The city agencies sometimes take the position that action by a local group implies that the city has not done what it could, and perhaps they are right. It has been our experience in Chicago and elsewhere that once a program is started, there is often immediate bureaucratic resistance by the municipal agencies. This usually takes a 180-degree turn when they try to take it over and run it as their program. You may have noticed that this has happened in the poverty program. Perhaps the most we can hope for is a armed truce with cities in which you continually push and see how your own leverage of money, publicity, and people can produce action from the city.

Finally, before I go to a meeting, my wife usually tells me not to say bad things about the FHA again. God bless their eighteenth-century heads but they just have not come to grips with the problems of the city. Sometimes I think it would be best to require all FHA employees to live in the city in which they operate. Most of them in every office all over the country live in the suburbs and like it — which in itself says something. It is like the story of the church group in which the president of the board of trustees says, "The pastor wants some new chandeliers, but number one, I do not know how to spell chandeliers, and number two, we do not have anybody here who can play them, and number three, what we really need is more light." Too often that typifies FHA reaction to a local group's request for assistance.

IRVING GERICK

Gil Feldman said "let there be light." But the question I must ask: Is it possible? At this moment not with the Federal Housing Administration. This is an agency organized in the 1930's to add liquidity to the mortgage market. Its traditional role has been to facilitate the building of single-family houses in the suburbs. It has none of the social orientation necessary for experimentation in the inner-city ghettos. In fact, FHA is an organization that has all the fear of risk characteristics of an insurance company and all the fear of mortgage foreclosure, characteristic of a mortgage company or bank. This combination makes them impossible.

Because of FHA, I had hoped that Vic DeGrazia would talk about rehabilitation. Without the FHA 221d3 below market-rate 3% interest program, rehabilitation would be impossible for moderate-income families. At this point there is no federal program I know of that can be used to upgrade housing for low-income families except that which occurs through public housing or through the public housing leasing program. Rent supplement, a program designed so that private developers can build or rehabilitate housing for low-income groups, is not workable in Chicago because of the high cost, the low levels set for rents, and the low amounts set to supplement the difference between the rent levels and the 25% of the low-income family's income alloted by law for the tenant's share of the rent.

Therefore, although Gil Feldman has committed me to say a few words about Old Town Garden Apartments, I think I can be most effective and most useful by talking about receiverships, a device which, if properly used, can serve to improve the housing supply available to low-income families. Further I would submit that it is this device that the Community Renewal Foundation, with the help of community organizations and tenant unions, will have to make work.

May I start with a little history of the Community Renewal Foundation, though many here know part of that history. We grew out of the Chicago City Missionary Society, which by the way will change its name to the Community Renewal Society. In organizing the Foundation, the specific purpose was to add a third and experimental force to the housing market. Most of the housing being developed in this country is by for-profit groups whose orientation is toward profit and higher income groups, and by various public housing authorities that over the years have moved from social purposes to bureaucracy. The CRF was organized to become an interdenominational, not-for-profit organization representing the various factions of the three major faiths. Our charter specifically directs us to engage in experimental housing for low- and moderate-income families. To accomplish this end we have (1) a new construction program; (2) a rehabilitation program; (3) a receivership program which is so successful that the City has copied it in at least its most obvious external manifestations; and finally (4) a legal assistance program for low-income families which Richard Newhouse, now a State Senator, fathered and through which he and Professor Julian Levi, of the University of Chicago Law School, brought the legally famous class-action suit by tenants against a slum landlord.

Receivership is designed to meet a very specific problem. There are 530,000 structures, not units, but structures, in the city. Over 75%, or about 400,000 structures, are more than forty years old and many of these were built prior to 1920. According to the 1960 census, over 150,000 of these structures were seriously violating the code and were in trouble. These old buildings are not like an old car; you cannot drag them off the street and into a junk yard. They continued to exist and to house people sometimes under most abysmal conditions.

I am not proposing – as some have stated here – that creating and maintaining slum housing is a conspiracy. I am saying it's part of the way our present economy operates. As we all know from personal experience, there is a limited supply of money. Investors, the government, etc., have to decide to put money in one place rather than another. So private money tends to flow into the safest place that yields the highest returns. Forty-year-old buildings in low income areas are not a safe investment. Consequently the people who invest in low-income areas are people who are willing to take a big risk for a big profit or people who make nickels and dimes from human misery. To put it in another way these buildings are not treated as an asset that will increase in value if properly maintained, but rather they are treated as a source of quick income. In short they are milked. When the most famous of Chicago slum operators, Mr. Winkler, finished with his building the joke was that Winkler had no buildings left; all he had was money in the bank.

The question is what can we do about it. Whe have over sixty years of experience to show that goodness of heart, civic virtue, publicity, and so on does not help. In order to solve the problem, by now it is abundantly clear that there has to be built into the economic system a way of preventing exploration of older housing. Receivership, I believe, is one of the techniques that can accomplish this.

Generally, in cases of housing, there are two kinds of courts, a court of law or housing court, and a court of equity or chancery court. The court of law, in effect, rules according to law and can only fine when there has been a history of building violations in the case of a slum building. It has been said that these fines are so low and are so long in coming that they act not as a deterrent, but rather as a license to operate for the slum owner.

The court of equity on the other hand can actually remove property from the control of a slum operator. This is done either by (1) ordering the building vacated and boarded up; or (2) ordering the building demolished as too dangerous for habitation; or (3) naming a receiver who takes possession of the building and all its income to make repairs and accomplish the necessary rehabilitation.

These buildings have usually been milked for so long that they cannot be repaired from current income. This point is important to understand. Once a building goes into receivership because of code violations, no income from that building goes to either the owner or the mortgage company. Yet all the income from the building is insufficient usually to make the necessary repairs. In order to properly repair the building, therefore, the receiver has to borrow money. In order to borrow, the court gives the receiver the right to issue notes of indebtedness called receiver certificates. These certificates, or notes of indebtedness, become a lien on the property paramount to all other private liens.

As a consequence, the receiver certificate in effect becomes the first mortgage and the first mortgage becomes a second mortgage. In the state of Illinois and in most other states, banks, insurance companies, savings and loan, etc., are not allowed to own or make second mortgages. This means that until the receiver certificate is paid off, not only does the mortgage company not receive any payment on its mortgage, but it has a mortgage that is worthless under the regulations of the State Examiner of Banks or Insurance Companies. This mortgage is no longer an asset and as a consequence, the institution owning it has to not only wipe it out, but increase its reserves to cover the loss.

With this procedure then, the building department has a valuable ally, for if the mortgage company does not inspect the property and keep it in repair, then the court appoints a receiver and the income from the property is removed from the owner and mortgage company for the length of time it takes to repay the receiver certificates. This is usually from ten to twenty years.

Two problems arise. One, before a building can go to equity court, it has to go into the court of law and the remedies in law have had to fail. Often, by the time a building gets to equity court and has a receiver named, it is fit only for demolition. Two, no one has even appealed a receivership case to the Illinois Supreme Court to test whether the requiring of the repaying of the receiver certificate prior to the repaying of the first mortgage is constitutional. Since the constitutionality has not been tested, no company will insure the certificates as a first mortgage and without this insurance, no bank is allowed to purchase receiver certificates. Therefore, we cannot sell receiver certificates on the private market. Within the last two months, however, two cases which may turn into test cases have been filed, so the necessary Supreme Court decision may be near.

In order to remove the first problem of length of time in law court, the class-action suit was developed. The Community Renewal Foundation and the University of Chicago Law School, through The Woodlawn Organization, found two tenants in a slum building in Woodlawn who filed a suit on behalf of all the tenants who lived in the same building. Until this action was filed by these two tenants as a representative of the class of tenants, no one but the city was recognized – had standing, to use the legal phrase – to bring a code violation suit. The purpose of this suit was to obtain legal recognition that two or more tenants acting for the class of tenants, or all the tenants in a building, have an equal right to bring a landlord into equity court in code violation cases. Once this right is recognized, then the low-income tenant has within his grasp the means to start to control his own housing destiny. If the recognition of the right of the tenant to bring such a suit is wedded to his right to ask for the appointment of a receiver to rehabilitate the building, then we have a union that, coupled with the growing strength of tenant unions can, I believe, upgrade and preserve decent housing for low-income families.

JAMES PHILLIPS

I will spare you the history of United States Gypsum and hopefully give you a direct answer to why a major industrial concern is interested in the problem which has been so ably identified here this afternoon, namely the problem of substandard housing in major American cities.

Essentially, United States Gypsum manufactures building materials. We are a profit-making corporation. We make a profit from the sale of products. United States Gypsum's major marketing effort is concerned with the sale of products for new housing. Two years ago, when interest rates were raised, sales began to suffer because the money available for new housing was restricted.

At that point, a marketing decision was made to look for a replacement market. Automobile manufacturers have a three-year, built-in replacement market. People buy new cars every three or four years, but they buy a new house once in a lifetime. With that in mind, United States Gypsum decided to investigate the sale of building materials to the urban rehabilitation market.

United States Gypsum has the long-range objective of solving the engineering and construction problems of the substandard housing problem. Our objectives are twofold. First, through involvement in pilot projects in major American cities, we intend to interest private developers to undertake urban rehabilitation for a profit. Second, through this involvement, we hope to make a profit from the sale of our products, and develop new products that reduce the in-place construction costs in urban rehabilitation. If this problem is solved the monies allowed under the total cost mortgage can be invested where they belong, in the rehabilitation of the existing structure.

I want to show you a nine-minute movie of our first building in New York City. It is one of six buildings on 102nd Street in the Metro North area of East Harlem. As Vic DeGrazia mentioned, we bought and rehabilitated this building under 221d3 as a builder-seller provision. Upon completion of the entire project of six buildings on 102nd and six immediately behind on 103rd, the building management and title will be transferred to the Metro North Housing Society of which the Maremont Foundation is a member. From a construction side, this short film shows the approach we are taking, which is to replace the entire insides of the building. When I started to explain how we got into this, I noted that we were literally forced into it. We had to open a new market. Now that we are in it, we see a great sales volume potential. Though I will not name them, many major American corporations have asked us to include them in the development of this market in various cities.

We did not and still do not know the requirements and attitudes of the people in local communities, and for this we must rely on our friends, the non-profit foundations to whom we intend to turn over these properties. Essentially we are construction people. We are not sociologists, and we are not attempting to identify all the requirements for the people who will live in these buildings after rehabilitation. Industry would be driven out of urban rehabilitation by the threat of demonstrations and pressures over not meeting the specific social requirements not accommodated in the total cost mortgage. We need a strong liaison of communication with the people living in these neighborhoods if we are to accomplish the job.

24

New Directions in Urban Housing

JOHN McCLAUGHRY

In 1964 when Charles Percy was running for governor of Illinois, his campaign travels took him to the slums of Chicago and East St. Louis. He began to see some of the difficult problems with which all of us here are quite familiar and, indeed which many have to live with day in and day out. As a result, he began to think of some ways in which he, as governor of Illinois, could fight the problems posed by the slums. As you know, in 1964 it did not work out quite the way he had in mind, but the campaign did give him much first-hand experience which was to prove most valuable later on.

In 1966, we prepared for the Senate race. I was the research director in the campaign, and Mr. Percy emphasized to the research staff that we had to develop ideas for solving the problems of housing, poverty, and motivation.

Of course, the first problem we focused on was housing in the physical sense – crumbling mortar, falling plaster, and peeling paint. But it soon became apparent that the housing problem was inseparable from the human problems of the ghetto, the slum, or even the run-down rural neighborhood. Too often our public housing programs, for example, have been designed only with the idea of producing safe, sanitary, sturdy dwellings. Poor people were then to be poured in to live there happily ever after, unless their incomes rose too far. I do not need to dwell upon the unhappy results with this group. There has long been a split, which is not a conspiracy of design so much as a reflection of different points of view, between those in the housing, mortgage, and credit-rating businesses, and those in the business of working with human beings and their problems, teachers, social workers, war-on-poverty officials – all those who day-to-day deal with people rather than with construction, housing, or finance, and the like. In our work we sought as best we could to heal that split.

Thus we changed our emphasis from housing as such to poverty and the economic conditions of slums, focusing on what we thought was one of the central elements, the problem of motivation. The poor person is kicked around by faceless, impersonal forces such as the power structure, uptown,

Mr. Charlies, and City Hall, which he cannot understand or often even recognize. Everytime he sticks out his neck and tries to take a step forward, he gets swatted down. As I am sure everybody here knows, the result is cynicism, despair, anguish, uncertainty, an unwillingness to invest today for tomorrow's rewards, and an unwillingness to defer gratification. It is a very familiar syndrome to anybody who has spent time working with very poor people, especially in urban slums.

How can we break this motivation barrier? For some people it is probably impossible. People who are beyond their productive years cannot, at the age of 80, get themselves a job as a welder. There is not much we can do for them or for mothers with dependent children, except to see that they are given the essentials of life in such a way that their dignity remains unimpaired – a condition too frequently unmet in welfare programs presently. However, this is not the case with a man between the ages of twenty and forty, with a stable family and without physical or mental disabilities which prevent him from getting ahead. Yet he may just be floating along unemployed or underemployed; for lack of a better euphemism, he is usually part of a multiproblem family. How do we get him to achieve his full potential?

We came up with an answer already being much discussed today. We think the answer is ownership, having the opportunity to own something important, to become an active participant in shaping one's environment. When he learns he can make a difference in the world around him, the seeds of independence, self-reliance, and dignity have been planted. This will accelerate the rise out of poverty into – I do not want to say middle-class status because in some circles that has a bad connotation – into a status of independence and identity, of knowing who you are and having some pride in what you are.

The next question is how to make a poor person an owner? There are more ways than one, of course, but the idea of home ownership fulfilled both the need to improve housing and the need to motivate lower-income people to climb the ladder. That was our first principle, and later, we added three others which together form the basis of the Percy Plan.

The first principle underlying the Percy Plan is ownership or, as Senator Percy frequently puts it, "having something and being somebody." This concept means something to him, for during the depression of the thirties, his family did not own a home and, at one time, they were on welfare. From his childhood, he remembers his mother saying, "Charles, when you grow up, save, invest, and try to own a home of your own." Though he never shared the plight of today's slum dweller, the value of ownership was impressed upon him at an early age.

The second principle was to bring into the slum the resources, the private sector, corporations, banks, people with money, the power structure if you will. A slum is a slum partly because they ignored it and partly because they exploited it; how do you turn around and develop it into a viable, living neighborhood with a spirit of its own? Government action is not enough – a way must be found for putting private sector resources to work.

The third was to generate grass-root, self-help participation by the people themselves instead of imposing from the top some fancy scheme thought up by somebody in Washington, Springfield, or the higher reaches of academia.

The fourth principle, to which I have already alluded, is to bridge the gap between the people who have to do with housing and the people who have to do with people, to make housing an aspect of human environment rather than a place to just keep out the rain and the rats.

As you can see from the printed description of the plan, the mechanics are rather intricate. I will not go into an explanation of who passes the papers to whom at what point except to say that our proposal involves a National Home Ownership Foundation which will be a private, non-profit, corporation. It will have two essential functions. First, it will have a loan fund, making direct loans to local, non-profit associations like many of those represented here. Second, it would provide technical assistance to aid those associations in wise management of that loan money and in conducting a viable rehabilitation or construction project in the slums.

In addition, the foundation would help local associations find the public and private resources to finance supporting activities necessary if lower-income people are to become home owners. This includes everything from basic education to job training to finding a job and moving up in it once you have it. It includes credit buying, counseling, money management, and all those things which community development organizations are trying to achieve in one way or another.

Finally, in Washington the Foundation would go to bat for community organizations which have suffered so long in trying to thread their way through the ponderous structure of federal programs.

Front money is one of the most serious problems facing the community organization. How are initial planning loans obtained for the project without having first delivered the project you are planning? We envision a foundation with money available for loans to local organizations which they can pay back later.

One of our main bottlenecks is the lack of trained manpower to run a sensible housing program at the grass-roots, neighborhood level. In 1964, Congress passed a section of the Housing Act authorizing federal-state grants to colleges for training professional people to work for city agencies dealing with these problems. This was three years ago, and to date the program never received a penny.

Senator Percy has said that he would introduce legislation to broaden that program, permitting training, not only of graduate-level people, but also of those with a good head even if they are not high school graduates, people who know how to work in slums and can understand mortgage financing and whatever else is necessary to conducting a housing program. Further, he would make it possible to train people who work not only for the city but also for non-profit organizations. These amendments would remove these two important restrictions and enable local organizations to acquire trained manpower to carry on a decent housing program in their neighborhoods.

Two years ago, an amendment to the Housing Act was passed which permitted the sale of detached or semidetached public housing units to tenants. Incidentally, this was a Republican amendment which was not sought by the administration and as far as I know, through perhaps someone can correct me, nobody has ever bought a public housing unit under the section 507 program. I suspect that very few people in public housing know that a unit of that nature can be purchased. The question remains as to whether or not anybody would want to buy a public housing unit, even one that is semidetached or detached. In any case, the Housing Assistance Administration has shown a lack of enthusiasm in making this known to people who might be interested in buying certain kinds of public housing units. In effect, they have not done much to implement this.

Another example is the Leased Housing Program, section 23, which has been discussed. It provides for a lease with an option to purchase, and recently we asked HUD to see if this has been used. As evidence that after two years it is finally moving, I was greeted with a newspaper clipping from St. Louis announcing the first family in the country to express an interest in exercising an option to buy a leased-housing unit. This did not seem sufficient in comparison to what might have been done. Another provision of the Act permits the sale of federally-owned public housing units to cooperatives. In fact, however, there is only one federally-owned public housing building in the United States of America, in Enid, Oklahoma. Thus I think the great promise of that idea is yet to be realized.

Finally, another section of last year's housing act which also has been mentioned, 221h, provides mortgage insurance to non-profit organizations for ownership projects. It was inspired by a very remarkable project in St. Louis which was conducted by what is now the Mullanphy Street Rehabilitation Corporation. Fifty-seven families were placed in homes located in a neighborhood which is adjacent to Pruitt-Igoe Public Housing. Without a doubt this is the cesspool of public housing. At last report, there was an entire building there which was completely empty, and the windows were broken as high up as the biggest kid in the block could throw a rock.

A non-profit association in cooperation with the St. Louis banks, which got very public spirited about it, placed fifty-seven families in those homes. Now after two years, fifty-three of those families are still there and making payments, which is a pretty good record. The other four families were divorce cases which distort the calculations. 221h was designed specifically for this project and was introduced by Mrs. Sullivan, a congresswoman from Missouri. As of two weeks ago, not one piece of paper on 221h had moved out of FHA. Fanny Mae will not pick up the mortgages, and no regulations have been issued. As far as any implementation is concerned, Congress might as well have rejected it 400 to 0.

Under existing federal programs, much more can be done to promote home ownership for low-income people. But the federal government has shown almost no interest in promoting ownership except for those who can buy in places like Hoffman Estates out in the suburbs. Senator Percy intends to work aggressively to implement what is already in the law and at the same time present a program which, on a national basis, will broaden the opportunities for home ownership by low-income people.

JOSEPH BURSTEIN

Though I have already spoken about all our new programs, there have been some direct statements about our programs and certain specifics which I should answer.

First, the Tower Amendment. It was drafted to apply only to detached or semidetached houses. We recommended that at least it apply to row houses, but for some reason it was not adopted. We tried to change it so that it would apply to the existing public housing program but unfortunately we were not successful. As a result, it is ineffective both because it applies only to detached and semidetached housing, which is practically nonexistent in the present public housing program, and because it is not applicable in projects where bonds are outstanding since such an amendment cannot affect the bondholders. St. Louis is the one place where a public housing unit is being leased with an option to buy, and it is under the Tower Amendment, not the leasing program. This project has been financed only recently; it is in an urban renewal area and consists of existing houses which happen to be detached. I hope I have clarified the factual situation on this amendment and the leasing of the one unit.

The section 23 leased-house program was introduced by Congressman Widnall as the Rent Certificates Plan. We were happy to work with Mr. Widnall in making this a very viable program. Although there was nothing in it which had to do with home ownership or rehabilitation, our regulation emphasizes that the leasing program should be used as much as possible for leasing with options to purchase. I do not know how many private owners have entered leases with an option to purchase, but I suspect that there are quite a few who have.

Another point has been made about cooperatives. The particular project in Enid, Oklahoma, referred to is the only remaining federally owned project in the program. It happens to be a leftover from the old TVA program, and we could not get rid of it because they did not pay the Housing Authority. In fact, Oklahoma did not have any housing legislation until a few years ago, so we had to retain that project. It still has to create a Housing Authority. The legislation referred to was our attempt to find a way to sell it to a non-profit organization in the absence of a Housing Authority. No non-profit organization will buy it and so we are still holding it.

Reference has been made to certain legislative proposals by Senator Percy. There are some programs of which Senator Percy does not seem to be aware. I would be happy to acquaint him with our self-help program on Indian reservations which Dr. Tax knows well. It is not under new legislation but is by administrative interpretation of a long-standing law. Indian families build their own houses, obtain an equity credit, and, over fifteen years, they can obtain ownership through self-maintenance. Over one hundred of these houses are occupied, many hundreds are under construction, and thousands are under contract.

We are expanding this program to involve private enterprise because the self-help program as supervised by the Bureau of Indian Affairs is moving too slowly. A South Dakota contractor and a private contracting corporation working with the Navajo, the Ibed Corporation in Oklahoma, have been induced to undertake this self-help program on a contract basis. I understand that the project on the Rosebud Reservation is moving much faster now that private enterprise is involved in prefabricating these units and supervising these people on their own houses.

Private enterprise is also involved under the turnkey method which we have developed administratively. Apprenticeship and training programs have been combined with OEO programs to help build houses on three Minnesota Indian reservations. This has proved so successful that it is being expanded to twenty-five others across the country as rapidly as financing can be found for it. By financing I mean private, not government, financing through which the families themselves are responsible for producing the completed house. The Housing Authority purchases it, entering a lease purchase arrangement with the participating families. And I could go on and on enumerating the possibilities.

Translating the self-help we have developed on Indian reservations into an urban setting can be accomplished legally and financially. Essentially it is a problem of working with labor unions and of the more difficult situation of building in an urban setting as against building on Indian reservations. Though it involves different problems, the basic system under which it can be accomplished is now well established under our programs. We are very proud of it, particularly because it involved private enterprise in direct contact with the poverty-stricken element in our population. In this instance, it has been restricted to Indians; hopefully it will be expanded to urban areas.

We welcome competition of ideas for helping the poor because it is the most helpful kind of competition in which this country can engage. As far as that goes, Senator Taft was probably one of the greatest advocates of housing for low-income families, so I do not intend to cast any aspersions on Senator Percy's efforts, because of his party affiliations or otherwise. I resent the aspersions because we are very proud of what we are doing. I think that if Senator Percy were fully aware of what we are doing in this area, he would agree with just about all of it.

Now we have a very flexible type of assistance under which private owners can lease their units to low-income families. The approval of the local governing body is the only condition for this assistance. A workable program is not required, and there are no other requirements. In Chicago now about 1400 units are approved which, of course, is far too few.

Let me reemphasize that in the leasing program it is not necessary to work through a Housing Authority. We can work through a state, city, or any public body authorized to engage in housing. Once they get the federal contract, they can work with almost anyone. As I mentioned earlier, a particular type of house can be financed conventionally, by FHA, or it can involve a cooperative.

Very soon we will be able to supplement a cooperator's rents or payments on the units. Whatever housing is involved, we can supplement the rent when necessary. It can be supplemented with respect to a unit under a lease-purchase arrangement. In other words, as I mentioned, if an owner or a non-profit organization is willing to lease the units with an option to purchase, we can supplement a family's rent until its income reaches the point where it can carry the full weight. Then, if the families choose to, they can exercise the option for purchase and obtain home ownership. There is no sale when the lease-purchase contract is entered into. Under home ownership plans where there is a sale, there is the disadvantage of having a mortgage because, in case the family cannot make it, you have legal expenses and so on. The lease-purchase arrangement is a simple way to subsidize the rents of families until they can acquire ownership.

As for housing which comes to be owned by the Housing Authority, we no longer talk in terms of monolithic public housing which has been criticized so often. We are talking about all housing, and we are talking about housing produced by private developers under the turnkey method. It can be produced where the developer buys or owns the structure, and rehabilitates it for sale to a Housing Authority, or it can be new, individual, multifamily, or any other kind of housing. Again, it utilizes the incentives, talents, and mechanisms which have created the market, the know-how, and the cost savings in the private enterprise system. This is an improvement on the methods used heretofore, a competitive and governmental bidding system, which loaded the cost of public housing.

I cannot possibly go into all the details, but the possibilities do exist. We have so many new and flexible tools that if you name the problem and have an interested local, government, non-profit, or individual organization, there is a way to work it out. Just ask our regional office, and if they do not know, they will ask us.

ANTHONY DOWNS

I. Some Basic Aspects of the Nature of Housing

A well-known author has written a book called *A House is not a Home.* We could also say that, "A house is not housing." In fact, I would say that the quality of any housing depends on three basic factors. The first is *the physical facility itself,* which includes design, layout, cost, construction quality, size, decoration, and furnishing as well as the structure and the state of its maintenance.

The second factor consists of *the people inhabiting the facility and their behavior.* This includes their number in relation to the size of the unit. No matter how well constructed or furnished it is, a two-bedroom unit is poor housing for a ten-person family. In addition, since housing is the space in which one lives, the behavior of people towards each other, including whether their relationships are excessively aggressive or reasonably tolerant, is an important ingredient in the way housing is perceived by the people in it. This is particularly the case with regard to their behavior towards the physical facility. No matter how well-constructed a house is, if they tear it down, knock holes in the wall, urinate on the floor, and throw garbage down the stairwell – and many people behave that way – then they will perceive it as pretty rotten.

The third factor is *the setting and surroundings of the facility.* This includes its location in relation to stores, churches, and workplaces; the condition of the neighborhood and how safe and friendly it is; the level of government services there; how fast snow is shoveled and garbage cleared, and the kind of police and schools there. These are all part of the housing problem.

I disagree with anyone who says that housing is a very simple problem, and all we need is money. I do not think it is quite that simple. There are two further aspects of housing we must keep in mind. First, the activity that goes on in housing is more complicated than that in any other structure. It is extraordinarily complicated in comparison to what happens in a school or office building. People sleep, eat, cook, make love, read plays, study, watch TV, sit around, are alone, have friends in, sew, do home carpentry and financial studies, build boats – almost any activity you could name is done in houses. Therefore, it is very difficult to design a house suited to all the activities of the people who live in it.

Second, with regard to urban housing problems, it is important to consider the longevity of the house. A house can last centuries. The White House, the Vatican, and the Palace of Versailles are quite old. Even if the inside of the house and some of the furnishings deteriorate, the frame can last for a very long time and thus be used by many different people. Therefore, a house cannot be personally designed like a shirt. A shirt is designed to fit you perfectly, and when it no longer fits, you throw it away. But a house will be used by many people and thus will not be very well-adapted to whoever lives in it at any particular time.

Furthermore, fashions change rapidly, particularly in this age of high-speed innovation. Because of the long time a house lasts, it will therefore become obsolete sooner or later. In this age of extremely rapid change, we can expect that any house built today will become obsolete quite quickly. About 20% of the existing dwelling units in Chicago were built before 1900; they are obviously very obsolete.

Longevity also affects the cost of building a house. Though most of the cost occurs immediately, the benefits are spread over many years. This results in a peculiar financing problem. The money must be put up at the outset, but the benefits are not received for many years. Hence money usually has to be borrowed to build houses, since most people do not have the money that will represent the future benefits to be derived from the structure. When people have to borrow money, their buying becomes very sensitive to even slight changes in interest rates. Such changes can significantly affect their ability to buy a house, even though they do not greatly affect their need for housing.

Thus, before we can understand city housing problems, we must recognize that housing is not just buildings, that houses are long lasting, and that they serve extremely complicated functions. With these things in mind, we can look at the so-called "housing problem," which is not quite as simple as it might seem at first.

II. The Varied Nature of the Housing Problem

It is useful to talk first about the scale of the housing problem, because scale is relevant to the solutions that the federal government has advanced and that Senator Percy and others are proposing.

In large cities, the housing problem can be defined in terms of four conditions. First there are substandard housing units which were poorly built or maintained, or which lack certain plumbing amenities. In 1960, there were about 58 million house units in the United States. About 15.2 million were either dilapidated, deteriorating, or of sound construction but without adequate plumbing. In other words, about one out of every four units in the United States was considered substandard.

In the central cities, there were 18.5 million housing units. Of these, about 3.3 million were either dilapidated, deteriorating, or sound without adequate plumbing. Most were in the deteriorating condition – about 2.2 million, or 12% of all the housing in central cities. About 1.8% were dilapidated, and about 3% were sound without adequate plumbing. These figures provide us with some idea of the great number of people who at this moment are living in housing which technically is substandard.

In addition, a lot of housing is extremely old, though technically it does not qualify as substandard. About 27 million housing units in the United States, or about 46% of the 1960 total, were built before 1930. In Chicago, 83% of the housing was built before 1930, and as I mentioned, 20% was built before 1900. No matter what condition it is in, a unit built before 1900 has some obsolete features. It has no parking facilities, and it is usually built on a 25-foot lot. Even if it has been updated, it does not have the bathrooms and family rooms that we now consider important. So to say that 3.3 million families live in substandard units in cities is an understatement of the number who live in relatively undesirable units.

Another group of people who have a housing problem are those who live in overcrowded conditions. In general, more than one person per room is undesirable. In central cities, 7% of all owner-occupied units and 14% of all rented units have more than one person per room. For Negroes, these percentages are about double. As of 1960, in central cities alone, 15% of all non-white owner-occupied units and 27% of all non-white rented units were overcrowded.

A further group of people who have a housing problem are those who live in undesirable neighborhoods. High crime rates, extremely high vandalism, and so forth produce very undesirable living conditions. Some people living in Chicago have as many as ten padlocks on their doors; it takes them about ten minutes just to walk out the door and pick up the newspaper. Many people live in this kind of situation, and they have a housing problem even if their physical unit is in good shape.

Finally, many people live in areas with very poor public services. Yesterday, in an area of Atlanta, Georgia, which is going to be nominated for the Model Cities Program, I saw a combination of poor private behavior and poor public services. Junk, autos, and tons of waste paper were all over; garbage had not been collected. Obviously, this area was not on the city's high-priority list for cleaning, and it was not being cared for by its residents. This also creates a housing problem even if the physical units are in good shape. If the housing problem is defined in this way, many more people are living in "problem" conditions.

III. The Relationship Between Housing Problems and Poverty

Clearly, most of these conditions are encouraged by poverty. So, to a great extent, we have more of a poverty problem than a housing problem. That is not to say that we do not have a housing problem; we do. But the poverty problem is probably a very large part of it. The economists at the University of Chicago, who are rather laissez-faire-oriented, sometimes define slums as "housing for low-income people." To some extent this is true, because there is a large demand for housing by people with very little money. They need low-priced housing and this is one reason why we have it.

Poor people have poor housing because they are afflicted with the following obvious disadvantages. They can pay only for the units in the worst condition among all those in existence, and these tend to be the oldest. They cannot pay for much space, but they have the largest families; this results in overcrowding. This perpetuates the problem by creating conditions in which children cannot study, internal family tensions increase, and so on. These conditions make it more difficult for them to get out of poverty. They are caught in the further squeeze of not being able to pay to maintain their property, even though it is the oldest and thus has the highest maintenance cost. They are less mobile and know less about where to look for better quarters, especially if they are old, crippled, disadvantaged, or have small children. They do not know where to find alternative supplies if any exist. They also tend to have the most destructive personal habits. And, of course, they may be discriminated against if they are Negro, Puerto Rican, or Mexican, and this tremendously reduces their choice of housing.

Obviously, the poor are at a great disadvantage. This is one reason why the housing problem is to a very large extent a poverty problem. If the cure to housing is not accompanied by a cure to poverty, it will never work. In fact, it seems to me that a cure to poverty is a prerequisite for any effective approach to the housing problem.

Our rising rate of aspirations is also relevant to the housing problem. Mr. Burstein referred to one of his programs under which Indians are building their own houses. Most of the people in the world live in houses which they built. In fact, in most countries the lowest-income families live in the newest housing; that is, shacks which they built themselves. These houses and those built by the Indians on their reservations probably would not meet our modern building code standards. One problem is that those standards are overblown by unions and material manufacturers.

In addition, our aspirations are rising much faster than we can change the built-in characteristics of the 58 million existing units. In a society where poor people spend a lot of time looking at television and seeing how rich people live, it is impossible to tolerate the gap between rich and poor that has been typical of most societies throughout most of history. The conditions of the poor are improving, but not as fast as those of the rich. Therefore, the gap between them is increasing. The poor watch television for several hours a day; it is one of the cheapest amusements they can find. They see others' living conditions far more now than they did when, once a week, they saw them portrayed in Hollywood movies. Therefore, they are certainly much less willing to accept standards far below those of the middle and upper classes. In spite of the fact that they see California ranch houses every day, they cannot have them, and this creates frustration.

Yet, unless we tear down 27 million of the existing, older housing units – which would leave quite a few people out in the street – we will have to live with and use these units for quite a while. As I mentioned, 46% of the units in the United States were built before 1930. In some way, we will have to use that stock of housing. It will most likely be used by lower-income citizens. Therefore, in considering "solutions" to the housing problem in our society, we cannot think in terms of everybody living in a brand-new, modern unit. Though we are the richest society in the history of the world, we are not so rich that we can throw away 27 million housing units and start over with all new structures. We just are not going to do it.

IV. The "Trickle-Down" Process

Since the poorest people live in the worst houses, the traditional way that more housing has been available to them was to increase the total housing inventory by building more new housing at the high-income end of the range. These units would eventually trickle down to the bottom. We are the only society in the world rich enough to do that. Throughout most of the rest of the world, no units trickle down because richer people stay in them. As I mentioned, poor people can get *new* houses only if they build shacks themselves.

The trickle-down system has the one great advantage that the people who live in new houses are able to pay for them without a subsidy. High- or middle-income groups buy the new houses and leave their older houses for the poor. In this way, everybody can pay for his unit without a subsidy.

However, there are some very severe disadvantages to the trickle-down process. First, all the oldest units are clustered together in the central cities. This causes de facto segregation of the poor. Since many of the poor are in minority groups, it also causes de facto segregation of those groups. Moreover, it puts a fiscal squeeze on central city governments. They have the people with all the expensive problems and none of the resources with which to pay taxes.

A second drawback is that housing lasts so long that is a wreck by the time it trickles down to the poor. So they live in pretty miserable conditions.

Third, the trickle-down process operates slowly, so a rapid increase in the number of low-income people in a given city causes a greater increase in population than in the local housing stock. This inevitably results in over-crowding. Such overcrowding is like congestion on an expressway. If more cars than the road can handle suddenly converge on a particular spot, the result is terrific congestion, and everybody has to slow down to two miles an hour. Yesterday in Atlanta the mayor said that 35,000 people a year are coming into Atlanta from surrounding rural areas. Certainly that many new houses are not being built each year. In the United States, the housing stock increases at the rate of about 1%, whereas people move at the rate of 20% a year. If that 20% or a large fraction of it decide to converge on one area, the increase in population there far exceeds that which can be handled by adding to the housing stock. Naturally, the result is overcrowding.

The final difficulty of the trickle-down theory is that racial discrimination obviously reduces the ability of Negro and Puerto Rican groups to "trickle up" into the supply. They are prevented from moving into better units and taking upward-mobile jumps even when they are financially capable of doing so.

Despite these weaknesses, the trickle-down process is and will probably continue to be the major method by which we provide housing for the poor. This is the case because we refuse to pay the price for subsidizing housing for the poor. We are certainly willing to have subsidies, in spite of the statements of many conservatives who in theory are opposed to subsidies. As a matter of fact, we have enormous subsidies in housing in the form of income tax deductions for interest and local property taxes. But these subsidies are only for those in upper income tax brackets. Alvin Schorr in the antipoverty program did a simple calculation which showed that the total subsidy for housing in the middle- and upper-income groups in 1962 was about $2.9 billion. For the lowest-income groups, including the cost of public housing, welfare rent payments, and tax deductions, the subsidy in 1962 was only $780 million. Members of the richest 20% of the population were getting double the per capita subsidy of the lowest 20%. Thus, our society is not against subsidy; it is only against subsidy for those who need it. Subsidy for people who do not need it is very well supported by Congress. Our unwillingness to put extensive resources directly into the housing problem of low-income people is the major reason why we are not making more progress in this area.

V. The Growth of Central-City Non-white Population

As I mentioned, the rapid increase in the non-white population of our central cities, and particularly of the Negro population, is an important factor relevant to our housing problems. You all know that neighborhood stability cannot be defined in terms of white and non-white groups, because the non-white population in central cities is increasing at a tremendous rate and the white population is decreasing. Any program aimed at stopping de facto segregation which assumes stability under these conditions is an ostrich program. The people who espouse it have their heads in the sand and cannot see what is happening.

The non-white population in most central cities is increasing even though the birth rate is decreasing quite dramatically. There is a great transition in the nature of the population as the non-white population increases and the whites leave. In Chicago, between 1950 and 1960, the non-white population increased by more than 300,000; while more than 700,000 whites left the city most people only see the *change* in the white population and conclude that the decrease was about 400,000. But that does not include the natural increase in the white population which would have occurred if people had remained in the city.

Though the housing stock stays the same, these tremendous movements in the population mean that standard, good quality housing for low-income people in central cities has to be made available at a much faster rate if we are to solve the urban housing problem. Ironically, one way that such housing becomes more rapidly available is by increasing the spread of massive transition from white to non-white occupancy. I presume that most of you would be opposed to this. For quite different reasons, many people in the white middle-class community are opposed to it too. Yet it is one of the fastest ways to provide better housing for low-income people.

VI. Possible Steps to Attack Poverty

What should be done about these complicated problems? Though I am a consultant to several government organizations, I am now speaking for myself, not for them. I think the first thing to do is attack poverty. The first major antipoverty step is to provide an income floor for everybody. This can be done through three devices. The first is a guaranteed annual income for people who cannot work. They comprise about three-fourths of those now on welfare. We should remove all the nonsensical controls and raise the minimum income level, making it uniform throughout the country. We should accept the fact that we have to support those people at a reasonable level.

Second, subsidized jobs should be given to the unskilled but ablebodied workers by paying employers to hire and train them. The employers, in turn, could hire them and pay them decent wages.

Third, I think we should have para-military service for those incorrigibles who are now unemployed. The Defense Department has made this suggestion, but its implementation has been stopped by certain Congressmen. I think this would help upgrade these people, change their environment, and enable us to make progress in areas other than those affected by my previous two suggestions.

Another major antipoverty step is to drastically improve education levels in poor areas through compensatory education. This might be done in combination with dispersal of low-income students into middle- or lower-class integrated situations. The Coleman Report seems to indicate that compensatory education does not work, but I think that is because we have never really tried it. Though there have been classrooms with less than thirty students, there have not been any with only four or five students. I believe this is where compensatory education begins to be effective.

I think the third major antipoverty step is dispersal of the poor population so that some are integrated into middle-class neighborhoods. Though some of you may think that creating a middle-class society is entirely wrong, I think that is precisely what we are trying to do. Many antipoverty, housing, and other programs are geared toward eliminating the lower class, not with gas chambers, but by upgrading them into the middle class. Many people are opposed to this, but I think that the consensus of opinion is that this is what should be done. Moreover, if any of the surveys of low-income opinion are accurate, these people have the same aspirations as most middle-class people.

In every society throughout history, segregation and discrimination have existed. The question is: What are the legitimate grounds for them? The Supreme Court and most people in our society agree morally (but not in fact) that race is not a legitimate ground. But socioeconomic level still is accepted as a legitimate ground for discrimination and segregation. I think that in the future we will move toward questioning that premise too. Possibly we will then be able to eliminate poverty, which no society in human history has ever done or even seriously tried to do.

In theory, poverty can be eliminated by one of two basic methods. A lot of money can be spent on improving the conditions of the poor where they now live, and they are now living with each other. But, as I am sure you know, one of the biggest housing handicaps for disadvantaged people is themselves. Many would claim that one of the main disadvantages of living in public housing projects such as those on State Street is that the residents must go to school with others who have the same background, the same broken homes, and so on. The Coleman Report claims, and perhaps it is true, that no matter how much money is spent on providing better teachers, using more people who are not professional teachers, and on special programs, we cannot upgrade the lowest income people without somehow integrating them with the middle class. Such integration is the second basic way to eliminate poverty.

Thus, the middle class is faced with a rather interesting choice. Its members will either have to spend much more money in massive subsidies to upgrade the lowest income groups, or they will have to live with them, accepting their dispersion throughout suburban and peripheral central-city areas. I do not think the middle class will do either of these things immediately. And I do not know which they will do in the long run. If the middle class is going to take housing programs seriously, they will have to choose between spending a lot more of their own money or becoming the neighbors of the poor and performing the upgrading function themselves. I do not think that middle-class whites are ready to do this yet. I wish they were, and I hope we can help move them along the road.

VII. Improving the Housing of the Poor

So far I have been talking about antipoverty efforts and I haven't said anything about improving housing. The first thing to do about housing is expand the total supply. Last year the total housing supply was augmented by only 1.2 million units. But 500,000 other units were destroyed; so in effect there was a net gain of only 700,000. Since more than 700,000 new households were formed, there was a net loss in housing, and crowding increased. Unless we build enough new units to at least maintain the status quo in housing supply relative to demand, the poor at the bottom of the inventory, who already get the worst units, will get increasingly worse off. Rents will increase, and maintenance will decrease. More new houses must be built so the "back-pressure" from the trickle-down process, however, poorly it works, will not cause the situation of the poor to get even worse.

Second, new housing must be made available not only at the top of the supply, but also near the bottom so it does not have to trickle-down so far in order to reach the poorest people. This means a massive increase in the 221d3 subsidy and integration of new public housing units throughout the suburbs and the central cities. Just today I suggested to the head of the Public Housing Authority in Washington that 10,000 new housing units on scattered sites be leased to people who want to get into public housing. He said that it was not possible to find 10,000 units in Washington. When I asked, "What if you could lease units in the suburbs?" he said, "Then I could make some progress." The Chicago Housing Authority should be able to rent existing units in Evanston, Arlington Heights, and anywhere else, and place in those units people from any part of the social stratum and from any racial group. Until we do, we will not make much progress in solving central-city problems.

A third housing improvement device is to take the worst units out of the supply through code enforcement, rehabilitation, and demolition. Though we are trying to do that, in order to take a unit out of the supply, the people living in it have to be placed somewhere else. Again we are faced with the problem of increasing the total number of units available to these people. We cannot destroy the worst units unless we have substitutes for them.

As I mentioned, a fourth housing improvement device is to disperse low-income families. Until both the white middle class and the central-city Negroes face the implications of a massive dispersal of Negroes to the suburbs, we will have to contend with the same ghetto situation we have had for a century. In fact, it would be a tremendous improvement if we could disperse enough Negroes just to keep the ghetto from growing. It is an illusion to think that the ghetto on Chicago's South Side will just disappear in the next thirty years. It will still be there because it is constantly growing. According to Don Bogue, in the last five years the ghetto population has increased by 140,000. Therefore, discussions about eliminating the ghetto are a bit naive. The question is how to open up enough non-ghetto housing channels for Negroes to stop the ghetto from growing at that rate. Whites and Negroes are not facing that problem, and until they do the ghetto and its housing conditions will stay with us. I am suggesting radical steps because we have a radical problem.

My last suggestion is to improve the neighborhood environment in the slums. Without going into detail, Senator Percy's private Model Cities Program is designed to implement rehabilitation, improvements in financing and counseling guidance. It is designed so that local, nonfederal agencies will do everything the federal government is doing now. However, ownership programs based on loans simply do not contend with the fact that poor people cannot repay loans. Over 52% of the people living in substandard units could never afford new housing even at a zero interest rate, on a forty-year mortgage, and with a 100% downpayment. Therefore, it seems rather unrealistic to assume that an ownership program will solve their problem. It might solve the problems of some, but not of the many with really low-income housing problems.

VIII. Conclusion

In summary, I think we should fight poverty and massively increase our housing subsidies for the poor. Are we going to do these things? Not in the short run. Most of us agree that Vietnam is forcing us to restrict what we are spending for the poor in our society. Our present taxes are not sufficient to solve problems in our own cities and fight in Vietnam at the same time. Though I am not necessarily opposed to the Vietnamese war, I believe it is no excuse for not spending enough money in our cities.

But even if the war in Vietnam ends, this problem is so large that we will not start programs on a scale adequate to solve it unless there is a significant change of opinion in Congress, the United States, and particularly in the suburban areas where the money is. More riots might produce the heightened sense of urgency that is necessary. But they might also produce a ferocious backlash that could create a situation similar to that in South Africa. In any case, until the middle class changes its views and is willing to make some large-scale sacrifices, it is unlikely that the necessary effort will be made to solve these so-called housing problems. We cannot eliminate poverty in this society by dealing only with the lowest-income groups. We must also deal with the middle- and upper-income groups to make them understand the situation and change their attitudes.

25

Planning Concepts and
New Directions – Housing

THOMAS DAVIES

I am here on fairly short notice, filling in for Mr. David Stahl, the mayor's Special Assistant on Housing. I have brought you summaries of Chicago's application for Model Cities planning money and several copies of the full application without the appended exhibits. I assume that you are all somewhat familiar with the Model Cities Program, and I understand that you are primarily concerned with housing. Since the Model Cities Program is an appropriate context in which to discuss it, I will concentrate on the two housing components in Chicago's Model Cities application.

I want to explain our approach to preparing the application so as to avoid any misunderstandings that might have resulted from the very elaborate nature of this document and the more elaborate process involved in asking for federal financial assistance in this case than is normally necessary when a municipality becomes involved in a new federal program. We have had to do a lot in a very short time to present what would be our approach to planning a Model Cities program if we were given the money. Therefore, this application does not represent a plan but rather an enlarged statement of what we would like to do and how we would go about planning if federal money were made available to us.

The sections that deal specifically with housing must be considered in the context of the application guidelines which call for a comprehensive approach to the problems that plague particular areas of the city. As you probably know, we have asked for planning money for four large areas of Chicago, one on the West Side, one on the North Side, and two on the South Side. There is a map of these areas in each application. Due to an apparent shortage of money, we do not know if planning money will be available for all four areas. As far as I know, our approach will be to work in all four areas, regardless of how much money we receive, which undoubtedly will affect what we will be able to plan for each area. Much has yet to be worked out, and I am sure that many of you with your community groups and agencies will be involved when we actually begin the hard business of planning.

We have divided housing into questions of supply and choice in accordance with the outline provided by the federal government, and have ourselves further divided the area of supply into housing for large low-income families and housing for large moderate-income families which provides a meaningful distinction in terms of approach.

To quote from the application: "Much of the housing in the proposed areas consisted originally of large, well-constructed apartments, many of which have since been converted into smaller units. One approach to increasing the supply of larger units for low-income families will be through a combination of code enforcement, rehabilitation, and the National Housing Act, Section 23 Public Housing Leasing Program. Another approach would be to acquire rehabilitable structures through urban renewal, write down their acquisition costs (which would be the cost to the public), rehabilitate them through either public or private action, and resell them to private parties . . ." Another approach would be for the Chicago Housing Authority to lease many of the buildings acquired, rehabilitate them, and make them available to tenants eligible for public housing.

In essence, this is calling for a new approach to providing housing for low-income families as an alternative to public housing as we now know it, and as I have tried to indicate, there are two possible ways to undertake rehabilitation. One is for a public agency to rehabilitate and sell units, and the other is for a public agency to buy and sell them to a private party, to someone who would carry out the rehabilitation. We hope that the Chicago Dwellings Association can expand its program of new construction as well as rehabilitation to provide moderate-income housing. Of course, we would also encourage other private, not-for-profit organizations, church and labor groups, to become active both in rehabilitation and new construction in the proposed Model Cities areas. As you may know, the Department of Urban Renewal is studying several possible renewal projects which for the most part will be in the Model Cities areas and should substantially add to the supply of moderate-income housing.

Due to the shortage of available land in many of these areas and the problems of displacing families which result from rehabilitation, we want to investigate the feasibility of building residential units on very large tracts of land over both the Dan Ryan and Eisenhower expressways. Many buildings in the Loop as well as in other cities are built over railroad air rights, and we think this is a possible way to substantially expand the inner-city housing supply without necessitating dislocation. Therefore, if we receive planning money, one of the things we will want to investigate is how this might be done.

A related aspect of the program is the question of the livability of high density areas. Many large family problems are associated with high-rise living as well as with crowded conditions in low rises. We hope to study the physical, social, and economic problems of high-density living. This will involve considerations of the sociological and psychological effects of high density living. We want to find out what can be done to improve the livability of such areas. By most standards, the Park Avenue apartments in

New York would be substandard in terms of light and air, the amount of land they cover, overcrowding and so forth. However, they remain some of the most desirable housing, and perhaps there is a secret we have not discovered. I suspect that in this case it is wealth or single-person families, but certainly other sociological, psychological, and physical design problems should be considered.

As to choice of housing, there are economic and social barriers to overcome throughout the metropolitan area and the state. However, a very significant aspect of choice is that there has not been a large-scale development of the condominium for other than upper-income families. I think there is a great potential for developing condominium units which could be made available to CHA on the rental program. This would enable families who, for example, are eligible for public housing, to move into apartment or town house units that technically were condominiums. As their income rises to the point where they would be no longer eligible for public housing, they could begin paying mortgage rather than rental payments. In fact, their rental payments might be credited toward a down payment so that as their economic situation improves, they might move toward owning their home.

Again I will read from our application: "The Chicago Dwellings Association and other not-for-profit organizations will develop a large number of condominium and cooperative housing units that will be made available to families who are eligible for public housing. These families will lease the apartments directly from the owner (which in this case would be the Chicago Dwellings Association or another private group) paying the same amount of rent that they would pay in public housing, but their leases would include options to purchase. The Chicago Housing Authority would make payments directly to the landlords to make up the difference between the amounts paid by the tenants and the economic rent of the units."

As a tenant's income increased, his payments would increase, though not in direct proportion. The full CHA supplement should be available until income limitations have been exceeded. By then a tenant should have built up sufficient equity in the unit to acquire a mortgage on his own or with the city's assistance. Thus he could continue living in the same unit and making payments which would ultimately involve fee ownership in the unit.

These are the highlights of our approach to housing under the Model Cities Program. Again I will say that they must be viewed in relation to other aspects of the Model Cities Program. Furthermore, this is all contingent on the amount of money that will be available for planning them. Everything in the application is subject to substantial additional alteration during the planning in which the communities will be involved. These are not intended to be final proposals but suggestions of what we think should be investigated so that the communities involved can make program proposals from a wider range of choices. We trust that we will be able to develop these programs on a joint basis when the time comes.

FLORENCE SCALA

The prospects of a Model Cities program for this city are disturbing unless either official or professional Chicagoans insist that its (the Model Cities Program) direction includes a concern for making a meaningful change in the life and environment of all the people of this city, not just the poor. Neither the Comprehensive Plan nor the Model Cities Program reveals that Chicago planners and politicians understand that we are heading toward a technological age which scares most of us who do not understand it or how we might fit into that new world. The newspapers discuss the mayor's plan for the Golden Age of Chicago, and I am more cynical and less hopeful than ever.

At the same time, I recognize that we must grapple with these plans since I am not willing to knock my head against the wall anymore. We must begin to speak to this city in a way that will impress them with the fact that we mean it. We must change our language and tactics; we must be revolutionary in the highest sense and act. If we do not begin to set forth some of our own plans, we will never get up to bat, much less to first base.

It is absolutely ridiculous to go on thinking that people cannot help to plan. Those of us who are not trained cannot decide how to reorganize the use of space or figure out densities. Professional people have to do the technical phases of planning, but people in the communities can and do plan when they have the opportunity. You can see the ingenious use some families have made of their blocks without the city's help. It only takes a little encouragement for people to begin thinking of how to best use the space in their area and how to make life a little more pleasant in their communities.

I still live on the Near West Side, and I hate it, even though I fought to make it into something. I have hated it since I was a child, and I hate it still. I did not fight for that area because I loved it. More than anything else, the people who live in the areas to which most people look with a sense of pity, concern, or dispassionate unconcern, do want an environment that dignifies their human spirit. They know that the area is ugly and bleak, and they know it better than Mayor Daley or the planners. We all know that much of the ugliness perpetuated in the area is an expression of hate for that environment.

We will be talking more and more about the Model Cities Program, and I have been heartened to find that some aldermen in the city are very anxious to become more familiar with what it may mean to them and their communities. They are concerned because they know the city has shown no sign that it is prepared. The mayor has established neighborhood service centers throughout the city which are supposed to help people meet the physical needs of their community. The building inspectors, code enforcers, rehabilitators, health people, and others are there. However, those centers are staffed by people who need jobs; not long ago many of them were cut out of the County Board's patronage list. But they are not qualified to service a community. Conscientious, concerned personnel in the Planning Department cannot imagine how to train them to go into these neighborhoods to do a job for the community.

In some respects, this is a frightening prospect because these people will not be welcome in certain areas, and they will not be able to discuss housing problems with the people in the areas they will visit. To be more specific, inspecting a building in Woodlawn or Englewood, for example, usually means looking at a pretty solid stone or brick building with set standards. Are those standards to be as rigidly applied to an older, frame building in Pilsen where the people involved are in a similar economic situation? What will happen if the people in Pilsen, who think their area is an ideal conservation area rather than a clearance area, find that the inspectors think the area should come down. It is filled with frame buildings that are over fifty years old, which is over-age according to the Department. The personnel who will be visiting us in the future will make a lot of trouble for us because they will be untrained and disinterested. As I see it, if the city does not meet this challenge, this will be one of the big chinks that will crack the armor of the city government in Chicago.

Though I do not intend anything personal, I want to tell Mr. Davies that I will never live in a house over a highway. If they are going to put us over a highway, they can gas me right where I am. Just look at the Post Office building over the Expressway and the Monoxide Island in Hyde Park which is a very nice apartment building in the center of a traffic turn around. I hope a lot more will be done about the automobile and the pollution before we decide to build over expressways.

I am also concerned about the language being used in planning. It is very frustrating to try to make sense out of the Model Cities information which speaks of Human Development Coordinators who will help develop and coordinate human development, Family Services Coordinators, Environment Improvement Coordinators, and the Urban Living Park where those who do not know how to live in the big city will be taught how to live, be human, and vote. I would be the first to admit that I probably look at these plans and programs with a jaundiced eye because I have a chip on my shoulder about such things. However, if I were challenged, I would say that there is something that excites me in the idea of a Comprehensive Plan and the Model Cities Program, but my main criticism of both is that neither excites me enough to be hopeful.

Reaction and Reconsideration

During the housing as during the welfare weekend, when representatives of various city and government departments were on hand, the participants seized the opportunity to ask for specific information as well as to voice their dissatisfaction with the existing system in terms of what it has to offer and how it offers it. Much of the discussion focused on the difficulties and possibilities involved in two major issues – segregation and community participation.

Public Housing

Before exploring more general issues of public housing, several participants asked for specific information.

Can CHA police enter an apartment anytime they choose? [community organization member]

We do not have any police, only guards who do not have keys for the apartments or the authority to enter them. [CHA representative]

Why doesn't the CHA return the interest received on the $50 security deposit to the leasee? [tenant in public housing]

[no answer given]

Has the CHA done anything about the suggested subsidizing of the flat rent of $55 per month for senior citizens and others living on about $90 per month who would prefer subsidized rent to going on welfare? [community organization staff member]

The subsidy referred to would not apply to elderly families who already receive a $10 a month subsidy from the federal government reducing rent to $45 per month. However, with regard to the others, most of the housing projects are on a flat-rent schedule. Anyone can be relocated from a flat-rent to a graded-rent unit where the minimum rent is $36 per month. [CHA representative]

Why doesn't CHA lease apartments for a year at a time? [community organization member]

We always have. Tenants have a lease on a month-to-month basis but this is based on a yearly operation. Although an apartment can be repossessed on thirty-days notice, tenants are cleared for eligibility, etc. and leases renewed only once a year. [CHA representative]

What about tenants asked to move out of public housing? [community mental health worker]

Of the 10% turnover, more than half move out of their own free will. Of the remainder, nonpayment of rent is the primary reason for which the Authority asks tenants to leave, and not more than ten or twelve families per year are asked to leave because of poor housekeeping standards. [CHA administrator]

I know of a case in which a family was rejected from entry into public housing because there was not both a father and mother present. Is public housing truly open to all, regardless of family structure? [community leader]

Public housing is open to anyone who meets the eligibility requirements. These are based on income but also stipulate that people whose morals are such that they would be a bad influence on their neighbors are not allowed in, which includes people such as drug addicts or local troublemakers. [CHA administrator]

The CHA is using arbitrary methods to control public housing tenants, specifically in the case of accusations made on the basis of alleged evidence without police or legal determination. [lawyer]

With regard to the difficulties large families, and particularly Negro families, have in getting public housing, would you clarify the point made that it could take thirty-five or so years to get four- and five-bedroom units in public housing. [community organization housing coordinator]

Undoubtedly there is a shortage of large-family units; there is a waiting list of about 8,000 for family housing. Out of the total 33,000 public housing units, the 235 five-bedroom units have a 1% turnover, making the statistical wait for them approximately thirty-five years. However, the situation for four-bedroom units is much better. For one and two-bedroom units there is not more than a six-month wait, which is a healthy market if a vacancy problem is to be avoided. The CHA and the city have recognized the need for about 2,500 additional units of public housing per year for the next several years and plan for the majority of these to be three-bedroom units. [CHA administrator]

Several participants raised questions about site selection for the projected 2,500 units per year. Some said they knew of plans for locating future public housing in all-Negro areas. Others referred to scattered sites throughout the city available for public housing construction.

No future sites have been selected. Furthermore, not only does site selection require City Council approval, but standard condition buildings cannot be torn down in order to build public housing. [housing administrator]

Why are public housing units concentrated in limited areas? [settlement house worker]

It is partly because the Housing Act now requires that for each newly constructed public housing dwelling unit, a dilapidated or substandard unit must be eliminated from the city. Furthermore, private developers cannot afford the land costs of lots with substandard buildings and thus purchase only vacant lots. [CHA representative]

Several participants deplored apparent discriminatory practices in assigning public housing applicants to certain areas.

Is it still the case that, as in the past, applications are coded A for white and B for Negro, and is it easier for A applicants to get into certain projects and B applicants into others? [urban researcher]

It is a federal requirement to code applications A and B for statistical purposes. In all our programs, we let applicants designate their first, second, and third choices for where they want to live, and we offer them their first choice if there is a vacancy. [CHA representative]

It is important for CHA to inform applicants about housing available in various areas of the city. [religious agency staff member]

The summit agreement states that the CHA will take every action within its power to promote the objectives of fair housing and that toward this end it would initiate a program of leasing housing for the poor in "good" neighborhoods. Has this program begun, and is City Council approval needed for leasing property in these areas? [member of the Archdiocese]

There are 400 units under the leasing program and because most of them are small units, the majority of tenants in them are elderly. We have approval of the City Council for the leasing program which applies to the City of Chicago as a whole. We can lease units anywhere within the City providing that they come within the maximum limits we can pay for a lease and that units are made available to us. [CHA administrator]

The summit agreement is not a signed document. It is an agreement resting on a moral commitment rather than a contract which involves a legal obligation and penalties for not fulfilling it, and thus is not enforceable. [community leader]

Can the CHA as an agency of the city government put pressure on those who do not want to lease to the CHA under the Fair Housing Ordinance or in conjunction with the Commission on Human Relations? [staff member of a private agency]

To the best of my knowledge, there is no way that the CHA or anyone else can force someone to lease any particular apartment to the CHA. In leasing apartments, the CHA enters into a contract with the owner of the building who can lease in one of three ways: he can take anyone sent by the CHA, select from those sent by the CHA, or send prospective tenants to the CHA to determine their eligibility for public housing. [CHA representative]

Several participants were seriously concerned with what constructive steps could be taken to help solve the city's housing problems.

Does the Catholic Archdiocese plan to build any low-income housing? [religious agency staff member]

There is a tremendous need for middle-income housing, and we intend to use 221d3. [member of the Archdiocese]

Do you have any suggestions for increasing the very limited understanding that the general public has of the problems that face tenants in public housing? [community organizer]

The reasons for the lack of understanding are tied in with the over-all attitude of prejudice throughout the Chicago metropolitan area. This will have to be faced again when the debate on open occupancy begins in the legislature. Deeply involved is the community's inability to face up to the social realities of community living. In our society, to be poor is to be a blighted person. Churches, educational institutions, the CHA and the city, aldermen, and others in the governmental structure must get off their dignity and do a better job of training people in terms of human values if things are to change at all. In facing the public housing situation in Chicago today, we are basically talking from ignorance. Sufficient money should be put aside to do top-to-bottom social research of all aspects of public housing. Although the CHA has studied certain aspects, what is needed is an outside study of the total situation because the general public needs to know the truth if there is to be any basis for changing their attitudes. It is tantamount to irresponsibility to continue the program with such needs as 2,500 units per year. [member of the Archdiocese]

Have there been any opportunities for discussing the Urban League's ideas about humanizing the CHA operation with CHA administration? [private agency staff member]

Although this issue and ways of changing CHA procedures have not been discussed with them, there have been discussions of more specific questions such as tenants' rights. Most of our energies have been directed toward preventing the intensification and extension of the ghetto pattern. [representative of the Urban League]

What specific suggestions should be made to the CHA? [civil servant]

The answer could be either in terms of what could be done or what should be done. Without real political muscle being put to work on the structure of CHA, the basic pattern cannot be changed. I do not think we need another study, and I think the sorts of things that should be done are: (1) halting further extension of high-rise concentrations; (2) increasing the number of public housing units, building them throughout the city, and preferably throughout the metropolitan area, in small numbers, low density, and attractive design; (3) convert some of the existing public housing to other uses such as office space which will also provide for employment; and (4) change the management procedures within buildings so that tenants' rights will be respected. In essence, change the CHA's policies and procedures. [representative of the Urban League]

Open Occupancy

Discussion with the panel on open occupancy was more charged with the tension of a divergence of views than was that on public housing because of the participation of several representatives of a white homeowners' association.

When confronted with the views of white homeowners such as these, community leaders, professionals, Jew and Gentile, Catholic and Protestant, middle-class and lower-class, black and white — all can unite, despite their differences, around the validity of and need for an open occupancy law in Illinois. [participant from a large county department]

But it is important to hear their point of view expressed because it represents forces in the community that believe a system of segregation and second-class citizenship for a racial or ethnic group is part of the American scheme. [state legislator]

The white homeowners' view is behind the times; people are now talking in terms of Negroes catching up with society. [unidentified participant]

The only way anyone will get ahead is by doing it himself; nobody can solve your problems for you. Whites as well as Negroes are robbed by businessmen, though admittedly Negroes more often than whites; the only way to change this is to start your own business. If you are not inferiors, you do not need others to help you. There is nothing in your living together that is wrong, but the fact that middle-class Negroes are moving out of ghettos indicates that even Negroes do not want to live in these areas because of the high crime rates, etc. [leader of a white homeowners' association]

What is your attitude toward integration? [unidentified participant]

I have no objections to integrated neighborhoods, and there are integrated areas where people can live. But I have found that the majority of those living in them do not practice the brotherhood they preach. I do not object to voluntary racial and/or economic integration, but I do object to planned integration which involves balanced neighborhoods, quota systems, etc. [leader of a white homeowners' association]

You say the Negro must do it for himself, but at every turn the Negro, the Puerto Rican, the poor white find so many walls to keep them in their place that it is almost impossible for them to do it on their own. Nobody can exist independently of others. Passing any bill on open occupancy providing for integration will not dissolve the problem in the hearts and minds of people, but it can give citizens of the country decent housing without waiting for the hearts and minds of men to change. That is why we need such laws. Too many people are being injured because of poor housing and too many children are dying because of poor housing, and this situation cannot be allowed to continue to exist. If it does, you will go right down the drain with me. [community leader]

People have the right to segregate or integrate, and it should not be the government or anyone else who tells them which to do. You cannot call it freedom to pass a law that takes away freedom because regulations mean somebody else is making the decision – to be free the individual makes the decision. [white homeowner]

Few can disagree that ideally integration should be an individual matter. Hyde Park is an example of successful integration because it was carried out by individuals rather than racial or economic groups, but this still leaves the problems of poverty, education, etc., to be resolved. [social scientist]

Is the paramount interest in property rights the right to own or the right to withhold from someone else? [lawyer]

One of the indicias of property ownership is the right to withhold or sell to whoever you wish; this is freedom and this is your right. [white homeowner]

It is important to recognize that there are rights on both sides; just as people have a right to sell property, others have right of access to it. [community organizer]

None of the housing bills restrict the right to make private transactions before property is placed on the open market. All these bills relate to property for sale on the open market, and that must be sold to the buyer who gives the price. One of the purposes of this kind of legislation is to set the atmosphere within which an owner who wants to sell is protected, by force of law, in the sale of his property. [state legislator]

One reason for having an open occupancy bill is to protect whites from their fellow whites by making it less possible for real estate companies to intimidate, pressure, and manipulate homeowners with threats of Negroes moving into their communities. [staff member of a private agency]

If there is any force involved it is under the present system. An open occupancy law would protect, rather than diminish, the freedom to sell to anyone the seller chooses. Although some people say the "fair" housing laws amount to "forced" housing laws, none of these bills say a person has to sell to anyone. They merely say that people may not discriminate on the basis of race, religion, etc., in denying a person the right to buy or rent property. [director of a metropolitan organization]

The activities of Negroes and white liberals over the past few years have set back the cause of integration more than five years by engendering hatred and a lack of trust in white communities. We were more prepared to accept integration five years ago than now. [representative from a white homeowners' association]

For four years Negro leaders have been threatening us with violence; and I can promise that if Negro groups come to us with violence, they will get violence. [lawyer in white homeowners' association]

These men are placing all blame for the hatred and antagonism engendered on Negro and civil rights groups while if the blame is to be placed, much of it rests with the hate groups that have devoted themselves to keeping down the Negro and maintaining the segregated system we had until the beginning of the fifties. Negroes in this country will not be content to continue to live in ghettos, and white segregationists, not civil rights groups, will be the cause of violence. [state representative]

Laws cannot prevent social pressure, but they can protect from violence, and there are already sufficient laws to protect people from violence. [lawyer from a white homeowners' association]

I agree that we do not need any more laws like open occupancy which only serve to protect people from violence. However, we want to live in white areas, not because we want to integrate or because we want to be accepted or liked, but because there is decent housing there. We are going to move into those houses and if there is a reaction outside the law, the law will punish those who violate it. [organizer who moved into an all-white neighborhood]

I respect such action when it is taken by individuals, but not when it is taken by groups. If you come in as individuals, you will get accepted as individuals, but if you come in as a group, you will get strong reactions. [property owner in all-white neighborhood]

Although marches will lead to violence, this is not the way to work out the problem. Property and homeowner groups were not represented at last summer's summit conference which only added to the distrust and doubt that has resulted from it. One's property and family are most important to any individual, and I am here to find out what we can do to solve these problems – not just to talk about them. [another property owner]

However, when a Negro participant asked to attend the next scheduled meeting of the homeowners' association, she was given a flat "no" despite the fact that she had indicated that she lived in the adjacent community.

Lack of understanding is the basis of this divergence of views and if we could get down to some grounds of agreement, we could come up with something constructive. By drawing on the past experiences of other ethnic groups in their struggle for freedom, a basis for mutual understanding might be discovered and become the grounds for accomplishing something constructive for the future. [state legislator]

It is misleading to view open occupancy in terms of individualism or as if one group were trying to get with another. It is for the common good – for white and black, poor and rich – to get together. White schools and students are also in bad shape. [clergyman]

The threat of the ghetto spreading outward and inundating adjacent communities is a real one and thus a statewide open occupancy bill is in the interest of those living in communities located on the edges of ghettos since it would guarantee housing on a metropolitan-wide basis, relieve the pressure on the communities in which Negroes are trying to get better housing, education, etc. [participant from a private agency]

There seemed to be no basis for reasoning together, despite this and other attempts by various participants to open bridges of communication with the white, property-owner spokesmen.

Federal Programs

Antagonism marked discussions of the city of Chicago and the housing situation, but in those discussions which focused on federal programs, the prime concern was with the specifics of what is available and how programs can be most effectively implemented.

How do federal housing programs fit into the Model Cities Program? [unidentified participant]

Presumably any of these programs would be available as tools for any designated Model Cities area. The Model Cities Program is an attempt to develop some positive models by turning the tables and saying to the cities, let us see what you can do. Whereas the federal government has been imposing systems down the line and defining how local cities should renew themselves, now they are asking cities to find a neighborhood and develop a total, interrelated plan for it, not just in terms of housing programs and other physical aspects but also in terms of youth programs, nondiscrimination, crime, all the way down to garbage collection, and involving all income levels. [federal government employee]

The interrelatedness of federal programs is important to effective utilization at the local level. I have always had the impression that one of the basic reasons for a workable plan is to increase local involvement. Formerly our agency developed plans and turned them over to consultants for implementation, but since that was not effective, we now develop both the plans and their implementation. [staff member of a government agency at the local level in a rural community]

This sort of thing is almost never done but it is a good idea since it provides expertise to those who most need it. [government employee]

We must recognize that politics are involved in using federal programs and monies. The money for federal programs such as Model Cities and Code Enforcement should not be channelled through the city and subject to the city's control. [participant working in a local community]

What we are talking about is how local people elect a man to go to Washington to write a law to be administered at the local level, and he writes that law so that the same people who saw that he got to Washington are helped by it — anyone who did not do that would be a fool. [government agency representative]

Loans

We would not have the slums that we do if those of us who live in the poor areas of the city could obtain bank loans. [community organization leader]

Two points: stereotype and discrimination. In some cases, there are also real economic considerations which must be taken into account. For example, it is difficult to receive loans on old homes, white or Negro, but this has always been especially difficult for the latter. Until very recently the FHA adopted the philosophy of protecting the taxpayer by only guaranteeing loans in "sound areas" – whatever that may mean. Some change in this thinking has been effected and to some extent the government realized that to really protect the taxpayer, the government must make funds available in slum areas. Only in this way can these areas be made healthier, thereby opening the door to private financing. [banker]

The inference that it is the attitude of the big banker which is responsible for the lack of mortgage money in certain parts of our city is an oversimplification. There are certain areas into which nobody would put his private money unless someone else assumed the risk. In order to do something in certain areas, it will take more than making mortgage money available since whoever assumes the risk must have the money available to pay off if it does not work. It is also necessary to insure that community facilities are adequate so the community will be viable and can stand on its own feet. [city administrator]

How can the pressure be put on FHA and others who are not doing the job? [participant from a national private agency]

The main difficulty is the magnitude of the problem of poor housing – 75% of the city of Chicago is deteriorating and some way will have to be found to get money into the ghetto areas. Rehabilitation is a scary business because you never know what you will run into. If FHA will not insure these loans, then new ideas have to be developed. The 312 government loan which is a 3% direct loan is one of the best for the small homeowner though the government is not pushing it and people are not getting the technical information about it. [private developer]

A revolving fund is one possibility. New York City and New York State have some of the best housing laws in the country and they are still a shambles. Wonderful laws will not change anything unless people and communities pressure city and federal agencies to make the possibilities work. [state legislator]

It is important to recognize that federal law has taken the position that it is up to the community to ask the government for federal money if it is desired. Housing authorities have great power and resources that they are not using. It is necessary to find a way to change this because the housing authorities are not pushing their programs or making information available. [federal housing agency representative]

The Public and Private Sectors

What is the possibility of the public and private sectors working together on community problems? [government agency staff member]

Most people, including businessmen, religious leaders, and government officials, do not understand the social revolution that is taking place or what it really means to live in a slum. They cannot get a feeling for what is going on by sitting in a downtown office or suburban home talking about it. As long as they do not understand they will not start working in this direction unless pressure is put on them from the community by, for example, tenant unions. Alternatively, we could get them to do something about these problems by raising their level of understanding, and the only way to do that is by talking in their language about the results of their inaction. If they realized how much of their tax money comes back into the inner city, they would understand that the social problems which exist there should be one of their major concerns. There are several ways to make the point. I believe in the use of the hook when I talk to people. When I talk to church people, I talk in terms of ethics and morality, but when I talk to businessmen, I must talk in terms of economic implications. We have to reach the real estate industry with the fact that they will be excluded from many markets as a result of their lack of participation in the stabilization of these communities. [banker]

It disturbs me to hear provisions being made for human concerns in order to continue the capitalistic system. I think the problem lies in examining the nature of the human concerns rather than in protecting capitalism if it will not provide for these concerns. [community organizer]

Historically, businessmen and industrialists have been notorious for driving nails into their own coffins. Whether or not they subscribe to the social ideology I enunciate, it would contribute to preserving capitalism which is in their interest. Instead they take paths that lead to continued and deeper social action throughout the community which will change the system that we have. [businessman]

The discussion turned to a consideration of some of the larger issues involved.

There are two different sets of people here — those who are talking about how to make capitalism work for poor people, and others, like me, who say capitalism does not work for poor people. We are not concerned with getting a piece of a cake we might not even like but with baking our own cake. [community organizer]

The difference lies in a concern for reforming capitalism vs. having revolution. Just as some things have not yet been tried, neither has the eradication of slums. Our society is the first to be anywhere near wealthy enough to try it. The existence of ghettos means the restriction of choice. By "ghetto," I mean an area in which people are forced to live and which is solely occupied by others like themselves. If this is a correct definition, then something must be done by both the Negro community and white middle-class suburban group to eradicate the ghettos in this country. The latter group is the dominant political force in this society and the force which will be even more dominant after reapportionment. [realtor]

We must take into account the fact that, in our society, the question of poverty is complicated by the culture of poverty which keeps people trapped in a cycle of poverty. [community agency staff member]

Manipulation of People

There was a division of opinion on whether dispersing ghetto populations into the suburbs is an acceptable approach.

The basic problem is that the ghetto is overcrowded and at least any increase must be dispersed. [unidentified participant]

I know of a 221d3 apartment building in an all-white area for which there were no Negro applicants, and I think organizations concerned with promoting integration in housing should be encouraging Negroes who are interested in moving into these areas. There is a big difference between integration and freedom of choice in housing. If open occupancy were declared in Illinois tomorrow, I doubt that there would be a shift of more than 0.1% of the population, but at least the choice would be there and that would have a stabilizing effect. [businessman]

The ghetto problem cannot be solved by the people outside the ghetto dispersing those living in it. [community leader]

I wish people concerned with real estate and building would forget about incidental programs designed to manipulate people and spread them out into middle-class neighborhoods and get about their own business of building decent housing in adequate amounts. [county employee]

Under the existing system people are being manipulated. Isn't there some way to help a poor person get what he wants as opposed to giving him what we think he ought to have? [white resident of a Negro community]

Given the fact that money is essential, if the poor are to get whatever it is that they want, the only way I can see to accomplish that is to give them money. [realtor]

This give, give, give to the poor attitude prevails in all federal programs and obviously does not begin to help solve the problems faced by the poor in this society. If anything it makes things worse because not only does it fail to consider what the poor themselves really want but it deprives those who receive it of self-respect and dignity. [private agency staff member]

The problem will only be perpetuated by giving hand-outs to the poor; it will be solved only when the poor take action. [community organizer working with a tenant union]

We have to give to the majority of poor who are incapable of supporting themselves – they are the old, the infirm, and mothers with many children. However, perhaps this is not the right approach toward those who are capable of potentially earning something. The housing problem would not be solved if all tenants simply took over their deteriorated buildings because money would still be needed to upgrade them. The cost of rehabilitation is a large one and to merely transfer ownership of a building will not pay that cost. [real estate broker]

Community Involvement

As in previous discussions of welfare and education, there was general agreement by most participants that an increase in community participation was the only way to begin to cope with some of these problems.

What can a community group do to become actively involved in the city's activities? [participant from a religious organization]

One way to get to the politicans might be to go through the good people who are high up. These people are far removed from what is really going on. While speaking of their concern over the agony which is going on in the big cities, they continue to support the city government and their programs. Community groups must prove to the city that they really mean business; there must be a show of strength. [local community leader]

There is an increasing recognition that community participation is necessary for success from both the community and business points of view. [agency administrator]

From the community point of view, it looks like less and less community participation in public housing rather than more and more. [community organizer]

What makes the City Department of Urban Renewal think they can solve all community problems and continue to perpetrate the same action on the people living in ghetto areas? [community leader]

Since 1953, Puerto Rican people in Chicago have been moving from one slum to another under pressure from urban renewal. Serious attempts are not being made to relocate them in decent housing before their homes are torn down. New housing is scheduled for our area, and I have not heard of priorities being set for people who have been living there from ten to twenty years, paying their rent, etc. [community leader in a Puerto Rican area]

We never thought we had all the answers; over the years we have only tried to take steps forward that would lead to a better community. In retrospect it is clear that we were naive in thinking that taking a few steps would be sufficient to solve the problems that face us in a society with ever-increasing stresses and strains. The greater the demands, the greater will be the stresses and strains, but when there are many and competing demands for improvements within a community, a set of priorities has to be established. [representative from a city department]

With regard to the possibilities described for expanding the urban renewal program, those who are working within that department ought to know that on the community level the discussion is about finding ways to stop the entire program. One reason for this is that urban renewal is not being used to clear land for parks or schools but to clear housing for parking lots for the business community. [community organizer]

The intended direction of expansion was from slum clearance to conservation to neighborhood information and service centers that would facilitate the use of federal programs. The Department's objectives were to develop and carry out a program that will make possible a stronger city and stronger communities. This involves providing not only for housing but for commercial and industrial development as well as public and private institutional development. This is important because it provides places of employment for people living in the neighborhood, and it maintains the tax base in the city. [representative, Department of Urban Renewal]

Tenant Unions

Why should the tenants, who have so many problems already, have to take the responsibility and initiative in acting against the irresponsibility of landlords? Other groups or experts and specialists should be doing something about the situation in which these people have been placed. [settlement house worker]

I know of no historical example of the rest of society reacting to a complaint of wrongs. As I see the problem, there is a tremendous vacuum of power in the hands of poor people, and the Welfare Department, Community Renewal, and others will not respond until the poor have sufficient power to exercise in making demands. Whether their power is in a tenant union or some other form is merely a question of strategy. Once they get power and learn how to use it, then you will see social change. [lawyer]

Although there have been some efforts by, for example, the union structure to put pressure on the building trades, they do not get very far. In working with a tenant union, I found that once tenants get together and get a start, with the help of community organization if necessary, get out of their way. When they begin to exercise the power they have, then they become effective. Though there are doubts at first, confidence and strength increases, and if anything the organizer has to put on the brakes so that they can take one step at a time more effectively. [community organizer]

It is necessary for people involved in tenant actions to do it themselves, even if it is at the instigation or with the guidance and assistance of someone from the outside. Otherwise, despite improvements that might be made, the tenants will not have any pride in the changes because they were not responsible for them and the building will again deteriorate to its former state. [community organizer]

It is necessary to go above code standards to build some future life into these buildings. As long as these old buildings are only fixed up to the building codes, only deferred maintenance is being taken care of. Furthermore, when tenants have a sense of control over their housing destiny, a morale is built, and they can begin dealing with the problems. [private developer]

I know of a case in which the Building Department sent out workers to repair a building. Since their contract stated only that their inspectors had to be satisfied, no real improvement was made. For example, one worker puttied the first floor windows only as far as he could reach and that passed inspection. [lawyer involved in the housing field]

With regard to rent strikes, if the Welfare Department sent public housing tenants their rent money so they could pay their own rent instead of the Department paying it for them, the recipient not only would have some dignity, but also would have his own whip on the landlord instead of having to go through the Welfare Department to withhold rent. [tenant union organizer]

Many people who receive assistance are afraid to participate in rent strikes and many caseworkers go so far as to even tell people they cannot participate. The Office of Community Relations in the Department of Public Aid is willing to help by informing recipients of their right to participate in rent strikes without fear of having their assistance cut off. [welfare employee]

Tenant unions do not get people into better housing because they continue to work within the existing social structure. The question is not "putting on the brakes" but putting on so much pressure that real changes can result. [housing coordinator for a community organization]

The Feasibility of Action

Perhaps there is a conscious conspiracy of existing agencies, corporate interests, etc. to perpetuate the present system of exclusiveness. [settlement house worker]

Personally I do not think it is a *conscious* conspiracy but, by its very complexity, this society is constructed for those who can take advantage of complexity and the poor lose out in dealing with complexity. Most groups are motivated to maximize their profit, and the easiest way to do that is by exploiting those who cannot defend themselves. Thus, they choose the path of least resistance to take from the poor everything they can get without giving anything in return. [lawyer]

It is more conscious than that. There is at least an implicit desire, not only to exploit people, but to keep them in a position where they can be exploited. For example, the fact that certain people and groups of people are found on the various boards which control different institutional structures within the city results in interlocking directorates with control or access to those who control a large number of institutions. [community organizer]

I do not disagree with the facts, only with the conclusion. In any case, if you are talking about social improvement, the point is not to place the blame but to take the facts as they are and try to change the situation because it is wrong. [lawyer]

Community people see the city's plans for community participation as meaningless structures which do not provide for large numbers of people living in these communities to express their concerns. The people do not see a way of getting a voice, of getting involved, and of seeing any change in what is happening in their neighborhood. You do not have to be a professional to be able to say what kind of neighborhood you want to live in. Is there any possibility of taking a new approach to the participation of people? [religious leader]

Bringing residents of these areas in on a representative basis to collaborate in developing a proposal that is suitable to everyone is the only workable approach to community participation. I do not think the right approach is to say that there are two sides which have to fight it out and that if you can get enough power, you will get what you want. [city administrator]

Hyde Park set a wonderful precedent. Because the University of Chicago was the power block, they were able to get money from the city, and with the community people, they hired their own planner and planned their own area. I think we should repeat this in other communities without cutting out all the community people. Why couldn't a federation of community groups be granted survey and planning funds, hire a planner, and develop their own plans? [local community leader]

Although programs such as 221d3 may provide rehabilitated buildings, many of the people now living in those buildings will not benefit under the existing laws and regulations. What we need is housing for *poor* people. [community organization housing coordinator]

Problems arise in situations that necessitate everyone in a building receiving subsidies but not when some can meet 221d3 rent. Other federal programs can provide rent subsidies for those who cannot pay the full rent. With regard to access to federal programs in general, the problem is not so much that of lack of information as of the complexity and newness of so many of these programs, and the possibilities in combining them, which necessitates the use of an expert. [federal housing administrator]

Talking with you directly has been very helpful. Is it possible to get federal representatives to come to local communities to provide the needed information and improve public relations? [public agency employee]

This is impossible but local people should go to the regional offices and if those staff members cannot work out what is desired, they can consult Washington. [housing administrator]

Not only does it seem to be impossible to establish direct access to information at the federal level, but it also seems clear that all federal programs must be channelled through the city administration. [community organizer]

The people must be recognized if the government is really going to do something for them. How can people get to know what is available when the federal government continues to multiply the programs and yet refuses to come to the local level to answer the people's questions directly? Part of the problem may be that the organizers and other professionals concerned with housing are influencing people to act on what they see as important. The problem is then determining that this is in fact what the poor see as important. [community leader]

Although the ideal situation would be for the people themselves to have the necessary expertise and information, vast training and educational programs would be required. As things stand, federal agencies, city officials, and organizers are needed to translate available programs into layman's terms. Not only do people have the right to organize but they also have the right to choose who they want to help them. The organizer's role should be to provide the people with the alternatives available so they can make their own choices and understand the implications of the actions they can take. [government administrator]

Although the people might need organizers to help them get resources, the problem is more complex than that. One of the biggest slumlords in the city is the city itself — the Department of Urban Renewal is tougher to fight than regular landlords. Eventually the poor will see that the issues concern not only race but a class situation as well. If there is ever real strife in society, it will involve the middle class of all colors fighting against the poor. Organizers and "do-gooders" must consider the possibility that they are feeding the dog that will eat them all up. [community organizer]

The question of access is not simply one of education and how much you earn but is one of putting on pressure because the so-called experts will not move until you push them. [community organizer]

It is the Government's obligation to state their programs in terms that the layman can understand so that the people will not have to go to others for interpretation. People should be informed of their rights and should not have to reach a certain status in order to learn of them. Furthermore, government officials must learn that they cannot lead the people as long as they do not know what the people want. [community organization staff member]

PART 4

Youth and the Community

26

Youth, the Community, and Mental Health

JEANETTE BRANCH

There has been some discussion in the field with regard to the need for agency workers to be more concerned about developing and maintaining meaningful collaborative relationships with the people who live in the communities where we work. In recent years there have been numerous conversations regarding this kind of agency-community involvement, and some agencies have quite actively sought the participation of community citizens as members of advisory groups. I should like to describe to you one such effort of collaboration between Woodlawn Mental Health Center and the Woodlawn community. I shall confine my remarks mainly to the development of our first major program and the ongoing support and sanction that the Advisory Board has given us to function in the community.

The Woodlawn Mental Health Center is a Chicago Board of Health facility. It also derives its support from the State of Illinois Department of Mental Health, and grants from the National Institute of Mental Health and the State of Illinois Psychiatric Research and Training Authority. As a center that performs both assessment and service functions, we have set about the tasks of (1) assessing the mental health needs of the area; (2) finding resources to meet those needs; (3) determining program priorities in collaboration with our Advisory Board; and (4) with community sanction and participation, developing programs to meet mental health needs.

Our commitment is to the total community of Woodlawn. It is a geographically defined area of about one and a half square miles, located on the South Side of Chicago. The population is approximately 82,000. Woodlawn is a Negro community. Although not a homogeneous group with respect to economic standards, in a large portion of the area, housing is poor, unemployment and delinquency rates high.[1]

Historically, the community has served as port of entry through which several ethnic groups have passed on their way to middle-class status. For

[1]Welfare Council of Metropolitan Chicago, *Chicago Community Area Profiles* (Publication No. 4006, 1964).

many of its Negro citizens a similar kind of passage through has not been without difficulty and some of the community's citizens have been actively involved in ways designed to increase the community's efficiency in supporting its people's efforts toward advancement.

The Woodlawn Mental Health Center has an Advisory Board which is made up of twenty to twenty-five people.[2] Most of the Advisory Board members are representatives from the major grass-roots organizations in Woodlawn. They represent many different points of view. As a board, they collaborate with us in determining program priorities and provide ongoing community sanction for the Center's operations. In addition, they assume an active role in some aspects of the programs and, most importantly, for us, they represent our commitment with respect to the community's right to be taken into account.

In the Center's relationship with the Board, the staff defines the technical aspects of a problem, and the Board shares with Center staff their views regarding the community's attitudes and aspirations in relation to the problem. For example, the Board pointed us toward the development of the first major program, which is one for first-grade children in the twelve elementary schools of Woodlawn. During the initial phase of the Center's development, preliminary studies were made on the acutely disturbed population and juvenile delinquency. The Board and other community leaders, however, continued to express interest in the very young children who represented for them the hopes and aspirations of the community's future. The fact that half of the children drop out of school before completing high school was of no small concern.[3] Programs of prevention and early treatment that would allow for early intervention were of critical importance, and since there were no technical considerations which would preclude beginning with young children, by consensual agreement between Center staff and community, this work was begun.

For the past three years, the Woodlawn Mental Health Center, in cooperation with the Chicago Board of Education and with the sanction of its Community Advisory Board, has been carrying out a combined research and service program aimed at assessing the mental health needs of 2,000 first-grade children, and providing a program of prevention and early treatment. I shall describe briefly how this has been done.

The initial task was to determine which children were in need of assistance from mental health workers. Each of the fifty-seven first-grade teachers in twelve elementary schools of Woodlawn was asked to make a list of the kinds of behaviors that she observed in first-graders which indicated to her that the children were having trouble adapting to the classroom.

---

[2] For an account of the Center's early history and formation of the Advisory Board see: S. G. Kellam and S. K. Schiff, "The Origins and Early Evaluation of an Urban Community Mental Health Center in Woodlawn," in L. Duhl and R. Leopold, eds. *Casebook on Community Psychiatry* (New York: Basic Books, Inc., 1967).

[3] Robert J. Havighurst, *The Public Schools of Chicago. A Survey for the Board of Education of the City of Chicago* (Chicago: Board of Education of the City of Chicago, 1964), pp.12, 57, 143—82.

From these lists, the information was classified into five major categories: (1) shyness, (2) hyperaggression, (3) immaturity, (4) underachievement, (5) restlessness. To these five was added a sixth category, which was designed to give an over-all view of the child's adaptational status. Using these categories on a four-point rating scale, each teacher was asked to rate every child in her room in all six categories as to whether he was adapting, mildly maladapting, moderately maladapting, or severely maladapting.

In addition to the teacher's view of the child's adaptational status in school, two other views of the child were obtained through (1) direct clinical observation, and (2) a home interview with the mother. The former procedure consisted of direct observation of small groups of children in a semistructured play situation. Two clinical raters, one male and one female, observed the children in groups of ten. At the beginning of the session, the children were asked to sit in a semicircle while the male rater had a brief "get-acquainted" conversation with each child. Then the children were allowed to play for a period of thirty minutes, after which time a second individual conversation took place. At the end of the session, the clinical raters made independent ratings on each child. These ratings reflected whether the child appeared to have overt signs of troubles in a more clinical sense.[4]

The interview with the mother took place in the home, and was for the purpose of getting the mother's view of the child as well as information regarding the family and its relationship to the community.

These views of the child in different situations have been important in the planning of a meaningful service program. For example, in their initial ratings of the first-grade children, the teachers saw 70% of the 2,000 children as having either mild, moderate, or severe troubles making the adaptation to the first grade. Psychiatric symptoms were observed in approximately 7% of the children seen by the clinical raters. Most of the latter group, however, were rated by teachers as maladapting. In consideration of this information, it was clear that a service program would have to be planned to meet the needs of a large number of maladapting children and also take into account the need for prevention in the smaller adapting population. The service program that was developed is as follows: The schools were divided into two groups of six, one group being the experimental and the other control. Mental health professionals were assigned to the six experimental schools. During the first year, the two major parts of the intervention program in the six experimental schools included:

1. A school staff meeting once a week, at which time the Center professional, principal, assistant principal, adjustment teacher, and all the first-grade teachers talked about any issues pertinent to helping first-grade children do better in school.

---

[4]For more detailed descriptions of the teacher rating and clinical rating processes see S. G. Kellam and S. K. Schiff "Adaptation and Mental Illness in the First Grade Classrooms of an Urban Community. I. Studies of Periodic Measurements of Adaptation" (Unpublished manuscript).

2. The classroom group meeting, which consisted of the teacher and the Center professional having a small group meeting in the classroom. In the group were included those children within the class who were severely maladapted. The discussion focused on problems the children were experiencing doing their best in school.

This program has continued for the past three years, each year beginning with the incoming group of first-grade children. During the second year there was one major modification and an important addition to the service program in the six experimental schools. The classroom group meetings were continued but modified so as to involve the entire class in discussing problems relating to doing their best in school. This approach came about as a result of the experiences in the first year's meetings when it became evident that the adapting children could be tremendously helpful in setting a positive tone for learning and in supporting attempts at change in children who were not doing well. The addition referred to is parent meetings. These meetings are for all parents whose children are in first grade in the experimental schools. Parents, teachers, and the mental health professional participate in periodic discussions on such concerns as the tasks of first-graders, the importance to the children of doing their best in school, and any problems in the classroom which may interfere with a particular child and/or children in the learning process.[5]

During the course of the year periodic assessments including teacher ratings and clinical ratings are done in order to measure time to time change in the children's adaptational and clinical statuses. This is done throughout the twelve schools and affords opportunities to observe changes in children in both the experimental and control schools. At the end of the third year these assessments are repeated providing a view of the children from a longer range vantage point.

Throughout the program we have been tremendously impressed by the magnificent effort put forth by the staff of the Chicago Board of Education as well as the Catholic Archdiocesan School System in this cooperative venture with Woodlawn Mental Health Center. This effort has been evident at all levels – central and local administrative, teaching and ancillary service staff.

Equally as important has been the continuous involvement of the Advisory Board with us each step of the way, not only in making critical decisions, but in actively supporting the program. When the first mother-home interviews were planned, Advisory Board members and other community leaders provided support and sanction by making it clear to mothers of first-graders and others that this was a community program, approved by community leaders. Ministers announced from their pulpits the

---

[5]For further information on the intervention program see S. K. Schiff and S. G. Kellam, "A Community-Wide Mental Health Program of Prevention and Early Treatment in First Grade," American Psychiatric Association Research Report No. 21 (April, 1967), 92-102

scheduled home visits and their purpose, reassuring parents that information shared with interviewers would be held in strictest medical confidence. It was indeed a real tribute to the commitment and dedication of the community to its young that the response from the mothers was overwhelmingly favorable.

Advisory Board members have participated quite actively in the parent programs, taking time out from their jobs to attend meetings describing the nature of center-community collaboration and how the Board functions with center staff. This is one example of agency-community collaboration in the growth and ongoing functioning of a mental health program for a subpopulation of young children living in a geographically defined community located in a large metropolitan area. Our experiences in this kind of collaborative relationship have been equally as rewarding and enriching as we have developed other programs.

THADDEUS KOSTRUBALA

I would like to tell a story about something I did two weeks ago at the American Psychiatric Association Convention where I discussed a paper on community mental health. The writer of the paper was a typical liberal psychiatrist who was interested in helping people and setting up community psychiatry programs. There was a great deal of talk and discussion at that convention about, among other things, how to organize relevant community programs. One issue that was avoided, as it very often is, was how to organize community mental health programs in relation to the people they serve.

One of basic premises of community mental health is that it should be truly subservient to the community it serves. In a sense, the professionals are employed by the community which should be their judge and tell them what to do. The professionals should not covertly manipulate to get sanction for whatever program they bring to the community. This immediately puts professionals with all their training, etc., on the defensive because they are not used to this. Their pride gets affronted, but this is perhaps the most important point in the whole area of community mental health. Programs must remain relevant and in order to be relevant they must be tied into the community in new and exciting ways. Without this relationship people will soon lose interest in the program.

At the meeting, I took an extrapolation of a mythical community mental health program in a ghetto of one of our large cities. I said there very well might be points of conflict. For example, what will happen when a truly representative community mental health board concludes that the mental health of their community does not necessarily have anything to do with the unconscious factors about which professionals talk but has to do with factors such as prejudice, discrimination, lack of jobs, and the activities of the police and others which are markedly discriminatory. If we are to improve community mental health, whatever it may be, it is irrelevant to see people on a one-to-one basis. If you look at the number of people in the ghettos and the problems they face, you will see that it is not only irrelevant; it is doomed to failure.

Or suppose this community said they had decided to stage a violent demonstration, to actually carry out something, maybe throw a Molotov cocktail. I asked the professionals if they would be willing to throw a Molotov cocktail, march, move with the community, and be subservient to it if they really understand their problems? I do not know if this has ever occurred, but it does highlight a conflict that may occur between a professional in a community and some members of the community who are concerned about what should be done to rectify the problems in their community, especially in the area of mental health. That is the first point I would like to make.

The second point has to do with youth. From two sectors of our society, I see something developing which, though perhaps not new on the American scene, is causing a great deal of concern. Not long ago, our young people were militant, angry, and willing to march and participate in political activities. This included people from the suburbs as well as from the inner city. It included those who backed Goldwater, wore the straw hats, played banjos, and carried on political campaigns.

Increasingly, this political activism seems to be substituted with political nonactivism. Apathy is growing within the ghetto as a result of the lack of significant progress for the majority of people, and it is beginning to appear in the suburbs where it is taking the new forms of the teenybopper group and the people in Haight-Ashbury in San Francisco as well as on the Near North Side in and around Old Town. In other words, the concept of "don't take action" is growing in both segments of our society. The concept of "dropping out" is beginning to take hold.

This has important consequences for what may happen to our culture in the immediate future. If this movement continues, it may mean an entirely new focus for political activities in the immediate future. By default there will be very little significant opposition, if there is any opposition at all, to the political policies of whatever party is in power. Furthermore, I think the concept of frustration, the inability to achieve genuine progress, is very closely related to delinquent behavior.

FRED STRODTBECK

Let me start my presentation by carrying out a group exercise. On a piece of paper, set up five columns from "strongly agree," on the left, to "strongly disagree," on the right with "neither agree nor disagree" in the middle. I will read a statement and want you to rate the degree to which you agree or disagree in terms of these five alternatives:

1) The idea of trying to adjust to society as now constituted fills me with horror.
2) There are sad and depressing times when the world strikes the eye as a huge, heartless, impersonal machine, almost devoid of understanding, sympathy and mercy.

3) I sometimes feel that I am the plaything of forces beyond my control.
4) I feel strongly how different I am from some of my closest friends.
5) I have very little in common with most of the people I meet.
6) I do not think I will ever find someone of the opposite sex who really understands me.
7) I have very little self-confidence.
8) I usually try to keep my thoughts to myself.
9) I sometimes wish I were a child again.

Add up your answers, giving from one for an "agree" to five for a "disagree."

Now let me explain why I have asked you this particular set of items. As I thought about my assignment today, my mind went through these steps. I wondered if twelve years ago there would have been consensus in a group similar to this one that the problem of urban living should be attacked first with a modification of housing? I doubt that, at that time, we would have been sensitive to the limitations of the large public housing constructions which have enlisted so much energy in the interim.

With that analogy in mind, I wondered if what we are doing now to increase local participation in matters relating to community mental health will seem equally inappropriate in ten or twelve years. Obviously I do not know the answer, but in phrasing the question this way, I want to juxtapose sets of materials relating roughly to adolescent delinquency so that you can share some of the uncertainty I feel when one is called upon not just to work on a problem, but to search for an answer.

I collaborated with Jim Short and the detached workers from the YMCA to produce the book, *Group Process And Gang Delinquency.*[1] Although this book was published several summers ago, the observations were made between 1959 and about 1964. I think that, at the time we completed this study, our explanation of the delinquency processes was superior to anything else in the literature. However, I am very aware that the interactions between gang organization and the politicalization of youth which has arisen from the freedom movement makes this book out of date in fundamental ways. Therefore, when I contrast Negro gang delinquency in the inner city with student activists at the great universities, I do it with an appreciation that radical changes may have occurred in the last two or three years in the inner city which I have been too remote from the scene to observe.

The source of the questions I asked is the book *The Uncommitted*[2] by Kenneth Keniston which is a study of alienated youth in American society. What puzzles me is, if we do produce alienated youth in upper middle-class homes and in the very finest universities of this country, then it may be that this alienation is generated by a process which is not understood. In general, rich people use social science to cope more than do poor, and this

[1] James F. Short, Jr. and Fred L. Strodtbeck, *Group Process and Gang Delinquency* (Chicago: University of Chicago Press, 1965).
[2] Kenneth Keniston, *The Uncommitted* (New York: Harcourt, Brace and World, Inc., 1960).

is one problem they have not solved. Those concerned about reducing the alienation of youth in the slum sections of the inner city may be guilty of oversights comparable to those made by persons who placed their confidence in the housing reforms of a decade ago. Understand, I am not talking about what I know to be true; I am raising questions which, if answered, could possibly change how we would go about our jobs.

I would like to get your scores on the alienation test you took by a show of hands. If you are not interested or willing to do this, just do not raise your hand.

	Scores	Number of Participants
Strongly Engaged	40-45	3
	35-39	12
Modal	30-34	20
Alienated	25-29	3
	20-24	3
	15-19	1
	0-15	0

If seven of forty-two who participate as community leaders are disenchanted, how is it for the ones they serve? How many of you are in direct contact with inner-city adolescents in your normal work relations? (About 50% of the persons there.) From your own experiences, would you think that the quality of alienation experienced by boys in privileged school situations (for example, the disillusioned Harvard student) and that experienced by inner-city boys who are frequently involved in delinquency (for example, the gang boy) would be similar or different? I am sure we would all be pleased if the boys we know in the inner city could be prepped and sent to Harvard. But if alienation can occur in both places, what is similar, or different, in the place of high and the place of low privilege?

When we started *Group Process in Gang Delinquency,* we thought that the so-called "opportunity theory for delinquency" merited particular consideration. The opportunity theory suggests that some middle-class boys who cannot stay in school are in sufficient contact with persons of similar values to persist in attaining goals through education, dutiful work, etc. Others strive for the same goals, but lack of cultural preparation, poor adjustment in school, etc., results in their frustration, and they turn their energies toward deviant and delinquent channels of achievement. One might conceive of an Al Capone as wanting the good things Chicago had to offer but being less constrained by the norms of the larger society in working for them.

Among Negroes, as among the whites of Capone's days, there are corner-boy adaptations in which a youth stays in his own achievement niche and has fun, but does not get into too much trouble. But also among the Negro out-of-school-adolescent who is frustrated and embittered, there are many who do not have sufficiently good contacts to enable them to enter even the rackets effectively. It was not surprising that Negro gang boys who were isolated from the chances of fencing stolen material, getting protection at the station house, etc., would demonstrate resentment in ways which would be viewed by the larger society as purposeless. An aspect of this theory leads Cohen to predict that persons who have opted for lower-class adaptations actually reject middle-class values. Miller, working in this tradition in the Boston area, suggested that a blue-collar adaptation leads to the rejection of many aspects of middle-class life.

We checked with about 500 gang boys in the city for their evaluations of people who studied hard, did well in school, read books, etc., and found that their evaluations were the same as the evaluations of the similar symbols by middle-class boys. However, we did find a much greater tolerance for the acceptance of pimping, strong arming, etc., and from careful work with our materials, we concluded that underprivileged boys in the inner city did *not* actively reject the "benefits" of middle-class adaptations.

We also worked with several drug-using groups and we did not find many stable gangs whose primary activity was drug use. In many of the groups, some members smoked marijuana, but only one or two sets of boys were greatly disposed to using all the available varieties of beanies, etc. At the first wade-in, our one chronic group of users got high on beanies, and played cards in a remote corner where they could see the action. They definitely took pride in differentiating themselves from what was going on. But even with these boys we did not find the same rejection of the larger society as that which is frequently manifested by the "in-burn" characters who are alienated from privileged schools.

In short, boys going from a very permissive and interested home into a controlled and bureaucratized educational setting react in some ways like boys going from homes with harsh discipline into the limited involvement, boredom, and community disinterest on "the corner." The in-burns want to help others while exploiting the dependency of others for their own psychological needs. The in-burns wish to give something for nothing as a result of long exposure to institutions which cared for them, though at times in a way which reduced their autonomy. On the other hand, the inner-city adolescent wants to get something for nothing at the lowest possible risk. He has adapted to an environment which has many threats; he has adopted by becoming "cool" and uninvolved. Beyond predicting that a gang boy would have difficulty understanding an in-burn, it is hoped that these remarks will also suggest that money, jobs, and better physical resources alone will *not* do the job. The community mental health job can probably *not* be done by indigenous personnel if they themselves are either too alienated, or so merely committed to the establishment that they see failures of poor people as arising because of character defects. The array of modal responses of the participants on the alienation scale probably shows some hidden wisdom in the institution: one has to doubt but not reject the larger society and the client if one is to make the best use of his opportunity to serve.

27

The Subculture of Youth

HUGH OSBORNE

I am not sure how to attack the subject of youth as a subculture, especially in light of what you probably have been talking about in other sessions. Rather than discuss youth in general, I will focus on that young person between the ages of sixteen and twenty-one who lives in a Negro community.

I am a bit confused about how to start because on this week's cover of *Time* Magazine we see our proud, young friend, Sgt. Clyde Brown, Jr., a young Negro man in Vietnam. This is perhaps the fourth time a Negro has taken a forward stride as a result of violence. The first was in the Civil War, the second in World War I, and in World War II the Negro took another giant step forward. Since that time he has moved very rapidly, and today, on the cover of *Time,* you see Sgt. Clyde Brown.

This spans a number of years and one way to describe my dilemma is by mentioning several cliches that are being attached to certain youngsters today. One is the "socially disadvantaged child," a second is the "culturally deprived child," and a third is the "victim of deprivation." I want to examine these in terms of the so-called "juvenile delinquent" and what he sees.

First, let's look at the community in which the disadvantaged child lives. We say it is largely inarticulate, nonvocal, very antagonistic, without any real ties or consideration of the community, and therefore it is nonproductive. There is, however, language and a system of communication. It is a very rapid one, and I submit that, if we do not know the language, and are left out because of our inability to communicate with the people in the community, we are apt to evaluate it as ineffective, disadvantaged, deprived, and say that there is no hope for the children in that community. We cannot make our evaluations from outside the community basing them on what we consider the norms, the basic participation numbers. If we plan programs and superimpose them on the people living in the community, we cannot expect them to participate simply because we say it is good for them. Nine times out of ten, they are laughing at us and at the number of times they have put us "in a bag."

Of course, there are other ways of looking at what a disadvantaged youth might be. I am afraid that if I go by the terms that are tagged onto our children now, I would have been a disadvantaged child, though I did not know it until about 1960. Even though I was gifted with a mother and father, both of whom spoke English, were God-fearing and contributing members of their community in a little Kentucky town, in 1960 I would be seen as a disadvantaged child.

I do not believe that, and my agency does not believe it either. We feel very strongly that if the forces of urbanization break Negro family ties, our families can be reunited through certain supportive experiences. We also feel that the child will be hypnotized by these continued references to his place in our new society. If he is disadvantaged because he lives in a particular community, if all of the parents in this community and all his associates are no good, then obviously we can say he is disadvantaged. But I challenge you to prove that the majority of families and young people living in Lawndale, Woodlawn, Grand Boulevard, Englewood, or any of the other so-called "disadvantaged neighborhoods" are not citizens who contribute to our city.

If we are to be selective in dealing with those people who are "acting out" as the sociologists might say, then let us work with the families that need help. We cannot work with them as if there were large differences; we cannot be patronizing or paternalistic if we want to maintain a system to support them.

On the other side, it is very difficult for a hard-working, young Negro family to move directly from the West Side into a middle-class neighborhood. In Chicago, there is a wide chasm between the middle-class Negro and the low-income Negro. This is one reason for the acting-out difficulties of our young people today. We need successful images to project before the young Negro child in a low-income family. We must reinspire and revitalize the hopes of our young people. Most of us who consider ourselves advantaged and middle-class stay away from those of our neighbors and friends who need help.

I submit that if there is a culture of youth in Chicago or any urban city, it is a stratified one; it has many layers which are based on the efforts of the Negro family to move upward. However, from examining the many problems exhibited by young people in Chicago and other urban centers throughout the country, one of the main hopes for reducing the amount of juvenile delinquency and the number of broken homes in the future seems to lie in the large, and ever-growing, Negro middle class in these cities.

In Chicago, there are now more than 85,000 Negro homeowners who have all the outward material appearances of being middle class. But in these same communities, there are no supportive services for dealing with less advantaged youngsters. There are no active members of boards or service and community centers in the neighborhoods that desperately need them. Apparently these people do not have the time. As a part of your Community Service Workshop session, I suggest revitalizing or moving toward the middle-income Negro families in Chicago to use their energy and strength to help the masses of our brothers. We can do something about our juvenile delinquency problems throughout this country and especially in the city of Chicago.

REV. JOHN FRY

If I were to characterize the organized and casual activities of youth today as exhibiting the marks of a "subculture," I would take the word "subculture" to refer to something existing within a main culture and generally characterized by some deviancy or delinquency. Perhaps our thinking of today's youth as existing in something so special as a subculture reveals the pressing problems of understanding them. From our standpoint as the old ones, we cannot understand and we deplore the quality of their remarkable ways of dressing and acting, and their peculiar language and music. When we see them bombing around on motorcycles, hot cars, and so on, we are bound to characterize them as displaying some kind of deviancy or delinquency.

As did Mr. Osborne, I want to confine my remarks to ghetto youth, and more specifically to one cluster of ghetto youth that I know best, the Blackstone Rangers. When you look closely at the structures, life styles, and activities of the Blackstone Rangers, you see that from where they are, as they look out upon the world, they see themselves as operating a politics of dissent, raising issues that otherwise might not be raised in our society or might be raised poorly. On the other hand, from the standpoint of the adult community and the prevailing culture, this is a very delinquent outfit. Therefore, the point of view is decisive, and I would not like to think of the Blackstone Rangers, or youth in general, as exhibiting anything like the marks of a subculture. Rather they form a dissenting structure in society which we are willing to abide momentarily.

Having raised this general terminological question, I have some particular comments to make. The first is that in the Blackstone Rangers there are 1500 young men for whom no adult models exercise power as ideals. If we were able to look inside their heads and, with our Freudian dialectics, find the contents of their ego ideal structure, we would not find any adult material. There would be all youth material. What a Blackstone Ranger wants to be is a Blackstone Ranger. He takes his model for a man in Chicago in 1967, not from looking at grown-up men, but from looking at Blackstone Rangers. What it means to be a man is to be a Blackstone Ranger. This incidentally solves many mental health problems immediately because the tension between the ongoing processes of the ego and the ego ideal system are not antagonistic or in any unfruitful tension. They are beautifully blended.

This also means that these young men have in that process rejected all the masculine possibilities that society has held out to them, as few and poor as they are. What is possible for a ghetto youth if he is lucky enough to get to a good high school, have somebody pumping motivation into him at the rate of about five gallons per minute, and if he has the essential brains to get into a high honor track and make it through high school? He is apt to go to a blue-chip college and then he can go back and be a white man's Negro for the rest of his life. As you see this is not a very attractive life opportunity which is held out for him, and it is the rare one who even has that opportunity. Most have the opportunity of being spun out of the ghetto environment into what is euphemistically called the "mainstream." When they get there, they find it is not the mainstream at all but only an eddy of the mainstream, where the little fish are. It is not out in the deep water where the real gold is.

Considering the opportunities for being a Negro man in 1967 that society has held out to them, they feel very fortunate to have rejected them. This is supportive material for the blend of their ego ideal material, for being what they are all the time. This has important implications for any consideration of this and similar groups of young men in ghetto communities. It is a phenomenon that has emerged very recently, and we shall have to consider it very carefully.

My second comment refers to the politics of power in which the Blackstone Rangers conceive of themselves as operating. They see themselves as a dissenting political structure. As they see it, they will get somewhere, not by simply registering dissent but by exercising the actual power they have accumulated in the maintenance of their organization. They do not see themselves as having anything, including life chances, beside their organization. Therefore, they perceive the first thing on their agenda as keeping their organization very strong and coherent, even as it evolves into new organizational patterns.

They do see, however, that they are operating in a power-force field, that the enormously powerful people in the ghetto are the syndicate, the Machine, the real estate, commercial structure, and the welfare establishments. They see quite clearly that, in order to have a significant voice among the many voices that will determine their destiny, and to have an important effect in the quality of their own lives, they will have to operate in a powerful way. I am here only as a reporter, and though their view disturbs many people, we will have to deal with it.

One example of their use of power took place at the height of last summer's West Side riots. On the basis of previous alliances between the Rangers and some West Side organizations, considerable pressure was put on the Rangers, not only to participate in the riots, but also to start one in Woodlawn. These young men decided that they could better use their power to inhibit riots in Woodlawn and Englewood. So they used the power and the communications network of the organization to keep hot characters out of Woodlawn. When one was found, he was hustled west of State Street and did not come back. This is an exhibition of genuine power wisely used, not to reduce violence as such, but to display an organization's stance in the community. This was their way of saying, "You have to reckon with us because, if we cannot stop one, well, you know the alternative." This was a naked display of power.

A second instance also occurred last summer, just before the Bud Billiken's Day parade. The Rangers enjoyed their usual notoriety, and particularly with the police. Rival organizations were looking forward to the possibility of severely embarassing the mighty Rangers by either drawing them into a fight they did not want and perhaps would loose, or drawing them into a fight in such a way that the entire Illinois constabulary would be arranged against the Rangers. Seeing this eventuality, the Rangers went to the youth welfare establishment and said, "From what you are and set yourselves out to be, clearly you do not want a lot of people to be shot and killed. Now, we do not want to be shot and we do not want to shoot a lot of people, so wouldn't it be best if all the Rangers just got out of town?"

It sounded like a glorious idea and everybody agreed to it, but who would pay? The Rangers did not have any money for things like picnics, so the youth welfare establishment, aided by the intricacies of that particular event, paid for taking the Rangers to play football at Notre Dame University on Bud Billiken's Day. We had a safe Bud Billiken's Day and everybody had a good time which would have been impossible without a display of power in a very intricate, successful way.

A third instance of their display of power is going on right now. The Blackstone Rangers are a legal corporation in the State of Illinois, and last week, along with Oscar Brown, Jr., they presented a musical review. At first, everbody laughed, not at Oscar Brown Jr., but at the Rangers for going into the musical review business. A few friends with newspapers gave the show some publicity, but it was not widely advertised. It was performed five times in a building which seats 1100 people, and there was standing room only for four out of the five performances. People who desperately wanted to see the show had to be turned away from three out of the five performances. It was a marvelous success, not only in terms of the number of people who came to see it, but also artistically. It left people in a state somewhere between astonishment and ecstasy. This is another display of power. It could not have been a smash hit had it been put on by an organization which was unaware of the dialectics of power in contemporary society. Thirty people would have shown up Friday night, and it would have died a slow death Saturday afternoon. The Ranger's show will be performed for the next two weekends and perhaps indefinitely. This is a third instance of operating genuine power politics in an environment which demands that, to get any place, you have to operate politically, as a power force in a power-force field.

My final comment has to do with reactions to the political activities of the Rangers. What does a society with a mainstream characterized by affluence, boredom, and general inability to deal significantly with novelty and vitality do with this almost naked, labidinal power which operates in a very political way? We have already seen that normal reactions destroy it as too incomprehensible, too novel, too destructive, too delinquent, etc. Having watched these reactions for about sixteen months, I think it is apparent to a great many people that there have to be other reactions. I believe that once we get past the first reaction, some of the next ones will be more creative and accommodating.

The Rangers do not want to get into the mainstream; they want a mainstream all their own. They want a separate society which is not a subculture in any sense. They want another culture alongside the main culture. This is obviously pretentious, arrogant, and probably hopelessly unrealistic. However, I think that the answer within our reaction patterns, accommodating as it will have to be, will mean something between what they want and what we are now prepared to give them. Then we will see that a dissenting structure won major concessions from the general American power arrangement which I would say is about the best you can hope for from any dissenting structure. It is my hope that these accommodations will be created, spontaneous, and quick in coming.

MALCOLM KLEIN

It is probably very dangerous for a panel member to start off his discussion by saying he is displeased, since that immediately alienates the entire host body; but I am displeased. Let me tell you some of the things that displease me. One of them is the sweetness and light which existed this morning throughout the panel discussion. A second is the sweetness and light in Mr. Osborne's portrayal of the situation of the "non-disadvantaged, disadvantaged" Negro. The third is the sweetness and light in Reverend Fry's talk about the Blackstone Rangers who sound very unlike any gang group I have ever known. I am displeased with your weather; I came here from Los Angeles in my winter suit!

I am not sure we can do what we are supposed to do this afternoon. I certainly cannot because I am from Los Angeles, a city very different from Chicago. I think that when Orville Luster talks, he will say the same about San Francisco which is also different in many respects. In addition, most of us are twenty years too old to talk about youth culture. At least I am, and I feel young in this experienced group.

However, let me make a few imprecise statements about youth culture. First, as Reverend Fry indicated, youth culture is a poor term; it is our lazy way of trying to put together a host of things we do not understand. We put it all together and call it the "youth culture," or "what is happening to youth," or the like, so we can deal with it conceptually. Frankly, I think that is the lazy man's way of going about our work. Obviously there is not one "youth culture."

There may be several, slightly distinct, youth subcultures which we could talk about, but again, each is probably nothing more than a variation on a wider culture. For example, the juvenile gang is said to exist in a distinct subculture. I do not find that to be the case. To the extent that a juvenile gang subculture exists, it seems to be nothing more than a variation on a much more diffuse culture which is generally associated with the

ghetto, or with delinquency, or with the lower class. Most of the characteristics of gang boys can be best explained by their class status rather than
by their racial, delinquent-gang, dropout, or any other status.

We used to speak about the beat culture as a separate and distinct
entity. A book was written on the beatniks of North Beach in San Francisco, but as I read it and as I talk to people, I find that the beat culture
is nothing more than a slight variation on a generally artistic culture or set
of values. We have already spoken about the "in-burns." This is a new term
to me, but it sounds like the seeds of the hippy culture of which we in
California have become very aware as you will be too as soon as we trans-
port it to you. But again, the hippy culture is nothing more than a
variation on a value-alienated, middle-class culture.

In order to understand these subcultures or slight variations, we have to
understand the larger value sets from which they come. I do not understand
those larger value sets. I am merely making the point that we must come
to understand them if we are to deal with the subsets. That is my first
point and perhaps it sets a context for us.

My second is that we identify these subcultures in terms of their alienation from or their antagonism toward our culture, or more specifically, from
middle-class adult life. However, if you talk to the members of these subcultures, often you will find they are far more concerned with alienation
from or antagonism toward their own peers. When the gang member talks
about what bothers him, he may not talk about the adult culture, but
about "those squares" at school. They are much closer to him, and he is
more likely to compare himself with his peers. He may talk about separation from non-gang boys rather than from adults, welfare people, the
political establishment, or Mayor Daley. We lose sight of this in our discussions when we try to understand and explain the behavior and value of
these boys in terms of their distinctness from what we know, what we are
(or think we are), or what we would like to be, rather than in terms of
their own immediate reference, which is other boys.

Third, as I indicated, there is a danger of lumping subcultures together.
Irving Spergel has recently written a book on detached work with delinquent
gangs. It was rather negatively reviewed by Yablonsky in *Trans-Action,* and I
fired off a letter to the editor for the first time in my life (which shows
how alienated I am). In that review, Yablonsky criticized Spergel for writing
a book on how to work with alienated youth culture in general, and the
hippies in particular, which is what Yablonsky happens to be interested in
right now. I was disgruntled with the review because I do not see gangs and
hippies as the same at all.

Let me describe a few of the differences I see. I know quite a bit about
gang boys and very little about the hippies, though I have been forced to
learn something about them in the last few weeks. They are very confusing,
but I think I know this much about them. The gang boy is by and large
an unconcerned boy. He is not concerned with politics, welfare, community
organization, or any of our other adult hangups. The hippy is very

concerned. He has chosen not to take action about his concern, but he has made that choice in a rational way. If you talk to him about what bothers him, he will tell you Vietnam, the draft, civil rights, the cops, and all the rest. He is very concerned while the gang boy is not. I think this is a distinct difference.

Second, the gang boy, of course, comes from a lower-class situation whereas, by and large, the hippy boy is middle class. As research that is being carried out indicates, he comes from a fairly comfortable home situation, at least financially.

Third, the gang boy is concerned with – and people are concerned about him because of – physical damage: assaults, auto thefts, purse snatchings, and the like. He lives in a world in which physical damage to property or person is an important matter. The hippy does not; he is concerned with moral damages and challenges. Suddenly, after going through the first eighteen years of his life, he is hit with the hypocrisy, the dry rot of our society. The gang boy lives with dry rot from his first day. The hippy kid does not know it until he gets to college and suddenly becomes aware of the rest of the world. In response, he withdraws from it. Even if we restrict ourselves to understanding the ghetto, the Negro or Mexican-American gang, we have to make these as well as many other distinctions.

Finally, a lesson on how to form a cohesive group or subculture. The subculture is a figment of our imagination; it does not exist until we identify it as such. There were hippies in San Francisco before last year, but somebody found the word "hippy" and the newspapers got hold of it. A cohesive group or subculture is formed, first, by labeling it. Once it is labeled, it is easier to deal with conceptually, and a subculture is in the making. Similarly with gangs.

Secondly, a subculture is formed by legitimizing it. Ordinarily it is legitimized by the sanctions which are applied to it. I do not think that the hippies were any particular problem until the San Francisco Health Department decided to be the instrument of society, and crack down on and sweep out the places where these youngsters were living. Suddenly there were legal as well as moral sanctions for the existence of a group of young people. We do the same with gangs. I believe that the worst thing the police can do is stop a boy and ask him which gang he belongs to. It is not so bad just to stop him; these kids are used to being stopped. But as soon as a policeman says, "Which gang do you belong to?" he is legitimizing his status as a separate entity, as something apart from society. We do it with beats, hippies, and occasionally with social workers. I question that any of these groups ought to be legitimized.

Third, and a corollary to this, is that we tend to reify the subculture once we can identify it. We call them "the hippies," and if there are 100,000 or 500,000 coming into San Francisco this summer, we will make them all hippies. Some of these people may be coming to see the Bay Bridge, but if they have long hair, they will be called hippies. They will be reacted to in this way because we have reified the concept of hippies, just as we have reified the concept of delinquent gangs. I am using "reify" to mean, to make real what is not yet real, to give it physical structure.

Finally, we help to form these subcultures by projecting, in the Freudian sense. I think this is one of the things the hippies are really bothered about. We say the hippies are homosexual because they have long hair. A good psychologist will tell you that there is no one who is purely hetero-sexual, but if we can say, "*they* are homosexual," that sets them apart and makes us hetero-straight, all right. We say they are immoral because they are living ten in one room or because they have sex relations without getting married. First, I do not dare do what Fred Strodtbeck did this morning and ask you to take a piece of paper and add up your "score," but I think the point is clear.

We say their trouble is that they were not spanked enough when they were children. What they need is a good firm hand, and, as many of you know, those who make the most noise about spanking are the unspanked. We say they are irresponsible, do not respect the law, represent a moral decline in society where the law and authority are no longer alive. But what may really underlie our reaction is the fear that they have caught onto the fact that one only abides by authority, and respects the law and good moral principles as long as there are sanctions, and not otherwise.

I think a subculture is created not only as the result of the behavior of certain sets of people, but also because adults or society react to that behavior. A vicious cycle is started which goes beyond the desires of the participants in the subculture. It is created and rigidified for them. These are some of the dangers that are the result, not of *their* behavior, but of *our reaction* to their behavior.

28

Youth Gangs

STANLEY NEWMAN

I only have a few points to make. The first is that we need to differentiate between "gangs," and more specifically "Negro gangs." I suggest that Negro gangs, in the sense that they have been treated in the literature, are obsolete since Mrs. Rosa Parks refused to sit in the back of the bus and gave rise to the Negro Revolution. One cannot talk about organizations of Negro youth without taking into account this very significant revolution which is still going on. It does not seem unreasonable to me to suggest that we must be aware of at least the possibility that where we had gangs, we now have organizations. Negro youths are undoubtedly very much aware of concepts such as self-determination, anti-colonialism, nationalism, and black brotherhood. They are familiar with Malcolm X, Kenyatta (Mau Mau), Karenga (U.S.), and Mohammed Ali. Evidence for this can be seen in the refusal of significant numbers of Negroes to process (straighten) their hair, the popular usage of the term *black* as opposed to Negro, and the continual talk of the war (Watts, Newark, Detroit) against "the Man" (the white man).

If this observation about the changed atmosphere in the ghetto is correct, then a second point needs to be raised. This has to do with what we think we know about ghetto youth. We can no longer easily go into a black ghetto and "study" whatever might be of interest. Because of the nature of teenage organizations, this has always been difficult, but it has become even more difficult today. Obviously this is particularly true for white people. Many people in the ghetto, and teenagers in particular, are fed up with whites who want to study or help them. This is related to the point I made earlier about self-determination and so forth. In short we have to take a very close look at the methods used for collecting data.

As an anthropologist I have always had a healthy suspicion of "scientific studies" carried out through the administration of questionnaires, once, twice, or three times removed from the source. While it is difficult enough to be a participant observer in a semisecret, hostile "society," it is nevertheless mandatory, in my opinion, to settle for nothing less. We have here a compounded problem of research being conducted in an area where it is imperative to be close to the source.

This leads to my final point, that perhaps we academicians know very little about the situation. Though there are people who know a great deal about it, by and large, they are not found on university faculties, nor are they concerned about publishing.

In sum, I am suggesting that we call for a moratorium on symposia of gangs and concentrate instead on going "where the action is."

FRANK CARNEY

I would like to return to some of the literature which Mr. Newman suspects is no longer valid. Not that I disagree with his contention, but I would like to review some of the literature on the efficacy of street-club work and work with delinquents in general, and pose a rather provocative question: Should we attempt to work with gangs and the so-called delinquent at all?

Berrelson and Steiner, in their monumental *Human Behavior,* reviewed some of this literature and concluded: "The efficacy of various treatments for the control of delinquency has not been established." This is to put it quite mildly.

Most of the projects directed at the reduction of delinquency are not researched, but I would like to outline some of those which have been. They are all reviewed in a very good work by Gold and Winter who divide them into two types: provocation-reduction projects and control-introduction projects. Provocation-reduction projects make the assumption that if the delinquent had an alternative to his delinquent behavior, he would take that alternative and become less delinquent. The control-introduction projects make the assumption that the delinquent is psychically disturbed to some extent, and if you rearrange his psyche and introduce controls, his behavior will be different.

One of the projects with a control-introduction orientation was the Cambridge Summerville project, carried out in Boston several years ago. In assessing the effectiveness of this program, the McCords, who researched it say, "The treatment program considered as a totality has been ineffectual as a preventative of crime."

Across the river the Roxbury Project was carried out from 1954 to 1957. Its goals were "intensive group work with adolescent gangs, casework with selected families who are persistent, long-term problems for city welfare agencies, research on the nature of community welfare." The project was a failure. Miller, who evaluated it, asked: "Was there a significant, measurable inhibition of law-violating or morally-disapproved behavior as a consequence of project efforts? The answer, with little necessary qualification, is no."

Caseworkers have also tried to prevent juvenile delinquency. In Washington, D.C., between 1954 and 1958, Tait and Hodge conducted a therapeutically oriented casework project called the Maximum-Benefits Project. They have published their results in a report called, "Delinquents, their Families, and the Community." The project was a failure, and the authors suggest that there are serious limitations in the usual casework treatment. The focus was on the multiproblem family, and the results of the casework treatment program were so dismal that the authors suggested that the multiproblem family should be classified as legally incompetent and placed in special therapeutic communities. Tait and Hodge do not go into detail on the constitutional questions which would be involved in such an arrangement.

The counselors and group workers also have had their try. For instance, a control-introduction project called "Youth Consultation Service" was conducted in a New York area high school and reported on in "Girls At Vocational High." In this program, 400 girls selected by their teachers were placed in small groups for special treatment. Cotrell, in his introduction to the work asked, "Is social work on the wrong track?" Meyer, Bogota, and Jones who researched the project do not say "yes" or "no," but "yes" is strongly implied, for this project was a failure. The authors imply that, "Change in client status may be a more promising approach than change in the client's psyche." Of course, this implies that provocation-reduction may be a more feasible approach than control-introduction.

For five years, I worked for the Chicago Youth Development Project, and we were rather thoroughly researched. Did we reduce delinquency among the youngsters or areas with whom we worked? The answer again, with little necessary qualification, is no. Lois Mock, a researcher who worked with us at the time, did a very interesting thing. In researching our project, she found that the intensity of the relationship between boy and worker was inversely correlated with the boy's conventionality. More simply stated, the workers worked the hardest with those youngsters who were least likely to change.

This is a very brief overview and many more studies could be cited. I checked with Malcolm Klein on the project he has been working with in Los Angeles for the past few years. Was there a significant reduction in juvenile delinquency among the boys served by the project? His answer, with little necessary qualification, is no. Recently in Seattle, Washington, Haeckler conducted a work-study program for selected boys in a housing project area. Was there a reduction in delinquency among the boys? The answer, with little necessary qualification, is again no.

Now I want to ask again, should anybody work with delinquents at all? It seems that those techniques which now are available for work with delinquents do not work. If we want to work with delinquents, we will have to develop some new techniques.

The delinquents with whom we want to work may be changing by themselves and may be involved in a project of their own making which will transform their lives. I have some intimation of this already. I was a street-club worker for eight years, and I never heard youngsters talking about an ideology. Now, however, I can see ideology developing among the youngsters I worked with and those who followed them. It is not widespread, but it is there, and it was not there in the eight years I worked.

GERALD SUTTLES

My main point is quite simple, and it is related to what Frank Carney has already said. My familiarity with gangs comes from the West Side and predates some recent developments and, to some extent, the development of the ideology that both previous speakers have suggested is on the way. However, from my own work, I would like to emphasize the extent to which gangs provide a social order within which the world is meaningful and orderly.

I spent considerable time among several gangs in which there were rather developed notions of each other's affairs and personal identities, of the territorial arrangements in the area where they lived, and the places to be at which time. There was an understanding of what would lead to conflict and trouble, and what to peace. There were standing definitions about interethnic relations, and here I might mention that these understandings extended to both Negro and white groups. Though, at that time, there were some differences between them, they did not seem to be very significant ones. There were local understandings about how girls, adults, and, among others, how social workers fit into the scheme of life. Information passed regularly within, and often between, groups. Within this order, members often could avoid trouble. It was a predictable order within which one could function and, to some extent, exercise self-determination.

At the outset, it was not an order which had been seriously disrupted. It seems to me that once intervention in this order was systematically practiced, it often disrupted the understandings that existed. In fact, often the explicit policy of those who worked with these groups ran counter to the dictates of the groups' own understandings. Commonly they were placed in association with groups toward whom they were somewhat ambivalent. They went along with the gang worker because of friendships with those who were working with them, but trouble was often the result. Perhaps the most frequent source of trouble was the violation of territorial boundaries. Despite such trouble between territorial groups, gang workers persisted in violating such boundaries, apparently because of an ideological commitment to "desegregation" and "cultural exposure."

The order that prevailed among these groups provided the individual boy with at least some chance of predicting the world around him. Mass media had not made any great inroads at the start. Nobody had seized upon the particular location and thrown additional rumors into the hopper so that the boys could anticipate possible future events. Though the conditions were similar, nothing happened to them which was similar to that which has happened to the Blackstone Rangers. It was not the press, but in some cases the social workers who played an important part in redefining the intentions of various groups. As a result, other groups had to react to them as a social movement with an ideology of racial or ethnic conflict rather than simply as the guys down the street who might have it in for them if they went into their territory. In other words, there was the inception of an ideology which took on much greater proportions than the previous conflicts.

The youngsters did not accept or reject that ideology because their main concern was to order the world around them and identify the intentions of others and behavior which would enable them to get something out of life. As outsiders took a more direct role in redefining the situation, they created an uncertainty where there had been some order.

Self-determination decreased as actions took on an ideological cast. One could no longer make choices as an individual; one had to choose as a group member: in this case, membership in an ethnic or racial group. Others had to be defined not in terms of local understandings but according to rumors that came through more formal sources. Self-determination in the sense of local determination became less possible as behavior was up in the air and one's responses had to be guided by unreliable headlines.

As Frank (Carney) has pointed out, the gang workers' record is not something to be very proud of as yet. I think that, whatever the social worker does, at least he should not contribute to this disorder and the relabeling of behavior to the point that such local self-determination as I observed simply disappears and people are caught in a national movement in which local considerations can play little or no role. Certainly there seems little point in introducing an ideology of racial or ethnic conflict which does not itself substitute a predictable order for the local set of understandings it tends to disrupt.

29

Juvenile Justice

ANTHONY PLATT

I would like to briefly discuss some general developments in juvenile justice during the last few years and then raise questions concerning the appropriateness and effectiveness of legal representation for youth.

As you may know, an important legal case was recently decided in the United States Supreme Court. The Gault case, as it is known, suggests that juveniles have a right to all the constitutional protections which are normally available to adults. This case suggests a dramatic change from the traditional principles of juvenile justice, beginning with the first juvenile court in Chicago in 1899. In delivering the majority opinion, Justice Fortas observed that "the condition of being a boy does not justify a kangaroo court."

In this decision, the Supreme Court seems to be suggesting that for the last sixty years juvenile courts have been perpetrating an enormous fraud on young people, especially the children of the poor and minority groups. Punitive and coercive policies have been disguised in the rhetoric of "rehabilitation" and "treatment." The Court was alarmed by the discrepancies between the ideal of rehabilitation and the depressing realities of juvenile prisons.

These efforts to "legalize" the juvenile court represent an interesting new social movement. The "child saving" movement, which implicitly recognized children as naturally dependent and corruptible, is suffering from the same kind of attacks which finally disarmed the supporters of temperance. Originally, child saving (of which the juvenile court was one example) was essentially a Protestant, middle-class antiurban reform movement. Its supporters were concerned about regulating and controlling the activities of youth rather than encouraging their independence and autonomy.

The juvenile court movement went far beyond a concern for special treatment of adolescent offenders. It brought within the ambit of governmental control a set of youthful activities that had been previously ignored or dealt with on an informal basis. It was not by accident that the behavior selected for sanctioning by the child savers – sexual license, drinking, roaming the streets, begging, frequenting dance halls and movies, fighting, and being seen in public late at night – was most directly relevant to the children of lower-class migrant and immigrant families.

The old policy of moral salvation, which until recently typified the juvenile court, has been replaced by the spirit of legalism involving representation and due process for juveniles. Juveniles are now said to *need* lawyers as well as social workers. This is the beginning of a new paternalism, a paternalism of legal representation. The pressure for these changes in juvenile court law has come mainly from the intellectual middle class – lawyers, academics, and sociologists. Young people themselves and civil rights organizations have shown little or no interest in this problem. The political revolution on the college campus may have had some indirect influence but certainly no direct influence because college students have very little contact with juvenile courts.

The Gault case and other changes in juvenile justice raise some important new questions. I would like to look at two problems now. First, is it possible to mobilize sufficient interest and resources within the legal profession so that juveniles can be properly represented? Second, are lawyers appropriately equipped to represent the interests and needs of young people, particularly ghetto youngsters in large cities?

As to the first question, my feeling is that the answer is "no," according to the present situation. Justice Fortas observed that juveniles need legal assistance to cope with problems of law, to ensure a proper review of the facts, to insist upon judicial regularity and order, and to prepare a competent defense. Where can we find the lawyers to represent the thousands of juveniles who are processed through the juvenile court in Cook County alone? Of the 13,000 attorneys in this city, only some 300 appeared in juvenile court in 1966. Most private attorneys avoid juvenile court because it is time-consuming, has little financial attraction, and is a considerable distance from downtown. The children of middle-class, suburban clients are usually represented as a favor to their parents. But these are just the children who least need an attorney. Negro children rarely use private attorneys and are usually referred to the Public Defender.

Even with the recent change to more formal procedures, lawyers still feel out of place in juvenile court because they do not consider it a regular legal institution. To them, it is still primarily a "welfare court," and they feel like outsiders who have to use humanitarian and sentimental tactics in their defense of a client.

Therefore, the burden of representation will fall upon the Public Defender and Legal Aid Bureau, which – as is widely known – are overworked and understaffed. There was only one Assistant Public Defender in the Cook County Juvenile Court during the last year, and yet he somehow managed to represent over 400 clients without secretarial or investigative help. Juveniles, however, are reluctant to trust a Public Defender and many do not even think that he is an attorney. Whether a Public Defender is equipped to do a competent job and whether he can properly represent the interests of youth are irrelevant questions if most young people from minority groups do not regard him as somebody who is on their side.

The second issue concerns the ability of lawyers to represent the broader interests and needs of youth, particularly Negro youth. Are lawyers equipped to represent young people at the community level, help them in their organized interests, and articulate their demands to the outside world?

A recent article by Edgar and Jean Cahn suggests that lawyers do have this competence in four special areas: (1) Lawyers can provide traditional legal assistance in establishing or asserting clearly defined rights. For example, defense of juveniles or clarification of pretrial rights would fit in this category. (2) Lawyers can exert pressure to reform vague and ambiguous laws, such as some of requirements of the Illinois Juvenile Court Act of 1965 which denies juveniles the right to bail or a jury trial. (3) Lawyers are useful where the law appears contrary to the interests of a community. An example might be truancy laws which discriminate against ghetto children by enforcing upon them a second-rate education. (4) Lawyers may also represent clients in contexts which appear to be nonlegal, such as "when a principal orders all boys to come to school dressed in coats and ties without regard for the economic burden this imposes upon the parents."[1]

In theory, the Cahns' plan is admirable but poses an immense challenge to the legal profession. It is difficult to find talented Negro lawyers who are willing to work in community action programs. There are also problems in recruiting young Negro attorneys into this kind of work. There is only one Negro student registered in the University of Chicago Law School this year. One alternative is the possibility of training nonprofessionals in lay advocacy to do some of the work that is presently being done by lawyers. But law schools and bar associations resist any encroachment upon their professional domain and are unlikely to approve of lay advocacy. Also, the courts are unwilling to allow nonlawyers to represent clients. Despite the practical problems of training lay advocates, it is a feasible proposition, but no law school would dare to be so innovative and no court would sanction it.

Although lawyers are potentially capable of mobilizing the interests and grievances of minority groups, it will take a long time before Negro youth make use of their services. Lawyers are generally unwilling to champion causes against police brutality, prejudiced teachers, and adult intolerance for the independence of youth. As Joel Handler recently observed, "the poor are more and more victims of ill-conceived substantive rules and maladministration. But, the traditional remedies – essentially the provision of legal services – are becoming less and less effective in coping with the issues. The development of sound social policy and proper implementation of that policy are beyond the competence of most lawyers, and outside the scope of most academic legal research. The crucial battlegrounds of social direction and control of the urban scene will not be the individual suits against bureaucrats or other court cases. From the worm's eye view, lawyers, law schools, and current legal research are geared to defending the downtrodden from the bureaucrats. From the bird's eye view, the activity generated by law schools is minor border skirmishing or sniper fire, as the vast public

---

[1] Edgar S. and Jean C. Cahn, "The War on Poverty: A Civilian Perspective" 73 *Yale Law Journal* 1317 (July 1964).

programs take shape and begin to involve the city populations."[2]

Another point worth noting is that lawyers in juvenile court are particularly susceptible to cooptation. Recent studies suggest that there is considerable cooperation in the legal system between defense and prosecution lawyers, the policy and judges – unlike the widely held stereotype of adversary battles. Abraham Blumberg suggests that the practice of law can typically be compared to a confidence game in which the client is the victim and the defense attorney is a shill. "The accused's lawyer has far greater professional, economic, intellectual and other ties to the various elements of the court system than he does to his own client. In short, the court is a closed community."[3] David Sudnow, in his study of a California Public Defender Office, also found that clients were assumed to be guilty of the crimes for which they were charged.[4] More recently, Edwin Lemert found that lawyers in juvenile court are more likely to become negotiators and mediators than adversaries.[5] Juveniles are perceptive about this duplicity and are unlikely to trust lawyers whose allegiance is obviously elsewhere. Claude Brown knew what it felt like to be degraded in court:

> When we got to court, the lawyer was already there. He spoke to Dad, and Dad yes-sirred him all over the place, kept looking kind of scared, and tried to make the man think he knew what he was talking about. When the lawyer came over to me and said, 'Hello Claude, how are you?' and shook my hand and smiled, I had the feeling that God had been kicked right out of heaven and the meek were lost. And when he started talking to me – not really talking to me, just saying the stupid things that white people say to little colored boys with a smile on their faces, and the little colored boys are supposed to smile too – nothing in the world could have made me believe that cat was on our side. We weren't even people to him, so how the hell was he going to fight our fight? I wanted to ask Dad why he went and got this guy, but I knew why. He thought all Jews were smart. I could have gotten all that shit out of his head. Anybody could see that this cat wasn't so smart. No, he was just lucky – lucky that the world had dumb niggers like Dad in it.[6]

LT. EDWARD BUCKNEY

Mr. Platt just mentioned that an enormous fraud on juveniles had been committed, presumably as a result of the new Supreme Court decision. To carry that a step further, I think an enormous fraud has been committed on

[2] Joel F. Handler, "The Role of Legal Research and Legal Education" *Discussion Papers*, 9 (University of Wisconsin, 1967).

[3] Abraham Blumberg, "The Practice of Law as a Confidence Game: Organizational Cooptation of a Profession", 1 *Law and Society Review* 15-39 (1967).

[4] David Sudnow, "Normal Crimes: Sociological Features of the Penal Code in the Public Defender Office," 12 *Social Problems* 255-276 (1965).

[5] Edwin Lemert, "Juvenile Justice—Quest and Reality," 4 *Trans-Action* 30-40 (July 1967).

[6] Claude Brown, *Manchild in the Promised Land* (New York: MacMillan, 1965) p. 930.

society in general as you may see from some of the things I will mention. However, I have been asked to explain my function first. Just over two months ago, a new unit called the Gang Intelligence Unit was created in the Chicago Police Department, Detective Division. It was created to deal specifically with criminal activities of street gangs. I was selected to head this unit, and, within the Police Department, I am responsible for immobilizing or neutralizing these activities as far as possible and for identifying those who are overtly or covertly responsible. Over the years, a problem with gangs had developed, and it was felt a new approach to this problem was needed. The Detective Division is organized into five general units: homicide, robbery, burglary, stolen auto, and a general assignments unit. Each of these units has an operation in the six police areas. As a result of this decentralization, someone in the first area might handle a homicide involving gang members, another in the second area might handle a robbery involving gang members, and another in the third area might handle an auto theft involving gang members, and so on. In each area, certain members of one unit had specific knowledge about certain gang activities, members, and problems, but in being spread over six areas and five units, it was very difficult to get a true reading of the extent of gang activity in Chicago.

A unit in the Youth Division of the Police Department called the Youth Group Intelligence Section maintains intelligence information primarily on juveniles. We found a gap existed here because most of their information deals specifically with juveniles rather than with the minor or young adult offender. Further, the Youth Division is primarily responsible for processing youthful offenders. We found that most members of street gangs are seventeen or older and not juveniles, and are thus susceptible to adult prosecutions. Therefore, my unit was created to bridge these gaps, as well as to carry on the work begun by the Youth Division. That is a thumbnail sketch of the responsibilities of my unit.

One of the specific areas of responsibility of my unit is to provide assistance to the court in the prosecution of those responsible for criminal gang activity. It is in this regard that I said a fraud has been perpetrated on society at large. We are finding that many people dangerous to society have repeatedly been brought before the juvenile court for punishment and are soon back on the streets to repeat the same sort of crimes for which they were originally brought to justice. Murder is the most serious of these. Every citizen has a right to relative freedom from gangs, and turning people who have committed more than one murder back on the society to murder again is not fair.

I want to assure you at this point that the Police Department is greatly concerned with the constitutional rights and freedoms of every individual in the society. We are concerned with their rights against unreasonable searches and seizures, self-incrimination, unreasonable bail, and other constitutional rights. Within our unit, we emphasize that, if and when we put someone out of action, we do so within the meaning of the law, which raises several issues.

First, the law should be vigorously enforced, not circumvented. Many problems have been created, particularly in cases of adults who commit serious crimes, and who are arrested and taken before the courts only after repeated continuances. Often it is one to two years before they go to trial, and the victim and other witnesses have to take off from their jobs to go to court each time. After sixteen to eighteen continuances and the loss of a minimum of $20 each per day, the day when a victim or vital witness does not appear is the day the attorney announces to the judge that he is ready for trial and nobody is there to prosecute. In the past, it has been suggested that an advantage of the English system of justice is that it saves time. I will not argue that point though it does have some merit.

We feel that the Juvenile Court may have a specific function which would be advantageous to everyone in the expeditious processing of minor offenses. However, when a juvenile commits a serious crime such as murder, rape, armed robbery, aggravated kidnapping for ransom, aggravated battery, or other serious offenses for which the punishment ranges from a minimum of a year in the penitentiary, he should not be prosecuted through the Juvenile Court. These cases should be called to the attention of the State's Attorney who should exercise his prerogative to process these cases through the Criminal Court. Once someone is exposed to indictment by a grand jury and stands trial, whether or not he is convicted, this will serve as a deterrent.

In most of the Juvenile Court cases, even if the person is convicted, he is remanded to the Illinois Youth Commission. According to law, the Illinois Youth Commission is entitled to retain the individual until he is able to return to his community as a useful member of the society. This may be anywhere from one week to expiration of Illinois Youth Commission jurisdiction. There should be a way to set more definite sentences, or there should be provisions for turning these men over to another institution which would keep them out of circulation for longer periods of time. As I mentioned, many of these individuals should be prosecuted as adults in terms of the seriousness of the crimes they have committed.

Though nobody should be oppressed, in certain situations it is necessary to create sufficient bail so that minor and young adult offenders in particular cannot be released to commit the very crime for which they are imprisoned. This may seem oppressive, but, day after day, people who are released on bond commit the same crimes again to get money for their defense or simply because for them, that is just their job. They see it as a calculated risk. "Pops," for example, takes great pride in the fact that he is probably Chicago's most celebrated burglar. He knows the risks involved and is willing to take them because that is his job.

In conclusion I want to mention one of the main problems in the area of justice. I believe that certain defense attorneys are overstepping their bounds. As a police officer, I was instructed a long time ago that a lawyer's basic responsibility was to see that his client received a fair trial. Today, many attorneys attempt to get their client off at all costs, which is not fair to the society or to the individual involved. He is not entitled to be free regardless of his guilt. I would suggest that perhaps attorneys and other representatives should recall the basic idea of a fair trial without going to the extremes of perjury, obstruction of justice, etc., in order to free their clients to the over all detriment of the society.

ARTHUR WILLIAMS

Our job at Legal Services to Youth (LSY) is to represent teenagers who cannot afford lawyers. Boys must be seventeen and under, and girls eighteen and under. We work in the area that runs from the tracks to Cottage Grove, and from 39th to 55th. When one of these young people comes to our office, he is interviewed. Then his case goes to Attorney McGee who will assign it to one of us.

My job is to find out what really happened. Lt. Buckney said that he thinks the lawyers go too far, but we think that, in many cases, his police officers go too far. This is our job. People come to us for help, and when I investigate a case, I report what I find to Attorney McGee. It is not my concern whether the person is innocent or guilty. Attorney McGee represents the client, so he does his best to do what he can for him.

I am at a disadvantage being on a panel with people like Tony Platt and Mr. Buckney because I am a nonprofessional and very new in my job. But my eyes have been opened in this Workshop, and I will keep working in the hope that perhaps we can do something to help juveniles as well as our society. It's time the juveniles should feel that they are on equal basis with the adults. There should be more Legal Services to Youth in and around Chicago, especially in the Lawndale area.

30

Planning Concepts and
New Directions –
*Delinquency and Crime**

SOLOMON KOBRIN

I intend to say very little about delinquency but somewhat more about the educational establishment. As I shall try to make clear, the two are not unrelated. In order to address the question of what can be done to improve our capacity to deal with the problem of unlawful behavior on the part of young people, we have to raise the question of what young people are up to, after all. To answer this question it is necessary to look at the relation of young people to society.

The educational institution is the principal means through which the young person is attached to, and ultimately becomes a working member of, the society. If we look at lawless behavior on the part of the young as an effect of the workings of the institutions through which the young are inducted into society, then we can begin to focus on what is required in dealing with this problem. That is not to say that the educational establishment is the only set of arrangements through which the young are inducted into society. I am not ignoring the family, but given an earlier experience through which the human being acquires his primary social capacities, which is acknowledged to be a function of the family, the question arises of what more has to be done to make it possible for the young to move toward establishing a position in adult society.

Here we must focus on the educational establishment, especially when we consider the adolescent, who comprises the segment of the youthful population which is most prominent in the delinquency picture. The school and, more particularly, the high school becomes the crucial institution in the experience of the adolescent. It becomes the major factor affecting the probability that he will make it, that he will avoid the personal and social destructiveness of a delinquent career. If there is to be any progress in the prevention of delinquency, it will come about primarily through the reconstruction of that institution which is most crucial to the process of the

*Editor's Note:

The following two papers were presented at the sessions covered in Part V. However, since their subject matter is more closely tied in with the papers and discussion on youth, we have included them here; the discussion following these presentations has been incorporated into the Reaction and Reconsideration on Youth and the Community.

induction of the young into adult society, namely, the school, and, more specifically, the high school.

When we look at the efforts that have been made to meet this problem, we see that the main focus has been on the development of so-called "quality education." There is a general idea abroad that an improvement in the quality of education, especially for low-income minority youth, will make for fewer youngsters running afoul of the law. I want to comment on the issue of quality education before discussing a set of additional considerations.

The general argument is that if quality education were available, it would be the effective agency through which the problems that confront low-income, minority youth could be overcome. I would argue that quality education operates not as a cause but as an effect; quality education is a result of the capacity to demand, and obtain, in terms of the public resources available, quality education. To put it bluntly, no quality education is made available to children unless their parents have the capacity to obtain it for them. This becomes painfully clear when we look at the distribution of quality education across society – it is roughly distributed in accord with income.

Furthermore, the prospects for constructive participation in adult society on the part of middle- and upper middle-class youngsters reflects more than mere access to quality education. Parents and other adults who are interested in their destiny regard quality education as necessary if these youngsters are to qualify for the occupations that these adults have in mind for them. A specific future is contemplated for youngsters at this level of the society, for which quality education is required. And so they get it. I am suggesting, therefore, that it would be futile to obtain quality education for low-income youth unless at the same time measures were instituted which gave reasonable assurance that future occupational slots were available that matched the enhanced educational opportunity.

It is significant that studies in the social psychology of delinquency reveal that those youngsters who tend more frequently to get involved in delinquency have less confidence that there might be some future stable and rewarding work career for them. Though these studies have not been altogether conclusive, they very strongly suggest that this is one factor on the basis of which it is possible to differentiate youngsters with a higher probability of getting involved in delinquent activity from those with a lower probability. It appears, therefore, one of the preconditions for developing the motivation to take advantage of quality education on the part of the youngster is a confident expectation of a rewarding occupational future.

In turn, a condition for the development of such expectations is that there be continuous, dependable, adult support for the young person during adolescence. Again, this is generally known, but it is not always easy to relate this element to other elements of the problem. The youth population is subject to a form of powerlessness peculiar to young people. As is well known, this is a product of their prolonged dependency which gives rise to defenses, which account for some forms of rebellion among young people with which we are so familiar. On the other hand, for those youngsters who are able to get through the adolescent period without excessive destructiveness, rebellion, or delinquency, there seems to be available a type of "sponsorhsip." This amounts to the simple fact that they have access to adults with a reasonable amount of power who stand behind them, interested in what will happen to them, and able to provide advice, help, psychological support, and so on. I would like to suggest that these two conditions, the first respecting expectation of a stable occupational future, and the second having to do with continuous and dependable adult support in the form of sponsorship as I have defined it, can be met if three concrete goals are achieved.

The first is perhaps the most difficult with which to deal. With regard to that segment of the population most involved in delinquency, low-income youth, it will be necessary to somehow restrict the scope of the professional educator to those aspects of education which are purely technical. The professional educator has captured the right to define the educational objectives of our society, and though I am not criticizing him for that, I am saying that perhaps education is too important to be left to the educator. When the purposes of education are left entirely to the professional educator, he forms his notions on the basis of his own perspectives and training. For the most part, these notions have been suitable for a situation quite different from that confronting low-income minority youth. Our educational establishment is class keyed and makes certain assumptions about the equipment that a youngster brings with him. Goals are established on the basis of these assumptions, and therefore the standard educational curriculum has never been sufficiently flexible to meet the needs of a wide spectrum of the population. It has quite properly been described and criticized as designed solely for middle-class youth. Though there is nothing wrong with an educational program designed for the middle-class youngster, it requires a thoroughly middle-class student body and is ineffective for those who do not have this background. Enrichment programs and similar methods cannot be expected by themselves to produce miraculous transformations. Such programs can be expected to produce only minor improvements in literacy and arithmetic competence. They cannot deal with the more important, unconscious equipment of attitude, point of view, perspective, expectation, and so forth.

Therefore, the first goal about which I am talking requires that the setting of educational objectives be recovered from the control of professional educators. If one can define what an educational system should produce, then it becomes possible to define the educational objectives. At that level of the problem, any organization should be able to engage the professional educator in a useful and possibly productive dialogue. However, I would warn that educators will offer the greatest opposition to attempts on the part of anybody who is not an educator to say anything about educational objectives. This insistence on monopolizing some of the most fundamental social values cannot and should not be tolerated. Any other professional group which attempted to tell the society at large what its values should be would be given short shrift. I think we are all somehow intimidated by early experiences with authoritative teachers and find it very difficult to talk back to educators.

A second goal which may help in meeting the conditions I outlined would be to reduce the transmission of social disabilities to many youngsters in the low-income minority segment of the population. These disabilities are many and serious, and nothing has been either proposed or done which offers any real prospect for reversing their destructive effect. I am referring to the effects on children of living in severely demoralized families. Many of those youngsters who fill our juvenile court dockets come from family backgrounds calculated to produce trouble, difficulty, and despair both for themselves and for those who must deal with them.

I would say that for those youngsters who are almost fated to become delinquent the only feasible expedient would be the establishment of all-day schools or boarding schools, or a combination of both. In our culture there is a notion of the sanctity of the family which insists that children should remain in the family even if there is none in any meaningful and effective sense of the word. Categorical insistence on the validity of this notion seems to me to be a way of avoiding an important public responsibility. A system of boarding or all-day schools could be developed in certain low-income areas, designed to give youngsters, at a reasonably early age, the consistent and meaningful socialization which they would not get if they remained in their usual living circumstances.

A third goal which might help create the conditions I outlined would be a drastic redesigning of the counseling function, especially in high schools. I would propose that it be transformed into sponsorship in the sense in which I defined it. These youngsters need much more than the often out-of-date information available to them in the standard counseling operation, frequently provided on a haphazard basis. They need someone who will take a real, continuous, dedicated interest in them as individuals and in their future as individuals.

Many of these youngsters know as well as we do that finding a place in the occupational world is very much a matter of one's contacts, associations, and affiliations. The jobs that one gets from the employment service are those left over after the affiliative networks have operated and the best opportunities have been preempted. It must be recognized that, in our society, a large part of occupational allocation is effected through relationships within kinship and friendship networks by means of which people may find their way to an occupation with reduced uncertainty. I am suggesting a principal virtue of the sponsorship program that, in addition to being more effective in helping these youngsters, it would have a feedback effect on the confidence with which the young person may envision his occupational future. It would also operate to reduce significantly the extent to which the low-income, minority group adolescent feels alienated from significant people in the adult society. A high school system oriented to such a sponsorship function would require the most drastic kind of overhaul of current educational purposes. The rigid and perfunctory purpose of advancing a mass of youngsters through a fixed and largely standard body of subject matter would have to give way to the new purpose of equipping each person with the knowledge, training, and orientation necessary for his successful absorption into the occupational world. To do this effectively might well entail much closer integration than now exists between educational establishments and the world of work. It would require as well the development of arrangements through which ultimate job placement had at least as high a level of certainty as does college placement currently for those who are college bound. The important difference envisioned by the sponsorship concept is that the high school would acquire the residual responsibility (in the absence of family and kinship resources) for the occupational future of each student.

I have described two conditions which must be met if we are to progress at all in the prevention of delinquency, and I have suggested three programs which might help us move in the direction of achieving these conditions.

JOSEPH LOHMAN

My remarks will focus on crime which is a very narrow aspect of the general social scene with which we are concerned here. I realize that crime is only one way, and in some respects a somewhat limiting way, of looking at more pervasive and basic problems. There is a crisis in the incapacity of institutions to deliver a condition of opportunity and promise for many of the people they seek to engage. The crisis of the service agencies is first and foremost their insensitivity to changes in the social world which have complicated their mission in establishing order, peace, and security. Accordingly, the police for example are under the necessity of effecting new and difficult adaptations. For example, the current polarization and confrontations of the police and the courts, and between various sections of the community, is tangible evidence of the disengagement and separation of the service institutions from great sections of the community – institutions which originally stemmed from and arose out of the life of the community in its needs. Now they address the community as something external to them, out of joint, and which they must bring to task and put in order.

To be very specific, the report of the presidential committee on the system of criminal justice in this country strikes a note which is not easily accepted by many elements of the system of criminal justice. All too frequently, certain of our police, our courts, and our correctional machinery generate the very tendencies they are designed to put down. I suspect that this in large measure reflects the disengagement of these institutions. In this they are one manifestation of the consequences of the large-scale, wholesale bureaucratization of our society. They are self-sustaining, self-serving bureaus whose objectives and purposes are at odds with the conditions of life in the changing community. Many of the problems which are confronting us today have a meaning and significance quite different from what we have traditionally ascribed to them or to the situations they represent. For example, there is much said these days about the estrangement of the young and the old; we speak of young people being "alienated," and estranged from the adult community. We refer to persons frequently as members of groups which do not identify with the general community, who live to themselves in some separate place according to their own standards. We see them at odds with the norms and values, with the law of the society. The point is that we see and explain the individuals we address through law enforcement as persons who, for some identifiable reason, are individually at odds with the conforming patterns of society.

I would like to suggest that this estrangement, this alienation, of individuals can be regarded in a quite different way. It will profit us, for a moment, to examine the agencies, institutions, and organizations to which we subscribe, and to apply the notion, which we are applying to individuals, to the institutions themselves. I think it might be properly suggested that even as we speak of persons as being estranged and alienated from the conventions and norms of society and from its institutions, we may be confronted in the current day by a crisis of these same institutions. For it can be seen that the institutions are not necessarily at one with the changing social scene. They do not reflect in themselves the trends, and so there are, indeed, stresses in education. There are stresses in welfare. There are stresses in law enforcement. It is these crises and the dilemma of our traditional services which need to be made explicit.

One might appropriately refer to the traditional services as alienated and estranged from some people, indeed, many people, rather than the reverse. We may state the problem differently: along with the revolt of the Negro and that of the youth, there are a whole series of specific revolts which are being expressed in various ways — in petitions for new legislation, for a new philosophy and orientation on the part of the organized society and its instrumentalities. There is, if you please, the revolt of the client, and this may very well be represented in what, at long last, the poverty program is awakening to and which we see reported in the daily press as the request by the poor for a role in the decisions which are affecting them.

We have given verbal service to this viewpoint in the past, but it is not generally the way in which the agencies and institutions of our society have organized and made available their services. The professional services have been made available on a worker-client relationship, and we are only now modifying our traditional practices in the light of protest and, shall I say, the talking back of these clients. There is a revolt of the clients. The revolt is manifest in the attitude they take toward the school, toward welfare, toward the police, and toward other agencies. The crisis of the helping services has been triggered by processes which reflect our society in major transition.

In speaking of these institutions as in some sense wanting, I am not attempting to indict anyone nor suggest that anyone or any institution is motivated by a spirit of malice. These remarks are not directed to any city in particular though you may make your own application if you see fit. As a matter of fact, these observations and generalizations I see as appropriate to the American scene, generally, and more specifically to the metropolitan centers such as Chicago, the Oakland-San Francisco complex, Los Angeles, New York, or Philadelphia.

Our current concern with getting through "the long hot summer" threatens to become a chronic preoccupation on the American scene. In the highest as well as the lowest places, everyone knows about "the long hot summer," and if that phrase is directed toward a particular place, it is regarded as an ominous remark that may encourage people to do what they would not do otherwise. In good conscience I must say that we will not get through this summer without a few places being disturbed. Enough places have already been disturbed to establish the record for this year so I cannot be blamed for inviting catastrophe by calling attention to its prospects without associating it with any particular place or time.

By and large, the posture of American society, with reference to the long hot summers, is epitomized in the present stance of the police systems. I have watched the evolution of their point of view and the way they have faced each summer with a redefinition of the problem, and the current police expression is that they will be ready next time. Though "being ready" obviously means something to everyone, whether it means the same thing to everyone is questionable. Whether the purposes of the police function with reference to our democratic society will be appropriately and adequately served is another question. Frankly, I very much regret our present preoccupation with mounting hardware resources with which to put down whatever may arise.

I do not think we have to debate the necessity for putting down a disturbance if it does arise. Nobody profits by an uncontrolled and unrestrained exhibition of violence which rends and destroys the very fabric of society and of the local community affected in particular. However, a preoccupation with seeing the problem mainly as a matter of control through repression directs the police function away from the essential quality of that function in a democratic society, namely the maintenance of the peace of the community.

Second, it immobilizes us with reference to accomplishing what needs to be done to establish a viable social structure and organization. In a sense, this relates to what Sol Kobrin has said, and what Dick Cloward has said in the past about our criminal justice and welfare structures. In my judgment there exists a widespread, general structural weakness on the part of our traditional institutions, among which law enforcement is one. This has been and, I am fearful, will continue to be conducive to expressions and over-expressions of hostility and violence within the community as a very direct consequence of their effort to establish order.

Difficulties such as an increasing crime rate, a spread of vice, and violence toward the social order by rebellious groups are viewed by those who manage and organize the law enforcement apparatus as evidence that there is a specific group of bad people loose in the society. There is an overcommitment to the idea that they are determined to do us ill and that they will lead increasing numbers of otherwise relatively decent, law-abiding individuals into some kind of snare. One instance of this idea is the current assertion that the ghost of communism is alive again and that a few communists are responsible for all of our difficulties, that there are people determined to do us wrong. The controlling effect of this idea is reflected in the way in which investigation, patrol, and other law enforcement resources are deployed.

The effect is to disregard the basic and relevant sources of our current difficulties, indeed to give offense to those whose discontent is a reflection of widespread grievance in American society. The young are excluded from the main stream of American life, and this grievance and protest is evidenced on many campuses, though with less celebration of the fact than Berkeley achieves. There is plentiful evidence of grievance on the part of those who live at the margin of American society with minority status, and the establishment has herded them together in the large-scale de facto segregation of nearly all our large cities. Notwithstanding their separateness and their powerlessness, there has emerged from the intimacy and togetherness of their ghettolike existence, a self-consciousness which has given them a new condition of collective action, hence a new power and influence.

That power is predicated upon the circumstances of grievance, and none of us should entertain the thought that reaction to grievance will only be expressed by those who are leaders or official spokesman. Indeed, a new leadership has emerged and rides the crest of the tides of grievance and protest. Undoubtedly, persons who have an axe to grind will seize upon such conditions to gain the followers for pursuing their revolutionary, subversive, or other purposes. But their role is dust in the wind alongside the fact that, within the body politic, there exists a condition which engenders widespread deviance and protest, ranging from delinquency and crime to radicalism and bohemian life styles. Therefore, our institutional structures should not be responding by merely mounting tactics, strategies, and inputs of resources designed to suppress the problems as subversiveness or suggesting that, by identifying and getting rid of the leaders and dissuading others from following them, the problem will be solved.

I submit that a commitment to this idea weakens and makes questionable the impact and effectiveness of the law enforcement structure and the system of criminal justice. Such critical weakness blinds us to what needs to be done as well as creates an input which further aggravates the situation. People quite rightly resent being characterized as subversive when they are calling attention to the fact that they have grievances, feel excluded and as outsiders with a right to be inside.

There are very conscientious and well-meaning police officers, correctional workers, judges, and other individuals who act with less than their potential effectiveness because of the way in which their behavior and roles are determined by outmoded and inadequate philosophies and structures of the institutions with which they are associated. They are so deployed, and their relationship with the community so structured that their activities become polarized with the police and the community in a relationship of hostility and confrontation. Under these circumstances, the police are seen as an "army of occupation," and we can understand how, in an attempt to control an incident, the very way in which we attempt to bring a situation under control more frequently than is realized, actually aggravates a situation which we are trying to control.

A second structural weakness which is conducive to an overexpression of violence and hostility is the fact that our communities are increasingly reflecting differing income levels, class interest, and ethnic groupings. This complicates the problem of exercising the police power and too often it is employed unequally in different segments of the social structure. As a result, the criminal justice system, often with the best of intentions, supports the custom and tradition of upper-income groups which does not have the status of law, as well as responding to the superior power and influence of private interests. This has the effect of producing a double, triple, and quadruple standard of criminal justice and law enforcement in the United States.

The NAACP has recently studied and analyzed the cases of persons who, under the Arkansas statute, have been convicted, found guilty, and sentenced to the death chamber for rape. The law provides a uniform penalty without reference to race or ethnicity. Though I do not favor the death penalty and apart from that question, the study established to the satisfaction of an Appelate Court that if a Negro man raped a white woman, the chances were disproportionately greater that he would be sentenced to death than if he raped a woman of his own race. Furthermore, if a white man raped a Negro woman, he would not be charged so as to be subject to that penalty, if he were charged at all.

Obviously this reflects more than the law; it reflects custom, tradition, private, economic, and social interests. The system of criminal justice in this instance grinds beyond the law to reflect the power and influence which seeps through the weaknesses of the structure to become a condition of the administration of justice.

As a student concerned with theoretical formulations of human behavior in general and crime in particular, I have become increasingly impressed by the absence of the concept of power in our theories of crime. We readily admit economic, psychological, social-psychological, and cultural concepts, but not the ubiquitous and pervasive fact of power. The law itself is formulated as a compromise of the complex of power within the society, and therefore, to some degree, reflects the superior power of some and the inferior power of others. In turn, its administration continues to reflect that fact. When we speak of the system of justice as being corrupt, it is not so much a question of venality or of bribery. These are instrumentalities of power; they are only two of the ways in which influence is exercised and the system corrupted. The degree to which the structured arrangements in society, from the local community to the very top, continue to express their power in and through established legal formulations, determines the quality and direction of criminal justice. This may be and often is in opposition to our professed democratic ideology, and the effect produces laws which are designed for its implementation. It serves no useful purpose to suggest that the so-called double-standard law enforcement does not exist.

I recently attended a law enforcement conference in an eastern city. The police officers in attendance were all committed to the support of their organization and their profession. Nevertheless, among them an aggravated and somewhat traumatic dialogue took place between the Negro and white officers as to whether or not there was, in fact, a double standard. The Negro officers made their point by informing their brother officers what had happened to them when they encountered white police while in civilian dress. This was the case par excellence of the legitimacy of the complaints raised about the unwitting commitment of individuals to a double standard without really being aware of the condition or its consequence. They were, as they saw their roles, simply fulfilling the mandate and philosophy of the organization. This is an essential weakness, not only of the police, but of the whole system of criminal justice, and we must come to grips with it.

If the police, the courts, prosecution, or corrections are to be a generally accepted arm of the whole community, they must inspire the whole community's confidence. Their support cannot come alone from those who see it as an instrument of their values and their interests. Again, this is not said to allege an indication of insensitive malice as perverse behavior of individual officers. The absence of total community confidence and support stems for the most part from the persistence of an outmoded, institutional, and organizational model in relationship to the changing community context within which the police must operate. A police department should be cognizant of the complex subcultures which make up our cities, anticipate the terms for engaging and relating to these subcultures. This will require an understanding of the population, the technological and the political processes which have transformed the form and substance of our metropolitan communities and the terms and conditions of life in the core cities.

Every time I return to Chicago, I marvel at how it has changed and how different my problems would be were I sheriff today. However, in 1954 and 1958, I was trying to persuade my political colleagues that there should be a Negro captain on the sheriff's force as a condition of its successful cooperation and in recognition of one man's talent which was equal to that of the others. The way it was done up to that time was to give to the Negro ward committeeman three low-rated jobs instead of that high-rated one. The high-rated jobs were reserved for candidates from the white wards. This was not done with malice or in secret; the minority leadership was party to the deal. Negro committeemen even came to me and said they would rather have the three jobs of the lower order and let others have the one big job regardless of a man's talent.

A police structure which is determined to resolve the problem in this antiquated and unfair manner and without understanding as to what confronts it is likely to aggravate and compound its own problems, even as it loses the confidence and support of aggrieved sections of the community. There is too little provision for differing sections of the community to discuss the appropriateness of their engagement by, and participation in, community-wide services and institutions. Any complaint about the double standard or about their grievances is answered with no more than rhetoric. There must be institutionalized channels to insure, first, that grievances and complaints will be received without negative consequences for those who voiced them, second, that these will be processed in a responsible manner and, finally, that the issue will be determined and reported to them.

I do not argue for a particular institutional arrangement that would solve such problems. In fact, I have serious reservations about any overcommitment to the idea that we must get it from outside the system as, for example, a Police Review Board. However, it is clear that the institutionalized system of criminal justice has many weaknesses, and the absence of channels for expression of grievances is a major one. The agencies of criminal justice are in need of reexamination. There must be flexibility and innovation with a view to providing a greater confidence in the system of criminal justice on the part of those groups within the community who feel excluded. Until this is achieved, the police will continue to labor under the greatest difficulty. The police must have the support of the general community if they are to be effective in the enforcement of the law on the marginal few who are violators of law.

I have been focusing on several themes which I suspect have brought to mind experiences in your own communities. I could say as much about the correctional system of the United States. At the local, national, and state levels, the innovations in the correctional system, which are so celebrated in the literature of the subject, have had little effect upon the traditional arrangements. For all practical purposes, the jails and penitentiaries are being operated in traditional and archaic ways. They generate more of the behavior they have been set up to repress or change. I am amazed when I see it reported that the Bridewell is still as it was in the thirties, forties, and fifties. When I was sheriff, and even as I administered the county jail, I found it necessary to acknowledge the grievances of the people who were confined there. It was then only a warehousing function as so many of our correctional systems remain today. They do not correct. They are more likely to confirm criminality. We need in this area, as in all the others, a greater and fuller dialogue between all the interested elements of the population, including those who are the accused.

Today we are putting great store in the development of a greater dialogue between the various elements of our communities and the agencies that would serve them. However, if the dialogue is to be meaningful in the resolution of our problems, it must be specific even as it is extended to all the places and elements of American social life.

31

Innovative Programs for Youth

DANIEL SCHEINFELD

I first would like to address myself to what I think is the most important hangup presently hampering youth workers in underprivileged areas. I am a victim of this mental obstruction and would suggest that nearly everyone in this room is its victim to some extent. The hangup is as follows: We tend to think in terms of the simple dichotomy of *delinquency versus non-delinquency.* This seems reasonable since delinquency is one of the most tangible problems in poor neighborhoods.

The tragedy of this dichotomy is that it consists of two negatives and therefore cannot be the basis of constructive programs. I would argue that a great many programs dedicated to the development of youth have floundered on this dichotomy.

The results of a family study recently carried out in Chicago's Lawndale area neatly point up the significance of a negative frame of reference. Parents were asked what attributes they would like most to see in a ten-year-old boy or ten-year-old girl. Some parents immediately suggest a list of negatives: For example, do not be sassy, be obedient (which frequently has a more negative than positive meaning), do not smoke, do not hang out with bad gangs. In such cases where the interviewer receives a list of negatives, the children of that type of family will be nonachievers. They will be losers in school, though some may make it on the streets if they have enough nerve and native ability. Conversely, the parents who offered a list of positive attributes were far more likely to have achieving children.

To return to our problem; in place of the construct *delinquency vs. non-delinquency* I would like to substitute the construct *competence vs. incompetence.* This construct allows for something positive to build toward, namely competence. I would argue that thinking in terms of competence is also important for the very obvious reason that delinquency is only a symptom of a sense of incompetence and inadequacy which makes youngsters feel that they cannot be successful within the traditional system. The theory that youngsters perceive that they do not have employment opportunity and hence become delinquent is partially valid. However, opportunity has an obverse side; namely, you need the competence to seize the opportunity. If you see yourself as an incompetent person, having been defined as such by the school and in your daily experience, you will try for a different type of competence, namely, on the street as a delinquent.

Then there are those who are incompetent both in school and on the streets. They are the crushed ones, at the bottom of the pile. Every successful hustler in the ghetto feeds off a number of such double losers. We must rid ourselves of the liberal backlash notion which purports that things are not actually so bad in the ghetto because everybody is hustling and making it in their own culture and so on. The majority of children living in the ghetto are being as much destroyed by the indigenous system as they are by the rejection from the legitimate world. They are not playing a satisfying role even within their own cultural context.

To return to my first point, the real issue in poverty areas is *competence vs. incompetence.* To talk about delinquency in a vacuum amounts to talking about treating smallpox with calamine lotion and will not result in effective programs. Why are we stuck in this conceptual rut? First of all, delinquency threatens those in power, while incompetence does not (at least to date). Secondly, to many people, it is threatening to talk about creating competence among the lower classes. Consciously or unconsciously, they fear that if competence is created among these masses, revolutionary things could happen. This is one reason why those who raise funds or make applications emphasize the double negative, *delinquency vs. non-delinquency.* It is less threatening, not to mention more exciting, in terms of vicarious experience.

Having set out competence as the major issue, I would like to discuss the kinds of competence about which we are talking, and I want, to speak briefly about two programs, the Sharper Minds Program and Operation Crossroads. Both hinge on six major areas of competence.

1) Academic competence.
2) Speech: the ability to express oneself through complex syntax and good vocabulary.
3) Problem-solving ability: the ability to conceptualize a problem, construe alternative solutions, bring to bear a system of standards with which to assess the alternatives, and take action to actually solve the problem. This complex of skills lies at the root of human autonomy. The kind of autonomy stressed by most youth in the slums today is really a pseudoautonomy, based on freedom from control rather than freedom to act effectively.
4) Goal orientation: the ability to project goals and construct action sequences that lead to their realization.
5) Social competence: the ability to relate to a wide variety of social types and utilize social institutions and bureaucratic structures, to be able to use something as simple as the yellow pages, to know how to act in a restaurant, and so on. If people do not have social competence, they are afraid and withdraw. This negative definition of self, a sense of incompetence in simple everyday social life, is most detrimental to the development of people trapped in slum communities. The final aspect of social competence is learning to work in teams which is, of course, related to problem solving, goal orientation, and so on.

6) Motivation to learn: this, we would argue, is based primarily on a sense of competence.

The Sharper Minds Program ran for two years and will be run again next year. It is a problem-solving exercise involving groups of boys ranging in age from nine to twelve. At the beginning of a session, the group is presented with a problematic situation. One such situation was taken from the short story "Leiningen and the Ants," in which a plantation in the Amazon Valley was being overrun by a huge army of carnivorous ants. Other problematic situations are taken from everyday life on the streets. For example, you are going to the store with 75c in your pocket, and in front of the store are six older boys. One of them steps out and says, "Give me your money."

Once the problematic situation is presented, the teacher acts primarily as a resource and guide. In the next step, the boys formulate a series of problems which they see in the situation. Then they decide which problem seems most interesting and try to formulate tentative solutions. Following that, they seek as much information as they can in order to test and build on their solutions. They then divide into teams to work out the best possible solutions. After the teams have thrashed out their individual solutions through rigorous examination of the alternatives, a representative from each team presents his team's solution to the other teams, who verbally attack the solution and force him to defend it.

The Sharper Minds Program builds on at least two aspects of the lower-income situation. First, an extreme emphasis on putting down the other guy which, as you know, occurs for hours and hours on every street corner. Second, it builds on a concept of group participation. I would maintain that the combination of exciting subject matter, verbal attack, and group participation can generate a tremendous amount of involvement at many age levels. It has already worked with teenagers as well as with younger children.

The Sharper Minds Program also utilizes men from the community who have attained competence in their occupational field. Each man presents the group with a problematic situation which he faces in his own work. The group then works out solutions to the man's problem and soon after visits the man at the work site in order to confront the concrete realities of the problem, see which solution was actually taken, and meet those involved.

The other program, Operation Crossroads, is currently taking place at the Better Boys Foundation under the direction of Gene Perkins. Through recruitment from schools and elsewhere in the community, Operation Crossroads has brought together seven incipient gangs. These include cliques of boys ranging from nine to twelve years of age who hang out in the alleys and on street corners, as well as several cliques that seem fairly respectable by standard criteria. These groups are brought into a leadership program. Nobody mentions the word "delinquency"; in fact, these boys do not even know that they are in a special program.

At the moment, Operation Crossroads consists of a series of activities in which problem solving, speech, goal accomplishment, and team work are heavily emphasized. Recently Gene ordered twenty-four telephone books. Every few days he gives the boys problems which necessitate looking up information in the yellow pages. For example, the problem may involve a dozen steps in building a house. Sometimes people have to be called for information, and so on. This is an effective technique for building vocabulary, reasoning, sequential thought, and for developing a sense of competence in dealing with the surrounding reality. In other words, Operation Crossroads consists of a series of activities which involve the gaining of *competence*.

ORVILLE LUSTER

I am going to talk about a small agency in San Francisco of which I am the Executive Director. It is called Youth For Service, and was started in 1957 by the Quakers in the person of a young man who was concerned about youth, especially members of what we call clubs rather than gangs. We started some weekend work projects which were a page out of the history of the American Friends Service Committee's High School and College Committee. These young people did weekend work projects for welfare recipients who were referred to us by churches, other agencies, and sometimes by the youngsters themselves. To date, we have completed close to four hundred work projects.

Those involved in Youth for Service are between the ages of sixteen and twenty-four, and represent all racial and ethnic groups. The Negro youngsters identify themselves as Bloods, the Spanish youngsters and their friends are known as Barts, and the Caucasians are known as White-shoes. We make our racial-ethnic identification on this basis too. In 1958, after starting the work projects, the youngsters decided to establish a council of all the representatives throughout the city where they could break bread and try to settle their disputes peacefully.

In 1960, we received a grant from the Ford Foundation; in 1965, we were admitted to the United Bay Area Crusade which was like going through the Pearly Gates, and now we are receiving funds from many sources. We are using the United Bay Area Crusade money as seed money to help get federal, private, and other grants.

I would like to present a thumbnail sketch of the many programs in which we are involved. One of the most exciting is the Neighborhood Youth Corps. We pay these young people $1.35 per hour to work in various public and private agencies as anything from clerks to custodians. We have not had to go through the CAP programs or get involved in board disputes and so forth. The money comes directly from the Labor Department, and we are our own sponsors.

We also have detached workers or street workers, some of whom have come from the clubs themselves. The present director of street work is a young man by the name of Percy Pinkney who was a former gang leader of the Aces in San Francisco. Last year he was voted the most outstanding citizen in San Francisco by the San Francisco Foundation and received a stipend of $400. Now he talks to the governor and the mayor as well as to the youth clubs. He is doing a terrific job and has gained great respect. Within the next three or four months, I hope to turn the agency over to him completely. He will be in charge of the professional as well as the nonprofessional staff. We have about ten street workers, and with the follow-up work for the special Impact Program, he will have thirty-five more people under him. As you can see, I feel very strongly about the role of the nonprofessional. This teamwork is very important if these young people are going to be able to move up. We have to develop new careers for them whenever we can.

To return to Youth for Service, our largest work project in 1958 was the building of a bridge on the Indian Reservation. This was very important in giving the young people an opportunity to develop some skills.

The second largest project was called the Big Double O, Operation Oasis. There was a real need for a park in the middle-class Richmond area of San Francisco. We wanted to build it next to the police station for a number of very subtle reasons. The lot was 98 by 100. The Police Department was afraid that if a park were built on this site, it would create problems. We wanted to create problems for them because we wanted to involve the citizens and build this park for them. This was civic property, but it took us four years to get it from the Police Department – three years to cut the red tape and one year to build the park. There were tremendous tensions between the various watches at the police station, but as the result of this, and of the labor and involvement of many people, we were able to build that park. There are benches and sandboxes there now. It is one of the most beautiful parks in San Francisco.

It is J. D.'s gift to San Francisco, juvenile decency. There are many things that people can do, even if they think they cannot, as long as they are organized and involved. These were the punks, hoodlums, and others with very little money; those, as Earl Rabb, noted sociologist says, who are "the x factor" – the participants rather than the recipients. They gave something to their city, and since this park was dedicated in May 1965, not one thing has been disturbed.

This is like motherhood; nobody is against it; not even Mayor Daley could be against building a park. We involved our mayor as well as others and as a result, we are now building more parks. When I return, we will build two parks in the Mission district, one in the Oceanview district, and we will develop property near the freeways. This will be a tremendous opportunity for positive recognition of many youngsters who ordinarily would not be noticed.

We are also asking the labor unions to let us into the Gardeners' Union. We are telling them that by building these parks, we are creating work for more gardeners. We are not only involved in the community but are also building up money in the bank. Like many of our other work projects, these parks act as a vehicle to rechannel energies into something constructive.

Furthermore, because of the tremendous publicity and involvement, new possibilities arise. For example, in Hunters Point which was the scene of last year's riots, young people were throwing rocks at the firemen and police. So we had a rock crusade to pick up rocks. As well as involving the community, we involved the housing authority, the police, and all the various city government departments. Supplied with two-gallon buckets and maps of the area, these delinquents and citizens picked up rocks, put them on a truck, and dumped them into the Bay. This involved a tremendous number of people who had never been to Hunters Point. We also got lunches for about 800 or 900 youngsters. We had difficulty raising money, and one foundation came forth with $10,000 for these rocks.

We have developed what is called an Order of the Rock. The mayor, governor, and others are fighting to have one of these rocks. This is just a common rock mounted on a plaque with the recipient's name and something nice about him engraved on it. We have had two rock crusades, and they have been very successful in capturing the community's imagination and getting people involved. It is very important to reduce these situations to the lowest common denominator. When we developed the Order of the Rock, everybody thought we were crazy, but now very important people proudly display their rock.

We also have what we call the ABC Seminar, Always Be Cool. Everybody thought we were crazy when we said we would invite the policemen for lunch, but this has created a tremendous impact. Our Chief of Police, who is on the National Crime Commission, has come to almost every one of these luncheons to meet with the delinquents. Two days after the San Francisco riots, he was faced by ninety-three young people. The first to come forth was a young man who had been shot by one of the police officers. The chief and this young man had a fine discussion. Later we talked to all but two of the captains, and we will continue talking with them and others. It is very important that we control this. We have the money, set the date, and we invite them. It is on our territory and our terms. The Police Community Relations Unit can sponsor it, but we control it. If this control were lost, it would become just another meeting.

We also have a program entitled Operation Spark Plug in cooperation with Standard Oil. Most of the youngsters do not want to be gas jockeys, but we are convincing a few. Standard Oil recruits on our premises, puts the youngsters through a five-day training period, and hires them at $2.30 or $2.40 an hour.

We have another program called Operation Minerva in conjunction with the City College of San Francisco. In this program, we pay our young people $1.35 an hour to go to school. If they receive their AA degree, they can take the civil service examination, for example.

In another program, the EDP course, we train young people to be computer programmers. Our instructor is a teacher who is donating his time free, and the various companies are donating the machines. Once these youngsters have completed this six month course, they can earn about $5.25 per hour. We are also conducting job seminars and a variety of other programs.

Before closing, I want to mention that, in addition to working with groups, our street workers work with the community. Some of the best and cheapest mass communication in any community is found by identifying and working with people like the barber who talks to nearly everyone in the ghetto community at least once a month. Others are the beauty parlor operator; the insurance man, especially if he works in a minority community; and the community mother, a mother on welfare who advises the young people on welfare. The pawnbroker, who is the banker of the ghetto, and the pool hall proprietor, who is the second banker in any ghetto, are other people that have been quite helpful in our program.

In conclusion I want to mention several of the many things we have learned about organizing. An organizer must be committed and know above all else that what he is doing is important to the people. He has to be persistent and willing to go door to door to talk with people. He must get people to work for him by involving them on a personal level which is what the rock did for us. An organizer must recognize self-interest as one of the most important motivations for human action, and therefore he must give his services which are needed and valuable. An organizer must have a sense of humor and be able to use it as a tactic and as a personal release. Often humor is the only way to cut through the tensions that develop. Finally, in organizing and working with our communities on anything from youth problems or housing, we have found that negotiation is very important.

JAMES DeBERRY

I will first give a brief background of Central Harlem to show the multiplicity of problems which I am sure are very similar to those here in Chicago, as well as briefly indicate the shift in the deviant behavior patterns of young people.

Central Harlem is located in the northern section of Manhattan and encompasses about three and one half square miles. It is crowded with about 230,000 people, which is about 100 persons per acre. Up to 3,000 people live on some blocks in Central Harlem. Ethnically, Harlem is composed of 94% Negro, 4% Puerto Rican, and 2% other; though I have been in Central Harlem thirty years, I have not located the "2% other" yet. The major demographic characteristics of the Central Harlem community are overcrowded and deteriorated housing. At least 40% of the houses were built before the turn of the century, and they are in pretty bad condition. Some of the characteristics which affect the social health of the community are a high rate of young people living with one parent, the mother; the low educational and occupational backgrounds of these youngsters; and low family income. As a result, there is a very high rate of juvenile delinquency, drug addiction, social disease, homicides, births out of wedlock, and felonious assaults.

We have already heard about Chicago gang patterns, and strangely, in Central Harlem, gang activity has subsided somewhat in the past few years. Gang activities were at their height in 1948 when there were forty active, fighting gangs in Central Harlem. In 1963 twenty-seven so-called "gangs" could be identified, fourteen of which were said to be potential fighting gangs. In 1967 there are about seven groups of which perhaps one or two could be considered fighting gangs. The last gang eruption took place in 1963. Of course, it involved police brutality, but it was considered a gang eruption.

The decrease in gang activity has not been related to the rate of juvenile delinquency which has doubled since 1962 throughout New York City. In 1962 the rate was 20.2% per 1,000 youths and now it is about 46%. In Central Harlem, in 1962, it was 46% and is now about 109%. To us this means that gang activity is not the key element in a high rate of juvenile delinquency. We found that when the gangs began to disintegrate, the youngsters turned to drugs, sexual promiscuity, felonious assaults, and other acts directed against property and what they considered the system.

In Central Harlem, there are now ninety-one social service agencies which provide recreational or leisure-time services to youth. I think we are coming to grips with the idea that the rate of juvenile delinquency can not be changed by getting youngsters off the streets and into recreational and other leisure-time group activities. This seems to have been the approach, and the rate of delinquency has continued to increase.

The Harlem Youth Unlimited program took as the basis of its approach the fact that these social problems have to be dealt with in a meaningful manner that involves young people. Rather than provide them with social services, we attempt to change the conditions with social action. In 1964, we recruited youngsters from a cross-section of the young population in Central Harlem and trained them as a cadre of technicians who would initiate a social youth movement.

Of course, one of the problems we faced was bringing the street-addicted youth, the potential punks, hustlers, dropouts, and drug users, together with high school and college youth who come from different socio-economic backgrounds. The common focus was bringing about change by dealing with the issues that affected the daily lives of each segment of the community. Our objective was to *mobilize* young people for *action*.

At first, we thought that, though the college-aspired youngster might get involved in this sort of program, the street-addicted youngster would not because he would not see anything in it for himself. However, after two months of the training program, the so-called dropout youngster with a third-grade reading level was the most positive, aggressive, and the most effective in reaching the youth. He advanced more rapidly in understanding the idea of change because he was more affected by the conditions with which we were dealing. Many of the college youngsters who, economically, came from the so-called upper echelon were rather marginal. When we actually went into the community, the so-called street-addicted youngsters were most productive in communicating to various segments of the youth population within the community.

We offer these youngsters training in five major areas which also involve a role in the functional operation, that is, getting the job done. One of our groups is called the Community Services Action-Oriented Workshop which involves the unwed mothers. Many of them in the past felt alienated from any type of participation in group activities. They entered the program, understood what we were trying to do, and became active participants. Their function is to recruit other young mothers to participate in the program. This group is anticipating being funded because of the uniqueness of the approach. The program includes holding small group discussion sessions on homemaking, returning to school, and public assistance. The girls remain in the program on an average of eight to twelve months. Many leave and return to public school or direct job placement. To date, approximately 125 girls have benefitted from the Young Mothers Program.

Another crucial program is the Small Groups Urban Development Project in which we deal directly with youngsters on the streets. In addition to the teenagers, we feel it is very important to deal with the eight- to twelve-year-olds. This is the age in which they begin to develop feelings of hostility and frustration and to identify with the illegitimate images in the community. This is the age where they identify themselves as nonachievers, someone who cannot learn. They begin to believe the system when it tells them they are stupid. After the process of playing truant, etc., they eventually drop out of school. More time is necessary to understand the details of this dynamic approach to reaching this group.

We also have training programs in the Public Relations Workshop, such as journalism techniques and methods, development of reporting and writing skills, etc. Through their efforts, the voice of young people in Central Harlem is projected through the largely noncensored bimonthly newspaper which they publish on their own.

During the development of Harlem Youth Unlimited programs, action projects, etc., youngsters are involved in the planning, decision-making, and action phases.

In our Personnel Workshop, the youngsters process all the youth in the Central Harlem community who are involved in the H/Y antipoverty program.

Our youngsters are paid $1.50 an hour, and to my knowledge Harlem Youth Unlimited is the only youth program funded by the Federal Government which does not come under the guidelines of Manpower and Neighborhood Youth Corps. We are now struggling with the city and with the Labor Department of the federal government to retain the concept of Harlem Youth Unlimited and not have it come under the Manpower guidelines. The obvious reason is because of the qualification restrictions placed on Neighborhood Youth Corps trainees.

The essence of the total program is in the Community Organization Workshop where young people are trained in understanding the nature of the conditions of poverty and the process of change. Over a six-month period, they participate in a training program which deals with the nature of political action, the political and power structure of the Harlem community, causes of the pathologies, black heritage, history of the poverty program, etc. They receive an orientation and education in health and welfare, methods of organizing, issues around education, employment, etc. They serve on many of the action committees in the community. This creates additional problems in the community because many adults are not prepared to accept young people even though they tend to be more knowledgeable of the issues and problems than the adults. They tend to be much more militant in their approach to problems, and, as a result, there is a tension between the adults and the youth of these committees. Nevertheless, the youngsters constructively participate in community activities with adults.

One of the problems we have to deal with is that many of the youngsters from the so-called street-addicted segment see the antipoverty program as a place to get easy money. However, for the most part, we have been very successful in getting youngsters who normally would have gone to the anti-social or illegitimate world for a livelihood, to take advantage of the limited opportunities made available through the poverty program.

One of our projects is called Operation Stop. In 1965 there was a series of jewelry and department store robberies, purse snatchings and the like. Some of the youngsters involved in our project were participating in these activities. We called a meeting which was chaired by peers of these youngsters. The purpose was to get the leaders to stop stealing, snatching purses, and other activities which get youngsters into difficulty with the police. The next question from those involved was what do you have to offer? Some of them accepted the $1.50 for twenty hours per week and worked with us. They became a priority group in helping find jobs.

Reaction and Reconsideration

When considering youth and youth problems, participants and some discussants admitted to being much less certain of what might be the significant questions and the meaningful solutions than was the case during the discussions which focused on problems in the fields of welfare, housing, and even education. However, there was an attempt to further define what is at stake, assess existing programs, and at least suggest the depth and seriousness of the issues at hand.

Continuing along the lines taken by several discussants in their consideration of underlying factors, participants suggested additional dimensions that must be considered if a fuller understanding of youth and youth problems is to be achieved. Participants inquired into such interrelated themes as what makes gangs distinctive from other groups, what factors contribute to the formation of gangs, what are the significant differences between the activities and problems of different gangs, inner-city and suburban, and Negro and white youth, between gang members and youngsters who do not join gangs, as well as the differences between the gangs of today and those of the past.

Family and Peer Relationships

Previous generations also have been faced with youth problems which in many ways are similar to those we are facing now, and it seems that to some extent youngsters simply "grow out of it." However, if we are to understand the more fundamental reasons why youngsters join gangs, we have to also look at those youngsters who are not in gangs and examine the reasons why. [participant from a community religious group]

It would also help if we knew whether or not there are real differences between Negro and white gangs. [former parochial school teacher]

We should examine whether or not the gaps between Negro and white youth, between white youth and white adults, and between Negro youth and Negro adults are widening. [community organization leader]

Poor communication between young people and their parents is an important aspect of the problems being raised. [community organizer]

One of the reasons many of these youngsters have problems in school at an early age and join gangs later is that they do not have good relationships in their homes. [teacher in an inner-city school]

384

Perhaps there is something in the family structure of these boys that makes peer relationships especially important. [community psychologist]

Sufficient information about the differences between family and peer relations of boys in gangs and boys not in gangs is not available. Consequently, at this point, there can be little more than speculation. [social scientist working with gangs]

On the basis of their experiences in Negro communities, a number of other participants expressed their concern for whether the importance of the family relations of these youngsters is given sufficient consideration by those working with gang members.

I doubt that there are serious attempts to involve the families of these youngsters in rehabilitation programs. [director of the Chicago committee of a national organization]

We can work with parents when there are at least the seeds of concern and interest even if there is not a complete understanding of the problems or a knowledge of how to deal with them on the part of the parents. Often a youngster is out on the street because his home is a very unsatisfying place to be. This has a significant effect on how he feels about himself and what he wants to do. [social scientist working with gangs in another city]

Youngsters often come together with no manifest symbols of structure or organization but simply spontaneously for the gratification of joining in peer relationships. [settlement house worker and sociologist]

One of the fallacies of youth work is the assumption that youngsters need groups. They need effective relationships with others but not necessarily in a group context. I would suggest that gangs and groups exist in response to a lack of opportunities and other pressures. [social scientist]

Simply providing opportunities for these youngsters is not enough. There must be supportive systems to counsel these youngsters about the opportunities available, particularly those which will meet their needs and satisfy them. [city administrator concerned with youth]

In Chicago, youngsters are getting paid $1.25 per hour for jobs that pay others $2.35 per hour. They might be getting a lot of satisfaction but no salvation. If mothers and fathers received a good wage, their children would be able to have summer vacations, instead of summer jobs. In any case, for most of them we should be providing permanent year-round jobs instead of temporary, summer jobs. [community leader]

Gangs and Groups

On the basis of extensive experiences with various gangs, a number of participants differed on the extent to which they thought outsiders contribute to the formation and expansion of gangs and gang activities. They indicated that outsiders, whether youth workers, newspapers, or other institutions including city agencies, by overreacting to gangs legitimitize their existence. However, there was general agreement that, as one participant put it, "gangs and hippies will not simply disappear if they are ignored."

A gang of youngsters and a country club "gang of bankers" are the same type of group. [mental health worker]

Though it might sound academic, not only is there a qualitative difference in the nature of these groups but there are also important differences in the kind of reinforcement their members provide for each other. These differences can only be understood within their social context. The significant difference between the gangs being discussed and the bankers' group is that the former becomes involved in delinquent activities and its members further isolate themselves from the mainstream. Their acceptance of antisocial activity reinforces gang cohesiveness resulting in a vicious cycle from which the individual finds it very difficult to break away. The delinquent boy follows an accepted pattern rather than acting out of personal, committed choice. His actions are for the most part impulsive and spontaneous with little consideration of the consequences, whereas the banker acts not only for his own personal gain but with a fuller knowledge of the context and consequences of his actions. This results in a more deliberate, intentional gamble. [social scientist]

I think there is a very significant similarity between these groups. The question of "delinquency" is a definitional one. In our community, there is a group called a businessman's association which takes $14 million worth of tax money and uses it for their own private purposes and nobody touches them. We beat up, throw in jail, and ostracize the one and call it a delinquent gang while we sit back, admire, and allow the other to operate and receive credit from the "good" people of society. [community organizer]

"Mainstream" and "Delinquent" Youth

There was further consideration of the differences between activities considered to be in the "mainstream" as compared to those considered antisocial or delinquent with specific reference to the differences between inner-city and suburban youth and the alienation they both suffer in present-day American society.

Underprivileged youth do not actively reject the aspirations and values of the larger culture. [social psychologist]

It is crucial to take into account their accompanying recognition that they have little hope of attaining these things, whereas the suburban youth sees what his parents achieved and knows that he can attain the same. He may perceive it as meaningless and insignificant, and apathetically continue in the same direction or see it as so negative in its consequences that he actively rejects it as a goal for himself. [mental health administrator in a private agency]

Underprivileged youth know they will not be able to earn an income sufficient to support a family. From their home experiences, they recognize that this ceiling on potential earnings is a persistent source of instability in family relations. On the other hand, the in-burn type boy who knows that all his life and all his father's life there has been enough money, also knows that if you go after professional objectives you will get trapped in the system. He feels that there are other more important values such as those relating to being oneself and living up to one's own aesthetic,   political,   and   religious   convictions   with   which   ordinary occupational adaptations interfere. [social psychologist]

Would you clarify what you mean by "in-burn?" [community worker]

These are boys who come from small, economically privileged families; their parents are in many instances even more liberal than the boys themselves and feel that it is very important to treat their children democratically. The boys go from this sort of home into a large, physically well-equipped, thoroughly bureaucratized high school, work hard to get into college which, they find, is just as sensible and humanly impersonal as their high school was. Increasing alienation is manifest in such behavior as oversleeping, sporadic class attendance, etc. [social psychologist]

More important than the matter of rejecting or accepting values is the similarity between the disenchantment of the lower-income youth who discovers he cannot make it, and the disenchantment of the in-burn's discovery of the dry rot of society and his refusal to get involved. [participant from a private agency]

The in-burn's refusal to get involved with political action is related to the inner-city youth's discovery of the failure of political action to produce genuine and tangible results, which produces the same effect. This "rejection of the whole business" is also evidenced in the increasing number of school dropouts from both groups who think you are crazy for expecting them to "get involved and do something" – both see that it does not do any good. [mental health administrator in a private agency]

The in-burn receives support from an intact, nuclear family who is very concerned about him, whereas the gang boy lacks the adult models who are concerned about him and his long-term career. Thus he must search for his own identity. [sociologist]

The alienation scores of the majority of participants on the test given during the Workshop fell in the category of "moderately alienated," which indicates that a lot of people carry out their jobs and make adequate adjustments to the corporate structure despite their being alienated to some extent. [participant involved in citywide activities]

Alienated students often perform adequately in college and many are among the better grade-getters, especially those who are recruited to activist programs. In contrast, being alienated and being lower class and in a very underprivileged position much more frequently results in failure to meet the requirements of the external society. Unlike the in-burn who feels secure in an organization because he has learned the ins and outs of its structure, the lower-class youth does not understand the implicit aspects of his position, feels persecuted and dissatisfied in, for example, his occupational situation. He finds it impossible to continue coping with the system which has such consequences as frequent job changes. The end result may be the same for the in-burn, but in his case it is the result of his suffering a disillusionment different from that experienced by the lower-class youth. [sociologist]

This amounts to a feeling of helplessness, in the one case with regard to one's personal fate and in the other with regard to the fate of the larger society. [community psychologist]

The in-burn knows he can reverse this trend whereas the person from the lower-class situation cannot. [agency staff member]

The test of courage for the in-burn is in resisting the system instead of playing by the rules. [social scientist]

The in-burn's discontent might be stimulated by his distaste for a society that produces this plight of the less well-off. [unidentified participant]

Many in-burns who were in college during the fifties now feel that working in underprivileged areas might be a meaningful career of service. They are trying to mobilize and help, but the question remains, "Are they doing any good?" [sociologist]

The Changing Context of Gangs

There are significant differences between gangs in their structure, organization, conception, and leadership. Instead of putting all gangs into one category, we must understand each gang in its own terms before beginning to work with its members in any way. [anthropologist working closely with a local gang]

The "traditional" view of a gang is limited to situations in which a youngster joins because he is looking for identification, a degree of gratification, and sometimes for protection; but I doubt that this type of gang still exists. Today, youngsters are joining because of an idea, or philosophy. They are joining a movement which goes beyond the need for belonging to a small gang. This is their positive way to become part of a system that has excluded them for generations. They are bursting out of ghettos, looking for a better way of life — which they do not call "middle-class" or "subculture" — than their fathers accepted. Dropouts, drug users, and what we call "street-addicted youngsters" are taking an interest in politics, job opportunities, and better educational systems. Young people today are involved in a movement which is not a gang — though the police may label it as such. They are talking about a revolution and about changing existing social conditions. [youth project director]

We have a cultural revolution going on whether we like it or not, and some people are ready to die. People in the ghetto are tired of being the subjects of research projects. They do not live their lives for demonstration; they live their lives daily, and they want a fresh urgency and permanency. These youngsters want permanent jobs, not summer jobs. Instead of sociological research, what is needed are new laws at city, state, and federal levels. If people keep writing those research papers, they will find that the social revolution just passed them up. The ghetto has more Ph.D.'s than anywhere else, and I am tired of it. Sociologists who write about the ghetto cannot understand it because they have never lived there. They do not know what it is like to live in housing projects and with cochroaches and rats. [director of another youth project]

Their work often fails to prove effective because their understanding, approach, and attitude toward the ghetto child is often naive. [youth worker]

They are not taking into consideration the cultural situation of the people with whom they are working, but basically are trying to meet their own emotional needs. Perhaps they are most helpful in the preliminary stages of work in these areas but they must get out if subsequent stages are to be achieved. [unidentified participant]

Several discussants pointed out that one of the important differences between gangs lies in the way they are viewed and treated by others.

When white hippies want to carry out one of their projects, high-level administrators are not only willing to meet with them but also assist them in their efforts. Negro gangs, on the other hand, are blocked in their efforts to make even initial contacts with city administrators. [youth project director]

When a gang of Negro youngsters gets involved in delinquent activities they are called savages, but when a group of white youngsters does the same kind of things, attempts are made to explain the circumstances that were the cause. Similarly, when Negro youngsters drop out of school, it is said they are uninterested and unreachable whereas when white youngsters leave school, all social forces go to work to try and deal with the problems they have. Negro youngsters understand that society does not categorize them in the same way that it does white youngsters, which further contributes to their alienation from society. [another youth project director]

The difference between the ways Negro and white gangs are viewed can be summed up by saying, "What is white is right." [participant from a community religious organization]

When the discussion centered on existing programs for youth, there was consideration of what is being done by the police and various social agencies, several comments on the schools, on "youth workers," and the new programs they have initiated. However, more significant than the specifics that were being considered was the underlying disagreement regarding the goals that were being striven for.

When we address ourselves to why there are gangs and what are the differences between them, we have to relate what we know about gangs not only to their elimination but also to how they can become 'useful' members of society. The Blackstone Rangers can produce a play but what about the youngsters they shot? [community leader]

How can we challenge these youngsters to get them back into the mainstream of society? [settlement house director]

On the other hand, many participants did not view the ultimate goal of work with these youngsters as either the breaking up of the gangs or insuring that their members adapt to society. Instead they emphasized the positive potential of these groups and suggested that the evident and over-all failure of gang work today indicates that the root of the problem has not even been approached.

Role and Attitude of the Police

The police figure that since some of the kids are junkies, all of them are, and they stop and search us all the time. [former gang leader, now a youth worker]

I can cite numerous examples of the difficulties we encounter when we try to get policemen to come out and talk with youngsters. The police hound them endlessly, and when they do come out to see the youngsters, they do not treat them as human beings. [community organizer]

That this Workshop is being used to present issues such as these is in itself indicative of impotence outside the conference room. [researcher concerned with criminal justice]

The police must recognize that the youngsters as well as the general public are entitled to protection and freedom. [member of a community organization]

These youngsters need lawyers to protect them from the police and other forces in society. They see that the police "serve and protect" only the middle class and carry out the letter of the law following orders from their superiors without questioning the validity and humanity of the laws themselves. It is questionable whether the things youngsters are convicted for are crimes to begin with. [community organizer]

Police are as human as anyone else, and we realize that there are ills among us. Though we do not always achieve goals such as "serve and protect," these are the ideas we are trying to instill in our men. There is a policy in the police department for just about every situation, but dealing with a person's heart is something entirely different. Many officers are sick and tired of the entire situation, which partly accounts for their attitude. [policeman]

Bail bonds are used to detain youths who have allegedly committed crimes. One of the functions of a bail bond is to assure that an individual who has been charged, but not convicted, of a crime will appear in court, but the attitude of the police department, as expressed by various of its representatives, that certain classes of people should be kept from getting back into the streets is unjustifiable. [staff member of a private agency]

I can cite many cases in which unreasonable and excessive bonds were set for youths on Chicago's West Side. What is "high" is relative to the individual in question; $250 is an impossible amount for certain individuals, especially youngsters. We must talk about decreasing rather than increasing the amounts set. [agency staff member]

This is not a question of a class of people. When anyone commits a serious crime, bail should be placed high enough so that, once apprehended, he cannot get out into society. [representative of an urban police department]

We should speak about the majority of cases, not specific and unusual ones. [lawyer]

It is not the police department itself which sets bonds. Furthermore, since the Constitution states that no unreasonable bails shall be set, it is easy to get into the position of depriving an individual of his constitutional rights. That is not what I am suggesting, but in some cases obstacles should be placed to make it difficult for an individual to get out. Admittedly, sometimes a lot of money is involved, but the situation today is a great departure from the days when everyone was forced to go through a professional bondsman. Overall, the arrested person today has a greater advantage than ever in the past. [policeman]

Although new laws have been passed in an attempt to prevent crime and unrest in Chicago, nothing significant is being done to accomplish this through rehabilitation programs for youngsters who get out of jail. [community leader]

Is any attempt being made on the part of the police to create a positive relationship with youngsters and work with them to alleviate existing problems? [community organization staff member]

These are not police functions. With regard to rehabilitation programs, personally I would like to see every youthful offender rehabilitated. As it is, they have to return to the same neighborhood and the same problems, and within three months they are right back in the same spot. But these are problems for social agencies. [representative of the police department]

Police and Community Relations

The existing community relations program is mere tokenism and cannot possibly do the job as evidenced by the lack of concern and even contempt for communities on the part of the police. [staff member of a community organization]

This is not the case. The community relations unit was created because the citizenry demanded that something be done about the situation. Things are far worse in other cities, and in Chicago at least some headway is being made. However, despite attempts to work out the problems of relations between the police and communities, the people are not responding. [representative of a police department.]

People are refusing to participate because they do not see these attempts as serious or meaningful. [the community organization staff member]

How adequate are the Citizen Review Boards in overcoming structural weaknesses in our system of criminal justice? [university professor]

We have suffered an eclipse of civilian authority and control as well as of responsible direction of the police department, and it is important to fill this gap. Community people are concerned with how grievances will be processed once they are filed. The basic problem is that substantial parts of the public lack confidence in the way the police relate to them. Though the important change has to come about within the police department itself, this must be encouraged and developed by those outside the department. Continuing the dialogue is one way to achieve this because there are a number of alternative approaches to the problem. The Citizen Review Board is one approach. When the police offer resistance to these Boards, as they are doing in many instances, it is important to persist in forcing recognition that there is a problem which has to be dealt with and that perhaps alternatives can be worked out. Another possibility is employing ombudsmen, and another is police departments making known that someone in their department is available to offer the kinds of answers the public requires. This approach could help in building confidence in the department and in diminishing the attitude that the police and the public are on opposite sides. [criminologist]

The police department where I come from is one of the most uncorrupt, honest, efficient, bureaucratic, militaristic, and uncompromising in the nation, and the community relations people there just do not know what to do because the program is so new. I have three suggestions for community people: (1) continue pressuring the police department to move into community relations; (2) help them define what community relations means for a police department since it is not one of their traditional functions; and (3) be patient with them — they cannot be expected to achieve success within a year. [out-of-state discussant]

We have implemented a program which has been successful in establishing fruitful contact between the community relations unit of the police department and gang leaders. It is important to help community relations units because one problem is that there is a lot of pressure from superiors within the department for the officers not to be associated with the so-called "social welfare worker." [another out-of-state discussant]

There is evidence which indicates that police are capable of dealing with people outside the system of criminal law by giving advice, acting as a resource when other agencies refuse, etc. If this evidence is valid, then the questions pertaining to race relations and dealing with young people and their rights must be recognized as matters of policy handed down from the top. The man on the beat cannot be blamed. [lawyer]

Approaches to Gang Leadership

If we consider the reasons for the existence of gangs and are really concerned with eliminating them, perhaps rather than leaving social problems to rehabilitation programs and agencies, there might be a way to combine that work with what the police know and better serve the youth of the city. [community worker]

That might be possible, but since we cannot deal with the thousands of gang members, we are trying to neutralize the leadership so that the majority of youngsters can be dealt with by the many agencies and programs which exist to help them. In many cases the youngsters do not take advantage of available programs because the leaders are keeping them from associating with sponsoring organizations. [police department representative]

Doesn't this amount to castrating the very leadership which could be the salvation of these youngsters? [lawyer]

Even projects involving very intensive and long-term gang work appear to be unsuccessful. Youth workers do not seem to be able to decrease delinquency on an individual basis, whether or not gangs continue to exist, so what is accomplished by creaming off the leadership and dissipating the little power that has been accumulated? In other words, how can you justify destroying a group that may have some structure when on the basis of available research, it is evident that then you will not be able to act constructively? [agency representative]

We are taking a calculated risk. Many of the criminal activities in which these youngsters become involved as well as their lack of freedom and need for protection are created by the gang structure itself. We know that many of these youngsters have to be in gangs to live in their community so our first step must be breaking up the gangs, neutralizing their activities. We have to get to the leaders if we are to prevail upon the majority of youngsters. Although no one group alone can be entirely successful in dealing with gangs or in eliminating delinquency, we will have served our purpose if we can prevent these gangs from bothering others. [policeman]

Assessing Existing Programs

The innovative programs described here are distinguished from most social programs in the ghettos because they are based upon a model of intervention. In other words, they are based on changing individuals or social situations with reference to an explicitly stated goal in contrast to most programs which are not guided by explicit and long-range objectives. [social scientist working with youth]

What sorts of changes in ongoing institutions are these programs designed to effect and what can they do for individual youngsters? [private agency staff member]

Some of them belong in the school system where either new curricula or new forms of old curricula are needed. [youth program leader]

Do these programs create new opportunities that would call for the new competencies they are designed to develop? [unidentified participant]

Work must be done on both fronts. [youth program director]

Disinterest in the programs offered by various agencies is paralleled in the schools. I can tell who the gang leaders will be by the way they lead the class. Their major object is to be seen, heard, and to attract attention, and they are not interested in what the school has to offer them. Despite my honest efforts, these youngsters do not respond. [new teacher in an inner-city elementary school]

Even if one is a good teacher with something to offer, these youngsters encounter too many of the others for it to make much difference. The schools do not hit on anything that is real to these young people. Considering what the schools offer them, if I were one of them, I would not be interested in going to school either. Young people do not drop out of school at sixteen – they are forced out in second grade. [experienced teacher]

Many dropouts are disinterested and get into trouble because they do not have any place to go or anything to do. We need playgrounds, gyms, and dance halls for teenagers. It is important that the older kids set an example for the younger ones. If your older brother is working out in the gym, that is what you will want to do, and if he is a junkie, that is what you will want to be. [former gang leader, now head of a large youth group]

We should make it possible for youngsters to clean, fix up, and use the vacant lots in these areas. Health problems are also a major concern with which we have to deal. Some of these youngsters have never been to a dentist in their lives or to a doctor until it hurts. These are issues like motherhood that nobody is against and are good ones to start with in any community. [out-of-state youth worker]

Something is wrong somewhere if in the three and one-half square miles of Harlem, there are ninety–one social agencies to cure the ills of the people. [member of a community organization]

A youth worker's prime concern is the welfare of gang members. His job is to offer them a range of things from trips to the beach to an adult who cares and who can do favors for them in court, find them jobs, and when asked, act as their spokesman and intervene on their behalf. Gang leaders can serve as adult role models because they are not too far removed from the youngsters. It is important for adults who are working with gangs to avoid too large a gap between themselves and the youngsters; Stokely Carmichael, for example, is an adult role model for these youngsters whereas Martin Luther King is not. Most gang workers are more concerned with the rehabilitation of young people than with delinquency prevention and law enforcement, but sometimes trouble even increases as a result of gang projects. Nobody seems to know how to reduce delinquency rates, and on the whole gang work is not successful. Not only do we lack the necessary tools, techniques and knowledge about human behavior, but gang projects are designed to change in a short time a situation that has developed over a very long time. [social science researcher]

A very evil paradox faces the gang worker. He is supposed to work with from twenty to one hundred youngsters. Obviously, he cannot deal with them on an individual basis so he deals with them as a group which serves to reinforce and make more cohesive already existing groups. [social scientist]

This is exactly what happened in the community where I worked. The groups worked with became more cohesive, more seriously delinquent, and remained delinquent longer. [former youth gang worker]

Another consideration in gang work is that underprivileged youth say different things about their values in group discussion than when they discuss them privately with detached workers. [social scientist]

The strategy of the traditional street work operation has been to take away the leader of so-called "delinquent gangs" on the assumption that the group will then fall apart. Though perhaps removing that fellow will "help," he has some potential for motivating those youngsters, and the deprived are deprived even further by taking away their leadership. It is decisive and revolutionary that the very bright and aggressive among them are refusing to have anything to do with the entire youth welfare establishment. They are refusing to be drained off and are staying to try and make it. If the youth welfare people want to be accepted by the young people, they will have to make themselves relevant to the new position taken by the youngsters. The reaction of people within the establishment to their lack of acceptance has resulted in a decrease in effort to even approach these young people. [youth gang worker]

This is also the attitude of others in the community. People in ghetto communities perceive all government administrators whose work focuses on their community, however well-meaning they may be, as representatives of an establishment they have learned does not provide either what it promises or what they need. [community organizer]

To what extent are the attitudes of these youngsters wrong in some empirical sense? [sociologist]

Our findings have a lot to do with the framework with which we start. Social workers tend to think of these youngsters as delinquents. I do not think of them in those terms. [researcher]

Perhaps some of the failure of youth work is due to the fact that workers try to operate in a political vacuum instead of considering the over-all political situation and the various factors which influence people. [settlement house worker]

"Delinquency" tends to decrease when the group has an ideological base with some objective toward which all their activities are directed. However, gang work seems to treat the symptoms rather than the basic causes. [community organizer]

The Wider Social Context

It is becoming increasingly evident that the work which has been done with gangs has not been successful, which indicates to me that a gang is just a symptom and that we should be trying to go beyond the gang and deal with the kinds of things in society that cause gangs and lead youngsters to want to join them. [community organizer]

One of the main reasons for the Mayor's Commission on Human Relations taking an interest in the gun bill was that our youngsters were killing each other. There was a need to protect them from the illegal possession of guns which are put into their hands by the irresponsible adults who help them procure weapons. [city administrator]

A large part of the gun problem exists because we are giving kids ideas by having guns all over the place; the solution lies in something other than a gun bill. [former gang member now working closely with gangs and the effect of the legal system on them]

The increase in gang activity can be attributed to society's unwillingness to give these youngsters the chance to prove to themselves that they are men. Society has lied to them, promised them so much and given them nothing. They are demanding recognition and a voice; and as long as they are kept down, gangs will continue to be created. [director of a community organization]

Youngsters are not interested in what this society is offering them. As Dr. Percy Julian, a Negro who by American standards has "made it," has said, "They tell all these pretty lies. They say excel and you will go forth. I excel, I get nothing." People do not live in a vacuum; you cannot talk about a youngster in a classroom or talk about a gang without taking into account everything that goes on around them. Even a sincere teacher is locked into what surrounds him; an exception does not change the rule. The youngsters have a certain knowledge about the way the world functions and their eyesight is uncluttered by rationalization. [counselor in a settlement house]

Charles Dickens focused on the problem of poverty, and programs for its elimination, in another social and historical context. He wrote about a "delinquent" gang in the London slums and commented on the social conditions that breed poverty and gangs, and his program for eliminating them was "more Christian charity." Karl Marx also saw the problem of poverty quite clearly, and his program for eliminating it and the ills which arise from it was a restructuring of society. I would submit to you that the real problem is not a question of identity and adult models or of getting young people to adapt to the school system or to fit into society. Given the structure of our society, we are wasting our time and money on present programs. What we need instead is a thorough restructuring of the priorities for this society, starting from the top down. [agency staff member]

Several participants raised questions about what we actually mean when we talk about "restructuring society," and although there was no detailed discussion of possibilities, a number of issues were brought out.

Although a restructuring of society would certainly result in changes, it would not necessarily result in an improved social situation. [director of a youth-oriented program]

I am concerned about possible negative effects of deep and far-reaching social changes, but if we are to even contemplate such an approach, one of the first priorities is ensuring that everyone in society, not just gangs, etc., be taken into consideration. [mental health worker]

I take a less skeptical view of what would be lost and what gained by a restructuring of society. Whereas in all previous Workshop sessions we talked about how sick society was, with regard to our discussions on gangs, and gang work in general, too much attention is paid to "saving" gang members, working with them to get them out of a gang and adjusted to society. What are we asking them to adjust to? Do we want to make them into "ghetto in-burns?" We should be talking about them in terms of human value. [staff member of a private agency]

The ultimate aim of work with gangs has been to get youngsters to conform to a society from which they feel completely alienated. They have been expected to adapt to a society toward which they have built up hostilities and anger because it has consistently excluded them from any meaningful opportunities to succeed within its system and benefit from the material things that should be open to all. The youngsters we have classified as "antisocial" and "juvenile delinquent" are beginning to collectively focus on that system which I think is a move in the right direction. [director of youth programs]

Simply working with individuals and their families will not motivate youngsters when they have nothing to move toward. No matter how well they do in school, they are still blocked when they get out. We must focus on restructuring society and dealing with questions such as power with regard to gangs. [former teacher]

Through their activities, gangs have begun to make some changes in the power structure. [community leader]

Stop Talking, Start Listening

You are not going to be able to lead these youngsters unless you stop talking to them and start listening to them. [director of a project involving youth gangs]

This is also what is necessary on the part of the police if their relations with these youngsters are to be improved. [staff member of a community organization]

It also holds for those carrying out studies of youth and youth activities – that is, those who are talking about youth as well as those talking to them. [researcher concerned with urban problems]

It is what is needed if we are to be able to understand and communicate with the young people of today. [director of a community organization]

It is more important to listen to youth in the ghetto than to talk to them outside the ghetto. Taking promises back to the ghetto from the outside only causes more frustration within. [community leader]

The place to start is listening to the kids themselves. [community leader]

PART 5

The City and the Community –
A Confrontation

(Suggested Courses of Action)

32

The City – A Look to the Future

DAVID LEWIS

I have been asked to summarize in a matter of minutes a program on which we have been working for more than three years. This program has developed to a point at which it is now recognized as involving a radical restructuring of one of the country's major cities – Pittsburgh, Pennsylvania, the center city of the twelfth largest metropolitan area in the United States.

Three years ago I was asked to be the urban designer in a team studying the city's schools. The purpose of the study was to achieve quality education for all students in the city, in a moment of dramatically changing social and technological needs. And this means achieving a situation in schools in which integration – irrespective of student origin – is a matter of course; and it also means, within the schools themselves, a radical restructuring of education itself as a result of new technologies and new educational goals. To participate in this task I formed a small team which we called Urban Design Associates. This team now includes, on a full- or part-time basis, a roster of planners, urban designers, and architects, supported by consultancies in urban economics and development, sociology, education, community relations, engineering, traffic, and landscape architecture.

No new high schools have been built in Pittsburgh for more than forty years. Although this is a somewhat shocking situation, it is apparently not uncommon in our major cities. The oldest high school still in operation in Pittsburgh was built over a century ago, before the inauguration of President Lincoln.

After six months of work, the Harvard University Center for Field Studies, which followed our first phase of the work, received a mandate from the Board of Education to replace every one of these old high schools with a new high school system. This is a very radical gesture. It means that five years from now every high school student in Pittsburgh will attend a new school which has not yet been built.

In approaching this problem of inserting a wholly new high school system into an old and rapidly changing city, we decided to look very critically at the city's basic structure, and see whether we could not use this rather large program (involving a capital expenditure of some $140 million) as a means of radically restructuring and reorienting for the better, its present shape and growth.

It's a truism to say that the modern city is totally different from the cities of the past. Today, cities are undergoing the first fundamental revolution in urban form since cities first began five thousand years ago. In the past, cities were based on the human foot: people walked everywhere, and the measure of space was the pedestrian. Because of the distances which separated one city from another, each city was autonomous, self-governing, and self-sufficient, with its own army, and its own temporal and divine princes. It is ironic how, today, we still hang onto the image of the traditional, walled city. For we still fight to maintain the political autonomy of our cities, in spite of the fact that we live in a nation – and even a world – that is really a vast lattice of interdependence.

The modern city is what one might call the "open-form" city, as opposed to the "closed-form" city of the past. The open-form city is based, not on the single measure of the pedestrian, but on a number of ever-widening time-space scales. When we look at the map we see that today's metropolises look like great inkstains, as cities grow outwards following the pattern of their radial highways. And a simple law may be stated for today's metropolis as follows: the more fluent and faster you make limited-access highways into the central areas of a city, the further out into the countryside the city will spread; for it is not geographic size, or population size, which today control the size and configuration of the city, but commuter time: the maximum time people are willing to spend traveling to and from work, schools, shops, recreation, and other amenities.

Of course, this has a significant impact on the traditional concepts of neighborhood or community. We continue to use these words but their meaning is becoming lost. Human relationships today are becoming a series of Chinese boxes: we have immediate relationships, we have intercity relationships, and we have intercontinental relationships. This continuing, outward progression of contact relations coupled with all the changes in cultural scales and identity implicit in communications media such as radios, television, newspapers, advertising, and paper-backs is undermining the traditional structure of the pedestrian-oriented community in its closed and autonomous form, as well as the very institutions which lie inside the neighborhood. For example, in what sense can we still speak of neighborhood schools? And, given these new dimensions, should an entire school system belong to what one might call a traditional neighborhood, when the neighborhood in the traditional sense no longer really exists?

Aristotle thought that the ideal size of a city was 5,000 people simply because he felt that everybody should know everybody else. By knowing everybody else's dirty linen it was impossible to get very far by political graft. Today, of course, it is impossible to know everybody else. A man's capacity for human relationships is obviously limited; however, those relationships are not inbred as they were in the city of the past. In an Italian hill town, one might know everybody else and the town might be entirely integrated; but it is very unlikely that the people I know personally will be known in any large percentage by most of the others I meet. We each have an outward progression of relationships which quickly compounds to an absolutely vast cluster of interrelationships.

This is reflected in the structure of the city. Pittsburgh is a typical radial city. Freeways radiate outward into the metropolitan region from the central business hub of the city, the Golden Triangle, like the spokes of a wheel. Thus Pittsburgh is gripped by the same chain reaction process which afflicts so many cities. As congestion in the center of the city increases, more freeways get built, causing more metropolitan growth which in turn results in more congestion at the city center. (See Figure 1)

To relieve this situation it becomes necessary to bypass the center of the city by siphoning off at least long-distance, through traffic through the construction of peripheral beltways. This in turn results in the construction of those gigantic interchanges which are today such a common sight on the edges of spreading metropolitan areas; and at these points land values increase, shopping centers and parks for light industry are built, and the virtually laissez-faire process of decentralizing the city is given added impetus. The new shopping centers form a series of interconnected subnodes around the city, and new suburban residential communities, inhabited by middle-class white families leaving the city to form white suburban enclaves, cluster around these new subnodes. (See Figure 2)

Simultaneously with this process, we are witnessing enormous influxes of rural populations into cities. Within the next generation some 95% of the total United States population will live in urban areas; and the top ten to fifteen metropolitan centers in this country will act as magnets of greater and greater concentrations.

Something of this influx is revealed in the statistics of agricultural employment over the last forty years. In 1929, 26% of the total population of the United States was employed directly in agriculture. By 1950 this had dropped to 15.3%. By 1960 it was 8.7%. And by 1975 it is expected to be a mere 4% – directly due to the high mechanization of agricultural production and processing, and a quiet revolution in distribution and marketing techniques. Of these migrating populations, a considerable percentage of the rural poor and deprived are Negro, who are moving into the central areas of our large cities – into those older residential areas of townhouses vacated by middle-class families moving into the suburbs – and most of these Negro migrants are without any of the skills needed for gainful employment and the fulfillment of aspirations in the cities.

Between 1950 and 1960 the number of Negros living in central city areas rose by 64%. Pittsburgh is more fortunate than most other major metropolitan areas, in that it has a relatively settled population pattern and has developed its problems at a slower rate. Even so, between 1950 and 1960 the number of Negros in the center city rose by 22.6%. Simultaneously there was a gross decrease of 10% in the over-all city population. In other words, while there was a 22% Negro influx, there was an even greater gross exodus of white families into suburban areas. As a result, the number of Pittsburgh schools which are de facto segregated has risen from eight to

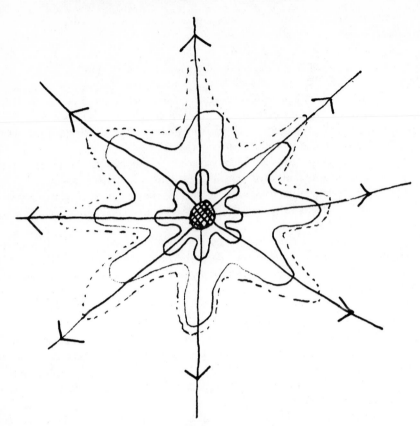

Figure 1

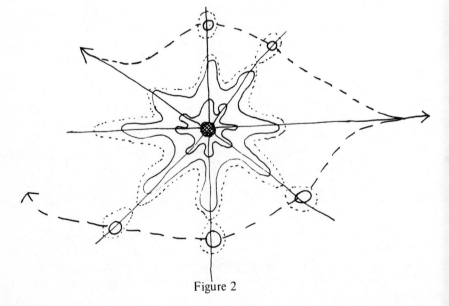

Figure 2

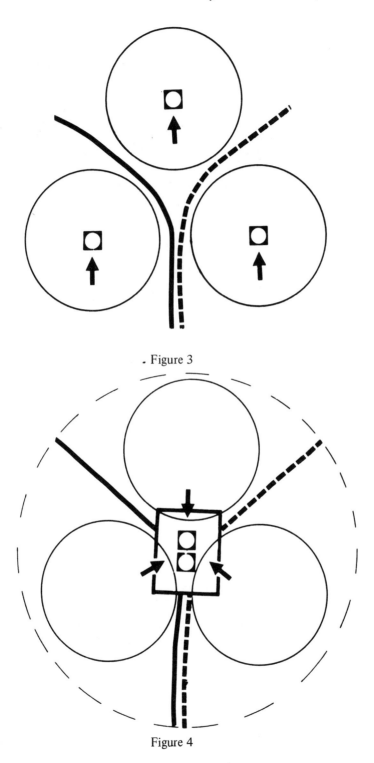

. Figure 3

Figure 4

The dark areas of this map show the areas
where elementary schools are 70-100 percent Negro.

Figure 5

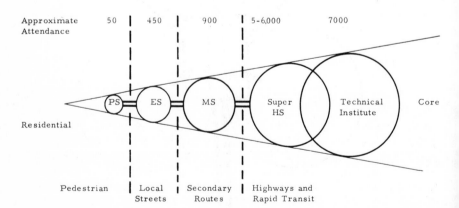

Figure 6

nineteen in fifteen years. And enormous pockets of socially circumscribed populations have thus developed in which the average male unemployment factor is now well over 20%.

In its physical form, Pittsburgh is a city of hills and rivers. Highways, railroads, and industry follow the valleys and river banks. On the high ground between these radials are the residential communities of the city. Traditionally these communities have been autonomous and inward looking – for each is separated from the next by valleys and rivers, and highways and industry – and each has its own traditional shopping street and school system. It is hardly surprising therefore to find the present boundaries of Negro ghettos in the city coinciding with these traditional topographic configurations, providing segregated populations by definite sector of 45,000 to 60,000 people; and whole school districts, each with, for example, a high school, two middle schools, and six elementary schools, being either white or Negro. (See figure 3)

Now in considering this total city and metropolitan situation, we adopted certain new and positive attitudes. We decided as a basic premise not to construct amenities within neighborhoods which would only further entrench circumscription. Our general thematic solution, reached in collaboration with the Department of City Planning and the Board of Education, was to treble the school district size so as to encompass several hitherto topographically separate and racially segregated communities, and create a series of completely new foci – not just education centers, but completely new cities within the old city, with new commercial areas, cultural, leisure, and entertainment facilities, parks and recreation areas, and housing for all incomes, in addition to the new great high schools. Thus the old pattern of segregated and inward looking communities would be reversed, and the new centers would become a dramatic focus of integration in the fullest sense of that term. (See figure 4)

In approaching this concept, we looked at the city as a whole, in economics, transportation, land use, land values, demography, topography, and so forth, and as a result of these studies chose sites where the new centers could be built to form a comprehensive "federation" of subcores constellating around the center city, each linked to all the others and to the center city by highways and rapid transit. (See figure 5)

To date, with full interagency participation, Urban Design Associates has now completed urban designs for four out of a total of five such centers, all of which have now been adopted as official city policy. Land has been acquired for the first three sites, and the site for the fourth is in active acquisition. Architects – the firm of Helmuth, Obata and Kassabaum of St. Louis – have already been appointed for the school system, and it is expected that the first great high school will be ready for occupation around 1972. In every case the sites for the new centers have been chosen on the edges of traditional communities, in positions where they can act as new and vital links between communities hitherto separated. Such sites have several advantages. Land values are low; being peripheral areas, there is very little relocation of families or public amenity; and, as we have said, this is precisely where the major highways are and where future rapid transit will be, so that every site is linked to all the others by the fastest limited-access systems, and to all parts of the city and the metropolitan region.

However, we in Urban Design Associates are beginning to have certain reservations. We feel we have not gone big enough. It would of course have been ideal to have considered not just the city but the whole metropolitan region as our basic unit. We could then have designed our subnodes in terms of the physical and demographic interrelationship of the region as a whole. It is absurd to leave the cities to bear the full brunt of urban poverty, while the surrounding counties accommodate exclusively white suburban enclaves. It is absurd that we cannot view the metropolitan region as a single economic federation, instead of as a series of competitive situations (commercial areas in competition, and taxing authorities in competition), particularly when one realizes that the radial highways and rapid transit configurations we have been describing give the region as a whole such a powerful weblike structure of communications on which to capitalize in the interests of balanced and rational interrelations. But metropolitan government, of the kind implied in these remarks, is apparently still a long way off.

Nevertheless, even in terms of a citywide federation of subcores, we in Urban Design Associates felt that we could and should have gone a lot larger. In our view, the Pittsburgh Plan would be much stronger with three centers instead of five. For with three centers, we could have concentrated far greater strengths in the way of housing and commercial development programs. The Board of Education was, however, more fearful than we were of great high schools of 7 or 8 thousand students instead of 6. In our view, the difference between 6 and 8 thousand students is not crucial. It all rests in the quality of architectural design. We have demonstrated without too much difficulty in our models how intimate, humanist scales and high characterization can be achieved in environments as large as these. After all, at the next level of education, colleges and universities, we do not cavil at sizes up to 20 and even 30 thousand students. And in terms of building costs and organizational efficiency, we could have made capital savings for the Board of up to $15 million.

The greatest effect of a three-center system may, however, have been felt in school districting and racial integration. Let us look at this. It is clear that if we want maximum integration, one school site – to serve the whole city – is the best possible solution. Unfortunately in Pittsburgh such a school would be so big (over 20,000 students) and site-acquisition problems so formidable as to render such a solution impractical. The next best solution is two centers; and the next best is three. We found that in Pittsburgh a three-school system would have produced balanced and integrated school districting on a simple geometric grid without any gerrymandering whatever, and could be built without any extra site-acquisition problems. It is unfortunate that our recommendations came too late. The Board of Education – apart from its uncertainties regarding size – had already been forced to make commitments to a five-school system as a result of political pressures.

But size notwithstanding, we have tried to show in our work how the new schools might be designed, not as institutions, but as "youth cities;" youth cities within the new city within the city. In other words, each youth city would be a focus where young people from very large areas of the city can come together irrespective of background, drawn to share centralized amenities such as theatres, jazz clubs, teen shops, debating areas, coffee shops, exhibitions, computer programming facilities, audiovisual equipment, and so forth.

We have also tried to show how the new centers can become a major catalyst for urban rehabilitation and the regeneration of community pride over wide areas. If a school system is viewed as an urban structure, we can quickly discern very particular urban qualities appropriate to each of these elements. For example, preschools and elementary schools are very much residentially oriented facilities. A mother or a grandmama brings the small child to school. And the school could be located at a small neighborhood center where there could be one or two corner shops as well, a branch library, a day-care center, clinics for prenatal, postnatal, and geriatric care, and a senior citizens' club, perhaps all grouped around a small landscaped plaza with benches under shade trees. Such an area could be protected from through traffic by a simple system of one-way streets and pedestrian malls. (See figure 6)

For middle schools, the situation is rather different. Instead of the pedestrian orientation which we find appropriate to elementary schools, at the middle schools level we find that at least 60% of the students are riders, mostly on public transit; and this places the middle school in a traffic hierarchy involving transit routes and collector-arterials. At the great high school level – designed to service a city sector of 120,000 people or more – we have something else again. The new city within the city is indeed a giant interface of all systems, pedestrian routes, local streets, collector-arterials, limited-access highways and rapid transit; for here are located schools and shops, cultural facilities, department stores, housing and recreation, restaurants and motels, served by rapid transit concourses and large-capacity parking structures.

In conclusion let me repeat that our approach is to overcome circumscription and the ghetto, and provide quality education, by building new facilities on an enormous scale. Clustered around these facilities are all the power the city can muster in housing, cultural facilities, and in commercial trade-offs, all of which increase the options of cluster. Nobody is telling anybody where to live, but we are beginning to provide the facilities which will allow people to live where they choose. We do this by endeavoring to meet the needs of people of all races and incomes in housing and through encouraging new mortgage proposals and a number of other new programs involving both public and private sectors. The Board of Education is attempting to gear education to new and integrated job opportunities, and we are applying these principles in a very localized, grass-roots manner.

We recognize that education cannot do the whole job of integration alone. Housing cannot do it alone. Highways cannot do it alone. Model

Cities cannot do it alone. We have to marshall all our forces into one comprehensive program. And then, with all the strength we can muster, we have to build new beginnings in our cities rather then try to shore up the rotten old fabric as we are doing now.

33

Model Cities

Citizen Participation and Politics

ARCHIE HARDWICKE

I grew up on Chicago's West Side and went to Tennyson Elementary School and John Marshall High School. I know the Lawndale area quite well because I worked in one of the supermarkets there. I am very familiar with some of the problems on the West Side and have seen the area change very drastically in fifteen years, and especially in the past six years.

For the last six years, I worked in the Watts community, and our agency was one of the primary community action-oriented agencies in that area. We became quite well-known during the Watts riots. The city power structure thought we had started the riots, but the federal government thought we had acted as a middleman trying to bring about constructive changes within that community. Our agency has worked with many federal programs to try to bring about change, and now that I am on the other side of the fence, I will be able to get a different perspective on how to deal with some of the problems that face us.

The agency with which I was working before I came to HUD, in addition to being a community organization agency, was concerned with bringing cultural enrichment and economic development into the area. It started as a direct action agency which tried to bring together various groups, from black nationalists to the ultraconservative elements, to confront the power structure which includes Mayor Yorty and other conservative elements. Even though the area had been practically burned down and there continued to be a great deal of militancy, black unity, and self-determination, the problems are still not being solved. After two and a half years, the buildings in Watts have not been rebuilt. There are very few new businesses in the area, and there continues to be a lack of communication between the police department and the city.

In my last few months at Westminister, we tried to develop a strong economic base and brought in a credit union and large businesses in the area, such as Lytton Industries which is one of the largest. Our two main problems were that we were too honest and too idealistic in dealing with the business people. At first we approached them because it was the right thing to do. We spent a lot of time at meetings, but that did not get us

411

anywhere. However, when we approached the problem in terms of their economic advantage along with our economic advantage, we began to communicate. Just before I left, we were in the process of bringing several small industries into the area. We also interested the federal government in helping many of the small businessmen in the area to develop a better financial base. In spite of their high ideals one of the problems that many community development agencies had to face was money. No matter how successful we were in starting programs, we had to come back to the fact that we did not have any money and that we had little communication with the people who control the money.

Since then I have been invited to work as a citizen participation advisor for the HUD Model Cities program. Because the guidelines give only a general idea of what a citizen participation program could or should be, I have been told that my role is to clarify and fill in those guidelines and to help citizen groups become more constructive in dealing with the power structure of the cities. At the same time, I am to help the cities understand their role in dealing more constructively with the citizens. This is a rather different role since I am supposed to be an unseen middle man, a catalyst setting up reactions. When I accepted the job, I told my superiors that someone like me would be most concerned about the neighborhoods and the citizens in the poverty ghetto area. I think that the very fact that a federal agency has taken the risk of hiring a person with my background and feelings about citizen involvement is a small step in the direction of trying to bring about some of the changes that many of us feel are needed.

From my experience so far, I would say that in case Chicago is chosen for the Model Cities Program, you should begin preparing an instrument to bring about the desired citizen involvement in the Advisory Committee – the policy- and decision-making body – and there are a number of ways that you can do this. First, organize so that you reflect the needs of those in the communities where you work. Second, set up instruments of communication with all segments of the community.

I have been in and around Chicago for the last two months, and from what I have seen, you are not really communicating with the needs of the community. I have been to several meetings and talked with residents in the areas where those meetings are being held. They had little understanding, concern, or interest in the organizations which purport to represent them. There is an awful lot of work to do, and until you begin to set up your own house as far as organization is concerned, you will be lost. Those in the power structure are probably very aware that you are not as powerful as you are supposed to be.

Another major problem that faces us is whether we, and the homeowners, should deal with black nationalist organizations, or include public agencies in our organization, or private organizations such as the neighborhood house in our organization? How would our Board react to my associating with black nationalists, and how would the black nationalists react to my relating to public and private agencies. You will not be successful until there is a broad selection of all groups in your organization and until they communicate with each other, because small organizations have the power to disrupt. Just when you think you are organized, three or four people, a power structure, will say you do not represent them. They will outshout you and you will be lost again. That is why I say it is important to have a comprehensive community-organization program.

Furthermore, it is necessary to relate to those in the power structure in a nonidealistic way because they definitely are not idealistic. You will have to use universities and get money to pull organizations together. Some organizations will join out of selfish interests and some because they are very much concerned, but all have to be pulled together.

Third, once organizations have joined together and are meeting with a power structure, a constructive comprehensive plan has to be developed as an alternative to what they are saying and doing. It is not enough to just be critical, angry, and militant. When you have an alternative proposal to offer, you have grounds for attracting federal and state governments as well as other interest groups even if your program is turned down.

Your organization can set up a non-profit corporation consisting of the different groups you represent. Along with developing a plan for what you think your Model Cities Program should be, your organization can hire a neighborhood planner who is concerned with your interests and can help you from a technical point of view. Though he might not know about your neighborhood, he is a technician and understands neighborhood planning so he can help you. You can also hire a community strategist who can help keep your organization together.

These are the sorts of technical advisors who can help you once your organization forms and develops as a non-profit corporation, because you will be confronted with people who know about the area from a technical point of view. One of my main problems wherever I work is the lack of communication when I talk about what I feel needs to be done and they talk from a legal or logical point of view. Therefore, my fourth recommendation is to begin developing effective lines of communication.

Finally, if this is to be an effective program, you not only have to ask to be involved in the planning, you have to demand it. You must be organized in your demands and plan an over-all strategy to get to the weakest link in the city, that person in the power structure to whom I can relate. In social work which is my field, we call it interaction, but after my experiences last year, I just call it plain old manipulation which is how we have to look at it if we are going to work effectively.

DAVID McMULLIN

For two million years, man has been living in a hostile environment and striving to make it less hostile. He developed cities. He could now specialize, and increasingly enjoy and become more dependent on the specialties of others. Some of these specialties are community services. They are not perfect. However, in our Workshop sessions, there has been a tendency to say that since all our community services and everything the establishment does can be improved, they are no good and we must get rid of them. I am suggesting that this goes against the way man has solved his problems in the past. Rather than getting rid of what he has already made, he has built and improved upon it.

We can make the city better because man can adapt. Even though a human being living in a city like Chicago is faced with more complex, demanding, and devastating problems than his ancestors faced, man can adapt and build on the foundations that have already been laid.

On page twenty-two of *Improving the Quality of Urban Life: A Program Guide to Model Neighborhoods in Demonstration Cities,* which is the only guideline for the Model Cities Program, is an example of how Model Cities Programs will be funded. It is built on the idea that there are many different federal funds which can be used to improve our urban environments. This is not simply another federal source of funds for solving the same problems. Model Cities funds are meant to supplement other currently available programs and are available only when other federal programs are used. Those cities selected will be given a program-planning grant, and once they have planned their program, money will be made available to carry out the plans according to the cities' participation in other federal programs. Urban renewal, Welfare, OEO, Manpower Development and Training, and other programs require that the local community make a certain financial contribution. The Government will grant up to 80% of this local contribution. If there is no local contribution, there will be no Model Cities grant. All of this, of course, assumes that Congress will make money available for Model Cities programs.

The expression "creative federalism" means that the government is waiting for the local community to accept maximum responsibility for conducting and planning programs. This has always been true in public housing which cannot be created unless a local group is willing to start it. This is also true of OEO and many other programs. Citizenship participation is also a requirement for the Model Cities Program.

"Maximum feasible participation" has been variously described during our Workshop, but most striking was its definition by the man from New York who said that for him "maximum feasible participation" meant "poor people participating in our total society." This is a very different idea from planning a small project in a community. I would like to offer an analogy to further clarify maximum feasible participation. Consider a hospital that decides that since the patients are most affected by what is done in the hospital they should participate in operating the hospital and in the diagnosis and treatment of their own case. So every day, they take their own temperatures, mark it on a chart, participate with the doctors in staffing their case, and so on.

This would not be a bad idea, provided, of course, that the patient is a medical doctor specializing in his own particular illness, and provided that he is not too sick to be objective about himself. I suggest that these two considerations are very relevant to participation in any program. Participation depends, first, upon the persons ability and competence in the field of concern, and second, upon his objectivity regarding the problem in which he has become involved.

In analyzing our urban problems, we must determine not only what we want, but also what we can achieve through our own efforts and what we must depend on others to give to us. It is very important to make this distinction. Throughout the Workshop, this group has been receiving information from experts, and if we could not develop a good plan, I think there is very little hope for maximum feasible participation or for community involvement in Model Cities programs. People in local communities will not be exposed to the wealth of information and expertise that we have received here which should enable us to be especially creative in working out practical and realistic ideas for a program as new and complex as Model Cities.

Case Presentation: St. Louis

DONALD BOURGEOIS

The four of us are here from St. Louis because some of the things that have been done there are relevant to your concern for developing a strategy on which to build a program that involves citizen participation.

The Model Cities legislation has three broad requirements. First, a city must conduct an in-depth analysis of itself. That does not mean a mere recital of the city's pathology such as its death rate from tuberculosis or its infant mortality rate. It means a city must understand the reasons behind its pathology. Second, a city must develop some techniques for dealing with its particular pathology. Third, a city must be able to provide the administrative machinery necessary to carry out its program. It is to the second requirement of techniques that I would like to address myself.

But first, a brief history of the St. Louis program. The St. Louis Model City Agency was created December 3, 1966. I am the director. And I have a staff of thirty-four and no budget. To get this many staff on board, we went to state agencies related to the problems with which we would have to deal – the Bureau of Employment Security, the Division of Vocational Rehabilitation, the Divisions of Health, Education and Welfare, and the Office of State and Regional Planning. We asked each of them to lend us a high-level person, which they did. These people began on January 1, and have been with us ever since. When their terms expired on April 20, they were renewed. All of our staff are paid, though a few are receiving barely enough to cover expenses until the Model Cities Program is funded.

Most of the staff are on another payroll. For example, Sam Dardick is an urban planner, and his salary is paid by the Office of State and Regional Planning. B. Ann Kleindienst is a social scientist from Washington University, and, though she was not paid for a long time, is now on the budget of the City Plan Commission. The Board of Education gave us a full-time man as did the Archdiocesan Board of Education, the City Plan Commission, the Human Development Corporation, our local community action agency, and various other groups.

We have submitted three applications, each one being a revision of the one preceding it. Prior to submitting our first, we adopted a certain theology with respect to our operation. Thirty-four of us from various disciplines did the initial planning, and I was one member of the planning team. At that stage no people from the neighborhood were represented, though we would have involved people from the neighborhood if we had known then what we know now.

With this as a brief background, let me turn to the planning process as we envisage it for the St. Louis program. Sam (Dardick) will describe certain aspects of the process in detail. Suffice it to say now that we have what we call a "top-down/bottom-up" approach. At the top-down level, many of our staff come from the state to work for us. I myself work directly for the mayor of St. Louis. On the bottom-up level, we have worked out the following approach which we gave a trial run in one section of our target area. We sent an interdisciplinary team consisting of an architect-planner, a real-estate economist, a social scientist, and a community organizer. Each was charged with various functions which Sam will describe. Basically, they were to serve as resource people for those living in the neighborhood.

Without federal funds, we have already established two such subcity teams. (We have divided the Model City target area or neighborhood in St. Louis into what we call "subcities," each containing 10,000 - 15,000 people. We would like to divide them into areas of 5,000 persons so that every-body might have an opportunity to know everyone else; but unfortunately, with a constraint of money, we could not afford the staff that would be necessary.) The architects come from the firm of Hellmuth, Obata and Kassabaum and others. (Gyo Obata is the architect for the Pittsburgh Great High Schools.) The real-estate economists, of course, come from various real-estate firms. The social scientists, who are hard to come by, come from Washington University, and the community organizers from the community itself. Sam will describe their functions, all of which culminate in a process which allows people to plan their own neighborhood.

But now to the techniques. Early in the planning for the St. Louis program, we adopted systems analysis as a tool of operation. We decided to look at things in much the same way as the aerospace industry. Under this system, and with the help of two persons from McDonnell-Douglas Co., we looked at the city as a system and divided it into a number of subsystems: housing, physical facilities, health, welfare, employment, education, transporta-tion, social services, economic development, vocational rehabilitation, crime reduction, recreation, and culture.

I will not go into detail on the systems analysis portion. We then adopted as a yardstick against which to measure all proposed programs the increase or maximization of personal disposable income. Income in this context meant real income such as the value of a better home to a family, the value of a decent transportation system or of improved health facilities. As a single criterion it subsumed many others. We felt at that time that all programs, whether they were hardware or software, that were brought to bear on the problems of the central city had to be measured according to this single yardstick. For example, a transportation program had to be viewed in terms of how much savings it effected, and this in turn was equated in terms of income.

It has become increasingly apparent over the past several weeks, however, that no single program approach is sufficiently strong enough or encom-passing enough to bring about a significant impact on the problems facing most American cities. As a consequence, our thinking has changed somewhat. We now talk in terms of reducing the disparities that exist between the central cities and the suburbs. For this we see four main approaches.

First, we could move central city residents to the suburbs. One hundred thousand white, middle-income people have left St. Louis since 1960. Today, the population is down from a high of 850,000 to 685,000. If this trend continues, St. Louis will become a predominantly Negro city by 1976. (One of the men from McDonnell-Douglas figured out that this will happen on July 4, 1976 at 8 A.M.) Presently our population is 89% white and 11% Negro. This would mean that in a fully integrated society a Negro should spend 11% of his time outside of his family with other Negroes and 89% of his time with whites. Conversely, whites should spend 89% of their time with other whites and 11% of their time with Negroes. This would be the healthiest kind of arrangement and would bring about new feelings toward the other race, a change of attitudes and a new set of values.

In order to implement the first approach of moving city residents to the suburbs, three programs are under consideration. The first bears on increasing harmony between the races. It is suggested here that a program be inaugurated to provide human-relations training on a mass basis through the use of the T-Group Method. Under this system we would bring together persons in groups of about fifteen divided between whites and Negroes. Under the direction of a trainer they would take part in a session of sensitivity training, preferably along the lines of a marathon session. In this case they would begin one evening, say a Friday, and go straight through the night and following day and evening. This method could be used by or promoted through church groups and other private social agencies who could be counted on to deliver participants in this kind of training. Before any moves can be made by central-city residents, mainly Negroes, into the suburbs, there would have to be this change in values and attitudes.

A second program facilitating the move of city residents into the suburbs would be the creation of a Metropolitan Housing Corporation. This would be designed to buy and acquire real estate outside of the central city boundaries, rehabilitate properties, prepare the receiving communities for these people and prepare those moving for their new environment. As we see it, the corporation would have a financial base of $3-4 million dollars funded by the Office of Economic Opportunity, the Department of Housing and Urban Development, private foundations, and labor unions. In an area the size of St. Louis, the corporation would be able to purchase suburban homes that have a direct bearing on job opportunities. Houses could be bought, rehabilitated, and sold; zoning restrictions could be fought and so on. The corporation would operate on the theory that it would move only one person of color into any particular block. And while it would not actively work against other Negroes moving into the same block, it would not lend its resources to such persons. In other words, if it had monies with which to purchase property or to loan to a Negro family, it would do so for only one family. It would not repeat the process on the same block lest new ghettoes spring up in the suburbs. It is my feeling that every standard metropolitan statistical area in the United States ought to have a program such as this in its central city. Wherever, as is the case in St.

Louis, the mayor's authority ends at the city's boundaries, there has to be a mechanism, metropolitan in scope, to deal with problems affecting the entire area.

A third program dealing with the move to the suburbs involves transportation. Subsidized bus transportation to outlying areas of employment is essential if the disproportionate unemployment of the inner city is to be corrected. Coupled with the two programs just mentioned, this would go a long way towards integrating the entire metropolitan area and reducing the disparities that exist between the central city and the suburbs.

The second main approach towards reducing these disparities is attracting higher socioeconomic groups into the central city. Since 1950, 250,000 middle-income whites have left the central city and now reside elsewhere in the standard metropolitan statistical area (SMSA). Most of these people live in St. Louis County. However, there are things we can do to attract these people back into the central city. One method is the educational park. The City of Pittsburgh has successfully tried this and is in the process of building some five such parks in the central city. Another is the construction of a major attraction such as a huge amusement center or some large state office building, something that would attract people and draw them into the central city. If, for example, the St. Louis Gateway Arch were located in the Yeatman area, one of the core ghetto areas of St. Louis, the area would then of necessity be a better place in which to live.

A third main approach towards reducing disparities is upgrading the central city itself. A prerequisite for such an approach, however, is citizen involvement. Resident planning must be a key ingredient in the entire process. And the use of simulation devices such as "Trade-Off," a game created in St. Louis, can be a valuable help. A little bit about this game might be in order since it was created in connection with preliminary discussions about the St. Louis Model City Program.

In its "indoor setting" the game is played on a board divided into street blocks, each of which has a flag describing what is in the block. For example, one block may have twenty units of housing that can be rehabilitated and twenty that cannot. Another block may have twenty vacant dwelling units. One flag may be for a one-hundred-year-old school with a very poor pupil-teacher ratio, another for a park that is not well lit and that is the scene of muggings and rapes, and another for a water tower in the neighborhood. (By the way, we are in the process of manufacturing this game but it is not for sale yet.)

The game is played by teams who remove the flags and replace them with styrofoam blocks which represent modifications such as rehabilitated or public housing, 221d3, or a community school. Someone might say, "We want a school here." "What kind of school?" "One which will attract people from outside the neighborhood and run adult training classes in the evening." They may ask for a health or recreational facility or to take down a water tower.

The game is played for about an hour, and whatever the players do is given a dollar value for which a total is added at the end. At the same time, they are asked to place a point value on what they do. The base is a unit of rehabilitated housing which is worth ten points. On a comparative basis a school may be worth 1,000 points, a recreational facility 500, and a health facility 250. Points are accumulated as dollars are spent. After the neighborhood is built, perhaps $3,800,000 has been spent on the neighborhood and 1,850 points have been accumulated. But when the team is told that it has only $2,000,000 to spend, the players must reduce spending while trying to maintain as high a point total as possible. By this process of "trading-off" desired improvements and costs, people at the neighborhood level learn priority-setting and decision-making with respect to their own neighborhood. Thus the name "Trade-Off."

Other measures intended to upgrade the central city would include replacing businesses like Scruggs with other new and vibrant businesses, building new office buildings, improving and increasing social programs in blighted areas and attracting new industry.

A fourth and final approach towards reducing disparities between the suburbs and central city is to decelerate the poverty buildup. This calls for the implementation of such programs as birth control and the deceleration of inmigration of the rural poor by improving agricultural programs in surrounding rural areas.

The Model Cities legislation calls for the coordination of federal, state, city, public and private agencies, and for what it terms a "total attack" on the causes of poverty. In all of this it is imperative that we give serious attention to citizen participation. The target neighborhoods must have something like information-sharing centers where residents may go to exchange ideas, make plans and in general let their voices be heard. In St. Louis, somewhat belatedly perhaps, we extended this principle to the final selection of the target neighborhood by inviting groups to attend a public hearing on the subject.

Whatever the form of involvement, the whole planning process of the Model Cities Program must be committed to total citizen involvement. We do not operate on any ratio or percentage system. Wherever there is action and decision making, the neighborhood people must be in a position where they can be making these decisions.

SAMUEL DARDICK

Don Bourgeois mentioned two aspects of the Federal Model Cities Program. One is maximum citizen participation and the other is coordinating the activities of various operating agencies and institutions in order to achieve the goal of eliminating problems in the inner city. I am going to focus on these two ideas in terms of the St. Louis Model City proposal.

Two types of planning activities will be underway at the same time. We call one the central-staff planning process and the other the subcity planning process. I will start by explaining the former. In central-staff planning, those principally responsible for the St. Louis Model City Program are the mayor and the Board of Aldermen. Both the federal and the St. Louis programs emphasize the importance of proposals designed for a target area being politically responsive. Thus, these people will make the most important decisions in the course of both planning and operational activities.

Directly responsible to the mayor are the executive and deputy directors of the Model City Agency. Advising them will be a steering committee of representatives from the metropolitan area and principally from the city of St. Louis. Most of the commissioners will be lay citizens appointed by the mayor, but representatives of other policy-making governmental units will also be appointed. As in many cities, the St. Louis school board has the power to make policy and carry out programs relevant to education in the City. The police department has separate powers given by the state to carry out its activities although its budget comes from the city of St. Louis. Representatives from each of these agencies will be members of the steering committee. The committee reviews the various planning proposals which are submitted, but most importantly, they are to determine whether and how their own policies can be adapted to the goals and programs of the Model City Agency.

The St. Louis Model City Agency will be a planning and coordinating agency rather than an operating agency. All the other agencies in the city will continue to carry on programs. Of course, part of the planning program, particularly the use of systems analysis, will assist planners in finding out which agencies are most suited to carry out specific problem solving programs.

The staff responsible to the director will include at the top two chief planners and a systems analyst. Their principal roles are the coordination of planning activities and the designing of work programs for the central staff operation as well as for the subcity teams. The systems analyst will insure that proposals submitted are measurable in terms of achieving various objectives of the program such as reducing the crime rate and, even more important, that they meet the single criterion which Don Bourgeois has already mentioned. The chief planners are in charge of coordinating all planning activities.

Directly responsible to them are a number of professionals, loaned from various state, local, and metropolitan agencies which operate in the target area. We divide these staff members into subsystem planning teams. There are eleven subsystem teams, each subsystem representing a problem area.

In addition to staff, a number of others will be involved in the planning process at the central staff level. Each of the subsystems will have an advisory committee made up of representatives from various institutions and agencies whose field of interest relates to a problem area. For example, in the area of education, the Board of Education, the Archdiocese, the Lutheran Church School Board, the Human Development Corporation (C.A.P. agency) and others will provide representatives to assist in designing the particular component.

what pur does the c. have?

Membership on the central staff and on advisory committees will be determined by the three areas shown on the matrix. They will be (1) city, metropolitan, local and private agencies and institutions: (2) state agencies: and (3) federal agencies such as representatives from FHA. The output from the central staff will be a complete plan for each component, designed by representatives of agencies who are familiar with the ongoing programs and who will know what the plan will mean in terms of their own future operations in the target area.

Two other important groups are also represented, namely residents from both the city at large and from the target area. These people will be in active dialogue with the various professionals who represent agencies. A member of the Board of Aldermen will also be on each committee to insure communication and dialogue with the legislators who determine final policy.

The federal government and the St. Louis MCA view planning as an incremental process. In the first twelve months a program package or comprehensive plan is prepared; then as programs are put into operation a continuing evaluation or monitoring period follows to insure that objectives are being achieved. If objectives are not being achieved, necessary changes will be made, e.g. modifying of some programs, phasing out others and adding new ones. The systems analyst and professional planners will continue to see whether the program is making any mark on the problems with which it is meant to deal.

During the twelve-month planning process which will begin after federal funding, the central staff and the subcity teams will carry out similar planning activities, the former in operations related to the entire target area, bringing together the various agency representatives that I mentioned, and the latter bringing together the citizens in the target area to design neighborhood plans. Of course, this will involve conflict between the planning proposals developed by the citizens and those developed by agency personnel, which is why the game of "Trade-Off" has been developed. It becomes an essential part of the entire planning process.

The central staff and subcity teams carry out the following planning process. Initially there is a period of reconnaissance. The federal program requires that no extensive research will be undertaken as part of the Model Cities effort. Surveys should be minimal, particularly in the area of physical problems. Certain surveys and studies can be undertaken to gather social data, but these should also be minimal and principally designed to include residents actually taught to use research techniques. Basically, the reconnaissance includes gathering existing data in order to provide a complete understanding of the problems and needs of the target area. The reconnaissance by central staff involves gathering information about the total city and the services performed within the target area. This information is passed on to other staff members and to the residents and planners in the field.

The subcity team is a group made up of planners loaned to the resident organizations within the neighborhood, as Don Bourgeois explained, the various agencies operating in the neighborhood such as settlement houses, development corporations, and so forth as well as the residents themselves. The subcity team also carries out a reconnaissance and passes on to the central staff specific information about the neighborhood. In addition, certain studies are undertaken by the subcity team designed to gather information about the neighborhood and involve people living there in various research efforts.

The second step of the planning process is the design of alternate solutions, and the last stage is when a plan is designed, which we call "optimum mix." The plan is a mix of the various programs to be fielded in the operation stage of the Model Cities program. To achieve optimum mix the exact expenditures for each program are determined, and through the use of systems analysis, dialogue, and compromise, a plan is produced which will have the greatest impact on an area's problems.

B. ANN KLEINDIENST

So far you have heard a rather detailed presentation of the complex planning and administrative structure of the St. Louis Model Cities program. Had you the leisure to examine it more fully, I believe you would gain an even better appreciation of the system of checks and balances which is built into this structure. It is magnificent, but rather than talk about it, I want to talk about what I have been doing as a subcity planner and share some of my experiences with you.

I cannot pretend to come to you as an expert. Six months ago, I was a graduate student of sociology, sitting in seminars on the problems of the urban ghetto and the like, at a high, rarified level of theoretical abstraction. Seeking a subject for dissertation research, I approached Sam Dardick with the idea of studying the decision-making process in the St. Louis Model City program. He approved, and invited me to join the staff as a subcity planner. I had anticipated a great deal of resistance to my wanting to come in and snoop around and was caught completely off balance. The same afternoon I was introduced to the neighborhood where I have been working ever since. As a social scientist, I am one of an informal subcity team which also includes an architect, a real-estate economist, and a community organizer, as has already been explained.

By any standard, this is the most depressed neighborhood in St. Louis. Almost no progress has been made there in memorable history. It is marked by an almost total lack of organization; there is not even a PTA. Fortunately, for a few months prior to our appearance there, around January 1, a citizen organization had been forming in the neighborhood, so we were not faced with the task of building one from scratch. Mac (Shephard) will tell you more about that organization. We spent some time searching for other groups or organizations which we were not able to find, but we could sit down and talk with members of this organization. At that time, they were largely concerned with the condition of the housing in the neighborhood.

One of the nicest things about working with the Model City Agency in St. Louis is that neither Don (Bourgeois) nor Sam (Dardick) are willing to wait for the complex planning to be complete or until the implementation money comes in 1968, if it does. The Model Cities schedule calls for programs to begin in 1969, but they both were very anxious to do anything possible, *now,* in the target neighborhoods. Both recognize what can only be described as a crisis situation in the neighborhood in which I have been working. Problems in housing, crime, education, health – all have reached crisis proportions.

We were not asked to go to the citizens with a little planning checklist and little committees to make big plans for two years from now. We were given some assistance. In late January, we were notified of a Housing and Urban Development, low-income housing demonstration program and set out to help the citizen organization present a proposal to HUD for money to rehabilitate housing in their neighborhood. A fancy term for what I have been doing is advocacy planning, which involves joining a citizen group in their often long and heated discussions and arguments. My principal role was taking notes because, when I began, I was totally ignorant of the operation of social service agencies in St. Louis, of this neighborhood's needs, and of urban planning. I began listening to the citizens' plan which sounded like a good one. We put it together; I helped write it into a proposal which we presented to Washington and which is now under consideration.

We have worked with this citizen group on several projects, which has gone a long way in gaining us some "acceptance" in the neighborhood. I cannot pretend that I use special skills and techniques for "gaining acceptance." There was no real problem here; I accepted them and they accepted me, so I cannot present you with a nice model for building citizen participation and the like. We sat down and talked. When they came up with a plan, in my ignorance I was able to say, "Gee, that is a great plan." It might take me three days of investigating to discover that it had never been done before and was probably quite unfeasible, but in some cases this turned out to be a slight advantage.

Since we do not have our money yet, we have not started the formal planning about which Sam and Don spoke or have we played "Trade-Off." However, at this point, I can tell you what I hope to do as a subcity planner for Model Cities. I strongly believe that planning has an enormous impact upon the people doing it; if citizens are involved in planning, then the planning process has an impact on their lives. You might say that it will be educational for them, and if you are open-minded, you might say that it will be educational for me, but in most cases, it ends when the plan is completed and all the professionals leave the neighborhood.

Some of what was said here earlier strongly reflects what I feel about the planning process. As is already beginning to happen in the Yeatman neighborhood of St. Louis, where I have been working, the planning process is a means by which a group of neighbors can begin learning to work the community system. Sometimes that involves threats of various sorts and sometimes it involves going through the normal due process and attending Board of Aldermen meetings. I think the planning process would be a failure if it did not involve things like this.

Mr. Shephard is the chairman of the board of a citizens' organization that, without much help from me, progressed to the point where they now attend Board of Aldermen meetings at which important decisions are being made. When there was a struggle in St. Louis about the location of the target area, this group brought two busloads that quite overwhelmed the hearing. They did this on their own, and, if Sam, Don, and I have anything to say about it, they will come out of the Model Cities planning process in precisely the sort of position that has been suggested. Communication will be established with a larger community and with other neighborhoods in the city: it will no longer be necessary to send planners down there as interpreters between the ghetto and City Hall.

I see my role in large part as bringing citizen planners into direct dialogue and confrontation with agency people and with the central staff people to whom Sam referred. The citizens would very much like to be a part of that, and I do not want to act as an insulator between them and the place where the decisions are usually made. In short, I am confident that citizens will play an important part in the decision-making of this program. If they do not, I will write a dissertation about it and publish it for all to see.

MACLER SHEPARD

I am not a member of the Model Cities staff but am one caught in the community the others have been discussing. Such a community is usually pressured into organizing. In 1948 the people in this area were forced to move for an urban renewal program. They were afraid to talk about urban renewal because the small owner was usually the one who lost. He had to sell his house for whatever the power structure offered, which was a small amount since they only wanted the land.

Urban renewal scares us because we always lose when they start swapping houses so when Model Cities came up with the idea of swapping and "Trade-Off," we began to go down in busloads. When a private owner went down on his own, he was told what he had to do in order to meet the minimum housing code. These laws were always enforced for private owners but not for the real-estate man or the absentee landlord of the place next door. An individual's property would lose its value because of the next-door real estate man. We fought individually for a long time but saw that we were going to lose the battle to another urban renewal project. If we asked the power structure what was going to happen in our area their answer was not to worry since there were not any plans yet. We went over the situation again and again but could not get insurance because we were too big a risk. FHA has a lot of excuses.

Then the businessmen start moving out, and we are easy prey for everyone that comes along. The businessmen who stay charge much higher prices than in other areas saying they have to pay more for insurance. Things that used to cost 90c sell for $1.50 or $2.00.

Some people are able to leave the area after earning money, probably on a job such as a large project which pays over $2.00 an hour. After being laid off six months later, a man is back again, and his large family has to stay in three rooms.

We found ourselves with absentee landlords, absentee representatives, absentee school teachers, and others coming in for eight hours a day to tell us what was good for us. We decided that the only way to get help was to help ourselves, and we became an organization called Nineteenth Ward Citizens Improvement Organization. The political power got scared at first; they did not know whether we were Republican or Democrat. Then, they decided that we were only a small group and that there was no need to worry about us.

Most cities receive money through a bond issue. When we asked our representative about our area, he told us that they had plans but no money. It was promises like these that kept us from organizing before 1948. Everyone kept telling us not to worry, just be quiet, and the government or somebody else will get us out. We thought the War on Poverty would be the way out. But outsiders rather than people in the community were hired. School teachers and others quit their jobs to help us in the community. The only staff working in the community were volunteers. It is rather difficult to ask someone to volunteer to tell his neighbor that the War on Poverty is good for them when he is not getting paid. This is the sort of thing that goes on in what is called the Negro ghetto.

The government tells us they can not put money in an area unless it is integrated. So, we decide to do what others do when they hire one colored person to show that they are integrated. We found a minister in our area who happened to be white. Once this type of thing gets started, the power structure starts to fight back.

The average person from an area such as ours will probably move out if he can. He does not come back to the area to help because he thinks that if he could fight his way out, others can do the same. But it is not that way, and this is the sort of thing that causes us to be skeptical of outsiders who come in to help us.

We questioned a lot of things about Model Cities. We wanted to find out who would actually be making the decisions. Since the mayor would handle the Model Cities program, we saw this as a way of getting to the top. Instead of going to our Alderman, we can go directly to the top man who can talk directly to the mayor. We attached ourselves to the Model Cities program because we would have access to the expertise we needed. In many cases we do not know how to solve our problems, but we do know what the problems are and what we want. We do not want outsiders to do the work and hand us the finished product. We want to become a part of the process.

One of the things we need most is housing. We want people in our area to be involved in rehabilitation which may mean nothing more than making mortar or laying bricks. We want to be sure that whenever such things start in our area, people from the area will be employed. If we do not like what is being built or how it is being built, we can catch it before it gets too far. We definitely do not want anyone making any more decisions for the community behind closed doors.

When it started open hearings, Model Cities seemed to be what we needed. Many people who have lived in our area for thirty-five years did not know that they had the right to attend open hearings. Since we were organized, we decided to attend and let them tell us if we were not supposed to be there. Whenever we find something going on which concerns the city of St. Louis, we think we should be involved. By attending these meetings in busloads, we let it be known that we want to play our part and that we are not satisfied to have everything handed down from the top. Even if we have to take it that way later, we definitely want them to know that we do not want it that way.

We discovered that a citizen organization could not do the job we wanted to do because money is not loaned to a city improvement organization. Therefore, we have become a chartered non-profit organization. To simply shout without having a solution was not the answer.

34

A Look at Community Problems

Community Development – Some Considerations

SOL TAX

I will start by reading some excerpts from a very interesting paper which is exceedingly relevant to the topic of our discussion.

The title of the paper is "Ecological and Political Perspectives on Community Development;" it is by a sociological ecologist, Paul H. Ray, an assistant professor at Michigan State University.

Ecology is simply defined as looking at political, social, economic, geographic, and other factors involved in the interrelations between people in a given situation. Any factor touched upon will affect all others and thus the result is circular. From this concept of ecology, Ray derives his understanding of what it means to change a community, and although he was primarily concerned with cities of about 100,000, what he says is easily translatable to a very large city like Chicago.

We started with the proposition that *because* all communities are crucial for sustenance of their members he who wants to change the community may actually *threaten* sustenance relations. And only fools talk of change, and being *fundamental* social change, and then do not mean altering fundamental ways of getting a living. If you *are* proposing to alter the sustenance base of a community, then realize that this alters a relatively comfortable status quo that the *majority* depends on. Even the inconveniences, or a slow downward slide, have a familiarity that a risky future darkens. Let us suppose, however, that even the masses can see beyond the ends of their noses – you still usually have to fight powerful vested interests. Those who are pillars of society and repositories of civic virtues are as often the enemies of change beforehand, as they are the beneficiaries of it afterwards. However laudable is virtually any reform attempt, as in trying to do away with fetid, crumbling slums, the reformer finds that some segment of the community makes a good living from someone else's inconvenience or miseries. Slumlords are often lofty institutions: especially major universities, banks, insurance companies and churches – through intermediaries of course. Interested in New York's air pollution? Just look at Con Ed and the New Jersey refineries. No such pillars of society ever need deal directly with a messy problem, or with the inconvenient reformer: a veto is enhanced by being passed at third or fourth hand. "No one" is then at fault, and those who man the redoubts of obstruction to change can operate thus for years – living comfortably all the while, and appearing elsewhere as benefactors of the community. It is an axiom of ecology that communities are webs of interdependence – and this is a political as well as an economic fact. One reason that a sub-standard situation remains so, is that it is *maintained*. Another is that communities are not any more the focus of American public life: our attention goes to the nation. We live as "limited liability" citizens in a community, not willing to invest very much in public goods, so long as life is not absolutely intolerable. With a low level of commitment to the public sector of a community it is seldom that the social movements can be created to rectify situations, and it is seldom that politicians can draw upon any basis of active citizen support. The community has become a *context* in which we get a living, we can take it for granted we think. So incremental reforms have little support and large reforms look risky. Social change that is only vaguely in the public interest has few interest groups, no constituency, and usually offends vested interests.

What really needs to be done in most cities is a very drastic step, and that is to break the veto power of the business establishment over the decision making that goes on in most middle sized and small cities. What that means is quite simply that businessmen don't have to be in elective office to get what they want. Businessmen want a progressive image in the community, that's good for business. They want clean streets, they want no race riots, but they don't necessarily want welfare, they don't necessarily care about avoiding pollution, and they don't necessarily care about the quality of education unless their particular workers are affected by inferior education. If you are going to make your city grow, you're going to have to make major changes to make it *really* different from other cities. It can't just be one more carbon copy of the 200 other cities of about the same size elsewhere in the country, for that offers no competitive advantage. To promote *real* structural change you are going to have to step on somebody's toes. Are you important enough to get away with it – mere community development specialists? Permit me to doubt it.

The role of the community development peoople *must* be a political role. In the political role of the community development specialist, who wants to plan a change, who wants to break up what somebody sees as a good thing, the first thing to investigate is political leverage. What can you do in the political process to make things any different at all? Let's say you're located as a community development specialist in an university, e.g., an associate professor, perhaps tenure (they can't fire you for saying unpopular things). Whom do you deal with first if you want to change something in that community? What have you to bargain with? What can you give to power figures in return for giving something up? Perhaps he is a slumlord who owns ten blocks of rotting apartment houses. What can you give him in return for giving up this nice profitable investment that doesn't require a lot of upkeep and requires only the misery of about 5,000 people? Are you allied with powerful politicians? Do you have access to the mass media so that you can broadcast ads everyday? (at a cost of only about $500 a minute on television) Where would your funds come from to foot the bill for all that exposure in the mass media?

The ecologist more and more is slipping into a problem of talking about how are the lines of communication organized in the community, because more and more of what people really are using to trade among themselves to survive is trading information, is trading ideas, is trading inventions, so you ask who talks to who, what kind of mass media have you got, what is the structure, how are the lines drawn so various groups can talk to each other in the community? They talk about the lines of communication between parts of the society and they talk about the lines of communication within a community; either way you look at it, the community development specialist is in a rotten position. Most networks are very centralized as in the diagram. All roads lead to Rome, and all roads lead out of Rome. Rome may be the local television station but its message goes just one way. Rome may happen to be the political machine in your city, sitting at the center of the spider web, because that's how it stays alive. Any political group keeps track of who owns who, and where the bodies are buried, and sees to it that all the little strings of communication and back scratching lead back to the center. The first thing the community development specialist has to find out is how far out of the center you are. I guarantee that you are not in the center, or you would be called something else – such as mayor, political boss, or member of the community power structures. So one of the things you can do to describe the way a community is organized, or a whole country is organized is to ask where the communication lines go, and how many people can be reached with a given dollar of effort. The first thing you find is that your communications position is very weak. You can't really get out great quantities of information to convince people to change themselves from any community development stand. And if you are a national figure trying to turn a community development project, the first thing you will discover is that the people who ought to be your best customers – those out in the provinces – *suspect* you as an outsider and won't listen. Perhaps the most critical idea to think about is the notion of political communications networks. Ask yourselves: where are you in it, how many people can you convince, how many people can you even talk to, how much does it cost you to get your message out? If you are out on the edge of a network it costs a fortune to get to the other parts of the network. If you're in the center, it doesn't cost very much at all. Try to move into the center, go where the power is, go where all the networks cross.

I would suggest that the historical, traditional, good-hearted community development is not where the action is. Historical, traditional, community development seems to be largely composed of people who have extremely good intentions and none of the muscle to put change through. They may even have extremely good ideas for changing society. But that doesn't matter in the face of political realities. I would suggest, that is what is wrong with community development from the standpoint of an ecological system to some other way of doing things. You have neither the skills, nor the ideas nor resources to promote change. I suggest that essentially, one of four things has probably been happening in community development (and I am going to put these harshly for a purpose – community development may be worth saving). Either: 1) community development has promoted no significant changes historically, produced no major changes of the fabric of modern communities; or 2) they have taken credit for changes that would have happened anyway; or 3) they have been bought out, coopted by power structures in the community, to be front men for the changes that the power people wanted; or 4) that their goals had been so vague that no matter what happened they would never be accused of failure. The classic example of the last case is in India, where village development teams go in to have a cultural revival: they are going to go in and help the people see how the government really is, by showing plays, they are going to give all sorts of information out, and have mass rallies, and to what end. Perhaps the nice thing about that is that there isn't one thing that you can do to measure how different the village was from the day you walked in. However, in developing areas the program is more straight forward because more severe. Massive doses of new technology and capital can succeed when they are put to the narrow goal of changing some portion of the way the environment works – it usually is the best way to get things going, because you can tell how much dollar value you got for dollars put in. I suggest that it is possible that community development to be fantastically successful will follow a Chinese Communist or Russian model. We can reject this gloomy prospect only if we are confident of the wisdom of the people (who have put themselves in a mess), or if we are confident of our skills of manipulation, or are willing to be political leaders. I would suggest that community development people need to find out that the most important thing to know is how to be a political figure who wants to promote economic ends. And then all the mechanisms we have talked about will do some good.[1]

Though we may not agree with everything Ray says, certainly there is a very strong truth in it.

I have become optimistic about community development because I have seen an extraordinary case in East Pakistan where the situation was as bad as it could possibly be – poverty, overpopulation, and so on, and the villagers were going downhill rapidly, paying 80% interest and losing their

[1]*Social Scientists View Poverty as a Social Problem*, **Proceedings of the Fifth National Community Development Seminar (Michigan State University, September 11-14, 1966), pp. 95-97, 100-103.**

land continually to the rich moneylenders in these little villages.

After U. S. aid programs and everything else had failed in this Moslem area, a local leader with charismatic qualities, Achter Hameed Kahn, who is a Moslem of course, using the Koran and every possible technique, went out as a Ghandi-like figure, walking through the villages and getting the people's confidence. However, from past failures he saw that what was necessary was to get to the power structure for the needed resources and money. He also saw that unless the money was somehow tied in at the grass-roots level, no amount could do any good whatsoever. He developed an extraordinary project called the Comilla Project in which he was able to tie together money power with the local grass-roots villagers.

He did this through developing a set of village cooperatives, and in each village, the cooperatives developed a new leadership. For obvious reasons, he started with a credit coop. As soon as someone joined, he could borrow up to six times the amount of money that he had invested. This borrowing and lending was done through local committees and was tied to an educational program. Immediately, the villagers were freed of the moneylenders because they could borrow from the coop at 6% interest instead of the 80% interest. By borrowing that money, they could get a start on improvements such as irrigation and were much better off almost at once. It was as if miracles happened. This spread from village to village and coop to coop. Butcher's coops, carpenter's coops, ricksha coops, and every kind of coop imaginable, aside from the village agricultural coops were developed. Each of the coops involved new leadership for the coop members, and the old leadership, as good or bad as it may have been, was left stranded.

No one coop could have done it alone. They formed a federation which helps to support each of the coops. As a result of developing this system, they could also get money from American sources, such as the Ford Foundation, and from Pakistan sources because as it turned out, all the money is repaid immediately. But you do not even need the foundations or the government because banks will lend money at a sure risk. This case is a remarkable success. In only seven years, these people have an entirely new leadership, a new life, and a new outlook.

Obviously the people who were involved were apprehensive about the reaction from the power structure, but because the villagers had gotten sufficient power fast enough to be able to be important politically, anybody who would try to stop this coop movement once it had spread so far would have a lot of trouble. I must confess that Achter Hameed Kahn was also a friend of the president of Pakistan; if he had not had that support, perhaps he would not have been allowed to start hitting the status quo. I doubt that now, even without that friendship, it could be easily stopped.

At any rate, economic factors were changed by getting outside, once large-scale support that was tied to the grass-roots organization. Schools came together once a week, and Achter Hameed Kahn insisted that the villagers make their own decisions. Even though this is a very Moslem country, he even got the women to work and developed women's programs. As soon as he said, "Here is your chance, do you want to do it?," they all seized the opportunity. It is hard to tell how much of it was him and how much was the system. Though it is verry difficult to separate out the accidents of the case, it does prove that it can happen given the right circumstances. However, in order for it to happen, it has to be dealt with politically. You have to get close to the center of some power structure that is important for your purposes in order to operate at all. That will not only help in getting the money, but it also will provide the support necessary to do the difficult things that have to be done against the presumed interests of some people. It will get you the help of whatever government agencies are involved. In short, it gives you the strength.

I would say that if you are going to get anywhere in the city of Chicago and the neighborhoods of this city, you will have to do something on a scale comparable to the one I have described for East Pakistan. As community leaders you can unite by accepting some notion of leadership among yourselves that will make this possible. Whether you do it or not is up to you.

Providing for Community Health

ROBERT SNYDER

There is a climate of change all around us, and I see this in the area of health as well as education. However, in these and other areas of concern, in order for there to be action, community leaders must agree on what should be done before they can expect to convince either the local neighborhood community or the larger central political power structure. Over a long period of time, leaders have reached consensus on some issues as to what should be done, and have recognized that the demands for change are irreversible.

Powerful social forces are at work which necessitate change. Thus, the opportunity to update social changes, and health care in particular, can be brought into line with the technical medical advances of the past several decades. This is a formidable task; it can be disheartening, depressing, and even frightening in view of the immensity of the problem, which sometimes seems insoluble. On the other hand, one can view these problems as exciting and challenging in terms of present opportunities to be innovative and creative, and to find an ally in large federal funds that were not previously available.

Fortunately, medical institutions in the country, and particularly in Chicago, view this as an exciting and challenging matter. Medical centers that traditionally restricted themselves to their own narrow commitments, primarily that of teaching, are turning to an interest in the community and accepting responsibility for taking inventory of the medical assets in their segment of the community. Along with local public health people, they are working out a plan that hopefully will meet the local needs which are so apparent in poverty areas of the city. A most striking example of this cooperation, coordination, and partnership are the Neighborhood Health Centers that, in their demonstration period, are being funded by the Office of Economic Opportunity. They are organized and directed by the local Board of Health and administered, staffed, and operated by the many private teaching hospitals and medical centers.

In the last two or three years much has been written about the need for cooperation in all areas. For example, as the result of a four-year task force, the National Commission on Community Health Services made readily available a report entitled *Health as a Community Affair*. There is also the AMA's Millis report on the graduate education of physicians, and Lowell Coggeshall, of the University of Chicago, has put out a report on changes in medical education. All these reports stress the need for developing a system whereby all citizens can obtain equal access to medical care. They also stress the need for turning our attention to changes in medical curricula so that physicians will receive the comprehensive training they will need in order to render effective, personal, high-quality care in the new centers that will have to be created. Since the Neighborhood Health Centers have also effectively utilized these concepts of comprehensive care, this is quite an exciting development from the standpoint of providing much needed medical care.

Good ideas often arise simultaneously around the country, and this idea of centers offering comprehensive care is not unique to Chicago. It had been similarly developed and implemented in Boston, Denver and Los Angeles, but its origin in Chicago is quite local. In the summer of 1965, the Board of Health commissioned Dr. Mark Leper, who was then the chairman of the Department of Preventive Medicine at the University of Illinois, and Dr. Joyce Lashoff, who was director of the Preventive Medicine Section at St. Luke's Presbyterian Hospital, to do a survey of Chicago's medical needs and make some recommendations. In their report, they outline the appalling deficiencies in medical care available to the poverty areas of the city in relation to the affluent areas. They delineate and describe twenty-four poverty areas in Chicago and prove that the needs in these areas are very great indeed. In the poverty areas, there was a 75% greater infant mortality and a 40% greater adjusted overall mortality. There were twice as many physicians in affluent areas as in poverty areas, and many other striking differences.

On the basis of their very critical study, they made two main recommendations. First, that an office of medical care be set up, directed and administered by the Board of Health, which would act as a liaison office between participating medical institutions and the federal program that would fund them. This was organized in March of 1966, and Dr. David Greeley was appointed as its director. The second recommendation was that a neighborhood health center be planned for each poverty area which would be directed and supervised by the large teaching hospitals and medical centers in the community in order to maintain high quality care. These neighborhood centers would be located in the poverty area, easily accessible, open during hours convenient to the patient, and in all ways be patient-oriented rather than doctor-centered as medical care so often is.

Several health centers, funded by the Office of Economic Opportunity, have been set up in Chicago. Dr. Herbert Abrams is the Project Director of the Mount Sinai neighborhood health center, and Dr. Joyce Lashoff is the director of one under the direction of the Presbyterian-St. Luke Hospital. Both the medical and dental schools of Northwestern University in cooperation with Children's Memorial, which already have a federal program under the Children's Bureau, are cooperating in organizing a neighborhood health center on the Near North Side, and Michael Reese Hospital is preparing one for the South Side. The University of Chicago is participating in one of Children's Bureau programs and other medical centers are following suit. Thus, at the medical center level there is a consensus of opinion that this is a good program which can result in a significant improvement in the deficient medical care currently available in poverty areas. The geographical area for each center includes about 20,000 to

25,000 people who can be served in a comprehensive and personal fashion. A center of this many people can be patient-oriented; each family's problems can be completely know to the teams of physicans, social workers, nurses, and community representatives who serve as nurse's aides. Whenever any member of the family comes to the center someone who knows that particular family well can treat and serve them. To a large extent, the nurses and the community aides will work outside the health center, extending services into the home and following through after visits to the center, as well as educating those not familiar with medical care about how to obtain it.

The health center will provide essentially what is now available in any good private group practice. Outpatient services, prenatal and postnatal care, pediatrics, internal medicine, geriatrics, dental care, etc., all will be provided in the same setting. When more complex laboratory work is necessary, patients will be sent to the laboratory of the sponsoring facility and transportation will be provided when needed. When hospitalization is necessary, insofar as possible, patients will be taken into the hospital of the sponsoring institution. Mt. Sinai and Presbyterian-St. Luke's hospitals are already receiving patients, and for Northwestern it will be Passavant and Wesley.

These programs will include in-training for community aides so that insofar as possible members of the residential community will be able to staff the center in the nonprofessional areas. There are also funds in the budget for training community people in secretarial work, and when they become proficient, they will be encouraged to seek jobs elsewhere. Thus, this is an effort directed toward correcting aspects of poverty in addition to health. As I mentioned, this program has caught the imagination of the traditionally conservative medical centers that are quite excited about these efforts which they feel will result in a significant advance in medical care.

OEO is extremely concerned that the community served be well-represented, and neighborhood advisory councils are activated long before the Health Center is in operation. Every effort has been made to achieve good community representation though admittedly we need more information on how to do this well. Officers are elected, and the OEO guideline quite specifically outlines their authority. One area of difficulty has come about through the OEO guideline which states that the Advisory Council shall have an analogous responsibility to lay Board of Trustees of the hospital. Since this refers to hospitals with already existing pay scales, personnel policies, etc., some difficulties have arisen. In one case, the Advisory Council wanted to set different pay scales which would have upset the entire salary range. These problems must be settled since they cannot be allowed to delay the great need for medical care.

To briefly mention some other health care efforts in Chicago, the Children's Bureau programs, which preceded the neighborhood health centers, though not as comprehensive, do meet a great need. These are of two main types. One is directed toward high risk pregnant mothers, which are primarily the young unwed mothers identified in the Infant Welfare stations. These and other pregnant women with complications are given special prenatal and postnatal care in an attempt to meet the greater incidence of difficulties they encounter. This program has been quite effective and is continuing. The second is a preschool and youth program which supplements the Board of Health efforts in prevention and adds actual treatment facilities for preschool children. It is this program that is in operation at the University of Chicago. The Board of Health also has $5,000,000 of bond-issue money, which was passed in 1966 for health centers. At present, these are not specifically worked out, but the hope is that they as well will be related to the large medical centers so they will be able to provide the same quality of care as is available in the neighborhood health centers.

An important problem that arises in almost every issue is the relationship of the community to the leadership. A lot of time must be devoted to this problem, and compromises will be necessary, rather than either group being asked to move all the way toward the other's position.

ROBERT KAHN

Although I feel a bit uncomfortable by the enormity of the topic, I hope that in these few minutes I can give you a sense of some of the issues and current directions in the field of mental health which will contribute to your discussion.

During the past ten or fifteen years there has been much ferment and excitement in the field, with the beginnings of a radical change in values and perspectives. This has entailed both a recognition of the inadequacy of existing patterns of care and the development of new conceptions of goals and practice. These changes have come about because of many factors, including the force of legislation such as Medicare and the Community Mental Health Centers Act as well as the more strictly professional reasons of research and clinical experience.

One of the most basic changes is in the approach to establishing services. Typically, the professionals have created mental health services that met their own needs for some special kinds of training or favored forms of treatment. The kinds of services thus established were limited both in the numbers and kinds of persons served, largely biased toward the young, white, and better educated. In our new thinking, instead of starting with the professionals' needs, we now ask first what does the community need and what kinds of programs must be developed to meet these needs.

This reversal of the basis for organizing services may sound rather elementary, but it has many important implications. For example, it now compels the professionals to deal with types of persons and problems that were previously ignored because of either the lack of interest or pessimistic expectations. The confrontation with such patients has presented a challenge requiring new methods of dealing with mental health problems.

What is perhaps even more significant are the changes in our notions of what is meant by providing services and the role of mental health professionals and institutions. Traditionally, we have tended to overemphasize the distinction between mental health and illness, with mental illness requiring treatment by professionals in special types of institutional settings, most often a hospital. Increasingly, we realize that the distinction between mental health and illness is not a simple medical question, but is related to complex social factors as well. It may not even be the doctor who is always the best person to determine whether or not a person requires treatment. Rather than evaluation by the standard psychiatric diagnostic system it may be more important to determine whether or not a person is "making it" using the community's definition of adaptation.

With the scarcity of facilities and trained personnel, it would be impossible to meet the mental health needs of all if programs were established in terms of the medical model system only. If one looks at the community, however, not as the cause of mental illness but as a therapeutic resource for dealing with adaptation problems, we can begin to think of interesting possibilities for program development.

One type of activity which has been used in hospital psychiatric wards in recent years is known as the "therapeutic community." By meetings and frank discussion between staff and patients it is hoped to overcome the more traditional role of the patient in which he is the passive recipient of treatment. Creating an artificial community in the hospital, however, can never be as meaningful for the patient as his real community. It can even create a problem of making the patient reluctant to leave the hospital environment, as he will have to break off relationships that are helpful to him.

In order to get the desirable aspects of the therapeutic community without the negative ones, what would happen if a similar program were based in the community itself rather than in the hospital. For example, in the Woodlawn Mental Health Center, part of the University of Chicago Department of Psychiatry, a social club has been formed which meets in church basements and to which patients are referred both before and after their hospitalization. In this setting it will hopefully be found that persons who might previously have been sent to a hospital are now maintained in the community. If a patient needs medication the physician can go directly to the social club to administer it, without requiring the patient to go to a hospital. These social clubs can take care of many more people, and at much less cost than would be possible if it were necessary for each patient to go through the complexities of admission to a hospital unit. The persons who will play key roles in this system will be nonprofessional mental health workers who actually live in the communities being served. The use of nonprofessionals is an important development in new mental health programs. It is not, however, just a question of their being a substitute for the scarce professional, but rather a recognition that they may be even more effective than the professionals in certain kinds of situations or with some patients. As these community based programs develop there will be need for fewer hospitals and institutions.

The difficulties that many programs have had in the past, particularly in working with the poor, is based on the relationship to the community. As with the antipoverty program, we realize that approaching a community as an enlightened do-gooder is not effective. The complaint has often been made that the poor were not using mental health services sufficiently even when made available to them. But to be effective and to be utilized, programs must be developed in collaboration with the community, and perceived by the community as meeting its needs. The community will have its own ideas about priorities and resources.

Another major new direction of the mental health field is the emphasis on prevention. This concern will necessarily lead to involvement with many other aspects of community life. An effective prevention system is importantly related to the quality of prenatal care, the educational system and housing. Breaking down the ghetto structure is as much a mental health measure as it is political or social.

At the University of Chicago, we have been meeting intensively for the last two years in an attempt to develop an extensive mental health program in the communities near the University. We are constantly frustrated by the problem of coordinating the participation of the federal, state, and city governments, the University, and the community. The state says the city should contribute, the city says it's the state's responsibility, and both say you should get a grant from Washington. Those of us in the professional field who are becoming interested, and making commitments to the community, are finding that the administrative problems may often be greater than professional ones. With all these concerns, I am enthusiastic and optimistic about the new ideas, interests and directions in the field of mental health. We are entering what I believe will be the most creative period in our history.

Cooperatives: Possibilities and Forms

HENRY ETZKOWITZ

I will tell you the story of how a completely new type of cooperative has been organized in Bedford-Stuyvesant to meet the needs of poor people in the ghetto. The basic idea of this community cooperative center is to sell goods, including food, gasoline, and pharmaceuticals, at drastically reduced prices, but still with a profit margin, and reinvest this profit in social services for the people in the neighborhood. These social services can include a child-care center, health and mental services, or any others that the cooperative decides upon. Thus, people can help themselves with their own money and do not have to wait for governmental or other programs.

I am a graduate student at the New School for Social Research. Last summer, 1966, I wass teaching at Brooklyn College where I met a fellow teacher, Gerry Schaflander, who had just come there from Harvard. After we had gotten to know each other, he told me his idea of organizing this new type of cooperative. For many years he had been active in reform Democratic politics, in the cooperative movement, and in the civil rights movement. He had seen cooperatives in poor areas which almost always failed, and compared the reasons for their failure to the reasons for the success of cooperatives in middle-class areas. In middle-class areas, people are able to put up money and buy shares to organize a cooperative, and at the end of the year, they receive dividends from the profits. This has worked very well in these areas because the people have sufficient money to begin their own cooperative. However, cooperatives have almost always failed in poor or ghetto areas because people there do not have enough money. There may be enough money to start but usually there is not enough capital to insure success.

Therefore, the first idea was to change the traditional cooperative. Instead of selling shares to people in a poor neighborhood, money would come from outside foundations and well-to-do individuals while people in the ghetto would pay only a nominal price for shares and membership in the cooperative. Since they would not be putting up the money to begin the cooperative, the second major change would be to eliminate individual dividends from the profits. Instead, any profits would be kept within the cooperative and spent on providing expanded social and health services.

This was the idea that Gerry presented to me last summer. At that time, I had been offered a grant to go to Nigeria, where I had taught in the Peace Corps for two years, to write my dissertation on the school system there. I had never gotten involved in any movement for social change in the United States because I had always found flaws in their ideas. But this idea for a new kind of cooperative seemed to be too good for me to leave the country without giving it a try. In the fall I moved to Hunter College while my colleague continued teaching at Brooklyn, and we began thinking about organizing it. We told some of our students about it and began having meetings to organize an integrated cooperative. As white students and teachers, we would join with black people from the ghetto on a fifty-fifty policy-making basis on a board of directors.

We invited students and a few people we knew from Bedford-Stuyvesant to one of the first meetings at a hotel in mid-town Manhattan where we had a bus waiting to take them to the First Baptist Church in Bedford-Stuyvesant for the meeting. We knew that if we told the students that they would be going to Bedford-Stuyvesant many of their parents would not have let them come. By just taking them there, they could see that there was nothing to fear. This was our first meeting in the community, and we explained the whole idea of the cooperative as I am doing now. Our first contact with the First Baptist Church took place a few weeks before when we saw an empty lot next to it, which we thought would be the right place to put up a tent to house the coop. We asked to speak to the Deacon and the Minister and told them about our idea. They were interested and allowed us to use the church's basement for our meetings.

During November and December we held more meetings, more people became involved, and by Christmas we were holding a three-day training session for the people who would be working with us. Those of us who had decided to work for the coop full-time asked the others to commit themselves to work with us, and some of them did. We had been talking about this theoretically for a long time and finally decided it was time to present the idea to the ghetto people of Bedford-Stuyvesant. With the help of a Negro girl from Bedford-Stuyvesant who was attending Brooklyn College, we planned a meeting for January 25.

At the beginning of January 1967, Gerry Schaflander and I had moved into Bedford-Stuyvesant because we knew that we could not have any feel for what it was like to live in the ghetto unless we were living there and fighting the roaches and the rats. We moved into a fourth floor tenement apartment in the heart of the ghetto and motivated our landlord who was a Negro realtor in the area. We interested him in working with us, partly because of a chance for a large commission if he found a building for the coop. We knew we would need a large building for all the activities we were planning, and he found us a 20,000 square foot garage, two stories, 100 feet by 100 feet on each floor.

While we were organizing, the money came from Gerry's and my teaching salaries and some small loans from our students. When the time came to put up the $5,000 for the building, we had to go to outside sources. When Gerry was at Harvard, he had met Charles Merrill, who had left Merrill, Lynch, Pierce, Fenner & Smith, where he made millions, to begin an interracial high school in the Boston area. We asked him to help us through his Foundation. As chairman of the Foundation, they had never turned him down, but this time they did. It seemed that a lot of the money for the Merrill Foundation came from Safeway Stores, and they did not appreciate our idea of drastically cutting the prices on food in the ghetto. In any case, he personally gave us a small sum and suggested other people to see. We went from one to the other and finally raised the $5,000 for the building. We have continued raising money in this way, and though we have been generally bankrupt, we have not been put out of business and now have enough funds to last through June.

When we were ready to hold a meeting in the community, we signed the lease for the building, and from a temporary office in the ghetto, we sent letters of invitation to ministers, leaders of block associations, people from the Youth in Action program in Bedford-Stuyvesant. This meeting was held on January 25 in the basement of the First Baptist Church. Gerry and I presented the idea for the cooperative and asked them to join us in building it. Anna Copeland, a Girl Scout leader in Bedford-Stuyvesant who was working with us, told about the social services which included a child-care center at drastically reduced prices. One of the Negro students who worked with us told how we would help initiate it and, at the end of this summer, leave to return to teaching and our dissertation. He presented our idea of getting people in the community to run the cooperative on a continuing basis. Out of the thirty-five people present, three came forward to join us. One was an itinerant Southern preacher, Reverend Amos Brown; another was a social worker, who was an assistant minister of the First Baptist Church; and the third was Butch Eccleston who was the leader of the Apostles for Truth, the new name for his former gang; at the time, he was a junior bureaucrat in the antipoverty program.

They joined us in forming a temporary board of directors which met to decide our policy. Some argued that people would not buy merchandise unless it had a brand name, but after long discussions, it was finally agreed that if trusted people in the community would test goods without brand names, people would buy them. We discussed the price for the child-care center. Middle-class oriented people wanted it to be fairly high-priced. They argued that people were spending $20 a week for a neighbor to watch their children, and if we were offering beautiful play equipment, teachers to take care of the children, lunch, and snacks, we should at least charge that amount. Others of us wanted to cut the price drastically to only $1.00 a day. We finally decided on $1.75 a day so it would not be charity. We also argued about which children should be included. Most child-care centers in New York City take children from ages two to five, but some of us thought the real problem was that someone was needed to take care of the young children of unwed mothers so they could return to school or get a job. Finally we decided to take children under two and now have children from three months to two years in the center.

After these discussions, we were ready to begin the cooperative center; we had the building and the board of directors. One of the graduate students and a member of Butch Eccelston's gang went to the pool halls and bars in Bedford-Stuyvesant and brought back thirty drop-outs and delinquents, most of whom were from the same gang. They gave the jobs to their friends, and we put them to work renovating, painting, and tiling the building. We found that about one-third of them were working for the first time in their lives; given the chance, they did want jobs. We planned that after they finished renovating the building, they would become the first workers in the supermarket and retail operation.

Our next step was to get the food for the supermarket. We began discussions with Mid-eastern Cooperatives, the regional cooperative marketing and warehouse in the New York, New Jersey, and Pennsylvania area. A committee of us met with the director and told him about our idea of organizing a cooperative. Though he did not think we could be called a cooperative because we were not following the Rochdale principles, since he was a businessman, he seemed interested in moving his merchandise. However, there was no decision to give us food in time for our opening which was planned for February 27, and we were not able to open the supermarket which would have given us the basis for making money to provide social services.

Instead of waiting for a source of food supply, we decided to begin the social service part of the coop center first. On March 1st, we opened the child-care center on the entire first floor, a great open space (10,000 square feet). We ordered toys from F.A.O. Schwartz because we wanted to bring the best upper-class toys to these ghetto children. They are getting good food, resting, reading, and playing. This center is well-organized and still continuing. We started with nine children and now have eighty-five.

We continued negotiations for food with Mid-eastern, and finally their board of directors, in principle, approved the idea of helping us. They set up a committee to look us over and make a recommendation to the Board. A few weeks ago three members of the committee finally came out to see us. One of the committee members was a conservative Republican Negro woman from Harlem, the only Negro member of the board. Her first reaction was that there had been another attempt to organize a cooperative in Bedford-Stuyvesant along traditional lines. They had tried to raise money from the members, and she had voted against their becoming a member of Mid-eastern because they were not able to raise enough money. On the other hand, she would not vote for us because a cooperative must raise money from people in the community and most of ours was coming from outside. Holding to the strict principles of the cooperative movement, as a good businesswoman she was not going to let us in even though we were raising money, meeting payrolls, and so on because we were getting it from the outside.

They were afraid to say yes or no. They did not want a new group which might not be conservative but were afraid of bad publicity if they said no. Though they are still considering us, we no longer count on getting food from the cooperative movement. At one point, we tried to put pressure on them by going to the national leaders of the cooperative movement in Washington. Gerry Voorhees, Charles Dryer, and Mr. Ihlenfelt of Minneapolis were all sympathetic to this way of organizing a cooperative in a poor area. They tried to influence Mid-eastern but we found that they had no real power over them. The power is on the regional level and the decision to admit a new member is made by the regional board.

It did not look as though we will become members of Mid-eastern and so we looked for another source for our food supply. We finally found it last week. We will go directly to canners, who will put up canned foods under the Bed-Sty label which we will begin selling at our planned Grand Opening on July 4. We also found a source of supply for pharmaceuticals. All we need now is $35,000 which we have to raise within the next ten days to buy our first order of food and drugs. Then we can sell goods to people in Bedford-Stuyvesant that, as in other poor areas in New York, are selling at prices that are 6% higher than elsewhere. We will still make a profit which will help run the child care center and the other social services which we will begin.

Even though we were not able to get food, we rented the gas station next door which was going out of business. We found a new independent source of supply for branded gasoline under an "economy" label and are now selling the lowest priced gasoline in New York City. Though we are not making enough profit to completely sustain the whole operation, the basic concept of making money by selling quality nonbranded goods at low prices, with the margin of profit supporting social services, is working. A month ago, we met with the parents of the children in the child care center and told them that the only way to keep the low price in the center was for them to buy gas from the coop gas station and give out gas leaflets.

If we can raise the money, we will have a Grand Carnival and Grand Opening on July 4, and by the end of summer, we hope to find the right man to be executive director. Then we can return to our teaching, and the C.C.C. will be a permanent, self-supporting institution able to provide social services for the people of Bedford-Stuyvesant.

WILLIAM STEWART

We are trying to mount a cooperative movement in Chicago – primarily in low-income areas, but also in certain middle-income areas. There has been a tendency in America to send people and money elsewhere to do what is needed at home. Last year the Cooperative League, through Worldwide Co-op Partners, approached the Hyde Park Cooperative Society with the idea of funding a program to start a cooperative movement in Chicago's low-income areas. The two major areas are both immediately adjacent to Hyde Park, namely Kenwood-Oakland north of 47th Street, and Woodlawn to the south. Since last summer we have been trying to interest local leadership in the cooperative movement and give them an idea of what it can do.

A major question is, "What is a coop?" A coop is just like any other business except that the people who use the coop also own it. There is no profit as such, only savings.

Another question is, "How does it work?" In general, the people have a need that is not being filled, or if it is being filled, it is not being filled to their satisfaction. When they decide to do something about it, they usually begin with study groups. Then they may apply for a charter, or they operate a buying club which is a simplified version of a coop. After the buying club grows, they apply for a charter.

Two of the major problems cooperatives face in low-income areas and in America generally are the American public's overconcern with the idea of competition and the impact of so much advertising. Thus very strong coops are in operation primarily in rural areas and in Canada. In Canada there are so-called "coop centers" with a grocery store, credit union, clothing, furniture, and appliance store, service station, and whatever else members need. Therefore, it is not necessary for the members to go outside the coop for most of their needs.

Though coops run counter to American teachings which stress competition, it would be most unfortunate if too many people were taught the idea of rugged individualism. Even the caveman learned that cooperation on a hunt meant getting the game instead of the game getting you. It seems that in America, we have been rather slow in learning that lesson.

Another question is, "What can coops do?" They can fill many needs from food, clothing, housing, and insurance to funeral services. They can bring dignity because no member has to go hat in hand to others. In low-income areas, coops will contribute to developing leadership and to building the community, because a coop means the ownership of a local community resource. When people tell me there is no money in poor areas such as Kenwood-Oakland and Woodlawn, I tell them that if there were no money, there would not be so many stores because businessmen go where there is a profit to be made.

Several forces thwart the development of cooperatives. The first are the vested interests. In time, any organization can become an opposing force, so some people will try to stop it before it starts. In addition, many religious leaders occupy strong positions and are consulted on many problems. For example, if a member of their church dies, the minister may tell the bereaved family of a mortician that he favors. Frequently the people in ghetto areas overpay for funerals. Sometimes they pay as much as $1,000 to $1,600. This would not be necessary if they joined a memorial society where the maximum would be about $650 or $700.

Many agencies are not free to move. Any time you start tampering with a community's economic resources, you interfere with others who may advertise in your agency's newsletter or paper, or who may be heavy contributors to the agency for which you work. For example, if the A & P has been contributing $500 or $1,000 a year to your agency, and you start a buying club for groceries, on one side you are accepting their money and on the other you are running an operation that is taking away their business. These are the sorts of local organizations you have to fight.

You also have to cope with the lack of social consciousness on the part of the "petty bourgeois set". They may have been born and reared in north Kenwood-Oakland or in Woodlawn and have gotten a job with the Chicago

Board of Education, Cook County Department of Public Aid, or another agency where they earn a decent salary. They move to Chatham, Hyde Park, or South Shore, and the local community is deprived of people who could have done a great deal for the community.

Another deterrent is the mass media. The philosophy there is that if you have something to offer, you will go out and compete, and they do not encourage these people to organize.

The system of the local community is also a deterrent. Many men who used to have good jobs will not respond to a movement that might change their present situation. They spend their time trying to figure out how to get back into their past groove instead of becoming involved in a movement that might provide local business and employment for them. Furthermore, many of these people are suspicious and skeptical of anything new. They wonder why we are offering it to them instead of advertising.

Another problem is that people are highly partial to brand names. In a discussion of the Negro market, the *Food Mart News* has this to say: "To begin with, may we say that the Negro customer is particularly conscious of brand names and high quality products." They also say: "Many factors contribute to Negro food buying preferences, but as in all of his other purchases, what he wants most is the quality image of a quality product. Quality is always put ahead of price since the Negro is determined to enjoy top products whenever he can and whatever the price." With regard to soft drinks they say: "Negroes consume about 41% of the carbonated drinks"; and they tell their members that they will not be able to sell these drinks by the carton because most people in low-income areas are willing to pay a few extra pennies to buy it cold.

A great variety of factors must be taken into consideration in stocking grocery items. The *Food Mart News* includes a chart on the types of foods Negroes purchase in excess of whites: 20% more bleaches, 60% more cereals, 10% more chile and tamales, 91% more corn meal, 49% more flour, 12% more food wraps, 27% more fruit juices, 26% more household cleansers, 60% more household insecticide, 12% more mayonnaise, and 113% more rice. Furthermore, Negro families generally buy more than other families because the Negro family averages 4.4 whereas other families average about 3.6.

Another problem arises from the difference in approach. Many people who can relate to people in these communities on a professional basis cannot relate to them on a human basis. Furthermore, there is too much top-down programming. Intellectual agency personnel develop their own idea for the community, hand it to the people there, and then wonder why they do not respond. One of the reasons is that they have not involved the people. The people do not see the program as meaningful. Though the other way may take longer, it is more likely that once something gets started, it will not collapse as soon as the instigator leaves the community. If you work with the people and program from the bottom up, programs are likely to last, be less dependent on an individual who is likely to leave.

As I indicated earlier, you must be willing to wait. I worked in a large, formal organization for a number of years, and I know that often the tallies rather than the real human result are what count as success. Many programs have a hidden failure to a degree. For example, a person who is moved off Welfare and put in the Manpower Development and Training program is still on public funds. If he is receiving a weekly allowance, he is being paid from the funds of the Division of Unemployment Compensation. Once he is trained, he still earns less than he would have received on welfare, which all reveals a few hidden problems.

Thus we need some organizations which are free to meet the needs of the people. They cannot be conservative but must be willing to go ahead and deal with the people's continuing needs. A client cannot be dropped as soon as he gets a job. Many women in these areas could get jobs if they could arrange for the child care. Because a cooperative nursery would operate on the basis of the profit providing a service to its members instead of on the basis of the profit motive, it could provide child care at a price they could afford. Community organizations could provide the meeting rooms and headquarters for local community groups to begin coop centers, and I say to these organizations, do it because it is a community service rather than waiting for the federal government to give you a grant.

Furthermore, more young people should be involved. Coops provide an excellent consumer education. In many areas young people have family responsibilities and need to learn how to get the most out of the dollar.

We also need to involve former low-income area residents, and I think we need more church involvement. Churches are an excellent place to start cooperative ventures, but one problem is that often they have a transient membership, including people who used to live in the area and only return on Sunday. However, the membership in some churches in these areas is largely composed of local residents. Furthermore, this is an area where you could cross church lines by involving a number of churches that do not have sufficient membership to support such a move on their own. For example, some cooperatives in Chicago are selling furniture to their members at substantial reductions. They are financing through the credit union which means they can get it directly from the factory. You can also have bargaining associations, and I think there is a move now to start housing cooperatives in this area. Churches can provide the necessary nucleus group of which the Antioch Foundation is a very excellent example.

People often ask about the savings from a coop. To give you an idea, these are some of this week's prices at a buying club in the Woodlawn area: center-cut pork chops at 59c a pound; pork steaks at 59c; lamb chops at 89c; beef tenderloin at 79c; sliced and slab bacon at 55c; t-bone steak at 79c; Boston-cut beef roasts at 79c; beef stew at 59c; grade-A fryers at 29½c; neck bones at 13c; pork tenderloin at 65c; grade-A eggs at 49c a dozen. This is just an idea of what a local group can do.

Reaction and Reconsideration

Having considered specific topics in previous Workshop sessions, in the last two sessions, participants focused on a general consideration of courses of action. During these discussions, many of the issues that had been raised previously were reemphasized and restated more explicitly. The approaches considered ranged from the citywide programs to possibilities for coordinated efforts between the city and local communities to independent community action.

Pros and Cons of Citywide and Individual Neighborhood Approaches

A number of participants expressed their doubts that the citywide approach could accomplish all that was being claimed for it and questioned some of its basic assumptions.

It is too late to start integration at the high school level unless something is done at the elementary level. [participant working with young children]

A comprehensive approach is of course what is needed. Education, at whatever level, cannot do it alone. Bussing does not deal with the situation because having to return to the ghetto adds new frustrations to already existing frustrations. We must change the urban structure that produces ghettos and to do that we have to think in terms of the total urban complex in a large-scale and comprehensive way. Instead of looking inward and patching-up, we must start looking outward to a shining example. [urban planner]

Do people really want economic integration? [community organizer]

People are suspicious of economic integration because of existing conditions of economic integration, but this would not be the case if the actual physical conditions were changed. People would be attracted to cluster near good schools and shops. Furthermore, if housing attractive to people of different income groups could be developed, they would be attracted to cluster because the options were increased, not because they had no other choice. [architect]

There was discussion of some of the pros and cons of dealing in terms of individual neighborhoods and with the city as a whole.

Your notions of creating anew do not go well with the Model Cities idea of refurbishing. [university staff member]

448

When you consider the direction of future urban planning, the Model Cities approach is already out of date becuase it is concerned with an obsolete urban structure. We can use the enormous public programs we already have to turn the orientation of the old, insular neighborhood outward to new cores rather than inward on itself. [urban planner]

Problems could arise from the lack of coordination which results from a policy, such as that of the Model Cities program, in which neighborhoods are treated separately. A community could decide to rehabilitate a building this year and next year the city might decide they need the land for an educational institution. Furthermore, coordination of efforts between neighborhoods could be to their mutual benefit. [participant working with a community organization]

For certain things such as education, health, and transportation, programs must be interrelated over the total city, and separate neighborhoods can come together to exchange information. However, at the beginning stages, there are obvious and pressing problems that can and must be dealt with in each area. In addition, due to the apathy of residents in these communities, something has to be started in order to capture their confidence and interest. In this, rehabilitation is not just getting better housing, but also achieving more visibility in the neighborhood. [Model Cities administrator]

There seems to be an increasing emphasis on programs dealing with the physical aspects rather than on programs for people. [social scientist]

It is not a question of emphasizing social or physical planning. Rather it is that the physical problems are easier and faster to solve. This results in an unfortunate imbalance which needs to be readjusted. [city administrator]

I do not think it is valid to deal with the physical problems prior to dealing with the social ones. [agency staff member]

Particularly in the area of mental health, the answer to problems is not simply a question of building more facilities and giving the poor what upper classes already have on the assumption that it must be good. This is a mechanical, simplistic conception which assumes they are effectively doing what they are supposed to do. [psychologist]

Ongoing programs in suburban communities may not even be best for the people living there much less for people in ghetto communities. [sociologist]

You cannot plan housing for people you know nothing about, and we are trying to avoid this. For example, along with a housing proposal, we had several closely related proposals. These included home maintenance programs and job placement and training to raise income levels since the ultimate aim of our rehabilitation proposal is home ownership. These people know what kind of housing they want and rather than high-rise public housing, they prefer the rehabilitation of old, smaller buildings, thereby retaining their neighborhoods. [urban planner with St. Louis Model Cities program]

Are attempts being made to bring business into the community? [unidentified participant]

We are trying to bring business into the community and match it with the labor force already there. [discussant from St. Louis]

Community Participation and Professional Assistance

It was generally agreed that the assistance of professionals is needed, but questions were raised concerning their relative importance and the relationship between professional and community involvement.

Where does community participation in working with professionals fit into this large-scale plan? Rather than needing more professionals in communities, we need involved people with expertise who are members of the community itself. Without such community participation, no amount of professional help will do any good or increase community involvement. [community organizer]

This confuses large-scale bureaucracy with large-scale architecture within which there can be community participation. [urban planner]

In our programs we have emphasized the importance of involving local professionals. Every doctor in each community is invited to work on the center's staff and is given assistance in upgrading his services if necessary. This not only maintains good relations with the private doctors in the area, but since the center also functions as a casefinding effort, there will be referrals of cases to these doctors. Thus the centers will not pose an economic threat to them. [doctor working with community health centers]

How handicapped are community people by their lack of expertise in what they can contribute? [community organizer]

Basic problems such as mental health should be seen as a part of what a community does. The people who do the important mental health jobs are not the mental health professionals but the clergymen, teachers, police, etc. They have the contact with people's fundamental problems and thus a far greater capacity for understanding them. Furthermore, in terms of people's long-run benefits, the closer outside professionals can work with them in their natural community context, the more meaningful and helpful they will be. [psychologist]

What can a community do on its own? [director of a community organization]

A community can identify its problems, define its needs, and attract attention to those needs, but to obtain the tremendous resources in expertise and money required, they will have to go outside the local community. [discussant concerned with urban problems]

Throughout this Workshop, we have been talking about how important it is for grass roots people to make their demands known, but sometimes, though they have ideas about what they want, they do not always know how to accomplish their objectives. They find that they need the expertise of specialists, and it seems that what is needed is a coordination of forces — grass roots people and experts must come together. [participant from a poverty area in the city]

Communication and understanding is what has to be achieved because it does not do any good to know what needs to be done if you cannot get it done. [out-of-state community representative]

The only workable relationship would be for community people to say to the experts, "You can work with us provided you allow us to take the lead and make our own decisions and mistakes. Though we might not know all the strategies of how to get what we want, and we may need your knowledge and resources, you can only take a leadership role when we ask for your advice and help in making our program workable." It is only if we make the decisions that we can be sure that our ideas, not theirs, will be implemented. [staff member of a community organization]

Direct funding of a not-for-profit citizens' organization, instead of more programs like urban renewal, would ensure that business concerns, political figures, professionals, etc., would help us but leave the control in our hands. [staff member of a community organization]

Though citizens' organizations could be funded directly, initially they need the expertise that professionals can give them in order to develop a base from which to work. [out-of-state city administrator]

Would you give us an example from the St. Louis Model Cities case of real opposition and conflict over a crucial issue that was resolved in favor of the community? [agency staff member]

Despite agreement that competent personnel were needed, there was disagreement over who would hire the staff that went into the neighborhoods. The community people felt that they could produce these people, and they now have the right to hire their own staff instead of personnel being sent from the top down. In this way we also avoid the danger of community people developing a plan which conflicts with the plan proposed by the "professionals." When that happens, the community's plan usually gets thrown out in favor of the other on the grounds that it is less workable. [St. Louis community representative]

When we talk about community involvement, we tend to restrict what we mean to resident involvement, but communities can no longer simply be defined geographically. Perhaps we should consider that teachers who work in the neighborhood as well as those with a financial stake in the area should be able to participate in these decisions and be just as involved as the residents. [administrator from a government agency]

It is worthwhile to have teachers and others who work in the ghetto take an interest and participate in helping the community. They can also help through discussions and political actions in the communities where they live which are either not informed about the ghetto or hostile to it.

This is very seldom done despite its importance to the total problem of community participation. [administrator from another government agency]

There is an important distinction to be made here. It is not valid for those from outside the community who have only a professional stake in it to become the spokesmen for that community. That is quite different from putting their expertise at the service of the community which is a meaningful way for teachers, social workers, agency personnel, outside businessmen with financial stakes in the community, and other professionals to participate. Community people must develop the broad policy outlines and make the final decisions. [participant concerned with city-wide community participation]

Involving the Private Sector

Further consideration was given to the role of the outsider in the community during discussion about involving the private sector.

With regard to the comprehensive approach to city planning, how can a working relationship be established between various agencies and the private sector? [university staff member]

I was able to achieve interagency participation because the separate agencies with which I worked could come together through me as an (academic) outsider. The private sector became involved because there was money to be made. [professor of architecture involved in urban planning]

What about the role of private interests in the St. Louis case? [agency staff member]

They have joined us on our invitation because they see their vested interests in this, especially over the long run. [discussant from St. Louis]

Are there programs to get low-income renters to become home owners? (government administrator)

In the St. Louis case, we involved the real-estate community, the slum landlords themselves. A situation had arisen where many houses in the area had been condemned and were scheduled for demolition. We got together with the absentee landlords (we stopped calling them slumlords when they began negotiating with us) and came to an agreement. Using rent supplement and low-income demonstration money, we offered to rehabilitate two properties in the neighborhood for every one they owned and would rehabilitate themselves. We promised to arrange for financing to rehabilitate their properties and rent subsidies to pay the differences in rent for the newly rehabilitated buildings. [discussant from St. Louis]

There was further consideration of the role of the private sector in community programs during discussion of cooperatives.

Though outside funds are needed in order to get started, if you can get people to work together, small businessmen in the area as well as low-income people can compete with those who are exploiting them and eventually put them out of business. [organizer of a new cooperative]

Do movements such as coops really fight the capitalistic system which is not solving the problems that face us? [settlement house worker]

Insofar as coops involve people doing for themselves, they are capitalism in its purest sense, without governmental control and based on free cooperation. Though they may not be the same type of system as the existing system in America, they are not in opposition to it as might appear. [lawyer]

We cannot expect the existing structure to open its arms to let us in. [social scientist]

Basic community needs from sanitation to social services are not being met, and we cannot count on the government and tax money to provide for them. [coop organizer]

The demand for low-priced food, entertainment, child care, etc., is there because poor people in ghetto areas have been denied so much because of high prices, and the possibilities of coops are fantastic once you get started. [volunteer worker in out-of-state coop]

By forming cooperatives we can meet these needs, and even if all the people in a ghetto get together, funding from the outside is still needed. [coop organizer]

Would such a coop have to continue depending on outside sources or could it become self-supporting? [university professor]

If we can show a steady growth, the coop will be able to become self-supporting, and once businesses that will support it are established, further social services can begin. [coop organizer]

A number of participants emphasized the importance of hiring community people along with experts from the outside so they will understand what is being done and why, and eventually will be able to take over the operation completely.

How do you build in the indigenous leadership necessary to perpetuate the coop? [settlement house worker]

To get started, we established a temporary Board of Directors which is half outsiders and half indigenous people, but eventually coop members will elect their own Board of Directors. In establishing a child care center, it was necessary to work outside the system at first in order to establish credibility. We went ahead and did it on our own with community people who are good with children and only the most essential facilities. Now it is blossoming and will probably get approval and an official permit soon, but even if it does not, the city will never close us down because they recognize the need and are afraid of community reaction. [coop organizer]

One thing that can be helpful in getting coops started is the growing attitude in poor areas that if we do not stick together, we will hang separately. [settlement house worker]

The politics of the situation is also important, especially at the beginning. If you have the neighborhood behind you, if they understand the possibilities of getting goods and services at reduced prices, and if they know what they can expect in the long run, they will not go somewhere else to save a few pennies. Establishing loyalty to the coop at the outset is essential to its survival. [community organizer]

Citizen Participation and the Politics of the Chicago Situation

The St. Louis example is a glowing report of citizen participation, but I doubt that this could ever happen in Chicago. I do not think it would be possible for citizens' organizations to receive direct funding, given Chicago's political structure. [community organizer]

We have experienced great difficulties in trying to convince the local power structure or the federal government of our need for grants to develop community action programs. [director of a youth group]

A lot depends on how the agency which serves as the intermediary is viewed, and it is important to have a close relationship with both community people and city officials. In terms of the actual money available, it seems that there is more than meets the eye since cities and states can and do supplement federal funds. [out-of-state city administrator]

What other alternatives were available in the St. Louis situation previous to the introduction of the Model Cities program, and what were the political realities that caused the people to be receptive to this kind of approach? For example, what percentage of the population is Negro, were they getting organized, were they threatening the mayor's reelection? [community organizer]

Nothing was happening and the situation was so bad that something had to be done. It could not have continued as it was. [St. Louis community representative]

St. Louis was way behind Chicago in terms of welfare, police protection, and public housing, and there were no major civil rights movements. [participant from Chicago]

Since Negroes are the only minority group of importance within the city itself, a lot of friction was avoided. As for the power structure, there was only one way to go since its popularity had reached such a low level. Things had gotten to the point where the power structure realized that they had to do something, and both state and city agencies were afraid of being left out. Initially there was a lack of confidence on the part of community people that anything could really be done, but the close relationship with the mayor and repeated demonstrations of his sincerity in getting what the people were asking for have been crucial to the change in attitude. [discussant from St. Louis]

This all seems rather inconceivable for Chicago. [community organizer]

Moving away from the specifics of the St. Louis case and to those of Chicago, several participants from agencies raised the objection, with which other participants voiced their agreement, that the city government evidenced their bad faith in community people by not consulting them in drafting the application for a planning grant.

Unfortunately community people have bad faith in the city administration. The application is only a broad outline and hopefully opens, not closes, doors for community participation in the actual planning. [city representative]

St. Louis did include community people in gathering information for their application, and I think that what was done here is typical of the Chicago approach. It is important that, although citizen participation may be provided for in Model Cities policy and in the Chicago application, the people here feel left out because this was done, whatever doors might open. [agency staff member]

The city should not be able to apply for federal money for programs without consulting the people living in the areas that will be affected. [participant from a community organization]

I do not think the Model Cities program will really contribute to change in Chicago. This city is divided colorwise, and perhaps we should ask that Chicago not be funded because it obviously has not fulfilled the requirements and shows no intention of doing so. [participant from a ghetto area]

It is naive to approach the city in terms of the face value of city programs. The city is trying to carry out Negro removal, not urban renewal. They want middle-class people to come back into the city so there will be more tax money in the city itself, and welfare expenses, etc., will be reduced. If this is a true picture of what is being planned, it would seem that any involvement on the part of community groups in government programs would amount to their being coopted by the city, and their strength diverted from what they really should be doing which is fighting the city planners. [public agency staff member concerned with citizen participation]

I know for a fact that the Model Cities program, for example, is definitely not set up for Negro removal, and the federal government will be looking very closely at any program it funds to insure that this will not happen. It will be up to the communities to also look very closely at these programs which is where lines of communication will have to be effective. [government official with extensive past experience as a community organizer]

If the mayor wants white people back in Lawndale, he will get federal support because the federal government needs him as much as he needs them. [agency staff member concerned with community participation]

In the need to be heard as an involved power block, citizen organizations have not given sufficient consideration to communicating with congressmen. Congress functions as a balance of power against the executive body, and it was Congress that passed the specific guidelines of the Model Cities Program. The policy of the Model Cities Program is to improve and rehabilitate a community, using all available resources – including state and city as well as private and neighborhood. [government official and former community organizer]

I do not think welfare, education, or urban renewal were originally conceived to do what they are doing. These and other programs start out being for all the people and end up being used by some people to their own advantage while others end up suffering because of them. What can we do to stop this from happening? [community organizer]

Ten years ago, communities were not as organized and outspoken as they are now. Previously most community people did not say anything and those who did were only small, ineffective groups. But now there are organizations which can act as watchdogs over what will affect their communities. This will enable them to constantly watch, interpret, and communicate through all channels, thereby preventing actions against their interests from being carried out. As long as there are powerful community organizations expressing their concerns and as long as they are organized, truly representative, and supported by the indigenous leadership, no power group can walk over them again. [community organizer]

Often putting pressure on those in control results in a negative reaction. [participant from an urban renewal area]

One of the main problems is that high-level federal, state, and city officials do not come into the community and talk with the residents. They always talk through a middle-man, the respectable, "responsible" citizen who looks, talks, and acts like they do. A responsibility of community organizations is to set up direct dialogue between the residents and concerned officials. Then they will not have to resort to rioting and burning down the place to say; "We want to be heard." [government official]

If a community organization without government money is successful in outmanipulating the city and the city knows it, how can the city be expected to allocate funds to that organization? We have submitted a proposal based on information from community people and have not gotten the type of response I think we should have. They are afraid to give us money because they know that with it we could do just that much more. [community organizer]

I am quite sure that they are afraid, but the Model Cities proposal explicitly stipulates that there must be citizen participation, and all the cities involved have stated, either in detail or in a broad sense, that they are willing to have citizen participation. If Chicago's proposal is approved and you are not satisfied that you will be directly involved, you have to be ready to confront them with an alternative proposal. [government official]

The fact remains that despite the talk about getting community participation in planning, there is no money available for it whereas a great amount of money is being spent on planning which is being done by the city without the involvement of community people. Given this situation, how can we even begin to get community people into the planning process? [agency staff member]

Though education is one of the most important aspects of changing the life of a ghetto, it is far from all that is needed to really solve the problem. Alternatively, an organized group that is asking for funds must have a dual purpose – its stated aims and its hidden agenda. For example, youth training and employment programs can achieve not only the hiring of youth for employment but such programs can also help in beginning to really organize a community. You can demand that the city, if it is really sincere, allocate funds to you, funds that you will control completely to hire the staff you need to help you develop a comprehensive plan in cooperation with the city. It constantly must be kept in mind that you are supposed to be doing this together, but it is important to emphasize that this would be a cooperative effort rather than one in which the city is on top and you are at the bottom, that community people should have a very strong voice in policy formation and decision-making, at least an equal voice if not more. [government official]

In several discussions, there were considerations of specific action that could be taken now.

It is very important for those who are interested in representing the citizens to convince the authorities that they actually do reflect the point of view of the citizens in the particular area in which they are working. Signed petitions may be one way of doing this. [university faculty member]

One of the problems is getting together homeowners, people who live in apartments, those receiving aid, and others in the community. A petition can be an effective instrument with which to confront the city if it is supported by a group of community people who can get together at any given time. [government official]

How clear are the guidelines with respect to citizen participation — do they define which citizens or do they leave this open to the discretion of the city administration? Would it be possible to take legal action in the event that citizen participation does not take place? [agency staff member]

The policy and guidelines are very nebulous on this point, but we are trying to help cities be more definitive in what they are actually going to do in these neighborhoods. We have to work closely with both the city administration and neighborhood groups to decide what needs to be done. If you feel that you are not directly involved in planning the program, you should use whatever effective instruments you can devise to demand that you are involved. [Model Cities staff member]

We have been talking about approaching sources of power through formal, i.e., legal, channels, but I think that whether we disregard these formal channels as being inoperative or try to use them, what is important is that we start by using the informal channels. You do not necessarily get to the mayor by talking to your ward committeeman, but you do get to him if you have frightened him. He has to talk to you if you have power which you can get either through direct action or by using the existing power structure. What we need to do is examine which of these courses is more effective. [community organizer]

Possibilities for Action

Although I agree with other participants that it is important to emphasize "reaching the people," I am distressed by the underlying theme that those with the badges of middle-class respectability must represent the poor and despised members of society. This ignores the important fact that the latter are the oppressed, and for anyone who has never been in that position, or who has gotten out of it, to propose that he will represent the interests of those people is preposterous. It means playing the same game and avoids confrontation with the real issues. If we are serious, all we can do is put ourselves at their service. They are perfectly capable of taking care of themselves once they understand that we regard them as human beings. What we must do is not represent them but get them to act and speak on their own behalf. We must train the black, poor, and despised members of this society in the kinds of skills they need in order to speak for themselves. [political scientist]

This raises a crucial issue that too often is avoided, namely can people who represent established organizations in a community be said to represent the poor who live in that community? One reason why we tend not to get down to the basic issues and the specifics of what can be done is that there are too many opposing philosophies. [community organizer]

One of the themes that has run through this Workshop, and one of the issues basic to the problems we are trying to deal with is the relationship between the oppressed and the oppressor, but we have never really come to grips with it because of our conflicting philosophies. Some think that we can work with the American system as it presently exists while others do not think the American capitalist system can work for the poor. We must address ourselves to the question of whether the existing structures can in fact serve either the poor or the middle class who are currently in another state of oppression. Oppression runs across American life and the servitude which people have to play to economic institutions is part of the theme and fabric of American life. [another community organizer]

After all these years of trying to go through the existing structure and failing, we cannot continue to talk about "change within the existing structure" because the oppressed just do not fit into it. We need to change the structure so it will include all. [an experienced community organizer]

We have to be willing to say we will subvert the whole structure to get money where it is needed. Churches and universities alike are hitting on nothing at all unless they are willing to deal with the real problems using any and every means to get the money into the ghettos where it is really needed. [another organizer]

Just giving money directly will not get to the root of the problem. We have to do more than provide for a limited, short-run solution which will not resolve the problems we are facing. Furthermore, if we are to think in terms of revolution, there are different kinds and ways of revolution which must be examined. Using strong words is not enough. [university professor]

The riots seem to indicate that it is easier to organize people against rather than for something, but what are the effects of the riots? [community organizer]

The first six months after the Watts rebellion were very emotional. People in the community expressed hostility toward all white people and would not let any of them into the community, largely because of the police brutality they had seen. During that period, the community was more unified than it had ever been before or has been since, but many of us permitted ourselves to be either bought off or carried away by publicity. This hurt us as did accepting too much government money instead of just enough for us to be effective. So far the rebellion has only solidified the resentment in both "camps." In other words, the white community is more determined than ever not to change, and the Negro community is more determined than ever to change. After the first six months we began to again set up communications with people we thought were interested in our goals, but it was a different type of relationship than it had been previously. A riot changes a lot of things in a community, and it will take years to bring back the former trust and sincerity. At this stage it is a rather pragmatic relationship without any of the idealism we had before. Though it is beginning to become an acceptable and working relationship, clear divisions still exist. [a former community organizer in the Watts area]

We need an organization to span the gap between the oppressed and the oppressor and react to the problems we have been discussing throughout the Workshop. We have been told ways to work with the power structure and ways to act against it, and though we all want the same sorts of changes, we disagree on how to achieve them. Something constructive could come out of the differences in our philosophies – if some can work within and others outside the power structure, perhaps through a combination of forces, we could solve some of these problems. [participant working with a local religious organization]

We need constructive suggestions and not just more discussion and criticism. It is important to recognize these problems but they do not amount to solutions. For those of us who are interested in seeing the oppressed rise up against the oppressor and taking what is there, we must look into how to change the status quo to the point where that may be possible. A community organization may want to destroy the welfare system, but in the meantime it will use that structure to ensure that more people live better by forcing it to support them. In other words, we must use the system as long as we have to while maintaining our concern with promulgating long-run change. [community organizer]

I think some of us came here hoping to find a clear panacea for bringing about an end to the problems we are trying to deal with, but that is not how it will happen. It will happen only as a result of a continual process of a variety of actions. What we have to focus on is eliminating the causes of the problems that concern us, and there are a variety of resources we can use to do what we feel needs to be done. We must go further than merely discussing the issues. [staff member of a community organization]

The real job that has to be done is organizing. [community organizer]

I think that in our discussions we are talking in terms of a very oversimplified idea of community organization. Even in Chicago where there are well-defined communities, they are not monolithic but are extremely complex structures. In every community, there are great variations in the desires, understanding, and interests of the people, and we have been saying that we would like to see more mixture in our communities. We have also been saying that we want to see more opportunity for expression of these differences, but we must recognize that people have the right not to participate and many want to exercise that right. Therefore, as community organizers, we cannot try to organize everyone in a community for if we did, we would end up with a group that could not act. We try to set up certain alliances and have to choose which ones we want. We may focus on those who are most vocal and willing to get involved or those who are most enlightened and see their community as part of the city, the country, and the world, or those who can get something done because they do not have any big enemies, or those within the power structure of each community. Though we do not even try to speak for all, we do try to understand all, and then try to bring together a group of people with enough goals in common so they can act. [community organizer]

Similarly with regard to leadership, there is never one leader in any community but different leaders for different situations. The black community is going through a revolutionary stage of leadership in which some people are asserting themselves, and there will be competition which can be good. [former community organizer]

Two important aspects of the East Pakistan project were that it took place in a universe of dialogue and that it was a very sophisticated process – a simplistic approach will not do if real social change is to be achieved. [agency administrator]

With regard to involving the people in the neighborhood, it is important to remember that most of them do not plan with an objective point of view but in terms of their own interests. Thus, in the planning process, as many individual points of view and objectives as possible must get onto the table, and the process must include the minority group that gets outvoted. The people that are hardest to reach are the ones you want to get to the most. They lack self-confidence and must be brought to the point where they are making the decision, which will only happen once you get down to the specific and concrete problems. The self-interests which are often said to disqualify people from engaging in the planning process are exactly what you want brought to the fore in the planning process itself. [out-of-state city administrator]

If the objective of citizen involvement is to be achieved, spreading the word is of utmost importance. We have stressed working with small areas so there can be intimate involvement of individuals on a neighborhood level. [administrator concerned with community participation]

Because the poor are more likely to attend meetings held in their own communities, it is important to meet in ghetto areas. [community organizer]

Since most community actions involve the political structure, community organizations need to increase their political power. [community organizer]

We need to understand the political set-up and operate with political leverage in order to have meaningful community participation and social action. [psychologist]

We feel health involves employment, adequate housing, and education, not just physical well-being, so if health services can be located where these other matters are also a matter of interest, for example in a settlement house, they, of course, will be more effective. Furthermore, we hope a total community outlook will eventually have a secondary effect on the health services provided by other institutions in the area such as hospitals. Overlapping existing services provides new opportunities for cooperation. [doctor involved in community health centers]

A lot of people shy away from settlement houses because they appear too official, and perhaps staff and patient participation would increase if health centers operated in conjunction with community organizations. [staff member of a community organization]

Cooperation with a community organization which is accepted by the people in the area as their organization would help get these services to the people who really need them. It is not enough to simply establish a center; an organizing job is also involved to get the word out by people known in the area. [another organizer from the same organization]

People go to clinics once trust is established and a good way to achieve that is through cooperation with a community organization and locating these services in familiar places. [another community organizer]

If we are going to deal with today's problems, we have to throw out all our traditional books on community organization and take a new look at and approach to them. At this stage in history, nobody is dealing honestly and pragmatically with the power structure. Getting ten or twenty people to yell at them or even burn down the city does not do anything more than solidify feelings. Unless community organizations begin to look at new and creative ways and means of approaching the problems that face them, nothing will get done. Community organizations have to begin to really involve indigenous people instead of just getting a little reputation, being bought off, and then forgotten. [former community organizer now working with a government agency]

Given the density of our cities, how do we ever achieve any other kind of real and meaningful citizen participation than the Watts kind of action? [community organizer]

I think many of us are very lazy when it comes to community organization. We get all tied up in public relations and sending out leaflets without the hard work which consists in knocking on doors and being able to convince people of our sincerity by returning over and over again. Initially it does not take a large number of people to bring about change, but it does take enough people who are coordinated and organized and have the same single-minded goals. It takes people who can communicate and act instantaneously when necessary. If you have ten people, each of whom is in close touch with ten others who understand your goals and policies, you can have a creative confrontation with the people you are trying to convince that changes are needed. [former organizer]

In order to go out to involve someone in a program, I have to really believe that there is something in it for him, and I am not sure I believe that this is so given the present situation. The people living in these communities know the facts much better than those who are trying to organize them, and I must admit that every day I become more convinced that nothing he can do will change anything. [community organizer]

You cannot build with the man in the ghetto in terms of intangibles; he wants to know "what is in it for me" and now, not two or three years from now. It is up to people on federal government staffs, good-intentioned people in the city, and people in the neighborhoods who are trying to organize, to begin defining what changes will really be in it for him which is especially difficult because they must be immediate, not long range. [former organizer]

The Community Service Workshop in Retrospect

The Participants' View

POST-WORKSHOP REUNION

The Workshop in Community Service valued highly the ongoing involvement of the participants in determining the very direction that the Workshop would take. In the initial project proposal, submitted by Sol Tax, these values were spelled out most clearly:

This proposal is an attempt to use the experience of the American Indian Center in Chicago as a major example in analyzing for others the problems, limitations, and potentialities of developing indigenous participation . . . Although American Indians to some degree represent an extreme case, anthropologists have observed and analyzed ways in which Indians develop an educative process designed to deal with their problems. This involves using people in the group to teach each other and creating a cultural continuum in which those who know more teach the others, and older members of the group teach newcomers. This institutionalization of the process of cultural diffusion does not seem to involve hierarchical structures or patterns of authority. It is obvious that much of what has been learned from this process may be transferred with advantage to other cultural groups in rural, urban, or suburban communities. (Title I Project Proposal)

Three of the project staff members, Sol Tax, Bob Rietz, and Len Borman, while they continued their association with the American Indian Center in Chicago were able to hold these values high in the operations of the Workshop. This approach, furthermore, was most congenial with the point of view favored by Earl Doty from his background and experience in community organization in the inner city. In many respects, the Workshop itself was an example of community development and organization. Through such features as ongoing feedback, high reliance on participation, self-determination, developing common positive objectives through the self-interest of members, the Workshop succeeded in becoming more than the usual training program or conference. Furthermore, there was no binding syllabus or preconceived unfolding of content or issues to be covered, no list of assignments to be done by student participants to be evaluated by faculty staff. Moreover, there was no assumption that experts, be they academicians or professionals, had a monopoly of the answers – or even the questions – involved in resolving the many thorny issues discussed.

In light of the very purpose and evolution of the Workshop, it seemed only natural to hold a post-Workshop reunion. If the Workshop participants could be asked – and they were – at the very beginning of the Workshop, "What is the most important benefit you expect from this Workshop?" then it seemed natural to ask them what they got out of their Workshop experience. There were many responses to the first question, some of which include the following:

To obtain ways and means of how to bridge the gap between the community and the resources of the community. [community organizer]

Exchange of ideas, information, fusion of community experiences with theoretical framework . . . using community conflict to advance goals, purposes, bringing about and accelerating social change. [community mental health worker]

Acquaintance and self-exposure to the changing concept of social welfare. [social service worker]

More knowledge of ways and methods that can be used effectively in the work of bringing about the product of the kind of politic necessary to develop programs to affect, and to be of service to the community and to our society. [director of a community organization]

Getting beyond the social service aspect of organization. [community organizer]

To become more effective in the role of leadership through a clear understanding of the community's perspective and through interaction with others who are seeking answers in relation to the needs of the community. [director of a public community organization]

A better understanding of tools and techniques that can be employed to unite dissident groups. [community organizer]

To better enable myself and to help the community help itself to become free of the slave yoke. [staff member of a community organization]

To find out how other community workers are attempting to organize their respective communities. [community. organizer]

Above all, to learn how to build a bridge between the inner and outer city for radical social change. [community organizer]

To discover means and methods of financing programs needed. [representative of a community organization]

Trying to involve the community in a meaningful way so that they can accept public welfare as a meaningful resource towards alleviation of the social and economic conditions that cause the poor to be poor. [staff member of a private agency]

To learn more about how to change a racially hostile community into a community willing to try integration. [staff member of a private agency]

Expect valuable details of how to keep tenants together while on rent strike. [community organizer]

On a Saturday in November 1967, five months following the last formal session of the Workshop, a reunion was called by the staff for all participants who could attend to reconsider the relevance and meaning of the Workshop. This reunion was held at the scene of the Workshop sessions themselves, the Center for Continuing Education at the University of Chicago. Following a luncheon, about forty participants gathered once again in the large assembly room where the earlier plenary sessions had been held. Again there was a great range of participants from agency administrators to neighborhood organizers. It was obvious from the informal luncheon conversation and initial greetings that a number of friendships had sprung up. Many of those who had returned for this reunion had been seeing some of the others — at block club meetings, new health centers, housing conferences, community action affairs, protest rallies, and especially the continuing organizational meetings of the ongoing Workshop. Some of the male inner city participants — both agency and neighborhood representatives — had sprouted new beards as symbols of their identity. A few faces had become very familiar from appearances on television and in the local newspapers. In the assembly room, each participant's name was displayed at a place on the green felt tablecover as before. Sol Tax welcomed the assembled group and noted the three items that had been placed before each person to review: (1) a proposed agenda for the reunion session; (2) a four-page table of contents describing the proposed book entitled *The People vs. The System: A Dialogue on Urban Conflict;* and (3) A nine-page draft for discussion of a proposal developed by the continuing Workshop group to establish Community Workshops for Citizens' Participation (see Appendix).

This reunion meeting was far from a backslapping session of self-congratulation. Even if it appeared that some highly prized academic objectives were being achieved — the collection of a number of incisive and articulate viewpoints to be published in a volume that may advance understanding — the community situations described, discussed, and debated seemed little affected. Many of those who gathered five months later came to remind everyone else of this fact. Moreover, during the interim, over eighty cities had been subjected to riots and disorders during the summer of 1967. Chicago was spared, but no one had suggested that the apparent peace that prevailed was related to the Workshop — even though some had suspiciously alluded to this as the main purpose of the Workshop! Rather, others in the reunion session explained the apparent Chicago tranquility during the previous summer months as resulting from an armed camp that was instituted and not as a result of the Workshop or other peaceable dialogues.

I have no truck for rioting and think that sometimes it is self-destructive. But I think what prevented people from rioting was not the programs but an armed camp provided by Daley. I saw it myself. People were kept from gathering in small groups. The entire network of the Commission on Youth Welfare, the Commission on Human Relations, the Building Department — everything turned into an intelligence network supplemented by the regular intelligence and subversive unit plus the large influx of FBI agents. There was a fantastic amount of police activity, all aimed at crushing dissent in the city and beginning to view the people as an enemy. [staff member of a private agency]

This wide polarization of positions often defined the route taken by many issues as they arose. The suggested title of this book, *The People vs. The System*, in attempting to characterize this dichotomy, caused a number of viewpoints to be expressed at the reunion.

I had the feeling that the Workshop was more concerned with maximum feasible participation, and that those three words describe it more than *The People vs. The System* which almost suggests that the system is not for the people. [representative from city housing department]

That is a fairly good assumption. [staff member of a private agency]

To me the title is appropriate because one of the things we were talking about was the system, and how you either could not get through to it or how it took so long to get through to it. [community worker]

It is so clear in my mind that the people vs. the system is exactly where we are that I am surprised to even hear it questioned. I thought the Workshop had brought this out very clearly but it seems that it has not. Until that is brought out clearly, we cannot understand what the revolution is about today. [staff member of a private, religious agency]

I agree that a large part of the discussion during the Workshop focused on the people vs. the system. Moreover, toward the end of the Workshop, there was some consideration of ways to work with the system and ways to take advantage of it. These were never fully explored or crystallized because the system so often frustrates these efforts which was very well expressed in the Workshop. Perhaps we should have discussed more fully and specifically where we could work best with the system and where we have to work against it. [staff member of a private agency]

This overlooks an important factor – some of us work in a different reality. Some people here operate from behind a desk, in a quiet place where a harsh word is never spoken. In another arena, some bloody battles are being fought. People are getting hurt and wasted, and they are going to do things differently. Their reality is immediate. When you talk about power structure, they are on one end of the stick. It is these people vs. the system. The system is operating and people are fighting it. [community organizer]

Perhaps it was the insight expressed here – "some of us work in a different reality" – that accounted at the same time for what some ascribed as the successes and failures of the Workshop: success in the sense of enhanced recognition of the genuine diversity of viewpoint and position, and failure in the sense of entrenched hostile stereotypes that continued to be perpetuated.

Perhaps one of the ways to characterize the participants might be through the coordinates of two axes. One axis represents the great range of community agency and organization: federal, state, city, private, neighborhood, religious, and other. The other axis represents a range of functions, roles, and positions in a series of hierarchies. Often these are correlated with professional education and training. Another distinction that became apparent throughout the Workshop, that was articulated again during the reunion, focused on the differences in the identities, careers, and constituents of the participants. For the most part, trained professionals working for established agencies ("the establishment") identified closely with their agency programs and functions and felt responsible to their boards of directors and superiors. Moreover, these were some of the key criteria by which their competent performance – by the agencies that hired them – was judged. On the other hand, those participants who represented area or neighborhood community organizations (the "grass roots") identified not so much with agencies, services, or supervisors, but more closely with their constituents. This was also apparent in styles of language, dress, and other outward symbols of identity, including hair styles, display of organizational buttons, etc. This difference accounted often for the "town meeting" quality of some sessions in which neighborhood participants launched critical attacks, in a sense grievance proceedings, against agency representatives. This was often frustrating for the agency professional who was not always able – nor allowed – to define the fine nuances of his position or that of his agency.

Throughout the Workshop sessions, practically every established agency, including some professional groups, was "up for grabs," so to speak. This is reflected in some of the presentations as well as in the "reactions and reconsiderations" reported in the body of this volume. If universities fared pretty well during the Workshop sessions, they were not ignored at the reunion, with some rising to their defense.

With regard to the universities dealing with urban issues, I do not think they do or want to. I think they have failed us all in that respect. I think there is a real lost opportunity with regard to university resources in urban problems. They could go in so many directions. It seems that in their devotion to scholarship and attention to detail, frequently universities do not come in where they would be welcome ... The concept of the ivory tower is not only in the mind of the beholder; it is a mentality within universities in general. It is a tragic flaw which possibly reflects the structural flaw in society which has already been mentioned. If our "intellectual leaders" cannot come to terms with a real commitment, I do not know who can. [staff member of a private agency]

University professors are humans like others and they want to get ahead in terms of their colleagues. The values in a university are for freedom, but freedom to learn new things. Precisely because we do value education, knowledge, etc., the professors themselves feel that their central job, and that which will get them the respect of their colleagues, is the learning of new things and writing them up. Therefore, from their point of view, every time they move into a community to do something (which they may want to do) they are in a sense diverting their attention away from the job which would get them the prestige. Most of them are not heroes anymore than others to do something which is against their personal advantage. [university professor]

How can we say that professors should be more responsible with regard to inner urban areas? They have not really been there so how can they be expected to understand and deal with these problems? Maybe they need some teaching too. [community leader]

Frequently some participants "crossed lines," and in so doing articulated the viewpoint of the "other side." This would also suggest that not all participants were agency or community bound. One participant, whose career ranged from grass roots to a position with a private agency, expressed some of this shifting in the reunion and even suggested that the "real power" lay in the hands of the neighborhood participant.

Within the participant group, the power was unequal which made for an awkward situation. We had people who are outside the system and want to operate outside it. The person from the community who has real power can go back to the community and get people to rally behind him. There were others who are inside the system, and though they do some good, they have no real power and cannot make a commitment. The bureaucrat can only go back to his boss with a report and his boss will make a report of it and on up the chain. Thus a problem which could be immediately acted upon on one side cannot be on the other. [community organizer]

A number of other comments were made at the reunion which reflect some omissions or deficiencies in the Workshop. Let me briefly note some of these here.

Failed to deal with the notions of power – the whole concept of what is our function professionally and nonprofessionally as social workers or actionists, or as "dirty workers." [community organizer]

One of the most important aspects left out was the thoughts and ideas of young people. [staff member of a private agency]

It would have been good if we could have gotten more volunteer community leaders as discussants ... They might not have been able to give as scholarly a presentation, but they do have something to contribute. [staff member of a community organization]

Trade unions are, can, and should be allies of community organization, and we did not get into that aspect at all. [staff member of a community organization]

We did not really get into the operation and strategies of the Police Department and how it regards the people. [staff member of a private agency]

One lack was the failure to have big business represented. Some of the large organizations which are totally within a community or are represented within a community should have been here to participate and show their profile. [director of a private agency]

We failed to dig into the dynamics and politics of religion in the city of Chicago. There is a Catholic structure here which is probably as powerful as the mayor. [staff member of a private religious agency]

The planning process is a very long and difficult one, and when you have to begin from scratch without the kinds of resources which are normally available to people who plan for cities, it is very difficult to come up with alternatives. [staff member of a private agency]

We didn't sufficiently cover the economics of the situation which is related to the issues of juvenile delinquency and crime. [community organizer]

We tried to talk about the ghetto institutionally, that is, in terms of housing, schools, etc. But we did not talk about it in terms of attitudes or structures. It's very hard to look at institutions when you are stewing about something somebody said that has to do with emotions and attitudes and structures that are not institutional and are not things that can be dealt with by programs. [staff member of a private agency]

Those of us working in communities organizing face tremendous obstacles and very difficult jobs and, of course, even by the end of the Workshop we were not anywhere near ready to say, "Now this is the way it should be done." [community organizer]

We should have organized ourselves into an organization so that as we discussed some of the issues and concerns, we could have taken some direct action on them which may have resulted in a much deeper learning process or experience. [community organizer]

As indicated in the presentations and discussions of this volume, part of the last phase of the Workshop was devoted to an examination of the Model Cities Program. The Workshop staff and planning committee, working closely with the numerous suggestions coming from participants, attempted to develop content and material that would have some immediate relevancy for community projects. Accordingly, specific sessions around the developing Model Cities Program were scheduled during the last phase. Panelists were invited who could serve as resource consultants for the Workshop which was divided into three groups representing the North, West, and South Sides of Chicago. Even though each group came up with a document recommending programs that might be considered for their Model City area, others felt this was fruitless activity.

Really what's implicit in the whole Workshop is the liberal assumption that somehow if we work within the system and reach the poor and get them into the system, more programming is going to help, that the real problem with the poor is that they have not been civilized yet and brought into this great consumer economy. Implicit in all our discussion is that what we are after is getting more training programs, better education and housing, etc., all of which are irrelevant to the real problem that exists in the ghettos and for the poor across the United States which is really one of injustice. And that is not solved by programming. So the people who are fighting against injustice and not necessarily for better programs are the ones who are being wasted because they are putting their finger on the heart of the problem and pushing at the crucial point. I don't think we need to waste our time developing more programs. That is not where the problem lies. The problem lies with the policies and the people who form them. [staff member of a private, religious agency]

In the last session, we were asked· to come up with alternatives, and despite all the information we received, we could not come up with a concrete proposal for action in any given area. It is easier to attack than to come up with positive solutions, and perhaps we should have spent more time thinking in the direction of creating positive solutions. [employee of a city commission]

My over-all reaction to the Workshop was tremendously positive, but I do not think it led into developing proposals in terms of the Model Cities Program. This was a jump which was contradictory to what we had been doing. Our approach had been the people vs. the power structure and then it was presumed that we could discuss what to do as though we were the power structure or knew what we wanted them to carry out. [staff member of a community organization]

I was against discussing Model Cities because, in the first place, I always suspect that the system will do what is good for the people who derive the most from it. Furthermore, in trying to come up with something in terms of the Model Cities Program, as inadequate as it started out to be, we had to slice it up even more. And without a power base from which to operate, we could only have a bit of rhetorical display. [community organizer]

Apart from the discouraging comments about the last Model City phase of the Workshop, a number of interesting and informative documents were prepared that focused on some of the pressing needs in the three crucial areas of Chicago. One of the summary papers ended on this note, which perhaps best captured the spirit of the Workshop, and charted a possible future course:

The approaches and the programs outlined above are not to be considered inclusive. They are a starting point for action. If change is to occur, the communities involved must be ready to come in with their own ideas of what is best for them. To do this, greater public awareness of the issues noted above must be generated. The important thing is that the community people know that they can bring about change and that they have a stake in their own society. Change by itself does not have to mean progress. Progress will only come if there is a positive attitude on the part of the community that it can make its environment better.

A Commentary

LEONARD BORMAN

This was an extraordinary Workshop in many respects. All of us in attendance – staff, participants, panelists – were variously concerned about issues involving community service and participation. Coming from a highly structured, diverse, and fragmented, professional and community scene, we were more used to talking with colleagues and cohorts than we were with the strangers across the hall or citizens at the other end of town. Or if we did meet with students or clients or citizens, frequently they were required to listen to us. Yet in coming together as we did for recurrent weekend sessions over the nine-month period, we found – or at least many of us did – that these citizens and strangers are connected to each other and to the rest of us in very significant ways. It was frequently uncomfortable – some even thought outrageous – but we were all required to hear viewpoints that we usually avoided. Unless we dropped out of the Workshop – and some did – we were not able to maintain our customary ritual distance from one another.

Let me illustrate some of the consequences of our fragmented concerns by relating a dramatic incident of a young man who appeared for a physical examination prior to his induction into the Army. As he made his way through an array of medical specialists, his physical examination chart began to look like a Christmas tree with many critical marks noted. His temperature was above normal. He had a sore throat. His pulse was unusually rapid. His hearing seemed impaired. His reflexes were markedly sluggish. He had a diffuse red rash over his skin, and so on down the line. At the end of the day after he had been subjected to a myriad of special examinations, he handed his chart to the final reviewing officer. The officer looked at the chart and then at the inductee and said, "My God, this boy has a contagious form of scarlet fever!"

In an analogous way we were all specialists of one kind or another – equipped with our specialized jargon – who rarely saw the forest for the trees. The Workshop revealed the larger, fuller picture, for it exposed all of us to the most critical and compelling testimony around the inadequacy not only of community participation but of community services, especially in the black ghettos of America. If our particular interest was housing, politics, education, welfare, youth opportunities, or whatever, the case of the inner-city ghetto remained before us. Each of us could become thoroughly concerned with a specific symptom, but these were all connected to a larger distressed whole. Yet in our usual activities we rarely had a link to a reviewing officer or an occasion where our piecemeal views could be related to others. Furthermore, this was no clinical pathology conference where we could gain further insight in examining an autopsy. The patient was far from dead. Moreover, he was manifesting a hold on life that he rarely exhibited in the past. There was an assertion on his part not only for greater involvement and participation in vital community affairs, but for a respectable identity and dignity and share in the abundance and opportunity of our nation. If this meant dismissing the professionals and programs that had failed to meet these conditions, then many felt this should be done.

As I reflect over these critical — even startling — impressions from my participation in the Workshop, I find that these were not biased or extreme views stemming from a conference composed largely of black ghetto residents and community organizers. For in terms of numbers, these repre-sentatives were in the minority. The voice of the ghetto resident was indeed expressed, but it was given greater credence through the observations and findings of many authorities drawn from a variety of disciplines. For example, some economists and political scientists cited the history of public housing for the poor in Chicago (and elsewhere) as an indication of how often such programs sought to contain poverty and manipulate its victims. Even the housing professionals who developed the original blueprints and guidelines were hard put to relate the final products to their recommended plans. Often influential community pressures and prejudice played key roles in determining the final outcomes. Many who reviewed the work of the Office of Economic Opportunity, including some former significant advisors, detected a kind of cynicism in the implementation of the legislation that provided maximum appropriation of funds for local political appointees with a minimum of service or feasible participation of the poor. Such programs, they suggested, contributed not only to a sense of futility but indeed to a sense of illegitimacy. A prominent criminologist indicated how the very notion of the "long hot summer" has become a battle cry perpetuated by many police departments as an opportunity to build up weapons and special forces to contain inner-city populations. He observed that many of these very programs of police action, enforced with greater zeal among the poor, are themselves conducive to overexpressions of hostility and violence in our ghetto communities As for education, few spoke from any conviction of accomplishment occuring in inner-city schools.

I am convinced that the Workshop provided an exceptional opportunity to bring together these various pieces of the community puzzle that few of us had an opportunity to hear about, let alone visualize, before. Our individual contributions were thus cast onto a larger canvas. But apart from the significance of bringing together such a rich diversity of resources from the university, the community, and across the nation, the Workshop succeeded in another crucial dimension. Furthermore, I would strongly highlight this dimension for any institution — higher learning or other — concerned with developing community service and continuing education programs.

Very simply put, this is the objective of aggressively seeking positive and creative solutions in a community atmosphere often charged with a dark and cynical reality. The trust and confidence expressed by the various community sectors for each other left much to be desired. It would be difficult to say who exhibited the greater cynicism: those who came to the Workshop from the black ghetto and elsewhere to criticize existing practices, to advocate black power and even bloodshed, or those representing established professional and community agencies who refused to appear at the Workshop at all. It became a routine announcement, during the various phases of the Workshop, to hear of the difficulties in getting panelists to appear from the local or national Office of Economic Opportunity, or from the mayor's staff in Chicago. But this lack of willing participation from some of the local and national offices concerned with poverty was not allowed to reinforce a hunch held by many that "they don't give a damn." Rather, the Workshop staff, through university and other concerned agencies, brought in government staff from Cook County, Michigan, downstate Illinois, St. Louis, and from other federal agencies in Washington. This was done in an effort to enrich the discussion and dialogue, although it also indicated that the "establishment" is no monolith that operates in lockstep against the poor.

I am suggesting that the University, through the Workshop, sought for realistic and creative solutions in an atmosphere that reaffirmed a faith and hope that they could be attained. On the one hand, the Workshop refused to become a sounding board or an apologist for what many regarded as the establishment, and at the same time did not succumb to the frequent despair and cynicism of the ghetto. I do not mean to suggest that the Workshop accepted or rejected these various postures in some simple or automatic way. I am convinced, rather, that this viable and productive posture was maintained through a variety of mechanisms that prevailed throughout the life of the Workshop. The periodic residential sessions allowed for intensive formal and informal interaction of participants with one another followed by - a month or two of interlude. Through these experiences many of us were able to add further helpful dimensions in the specific round of life of our agency, community, or professional activities. Some professional agency representatives were stunned, even angered, by the forthright testimony on the inadequate representation of inner-city voices in community programs. If we could not incorporate in various ways what we were hearing and learning — and for most of us, this was out of the question — we certainly had to think about it. We could react and test out what we had heard or what we had learned and come back for a clarification, restatement, or reaction. At the same time, many of us became acquainted with a greater range of community workers and residents with whom we continued to maintain some contacts after the weekend sessions. Perhaps the glaring deficiency of such regular means for two-way communication was high on the list of what we were all learning about.

Both the "open agenda" of the program as well as the value placed on the active involvement of the Workshop participants contributed to this viable posture. By the open agenda of the Workshop I mean to point to the absence of any star-chambered sessions whereby a small group of staff or experts decided what was to happen. We were not about to recapitulate in microcosm what was being so severely criticized in the larger community. A planning committee was elected at the plenary session of the Workshop to meet with the staff and to help provide reactions to what was occurring, indicate suggestions for procedure, future topics, and participants, and generally to create some ongoing linkage between the staff, the participants, and the residential sessions. But even these staff-planning committee meetings were not sacrosanct, since all issues and proposals raised during the occasion of these meetings were subsequently presented to the plenary session of all participants. Topics, panelists, and future weekend dates for meetings were always voted upon. Furthermore, ongoing feedback from all participants was encouraged at all times. Initially, much of this was written following specific sessions, and eventually feedback was encouraged through correspondence, personal discussions, and the use of questionnaires. In these ways, the particular interests and concerns of all participants could be channeled into some larger, common objectives – not by superimposition but from a high degree of self-determination. This stemmed from the approach of the principal convener of the Workshop, Sol Tax, who minimized the importance of hierarchial patterns of authority in favor of strong reliance on people learning from each other through a cultural continuum.

And finally, I think that one of the crucial elements that kept the Workshop in a positive, creative dimension was the incorporation of reasonably successful case material drawn from throughout the country and presented directly by members of the specific projects involved. On almost every major topic presented – welfare, housing, youth, health, education, etc. – some case of creative innovation was presented before the Workshop. And these were diverse in their auspices, setting, and funding. There was no stacked deck here suggesting that only programs in the War on Poverty can really save the cities, or that only Saul Alinsky-type programs will work. The cases brought before the Workshop covered some of these categories and others as well. We heard from the Model Cities people planning programs in St. Louis, as well as from Students For a Democratic Society organizing social action programs among Southern whites in Chicago. We learned of the Child Development Program in Mississippi, with its strong emphasis on involving mothers in a nursery program, as well as the attempts to organize a struggling cooperative by two social science graduate students in Bedford-Stuyvesant, New York. We heard how Public School 201 in New York City had literally been taken over by its community, with the assistance of an able social worker, and we received the details from the former Superintendent of Evanston on their unique community program for integrated, high-quality education. One might say that the cases presented were cafeteria style – you could pick the example or case that suited your own needs, while you remained cognizant of people and programs somewhat remote from your current interests. It was like learning in the one-room school house that provided something for everybody. Often the form of dialogue or presentation resembled an old-fashioned town meeting. Fortunately, most of those who presented cases were encouraged to make their presentations brief and their weekend stay long. This allowed for a maximum amount of time to be devoted to informal discussions at meal times, party times, and other times. It also afforded the panelist an opportunity to learn as well.

Let me attempt now to characterize some other outcomes of this Workshop that I felt were significant. First of all, the Workshop succeeded in tape-recording over one hundred presentations made by panelists as well as the discussion that followed. This accomplishment is far greater than it might appear. For often the issue of the taperecorder and the trust or distrust that it aroused provided an occasional stormy issue for discussion. The Workshop staff always took the position that the recorder would be turned off whenever the majority of participants agreed on that decision. For this Workshop was not a guinea pig to be prodded, probed, and studied by outside researchers. As with other major dimensions of the program, recording and evaluation were to be carried on only through the ongoing cooperation and assistance of the participants themselves. Nor was there some predetermined set of outcomes to be checklisted along the way. For even these were to be derived from the participants. Accordingly, the presentations and discussions that have been recorded and since transcribed attest to the overwhelming climate of trust and confidence that prevailed throughout the Workshop. Furthermore, many participants following the formal termination of the Workshop voluntarily agreed to read the rough transcripts of the discussions and help to summarize the crucial points. If they had learned from these discussions, certainly others might equally profit. The volume of presentations and discussions that emerges into publishable form indeed becomes a product of the Workshop participants themselves.

These presentations, moreover, are a result of the Workshop in another sense. Often each panelist in his formal presentation was able to take into account the presence, if not the viewpoints of those appearing on the weekend session with him. Frequently a panelist sat through an entire plenary session before he was called upon. Some panelists returned at subsequent sessions to present more specific proposals, or suggested strategies, or to react in other ways to earlier discussions or presentations. More were desirous of doing this than the program could accommodate. The Workshop, then, served a dual purpose in providing a greater range of alternatives, strategies, and techniques to the community resident and organizer, at the same time that academic and other community experts were able to clarify their own findings and concepts. Most significant in the latter process was the opportunity to hear at great length representatives from inner city communities.

I was particularly impressed with the opportunity provided by the Workshop for a great number of panelists and participants to present some of their ideas, drawn from their current research or activities, that would not otherwise be shared so soon. The time that usually elapses between the completion of some research or action program and its publication in a professional journal is often considerable. The Workshop helped to accelerate this process by not only making the presentation available for publication, but allowing the researcher to present his findings to a broader community audience — with the possibility of more rapid implementation as well. This might present a most useful model to be emulated by other agencies, universities, and departments as they relate to community interests. At the same time, and this may be my own professional bias, such community workshop presentations would encourage greater intelligibility on the part of the scholar, and less professional jargon. It might also serve to redress one grievance expressed by inner-city residents to the effect that academicians "rarely come our way, so how can they help us?"

Another significant outcome of the Workshop was a continual questioning of basic premises. I do not mean to suggest that this ran over to the side of cynicism and despair — which frequently occurred — but rather that concepts and programs and cliches got thoroughly examined. While many of us focused initially on problems of indigenous involvement and the issues around maximum feasible participation of the poor, other perhaps more basic issues were revealed. Are we, for example, confronted with a racist core that permeates a great deal of thinking and action in America? And, if so, what steps might be taken and by whom? Are not basic revisions in the very system of providing housing and welfare and education required? And how might this be done in a specific community or in relationship to a specific school? Should political strategy center on the organization of special communities or neighborhoods, even requiring all black memberships? Or should there be a concern with political alliances and pressure groups that seek more widespread coalitions? What was then added to the creative solution of community problems by the Workshop was a continual dialogue and questioning of basic premises upon which many programs and proposals stand. What followed, then, were the obvious necessities for newly suggested lines of thought or action.

A third significant outcome of the Workshop were the many and varied opportunities for continuing Workshop activities under different auspices. Very few of us were unaffected by our Workshop experience. While the formal Workshop ended in June of 1967, a group of participants continued to meet during the summer and fall of that year. This ad hoc group drew up proposals for funding educational programs similar to the one just completed in their Workshop. It was suggested that these programs be conducted in the Model Cities areas or with specific inner-city populations, such as the Puerto Rican community. The proposal which was developed and funded during the Workshop, providing legal services to community organizations, was also a great boost to the efforts of this ad hoc group. (See Appendix)

What is suggested here is that the Workshop began or at least encouraged a process of facing community issues head on, bringing together a great range of agency functionary and community resident, and enhancing the role and the right of the individual to participate in the formulation of decisions affecting his destiny. These were not insignificant outcomes. For they may constitute the only visible hope for meeting the community and national crises of our time.

Appendix*

*Editors Note:
Included are three of the concrete results which arose from the Workshop: (1)
two descriptive statements on the progress of a proposal presented to the Workshop by one of the participants (the first at the beginning of the Workshop, the
second at its conclusion); (2) a proposal developed by the continuing Workshop
group which met during the summer months following the Workshop; and (3) a
proposal initiated by one of the participants in his community directly as a result
of his experience with the Workshop.

Reports on a Proposal, I and II

WILLIAM MARSH

I

During our October meeting, there was an expressed interest in developing a new approach toward legal services for the poor. We discussed a proposed legal service program which would provide legal counsel to community organizations. I advised you that there is no existing legal aid program oriented specifically to organizations rather than individuals, but that the Office of Economic Opportunity would be very interested in such a program if it were developed and submitted to them.

I agreed to investigate the possibilities of getting a grant from OEO. The next week I had an opportunity to speak with Earl Johnson, the director of OEO services in Washington, and presented the general proposition to him. He gave a very, very favorable reaction. He said it was the most exciting proposal he had heard of. Armed with his reaction, I went to my own agency, the National Legal Aid and Defender Association (NLADA) and began to develop support for the project. I hoped they would sponsor the program as a demonstration project which would benefit legal services throughout the country.

NLADA's Board of Directors met very recently and considered the proposal. I am pleased to report that they voted unanimously to act as the applicant agency to sponsor the project and authorized me to go to OEO with a written proposal. Shortly after our Board's approval, I received a telephone call from OEO telling me that money was very, very short. As most of you well know, there is not much money available this year for new programs. OEO advised me they wanted to fund the project and told me that they needed the proposal within a few days. I completed the application and forwarded it to Washington, and it is now being processed.

As far as I know, it seems likely that funds will be made available within two to four weeks. It has been given top priority in the Legal Services Office. I am going to Washington on Monday to meet with them and to see if any problems have arisen. Though I have not heard of any, I think it is important to stay very close. After we get the grant, I want to follow it through and see that it is implemented here in Chicago.

Now that you know the status of the project, I want to briefly review its scope and objectives. There are two basic principles upon which it will operate. It is assumed that there are effective and timely legal processes which either exist or can be developed to implement needed social and economic changes. Furthermore, it is assumed that individual communities must be strengthened and, in fact, made capable of shaping their own destinies, controlling their inhabitants, and planning means for social and economic change.

As I mentioned, the project is oriented toward community organizations as opposed to individual action. The lawyers would work very much like corporate counsel for private or public corporations. Most of you are probably aware that most private corporations have legal counsel who meet regularly with the corporate boards of directors to advise and consult with them regarding goals, strategy, procedures, and general planning. Hopefully, the lawyers from the proposed project will be invited to participate in the community organizations' planning sessions. They could meet in the evening or during the day, whenever the organizations meet.

We should briefly consider some of the things lawyers can do. First, as I have mentioned, they could assist organization leaders by giving them legal advice and counsel on the planning of goals, tactics, and strategy. They are especially well equipped to interpret available legislative programs and work out problems of eligibility.

Second, they can help tremendously by adding some new tools to the arsenal of the community organizations, including injuctions, test cases, declaratory judgments, class actions, and other forms of legal and equitable relief.

Third, they can serve as a community advocate in negotiations with public and private agencies.

Fourth, they can assist by studying existing laws and regulations, and devising effective procedures to insure the implementation of benefits and protections. You probably know that too often there are laws which are not enforced and will not be enforced until communities find effective ways to enforce them.

Fifth, lawyers can assist in planning for the expansion of the economic base in communities through development of credit unions, cooperatives, buying clubs, redevelopment corporations, and small businesses. Such action is necessary to hold the funds that are being drained out of the slums to outside interests, so that they may be used for redevelopment or reinvestment within the community.

Sixth, attorneys can assist in development of more viable community organizations and help to establish democratic processes to attract individuals, organizations, and ethnic groups to participation in them.

Seventh, lawyers can aid in developing public support for community efforts in a number of ways: they can develop legal and moral arguments to support group activities, promote publicity of organizational objectives, and lend the prestige of the legal profession to those seeking to organize and promote projects which will promise benefits to the poor.

With regard to this prestige angle, I should call to your attention that the governing board which will be administering the project will include several national figures as well as local leaders. The president, president-elect, and president-elect nominee of the American Bar Association have agreed to serve as directors, and lend their support in planning and implementing the project. The former director of OEO legal services has also agreed to serve on the project, as have several other leading lawyers.

Locally, we hope to establish a Chicago Council of Community Organizations. I hope that many of the organizations represented here would serve as the nucleus for the creation of this council. It would serve as a forum for the development of consensus on the types of problems which will be attacked. It could also try to establish some priorities and means of coordination to assure maximum utilization of the project legal resources. It should meet regularly and often. Representatives of this Council could also serve on the board of directors of the legal service program.

II

It is a pleasure to announce that funds are now available to hire attorneys to provide community organizations with legal counsel. The money has been provided in the form of a grant by the Office of Economic Opportunity. The grant was made directly to the National Legal Aid and Defender Association and as such did not go through the local War on Poverty office. The project is now in the process of hiring attorneys. There will soon be a staff of eleven lawyers and the project headquarters will be located at the Church Federation Building, 116 South Michigan.

When we started discussing the problems of community organization about seven months ago, I spoke to you about the need for lawyers to work as house counsel for action-oriented groups. At that time, I spoke of a role for lawyers in assisting to plan community development. I would now like to expand the discussion and present some examples. For the past few days, I have been attending the Lawndale People's Planning Conference. I have been disappointed to find that there is not more truly grass-roots participation. When the planners finish, they will make a recommendation to the mayor, and he will say that they have done a fine job. He will assure them that the interest of all will be served and he will then proceed to implement the plan for the Lawndale area which he now denies to be in existence. Meaningful participation is part of any renewal program. The problems of areas like Lawndale will not be solved by this kind of superficial participation.

There is a better way. Development of slum areas has to be done from within. The answer is not to be found in going to Mayor Daley to give him guidelines to follow. The guidelines are too easily subverted. People in redevelopment areas should decide what they want in their community and develop the areas themselves. The structures and resources are available to make this possible.

If you, as community leaders, are willing to help locate rundown tenement buildings we will provide the lawyers to take the legal actions necessary to have the buildings restored to livable conditions. The scope of legal action can include criminal management actions and code violation complaints, or the lawyers are available to work with you in setting up tenant unions, tenant strikes, and rent withholdings. These are some of the more traditional legal approaches. They are effective in some instances, and completely ineffectual in others.

As you well know, there is a problem of overcrowding. In some buildings, ten families may be living where only five should be accommodated. Too often, we find that the five who are complaining are the last five to move into the building, and the first five to be evicted due to code enforcement.

A community organization can set up a non-profit housing corporation to develop low-income housing, or the tenants living in a building can organize into a cooperative. In either instance, money can be obtained to cover the cost of acquisition and rehabilitation of property. If planned properly, the loan will cover 100% of the acquisition and rehabilitation costs. Repayment can be spread out over a forty-year period at a rate of interest of three per cent. The difference, between 3% and the 6½% you would have to pay a bank, amounts to a $23 per month reduction in rent or payment of a $10,000 unit. Due to construction costs in the city of Chicago, it is not economically possible to build low-income housing for rent or sale, unless there is a government subsidy in the interest rate, and/or the cost of acquisition. The urban renewal program is presently the only program capable of subsidizing acquisition costs. Unfortunately, urban renewal has seldom, if ever, been used for this purpose.

In any type of project to develop or rehabilitate low-income housing there is need for legal assistance. Lawyers are needed to draft articles of incorporation and plan financial and management controls necessary in order to qualify for loans of any type. When a building or lot is selected there is need for title searches and review of building and zoning problems. Before construction can be commenced, there is need for drafting of construction contracts. These contracts, if properly drawn, can provide training programs in building trades and management of buildings for area residents. Community organizations can pick their own contractors, and can decide whether whites, Negroes, or other minority groups should participate in development of these programs.

You do not have to go to the city to ask them for sites; you need only look for them yourself. If a question with the city or with urban renewal arises, staff lawyers will be available to represent your interests and push for approval of your program.

For the purpose of this discussion, I have chosen one area, the area of housing, as the example. This is because I think it is very important to you. Once you decide what problems you want to deal with, lawyers will be able to help you find the legal process by which you can get the quickest and best results.

I do not argue against working with the present urban renewal program. You should, by all means, work to achieve participation in the program. However, as community organization leaders you have a responsibility to your community to utilize your own individual initiative in achieving community redevelopment. You should make the most effective use possible of all services available to you.

Before the end of the year, we will have thirty lawyers available to work with you in community organization activities. Their assistance will not be limited to housing matters. They should be used in finding procedures to solve all types of community problems. They will have expertise in developing small businesses, credit unions, cooperatives, and other enterprises needed to develop the economic base of low-income communities. They can provide guidance in tailoring your public schools to become more responsive to the people of the neighborhood, and they can work with you in solving social problems such as police-community relations, juvenile problems, and the problem of crime.

I invite you to take advantage of their services.

Community Workshops for
Citizens' Participation

CONTINUING WORKSHOP GROUP

The ad hoc organization, to be known as The Community Services Workshop Group, proposes to enable one hundred people in a geographical community to participate in a Community Workshop designed to prepare them to intelligently participate in governmental programs which are, and will be, entering their communities to effect economic and social change.

Introduction

Citizens' participation is a byword in almost every federal and local governmental program. It has been written into almost every piece of legislation designed to bring about progressive social change in decaying communities. Too often, however, this word has become a bone of contention between neighborhood groups and local and federal governmental officials as they wrestle with its definition and with the practical problems involved in bringing about participation. One of the charges frequently leveled against local groups is that they are "uninformed" or that "they do not know what they want and have not come up with a constructive alernative."

Participation, then, is not an easy word to define in its application to governmental programs in general and particularly difficult in application to specific programs (e.g., the War on Poverty). However, it is the consensus of the Community Services Workshop Group that one ingredient needed for intelligent participation is information. The information should be of two kinds: specific information regarding the specific programs under discussion and information beyond the specific which sheds light on local projects by opening up a new range of alternatives.

At present, there is no vehicle that exists in the city of Chicago to accomplish a program of this nature. Most workshop programs are general in nature and do not address the hopes and desires, the burning issues, in local communities. Consequently, the citizenry is not informed to the extent needed to intelligently participate in the planning of their own communities.

It is for the above reasons that the Community Services Workshop Group voted to develop this proposal with the intention of facilitating citizen's participation in governmental programs by involving local, grass-roots community organizations in the development of comprehensive workshops designed to provide local communities with the information needed to understand the governmental programs, and to provide them with the opportunity

488

to begin developing models of involvement.

Through this method of involvement in actively discussing specific problems which are most pressing the community, hopefully the feeling of alienation which many slum residents have, will be lessened.

Also, while there is not any specific relationship between this project and other governmental programs, the project will require active cooperation by governmental agencies to bring it to a successful conclusion.

The Community Services Workshop Group

The Community Services Workshop Group is an organization which developed out of the Community Service Workshop sponsored by the Extension Division of the University of Chicago. The Group is composed of individuals representing almost every facet of community service, including administrators of public and private agencies as well as local grass-roots individuals from the Workshop. This Group had the opportunity of hearing experts on every facet of community development, and had the opportunity of discussing in detail the ideas put forth by the various speakers. The speakers were from a variety of professions, and from various parts of the country, and, again, included people from governmental and private agencies and business, as well as local grass-roots community organization representatives. The Group came together on seven different weekend sessions, with the last two sessions being largely devoted to evaluation, model building, and discussion of the future of this Group. At that time the Group voted to continue as a Workshop, and to devote itself to attempting to define the role of the citizen in governmental programs.

Target Area

The target area shall have two important criteria for its selection: it shall be an area that is included in the city of Chicago proposal for a planning grant from the Department of Housing and Urban Development of the federal government, and it must have strong grass-roots organizations with an awareness of the problems of the urban poor. (This latter qualification will be decided upon by discussion and evaluation of the entire Group; i.e., it will be decided democratically). An alternative criteria might be that the area be an urban renewal area and/or an area designated a poverty area by the Chicago Committee on Urban Opportunity.

Method

A period of six months shall be projected as a maximum for a Community Workshop in this community. The project shall be developed in three phases.

Phase I – Planning

1. The Group Steering Committee (elected) shall meet with local community organizations in the selected area to explain the purpose of the project and to enlist the cooperation of the organization in setting the Workshop agenda.
2. In discussion with the Steering Committee the areas of interest will be

defined by the community organization as they apply to the local community.

3. The concerns shall be broken down into four categories: economic development, housing, education, and citizens' problems. These shall be referred to four standing committees of the Group paralleling the areas of interest. These committees, which are composed of the constituents of the Group, will, in conjunction with representatives of the local organizations, develop the curriculum for that area and develop the needed resources.

4. The Steering Committee shall make the final schedule arrangements, serve as the coordinator of the project, and proceed to administer the program.

Phase II – Selection of Conference Participants

One of the requirements for the success of this program will be the broadest possible geographical distribution in a given area.

Another will be a heterogeneity among conference participants. These should be selected from different occupations, different community relationships, and inasmuch as possible, different ethnic and racial backgrounds.

Also, those coming to the Workshop must be able to share information with their neighbors. That is, they must have rapport in the neighborhood and have some leadership potential. This criterion is seen as crucial in the success of the program. For it will be the ability of the conference participants to reflect the feeling of that community and to articulate first its concerns, and then articulate to their neighbors the information and conclusions arrived at in dialogue with others, that will guarantee the broadest possible impact in the community.

Finally, continuous Workshop participation must be insured for maximum benefit of the project.

In order to accomplish the above, it will be necessary to have a paid staff in the local area to organize the participants in the Workshop to insure their participation and attendance. There are many important reasons why people in low-income areas do not participate in programs of this kind which, if given the proper attention, can be worked out. Therefore:

1. The area selected for the Workshop will be broken down into zones.

2. Each zone shall have assigned to it a paid, indigenous worker. This worker is to be selected by the community organization in conjunction with the Steering Committee and the project director. This worker shall have the responsibility of finding people to participate in the Workshop, people who fit the above qualifications. Each worker shall have a quota of people for the Workshop. There will be a maximum of four workers for each area, and they will be under the supervision of a local community organization director.

3. The Workshop participants will have many practical problems in getting to the Workshop. It will be the responsibility of the worker to help the participants surmount the problems and attend the Workshop. Many of these practical problems are often connected with large family life, and it may be

necessary to organize such services as baby-sitting.

4. Another practical problem that often occurs is that of people becoming disinterested for a variety of reasons: confusion, fear of speaking, etc. It shall be the responsibility of the worker to do follow-up supportive work during the gaps in between sessions, in order to deal with problems of this nature. The conference participants in his zone shall be his "constituency," and he shall be responsible for their continuing participation.

5. Lastly, the worker shall act as discussion leader for small group discussion as necessary.

Phase III

The last phase of the development will be the actual Workshop itself. The Workshop itself will run for four months. Of the six month total, two months will be given over to identifying the participants, planning the conference, and making the arrangements before beginning the actual Workshop. The Workshop will meet once a week.

The method of the Workshop will be a simple one. Every speaker shall make a presentation of his point of view with respect to the topic at hand. The Workshop participants will respond as they choose, in a nondirected, freeflowing dialogue. The Workshop participants themselves shall choose the alternatives they feel to be in their own self-interest through "democratic dialogue."

Workshop Coordination

In order to achieve a smoothly running coordination of the Workshop, a Workshop Coordinator will be hired. This person's responsibility will be to staff the Workshop Group itself, including the Steering Committee and the four standing committees.

Specifically, the coordinator will be responsible for the following:

1. Contacting the community organizations and setting up the meetings with the Steering Committee for initial negotiation and ongoing planning.

2. Scheduling the meetings of the four standing committees of the Group, working with the chairman of same in the development of Workshop agenda and resources for same. The coordinator in effect will staff the four standing committees.

3. Contacting resource personnel and arranging for resource materials for the Workshops.

4. Carrying out all administrative matters with respect to location of the Workshop, field trips, meals, etc.

5. Carrying on liaison with local Community Organization and local Workshop staff during the course of the Workshop, specifically conferring with local staff participants with regard to the selection of resource staff.

It is anticipated that this will be able to be done by a part-time Coordinator, with secretarial services.

Project Evaluation

While a research scheme is not projected for this project, an evaluation can be projected in two areas which are part of the over-all proposal.

1. The proposal aims at relieving isolation and alienation through providing participants with an opportunity to discuss concrete problems which they have chosen to discuss, and to provide resources which can guide them to an understanding of all facets of the problems. Therefore, a large part of the evaluation will have to be done by the participants themselves. They will have to decide whether or not the Workshop accomplished their objectives.

2. Actual participation in the planning or implementation of some governmental programs which are currently in operation in the community is a possible means of evaluation.

3. A more concrete mode of evaluation is the extent to which the group itself feels itself to be part of an ongoing project for the community, as a sort of information clearinghouse, and devotes itself to the task of helping the community understand the problems facing it.

A Proposal to Develop an Urban Service Training Center

SPANISH ACTION COMMITTEE OF CHICAGO

The Spanish Action Committee of Chicago, Illinois was formed by leading Puerto Rican citizens in June 1966. Following the massive civil disorders which occurred in the Puerto Rican community during the summer of 1966 groups of concerned residents and local business men met to form a community organization. The express purpose of the Spanish Action Committee is to enable local residents to identify in an organized manner the physical and social problems of the community, to interpret these needs to city agencies, and to work toward implementing sound community-based programs.

The Spanish Action Committee, administered under the direction of its executive director, Juan Diaz, .and a board of directors composed of local residents, has focused its program in two broad areas. First the committee has brought together Spanish-speaking citizens to discuss and identify neighborhood problems; second, the committee has attempted to bridge the cultural gap between the Spanish-speaking community and the English-speaking community. Through a volunteer program, educational workshops, and a host of social service projects, the S.A.C.C. has been able to help local citizens to examine community problems, train community leadership in assessment of problems, and mobilize the informed and trained leadership to work cooperatively.

A most notable success has been S.A.C.C.'s sponsorship of weekly training workshops for local residents. Through the use of university resources and experts in the field of urban problems, the workshops have helped local citizens to: (1) develop the skills and techniques needed for effective leadership in the community; (2) broaden participants' interest in the knowledge of community problems; and (3) involve other local groups and organizations in vital community programs through their individual representatives. The creation of such a reservoir of leadership talent can be useful not only to S.A.C.C. but also to other public and private community service organizations which must deal with the increasing number of Spanish-speaking people in Chicago.

The Problem

The Puerto Rican population within the target area of Ashland to Kedzie and Chicago Avenue to North Avenue is roughly estimated to be as high as

493

25,000 or over 50% of the Spanish-speaking population in Chicago. In addition, the target area's population is composed of small ethnic enclaves of Italian, German, Polish, Croatian, Serbian, and other Central European national groups, as well as Negroes, American Indians, and Southern whites.

The problems of this community, which can be classified as lower income, are multiple and varied. Although the deteriorated housing and meager health and welfare services affect the total community, this proposal will only discuss those problems unique to the Puerto Rican population.

The Puerto Rican's adjustment to a complex urban city is at best difficult, and often is never totally achieved. In-migrants from Puerto Rico, are for the most part accustomed to life in a rural area and come to Chicago with no financial resources, little education much of which is not applicable in our modern city, and an inability to speak English. The complexity of Chicago coupled with the meager services available for these new arrivals creates a situation which is overwhelming, frightening, and often results in an inability to function properly. These American citizens come to Chicago with high educational aspirations for their children and professional ambitions for themselves. What occurs, in many instances, is an inability to "plug into" the urban systems (education, employment) and results in alienation and frustration.

The problems of this Puerto Rican community are no better symbolized than in the extreme difficulty the individual encounters as he attempts to involve himself in the employment, education, health, and welfare systems of the city. The obstacles which appear to impede the delivery of services to the people, especially the socially and economically disadvantaged, are bureaucracy, a market-exchange philosophy, and community isolation.

Obstacles to service are indicated by the following situations:

1. The client or applicant for employment or welfare is unable to be clear on what he needs. The language barrier often inhibits free expression of need.
2. He does not know where to go for what he needs.
3. He is too anxious and distrustful to deal with staff or public school personnel, who may be indifferent or hostile.
4. If the applicant is a woman, she can not always manage baby sitting or day care arrangements, carfare, clothing, and energy for a trip to make an appointment, probably at a distant spot in the city, to obtain service.
5. Modern urban agencies and schools operate within complicated bureaucracies thus causing delays in the delivery of services. Those who do not understand the system will become impatient and frustrated and not wait for services.
6. Service is not always offered in a way and form which is acceptable.

The following expressions from neighborhood people clearly illustrates service failures in education, welfare, and employment. Concerning the public school system, several adults claimed, "Teachers do not understand our children – they (the teachers) claim kids do not pay attention in classes." Further discussion revealed that many Spanish-speaking students cannot speak

English until the third grade, and some cannot read until the eighth grade. Teachers often become frustrated and respond insensitively. Parents claim teachers shame the youngsters by implying that their parents are stupid, and now that they are in America they should speak English all the time.

The language barrier of the young Puerto Rican coupled with a complete communication breakdown between the school system and the community results in a high percentage of absenteeism, truancy, and a high drop-out rate. Young Spanish-speaking students cannot adequately compete with other students, and parents will not explain family needs to the school because of the shame of not being able to speak English, which results in fear of the system and apathy.

The adequacy of the employment service approach and program in reaching people who need it most is open to question. Puerto Ricans have difficulty in filling out applications, being interviewed, and following through on a recommended job placement. Often because of a lack of understanding of the applicant's interest and needs, inappropriate placements and counseling are given.

Many similar problems are also evident in the relationships Puerto Ricans have with local welfare offices. Difficulty in dealing with the organizational, language, and cultural barriers between the recipient and caseworker often results in a breakdown of communication and inability to provide services.

These failures, which are clearly evident in the target area, severely affect the spirit of urban living by:

1. Deepening the Puerto Ricans' belief that nobody cares.
2. Encouraging deception of school personnel, employment service counselors, and welfare caseworkers, by creating an illusion that adequate service is being given since those who come usually do not complain.
3. Contributing unnecessarily to the deterioration of community life.

A fundamental assumption of the project can best be stated in the language of economic analysis since a developmental program is finally concerned with the mobilization of economic resources and labor power.

In the past, the approach, particularly in the social welfare and employment service fields, has been to apply capital intensive procedures; that is, to use highly trained personnel in intensive practice procedures. The emerging trend we will seek to facilitate is a shift from capital intensive procedures to labor intensive ones. Labor intensive procedures involve a recognition of the full range of tasks in community mobilization so that minimum skills and competence can be developed on a widespread basis to achieve maximum impact. Under such procedures, the highly trained professional not only renders services, but above all, acts as a manager-trainer and mobilizer of community resources. What will be sought is a proper balance between a reliance on the professional, the sub-professional, and the volunteer.

The Proposal

The aforementioned problems indicate a serious breakdown in communication and the delivery of services between the Puerto Rican people and the service agencies. It is proposed to establish an urban service training center within the Spanish Action Committee. The training center will be designed to provide a long-range and immediate, comprehensive, multiprofessional training service to public and private health, education, and welfare agencies within the target area. Specifically the training program will involve members of the Puerto Rican community and professionals in the public school, employment service, and welfare systems. The nonprofessional community worker will work along with the professional for the purposes of learning the job, interpreting the needs of the community to the specific agency, and interpreting the agencies function and responsibilities to the community. Through the use of short term in-service training, consultation seminars, and conferences, the learning needs of both the professional and community worker will be enhanced.

Training Content

The training needs for the professional and the nonprofessional worker have not been clearly differentiated. We do know that the nonprofessional or indigenous person, relatively poorly educated – at least in a formal sense – is called upon to do a complex job which would tax the skills and resources of professionally trained and experienced workers. Our hopes for the indigenous worker would appear unrealistic except for the fact that the life circumstances of a sensitive and bright person raised in a slum may well constitute the most relevant preparation for the job. Thus the task for the trainer would be to identify concrete aptitudes of the indigenous leader and provide a curriculum which would sharpen the understanding and skill of relationships they already possess. The professional may or may not possess the natural aptitude for relating to those from low income neighborhoods. His major skill may be in a theoretical awareness of community dynamics, but with little skill in transforming this knowledge into a viable neighborhood or community program. It is assumed both the professional and nonprofessional are lacking, perhaps in different ways, in a service component of community work. The indigenous worker may have strengths in being able to relate to neighborhood people, but may be weak in administration and planning ability. The professional may have planning ability, but lacks ability in relating to culturally different people. As a result, the service given to communities is hindered, as at one point or another the workers may not be able to adequately help the client.

It is for these reasons that the Spanish Action Committee of Chicago proposes to develop training content for both professional and nonprofessionals in the employment, education and welfare fields.

Specifically, this proposal will outline training content for the nonprofessional and professional. Training content can be significantly altered as community needs change.

The following is an abbreviated outline of major content areas for the proposed training program:

I. Problem Identification

A. The specific problem areas a worker can use as a base for his activity.

B. Assess procedures for specific aspects of the home environment, home management, health, education, and employment. A specific problem may be one which is perceived by any one of the following persons:
1. The client himself
2. Other significant persons with a relationship to the client
3. The welfare worker
4. Other professionals who work with the client

II. Some Problem Areas

A. Interpersonal
1. Parent-child relationships
2. Emotional problems
3. Parent-teacher problems
4. Client-worker problems
B. Developmental problems
1. Children leaving home
2. Children reacting to poverty by acting out – i.e. joining gangs, quitting school
C. Crisis
1. Husband deserts
2. Husband dies
3. Unemployment
4. Trouble with law
5. Illness
D. Motivation for change
1. In relationship to employment
2. In relationship to training
3. Community subcultural; does not permit change to take place

Trainers can use this as a base for helping workers be more specific as to presenting problems, establishing their own activities (in relationship to seriousness of problem, amenability of problem to change).

The following is a listing of the objectives of problem identification:

1. To enable the community worker to better understand the rationale and objectives of services in education, employment, and welfare.
2. To enable the workers to understand the relationship of social study to provision of services.
3. To enable the workers to see the relationship of their problem formulation to community development.
4. To help the workers to gain understanding of what constitutes a problem.

5. To help the workers relate understanding of the Puerto Rican family in ascertaining the problems of the family.
6. To help the workers to identify the legitimacy of their activities in helping poor families solve problems.
7. To assist workers to understand how to assess the accuracy of information secured in identifying and formulating problems.

Utilization of Community Resources

The emphasis will be to develop three areas of skill. First, the worker's awareness of the differential utilization of health, education, and welfare resources. Second, the worker's skill in working with these resources on a teamwork basis, where necessary, and enabling the client to approach and use such resources. Third, to help workers become aware of how to work with community social systems.

Helping the Worker Deal with the Environment

This portion of the curriculum will deal with real problems resulting from the environment itself, and not necessarily community behavior which affects the environment.

The objectives for the unit are:

1. To identify and list main possible environment problems.
2. To develop greater understanding of the importance and effectiveness of environmental change.
3. To clarify techniques for changing environment.
4. To develop confidence and competence in changing environment.

This unit will concentrate on the following five major areas of environmental study: physical, economic, mental health, cultural, and social.

Evaluation

Inasmuch as this is a project concerned with development and refinement of training techniques, the evaluation process will be initiated during the initial stage of the program. Methods and techniques of the training process and its effectiveness with professionals as well as nonprofessionals will be evaluated, and based on such evaluation appropriate revisions will be made.

Goals

The major goal of the training program will be to develop, based on actual practice, experience, and evaluation, better techniques in helping nonprofessional and professional service workers serve the Puerto Rican community.

Job Description

Director

This position calls for a highly skilled person who is articulate in both Spanish and English. A basic requirement of the position is the ability to understand and empathize with people in the target community. He must be able to identify and articulate their needs to the directors, principals, professional and nonprofessional workers in welfare, employment, and educational agencies. He must be able to develop the trust and confidence of the community and the appropriate service systems. In addition he must:

1. Implement the program as stated in the proposal.
2. Supervise and train staff.
3. Initiate contact with social service agencies and act as liaison between these agencies and the community.
4. Interpret and develop appropriate programs and services with the Illinois Employment Service, Cook County Department of Public Aid, and the Chicago Public Schools.
5. Make regular and detailed reports to the Board of Directors and to the funding agency.
6. Administer all project funds.

Assistant Director

The assistant director's areas of responsibility will include working with the director in developing content materials for in-service training, developing cooperative training programs with the appropriate agencies (employment service, welfare department, and school system).

In addition, he will be responsible for evaluating the program and developing appropriate research projects.

The assistant director should have a master's degree in either social work, education, or the behavioral sciences. He should have a working knowledge of training and community organization.

Field Worker in Employment, Education, and Welfare

Six field workers are necessary to work with community people and agency workers in order to effectuate better service. A field worker must be bilingual and be familiar with the community and its residents. He must be comfortable in community homes, taverns, grocery stores, barber shops, etc., as these may be the places where his best work will be done. Duties will include:

1. Interviewing clients (generally in Spanish) who are experiencing difficulty in getting adequate service.
2. Determining and recording all the necessary facts.
3. Connecting client with appropriate service agency.
4. Recording all action taken.
5. Doing the necessary follow-up with client and agency to maintain services.
6. Attending all project planning and staff meetings as called by the director.
7. Attending a qualified center of education to expand the broaden his academic background.

Administrative assistant

The administrative assistant must be able to set up and maintain the office for the project. She must speak Spanish and English in order to deal with clients' personally and on the phone. Her duties include:

1. General office routine: typing, answering the phone, correspondence, mimeographing and duplicating, filing.
2. Ordering office and program supplies.
3. Keeping appropriate records of all expenditures.
4. Using and training a core of office volunteers.

BUDGET

STAFF		TIME	COST (Per Annum)
1	Executive Director	Full Time	$12,000
1	Assistant Director	Full Time	10,000
1	Administrative Assistant	Full Time	7,000
6	Field Workers	Full Time	
		($7,000 per worker)	42,000

PROGRAM COSTS	12,000
Conferences	
Seminars	
Trips	
Supplies	
CONSULTATION	2,000
OFFICE RENTAL	3,000
UTILITIES	2,000
Total	$90,000

Community Service Workshop Participants

Thomas Angeli
Field Coordinator, Economic Development Administration
U.S. Department of Commerce
Iron River, Michigan

Martin Baker
Executive Committee Member
Englewood Civic Organization
Chicago

Mike Barreto
Youth Program Director
Latin American Boys Club
Chicago

Curtis Lee Beard
Assistant Director, Lawndale Welfare Union
West Side Organization
Chicago

Lou Bobka
Community Consultant, Community Development Services
Southern Illinois University
Edwardsville, Illinois

Leonard Borman
Director of Program Development
Stone-Brandel Foundation
Chicago

Harold Boysaw
Area Supervisor
Cook County Department of Public Aid
Chicago

Steven Bracker
Tenant Union Director
Englewood Civic Organization
Chicago

Thomas Brittenham
Director
Franklin County Welfare Department
Columbus, Ohio

Margaret Brooks
Representative
Martin de Porres House
Chicago

Rev. William Brooks
Executive Director
Gary Neighborhood House
Gary, Indiana

Lucille Brown
Youth Director
Mile Square Federation
Chicago

Mildred Buck
Community Psychologist, Chicago Board of Health
Mental Health Division
Chicago

Clifford Burke
President
Mile Square Federation
Chicago

Donna Burrows
Human Relations Officer
Chicago Commission on Human Relations
Chicago

James Cage
Director
West Side Committee for Education and Direct Action, CORE
Chicago

Louis Carter
Community Organizer
East Garfield Park Community Organization
Chicago

Lenora Cartright
Supervisor, Community Relations Department
Cook County Department of Public Aid
Chicago

Clare Conine
Director of Social Service
Chicago Osteopathic Hospital
Chicago

Phyllis Connors
Principal Psychiatric Social Worker
Lakeview Uptown Mental Health Center
Chicago

John Crawford
Staff Member
West Side Organization
Chicago

Irene Darling
Assistant
Aldridge PTA
Chicago

Mel Diamond
Director
Notre Dame Information Center
South Bend, Indiana

501

Juan Diaz
Executive Director
Spanish Action Committee of Chicago
Chicago

Norman Dineen
Community Consultant
Division of Mental Hygiene
Madison, Wisconsin

Greta Edwards
Community Organizer
Agency, Business, Community Planning
    Association
Chicago

William Fischer
Director
Milwaukee Youth Opportunity Center
Milwaukee, Wisconsin

Jeanne Fox
Community Organizer
Newberry Center
Chicago

Meredith Gilbert
Assistant Coordinator
Lawndale Union to End Slums
Chicago

Jacob Ginsburg
Director
Bureau on Jewish Employment Problems
Chicago

Jacob Gold
Executive Director
Jewish Home for the Aged
Chicago

Sherry Goodman
Assistant Director of Program
National Conference of Christians and Jews
Chicago

Waldo Graton
Executive Director
Evanston Community Relations Commission
Evanston, Illinois

Eugene Harris
Volunteer Staff
West Side Organization
Chicago

Ralph Henry
Field Staff
West Side Organization
Chicago

William Hollins
Field Staff
Southern Christian Leadership Conference
Chicago

Maggie Holmes
Welfare Union Member
The United Friends
Chicago

Ben Hughes
Community Representative
East Garfield Park Community Organization
Chicago

Marge Hunter
Former School Teacher and Graduate
    Student
Saint Xavier College
Chicago

George Jefferson
Consultant
State Board of Vocational Education
    and Rehabilitation
Springfield, Illinois

Nancy Jefferson
Community Service Representative
Midwest Community Council
Chicago

Alan Kardoff
Executive Director
Lakeview Citizens' Council
Chicago

Karen Kelly
Assistant Director
Catholic Interracial Council
Chicago

Eleanor Kempf
Executive Director
Chicago Area Council Campfire Girls
Chicago

Adele Kinghorn
Director
Englewood Mental Health Center
Chicago

Richard Lawrence
President
Englewood Civic Organization
Chicago

Michael Lawson
Assistant Director
Catholic Interracial Council
Chicago

Christine Leak
Section Leader
Christian Family Movement
Chicago

Lena Linnear
District Director
Chicago Area Council Campfire Girls
Chicago

William Marsh
Field Representative
National Legal Aid and Defender
    Association
Chicago

Sister Mary Patricia
Field Consultant
Urban Apostolate of the Sisters
Chicago

David McMullin
Community Services Officer
Department of Housing and Urban
    Development
Chicago

Leslie Montie
Community Consultant
Division of Mental Hygiene
Madison, Wisconsin

William Moore
Division Director
Commission on Youth Welfare
Chicago

Willie Morris
Project Chairman
Maple Park Methodist Men
Chicago

Masaru Nambu
Social Service Worker, Japanese-American
    Service Committee of Chicago
Chicago

Will Nunnally
Group Worker
Beacon Neighborhood House
Chicago

Velmae Olieff
Advisory Board Member
District 8 PTA
Chicago

Lena Phifer
Treasurer
Improvement Club
Chicago

Faye Price
Associate Director, Chicago Board of Health
Mental Health Division
Chicago

Vernon Pohlman
Chairman, Department of Sociology
Illinois State University
Normal, Illinois

Louis Randall
Caseworker
St. Leonard's House
Chicago

James Rea
Consultant, Community Development Service
Southern Illinois University
Carbondale, Illinois

Evelyn Reed
President
Aldridge PTA
Chicago

Sister Mary Ronald
Clinic Director
Mercy Hospital and Clinics
Chicago

Lois Ann Rosen
Executive Secretary
South Lynne Community Council
Chicago

Matthew Scherer
Caseworker
Independent Union of Public Aid
    Employees
Chicago

Joseph Scime
President
Kane County Council of Economic
    Opportunity
Elgin, Illinois

Faith Smith
Social Service Worker
American Indian Center
Chicago

Judy Smith
Preteen Director
YWCA
Chicago

Samuel Smithe
Coordinator
Lawndale Union to End Slums
Chicago

Vivian Toban
Postdoctoral Trainee in Community Men-
    tal Health
University of Illinois
Chicago

Arthur Vazquez
Assistant to the Program Director
Community Renewal Society
Chicago

Noreene Walsh
Psychiatric Social Worker, Chicago Board
    of Health
Mental Health Division
Chicago

Rose Wheeler
Social Worker, Chicago Board of Health
Mental Health Division
Chicago

Jean White
Housing Chairman
Together One Community
Chicago

Mary Widman
Treasurer
Martin de Porres Workers
Chicago

James Williams
Relocation Officer
Department of Urban Renewal
Chicago

Sigemond Wimberli
Community Organizer
Committee on Community Organization
Chicago

George Zilliac
Associate Director
National Conference of Christians and Jews
Chicago

Community Service Workshop Guest Discussants

Herbert Abrahams, M.D.
Physician
Mt. Sinai Hospital
Chicago

Warren Bacon
Member of Chicago Board of Education
Assistant Director of Industrial Relations
Inland Steel Company
Chicago

John Ballew
Former Acting Director
Cook County Department of Public Aid
Chicago

Harold Baron
Director of Research
Urban League
Chicago

Bernard Berkin
Assistant Director, Race and Education
Study
U.S. Commission on Civil Rights
Washington, D.C.

Ezra Birnbaum
Mobilization for Youth
New York, New York

Timuel Black
National Teachers Corps
Chicago

Richard Boone
Executive Director
Citizens' Crusade Against Poverty
Washington, D.C.

Eugene Borucki
Teacher
Chicago Public Schools
Chicago

Donald Bourgeois
Director
St. Louis Model Cities Agency
St. Louis, Missouri

Jeanette Branch
Chief Social Worker
Woodlawn Mental Health Center
Chicago

Rev. Arthur Brazier
President
The Woodlawn Organization
Chicago

Lt. Edward Buckney
Director, Detective Gang Intelligence Unit
Chicago Police Department
Chicago

Willie Burns
Child Development Group of Mississippi
Jackson, Mississippi

Joseph Burstein
General Counsel
Housing Assistance Administration
Department of Housing and Urban
Development
Washington, D.C.

Nathan Caplan
Associate Director of Research, Institute
for Social Research
University of Michigan
Ann Arbor, Michigan

Frank Carney
Director, Seminar Studies Center
JOBS NOW
Chicago

Oscar Chute
Former School Superintendent
Evanston, Illinois

Richard Cloward
Professor, School of Social Work
Columbia University
New York, New York

Samuel Dardick
Chief Planner
St. Louis Model Cities Agency
St. Louis, Missouri

Thomas Davies
Planner
Department of Development and Planning
Chicago

Rennie Davis
JOIN
Chicago

James DeBerry
Coordinator
Harlem Youth Unlimited
New York, New York

Victor DeGrazia
Kate Maremont Foundation
Chicago

Dennis Deshaies
Assistant Study Director, Institute for
   Social Research
University of Michigan
Ann Arbor, Michigan

Leon Despres
Attorney
Alderman, 5th Ward
Chicago

Anthony Downs
Real Estate Research Corporation
Chicago

Pearl Draine
Associate Director
Child Development Group of Mississippi
Jackson, Mississippi

E. Babette Edwards
I.S. 201
New York, New York

Monsignor John Egan
Office on Urban Affairs
Archdiocese of Chicago
Chicago

Rev. Thomas Ellis
Lincoln Memorial Congregational United
   Church of Christ, Woodlawn
Chicago

Henry Etzkowitz
Treasurer
Bedford-Stuyvesant Community Cooperative
   Center, Inc.
Brooklyn, New York

Gilbert Feldman
Attorney
Kleinman, Cornfield & Feldman
Chicago

Gerald Fitzgibbon
Education Specialist, Community Action
   Program
Office of Economic Opportunity
Washington, D.C.

Richard Flacks
Assistant Professor, Department of Sociology
Director, Youth and Social Change Project
University of Chicago

Rev. John Fry
First Presbyterian Church, Woodlawn
Chicago

Irving Gerick
Director
Community Renewal Foundation, Inc.
Chicago

David Greenstone
Assistant Professor
Department of Political Science
University of Chicago

Archie Hardwicke
Citizen Participation Advisor, Model Cities
   Staff, Regional Office
Department of Housing and Urban
   Development
Chicago

Archie Hargraves
Director of Mission Training
Urban Training Center for Christian
   Mission
Chicago

Philip Hauser
Professor of Sociology
Director, Chicago Community Inventory
University of Chicago

Robert Havighurst
Professor, Department of Education and
   Committee on Human Development
University of Chicago

Edward Holmgren
Executive Director
Leadership Council for Metropolitan Open
   Communities
Chicago

C. E. Humphrey
Deputy Executive Director
Chicago Housing Authority
Chicago

Solomon Ice
An Original Staff Member
The Woodlawn Organization
Chicago

Robert Kahn
Associate Professor, Department of
   Psychiatry
Billings Hospital
University of Chicago

Malcolm Klein
Youth Studies Center
University of Southern California
Los Angeles, California

B. Ann Kleindienst
Social Scientist
City Planning Commission
St. Louis, Missouri

Willey Klingensmith
Director, Industrial Arts
Chicago Public Schools
Chicago

Solomon Kobrin
Youth Studies Center
University of Southern California
Los Angeles, California

Thaddeus Kostrubala
Former Director
Stone-Brandel Center
Chicago

Leontine Lemon
Supervisor, Robert Taylor Homes
Cook County Department of Public Aid
Chicago

David Lewis
Professor of Urban Design
    Carnegie Institute of Technology
Director, Urban Design Associates
Pittsburgh, Pennsylvania

Jan Linfield
Pediatrics Children's Clinic, Woodlawn
Formerly, Social Service Department
Billings Hospital
University of Chicago

Joseph Lohman
Dean, School of Criminology
University of California
Berkely, California

Theodore Lowi
Associate Professor
Department of Political Science
University of Chicago

Orville Luster
Executive Director
Youth for Service
San Francisco, California

D. E. Mackelmann
Deputy Commissioner
Department of Urban Renewal
Chicago

Robert Mann
Illinois State Representative
Chicago

Hans Mattick
Associate Director, Center for Studies in
    Criminal Justice
University of Chicago

Henry McCarthy
Chief, Division of Community Service
Illinois Department of Public Aid
Chicago

John McClaughry
Special Assistant to Senator Charles H.
    Percy, Jr.
Washington, D.C.

John McKnight
Director, Midwest Field Office
U.S. Commission on Civil Rights
Chicago

Bruce McPherson
Secretary, Committee on Urban Education
Department of Education
University of Chicago

Curtis Melnick
Superintendent, District 14
Chicago Public Schools
Chicago

Jack Meltzer
Director
Center for Urban Studies
University of Chicago

Abner Mikva
Former Illinois State Representative
Chicago

Daniel Morris
Assistant Executive Director
Mobilization for Youth
New York, New York

Clyde Murray
Social Welfare Consultant
Welfare Council of Metropolitan Chicago
Chicago

Thomas Nader
Secretary – Treasurer
Cook County Building and Construction
    Trades Council, AFL-CIO
Chicago

Richard Newhouse
Illinois State Senator
Chicago

Stanley Newman
Assistant Director
Center for Inner-City Studies
Chicago

Raphael Nystrand
Research Associate Midwest Administration
    Center
Department of Education
University of Chicago

Gary Orfield
Brookings Institution
Washington, D.C.

Hugh Osborne
Deputy Director
Commission on Youth Welfare
Chicago

Paul Peterson
Assistant Professor
Departments of Education and Political
 Science
University of Chicago

James Phillips
Construction Manager
U.S. Gypsum Company
Chicago

Alvin Pitcher
Associate Professor
Divinity School
University of Chicago

Edward Pitt
Mobilization for Youth
New York, New York

Anthony Platt
Research Director
Center for Studies in Criminal Justice
University of Chicago

Daniel Reid
Minority Group Specialist, Regional Office
Department of Labor
Chicago

Edward Riddick
Assistant Director, Department of Social
 Service
Church Federation of Chicago
Chicago

Chester Robinson
West Side Organization
Chicago

Mary Robinson
Tenant Union Member
Chicago

William Robinson
Director
Cook County Department of Public Aid
Chicago

Joseph Rosen
Principal
Howland Elementary School
Chicago

Joseph Sabella
Housing Assistance Administrator
Regional Office
Department of Housing and Urban
 Development
Chicago

Erwin Salk
Banker
Salk, Ward and Salk, Inc.
Chicago

Rev. Albert Sampson
Southern Christian Leadership Conference
Chicago

Florence Scala
Citizens Housing Committee
Chicago

Daniel Scheinfeld
Operation Crossroads
Institute for Juvenile Research
Chicago

Edward Schwartz
Professor
School of Social Service Administration
University of Chicago

Macler Shepard
Citizen Representative
St. Louis Model Cities Agency
St. Louis, Missouri

Ashby Smith, Jr.
Director, Apprenticeship Project
Chicago Urban League
Chicago

Robert Snyder, M.D.
Chicago Board of Health
Chicago

Irving Spergel
Professor
School of Social Service Administration
University of Chicago

Rev. Lynward Stevenson
Former President
The Woodlawn Organization
Chicago

William Stewart
Cooperative League of the U.S.A.
Chicago

David Street
Assistant Professor
Department of Sociology
University of Chicago

Fred Strodtbeck
Associate Professor
Departments of Sociology and Psychology
University of Chicago

Rev. Robert Strom
West Side Organization
Chicago

Gerald Suttles
Assistant Study Director
Chicago Youth Development Project
Institute for Social Research
University of Michigan
Ann Arbor, Michigan

S. T. Sutton
Attorney; President, Operation Crescent
Chairman, Property Owners Coordinating
    Committee
Chicago

Elaine Switzer
Associate Professor
School of Social Service Administration
University of Chicago

Sol Tax
Professor, Department of Anthropology
Dean, University Extension
University of Chicago

Helen Testamark
President
PTA I.S. 201
New York, New York

Herbert Thelen
Professor
Department of Education
University of Chicago

Alan Wade
Associate Professor
School of Social Service Administration
University of Chicago

Richard Wade
Professor
Department of History
University of Chicago

John Waner
Republican Candidate for Mayor, 1967
Waner Heating & Air Conditioning Corp.
Chicago

John Wedemeyer
Project Director
American Public Welfare Association
Chicago

Meyer Weinberg
Chairman, Education Committee
Coordinating Council of Community
    Organizations
Chicago

Jean White
Chairman
Together One Community
Chicago

Preston Wilcox
Professor, School of Social Work
Columbia University
New York, New York

Doxey Wilkerson
Associate Professor
Department of Education
Yeshiva University
New York, New York

Arthur Williams
Legal Services for Youth
Chicago

Livingston Wingate
Associate Director
Citizens' Crusade Against Poverty
Washington, D.C.

Title I, The Workshop, and This Book

Title I, The Workshop, and This Book

Land grant colleges, agricultural extension, and universities have played an important role in rural development in America. With the country having shifted from rural to urban, it is not surprising that President Johnson and the Congress should think some equivalent desirable and necessary. Why shouldn't universities concentrate some of their resources to help understand and resolve problems of urban life? The response to this question was Title I of the Higher Education Act of 1965. (see back cover). Let the federal government provide a little money to encourage universities to think imaginatively about how their intellectual resources might be put to the service of the community.

In response, and under the direction of Jules Pagano of the Adult Education Division of the Office of Education, each state set up its own administration, bringing together its universities in different ways. In Illinois, the Governor placed the program under the Board of Higher Education (Ben Heineman, Chairman; Lyman Glenny, Executive Director; Keith Smith, Associate Director), which on April 24-25, 1966, convened a statewide conference to establish a Council of Community Service and Continuing Education. Under the direction of Glenny and Smith, and of Bruce Trester who was appointed specifically for the purpose, Council membership consisted of:

1. Institutional Members
   Public Universities and Colleges
      Roger Axford, Northern Illinois University
      Norman Britan, Northeastern Illinois State College
      Cameron Merdith, Southern Illinois University
      Louis Volpp, University of Illinois[1]
   Private Universities
      James Banovetz, Loyola University
      Dan Lang, Northwestern University
      Otto Snarr, Bradley University
      Sol Tax, University of Chicago[2]
   Public Junior Colleges
      Doyle Bon Jour, Chicago City College
      Ronald Hallstrom, Rock Valley College
      Clifford Hayes, Belleville Junior College[3]
      Robert Jensen, Blackhawk College[4]
2. Public Members
      William Besuden, International City Managers' Association[5]
      John Dever, City Manager, Decatur[6]

[1] Replaced (7-67) by Louis Wetmore, University of Illinois
[2] Replaced (2-68) by Julian Levi, University of Chicago
[3] Replaced (7-67) by Albert Martin, Illinois Junior College Board
[4] Replaced (4-68) by Philip Walker, Parkland College
[5] Replaced (7-67) by Jerome Kaufman, American Society of Planning Officials
[6] Replaced (7-67) by Robert Morris, Village Manager, Glencoe

Lynford Keyes, State Department of Public Health
William McDaniel, Illinois Department of Business and Economic
  Development[7]
David Larson, Department of Urban Renewal, City of Chicago
Roger Nathan, Illinois Commisssion on Human Relations
Mrs. Dorothy Rubel, Metropolitan Housing and Planning Council
Louis Wetmore, Director of Planning, City of Chicago[8]

The Council set up a means for reviewing projects. Since I was involved from the beginning, I had perhaps more chance than most to think about what might be an "imaginative" and useful project. I developed a proposal more as a sample, hoping that others would learn from it and improve upon it. When the Council included my proposal with those to be funded, I was surprised as well as challenged.

The Economic Opportunity Act of 1964 states that under the Act programs should be "developed, conducted, and administered with the maximum feasible participation of residents of the areas and members of the groups served." It has been discovered that this is easier said than done. Our proposal — "Methods of Providing Opportunities for Indigenous Autonomy of Social Service Centers" — was designed to analyze the problems, limitations, and potentialities of indigenous leadership and participation. This was to be accomplished through the participation of 100 selected men and women, representative of every level of administrative, supervisory, research, and line staff; volunteers, and local community leaders; and educators involved in training programs.

Time was exceedingly short, and we had to round-up the participants quickly. I wrote letters to the relevant cabinet members in Washington, to the governor of Illinois asking his cooperation, and to the mayors of a number of cities and especially to the mayor of Chicago. Governor Kerner was the first to respond; he asked all state departments to provide opportunities to appropriate people to participate in the program and indeed they did. The response at the federal level was also encouraging, especially from OEO under Sargent Shriver, HEW under John Gardner, and HUD under Robert Weaver.

When it came to enlisting appropriate people from the grass roots, I sought the help of Frank Carney and Earl Doty who had just completed a five-year, action and research project launched in three inner-city areas of Chicago. Eventually Mr. Doty joined the staff of our program and, having the confidence of the grass-roots people, did more than anyone to bring them into the program.

The Community Service Workshop was conducted during seven residential periods of from two to five days each. The group of 100 participants, including representatives of all levels of public and private agencies, grass-roots community organization leaders and representatives, and university faculty involved in related research and training programs, were brought into close and continuing contact on questions of greatest concern and mutual interest with other agency professionals, academicians, community organization leaders, and one another. They heard presentations on, and discussed issues in community organization, politics and the welfare system, dominant issues in urban education, major developments in the field of housing, and

---

[7]Replaced (2-67) by Charles Kirchner, Illinois Department of Business and Economic Development
[8]Replaced (9-67) by Rev. H. Kris Ronnow, Interreligious Council on Urban Affairs

the complex nature of youth and youth problems. Discussion around the Economic Opportunity Act raised the issue of maximum feasible participation of the poor which was a major interest of the Workshop group, and an early and primary focus was on the inner-city Negro community as a case in point. The Workshop enabled the participants to face controversial problems directly and realistically; the result was a powerful, emotional, and sustained confrontation between professional and indigenous people.

On the program that resulted, the book will have to speak for itself. But it makes so evident the value of the Title I approach which brings universities into contact with the community that this report is being distributed widely among persons interested in and administering Title I itself as well as to those who participated in the Workshop.   Sol Tax

Public Law 89-329
89th Congress, H. R. 9567
November 8, 1965

An Act

79 STAT. 1219

To strengthen the educational resources of our colleges and universities and to provide financial assistance for students in postsecondary and higher education.

Be it enacted by the Senate and House of Representatives of the United States of America in Congress assembled, That this Act may be cited as the "Higher Education Act of 1965".

Higher Education Act of 1965.

TITLE I—COMMUNITY SERVICE AND CONTINUING EDUCATION PROGRAMS

APPROPRIATIONS AUTHORIZED

SEC. 101. For the purpose of assisting the people of the United States in the solution of community problems such as housing, poverty, government, recreation, employment, youth opportunities, transportation, health, and land use by enabling the Commissioner to make grants under this title to strengthen community service programs of colleges and universities, there are authorized to be appropriated $25,000,000 for the fiscal year ending June 30, 1966, and $50,000,000 for the fiscal year ending June 30, 1967, and for the succeeding fiscal year. For the fiscal year ending June 30, 1969, and the succeeding fiscal year, there may be appropriated, to enable the Commissioner to make such grants, only such sums as the Congress may hereafter authorize by law.

DEFINITION OF COMMUNITY SERVICE PROGRAM

SEC. 102. For purposes of this title, the term "community service program" means an educational program, activity, or service, including a research program and a university extension or continuing education offering, which is designed to assist in the solution of community problems in rural, urban, or suburban areas, with particular emphasis on urban and suburban problems, where the institution offering such program, activity, or service determines—

    (1) that the proposed program, activity, or service is not otherwise available, and

    (2) that the conduct of the program or performance of the activity or service is consistent with the institution's over~~~ ~ducational program and is of such a nature ~ ~~ effective utilization of the institution' competencies of its faculty.

Where course offering~ ~ invol~
extension or conti~
    (A) f~~

See page 511